Roosevelt to Roosevelt

Presidential Nominating Conventions from 1904 to 1944

Stan Haynes

Roosevelt to Roosevelt
Presidential Nominating Conventions from 1904 to 1944

Copyright 2024 by Stan Haynes

All rights reserved

No part of this book may be reproduced or transmitted in any form or by any means, electronic or mechanical, including photocopying or recording, or by any information storage or retrieval system, without permission from the author.

Cover design by White Rabbit Arts

ISBN: 978-1-7377669-5-7 (print)
ISBN: 978-1-7377669-6-4 (e-book)

Printed in the United States of America

Other books by Stan Haynes:

The First American Political Conventions

President-Making in the Gilded Age

And Tyler No More

And Union No More

To Anna Louise

Contents

Introduction 1

1. 1904: Perdicaris Alive or Raisuli Dead 5
2. 1908: The Wise Custom 35
3. 1912: We Stand at Armageddon 56
4. 1916: Too Proud to Fight 92
5. 1920: Best of the Second Raters 111
6. 1924: Keeping Cool 147
7. 1928: I Do Not Choose to Run 174
8. 1932: Cloudy Gray Times 195
9. 1936: Rendezvous with Destiny 228
10. 1940: No Ordinary Time 252
11. 1944: Clear It with Sidney 280

Conclusion 306
Selected Bibliography 311
Index 316
Acknowledgments 319
About the Author 320
Chapter Notes 321

Introduction

The stately, six-columned house on the six-hundred block of Delaware Avenue in Buffalo still stands. Originally built in the 1840s as officers' quarters for a United States Army outpost located on the site, it was later converted into a private residence. In the 1880s, it became the home of a young Buffalo attorney, Ansley Wilcox, and his wife, Mary Grace. Tragedy would make this home a part of American history. Wilcox had been a friend of Theodore Roosevelt since the first administration of President Grover Cleveland, when the two Republicans were appointed by Cleveland, a Democrat, to serve on a commission studying civil service reform. In the summer and fall of 1901, Buffalo hosted the Pan-American Exposition, a world's fair celebrating the cultures of the nations of the Western Hemisphere. The exposition drew millions of visitors to the city and, in September, the president of the United States, William McKinley, came for a two-day visit to give a speech and tour the grounds. On September 6, while shaking hands in a receiving line, McKinley was shot twice in the stomach by an anarchist, Leon Czolgosz. After initial concerns that his wounds would be fatal, McKinley's condition improved over the next few days. His vice president, Roosevelt, came to Buffalo to pay his respects. By September 10, with McKinley seemingly out of danger, Roosevelt left the city to join his family on a previously planned vacation in the Adirondacks. It was there, on September 12, that the vice president received a telegram, delivered by a special messenger on a soggy mountainside, advising that McKinley's condition had worsened.

First by wagon, and then by train, Roosevelt rushed four hundred miles back across New York State to Buffalo, learning en route that McKinley had died. He arrived on a Saturday afternoon, September 13, and went to the home of his old friend, Wilcox, where he had stayed during his visit earlier that week. After viewing McKinley's body and comforting his widow, Roosevelt went back to Delaware Avenue and, in the home's small library on the first floor, in the presence of six of the eight members of McKinley's cabinet, and a few guests and reporters, forty-two-year-old Theodore Roosevelt took the oath of office and became the nation's twenty-sixth president. American politics would forever be changed. The "cowboy" who New York political boss Thomas Platt had pushed onto the Republican ticket as McKinley's vice president only a year earlier at the Republican convention in Philadelphia, as a way to get him out of the New York governorship, would now lead the nation.[1]

Thus began the era of the Roosevelts. Theodore, along with his fifth cousin, Franklin, who entered the political stage more than a decade later, would dominate American politics during the first half of the twentieth century. There have been other families with more than one member rising to the White House—the Adamses, the Harrisons, and the Bushes—but none controlled American politics and government, or stayed in the public arena as long as, these two distant relatives from different branches of the Roosevelt clan of New York. In the eleven presidential campaigns between 1904 and 1944, one of them would be their party's nominee for president or vice president in six, winning all but one. Of the remaining five, Theodore's handpicked successor was nominated and elected president in one and he headed a third party in another that, for the only time in American history, finished ahead of one of the two major parties. In the other three, Theodore was a likely nominee in one and Franklin made major speeches in two. One way in which the political dominance and staying power of Theodore and Franklin Roosevelt can be seen is from studying the Republican and Democratic presidential nominating conventions of their era. They left their marks not only on the presidency, but also on the quadrennial gatherings of their parties to select candidates for that office.

In addition to exploring the influence that the Roosevelts had over the conventions during the first half of the twentieth century, this book chronicles all of the conventions and candidates of the era—the frontrunners, the surprise nominees, and the also-rans. Each convention had its own twists, interesting anecdotes, and stories of victory and of defeat. William Jennings Bryan, a two-time Democratic loser in presidential elections, came back to win his party's nomination in 1908. Woodrow Wilson, who had decided to withdraw after being stuck in second place for multiple ballots at the 1912 Democratic convention, only to be talked out of it, went on to win the nomination. The 1920 Republican convention was the classic example of men in a "smoke-filled room" selecting a nominee, when a divided convention turned to Warren Harding after several ballots. In 1924, the Democratic convention went on for one hundred and three ballots before selecting a relatively unknown dark horse, John W. Davis, as its nominee. At the 1932 Democratic convention, Franklin Roosevelt struggled to reach the threshold required to win the nomination and, if the voting had extended for one more ballot, likely would have lost. In 1940, Wendell Willkie, a political novice, won the Republican nomination, even though he had been an active Democrat for most of his life. At the 1944 Democratic convention, Harry Truman was named FDR's running mate for his fourth term, replacing the incumbent vice president, Henry Wallace, who fought hard to maintain his place on the ticket. Each of these conventions, and others, could easily have resulted in different nominees for president or vice president. If they had, American history would have been dramatically different.

The composition of and the procedures followed by presidential nominating conventions, established in the mid-nineteenth century, continued to be used in the early twentieth century. A state's population determined its allocation of delegates, based on its number of congressional districts. Each state had two delegates per district (selected at district conventions) and four "at large" delegates (selected at statewide conventions). The more populous the state, the more delegates it had, and the more power it could wield at conventions. The agenda of conventions followed a standard formula, much of which continues to the present. At the opening session, a temporary chairman was approved, based on a recommendation from the party's national committee, who gave an opening speech, known as the keynote, to rouse and inspire the delegates. The various committees were selected, with one member from each state and territory, to review credentials of the delegates, to set the rules and permanent organization, and to draft the party's platform. Once committee reports were received and voted upon, the convention moved to nominations of candidates for president, followed by nominating speeches and voting. While Republicans required only a simple majority to win their nomination, Democrats required a vote of two-thirds of their delegates. Balloting continued until a winner was declared. A vice presidential nominee was then selected. Candidates generally did not attend conventions, it being considered unseemly to do so. The office of president sought the man, it was said, the man did not actively seek the office. There was no acceptance speech at the convention by the presidential nominee. A committee was appointed to formally advise him of his selection. The candidate received the committee a couple of weeks after the convention, usually at his home, and delivered at that time prepared remarks accepting the nomination. Conventions usually lasted four days, unless there were multiple ballots for the nomination, which would cause an extension.

It must be noted that the conventions discussed in this book mirrored the politics and American society of the era. Presidential politics then was an enterprise engaged in by white males, as all politics had been since the founding of the republic. Although Black males had the right to vote since the passage of the Fifteenth Amendment to the Constitution in 1870, by the turn of the century, Jim Crow laws enacted in southern states effectively barred most of them who lived in that region from voting and political participation. Those Black men in the South who were politically active were Republicans and they did make up a significant percentage of Republican delegates from southern states, at least until the 1920s, when that party modified its formula for allocation of delegates. Black Republican delegates, including those from outside of the South, however, rarely had any leadership roles at conventions and their votes were usually determined by the political bosses of their state. The same can be said of many of the white delegates of the era. No Black would represent a state as a full delegate to a Democratic convention until 1936.[2] To Blacks, until the 1930s, Republicans were the party of Lincoln, and Democrats the party that had sympathized with the southern cause and pro-slavery during in the Civil War. That said, neither party actively pursued civil rights for Blacks in this era and their plight was generally not a part of political discussion.

The era covered by this book encompasses the women's suffragist movement and its success. Several western states entered the Union with constitutions that permitted women to vote, and other states passed suffrage laws prior to the enactment of the Nineteenth Amendment in 1920. Like Black men, however, voting rights did not translate into power for women in presidential politics. While a handful of women began to appear as delegates at conventions of both parties early in the twentieth century, with their numbers significantly increasing after 1920, through the last conventions in 1944 covered by this book, convention delegates, in addition to being overwhelmingly white, were also mostly male.

Chapter 1

1904: Perdicaris Alive or Raisuli Dead

Hear the call throughout the land
Come and proudly take your stand.
Now uphold your chieftain's hand
ROOSEVELT THE CRY . . .

Roosevelt, the soldier true
Roosevelt, the statesman too.
Sane for me and safe for you
ROOSEVELT THE CRY
—**Republican campaign song, 1904**

After assuming the presidency upon the assassination of William McKinley in 1901, Theodore Roosevelt kept his pledge to pursue the policies of his predecessor, but also showed reformist tendencies that troubled those who ran the Grand Old Party and who favored the status quo. Roosevelt became involved in the settlement of a strike by coal miners in Pennsylvania, strong-arming the parties to agree to the formation of a federal commission, which sided more with the demands of the miners than with those of the mine owners. Utilizing the Sherman Antitrust Act, his Department of Justice pursued an antitrust suit against the Northern Securities Company, the nation's largest railroad conglomerate, and prevailed, with the Supreme Court ordering the dissolution of the company. He signed legislation creating the Department of Commerce and Labor, viewed by business and industry as a step toward more federal regulation. His speedy recognition of Panama as a separate nation, after its breakaway from Columbia, and the negotiation of an American-owned canal across Panama, showed a president who was willing to bend the rules to accomplish his goals.

Wildly popular with the public, Roosevelt was the clear favorite in 1904 to win his party's nomination and election to a full term of his own in the White House, but that did not mean that Republican party leaders liked it.

Republican Convention

There was irony in the weeks leading up to and at the 1904 Republican National Convention. The party was certain to nominate its incumbent president, Roosevelt, but party leaders remained decidedly cool toward him. By 1904, Roosevelt was looking less to the party's Old Guard for advice and for the staffing of his administration. They felt their power slipping away. As one reporter noted, their "unimportance is irritating to them."[1]

At the 1900 convention in Philadelphia, Roosevelt, then a reform-minded governor of New York, had been placed on the ticket with McKinley, largely due to the desire of New York party boss Thomas Platt to get him out of Albany and into the powerless position of vice president, where he could do no harm. But his pairing with McKinley was also due to a groundswell of support among the party's rank-and-file for the popular young hero of the recent Spanish-American War. Instead of Roosevelt presiding over the Senate, an assassin's bullet put, in Mark Hanna's words, "that madman" in the White House. Hanna, a wealthy Ohio businessman who headed the successful campaigns of his good friend McKinley in 1896 and 1900, had fought hard to keep Roosevelt off the ticket, but had finally relented. After that convention, Hanna continued in his roles as chairman of the Republican National Committee ("RNC") and as a senator from Ohio. Once TR was in the White House, he and Hanna never feuded publicly. Although their private dealings were amicable, the tension between them was palpable. Hanna was by nature a conservative; Roosevelt was a reformer. By 1903, many thought that the Ohio senator would challenge the president for the 1904 Republican nomination. More likely, astute political observers believed that Hanna planned to withhold any endorsement of TR, hoping to prevent a first-ballot victory at the convention, and to be a kingmaker and steer the nomination to someone more acceptable. This speculation ended, however, just as the presidential campaign season was getting underway in early 1904. On February 15, Hanna died unexpectedly of typhoid fever. Once again, Roosevelt's career benefitted from the untimely death of another.

In the delegate selection process that took place in the winter and spring, no opposition to Roosevelt emerged. The formula for choosing delegates remained the same as had been used by both major parties since the mid-nineteenth century. Each state was allotted delegates equaling twice its number of votes in the Electoral College—with two delegates per congressional district (selected local district-level conventions), and four "at large" delegates (selected at statewide conventions). The more people a state had, the more delegates. In 1904, New York was the most populous state, as it had been for years, with 78 delegates out of a total of 994, and it wielded the most power at conventions.

The Republicans selected Chicago as the site of their 1904 convention, returning to the city that had hosted several of their prior gatherings, the last time being in 1888. Its central location and ease of access by railroads from around the country made Chicago a popular convention locale. The convention was held in the Chicago Coliseum, located at Fifteenth Street and Wabash Avenue. Built in 1899, it was the third exposition hall in the city to carry that name and had a seating capacity of nine thousand. The arched-roof structure, which stood until the early 1980s, is remembered for its distinctive front façade that had been part of a Confederate prison during the Civil War. The Libby Prison, in Richmond, Virginia, had been dismantled stone by stone and rebuilt in Chicago, originally as part of a war museum. A special telegraph wire was installed in the White House, connected to Chicago, so that the president and his staff could closely follow the proceedings.[2] This would be the first of five straight Republican conventions to be held at the Chicago Coliseum, a record for convention halls of both parties.

In the days before the convention opened, the center of activity in Chicago was at the Auditorium Annex, an eleven-story hotel, opened in 1893, and located on South Michigan Avenue across from Grant Park. The building still stands and is now known as the Congress Plaza Hotel. Delegations from several states lodged there, and the hotel's conference and banquet rooms served as hospitality rooms. The California suite was among the most popular, serving fresh California fruits and wines, and cigars to all comers. The Auditorium's lobbies were full of crowds gossiping about the convention and spreading the latest rumors. The Alaska delegation moved about town marching behind two large totem poles, topped with stuffed bald eagles. Delegates from the Indian Territory were accompanied by a sixteen-member band of Native-American boys, who were "objects of great interest" on the streets.[3]

There were more than one hundred Black delegates at the convention, almost all from southern states. The delegations from South Carolina and Mississippi had Black majorities, while Blacks made up more than forty percent of the delegates from Texas, Florida, and Georgia.[4] Black delegates had been fixtures at Republican conventions since Reconstruction. In contrast, conventions of the Democratic Party in the era had none. The South was still solidly Democratic and state Republican organizations in that region were weak, almost never electing officeholders. Their power existed mainly as recipients of federal patronage jobs from Republican administrations in Washington. At past conventions, rumors of bribery for their votes often swirled around Black delegates and they were not treated by their northern colleagues, nor by reporters from the nation's newspapers, with much respect. The discrimination and insults continued at the 1904 convention. Newspapers carried a story of a white administration official from New York who arrived to check in at the main convention hotel. Two Black men were standing by the front door and the official handed his suitcases to one with instructions to take them to his room. The outraged man responded that he "ain't no bellboy" and that he was a delegate from Alabama. The event was reported as one of humor only, with no sympathy for the man wrongly assumed, because of his race, to be part of the hotel staff.[5]

As at past conventions, suffragists were in Chicago. The National Women's Suffrage Association sent a flier to all delegates seeking their support for a constitutional amendment for nationwide voting rights for women. Once again, their pleas would be unsuccessful and their cause would not be included in the party's platform. On the state level, however, the constitutions of several western states, as they entered the Union in the late nineteenth century, had given women voting rights. There were four female alternate delegates at the 1904 Republican convention, two from Colorado, and one each from Idaho and Utah. One of them, Mrs. J. B. West of Idaho, had also been an alternate delegate four years earlier in Philadelphia.[6]

The enthusiasm and hoopla that usually surrounds presidential nominating conventions was noticeably absent in Chicago in 1904. "Apathy Among Delegates" read a headline in the *New York Times* the day before the convention opened. The primary reason was that the Republican National Committee ("RNC"), which organized and put on the convention, was still controlled by Mark Hanna's friends and cronies, a conservative establishment that was stoic, if not hostile, toward Roosevelt. Weeks before the convention, the president had further antagonized the party establishment by announcing George Cortelyou as his choice to be the new RNC chairman, and the man who would head the general election campaign. Cortelyou was in Roosevelt's cabinet as the secretary of the newly-created Department of Commerce and Labor. The pick outraged some, as Cortelyou did not have a history of working for the party, nor of having a political background. He had served as the personal secretary to Grover Cleveland, the last Democratic president, and had continued in that role under the Republican administrations of McKinley and Roosevelt, until moving to the cabinet in early 1903. When TR heard of RNC opposition to his choice, he was defiant: "I will not have it any other way . . . . The choice of Cortelyou is irrevocable and I will not consider any other man for the position, and shall treat opposition to him as simply disguised opposition to the republican party."[7] Roosevelt got his way, but resentment over the choice lingered. The bad blood between the RNC and Roosevelt extended to the decorations in the convention hall. Above the podium, where one would expect to find a portrait of a sitting president who was about to be nominated, there was, instead, a huge portrait of the recently-deceased party chairman, Hanna. Much smaller posters of Roosevelt were placed amidst the bunting, hardly visible from the convention floor. Roosevelt's close friend, Senator Henry Cabot Lodge of Massachusetts, wrote to the president from the convention that the hall's décor showed the stubbornness of the old guard "making their last struggle with the inevitable . . . . They had in the centre of the hall over the platform a perfectly colossal oil painting of Hanna, nothing of McKinley and little bits of lithographs of you stuck about in the flag clusters on the top gallery."[8] A not so subtle dig at the president was seen in the campaign buttons being worn on the lapels of some in Chicago, which featured playing cards with four aces and Roosevelt's face, and the words "Stand Pat." The phrase had been coined by Hanna a couple of years earlier in opposition to Democratic attempts to reduce high tariffs, which were a key Republican policy in that era. It referred to a poker player liking his hand and standing pat, or not taking any new cards. Hanna and his supporters became known as "standpatters." The message to the president and to the country was clear—who needs reform when things are already going so well? Newspapers the weekend before the convention were full of stories of the "indifference" and "apathy" of party leaders to the president, and of him being "spoken of slightingly" in the hotel lobbies. Said one party official, "Our smiles are fastened on."[9]

The agenda followed by conventions in that era was standard, and similar to that still followed today. Usually lasting four days, the opening session featured the selection of a temporary chairman, who gave a speech that was the equivalent of what is known today as the keynote speech, followed by the appointment of various committees to resolve disputes as to the seating of delegates, set the rules of the convention, its permanent organization, and draft the party's platform. On the second day, a permanent chairman was selected and the reports of the committees were received and debated, followed on the third day by nomination speeches and, on the fourth day, by voting for candidates for president and vice president. If there was no first ballot victory, the convention could be extended for days. As of 1904, the record for Republicans was in 1880, with James Garfield nominated in Chicago after a week and thirty-six ballots. For the Democrats, it was in 1860, with Stephen Douglas nominated after more than two weeks of sessions in both Charleston and Baltimore and fifty-nine ballots. Active candidates did not personally attend conventions, it being considered unseemly to do so. Thus, there was no acceptance speech at the convention by the nominee, an event that is the highlight of modern conventions. In that era, a committee was appointed to formally notify the candidate of his nomination, usually in his hometown a couple of weeks after the convention, and his remarks then were his formal acceptance.

The first Republican convention held in the Chicago Coliseum was called to order shortly after noon on Tuesday, June 21, 1904, by Henry Payne, the acting RNC chairman, who had taken over after Hanna's death. A band in the upper seats played patriotic and popular tunes of the day. By the scheduled opening time, the galleries still had thousands of empty seats. There was little reaction from the crowd as familiar faces of the party took their seats. The singing of "The Star Spangled Banner" drew such a poor effort from the crowd that a Kansas delegate jokingly told a reporter that he was going offer a plank to the party's platform that the American people either learn the words, "or else refrain from any attempt to sing it in public." Elihu Root, a prominent New York lawyer and former secretary of war under McKinley and Roosevelt, was named temporary chairman. The standard committees were appointed. Root gave a long speech reviewing and praising the last eight years of Republican rule, which generated little enthusiasm from the crowd. The longest applause came when he mentioned McKinley and Hanna. His one reference to Roosevelt at the end of his remarks, intended to stir the audience, did not cause any great outburst. By mid-afternoon, the opening day was over. Noted a reporter from the *Baltimore Sun*, the convention "opened today with a yawn and closed with a chill."[10]

On the convention's second day, some delegates were hoping to rush through the agenda and wrap up the convention by early evening, in order to save an extra day of hotel and other expenses. The officials in charge, however, were not about to let the convention end early. Chicago's hotels and restaurants had been promised at least a three-day convention—and the revenue that it generated—and that is what they would get. A prolonged debate over a minor issue, likely contrived to kill time, made an early adjournment impossible.

Temporary Chairman Root called on the Committee on Credentials, whose chairman presented his report. There were delegate disputes in a handful of states, including Wisconsin. There were two competing delegations from the Badger State, one of which was headed by Robert La Follette, the sitting governor, whose delegate slate had been rejected by the RNC. La Follette had bypassed the credentials committee, alleging that it was biased against him. The irritated committee chairman (perhaps proving La Follette's point) advised that his committee took it upon themselves to review the evidence presented before the RNC and determined that the exclusion of the La Follette faction was, in their opinion, clearly correct. This would not be the last time that Robert La Follette and his followers would play the role of gadfly at a Republican convention. The report of the Committee on Credentials was approved on a voice vote.[11]

The Committee on Permanent Organization recommended Joseph Cannon of Illinois, the speaker of the House of Representatives, as the convention's permanent chairman. This was quickly approved and Cannon took the gavel from Root. The sixty-eight-year-old Cannon, known as "Uncle Joe," had been, with the exception of one term, a member of Congress for more than thirty years. In 1904, he was still in his first term as the presiding officer in the House, a post he would hold for more than a decade, and he would become one of the most dominant speakers in history. Crusty, but likable, Cannon was firmly in the camp of the Republican standpatters and was wary of Roosevelt, but knew that the popular president made the party stronger in the coming campaign. By tradition, as permanent chairman, Cannon gave a speech. Although a written copy of his remarks had been distributed to the press for publication, Cannon, as was his custom, substantially departed from it in his delivery. "Now let me go on and ramble," he began. He noted the reports in newspapers of lack of enthusiasm at the convention. Said Cannon, "It is a contest which makes enthusiasm" and, as the party was united, he declared, lack of enthusiasm was a blessing. Referring to the upcoming Democratic convention, with its nominee uncertain, he said, "Our friends, the enemy, will have the enthusiasm; we will take the votes in November." He reviewed the history of the Republican Party since it first assumed power in the 1860s, its role in winning the Civil War, in the restoration of the Union, in the abolition of slavery, its support for strong tariffs and the gold standard, and the prosperity of the country under the party's watch. Roosevelt was mentioned as "the young, enthusiastic, true man, who succeeded McKinley," who carried out the latter's policies, and who would be elected in his own right. Cannon's ramblings had little direct praise for the man the convention was about to nominate as its presidential standard-bearer.[12]

The report of the Committee on Rules and Order of Business was then presented. Usually a non-controversial agenda item, it was not at this convention. The tradition of both parties was to allot a small number of delegates to territories and possessions of the United States. The committee proposed that six delegates each be seated from Arizona, New Mexico, Oklahoma, the Indian Territory, and two each from Hawaii, the District of Columbia, the Philippine Islands, and Puerto Rico. An Ohio delegate proposed an amendment giving Hawaii six votes, noting that it was a territory and the other territories had been given six votes. Moreover, it was noted, the RNC's call of the convention had invited Hawaii to send six delegates, and twelve Hawaiians (six delegates and six alternates) had traveled more than five thousand miles to Chicago for the convention. An Illinois delegate objected and a long debate and roll call vote followed, lasting more than two hours. The outcome was a substitute amendment under which Hawaii was given only two delegate votes, but all six delegates present could participate, with one-third vote each. This revised resolution narrowly passed with 495 yeas and 490 nays. By the time it was over, there was no way that the convention could finish its business that day. Many believed that this had been the true purpose of the debate, and that it had been manufactured to take up time. The *New York Times* called it a "fake five-round fight" staged by Cannon to ensure a third day for the convention.[13]

The convention's proposed platform was presented by Senator Henry Cabot Lodge of Massachusetts, the chair of the Committee on Resolutions and a close friend of the president. Roosevelt and Lodge had attended their first Republican convention in 1884 as young men opposing the frontrunner for the nomination that year, James Blaine, whom they viewed as tainted by corruption. They lost that battle, and while others opposed to Blaine had bolted the party, they stayed and worked within the party for change.[14] Two decades later, one was president and the other a prominent senator. The proposed platform noted the dominance of the Republican Party since Lincoln's first election in 1860 and stated that this was not due to chance, but to the confidence of the people in its "high capacity for rule and government." In foreign affairs, it noted that the country, under Republican rule, had seized Cuba from Spain and had set it free, had suppressed insurrection in the Philippines and set up a civil government there, and that the dream of American ownership of land for an isthmian canal connecting the Atlantic and Pacific, through "prompt and vigorous action" by Roosevelt, "is now an accomplished fact." In domestic affairs, it proclaimed that the party enforced existing laws and had enacted new ones protecting the public against "vast aggregations of capital." It called for upholding the gold standard, for enforcing civil service laws, and for continued exclusion of laborers from China, a longstanding issue on the West Coast. Prior to the convention, there was discussion in the press as to whether the party would waver from its historical stand favoring high tariffs, which protected American business and industry from foreign competition, but which also caused higher prices for many items that were the staples of consumption by the American public. As has so often been the case with party platforms, the issue was straddled. Calling protection "a cardinal policy" of the party whose maintenance must be insisted upon, it provided some room for revision, but noted that "rates of duty should be readjusted only when conditions have so changed that the public interest demands their alteration."[15]

One plank addressed the plight of Blacks in the South, where Jim Crow laws enacted in the past several years had effectively taken away their voting rights. A previously never-used part of the Fourteenth Amendment provides that a state's representation in Congress is apportioned based on its population, but that whenever a state denied the right to vote in federal or state elections, its "basis for representation . . . shall be reduced in the proportion which" the excluded voters bear to the whole number of voters. The platform called for action in Congress to determine whether "special discriminations" by any state had unconstitutionally limited the franchise and, if so, demanded a reduction in that state's members of Congress and its votes in the Electoral College.[16] Since taking office in 1901, Roosevelt had reached out to Blacks with appointments to jobs, mainly in the South, and by a famous dinner with Booker T. Washington, actions that angered white southerners. After the convention, a Democratic state senator from Virginia fumed that the "Negro Plank" in the Republican platform was added as "a compliment to the president on account of his being such a rampant negrophile" and that it would ensure that the South would be solidly Democratic once again in the coming election.[17]

The platform ended with praise for Roosevelt, noting that he had "brought to the great responsibilities thus sadly forced upon him a clear hand, a brave heart, and earnest patriotism, and high ideals of public duty and public service." It endorsed his record "without reservation to the considerate judgment of the American people." The reading of the platform was met mostly with silence from those assembled in the Chicago Coliseum, reporters noting that the references to Roosevelt were only "perfunctorily cheered and applauded," and cited this as another example of the lack of enthusiasm at the convention. The proposed platform was approved unanimously, without debate, on a voice vote.[18]

With the adoption of the platform, the second day of the convention was drawing to a close. Like the first, it had been a dull show. Ticket scalpers, facing a dwindling demand for seats in the galleries, had dropped their prices to only a dollar, a fraction of what they had been seeking a few days earlier. Party leaders, at best indifferent to Roosevelt's nomination, were unwilling to stir up their troops in vocal displays of support for him. One reporter jokingly predicted that the delegation from New York, Roosevelt's home state, acted with such coldness to the proceedings in Chicago that they would return home with pneumonia.[19] Something was needed to invigorate the crowd in the Coliseum. Roosevelt and his team found just the right thing.

In the month before the convention, an international crisis was playing out in Africa. In a foreshadowing of what would become all too common in the latter part of the twentieth, and the early part of the twenty-first, centuries, an American was kidnapped and held for ransom by a man who would today be called a terrorist. Ion Perdicaris was a wealthy sixty-four-year-old American expatriate of Greek descent who had been living in Tangier, Morocco, since the 1880s. In May 1904, Perdicaris and his adult stepson, a British citizen, were brazenly taken as hostages by Mulai Ahmed er Raisuni, a Moroccan renegade, who was known by the name of Raisuli. The kidnapping was part of a battle between Raisuli and the young Sultan of Morocco, who was the puppet of a corrupt clique backed by the French and the British. When the American consul in Tangier, Samuel Gunmere, requested that a warship be sent to enforce America's demand for the release of Perdicaris, Roosevelt sent four. It was a classic show of his "big stick" diplomacy and the affair was heavily covered in the nation's newspapers. For the release of his hostages, Raisuli made demands of cash, a title for himself, and revenge against his Moroccan rivals. The government of Morocco, under pressure from the French and the British to end the crisis, agreed to the ransom. When Raisuli, sensing weakness by his opponents, upped his demands, the American government had had enough. On June 21, the day that the Republican convention opened, Gunmere asked for authority to deliver an ultimatum to the Moroccan kidnapper. Roosevelt and his secretary of state, John Hay, responded with a concise statement of American policy that was heard around the world. The terse telegram to Gunmere, under Hay's name, which was immediately released to the public, read: "We want either Perdicaris alive or Raisuli dead."[20] By releasing the telegram, Roosevelt was able to adroitly use it to his advantage. The White House requested that the convention's permanent chairman, Speaker Cannon, convey the American ultimatum to the convention. Just as the convention was about to adjourn on its second day, Cannon complied, and had the clerk read the telegram. It was a political masterstroke—Roosevelt to terrorist: release our hostage or you are a dead man. The convention ignited with a show of patriotism and support for Roosevelt. Thus, the day ended on a high note. Said a prominent senator at the convention, "Magnificent, magnificent! The people want an administration that will stand by its citizens, even if it takes the fleet to do it." The *New York Times* commented that "Roosevelt and Hay at last had succeeded in creating artificial respiration and heart action in the convention through saline treatment."[21]

Within days, Perdicaris was released, and Roosevelt's bluster seemed to have worked. In fact, the final terms of the release had been worked out before receipt of the telegram and Raisuli, far from dead, got his ransom. Cinema buffs may recall a version of this story from a 1975 movie, *The Wind and the Lion*, with a bully Roosevelt played by Brian Keith and a dashing Sean Connery as Raisuli. In a significant departure from reality by Hollywood, the aging male hostage, Ion Perdicaris, was transformed into a young and beautiful woman named Eden Perdicaris, with Candice Bergen starring in the role.[22] Roosevelt would have loved it. The Perdicaris affair has an interesting postscript. In 1933, when a biography of Hay was published, it was revealed that the State Department had learned early during the crisis that Perdicaris was no longer an American citizen. In 1862, while living in Greece, he asked for and was granted Greek citizenship, effectively renouncing his American citizenship. He did so to prevent the Confederate States of America from seizing land that he owned in South Carolina, as they would not take land owned by foreigners. This was something he had never publicized. Roosevelt and Hay did not change their policy upon receipt of this information. Raisuli *thought* he had kidnapped an American for ransom and he *did* make threats. It would have been embarrassing for the administration to turn the fleet around and say, never mind, he's not one of our citizens.[23]

The convention's third day began with the highlight of every convention, the nomination of the party's candidate for president. In contrast to the first two days, the Coliseum was packed, with more women present to observe the speeches and the festivities. There would be only one name placed in nomination. As the alphabetical roll call of the states began, Alabama deferred to Roosevelt's home state of New York, and Frank Black, a former governor of the Empire State, made his way to the podium. Roosevelt's choice of Black to deliver his primary nominating speech was, a reporter noted, "one of those curious turns in politics which excite both interest and wonder."[24] The two men had an awkward history. In 1898, Black was governor and wanted a second two-year term in the office. The New York Republican boss, Thomas Platt, was concerned that Black could not win re-election, due to a scandal in his administration related to overspending and corruption in repairs to the Erie Canal. Tossing Black aside, Platt had turned his support to the young Roosevelt, fresh from his heroism a few months earlier in Cuba during the Spanish American War. Roosevelt won the nomination and the election as governor. Now, six years later, Black was being asked to nominate for president the man who had been used to push him aside and replace him as governor. By all accounts, Black did so without reservation.

Tall and gaunt, Black reminded some of a young, beardless Lincoln. Holding a handkerchief in his left hand and gesturing with his right, Black began his remarks by mocking the disunity of the Democrats, who that year were torn between liberal and conservative factions, proclaiming, "They have neither guns nor ammunition, and if they had they would use them on each other . . . the boomerang has been substituted for the gun." In their search for an identity, said Black, Democrats were looking to the past and had no plans for "the conduct of the fall campaign. Their zeal is chiefly centered in discussion as to what Thomas Jefferson would do if he were living." Republicans, in contrast, said Black, were united in the causes that had motivated them from the beginning: "The name of the Republican party stands over every door where a righteous cause was born . . . . Its flag for more than fifty years has been the sign of hope on every spot where liberty was the word." It is a party that "needs no new name or platform to designate its purposes."[25]

Moving on to the man he was about to nominate, Black declared that Roosevelt was the "single choice to fill the most exalted office in the world." In a few sentences, Black captured the essence of Theodore Roosevelt as president and America's new role in the world:

> [N]o man in that exalted place since Lincoln has been better known in every household in the land. He is not conservative, if conservatism means waiting till it is too late. He is not wise, if wisdom is to count a thing a hundred times when once will do . . . . He believes in going ahead. He believes that in shaping the destinies of this great republic, hope is a higher impulse than regret . . . . A profound student of history, he is to-day the greatest history maker in the world.

A new century, with America an emerging world power, declared Black, demanded that Roosevelt remain at the helm:

> This is the time when great figures must be kept in front. If the pressure is great the material to resist it must be granite and iron. Whether we wish it or not, America is abroad in this world. Her interests are in every street, her name is on every tongue . . . . And in the man whom you will choose, the highest sense of every nation in the world beholds a man who typifies as no other living American does, the spirit and the purposes of the twentieth century . . . . [A]bove all things else he stands for progress, courage and fair play, which are the synonyms of the American name.
> Events sometimes select the strongest man, as lightning goes down the highest rod. And so it is with those events which for many months with unerring sight have led you to a single name which I am chosen only to pronounce: Gentlemen, I nominate for President of the United States the highest living type of the youth, the vigor and the promise of a great country and a great age, Theodore Roosevelt of New York.[26]

Black's speech for Roosevelt was an overwhelming success. One newspaper observed that his remarks were "pointed, witty and enlivening" and made the party's Old Guard "look as if they might take an interest in things." Another said Black's "epigrams were as draughts of wine to the delegates." The absence of enthusiasm at the convention was no more. Chairman Cannon led the cheering, shouting to the crowd, "Get up boys, and yell!" Cannon was one of the GOP's conservative leaders and was personally less than enthusiastic about Roosevelt and his reformist tendencies. A few years later, he would utter one of his most famous quotes: "I am god-damned tired of listening to all of this babble about reform. America is a hell of a success." Despite this, "Uncle Joe" was all in for Roosevelt and stirred up the convention. He waved a tattered American flag with holes in it, one that had first been waved at the 1860 convention that had nominated Lincoln. When the cheering started to lull, Cannon kept it going. Noted a reporter, Cannon "waltzed about the platform like the leading spirit at a country dance . . . [until it] brought blood to his face." Four men came to the stage and unveiled a huge portrait of TR, done in crayon, and slowly turned it for all to see. Shouts of "Roosevelt!, Roosevelt!" filled the air. The demonstration lasted for twenty-three minutes. It was all a little much for Tom Platt, the New York Republican boss whose efforts at the last convention to rid himself of Roosevelt as governor by making him vice president had taken turns he did not foresee. With pandemonium going on all around him, a reporter noted that a stoic Platt "sat with the look of a martyr on his face." Following the demonstration, there were six seconding speeches, including one, per Roosevelt's request, by a Black delegate. The man selected for this was Harry Cummings of Maryland, a respected lawyer and member of Baltimore's city council. His remarks were well-received by the entire convention, especially by his fellow Black delegates, who, a newspaper noted, were "wild in their enthusiasm" over the honor given to one of their own.[27]

The voting on the nomination of Theodore Roosevelt as the party's standard-bearer for president was a formality. A request for a nomination by acclamation was denied, as most delegates wanted to be on the record with their votes and experience the roll call of the states. When the formal process was completed, Chairman Cannon announced that Roosevelt had received all of the 994 votes cast.[28]

The president, during an outdoor lunch with his wife and other family members at the White House, received news of his nomination from his personal secretary. He rose, accepted congratulations from all and, after a few minutes, went back to his office in the Executive Office Building and held court before a throng of reporters. Nothing else was required at that time from him. By tradition, a few weeks later, he would receive a committee appointed by the convention and would then issue a lengthy written statement formally accepting the nomination and laying out his views on the issues and why he wanted to continue in office.[29]

The only thing that remained for the convention was the choice of Roosevelt's running mate. There was no incumbent vice president, as the office had been vacant after Roosevelt assumed the presidency on McKinley's death in 1901. TR had made it known that he favored Robert Hitt, a seventy-year-old congressman from Illinois. Hitt was ready and willing, but it was not to be. Unlike modern times, the presidential nominee at that era had little say in the choice of running mate and it was party bosses, or the delegates, who usually decided the bottom half of the ticket. Roosevelt's support was the death-knell of any chance that Hitt might have had.

Party leaders were not about to appease the president. In their minds, having held their noses and supported Roosevelt, they wanted one of their own a heartbeat away from the presidency. Many members of the Republican establishment favored Charles Fairbanks, a senator from Indiana who was just beginning his second term. Solidly conservative and respected in the Senate, the fifty-two-year-old Fairbanks had been a close ally of McKinley and Hanna. Before fate had intervened and put Roosevelt in the White House, some had viewed Fairbanks as McKinley's likely successor. In many ways, Fairbanks was the antithesis of Roosevelt—tall and lean while TR was short and solid, Fairbanks was "cautious, conservative and . . . does not believe in disturbing the existing order." He was also the opposite of Roosevelt in personality, some in the press referring to him as "the human iceberg." Other names had been tossed about for the bottom of the ticket. Weeks before the convention, a boom for Speaker Cannon lost traction when he renounced any interest in being vice president and made a firm statement that he would decline the nomination if it were offered to him. An effort in Chicago the weekend before the convention to revive a Cannon candidacy was again quickly shot down by him. As the convention's permanent chairman, Cannon vowed that he would never let it adjourn with his name on the ticket. The name of William Howard Taft, then serving as secretary of war in Roosevelt's cabinet, was floated, but got little support from his home state of Ohio. An informal poll among delegates found almost five hundred supporting Fairbanks, with Hitt far behind at just over one hundred. When the New York delegation, some of whose leaders had been promoting Cannon, met the night before the convention and agreed to cast all of its seventy-eight votes for Fairbanks, any chance of a contest for vice president was over.[30]

In the afternoon of its third day, the convention began the process of selecting a running mate for Roosevelt. As with the contest for president, only one name would be formally placed in nomination. A delegate from Illinois announced that he had received a telegram from Congressman Hitt asking that his name not be placed before the convention, "as the sentiment of the country seemed so unanimous for Senator Fairbanks." The main nominating speech for Fairbanks was made by Senator Jonathan Dolliver of Iowa. At the last convention in 1900, Dolliver, considered a rising star in the party, had himself been a prominent candidate for vice president before the Roosevelt deluge overwhelmed that convention and Roosevelt had been nominated as McKinley's running mate.[31] One wonders what thoughts ran through Dolliver's mind, and if he speculated how different this convention might have been, if he had been on the ticket with McKinley in 1900. Dolliver noted that, with Roosevelt's nomination, the leadership of the party was transferring to a younger generation and that Fairbanks was the perfect choice among the new leaders to stand by Roosevelt's side. Fairbanks was praised as a "leader of the senate," and a man in whom the "whole business community" had confidence. Dolliver's speech was followed by four seconding speeches for Fairbanks. Unlike with Roosevelt's nomination an hour or so earlier, the roll call of the states was dispensed with and Fairbanks was nominated by acclamation. It was mid-afternoon and there were trains to catch. After some housekeeping matters, the thirteenth convention of the Republican Party adjourned shortly before 2:30 p. m.[32]

Fairbanks, a delegate to the convention, had stayed in his hotel during the voting, thinking it inappropriate to attend a session in which he would be voted upon for national office. In contrast, Roosevelt had sat through the voting at the 1900 convention on his nomination for vice president. He cast an abstaining vote, while every other delegate had voted for him.[33] After Fairbanks's nomination, he refused an offer to go back to the convention hall riding a circus elephant that had been rented by some of his supporters. Then, as now, the elephant was the symbol of the Republican Party. "No, no, boys—that wouldn't be dignified," said the human iceberg.[34] In this, he was undoubtedly correct.

One man had come to Chicago confident of the makeup of the ticket. Myer Bimberg, known as "Bim the Button Man," a New York trinket dealer, had been a fixture at conventions since 1896, when he showed up at the Republican convention in St. Louis with trunks filled with "McKinley and Hobart" buttons, having correctly predicted that a relative unknown, Garret Hobart of New Jersey, would be nominated as McKinley's running mate. Campaign buttons in that era had to be manufactured well before the start of a convention. A correct guess meant a financial windfall from being the first on the streets of the convention city with buttons touting the two names on the party's ticket; an incorrect guess meant a bad investment in thousands of buttons that could not be sold. In Chicago in 1904, Bimberg arrived with "Roosevelt and Fairbanks" buttons, telling reporters "Guess I've got it right" and "I have staked a bunch" on the prediction. As fate would have it, Bimberg was correct again and, as the convention ended, was a happier and wealthier man.[35]

The Republicans left Chicago having nominated their popular president and, despite some misgivings from the party's Old Guard, were united for the fall campaign. As the nation's political eyes turned to the upcoming Democratic convention, the identity of Roosevelt's opponent in the general election was eagerly awaited.

Democratic Convention

Chauncey Depew, one of the era's Republican senators from New York, was one of the most entertaining speakers of his generation. Always good for a quip or a quote, if alive today, he would be the master of the televised sound bite. During a speech in June 1904 to the Republican convention in Chicago, Depew speculated about the upcoming Democratic convention. "I cannot help thinking," he said, what will happen "when our Democratic friends meet on July 6 . . . . On the one side will be their only president, rising and saying, 'Be sane,' while on the other side, in opposition will come their last candidate for president saying, 'Be Democrats.' The two are incompatible." Depew's joke drew laughter and applause in a hall filled with Republicans, but he had concisely stated the dilemma of the Democratic Party as it headed into its 1904 convention.[36]

In the late nineteenth and early twentieth centuries, the Democratic Party was badly split between conservative and liberal factions. The conservatives were allied with Grover Cleveland, the only Democrat to win the White House since the Civil War. A three-time nominee of his party, Cleveland had served two non-consecutive terms as president, elected in 1884, losing in 1888, and elected again in 1892, winning the popular vote all three times, and the only man in American history to have reclaimed the presidency after having lost it. An economic downturn during his second term made him unpopular, even among many Democrats, and he did not seek another term. He lost control of the party and it turned on him. At the 1896 Democratic convention, a proposal to include in the party's platform a recognition of the "honesty, economy, courage and fidelity" of Cleveland's administration was soundly defeated. His supporters were consistently booed, hissed, and viewed as little better than Republicans by the majority of the delegates and the crowds in the galleries. That convention turned to a relatively unknown former Nebraska congressman, William Jennings Bryan, as its presidential nominee. Then only thirty-six years old, Bryan had electrified the convention with his famous "Cross of Gold" speech, arguing for a plank in the platform favoring the unlimited coinage of silver currency. He came out of nowhere to win the nomination on the fifth ballot. With Bryan's victory, the liberal faction took control of the Democratic Party. Despite being soundly beaten in the 1896 election by the Republican nominee, William McKinley, Bryan was re-nominated in 1900, only to lose to McKinley again, by an even greater margin.[37] As has often occurred in American history, the reputations of unpopular presidents improve once they are out of office, and with the passage of time. By the time that the 1904 campaign season began, with Bryan's two losses, Grover Cleveland was viewed more fondly, was considered an elder statesman, and the Democratic Party's conservative faction, which still viewed him as its leader, was poised to reclaim control.

Cleveland, sixty-seven years old in 1904 and not in good health, had retired to Princeton, New Jersey, and was living a quiet life away from politics. He announced that he would not actively seek the nomination and could not conceive of any circumstances where he would get into the race. Some of his die-hard supporters hoped they could get him to accept a draft, if the convention deadlocked. Bryan, much younger than Cleveland at the age of forty-four, and living in Lincoln, Nebraska, had also stated that he would not seek the 1904 nomination, although he remained active politically, publishing his own weekly newspaper, *The Commoner*, and was a frequent speaker on lecture circuits. With Cleveland and Bryan out of the race, both factions of the Democratic Party would have to look beyond their leader for a nominee. Cleveland's conservative faction, led by two New Yorkers, August Belmont, a wealthy financier and son of a former party chairman, and David Hill, a former governor and senator, turned to a political unknown, Judge Alton Parker, another New Yorker. With Bryan out, there was a void in the leadership of the liberal faction, which publisher William Randolph Hearst hoped to fill and become the party's nominee.

Alton Parker, fifty-two years old, a judge on various New York courts for almost twenty years, had been serving since 1897 as chief judge of the Court of Appeals, that state's highest court, which was an elected position. Parker had dabbled in politics prior to taking the bench, being a delegate at Democratic conventions and heading the statewide gubernatorial campaign of his friend, Hill. As a judge, he had a reputation for being conservative, but did not publicly express his opinions on political matters. Even after agreeing in late 1903 to having his name put forward as a presidential candidate, during the delegate selection process that began in early 1904 and up until the convention, Parker stayed mum on all of the issues of the day. His attraction, according to his backers, was that he was above the political fray and would govern that way as president, although there was little doubt that his views lined up with the conservative faction of the party that was promoting him.[38]

Donald Trump was not the first multi-millionaire businessman and celebrity to seek the presidency. In 1904, a young William Randolph Hearst, at the age of forty-one, was convinced that he was the heir to Bryan as the leader of the liberal wing of the Democratic Party and spent part of his fortune in a quest for the presidency. The similarities between Trump and Hearst are almost eerie. Both had rich fathers and parlayed their inheritances into much greater wealth, both had concerns raised about their morality, both flaunted their wealth, were bluntly critical of their political opponents, were uninspiring orators, and appealed to the masses for their political support. President Theodore Roosevelt, who would later be accused himself of being a demagogue, viewed Hearst as a menacing threat to American politics. The publisher, Roosevelt wrote to a British friend in 1906, "preaches the gospel of envy, hatred, and unrest. His actions so far go to show that he is entirely willing to sanction any mob violence if he thinks that for the moment votes are to be gained by doing so . . . . He is the most potent single influence for evil that we have in our life."[39] There was one key difference between Hearst and Trump—while Trump consistently attacked the media, Hearst *was* the media. The son of a self-made wealthy California mine owner, who late in life managed to buy a seat in the United States Senate, Will Hearst had a checkered past, having been expelled from Harvard (for mailing chamber pots to his professors) and living many of his young adult years as a playboy. Having inherited the *San Francisco Examiner* from his father in the late 1880s, he had an uncanny sense of what would sell newspapers and began a brand of sensational news that became known as yellow journalism, featuring bold headlines, aggressive reporting of government corruption and horrid crimes, extensive use of comics and graphics, the promotion of liberal causes, and not always having an affinity for the truth. Known to his employees as "The Chief," Hearst became wildly successful in the news business, moving into the New York market in 1895 with the purchase of the *New York Journal*. The *Journal* was one of the few major eastern newspapers to support Bryan in the 1896 election. Hearst idolized Bryan. In 1900, largely to support Bryan's run for president that year, Hearst opened his first Midwest newspaper, the *Chicago American*. By 1904, he also had newspapers in Los Angeles and Boston and was well on his way to building a media empire that would eventually include almost thirty newspapers, as well as magazines, news services, and radio stations. After moving to New York, Hearst began a political career and, with the support of Tammany Hall, was elected to Congress from a Manhattan district in 1902. Despite his celebrity status, as a freshman in Congress, Hearst got no important committee assignments, few in Washington paid attention to him, and he soon became bored with congressional sessions and seldom attended. He already had his eyes on a bigger prize—the White House. To run for president, he needed a wife and, in

1903, he married a former chorus girl half his age, whom he had been dating for years. After officially announcing his candidacy in January 1904, his papers began touting Hearst and his agenda. He favored, among other liberal causes, government ownership of railroads and telegraphs, the breakup of monopolies, a graduated income tax, and an eight-hour workday. The Eastern establishment of both parties was aghast at the thought of Hearst as president. In their view, at least Bryan, a deeply religious man, was moral. Typical was an editorial entitled "The Unthinkable Hearst" in the *New York Evening Post*: "The country cannot afford to have its insignia of honor trailed in the mud . . . . We have not yet reached the point where we can be indifferent to the spectacle of an aspirant for our highest office being an Alcibiades without talent or courage or charm . . . . An agitator we can endure; an honest radical we can respect; a fanatic we can tolerate; but a low voluptuary trying to sting his jaded senses to a fresh thrill by turning from private to public corruption, is a new horror in American politics."[40]

Other than Parker and Hearst, the other contenders for the nomination were minor players. Senator Arthur Gorman of Maryland, a conservative and the minority leader in the Senate, had his state's delegates pledged to him, as well as most of those from West Virginia, but never actively entered the race and, as the convention approached, appeared more interested in making sure that the party adopted a conservative platform, than maneuvering for the nomination. A few states had favorite son candidates, lining their delegations up behind home-state politicians who, unless lightning struck, had no hope for the nomination. These included Senator Francis Cockrell of Missouri (a former Confederate general who had been in the Senate for almost three decades), Richard Olney of Massachusetts (a former member of Cleveland's cabinet), Edward Wall of Wisconsin (a businessman and former DNC member), and George Gray of Delaware (a federal judge and former senator). Most were part of the conservative faction of the party and their states would likely go to Parker if more than one ballot was required for the nomination.[41]

The Democrats chose St. Louis over Chicago and New York as the site for their convention, in part because St. Louis did not have a Hearst newspaper and party leaders were concerned that the rantings of a local paper owned by Hearst during the convention could influence its outcome.[42] St. Louis, then the nation's fourth largest city, was also chosen because 1904 would be a banner year for the city, with the eyes of the nation, and of the world, focused on it. The St. Louis World's Fair, officially known as the Louisiana Purchase Exposition, was held in the city's Forest Park from the spring until the fall, and had exhibitions from forty-three states and almost fifty foreign countries. Starting a year late due to logistic and planning delays, the exposition celebrated the centennial of the purchase of the Louisiana Territory from France in 1803 by President Thomas Jefferson. The fair attracted almost twenty million visitors, who marveled at newly-introduced products such as the ice cream cone, hot dogs, hamburgers, Dr. Pepper, and cotton candy. The city also hosted the Olympic Games in 1904, only the third games of the modern Olympic era, and the first held outside of Europe. Much smaller in scope than what the Olympics would become, the St. Louis games had athletes participating from more than a dozen countries and brought international attention to the city.[43]

The convention was held in the St. Louis Exposition and Music Hall, located at Olive and Thirteenth streets, and it was the second time that the Democrats had met there. In 1888, they had convened under the same roof and nominated Grover Cleveland. Away from the convention hall, the center of activity was the Jefferson Hotel, which had opened only a couple of months earlier. With an impressive white marble columned lobby, twelve floors, over four-hundred rooms, and luxurious accommodations, the Jefferson was the talk of the town. In the days before the convention, supporters of some of the minor candidates proselytized in the hotel's lobby, sometimes attracting a crowd, sometimes ignored. High prices in St. Louis shocked some. Two enterprising Michigan delegates, not willing to pay the going price of fifty cents for a shave, took bids from local barbers and found one who, in exchange for volume, agreed to dewhisker the entire fifty-two members of their delegation at a discounted price, and would come to their hotel to perform the service. Local beverages were suspect to some. "St. Louis beer is not like Milwaukee beer," warned a Wisconsin bandleader to his band's members, "When you go to a strange country it is best to go light on the native beverages till you get acclimated."[44]

In the district and state conventions held in the winter and spring, no clear favorite for the party's nomination emerged. Almost half of the approximately one thousand delegates were uncommitted. Of the committed delegates, Parker led with 298, Hearst was second with 138, and Cockrell, Olney, Wall, and Gray far behind, with support from only their own state's delegations. Democrats used two rules at their conventions, both in effect since their first convention in 1832, which complicated their contests. Unlike Republicans, who required only a simple majority to win their nomination, Democrats required a two-thirds vote. Also unlike Republicans, who let each delegate cast his own vote, Democrats permitted a state (if it chose to do so), to impose a unit rule on its delegation, under which all of its votes were cast as a unit for the candidate favored by the majority. Historically, the two-thirds rule gave the South, which had about a third of the overall delegates, a veto over nominations, and the unit rule gave state party bosses more power, since they could ignore the minority in their delegations and negotiate deals and favors by delivering all of their state's votes. In the days before the convention, the momentum was all toward Parker, as uncommitted delegations announced their support for him. By the time the convention opened, it was clear that the conservative faction of the party was back in control. "Old-Timers Are Back" proclaimed a prominent pre-convention headline. With the opposition unable to agree on any single alternative, Parker's nomination appeared to be inevitable.[45]

William Jennings Bryan, the nominee of the last two Democratic conventions, arrived in St. Louis on July 3, set up shop in a suite of rooms on the second floor of the Jefferson Hotel and immediately began seeing a stream of visitors. He was accompanied only by a young assistant, who served as his gatekeeper, and who stood outside of Bryan's rooms to usher in all who wanted to see one of the most famous men in America. Among the first in line were Mr. and Mrs. F. L. Taylor of St. Louis, along with their three-year-old triplet boys. The parents proudly introduced the lads, named William, Jennings, and Bryan, to their namesake. A jovial Bryan patted the boys on the head and told the parents that he was aware of two other sets of triplets who had also been so named. At the day's end, Bryan made it known that he was not going to have his liberal faction of the party go down without a fight. He released a statement asserting that he found it "highly improbable, if not impossible" for Parker to be nominated, noting Parker's failure to have publicly stated his positions on the issues, his having placed his fate in the hands of Wall Street financiers like August Belmont and David Hill, and the widely-held belief that Parker could not beat Roosevelt in the general election. There was gamesmanship in Bryan's statement because, by then, opinions were almost universal that Parker would be nominated, if not on the first ballot, then on the second or third. Bryan, a delegate from Nebraska, noted in his statement that he would be his state's representative on the committee drafting the platform. On the Fourth of July, the Great Commoner, as Bryan was known, was the featured speaker at the World's Fair, the type of event in which he thrived. Otherwise, he kept up his pre-convention meetings and, as the *Baltimore Sun* observed, "endeavoring to make trouble."[46]

Tammany Hall always provided an interesting side script to Democratic conventions of the era. The New York City political organization, made up largely of working men and immigrants, controlled many local offices and was a powerhouse within the city, but was always battling for statewide control of the party. If the establishment New York Democrats took one position, Tammany reflexively took the other. In 1904, with David Hill and other leaders of the statewide party supporting Judge Parker, Tammany's leader, Charles Murphy, lined up his organization behind a former president from New York, Grover Cleveland, who had flatly declared that he was not in the race. This support for Cleveland was ironic, since Tammany had vehemently opposed him when he was New York's governor and in his prior runs for president. Trainloads of Tammany's rank-and-file members, called "braves," always descended on Democratic convention cities to have a good time, whoop it up, and could be counted on to find a way to pack the galleries at the convention hall, tickets or no tickets, and vocally support whatever cause or candidate their leaders favored. Well over a thousand of Tammany's braves left New York for St. Louis, having loaded cases upon cases of "varied stock of drinkables" onto their trains. Upon their arrival, many who had never left the confines of New York City, had difficulty understanding that there was a time difference between New York and St. Louis. Whatever time it was, one proclaimed, "It's time for a drink!" They had already gotten a head start en route. A reporter at the train station noted that "Beer simply oozed from them in the sultry St. Louis weather" and, with their leaders already in town, commented that "the brains had come yesterday. It was the lungs and feet which arrived today."[47]

The Hearst team arrived in St. Louis and, as might be expected from the campaign of a man with immense wealth, planned to make their man's presence in the race known. They had an unlimited supply of lithograph posters of the famous publisher, which they gave away to any shop owner or person on the street who would take one. Hearst's mother sent a train car filled with California fruits from her own farms for the hospitality suite of the Golden State's delegation, which was firmly behind her son's candidacy. Hearst, estimated to have spent more than $600,000 of his own money on the campaign, came to Chicago to woo more delegates, a move that was considered unseemly in an era when candidates did not attend conventions, but observed from afar. His presence had little impact on the race.[48] A couple of days before the convention, a salesman in the lobby of the Jefferson Hotel was hawking new-fangled noise-makers, a combination of a horn and a cowbell, which he bragged "beats all ear-splitters since the Deluge. . . . It's enough to drive 'em crazy." A man suggested that he go up to the tenth floor, where the Hearst campaign managers were staying. A few minutes later, the salesman returned with a smile on his face and bought his tipster a drink. The Hearst men had purchased his entire inventory. Lacking votes, the Hearst supporters at least intended to make some noise at the convention.[49]

The convention was called to order by James Jones, the chairman of the Democratic National Committee (DNC) at noon on Wednesday, July 6. The heat in the arena bordered on oppressive and, to cool themselves, thousands waved palm leaf fans that had been placed on their chairs, as a promotion, by a St. Louis newspaper. Jones introduced his committee's choice of John Sharp Williams of Mississippi, the party's minority leader in the House of Representatives, as the convention's temporary chairman. Williams then launched into a two-hour speech, the equivalent of the keynote speech at a modern convention. He went through a point-by-point criticism of the speech that his counterpart, Elihu Root, had given at the recent Republican convention, but the loudest applause came not from his denunciation of Republicans, but from his praise for a former Democratic leader. Williams proclaimed that it was due to the "dogged persistency and indomitable will of Grover Cleveland" that the gold standard had initially been adopted and that the other party was now trying to "steal his thunder." At the two prior Democratic conventions, where support for the free coinage of silver had reigned, such a statement would have gotten a speaker hissed off of the stage. Instead, this convention erupted at the mention of the name of the former Democratic president, a demonstration that lasted for fifteen minutes. If any evidence was needed that the conservatives were now back in charge of the party, this was it. One could see it in looking around the convention hall. A reporter commented on the change in the appearance of the delegates and the galleries from the 1900 convention in Kansas City: "This convention is made up of men of a distinctly more substantial and thoughtful character than that of 1900 . . . . The people who think it is a crime to have succeeded and made money do not throng the galleries . . . and it is not considered disreputable to be a banker. At Kansas City, they were called 'money changers.'" After Williams' speech, an invitation was read to all of the delegates to attend the World's Fair while they were in St. Louis. The convention then formed its standard committees (for credentials of the delegates, for permanent organization, for rules, and to draft the party's platform) and adjourned for the day.[50]

The highlight of the convention's second day was a battle over the report of the credentials committee concerning the seating of delegates from Illinois. There were two competing factions, one headed by John Hopkins, a former Chicago mayor, and one by Carter Harrison, Jr., the Windy City's sitting mayor. The Hopkins faction was allied with Roger Sullivan, Chicago's Democratic political boss. At the state convention, the Hopkins forces had delegates to St. Louis chosen by a committee it controlled, rather than having the delegates selected at local conventions held in congressional districts, which was the method generally used. The majority of the Committee on Credentials recommended seating the Hopkins faction. Both factions were pledged to Hearst, so the dispute was irrelevant to the outcome of the presidential nomination. William Jennings Bryan, who was not a member of the committee, decided to lead the credentials fight before the entire convention on behalf of the minority Harrison faction. Hopkins and his political ally, boss Sullivan, had opposed Bryan in his 1896 run for the White House, so Bryan's action was no doubt, in part, revenge against them over past actions. Perhaps he sincerely thought a wrong had been committed that warranted his personal intervention. More likely, Bryan knew that taking the lead in the Illinois credentials battle would give him an early opportunity to address the convention. Eight years earlier, in Chicago, he had wowed that convention and the nation with his "Cross of Gold" speech in a platform debate over the free coinage of silver, which had propelled him from a dark horse candidate to the party's presidential nomination. Now, he had to be thinking, another oratory masterpiece could sway this convention, if not to him, at least to a nominee more acceptable than Alton Parker.[51]

Bryan was encouraged by his reception upon entering the hall that afternoon and the New York brain trust for Parker had to be concerned. A convention that had given a thunderous ovation the day before at the mentioning of the name of Grover Cleveland now gave Bryan, Cleveland's nemesis in the party, an even louder demonstration. While partially out of respect for a two-time nominee, the cheering for Bryan in the galleries seemed to be orchestrated. It was. Tammany and the Hearst campaign had packed the galleries, with instructions to their men to go wild for Bryan. The two groups did not agree on much, but their leaders knew that cheering for Bryan gave the appearance that the Parker forces did not control the convention. For twenty minutes, the hoopla for Bryan went on. The loud noisemakers purchased by the Hearst campaign a couple of days earlier at the Jefferson Hotel no doubt added to the frenzy. When Bryan walked to the podium to speak on the Illinois contest, it began again.[52] Despite having a cold, Bryan's strong voice reached all areas of the hall, the first speaker to do so. As the man who had given the most famous speech of his generation began his remarks, a reporter wondered, "Is he going to do it again?" The speech was classic Bryan—emotional, energetic, and captivating. Early on, he lost a cuff link due to the waving of his arms.[53] He spoke, he said, not for himself, but for the principle of majority rule. Hopkins and his cronies who controlled the Illinois state convention, he charged, were no better than train robbers:

> That Convention was dominated by clique of men who deliberately, purposely, boldly trampled upon the rights of the Democrats of Illinois. The evidence shows that no band of train robbers ever planned a raid upon a train more deliberately or with less conscience than they did. And the men who planned it and who carried it out, have the audacity, the impudence and the insolence to say that, because they certified that what they did was regular, you cannot go behind their certificate . . . .
>
> But what will you tell these men? Will you indorse the action of that Convention? . . . . If they had a majority of the Convention, why did they not permit roll calls? . . . . Men do not do wrong, as a rule, unless they think it is necessary to do so to carry out some object . . . . Their whole conduct shows that their purpose was conceived in sin, brought forth in iniquity and carried out to the destruction of Democratic hopes in that State . . . .

Now their sin rests upon them; you do not bear it. But if you decide to seat these men . . . you take from the shoulders of [the Hopkins faction] the odium that they ought to bear, and put in upon the Democratic party of the nation.[54]

The debate over the Illinois contest went on for four hours, and it was bitter. As Bryan's opponents spoke, they were jeered and interrupted by the Tammany and Hearst shouters in the galleries. Bryan spoke again, in rebuttal. While the galleries again voiced their support for him, a reporter noted, the delegates, most of whom supported the party's conservative faction, sat "quiet but spellbound." The roll call vote on the minority report to seat the Illinois delegates that Bryan favored resulted in a resounding defeat for him, with only 299 votes supporting his position and 647 against. The delegates had appreciated a good speech, but had not bought his cause. A headline about Bryan in a Chicago newspaper—"Stampedes the Galleries, But Fails to Move Delegates"—accurately summarized his dilemma. The vote was a sign of the strength of the Parker forces at the convention. It showed that, despite the ability to make a lot of noise from the galleries, those opposed to Parker could not muster more than one-third of the delegate vote and were therefore unlikely to block his nomination.[55]

After the Illinois fight ended, the dinner hour was approaching. The Committee on Permanent Organization gave its report, recommending Champ Clark, a member of Congress from Missouri, as the convention's permanent chairman. Clark had a long speech prepared, which had been released to the press. However, as he began speaking, many in the galleries, having sat through hours of the Illinois debate and getting hungry, began to leave, and even some of the delegates headed for the exits. Sensing that the crowd was in no mood for another long speech, Clark wisely cut his remarks short after five minutes and the convention's second day came to an end.[56]

When the convention met on Friday for its third day, Chairman Clark called for the report of the Committee on Resolutions. When told that the committee was still meeting, Clark appointed his own committee to find out the reason for the delay. Sometime later, Clark's committee reported back. The good news was that the Committee on Resolutions promised to bring a unanimous report on the party's platform to the convention for its consideration; the bad news was that it would not be ready until eight o'clock that evening. With that, the convention adjourned at noon, for eight hours, for the committee to finish its work. While waiting to hear back on the status of the Committee on Resolutions, Richmond Hobson of Alabama, a prominent figure from the recent Spanish-American War and who would later be awarded the Medal of Honor, was called upon to speak. He delivered what can only be described as a racist tirade. The plank in the Republican platform threatening to reduce representation in Congress of states that had denied voting rights to Blacks had struck a nerve with southern Democrats. The white race, said Hobson, must remain "absolutely distinct" from all others, or it will "commit suicide." Hobson condemned President Roosevelt's appointment of a Black man to a federal office in South Carolina, a man who, said Hobson, "is out of the class that should dominate." Southerners, by passing Jim Crow laws to restrict the voting rights of Blacks, argued Hobson, were only trying to resolve "how the men who care for those that are charged to them may work out their salvation the best." Following Hobson's speech, the band in the hall played Dixie, a frequent tune at Democratic conventions but, a reporter noted, this time, it was received with "more than the usual tribute." Interestingly, although Hobson's speech was widely reported in newspapers, it was omitted from the official transcript of the convention, party leaders obviously concerned how it would play to northern audiences during the coming campaign.[57]

Meetings of the Committee on Resolutions lasted all night and continued throughout the next day. Monetary policy, the issue that had so divided the party for a decade, was the main point of contention. The opponents in the committee were David Hill of New York, a leader in the Parker campaign, and William Jennings Bryan, the man who seemed to be in the thick of every battle in St. Louis. Bryan wanted a statement reaffirming the party's last platforms in 1896 and 1900, which had supported the free coinage of silver, and upon which he had run as the party's nominee. Hill wanted a statement strongly supporting the gold standard. A compromise position, which had been adopted in the spring by some state parties in their platforms, most notably in Mississippi, conceded that the gold standard was law and would remain, but without admitting that the Democrats had been wrong in their past support of silver. This Mississippi alternative stated that the discovery of additional gold reserves around the world in the last few years had increased the money supply to the extent that the unlimited coinage of silver was no longer a relevant political issue. The Parker men could live with this cleverly worded alternative. Bryan did not like it. There were also battles over other planks, with Bryan wanting a stronger statement for tariff reform than Hill, stronger language opposing trusts, and with Bryan favoring a constitutional amendment for an income tax, which Hill opposed. Unexpectedly, Bryan won on almost every point. As one author has commented, "Bryan mopped the floor with Hill and tore the platform to shreds. For sixteen hours . . . Bryan took up the platform plank by plank, moving to strike out phrases and planks and substitute his own. Surprisingly, for a man who was supposed to be dead and buried, he carried a majority of the committee with him on each point . . . Bryan won, in the face of what should have been overwhelming opposition, one of his greatest victories."[58] The committee decided, by a vote of thirty-five to fifteen, to totally omit *any* reference to the gold standard from the platform, even the Mississippi compromise language that the conservatives supported. Bryan's language on tariffs and trusts was adopted. Hill did manage to keep support for an income tax out of the platform, but had little else to show for his efforts in the committee. Many conservatives were furious with Hill over rumors of the concessions made. We are "simply benumbed," said one.[59]

On Friday evening, the convention resumed. The hall was packed, as the nominations and voting for president were on the agenda. Newspapers reported that the rules for admission to the galleries were "utterly ignored," with multiple people allowed to enter on a single ticket, or with no ticket at all. A Tammany man proudly told a reporter "we don't need tickets, we've got a doorkeeper," *i.e.*, a bribed official at the gate who would let the "braves" in at will. The size of the crowd added to the intense heat in the hall. They were boisterous and they "came to participate."[60]

Before the featured event, the platform had to be approved. It was read by the chairman of the Committee on Resolutions, Senator John Daniel of Virginia. He announced at the outset that his committee had unanimously approved its final product, pleasing those who wanted to avoid conflict, but worrying those who wondered what compromises had been made to reach a consensus. Daniel, his voice weak from hours of meetings and drowned out by noise in the overcrowded hall, was "but a silent figure with moving lips" to those sitting more than ten rows from the podium. Despite the conservative faction's control of the convention, the proposed platform was one on which the liberal Bryan could have run, not surprisingly, since it was he in the marathon committee sessions who had the most influence over its writing. It condemned imperialism, favored direct election of senators, and immediate independence for the Philippines. On tariffs, it denounced "protectionism as a robbery of the many to enrich the few" and called for revisions and reductions "by the friends of the masses." Trusts and monopolies were denounced as "indefensible and intolerable." There was a strong response to the plank of the Republicans calling for a congressional investigation to determine if the South had unconstitutionally limited the voting rights of Blacks by the passage of Jim Crow laws. Democrats, the party of white supremacy in the South, regretted the "reopening of wounds now happily healed" over the race issue and condemned the "Bourbon-like, selfish, and narrow spirit" of the Republican platform, "which sought to kindle anew the embers of racial and sectional strife." The sitting Republican president, Theodore Roosevelt, was criticized for his repeated "executive usurpation" of power. One of these, alleged the platform, was the yet to be built Panama Canal, a product of what the Democrats called the president's violations of the Constitution, of laws and treaties, but which they nonetheless pledged, if elected, to proceed with and build. In general, the Roosevelt administration was denounced for its "spasmodic, erratic, sensational, spectacular and arbitrary" actions. Notably absent from the proposed platform was any reference of support for the gold standard, given the compromises agreed to by the committee. The silence on this issue was deafening to many in the party's eastern establishment, who were dismayed that this key issue had been totally left out. Despite this, the proposed platform was approved on a voice vote without any discussion.[61]

As the clock struck nine, the agenda moved to nominations for president, and a night of seemingly endless speechmaking began that would last until dawn. The roll call of the states began with Alabama, which yielded to New York, and Martin Littleton went to the podium to nominate the frontrunner, Judge Parker. A lawyer and the borough president of Brooklyn, the thirty-two-year-old Littleton had a reputation as a spirited orator, and would go on to have a long career as a prominent criminal defense attorney. He began with a plea for party unity, arguing "we are together again." In a clear reference to the party's losses under Bryan in the last two elections, and the free silver platforms on which Bryan had run, Littleton argued for that it was time for a change and for victory: "It is better to give up some untimely doctrine and occasionally succeed, than to hold them all faithfully and always fail . . . . Winning is not wicked, strategy is not a sin." He criticized Roosevelt for multiple alleged abuses of power. In contrast to the current president, New York, he said, was offering, in Judge Parker, "a man who puts against the strenuous sword play of a swaggering administration, a simple faith in the perfect power of the Constitution; a man who puts against an executive republic the virtue of a constitutional republic; a man who puts against executive usurpation a knowledge of and a deep love for the poise and balance of its three great powers." Portraying Parker's silence on the issues of the day as a virtue, Littleton proclaimed:

> If you ask me why he has been silent, I tell you it is because he does not claim to be the master of the Democratic party, but is content to be its servant. If you ask me why he has not outlined a policy for this Convention, I tell you that he does not believe that policies should be dictated, but that the sovereignty of the party is in the untrammeled judgment and wisdom of its members; if you ask me what his policy will be, if elected, I tell you that it will be that policy which finds expression in the platform of the party.[62]

After Littleton's speech, newspapers reported that a "hurricane broke out" and shouting and flag-waving for Parker began, which lasted for twenty-five minutes. As with most convention demonstrations of that era, it was orchestrated. Men and boys were usually stationed around the arena to spur them on and to keep them going. Reporters timed them to the minute and the next day's newspapers would duly note which candidate's uproar was loudest and lasted the longest. As one cynical observer noted, the spectacle was one of "Men dancing and jumping on chairs, parading about with banners and flags, drunk with the unintelligent, emotional frenzy of a campmeeting." It all suggested that, in choosing a candidate for the highest office in the land, "the longest fit of childish and senseless yelling should be the decisive factor."[63]

William Randolph Hearst was nominated by Delphin Delmar, a prominent California attorney known as "the Silver-tongued Orator of the West," who focused on the publisher's appeal to the masses. The overriding issue in 1904, said Delmar, "is whether this Government shall be carried on for the benefit of the people, and of the whole people, or whether it shall be manipulated for the benefit of a privileged class." There was much support for Hearst in the galleries, which his team had packed, and, as a result, the demonstration following Delmar's speech was more vocal and longer than the one for Parker. A seconding speech for Hearst, by Chicago attorney Clarence Darrow, was much more grounded in reality than in hope. Darrow acknowledged that Hearst's cause was lost and bluntly criticized the conservative majority that had once again taken over the party: "It seems to have been decreed by fate," said Darrow, "that the men who scuttled the Democratic ship shall once again be placed in charge." The time will one day come, he hoped, when the party will turn away from those who love the "golden God and the flesh-pots of Egypt" and it will "come back once more to the common people that it served so long." [64]

The night wore on. Many in the galleries, who had been vocal and mostly pro-Hearst, began to leave. There were more nominations, of George Gray by Delaware, Nelson Miles by Kansas, Francis Cockrell by Missouri, Richard Olney by Massachusetts, Edward Wall by Wisconsin and John Sharp Williams by North Dakota. It seemed as though every delegate wanted to give a long seconding speech for one candidate or the other, until finally, as night inched toward daybreak, the rules were amended to limit the speeches to only four minutes each. Still, they continued.⁶⁵

Hours into the speechmaking, around half past four in the morning, Bryan was recognized to give a seconding speech. For whom, he did not say. He asked for and, as a courtesy to the party's former presidential standard-bearer, was given an exemption from the four-minute time limit. His remarks were more about himself and his past two campaigns than any candidate in the current contest. Noting that he had been ill and had been without sleep for two nights, he requested patience with his strained voice, and, once again, William Jennings Bryan addressed a Democratic convention, still proud and defiant:

> Eight years ago a Democratic National Convention placed in my hands the standard of the party and commissioned me as its candidate. Four years later that commission was renewed. I come to-night to this Democratic National Convention to return the commission. You may dispute whether I have fought a good fight, you may dispute whether I have finished my course, but you cannot deny that I have kept the faith . . . .

He noted the emphasis by Republicans at their convention, in their support for Roosevelt, on militarism, manliness, and the willingness to fight wars, and compared it with the wealthy eastern elite that had resumed control of the Democratic Party in St. Louis: "Must we choose between a god of war and a god of gold? Is there no choice between them? If there is anything that compares in hatefulness with militarism it is plutocracy, and I insist that the Democratic party ought not to be compelled to choose between militarism on one side and plutocracy on the other side." He noted with pride the platform that he had a large role in drafting, during hours of meetings at which many of his views had been adopted: "We were in session sixteen hours last night . . . . But, my friends, I never spent sixteen hours to better purpose in my life—because I helped to bring the party together, so we could have a unanimous platform to go before the country on in this campaign."

Bryan moved on to the candidates for president, saying, "I have not asked the Democrats of this nation to nominate any particular man . . . . We have a platform on which we all can stand. Now give us a ticket behind which all of us can stand." He then reviewed some of the candidates. Of Hearst, he said, "though he has money, [he] pleads the cause of the poor." But there was no endorsement of the man in the race whose views on the issues were closest to his own, and who had lavishly supported him in 1896 and in 1900. The Great Commoner was not yet ready to pass the baton of leadership of the liberal wing of the party to anyone. Bryan, undoubtedly, was already thinking about a comeback in 1908. He never mentioned Parker by name. Bryan ended up seconding the nomination of Senator Cockrell of Missouri, because, "He is known; he has a record, and can be measured by it," an obvious dig at Parker, who had no political record and had refused to state his views on the issues. Knowing that a candidate of his liking would not prevail, Bryan said he had come to St. Louis to represent the more than six million people who had voted for him in the past two elections, and "I came to get them as good a platform as I could . . . . I came to help to get as good a candidate as possible."⁶⁶

The roll call of the states to decide the party's presidential nominee finally began. Parker jumped out to an early lead and it was never close. After all had been called, the tally was 658 for Parker and 200 for Hearst, with the rest far behind. Cockrell had 42, Olney 27, Wall 27, Gray 12, and rest were in single digits. Parker was only nine votes short of the two-thirds required for the nomination and, before the first ballot was made official, Idaho, Nevada, West Virginia, and Washington switched some of their votes to the judge from New York, making him the official nominee with 670 votes, and with Hearst dropping to 181. Other than his home state of California, the only states where Hearst won more than ten votes were Illinois and Iowa. The nomination was then made unanimous and, as dawn broke over St. Louis, shortly before six o'clock on a Saturday morning, the convention adjourned until the afternoon. The usual demonstration for the new nominee was dispensed with and most of the weary delegates went to their hotels and to bed.[67]

While the convention may have been satisfied with the compromises reached to unanimously adopt its platform, one man was not. And it was his opinion that mattered most. During the convention, Judge Parker was at his home near Esopus, New York, on the Hudson River. His court was in summer recess and he spent his time taking morning swims in the river, doing chores around his farm, and working on judicial opinions. He had no campaign aides with him, had declined a special telegraph line to the convention hall, and told reporters that he would keep up with events in St. Louis as most others did, through newspapers. Despite this, it did not take long for the contents of the platform to reach him. Having been assured that some version of a plank supporting the gold standard would be in it, Parker was shocked to learn by telephone on Friday night that it had been removed. After a restless night and review of the Saturday morning newspapers, he decided to, in effect, toss a hand grenade into the convention. Parker fired off a strongly-worded telegram to William Sheehan, his personal representative in St. Louis, threatening to withdraw as the party's nominee: "I regard the gold standard as firmly and irrevocably established . . . . As the platform is silent on the subject my views should be made known to the convention, and if they are proved to be unsatisfactory to the majority I request that you decline the nomination for me at once, so that another may be nominated before adjournment." The telegram was sent from the Western Union office in Esopus at noon and, after some delay, arrived in St. Louis in mid-afternoon.[68] It was contrary to all that Littleton had said in his nominating speech for Parker hours earlier. Parker would not be a silent servant of the party and accept whatever the party dictated. Was he demanding that the platform debate be reopened and that a pro-gold plank be inserted and, if this was not done, would he really decline the nomination? After its all-night session and with the convention set to resume that afternoon to wrap up its business, things suddenly became more interesting.

Chairman Clark gaveled the convention to order for its fourth day, in the early afternoon on Saturday. Telegrams were read from two of the defeated candidates, Hearst and Cockrell, pledging their support for Parker. A North Dakota delegate then offered a resolution of condolences to the family of a delegate from his state, Jacob Birder, who had died from injuries sustained a few days earlier in a train accident while en route to the convention. The resolution was unanimously adopted and an Alabama delegate quickly moved for a recess due to the "sad news" and "to give the delegates an opportunity to confer" over the tragedy. Clark ruled that a voice vote on the motion had carried and, no sooner had the session begun, it ended. Things at conventions are not always what they appear to be. Grief for the recently departed Mr. Birder had nothing to do with the recess. Party leaders were still trying to agree on their choice for vice president, which was the next item on the agenda, and, moreover, rumors of Parker's telegram had begun to swirl.[69] Political parties want smoothly-run conventions with as few surprises as possible. Democrats had a potential disaster on their hands. Said South Carolina Senator Ben Tillman upon hearing the news from Parker, "The Democratic party can always be relied on to make a damn fool of itself at the critical time." Its newly-minted presidential nominee was threatening to decline his nomination, not over something in the platform, but over something *not* in the platform. Panicked party leaders huddled to deal with this unexpected crisis. What to do? The convention had yet to nominate a running mate for Parker; maybe it would also have to select a new presidential nominee. In a meeting at the Southern Hotel, the Missouri delegation developed a plan to withdraw Parker's nomination. Initially, party leaders had hoped to deal with this bombshell quietly, keep it under wraps, and continue with the selection of a nominee for vice president. It was not to be.[70]

When the convention resumed three hours later, in the late afternoon, it moved forward with nominations for vice president. Speeches were made. Illinois nominated John Robert Williams, Colorado nominated George Turner, West Virginia nominated Henry Davis, and Kansas nominated William Harris. Few listened. All around the convention floor, delegates were huddled in small groups, all talking about the rumored Parker telegram. Party leaders had by then decided that Davis would be their choice for vice president, but were still huddling in the back of the hall about how to deal with the Parker situation. In the galleries, most of the public was unaware as to what was really going on. After the nominating speeches ended, when Chairman Clark called for a roll call vote for vice president, a Texas delegate, who had had enough of the charade, strongly objected, stating "[I]t seems to me we ought not to proceed to nominate a candidate for Vice-President at this time." Moving for a recess, he continued, "I think the delegates understand what I mean." Citing "the present exigency confronting the Convention," he declared that he and others "want to know, before a candidate for Vice-President is nominated who will be the nominee of this Convention for President." The cat was now fully out of the bag, the motion carried, and the convention recessed in disarray. Upon hearing the news of the Parker telegram, Hearst, who had left St. Louis by train hours earlier, reversed course and headed back, hoping against hope that the contest for the presidential nomination would be reopened.[71]

When it began its third session of the day, at 8:30 p.m., Parker's telegram had still not been released. Confusion and anger reigned in the hall. At the outset, Governor Vardaman of Mississippi rose and demanded answers: "[L]et us find out what is that rumor which . . . has seemed to create almost disorder in this hall. Let the gentleman from New York, to whom the telegram was addressed, if it is a matter which the Convention should consider and which affects this Convention—read the telegram; let the truth be known; and then let us proceed to business." Another purported telegram from Parker, published in an afternoon newspaper and allegedly sent to Senator Carmack of Tennessee, was read to the convention and in it Parker demanded that a pro-gold plank be put in the platform, or the convention would have to nominate someone else. When it was learned that the chairman of the New York delegation was not in the hall, there was more confusion and stalling. Finally, around 10:00 p.m., the full text of Parker's telegram to Sheehan was read to the convention, and it was less stinging than what had been reported. It was also revealed that the Carmack telegram was a fraud, created by some reporters that afternoon to cause a stir. John Sharp Williams of Mississippi, who had been the convention's temporary chairman, argued that, in the legitimate telegram, there was not "one word about 'requiring' or 'demanding' or asking or requesting, that anything shall be placed in the Democratic platform" and that, at worst, Parker was simply acting from "a too sensitive spirit of honor," not wanting to be misunderstood as to his personal beliefs on the monetary issue.[72]

After hours of meetings, party leaders had decided that the best strategy was as little action as possible. A telephone conversation between Sheehan and Parker had assured Parker's consent to the plan. Williams read to the delegates the draft of a response telegram that had been prepared, telling Parker, in effect, thank you for your concern, but don't worry yourself over nothing. It read: "The platform adopted by this convention is silent on the question of the monetary standard, because it is not regarded by us as a possible issue in this campaign, and only campaign issues were mentioned in the platform. Therefore, there is nothing in the views expressed by you in the telegram just received which would preclude a man entertaining them from accepting a nomination on said platform." There then followed a debate on whether to send the response. Bryan, who had been sick in bed most of the day, having just been diagnosed with pneumonia, roused himself, came to the hall against his doctor's advice, and weighed in. He recounted the long hours he spent in the meetings of the resolutions committee and the compromises that all had agreed upon that led to the platform's silence on the monetary issue. He put the blame for the current crisis directly on Parker, for his repeated failure to address the issues in the months before the convention. Said Bryan, "I think it is a manly thing to express his opinion before the delegates act finally upon his position, but it would have been a manlier thing had he expressed his opinion before the voters throughout the country went to their caucuses and their primaries and sent instructed delegates here . . . . It is the Judge's fault that he did not speak sooner, and not our fault. He has been invited to speak on numerous and sundry occasions." Bryan stated that he was opposed to sending the proposed response to Parker because, in doing so, he felt that the convention would, in effect, be endorsing the gold standard. As a free silver advocate who had ridden that issue to the party's last two presidential nominations, Bryan advised that he would not be a party to such an action. If that is what was desired, he said, the convention should be honest with the people and formally put it in the platform. Long and heated exchanges followed, with most speakers favoring sending the proposed response to Parker, and with Bryan pushing back, but making it clear that he would not bolt the convention if his view did not prevail. Finally, at one o'clock in the morning, a roll call was held and the convention voted by a resounding margin, 794 to 191, to send the response. As with the Illinois credentials debate earlier in the convention, Bryan had his say, but he had lost badly.[73]

As an anticlimax, the convention then voted on a running mate for Parker. On the first ballot, Henry Davis of West Virginia led with 654 votes, with his closest challenger, John Robert Williams of Illinois, receiving only 165 votes. Davis was only thirteen votes shy of the two-thirds vote that was needed. With everyone tired and ready to go home, a motion to make Davis's nomination unanimous was carried, and, after four days and one all-night session, in the wee hours of a Sunday morning, the convention adjourned.[74]

Parker received news of the convention's final outcome in the middle of the night and, after a brief rest, attended church that Sunday morning and received guests in the afternoon. Generally, the reaction in the press to his telegram, at least in the East, was positive. A "Chorus of Approval" read a headline in the *Baltimore Sun*. A "master political stroke" wrote the *Washington Post*. He was praised as having taken a "sublime moral stand" in making sure his views were known. Parker was also credited for having shown independence from David Hill, his main promoter, who had agreed with Bryan during the negotiations over the platform to remove any support for the gold standard. Some compared him to Henry Clay, who, in another era, had declared "I had rather be right than be president." The *Wall Street Journal* was less kind, arguing that "The platform is Bryan's; the candidate is Hill's" and that the two were irreconcilable.[75]

While the conservative faction had won the battle of 1904, the war for the soul of the Democratic Party was not over. William Jennings Bryan, far from being humiliated in St. Louis, had played a prominent role at the convention. He was well-received by the galleries and had bested his opponents in drafting the platform. He would later write, while "I did not get into the platform all that I wanted . . . . I kept out of the platform everything to which I objected."[76] In each of the key events of the convention, Bryan had loomed large. Commented one observer, "[W]hen Mr. Bryan retired from the convention, exhausted, sick and defeated, he was and is the biggest man in the party, and more a power than ever. Nor is the reason a secret. He has the courage of his convictions. He is outspoken. He uses no trickery or subterfuge, but all men may plainly see his course and hear his views. He stands for the plain people—the masses."[77] Even a Republican who attended the convention, and who wrote a review of it in a national publication, had a grudging respect for the man Republicans loved to hate. Of Bryan, he observed, "the one strong, commanding personality of the convention, in my judgment, was, strangely enough, William J. Bryan of Nebraska . . . . [I] came away from St. Louis with a greatly heightened opinion of Mr. Bryan's character, and with a new respect for his sincerity and courage . . . . He was honest with the convention and he wished the convention to be honest with the people."[78] The conservative faction of the Democratic Party had won the battle, but it had not won the war. It had not, as it had hoped to do in St. Louis, driven a stake through the heart of Bryanism. The Great Commoner and his cause would survive and would live to fight another day.

The Democrats left St. Louis with some optimism but, with Alton Parker, a relatively unknown political newcomer as their nominee, and uncertainty as to whether the rift in the party's two factions had truly healed, they entered the fall campaign as decided underdogs to a popular incumbent president, Theodore Roosevelt, and the Republicans.

The Campaign and Election

Two New Yorkers were the nominees, only the second time in American history (Lincoln and Douglas of Illinois in 1860 being the other) that the two major parties had standard-bearers from the same state.

From the outset of the campaign, Roosevelt was seen as the favorite, although he professed several times to friends and family that he had "not the vaguest idea" if he would win or not. As the incumbent president, he followed tradition and stayed mostly at the White House, which he hated. He preferred traveling the country, as he had in 1900 when running for vice president, making multiple speeches a day and being before admiring crowds. Although confined in Washington, he was actively involved in the details of the campaign, plotted strategy, and corresponded with reporters.[79]

Parker and the Democrats focused on the large contributions that corporations were making to the Republican cause, charging that the administration had gone soft on antitrust enforcement and that Roosevelt, despite his reputation as a trust buster, would do nothing to rein in big business if he continued in office for another term. Late in the campaign, Parker called the campaign contributions "blackmail" by the president and his administration in exchange for promised favorable treatment. The allegation enraged TR and he went on the attack. "The assertion that there has been made," he declared, "any pledge or promise or that there has been any understanding as to future immunities or benefits, in recognition of any contribution from any source is a wicked falsehood." He demanded evidence to support the allegation and, absent any, he said of Parker, "Heavy must be the condemnation of the man making them."[80]

On election day, the voters gave Roosevelt a resounding victory. The Electoral College tally was decisive, with Roosevelt winning thirty-two states and 336 electoral votes, compared to Parker's thirteen states and 140 electoral votes. Parker won no states outside of the South. In the popular vote, Roosevelt had 7,628,785 (56.4%) votes, compared to 5,084,233 (37.6%) for Parker. The margin of more than two and a half million was much larger than McKinley's two wins over Bryan in 1896 and 1900. In fact, it was the biggest winning percentage in the popular vote since James Monroe had run unopposed for reelection in 1820. The only third party of note in 1904 was the Socialist Party, which had Eugene Debs as its nominee, and who received around 400,000 (3%) votes. In Congress, Republicans increased their majority in the House by more than forty seats and maintained their almost two-to-one majority in the Senate.[81]

Americans loved Teddy. He was the first vice president who had assumed the presidency upon the death of his predecessor to win a term of his own. A relieved Roosevelt happily declared "I am no longer a political accident." Freed of any obligation to the memory of McKinley, and with a mandate behind him, he was ready to pursue his own agenda.[82]

Chapter 2

1908: The Wise Custom

Get on a raft with Taft, boys
Get on the winning boat.
The man worthwhile, with a friendly smile,
Will get the honest vote.

He'll save the country sure, boys
From Bryan, Hearst, and graft.
So all join in, we're sure to win.
Get on a raft with Taft!
—**Republican campaign song, 1908**

On the night of his greatest political triumph, Theodore Roosevelt made a statement that he would regret for the rest of his life. On November 8, 1904, as the election returns came in showing that he had decisively beaten the Democratic nominee, Judge Alton Parker, and had won a term of his own in the White House, the president spoke to reporters assembled in his office. After expressing gratitude to the American people for their confidence in his leadership, he then added that it would be his last election night. "On the 4th of March next," Roosevelt said, "I shall have served three and one half years and the three and one half years constitute my first term. The wise custom which limits the President to two terms regards the substance and not the form, and under no circumstance will I be a candidate for or accept another nomination." The no-third-term tradition that had been honored by all presidents since George Washington had stepped down after eight years would continue, although arguably, as Roosevelt noted, it did not apply to him in "form," since he would not serve two full four-year terms, although in "substance" he in effect would do so by serving for seven-and-one-half years.[1]

Over the next four years, Roosevelt went on to have what many consider one of the most successful terms of office of any president. He promoted and signed legislation increasing regulation of railroad rates and establishing federal inspection of food and drugs. He established national forests and national monuments, including the Grand Canyon. He mediated the end of the Russo-Japanese War and, in so doing, won the Nobel Peace Prize. He visited Panama to inspect construction of the American canal there, the creation of which he had forced during his first term. He launched the Great White Fleet, projecting American naval power around the world. Although Democrats and conservative Republicans in Congress resisted many of his policies, the young and energetic Roosevelt remained widely popular with the public and, but for his pledge on election night in 1904, would likely have won another term in the White House in 1908.[2]

Republican Convention

Very few presidents have remained so popular at the end of their time in office that they could dictate their successor in the White House. Thomas Jefferson had done so in 1808 with James Madison, and Andrew Jackson in 1836 had handpicked Martin Van Buren as his heir. As the 1908 election approached, Roosevelt was in a position to do as Jefferson and Jackson had done. After some consideration of his secretary of state, Elihu Root, Roosevelt decided upon another member of his cabinet, Secretary of War William Howard Taft, as the man whom he wanted to follow him in the presidency. The two had been acquainted for more than a quarter century, when both had served in Washington in the early 1890s as appointees in the administration of President Benjamin Harrison. An Ohioan, Taft had a distinguished judicial and legal résumé, having served as a state judge, as solicitor general of the United States, and as a federal appellate judge. In 1900, President McKinley named Taft to the American commission overseeing the Philippines, which the United States had taken control of after the recent Spanish-American War and where an insurrection against American rule had broken out. Intelligent, an effective administrator, and known for his amiable personality, Taft won praise for his work in the Philippines, became its governor, promoted the restoration of civil authority and oversaw the gradual defeat of the rebellion. In 1903, Roosevelt brought his old friend back to Washington to be his secretary of war and, over the following years, Taft became one of TR's most trusted confidants and advisors. With his judicial mindset and temperament, Taft's career goal was to be chief justice of the Supreme Court, not president. However, with pressure from his ambitious wife, Nellie, and at Roosevelt's urging, Taft agreed to enter the political arena as a candidate for the 1908 Republican presidential nomination.[3]

As president and the titular leader of the Republican Party, protocol required that Roosevelt remain publicly neutral, and he did not issue a formal endorsement of Taft for the nomination. In his private correspondence and in his meetings with influential Republicans, however, he left no doubt where he stood and vowed that he would "do all in his power" to promote Taft. Soon, it was no secret and his views were widely reported in the press.

Despite Roosevelt's known preference for Taft, several other candidates contended for the 1908 Republican nomination.[4]

One of the potentially most damaging opponents to Taft came from his home state of Ohio. Lack of solid support at home handicapped any potential presidential nominee. Senator Joseph Foraker of the Buckeye State, a conservative, had been a thorn in Roosevelt's side for years. Foraker had lost his best shot for the presidency years earlier when his one-time mentor, Ohio industrialist Mark Hanna, decided to back William McKinley over him as the Ohioan for whom he would devote his time and money to make president. In March 1907, Foraker announced that he would be seeking an endorsement for president from the Republican State Committee in Ohio. Taft fought back, demanding a primary election to gauge the sentiment of the state's Republican voters. In July 1907, the state committee endorsed Taft for president by a vote of fifteen to six and, a few months later, in a primary held to select delegates to the state convention, Taft won decisively. That convention, held in March 1908, endorsed Taft for president and the overwhelming majority of Ohio's delegates to the national convention were pledged to him. Although beaten badly, Foraker vowed to stay in the race.[5]

In addition to Foraker, there was much talk about Charles Evans Hughes, the governor of Roosevelt's home state of New York, as a serious contender for the nomination. Hughes had won the governorship in 1906 in a much-publicized race against publisher William Randolph Hearst, the Democratic candidate. Hughes was a reformer in the Roosevelt mold, but the two had a falling out. The president felt that he had been a mentor to Hughes and that Hughes, as governor, had been ungrateful, largely over patronage issues. Friends and supporters of Hughes formed clubs around the state promoting him for president. Hughes himself did not actively seek the nomination, but did not renounce the efforts being made on his behalf. Roosevelt and Taft decided to not take on Hughes directly in New York and became resigned to him being that state's favorite son candidate. They worked successfully, however, to minimize his support both inside and outside of New York. In late January 1908, when Hughes delivered a major policy speech to a club of New York Republicans, Roosevelt, on the same day, issued a feisty special message to Congress, which grabbed front page headlines in newspapers around the country and relegated coverage of Hughes's remarks to the back pages. A famous cartoon in the *New York World* depicted a meek Hughes in the window of a building trying, in vain, to speak, while outside Roosevelt beat a huge bass drum, attracting all of the attention. "If Hughes is going to play the game," the caricature of Roosevelt proclaimed, "he must learn the tricks." By April, any boom for Hughes had withered. Roosevelt's supporters controlled the state convention to select delegates to the national convention and, although Hughes was supported as a favorite son, it was a "lukewarm endorsement" that did not carry with it a commitment to support him much beyond the first ballot.[6]

Several other candidates entered the race for the Republican nomination against the frontrunner Taft, but none had much support outside of their home state. Most were conservatives and no fans of Roosevelt, nor of the president's presumption to handpick his successor. Philander Knox of Pennsylvania had been a prominent corporate attorney in Pittsburgh when he was named Attorney General in 1901 by McKinley, his college friend. Roosevelt kept Knox in his cabinet until 1904, when Knox resigned to accept an appointment to the Senate. Charles Fairbanks, Roosevelt's sitting vice president who, like most of his predecessors, had been frozen out of any influence in the administration, was supported by his home state of Indiana. Joseph Cannon, the cantankerous and conservative speaker of the House, who had a tense relationship with Roosevelt and had blocked some of the president's reform legislation in Congress, had the support of his home state of Illinois. To the political left of Roosevelt and Taft, the progressive Senator Robert La Follette of Wisconsin made the first of his many runs for president in 1908, but like the other candidates, had little or no support outside of his home state.[7]

While Taft and the others spent most of 1907 trying to build support among Republicans around the country, there were persistent rumors that Roosevelt, despite his election night vow in 1904, might still decide to run again, and calls from many of his supporters for him to do so. TR did have some second thoughts, but ultimately decided, although he believed that the nomination could be his for the asking, that his reputation for integrity demanded that he stand by his word. On December 11, 1907, just as the 1908 campaign year was about to begin, he issued a statement repeating his 1904 promise and adding, "I have not changed and shall not change the decision thus announced." Many party leaders, who had been holding back their endorsements, hoping that Roosevelt might get into the race, began to openly declare their support for Taft. The secretary of war, who had been out of the country since September on a world tour traveling to the Philippines, Japan, China, and Europe, received word of TR's confirmation of recusal just as he was about to return home. Taft's wife, Nellie, who never trusted Roosevelt and had always feared that he was using her husband as a stalking horse, was the Taft most relieved by the news. Still, some of the president's supporters planned to go to the convention and force a movement to draft him, convinced that he would ultimately accept. Said one pro-Roosevelt senator, TR will "not run away from duty" and, if the party failed to nominate him, it "will wantonly throw away the most valuable living asset of the nation and of the world."[8]

As the delegate selection process played out the winter and spring of 1908, none of the candidates opposing Taft, who were collectively referred to in the press as "the Allies" (although they did not coordinate their campaigns), made any headway. They were and remained favorite son candidates of their own states, with little support elsewhere. Roosevelt worked to help Taft, focusing on the South, where almost half of the delegates needed to win the party's nomination could be obtained. With Taft's approval, he put Assistant Postmaster General Frank Hitchcock (who had post office patronage at his disposal) in charge of lining up southern support for Taft. Hitchcock would later become Taft's campaign manager. The system in the South had long been criticized by many northern Republicans, who viewed the southern states as "rotten boroughs," rife with corruption and having unjustified power in deciding the party's nominee. Delegate seats were allocated based on a state's number of votes in the Electoral College. Yet, after the end of Reconstruction in 1877, no Republican presidential nominee had won *any* electoral votes in the South. Most Republican voters in the South (what few there were, especially after the passage there of Jim Crow laws around the turn of the century) were Black, as were a significant number of delegates from that region to the party's national conventions. There were always rumors of bribery of Black delegates for their votes. For years, there had been proposals to adjust the number of delegates allotted to the states at Republican conventions to a formula based on the number of votes cast in that state for the party's nominee in the previous election. Such a reform would shift well over one hundred delegates from the South to the North and West. The issue had been raised at the 1900 convention by the Republican boss of Pennsylvania, Matthew Quay, but was dropped as leverage to get southern delegates to support Roosevelt for vice president on that year's ticket with McKinley. In 1904, as president, Roosevelt was the beneficiary of the existing system and quashed any efforts at reform. In 1908, he used it to line up support for Taft. By May, 128 of the 194 delegates from the South, most of whom were Black and/or federal officeholders, were solidly pledged to Taft. The Allies planned to bring a delegate reallocation proposal before the 1908 convention, hoping to use it to sow division among northern delegates supporting Taft and peel off some of his support.[9]

Four states held some form of a primary in 1908, an electoral reform pushed by progressives that was in its infancy. Most did not involve direct voting for a presidential candidate but, rather, voting for delegates to a state convention who were known to favor a particular candidate. Three of the four primaries were won by home state candidates, with Taft winning in Ohio, Knox in Pennsylvania, and La Follette in Wisconsin. A pro-Taft slate of delegates was chosen in California. From this seed planted in 1908, primaries would gradually grow in number and importance over the next several presidential elections and would eventually revolutionize the delegate selection process for presidential nominating conventions of both major parties.[10]

There were 980 delegates to the 1908 Republican national convention, with a simple majority of 491 needed to win the nomination. Among the delegates was Lucy Clark of Utah, the first woman to be a voting delegate at a Republican convention. She was initially an alternate, but when a male delegate from Utah was unable to attend, she filled his seat. By mid-May, Taft had all but locked up the nomination, with 454 delegates pledged to him, 227 for all of his opponents combined, 171 not instructed for any candidate, and 128 yet to be selected. Faced with these grim numbers, all that the Allies could do was to vow that they would remain in the race and try to challenge the credentials of Taft delegates at the convention.[11]

Once again, Republicans chose Chicago as the site for their convention in 1908 and would meet in that city's Coliseum, the second of five consecutive GOP conventions that would be held under its roof. The hall was decorated from "end to end" with flags and bunting, so much so that "no matter where one looked red, white and blue met the eye." There were no portraits of the retiring Roosevelt on the walls or hanging from the roof, nor of any of the party's prior presidents. With Taft's nomination thought to be assured, excitement on the streets was lacking. Said one veteran observer of past conventions, there "isn't any fun here, with everything run from Washington." The main convention hotel was again the Auditorium Annex (still standing and now known as the Congress Plaza Hotel), where most of the candidates had their headquarters and hosted guests in hospitality suites. Impressions made at such events mattered.

The *New York Times* reported that any hope of increased support for a candidate seeking to be vice president, John Hays Hammond of Colorado, faded after the "injudicious distribution of extremely bad cigars" at his suite. The next day, better tobacco was on hand, but the damage had been done. The hotel's management turned off the water and boarded up the base of a large fountain in one of the public rooms, having learned from past conventions that tipsy convention-goers sometimes jumped in. The convention attracted international attention. The British and French ambassadors, the latter a frequent tennis partner of Roosevelt at the White House, were on hand. The Bureau of American Republics invited diplomats from many countries in Central and South America to attend, to observe how the United States went about selecting its leaders. When twenty-five accepted, the director of the organization panicked when he learned that the RNC had no additional VIP seats available. He appealed to the State Department and Roosevelt donated twenty-five seats that had been personally allotted to him, averting a diplomatic embarrassment. Among those in the front row of the VIP section (located behind the platform) were Alice Roosevelt Longworth, the president's twenty-four-year-old daughter from his first marriage, who sat with her husband, Congressman Nicholas Longworth of Ohio. The often-outspoken Alice would become a celebrity at conventions of both parties over the next sixty years.[12]

Scammers are not unique to modern times. A man showed up at the headquarters of several of the candidates, professing his loyalty but explaining that he had to get home due to the sudden illness of his wife. Alas, he tearfully said, he had lost his train ticket and wanted to know if a fellow supporter of his candidate could lend him twenty-five dollars, which he would gladly reimburse by mail as soon as he reached his dearest's bedside. There were no known takers. The telephone, which by 1908 was in widespread use in large cities, provided new opportunities for pranksters. As he hurriedly rushed through a hotel lobby, the manager of Speaker Cannon's campaign was handed by a clerk a note with a phone number on it. The clerk explained that he had been told it was urgent for the manager to return the call. Dutifully, the manager picked up a phone in the lobby and, with the assistance of an operator, the call was placed. He was none too happy when the person on the other end of the line explained that he had reached the Cook County Insane Asylum.[13]

In the days before the convention, the RNC held meetings to hear the challenges of the Allies to well over a hundred delegate seats. Many of the contests were from the South and almost all were decided in favor of seating Taft delegates. By the end of the process, Taft had more than seven hundred delegates, two hundred more than needed for the nomination, with his closest competitor, Knox, at fewer than seventy-five. Foraker's manager denounced the "star chamber methods" used by the RNC, accused it of being a "steamroller" for Taft, and vowed to take the fight to the floor of the convention. The dire outlook caused the Allies to consider the unthinkable. If they could not stop Taft, maybe, some proposed, they should join Roosevelt's die-hard supporters in trying to stampede the convention for TR. The idea was to create chaos and then see where things went. According to one report, representatives of the Allies met in Chicago just before the convention and most agreed to this plan. It was rejected only when

Speaker Cannon, who arrived late to the meeting, vowed that he would have nothing to do with any strategy that could end up with another four years of TR in the White House. If the others attempted to carry it out, the speaker vowed, he would withdraw from the race, endorse Taft, and nominate him personally. Cannon *really* disliked Roosevelt.[14]

The fourteenth national convention of the Republican Party was called to order shortly after noon on Tuesday, June 16, by RNC Chairman Harry New of Indiana, who was presented with a gavel made from a log of old Fort Dearborn, which had been located nearby at the mouth of the Chicago River. New announced his committee's selection of Senator Julius Burrows of Michigan as temporary chairman, which was quickly approved. The primary function of the temporary chairman was to deliver the convention's keynote speech. The choice of Burrows, who was a conservative, was a win for the Allies, who had objected to the man that the Roosevelt/Taft members of the committee had wanted, Senator Albert Beveridge of Indiana, who was a progressive. Burrows then proceeded to deliver what has been described as "one of the longest, dullest keynote speeches on record," which was "heavily laden with financial and product statistics and quotations from various speeches and reports." He mentioned Roosevelt by name only twice, in passing, and never said Taft's name. He did praise "the President" for his role in the peace treaty that ended the Russo-Japanese War, adding that "nothing has added so much to his just fame as his persistent and irrevocable refusal to break the unwritten law of the Republic by accepting a nomination for a third term. By this act of self-abnegation, he places his name and fame in the secure keeping of history by the side of that of the immortal Washington." Likely suspicious of a later attempt by Roosevelt's supporters to stampede the convention for him, which had been rumored in the newspapers for days, Burrows wanted the record clear that he and the Allies intended to hold the president to his vow. After Burrows finished his speech, the convention moved to the appointment of its various committees, with the traditional one member from every state and territory on each, and then adjourned for the day in the early afternoon.[15]

The convention's second day began with the report of the Committee on Credentials. Even though the Allies had lost almost all of their challenges to Taft delegates in preliminary hearings before the RNC, and also before the committee, none of these were taken before the full convention and the committee's recommendations for all of the permanent delegates were approved without debate. The bark of the Allies had been much louder than their bite.[16]

Senator Henry Cabot Lodge of Massachusetts, a longtime friend and ally of Roosevelt, assumed the podium as permanent chairman. During his speech, one of the most dramatic moments of the convention occurred. In reviewing the accomplishments of Roosevelt, Lodge noted that entrenched financial interests had opposed the president, making him "the best abused and the most popular man in the United States today." The line ignited a demonstration for Roosevelt, so loud that Lodge was unable to continue. It came almost entirely from the galleries, as shouts of "Teddy, Teddy, we want Teddy!" and "More, more, four years more!" rang out. As the cheers began to wane, they were revived again. Some thought it had all been orchestrated. About thirty minutes into the bedlam, a large brown Teddy bear was thrown down to the convention floor and tossed around. A reporter noted that the heavy bear, "being fully equal to a fat boy about ten years of age," was not easily handled. It finally made its way to the Oklahoma delegation where a delegate sat on it and refused to budge, putting an end to the bear's adventure. It all lasted forty-nine minutes, longer than most demonstrations at prior conventions. If this convention was going to abandon Taft and turn to Roosevelt, this was the moment. But it did not happen. Taft's manager, Frank Hitchcock, looked on, but did not appear to be concerned. As the *New York Times* reported, "it was very noticeable that the great body of delegates took no part . . . . They remained somewhat blase throughout it all, and their attitude indicated that all chance of a stampede resulting in the renomination of the President had failed."[17]

The demonstration caused anxious moments in Washington, where both Taft and Roosevelt were getting regular updates from Chicago by telegraph. Taft (along with his wife and several friends) was in his office in the Executive Office Building, adjacent to the White House, where Roosevelt was working in his private office. The initial bulletins of a massive show for Roosevelt at the convention caused concern, especially from Nellie Taft, who was always fearful that TR would snatch the nomination from her husband. She was somewhat relieved when Hitchcock telephoned from the convention floor to assure that he was "not at all alarmed." Later bulletins confirmed that it was mostly those in the galleries, not the delegates, who had been shouting for Roosevelt. It was decided that no statement from the president was needed. The crowd just needed "to blow off some steam" and all was good, Roosevelt's secretary, William Loeb, assured reporters.[18]

When the crowd finally quieted, Lodge sought to quash any "draft Roosevelt" movement once and for all, sternly telling them that the president's "refusal of a renomination, dictated by the loftiest motives and by a noble loyalty to American traditions, is final and irrevocable. Any one, who attempts to use his name as a candidate for the presidency," Lodge continued, "impugns both his sincerity and his good faith . . . that man is no friend to Theodore Roosevelt . . . he says what he means and means what he says, and his party and his country will respect his wishes as they honor his high character and great public service."[19]

When the committee on the convention's rules presented its report, a minority report was also offered. Endorsed by seventeen states, this was the much-anticipated proposal by the Allies to change the delegate allocation for future conventions, which would result in a massive shift of delegates from the South to the North and West. It provided that each state would have four at-large delegates and "one additional delegate for each 10,000 votes or majority fraction thereof, cast at the last preceding presidential election for Republican electors." A long debate followed. A Pennsylvania delegate spoke for the proposal, arguing that it was "as fair as ever was presented to a political body for its adoption." Under the current system, he noted, South Carolina received one delegate vote at the convention for each 136 votes cast by its citizens for the Republican nominee in the last election, while many of the large states in the North had only one delegate vote for every 11,000 votes so cast. An Arkansas delegate opposed the resolution, noting that, if adopted, only eight states in the North and Midwest would have sufficient delegates to name a presidential nominee and write the party's platform, while thirty-eight states "would be absolutely voiceless in the convention." A vote to add the minority report to the rules of future conventions was narrowly rejected, with 471 in favor and 506 against. The South solidly opposed it and most, but not all, of the North favored it. A shift of 18 delegates would have changed the outcome. Taft's home state of Ohio had been the key, voting against the rule change by 38 to 8. Roosevelt had strong-armed enough delegates in the North to ensure its defeat. He sent a message to a friend at the convention, which was circulated, wherein he stated that the resolution "was but a ruse on the part of the 'Allies' to wrest certain southern delegates from Taft, and that it must not be adopted under any circumstances." He would live to regret this victory. Four years later, when he was battling Taft for the Republican nomination at the 1912 convention and lost in a close race, he likely would have won if the delegate reallocation formula had been in effect.[20]

Nomination speeches for president were delivered on the afternoon of the third day. Taft's name was placed before the convention by Representative Theodore Burton of Ohio. Not surprisingly, Burton had lavish praise for Roosevelt ("The story of his achievements will make up one of the brightest pages in the history of this or any age") and tied Taft to Roosevelt at the hip (who else, he asked, but Roosevelt's "great War Secretary" was "fit to take up the task which this wondrous generation demands.") He reviewed Taft's friendship with Roosevelt going back to the early 1880s and Taft's career as a judge, as an administrator in the Philippines, and his work in the cabinet. It was Taft, he noted, who had taken charge of construction of the Panama Canal, a "colossal enterprise" that "under his directing hand . . . is no longer a vague and distant hope, but an imminent reality." In personality, Burton praised Taft for "his equable temperament" and his "infinite good nature, a charm of manner and poise which have made him a model for exalted station . . . . Secretary Taft is now and will ever be known for his broad sympathies with every grade of humanity and as one invariably actuated by that democratic spirit which should characterize a progressive American."[21]

Six other candidates were nominated. Speaker Cannon, despite having blocked in Congress some of Roosevelt's more progressive proposals, was described as one who "stood by the President and helped to crystalize his policies into law." The speech for Vice President Fairbanks stressed his ties to the stoic McKinley, rather than to the temperamental Roosevelt. "It is said," of Fairbanks, the speaker noted, "'He is conservative,' and so he is . . . . His sense of right . . . and not his 'indiscretions,' make him great. As President he will build up and not tear down, create and not destroy." Governor Hughes was promoted as the only candidate who "without the question of a doubt" would carry the large and key swing state of New York. Senator Foraker was praised as a man with common sense, one who "is not too radical to be safe, nor is he too conservative to be progressive. His statesmanship is of the constructive kind." Senator Knox was nominated as a lawyer of "intellectual greatness" who had been named Attorney General by "the lamented McKinley" and who continued in that office under TR. "[N]o man had done more," the speaker proclaimed, in contributing to "the triumphs . . . and they are many" of Roosevelt's administration than Knox. The liberal senator from Wisconsin, La Follette, was put before the convention as the only man in the field who would "plant the flag" of progressivism "further and yet further forward, until justice shall come." In a slap at Taft's friendly nature, the speaker proclaimed, "This is a war, a war in which modern industrialism is on trial . . . . In this contest there is no place for the genial and gentle art, or men of peace, for compromise today spells death." La Follette, the "man of iron with a heart of gold" was the only one, the speaker asserted, "who justly should be" Roosevelt's successor.[22]

The first and only ballot for the presidential nomination had no surprises, with William Howard Taft the overwhelming choice of the convention. The tally was 702 for Taft, 68 for Knox, 67 for Hughes, 58 for Cannon, 40 for Fairbanks, 25 for La Follette, 16 for Foraker, and 3 for Roosevelt. The nomination was quickly made unanimous.[23]

As the voting began, there were additional anxious moments, as another demonstration for Roosevelt broke out, similar to the one during Lodge's speech the previous day. This one started with a large portrait of Roosevelt being lifted and carried around the platform. Soon, an American flag with TR's face on it was being waved and paraded through the aisles in the galleries, visible to all. Chants of "Four, Four, Four Years More!' rang throughout the hall, once more coming mostly from those in the galleries than from the delegates. When a telegraph advising of the renewed clamor for Roosevelt reached the War Department in Washington, Nellie Taft picked it up, read it, and turned "white as marble," again concerned that TR would grab the nomination from her husband at the last minute. She was not alone. There was silence in the room for fifteen minutes, as "[m]en who ordinarily are not affected by nervousness hung over the telegraph instrument as though their lives depended upon the words" that would soon be conveyed via Morse Code. The next bulletin relayed that Massachusetts had cast all of its votes for Taft, evidence that there had been no stampede for Roosevelt, that the roll call had begun, and that it was proceeding. It was later learned that Lodge had ignored the crowd's chants for TR and had moved on with the roll call while the bedlam was going on. "Pay no attention to the crowd," he had told the convention's clerk, "I shall not have the president made by a Chicago mob." The clerk had to use a megaphone to call out the names of the states. An article in the *Washington Post* the next day, under the headline of "Taft Wins While Stampeders Yell," described the scene as one of "intense confusion" as had never occurred at a convention: "A ballot was taken to nominate a candidate for President while the convention was cheering frantically for a man whose name had not been presented to the convention. The votes were being counted for Taft while the people were cheering for Roosevelt." Taft was nominated, but the people still loved Teddy.[24]

When word of the nomination was telegraphed to the War Department, Taft handed the message first to his wife, who cried out "Oh, Will!" and dropped it to the floor. The couple embraced as Taft "laughed with the joy of a boy." Colleagues from the War Department, at least fifty in number, soon dropped by the office with their congratulations. Taft then left for a meeting, telling reporters that he was still too excited to give them a formal statement. "Words don't frame themselves for me now," he advised, "but I don't deny that I am very happy." That evening, from the porch of his home in Washington, the new nominee greeted an enthusiastic crowd that had gathered. Roosevelt, who had been playing tennis at the White House that afternoon when he got the news, had prepared a formal statement, which was promptly released to the press. "The country is indeed to be congratulated upon the nomination for Mr. Taft," he said. "I have known him intimately for many years and I have a peculiar feeling for him, because throughout that time we have worked for the same object with the same purposes and ideals. I do not believe there can be found in the whole country a man so well fitted to be president."[25]

That morning, before the nominations, the party's platform had been presented. It was approved after several minority planks (all more progressive than the party was willing to go) proposed by one of La Follette's Wisconsin delegates had been voted down by huge margins. The platform, as adopted, had high praise for Roosevelt's administration and vowed "unfaltering adherence to the policies thus inaugurated, and pledge their continuance." Two issues—what to do about judicial injunctions against labor strikes and how to further control monopolies—had taken up most of the discussions in the committee. The final product was largely what the Roosevelt/Taft forces had wanted and were progressive in nature. On injunctions, the issue was one of due process, with the platform calling for the right of labor unions to receive notice of and have the right to a judicial hearing before a court declared a strike illegal. On monopolies, it called for strengthening the Sherman Antitrust Act to "give the Federal government greater supervision and control over . . . that class of corporations . . . having power and opportunity to effect monopolies." The platform called for limited revisions to tariff rates. It had a strong civil rights plank for Blacks, demanding strict enforcement of the "letter and spirit of the Thirteenth, Fourteenth, and Fifteenth amendments to the Constitution." It also denounced Jim Crow laws that had arisen in the South, stating "we condemn all devices that have for their real aim his [Black] disenfranchisement for reason of color alone, as unfair, un-American, and repugnant to the Supreme law of the land."[26]

On the convention's fourth and final day, a running mate for Taft was nominated. Taft had wanted a progressive for vice president and first offered the spot to Governor Hughes of New York, who declined. His second choice, Senator Johnathan Dolliver of Iowa, also turned him down. After a couple of others were consulted and declined, Taft decided to let the convention decide without any recommendation from him. The night before, the New York delegation had caucused and endorsed one of its own, Congressman James ("Sunny Jim") Sherman from Utica. Sherman was aligned with the conservative wing of the party and Speaker Cannon also supported him. By dawn, several states in various regions, including Pennsylvania, Indiana, Texas, Kansas, and Colorado, had jumped on the Sherman bandwagon. It was all a formality by the time the convention was called to order. In addition to Sherman, two other candidates—Governor Curtis Guild of Massachusetts and former Governor Franklin Murphy of New Jersey—were nominated. Sherman won on the first ballot with an even larger tally than Taft had received the day before, getting 816 votes, compared to 77 for Murphy, 75 for Guild, and a handful scattered among others. The choice of Sherman gave the party balance between its progressive and conservative factions, as well as geographic balance. With its ticket in place, the convention adjourned.[27]

Republicans left Chicago as the majority party in the country, with the man their popular president had wanted as their nominee. They were relatively united. If predictions in the press about the upcoming Democratic convention were correct, they would be facing an old foe in the general election, one that was sure to unite them even more.

Democratic Convention

Isaac Newton's third law of motion holds that for every action there is an equal but opposite reaction. To the extent that laws of science can be applied to politics, perhaps Newton could have predicted the outcome of the Democratic Party's 1908 nomination contest. After the conservative faction of the party prevailed at the 1904 convention and nominated one of its own, Alton Parker of New York (who lost in a landslide to Theodore Roosevelt), a reaction—a change of strategy—was likely inevitable. As the 1908 campaign season began, Democrats were ready to reverse course and go back to their liberal faction for a nominee. Surprisingly, the man who emerged as the favorite for their nomination was the same one who had led them to crushing defeats in 1896 and 1900, by margins almost as large as Parker's loss in 1904.

In 1908, William Jennings Bryan was not yet fifty years old. Although he had twice been the nominee of his party, he was just approaching the years in life when men were considered to have the experience needed for the presidency. After giving perfunctory speeches for Parker during the fall campaign in 1904, and earning credits for being a party loyalist, Bryan took several steps that kept him in the public eye. A great orator, he became one of the leading speakers of the Chautauqua Movement, which had begun in the 1870s as a series of lectures on various topics at Lake Chautauqua in western New York, and spread through organized lecture tours to small towns and rural communities around the country. Each year, throughout the summer months, Bryan took to the road and gave hundreds of speeches to crowds of thousands, on topics ranging from politics and religion to social responsibility and education. Not a wealthy man, the fees from his speeches supported his family. He bought farmland near Lincoln, Nebraska, and built a comfortable home there, which he named Fairview. He also continued to publish, from Lincoln, his own weekly newspaper, *The Commoner*, which had tens of thousands of subscribers, mostly in the West and the South, in which he editorialized against corporations and imperialism, and for progressive issues that formed the basis of his political creed.

In 1905, Bryan and his family began a year-long world tour, departing from San Francisco and traveling first to Japan, on to the Philippines, China, India, and Russia, and then throughout Europe. It was reminiscent of a similar trek by Ulysses Grant, then a former president, in the late 1870s. Grant's tour lasted more than two and a half years and kept his name in the headlines. By the time he returned to the United States in late 1879, he was the favorite for nomination by the Republicans to a third term in 1880.[28] Similarly, when Bryan's ship docked in New York in August 1906, he was met by prominent Democrats from around the country and gave a rousing speech to a packed Madison Square Garden. In his remarks, he focused on his familiar theme of oppression of the poor by the rich, called for government ownership of railroads, and prohibition of monopolies by the federal licensure and control of corporations. After being shunned in 1904, "The Great Commoner," was once again viewed as the frontrunner for his party's presidential nomination.[29]

The Democrats selected Denver as the site for their twentieth national convention. The choice reflected the shifting population of the country and improvements in continental rail transportation. It was the farthest west that either major party had ever held a convention. Kansas City, six hundred miles to the east, and where the Democrats had met in 1900, was the previous western milepost for conventions. Founded during a gold rush in the late 1850s, Denver was, by 1908, the second largest city in the west (after San Francisco) and was home to 200,000 people. Near the Front Range of the Rocky Mountains, it had spectacular views of snow-tipped mountains which awed locals and visitors alike. The city's Democratic mayor, Robert Speer, attracted the convention with a pledge of $100,000 to the party and a promise (which was kept) that a new meeting hall, then under construction, would be completed in time. The Denver Municipal Auditorium, located at Fourteenth and Curtis Streets, had seating for more than 12,000, making its capacity second in the country to only Madison Square Garden. The Democratic convention was its inaugural event. The still-standing arena is now known as the Ellie Caulkins Opera House. Other civic projects in Denver opened in time for the convention, including a dazzling electric fountain on a lake and a new amusement park. Local citizens took pride in hosting the convention. Residents wore badges stating, "I Live in Denver. Ask Me." As with most conventions, alcohol flowed freely. One hotel featured a bar a half-block long, with more than forty bartenders and seating for three-hundred. Railroad cars of snow were brought from the nearby mountains and placed around the entrances to the Auditorium. The original intent had been to put the snow in barrels strategically located throughout the arena as a primitive air conditioning system. This appears to have never been implemented and, instead, huge piles of snow were deposited around the building. The site of the white stuff, which most visitors had never experienced in July, resulted in the inevitable snowball battles, at least one of which was reported to have gotten out of hand and resulted in numerous arrests.[30]

Keeping with the tradition of the era, Bryan, as the frontrunner for the nomination, did not travel to Denver, but remained at his home near Lincoln, Nebraska. In the days before the convention, he received visits from numerous party officials and delegates as they headed westward by rail. One of the last visitors was Theodore Bell, the convention's temporary chairman, who arrived the weekend before the convention to go over his keynote speech with Bryan. Massive rainfall in the area while Bell was meeting with Bryan resulted in near record flooding, canceling all trains from Lincoln. Bell was forced to make his escape, along with a couple of others, on a railroad push car. With the water rising above the floor of the car at times, Bell helped with pumping the car during the eight-mile journey to the nearest operating train station. There, he was able to catch a train that got him to Denver just in time for the opening of the convention.[31] A telegraph receiver was installed in Bryan's home, assuring that he would be in constant contact with his team at the convention. He sent a draft of the platform that he desired to Denver, closely followed the deliberations on it, and privately made his views known on who would be acceptable, and who would not be, as a running mate. Honored guests at the convention included Bryan's daughter, Ruth Bryan Leavitt, who, later in life, would become the first woman elected to Congress from the South and the first of her gender to serve as minister to a foreign country. Also present was Alice Roosevelt Longworth, the eldest child of the incumbent Republican president, Theodore Roosevelt, who would go on to be a fixture in Washington society for decades.[32]

Any hope that the anti-Bryan forces had of stopping him rested upon the party's two-thirds rule for nominations. Bryan had a majority of the delegates, either through instructions from their state conventions, or who had otherwise pledged their support or were leaning to him. If the Nebraskan could be kept below two-thirds on the first ballot, then, it was hoped, his support would lessen on succeeding ballots and the party would turn to someone else. It was a long shot, at best. In the weeks before the convention, two men were most discussed in the press as potential alternative nominees. The conservative faction of the party looked to George Gray of Delaware as their man. The sixty-eight-year-old Gray had served more than two terms in the Senate and had then been appointed in 1899 by a Republican president, McKinley, to be a federal appellate judge, a position in which he was still serving. In his politics and in his judicial decisions, Gray was conservative to the core. Although he had issued statements denying any interest in the nomination and took no active steps to seek it, he did not forbid others from working on his behalf and the Delaware delegation at Denver was pledged to him. The second candidate of the anti-Bryan forces was a man who was the opposite of Gray. Governor John Johnson of Minnesota was young, handsome, progressive, and a rising star in the party. He had wowed official Washington in a speech at the Gridiron Club dinner in December 1907. Wrote one prominent journalist after that speech, "Here is a Democrat without demagogy. A leader whose head is not in the clouds. A sober thinker with the saving grace of humor. A right-doer whose temperature is perfectly normal. A man of action without strenuosity." In other words, Johnson was not Bryan, whom many viewed as a demagogue, sanctimonious, and humorless.[33] Liberal Democrats who did not believe that Bryan could win the general election, and conservative ones who were looking for anyone who could keep Bryan from the nomination, threw their support to Johnson, who made no effort to stop them. Official campaign headquarters were opened in Denver hotels for both Gray and Johnson in the days before the convention, but no booms for either man developed and, by the time the convention opened, it was generally agreed that Bryan was unstoppable. Much of the eastern press remained convinced that Bryan, a two-time loser before, still could not win a general election. "Denver is no place for logic just now," opined the *Washington Post*, with the Democrats about to put on a performance filled with "misinformation and misplaced enthusiasm." In time, the paper predicted, the party will realize that its convention show "has been . . . a tragedy, with itself the soul of the plot."[34]

The ghost of Grover Cleveland, the only Democratic president for almost a half century, hung over the buildup and opening of the convention. Cleveland had become a divisive figure in the party, loved by its conservative faction and loathed by its liberal faction. Two weeks before the convention, Cleveland died of a heart attack at the age of seventy-one. He had been in poor health for months. Several days before the convention, Alton Parker, the party's 1904 nominee and a leader of the conservatives, let it be known that he wanted the convention to honor Cleveland and he released to the press a lengthy thirteen-paragraph resolution praising the former president. In it, Parker noted Cleveland's "lofty character, his commanding ability, and his unfailing wisdom." It commended him for "his faithfulness to the settled traditions and policies of the Democratic party," his respect for "the integrity of our constitution," and for "strict enforcement of the laws."[35] Some Bryan supporters, and likely Bryan himself, viewed Parker's resolution as a backdoor attempt to criticize Bryan. It was by opposing the "settled traditions and policies" of the party that Bryan had won his nominations in 1896 and 1900. Further, Cleveland's "strict enforcement of the laws" included his use of federal troops to enforce a court-ordered injunction against railroad workers during the 1894 Pullman Strike, which Bryan had opposed. Bryan's brain trust was determined that the convention would not open with a love-fest for Grover Cleveland, especially one that implicitly criticized their man.

The convention opened at noon on Tuesday, July 7, with Thomas Taggart, the party's chairman, at the podium. Amid an abundance of American flags and bunting, portraits of Washington, Jefferson, and Jackson hung above the rostrum on the front wall. Cleveland's likeness, draped in black, was at the rear. The call for the convention was read, which provided that the forty-six states in the Union would be allotted their standard number of delegates at twice their votes in the Electoral College and that the territories (Arizona, New Mexico, Alaska, Hawaii, Puerto Rico) and the District of Columbia would each have six delegates. In all, there were 1,002 delegates. Most states also sent full slates of alternates. Among the delegates were Mary Bradford of Colorado and Elizabeth Hayward of Utah, the first female delegates to a Democratic convention, as well as three female alternate delegates. Colorado and Utah were among those western states in 1908 that had women's suffrage. There were no Black delegates. No Black would serve as a full delegate at a Democratic convention until 1936. Also, almost no Blacks attended the proceedings in Denver. The *Washington Post*, commented that Blacks at the convention "are scarcer than hens' teeth . . . . Not only are they missing as delegates, but you cannot find any among the spectators." Black leaders had recently been critical of President Roosevelt for his 1906 dismissal of an entire regiment of Black soldiers in Brownsville, Texas, after a fracas that the soldiers had been accused by whites of starting, but the incident did not overcome the fact that Republicans were the still party of Lincoln and Democrats still the party of former Confederates, as well as the reality of treatment of Blacks in the South, where the Democrats ruled. As one Black-owned newspaper in Denver declared, "As long as we are treated as we are in the South, the Democrats cannot expect our votes."[36]

Taggert named the temporary officers of the convention, including Theodore Bell of California, as the temporary chairman. Bell then launched into a lengthy keynote speech. He wasted no time in getting to his theme: "Foremost among the great evils that afflict the country," he proclaimed, "is the abuse of corporate power." He derided the platform of the recent Republican convention for its pledges of corporate reform. Noting that the Republicans had been in control of the presidency and both houses of Congress and had failed to pass the reform items listed in their platform, he asked if the opposing party could "be absolved from its dereliction of duty by an empty promise to do in the future what it has willfully failed to do in the past?" He noted that their platform failed to call for additional reforms that their own president, Roosevelt, had been urging Congress to pass during his current term in office. Bell's speech revealed the tightrope that Democrats planned to walk during the coming campaign—commending the popular incumbent Republican president for the reforms that he had championed, but arguing that Bryan (whom Roosevelt detested) was his proper heir. Taft, said Bell, was no Roosevelt: "[N]o man can transfer his personal popularity to another . . . natural children, as well as proteges, often suffer a distinct loss from their relation to greatness. Especially in America will the people do their own thinking and make their own choice of Presidents." He derided as un-American the notion that Taft was an acceptable commander-in-chief because Roosevelt would be controlling him behind the scenes. There could only be one president. "The American people," he said, "are sticklers on some things . . . they will not stand for divided responsibility in the White House. They will demand, and they have a right to demand, that the heart that conceives, the brain that plans, and the hand that executes shall be directly answerable to the sovereign power that built the White House and selects one man at a time to occupy it."[37]

Bell's speech was well-received and he then presided over the appointment of the various committees, each with one member from each state and territory. At least thirty-six delegations had a majority of Bryan delegates, meaning that Bryan's supporters would control all of the committees.[38] Bell recognized Ignatius Dunn of Nebraska, one of Bryan's floor leaders in Denver and the man who would put his name in nomination. Dunn advised that he was offering a resolution in honor of the recently deceased Grover Cleveland. The resolution was brief, recognizing him as "one of the strongest and ablest characters known to the world's statesmanship" and for "his able, conscientious and forceful administration of public affairs." It called for adjournment of the convention for the rest of the day, as a "mark of respect to his memory." After delegates from Missouri and Kentucky seconded the resolution, in response to shouts from the crowd of "Parker! Parker!," Bell then recognized a flustered Alton Parker, who advised that "it was my purpose, had I been fortunate enough to have first secured the attention of the chair, to have offered the following resolutions." Parker then read a watered-down version of his draft resolution for Cleveland that had been published in the newspapers a few days earlier, having removed most of the points he thought might be objectionable to the Bryan men. Parker did not push for adoption of his version but, instead, sheepishly seconded the resolution offered by Dunn. The resolution was approved and the convention's first day ended. Newspapers described the scene as the Bryan men having "humiliated" Parker, the party's last nominee, before the entire convention.[39]

When the convention resumed for its second day, word was received that the Committee on Credentials had been meeting round the clock but would not likely have a report until the evening. No substantive business could be conducted until this committee reported. Such a delay was not uncommon in the era and, as at other conventions, to kill time, calls were made for various prominent politicians to address the crowd. The first speaker was Senator Thomas Gore of Oklahoma. Gore (who would later in life be the grandfather of author Gore Vidal) had been blind since childhood. Oklahoma had become the newest state in the Union the previous year and there had been controversy over its constitution, which contained many progressive provisions. Bryan had wholeheartedly endorsed the constitution, while William Howard Taft, at the behest of President Roosevelt, had gone to Oklahoma and spoken out against ratification, calling the proposed document a combination of "Bourbonism and despotism, flavored with socialism."[40] Gore wasted no time in flaying Taft, now the Republican nominee for president, and praising the man the Democrats were about to nominate. Stating that Oklahomans had followed the advice of Bryan, the "greatest living apostle of human liberty," over that of Taft and had overwhelmingly approved the constitution, Gore, perhaps without realizing the consequences, spoke Bryan's name. During that era, the first time a likely nominee's name was mentioned from the convention's podium, it guaranteed a vocal demonstration would follow. It was as if all in the convention hall sat on the edges of their seats earnestly waiting for the name to be heard, so that they could pounce into action. And pounce they did. Before Gore could speak another word, the crowd erupted and pandemonium ensued. Despite attempts from the presiding officer, Bell, to gavel the proceedings to order, wave after wave of cheering, aided by the band in the hall playing various tunes, continued. The poles with signs on them designating each state delegation were lifted and their bearers led a sea of delegates up and down the aisles, with most on the floor and in the galleries shouting at the tops of their lungs, and waving hats, flags, and handkerchiefs. It continued for an hour and twenty minutes.[41]

The sightless Gore, who stood at the podium the entire time, later explained his own feelings during the demonstration. "Eyesight," he said, "is not so valuable as the magnetism which every blind man possesses. We feel what is going on, not only in the sense of being independently affected by it, but we enjoy a sensation unknown to others . . . . Today I faced the crowd and 'saw' what was going on, and I believe my picture of it was as vivid as that of any man or woman present." Democrats proudly noted that the hurrahs for Bryan lasted a half hour longer than those that had followed the mention of President Roosevelt's name at the recent Republican convention. The *Baltimore Sun* suggested a possible explanation why Democrats were louder at conventions, noting, "Whether the Democrats can naturally make more noise than the Republicans, or whether they have to do all of their cheering in the conventions (having for some years had little use for cheers at elections), we do not undertake to determine."[42]

When the convention resumed in the evening, the Committee on Credentials presented its report on the seating of disputed delegates in a handful of states. The most controversial portion concerned the Pennsylvania delegation, where the majority of the committee recommended the unseating of eight anti-Bryan delegates. The impetus for this came from outside of Pennsylvania. The delegates were affiliated with James Guffey, a Pennsylvania oilman, who had, in a blistering speech a week before the convention, denounced Bryan as the most "impudent, domineering, devastating boss" that ever held influence over the Democratic Party. After much debate, the full convention, by a vote of 605 to 387, agreed to exclude the anti-Bryan men and replace them with pro-Bryan delegates. Usually, a convention in that era deferred to a state's own recommendation for the makeup of its delegation. The incident (along with the rift over the Cleveland memorial the day before) was viewed by the mostly anti-Bryan eastern press as showing the extent to which the Bryan forces in Denver were willing to go to silence dissenting voices and to steamroll any opposition.[43]

The convention's third day was the one that all had been waiting for. If all went as planned, by its end, the party would have voted on its presidential nominee. Congressman Henry Clayton of Alabama took over the podium as the convention's permanent chairman. He presided over the proceedings with a gavel made of hickory from a tree on Andrew Jackson's estate in Tennessee. Jackson is considered the founder of the Democratic party. After a lengthy speech by Clayton, others were invited to take the podium, as the report from the platform committee, the next item on the agenda, was not ready. By mid-afternoon, the committee was still meeting and the convention adjourned until the evening.[44]

In the evening, after more speeches to kill time, and with the platform still not finalized, the rules were suspended to move forward with nominations of candidates for president. The roll call of the states began and Alabama yielded to Nebraska. Ignatius Dunn, described in newspaper reports as "a youthful orator of fire and eloquence"[45] delivered the main nominating speech for Bryan. He began by focusing on the Democratic theme of corporate greed. "The question is," he asked, "whether this government shall be restored to the control of the people and be administered in the interest of all, or whether it shall remain an instrument in the hands of the few for levying tribute upon all the rest." Attempting to win over Roosevelt supporters frustrated with the Republican Party, Dunn noted that the recently adopted Republican platform had rejected many of the reforms that Roosevelt had supported—"Republicans who really desire reform are powerless; the efforts of the president have been futile." Come to the Democrats, he said, and support the one man "whose nomination will leave no doubt as to where our party stands on every public question." His candidate, he said, "has never inquired whether a political principle was popular; it has been sufficient for him to believe that it was right." Dunn continued:

> He favored the election of senators by direct vote before the House of Representatives ever acted favorably on the subject. He championed tariff reform when the West was the hot-bed of protection.
> He favored an income tax before the income tax law was written. He attacked the trusts when Republican leaders were denying that any trusts existed. He advocated railroad regulation before the crusade against rebates and discrimination began.
> He has always been the friend of labor, and was among the first to urge conciliation between labor and capital.... He announced his opposition to imperialism before any other man of prominence had expressed himself on the subject, and without waiting to see whether it would be popular....
> Nebraska's Democracy which saw in him, when a young man, the signs of promise, places in nomination as the standard bearer of our party the man who in the thrilling

days of '96 and 1900 bore the battle-scarred banner of Democracy with fame as unsullied and fidelity as spotless as the crusaders of old. Nebraska presents his name because Nebraska claims his dwelling place, and proudly enrolls him among her citizens; but his home is in the hearts of the people . . . . I offer the name of America's great Commoner, Nebraska's gifted and incomparable son, William Jennings Bryan.[46]

At the conclusion of Dunn's speech, just as when Bryan's name was mentioned the day before by Senator Gore, the hall erupted in "a perfect pandemonium of sound and motion." Small American flags, which had been placed on each seat before the session began, were waived. Portraits of Bryan were held aloft and carried around the convention floor. The band played and the galleries cheered. The standards of the states were carried up and down the aisles, leading a parade of delegates. A reporter described the sight: "The scene was vivid, the din deafening. The wave of sound that rose became a roar . . . . 'Bryan!' they shouted; and again, 'Bryan!' A rip-roaring shout that burst and boomed with the might of a cannon shell. It stirred the pulse and sent the blood coursing through the veins." The fervor was less impressive to a reporter from the *Philadelphia Inquirer*, who observed, "Bryan craziness seems to demand the noisiest of noises and the most ear-splitting of yells, with brass instruments of all degrees of torture going on all the time." Only six state delegations declined to join in, and sat and watched—Delaware and Minnesota (the home states of the two men who would later be placed in nomination against Bryan), as well as New York, New Jersey, Georgia, and Maryland. To quiet the crowd, some of the banks of electric lights were turned off, which worked to some extent. Finally, after an hour and ten minutes, order was restored.[47]

Although the convention remained in session for five more long hours, the rest of the proceedings were anticlimactic. Minnesota nominated its governor, John Johnson, lauded as being "in the prime of life, courteous, kind and unpretentious, strong, resolute and virile . . . [of] high character and winning personality."[48] A much less intense demonstration followed, lasting twenty minutes. By this time, the crowd in the galleries had thinned out, unwilling to wait for the voting to begin. There were more seconding speeches for Bryan, which were supposed to have a five-minute limit. Shouts of "Time!" from the crowd greeted many of the speakers after only a couple of minutes, with most wanting to move things along.

Around midnight, the platform committee finally reported, with the reading of the platform taking an hour. It called for an immediate reduction of tariffs; for federal licensure of corporations with more than a quarter of the market for their products, and forbidding them from controlling more than half of that market; increased regulation of railroads; a guarantee fund for bank deposits; constitutional amendments allowing a federal income tax on individuals and corporations, and for the direct election of senators; limited use of judicial injunctions in labor disputes; for an eight hour workday and workers' compensation for injuries for federal employees; and against immigration from China. The platform was unanimously approved without debate.[49]

In the early morning hours, the nominating speeches continued. George Gray was nominated by Delaware, and there were numerous seconding speeches for Bryan, Johnson, and Gray. It was not until three o'clock in the morning that the roll call began. On the first ballot, William Jennings Bryan, with 888½ votes, was named the presidential nominee of his party for the third time. It was an achievement that had previously been accomplished only by Grover Cleveland. Bryan's two opponents were far behind, with 59½ votes for Gray and 46 for Johnson. Given the hour, there was no demonstration in the hall and, at almost four o'clock in the morning, the convention adjourned.[50]

The convention resumed for its fourth and final day to nominate Bryan's running mate. Bryan's strength in the party was sufficient that he could name his vice president. He chose John Kern of Indiana, a longtime friend and supporter. Indiana was a pivotal swing state in that era. Kern was an Indianapolis attorney who had lost races for governor of Indiana in 1900 and 1904. Three other candidates, from Connecticut, New York and Georgia, were formally nominated, but it was no real contest. Bryan wanted Kern and the convention obliged. As the roll call of the states continued, state after state seconded the nomination of Kern. Before the voting began, the other candidates were withdrawn and Kern was nominated by acclamation.[51]

Democrats left Denver, after a relatively united convention, with Bryan again their nominee. Republicans wasted no time in pointing out that, in selecting a ticket of Bryan and Kern, Democrats had paired a two-time loser for president of the United States with a two-time loser for governor of Indiana. Most political observers felt that Democrats would have an uphill battle in the general election. As one of the party's disgruntled conservatives commented, "The Democrats will now resume their accustomed occupation of electing a Republican President."[52]

The Campaign and Election

Unlike his past campaigns, Bryan did not focus on one issue. In 1896, he had run mainly on free coinage of silver and, in 1900, on anti-imperialism. In 1908, he supported a host of reforms—lower tariffs, curbing corporate greed and influence, limits on judicial injunctions in labor disputes, direct election of senators, and publication of campaign contributions. His slogan was "Shall the People Rule?" As he had before, Bryan took to the road, campaigning mostly in New York and the Midwest. He often gave more than twenty speeches a day and drew large crowds. Most of the Eastern newspapers opposed him. By 1908, Bryan was a known quantity. People loved him or hated him.[53]

Initially, Taft resisted active campaigning, partially due to his belief that he was ahead in the race and did not need to, but also due to his distaste for it. "A national campaign for the Presidency," he said, "to me is a nightmare." Roosevelt wrote to Taft and urged him to take to the campaign trail: "[Y]ou ought to be on the stump.... Do not answer Bryan; *attack* him. Don't let him make the issues." Taft decided to hit the road, making about four hundred speeches, traveling in October from Indiana to Colorado and finishing the campaign in the Midwest and New York. He focused on the good economy and promised continuation of Roosevelt's progressive policies. To draw attention to Bryan's losses in prior races for the White House, Republicans joked, "Vote for Taft now, you can vote for Bryan anytime."[54]

There were several third parties of note in 1908. The most prominent was the Socialist Party, which nominated Eugene V. Debs, for the second time, as its candidate for president. The Prohibition Party nominated another Eugene, Eugene W. Chafin of Wisconsin. A revived version of the Populist Party nominated Thomas Watson of Georgia. The candidate of the Socialist Labor Party was August Gilhaus of New York. William Randolph Hearst, a strong supporter of Bryan in 1896 and 1900, got revenge for Bryan's failure to endorse Hearst in his own run in 1904 for the Democratic nomination. Hearst formed the Independence Party, based mostly in New York, which named Thomas Hisgen of Massachusetts as its candidate for president.[55]

On election day, Taft won decisively. The Electoral College tally was 321 for Taft and 162 for Bryan. As expected, Bryan carried all of the southern states. Outside of the South, however, he won only in his home state of Nebraska, in Colorado, in Nevada, and a majority of Maryland's electors. Taft won the popular vote with 7,677,788 votes (52%), compared to Bryan's 6,407,982 (43.5%). Bryan's percentage of the overall vote was less than he had in 1896 and 1900, although he did better than Parker had in 1904, getting well over a million more votes than Parker. The third-party candidates with the most votes were Debs of the Socialists with 420,890 (3%) and Chafin of the Prohibitionists with 252,511 (1.7%). In the congressional races, Democrats made slight gains (picking up five seats in the House and one in the Senate), but Republicans maintained their solid majorities in both bodies.[56]

Theodore Roosevelt had selected the man he wanted, William Howard Taft, to take his place as president and had succeeded in having Taft nominated by the Republican Party and elected by the American people. Once the election results were known, each man sang the praises of the other. "I pledge myself . . . to make the next Administration a worthy successor to that of Theodore Roosevelt," Taft proclaimed, adding "I could have no higher aim than that." Roosevelt expressed his confidence in Taft, telling reporters "The result is a great victory and a mighty good thing for the whole country. . . . Naturally I am greatly pleased." Little did anyone then know that, four years later, the two of them would face off in one of the most bitter and personal political battles in American history.[57]

Chapter 3

1912: We Stand at Armageddon

Now convention days are over,
And election time is near,
From East to West, from North to South,
There's just one name in every mouth.

Wilson, that's all, Wilson, that's all!
Who strikes the public sentiment,
Say, who will be our President?
It's Wilson, that's all!
–Democratic campaign song, 1912

They had been the best of friends. Although men of divergent personalities and interests, Theodore Roosevelt and William Howard Taft had first formed a personal bond in 1890 when both were eager young Republican political appointees serving in the administration of President Benjamin Harrison. The thirty-two-year-old Roosevelt had come to the nation's capital as a commissioner on the Civil Service Commission, hoping to bolster his reputation as a crusader against political corruption. Previously, he had served a brief time as a reformist member of New York Assembly, but took a sabbatical from politics in the Dakota Territory after the death of his first wife. Taft, one year older, had a more prestigious appointment from Harrison, as solicitor general of the United States, and had previously been a judge on the Ohio Superior Court. The two were neighbors in the Dupont Circle section of Washington and were often seen walking together to work in the mornings. Taft, taller and stouter than his friend, was more sober in appearance as they strode along, with Roosevelt usually in conversation and animated.[1] After Harrison's term ended, they went their separate ways, but remained friends.

When Roosevelt became president in 1901 after McKinley's assassination, Taft was then serving as governor general of the Philippines and, in 1904, Roosevelt brought him back to Washington to be secretary of war in his cabinet. Taft became one of Roosevelt's closest advisors during his second term and, when Roosevelt kept his promise not to seek another term in 1908, he handpicked Taft to be his successor. Taft, whose career path had included a stint as a judge on a federal appellate court and who was more interested in serving on the Supreme Court than in the White House, reluctantly agreed to run for president, with strong encouragement from his ambitious wife, Nellie. With Roosevelt's support, Taft won the Republican nomination in 1908, and the general election.

After Taft's presidency began, Roosevelt went on an extended African safari, followed by a tour of Europe, and was out of the country for more than a year. While he was away, in-fighting between the progressive and conservative factions of the Republican Party became more intense and Taft increasingly aligned himself with the conservatives. This infuriated the progressives, who had viewed Roosevelt as their champion during his years in office.

Republican Convention

Roosevelt, after initial reluctance and months of indecision, at the urging of prominent progressives in the party, and his own desire to return to the political arena, announced publicly in February 1912 that he would challenge his old friend Taft for the Republican nomination. "My hat is in the ring," declared the former president. He gave speeches favoring progressive views on the issues of the day, some of which he had opposed when in the White House. In his zeal for all things progressive, TR announced that he favored the right of the people to call for elections to overturn unpopular judicial decisions. Although his proposal was limited to cases in which state judges had decided cases on constitutional grounds, it was interpreted more broadly. By endorsing recall of judicial decisions, many branded Roosevelt as a radical. Even under a narrow interpretation, opponents noted, TR's proposal would make the final determination as to which laws were constitutional, and which ones were not, subject to the whim of a majority of voters at a given time. As one author has noted, "It was an egregious political error. Judicial recall was anathema to many Republicans," including some of Roosevelt's former closest advisers. TR's endorsement of this policy had the effect of driving many wavering Republicans into the Taft camp.[2]

In deciding at virtually the last possible minute to run against Taft for the 1912 Republican nomination, Roosevelt offended and eclipsed Senator Robert La Follette of Wisconsin, who was viewed as a leader of progressives in the party, and who had been actively planning his own campaign for the nomination ever since the 1910 midterm elections. Known as "Fighting Bob," he had been in the United States Senate since 1906 and had also served six years as Wisconsin's governor. In both positions, he championed policies that were at the forefront of the progressive movement, including increased regulation of business, breaking up monopolies, a graduated income tax, workers' compensation, minimum wage laws, primary elections, judicial recall, and referendums. Although a powerful orator, La Follette's prickly personally and his uncompromising views had made him many enemies. Like William Jennings Bryan, the most liberal prominent Democrat of that era, many viewed La Follette as "too much the crusader, too much the evangelistic reformer" to ever win the presidency. In April 1911, the National Progressive Republican League endorsed La Follette and he formally announced his campaign two months later. La Follette became increasingly miffed at Roosevelt's failure to endorse his candidacy, which kept many congressional progressives on the sidelines, who were waiting to see if TR was going to enter the race. Roosevelt, keeping his options open, worked behind the scenes to undermine La Follette's candidacy and told supporters that the Wisconsin senator was too temperamental to be president. Around the time Roosevelt was set to formally announce his candidacy, La Follette self-destructed and virtually destroyed any chance he had of winning the nomination. In a speech before magazine publishers in Philadelphia in February 1912, he lost his composure (some believe he had a nervous breakdown at the podium), repeated himself, harangued his audience, and abused them as they walked out of the hall in disgust. His incoherent remarks dragged on for two-and-one-half hours. His campaign continued, but it was mortally wounded. Within days, TR formally entered the race, and many progressives deserted Fighting Bob for the Rough Rider.[3]

The election of 1912 saw more widespread use of a new system for selecting delegates to presidential nominating conventions—the primary election. Previously, delegates were selected at local conventions held at the congressional district level (two delegates per district), with four additional delegates named at statewide conventions. Often, political bosses controlled these conventions. Primaries were a reform that progressives had been advocating to give the people a direct voice in choosing delegates through an election. The first primary laws were passed in a couple of states around 1905 and, in 1908, there were Republican primaries in four states. The 1912 election was the first in which primaries were widely used. As the year began, six states had primary laws to select convention delegates and, by the early spring, seven more states had joined them. Prior to 1912, Roosevelt had been, at best, a lukewarm supporter of primaries. Once he began to seriously think about running in 1912, however, he became their champion and saw primaries as the best way to weaken the firm grip that Taft held, as incumbent presidents always did, on the delegate selection process when seeking re-nomination.[4]

With primaries came a new way of campaigning. Candidates had to appeal directly to the people with speeches and rallies in the primary states. Presidential campaigns were forever changed. Active campaigning by nominees in the general election had become an accepted practice only in the prior generation. Before then, it was deemed undignified. Now, candidates would also have to hit the campaign trail in the late winter and spring to round up delegates to win their party's nominations. As the challenger to an incumbent president of his own party, this new system favored Roosevelt. It opened up the delegate selection process to more people, instead of to just the political insiders and bosses who often controlled local and state conventions, and Roosevelt (with the possible exception of Democrat William Jennings Bryan) was the most energetic and effective campaigner of his generation.

TR hit the campaign trail early and often, as did La Follette. Both attacked Taft as a tool of political bosses, as too conservative, and as out of step with the times. La Follette also denounced Roosevelt as a pretender to progressivism, allowing TR to be viewed by some as the moderate candidate between two opponents on the extremes of the political spectrum. As expected, in states where the traditional method of conventions was used to select delegates, Taft usually came away the winner. This was especially true in the South, where the patronage power of an incumbent Republican president always commanded loyalty. In primary states, however, it was a different story. La Follette did well early on, with victories in North Dakota and his home state of Wisconsin, but then quickly faded and became a non-factor in the race. Roosevelt then won a couple of primaries, forcing a reluctant Taft to take to the campaign trail. He was the first incumbent president seeking re-nomination to do so. "An indignity," he fumed. Taft won in TR's home state of New York (amid allegations of fraud by Roosevelt's supporters) and campaigned extensively in Massachusetts, where he also won. Elsewhere, however, Roosevelt ran the table, winning primaries in nine states from March to early June, including a humiliating defeat of Taft in Taft's home state of Ohio. TR could rightly claim himself as the people's choice, racking up more than 1,100,000 votes and 278 delegates in the thirteen primary states, compared to 760,000 votes and 48 delegates for Taft, and 350,000 votes and 36 delegates for La Follette. But delegates selected in primaries amounted to only a third of the total number of delegates to the convention. Taft's strength in the South and in the rest of the convention states left him with a slight edge over Roosevelt in delegates going into the convention, which was set to begin in Chicago on June 18. Roosevelt's campaign team announced challenges to 254 of Taft's delegates, alleging irregularity and fraud at various local and state conventions, as well as in the allocation of delegates in primary states. The outcome of those disputes at the convention would determine the nominee.[5]

The contest in the spring of 1912 between Taft and Roosevelt, former best friends, became bitter and personal. Both said things they would come to regret. Roosevelt's charges put Taft on the defensive. In response, he declared, "I do not want to fight Theodore Roosevelt, but sometimes a man in a corner fights. I am going to fight." Taft called his predecessor in office "a demagogue" and a "dangerous egotist." Roosevelt gave as much as he got, calling Taft a "fathead" and a "puzzlewit." Taft was determined that he was going to defeat TR for the nomination, which he viewed as a fight for the soul of the Republican Party and for the continuance of constitutional government, even if he went on (as he expected he would) to lose the general election to the Democrats. But personally, the campaign hurt Taft and he was upset and conflicted. After a particularly tough speech in Boston attacking Roosevelt, a reporter spotted Taft slumped in his seat on a railroad car. Taft looked up at the reporter, plaintively stated that "Roosevelt was my closest friend," and the president of the United States began to weep.[6]

On June 7, more than a week before the opening of the party's convention, the Republican National Committee ("RNC") began its meetings in Chicago. The main issue before it was to determine the temporary roll of delegates, which would be subject to revision by the credentials committee, and by the full convention, after the convention began. This necessitated lengthy hearings, at which the Roosevelt forces presented their evidence contesting the 254 proposed Taft delegates and replacing them with Roosevelt supporters. The RNC consisted of fifty-three members, one from each state and territory, who had been chosen at the last convention in 1908 to serve until the conclusion of the 1912 convention. Victor Rosewater, a newspaper owner from Nebraska, was the committee's chairman. As would be expected of a committee appointed by the 1908 convention that had nominated Taft, a solid majority of the committee, almost forty, supported the president's re-nomination. Even some of Roosevelt's supporters on the committee admitted that they did not have substantial evidence to support more than two-thirds of the 254 delegate seats that they were contesting. The number had been inflated to keep Taft's pre-convention count of non-contested delegates below the number needed to win the nomination, in order to make the race appear closer than it actually was. The RNC's hearings stretched on for several days and, at the end of each day's session, Roosevelt, from his Long Island home on Oyster Bay, denounced the committee as stealing votes from him and thwarting the will of the people. By the end of the hearings, Taft had been awarded 235 of the disputed delegate seats, compared to only nineteen for Roosevelt. Almost 150 of the seats were awarded to Taft delegates unanimously, or by a voice vote that went unchallenged by any of Roosevelt's supporters. Of the remaining contests, modern observers differ in their count, but agree that there was credible evidence to support the Roosevelt position on somewhere between thirty to fifty delegates seats that were awarded to Taft. The methodology used by the RNC in its 1912 hearings, however, was the same that had been used in the past, and which Roosevelt had supported when he was president. After the hearings ended, Roosevelt's managers advised him that there were twenty-eight seats that clearly should have gone to him and they recommended pursuing challenges to those seats at the convention. TR was incredulous at the small number, correctly pointing out that it would not change the outcome. He demanded that they challenge at least one hundred seats. After some discussion, they compromised and it was decided that the campaign would publicly announce that it would be contesting seventy-two seats. That figure was enough to narrowly put Roosevelt over the top, but as the challenger and the perceived underdog, the Roosevelt campaign needed to do more than just announce its delegate contest. It needed to seize the moment and grab headlines.[7]

Roosevelt announced, on June 14, a bold decision—he would go to Chicago himself to rally his supporters and lead his campaign team in fighting what he called the RNC's "theft" in deciding the temporary roll of delegates. It was a precedent-shattering move. Never before had a leading contender for a major party's nomination gone to the convention city. It was considered unbecoming and in poor taste. Surrogates went to conventions and cut deals and rounded up delegates, not candidates. A few prior candidates of both parties had been delegates at conventions that nominated them (notably James Garfield in 1880 and William Jennings Bryan in 1896), but they had been dark horse candidates when their conventions began and were thought to have little or no hope of winning the nomination. The Taft team portrayed the TR move as an act of desperation by a losing campaign, but they were concerned. Could the legendary Roosevelt charisma, on display in person in the convention city, sway enough delegates to swing the nomination to him? TR arrived in the Windy City on the afternoon of Saturday, June 15, three days before the convention opened. The famous Roosevelt toothy grin was present as he shook hands with supporters. "[H]is teeth continually clicked in pure ecstasy" reported the *New York Times*. Thousands cheered the former president as he arrived at the train station, and as he stood in his open automobile the entire route to the Congress Hotel, where his team had its headquarters. TR's nephew, Nicholas, witnessed the scene and described the motorcade in his diary: "Everyone was howling with delight, and cries of 'Teddy!' filled the air. At the cross streets, as far as we could see to either side, or back or forward, people were wedged in like pins. Everyone cheered. Everyone screamed." Once inside the hotel, the Colonel, as the former president preferred to be called, stepped through an open window above the entrance onto a small balcony and addressed his supporters below, shouting that "Chicago is a mighty poor place in which to try and steal anything." A reporter noted that he "simply radiated hostility" toward his opponents and was in a fighting mood. Taking off his trademark hat (he favored a cross between a slouch hat that he wore as a Rough Rider and a sombrero) and shaking it with his hand to punctuate his remarks, he declared, "This is no factional fight. It is a contest between the people themselves and the perpetual politicians who represent all that is worst with corrupt politics and business, and the people will win . . . It is a fight against theft, and the thieves will not win." He then met the rest of the evening with his campaign managers to plot their strategy.[8]

There were 1,078 delegates at the convention and a simple majority of 540 was needed to win the nomination. Independent tallies of delegates gave Taft a lead, but not an insurmountable one. In addition to Taft and Roosevelt, La Follette was still in the race, but had only thirty-six delegates. There was also a favorite son candidate from Iowa, Albert Cummins, who had ten. Both were progressives, like Roosevelt, but were hostile to his candidacy and vowed to never throw their support to him, viewing him as a late-coming pretender to their cause and hoping that a deadlocked convention would turn to them. Other than challenging the RNC's temporary roll of delegates, this left only one place for the Roosevelt team to look for the votes needed to overtake Taft—the South. The role of delegates from southern states at Republican conventions had been controversial ever since Reconstruction. Under the party's rules, delegates were allocated to states based on twice their number of votes in the Electoral College. The bigger the state, the more delegates it had. A state's level of support for Republican presidential candidates, or its number of Republican officeholders in state and local contests, were not considered. All across the South, Democrats firmly controlled state and local governments and the Republican Party in the region was, at best, a fledging organization that existed more to receive and control federal patronage appointments from Republican administrations in Washington than to field competitive candidates in elections. Over time, hostility grew among Republicans in the North and the West to the existing system. Almost a third of the delegates to their national conventions came from states in the South that had no hope of ever contributing a single electoral vote to a Republican in a presidential election, and where the party's support was almost non-existent. Beginning in the 1880s, there had been proposals to do away with the Electoral College-based system for delegate allocation and replacing it with a system that considered a state's level of support for the Republican presidential nominee in the last election. Such a change would result in a massive shift of delegate votes away from the South and to the North and West. The proposals always failed, in part due to the opposition of Republican presidents who, when seeking reelection, could count on solid support from southern delegates, since they controlled the federal patronage upon which most of those delegates had obtained their local power and influence. Roosevelt had used and benefitted from this system when he ran for a second term in 1904 and also when he arranged for Taft to succeed him in 1908. Now, in 1912, as the incumbent president, Taft was its beneficiary.

In addition to its challenge to the seating of some delegates, another way for the Roosevelt team to gain support was to change the votes of southern delegates, almost all of whom were pledged to support Taft. Among them, Black delegates were viewed as most likely to desert the president and shift their votes. Newspapers portrayed them in racist terms and as readily willing to accept bribes. The *Baltimore Sun* headlined "Negro Holds Key" and commented "Nobody is willing to believe for a minute that any negro deserter [of Taft] was activated by patriotic or political motives." According to the newspaper, "the balance of power of a great political party is held by half a hundred negro voters" and the presidential nomination would be determined "with cold cash." Estimates of the number of Black delegates at the convention vary from around sixty to one hundred, with most from the South. Since Reconstruction, it had been a common practice for the campaigns of Republican candidates to pay the expenses of Black delegates who supported them to attend conventions, including travel costs, hotel rooms, etc. Where legitimate expenses ended and bribery began was often difficult to determine. Over the weekend before the convention, both the Taft and Roosevelt campaigns released affidavits from Black delegates alleging that the other side had offered them bribes. Although TR expressed outrage against the Taft campaign, the available evidence shows that his campaign, which was the one in need of votes, was more active in offering cash incentives. Later, one of Roosevelt's managers at the convention confessed, "I never told Roosevelt about this strange little backwater in the river of righteousness on which the progressive craft was sailing so gallantly, and I doubt that he ever knew of it." Whatever the extent of the bribery efforts, they failed and almost all of the Black delegates voted at the convention for Taft, the candidate they had pledged to support.[9]

The convention was held in the Chicago Coliseum, located on Wabash Avenue between 14th and 16th Streets, a building that was hosting its third straight Republican convention. As set up for the convention, the Coliseum could seat more than 11,000 people and it had the latest technology in telephone and telegraph equipment and lines. Given the divisiveness of the campaign, there were fears of violence, particularly coming from angry Roosevelt supporters. A police station was placed in the hall and a temporary hospital was set up nearby. The RNC made sure that no Roosevelt supporters were selected as doorkeepers or as assistants to the convention's sergeant-at-arms. To guard against counterfeiting, tickets to the convention's sessions were kept under lock and key until the day before the convention opened. The arena was decorated with the usual American flags and bunting, but there was a security item that prior conventions had not had. Underneath the bunting surrounding the podium, the railing was wrapped in barbed wire, to impede any would-be rushers of the stage. Reporters noted the lack of a festive atmosphere that was normally associated with conventions. Still, there were plenty of bands marching to and fro. One frequently played tune was "There'll Be a Hot Time in the Old Town Tonight," which most felt was appropriate. Both campaigns had their public headquarters in opposite wings of the Congress Hotel, Taft in the Gold Room and Roosevelt in the Florentine Room, where speeches could be heard at all hours of the day. In the Gold Room, a sign in electric lights spelled out "Preserve the Republic," expressing Taft's theme that Roosevelt was a radical and his nomination would be a danger to constitutional government. Across the hall from the Florentine Room, a steady stream of visitors went in and out of TR's suite of personal rooms, where he was holding meetings and plotting strategy. Outside, the Roosevelt supporters were boisterous, many sporting buttons depicting a hat surrounded by a circle, symbolic of Roosevelt's declaration announcing his candidacy few months earlier by stating "My hat is in the ring." When TR heard a band pass below, he often could not resist sticking his head out of a window and waving his hat to supporters. The day before the convention, the *Baltimore Sun* reported "Anything is possible, for conditions defy analysis." Taft, the newspaper said, could win by a few votes, but so could Roosevelt, or there could be a stalemate and a dark horse nominee emerge, or the party could split and there be two conventions. Whatever the outcome, few Republicans saw a united party after the convention and held little hope of beating Democrats in the election. Upon arriving in Chicago, Chauncey Depew, a former senator from New York, who had played a leading role at several past Republican conventions, was asked to comment on the situation between Taft and Roosevelt. Known for his wit, Depew responded, "Situation? There is no situation. It is simply a question of which corpse will get the most flowers."[10]

The night before the convention opened, Roosevelt addressed a rally at the Auditorium Theatre, which had been the site of the 1888 Republican convention. More than five thousand people packed the room, with more than twice that number outside and unable to get in. In a fiery speech lasting over an hour, Roosevelt urged his supporters to fight "from the moment the convention opens." He alleged that the RNC had stolen his delegates and that the theft must be avenged. Declared the former president, "It is not a partisan issue; it is more than a political issue: it is a great moral issue. If we condone political theft, if we do not resent the kinds of wrong and injustice that injuriously affect the whole nation, not merely our democratic form of government but our civilization itself cannot endure. If the methods adopted by the national committee are approved by the convention, which is about to assemble, a great crime will have been committed." With "deliberate dishonesty," he charged, some "sixty to eighty lawfully elected delegates" had been excluded from the convention by the RNC and replaced with "an equal number of fraudulent delegates not elected by the people." He then announced his remedy—none of the contested Taft delegates placed on the temporary roll by the RNC should be allowed to cast votes on the makeup of the temporary roll of delegates. "It is for the convention itself to decide these cases," with only uncontested delegates permitted to vote. TR knew that he had a thin margin over Taft among the uncontested delegates and his proposal would get his contested delegates seated, allow his choice for temporary chairman to be elected, and give him control of the convention. Otherwise, he stated, the convention's nominee would be tainted and his followers would not be bound by the outcome. Implicit in his remarks was the threat, which had been reported in newspapers for weeks, that if the convention did not go their way, Roosevelt and his supporters would bolt the Republican Party and set up a third party with the former president as its nominee. The rally had the feel of a revival meeting, with Roosevelt proclaiming that the convention would be a battle between good and evil. He ended his speech with stirring words and a final line that would go down in history:

> It would be far better to fall honorably for the cause we champion than it would be to win by foul methods, the foul victory for which our opponents hope.
> But the victory shall be ours, and it shall be won, as we have already won so many victories, by clean and honest fighting for the loftiest of causes.
> We fight in honorable fashion for the good of mankind; fearless of the future, unheeding of our individual fates, with unflinching ears and undimmed eyes; we stand at Armageddon and we battle for the Lord.[11]

The crowd was electrified. The *Baltimore Sun* called it "an epoch-making speech, made under circumstances unparalleled in the history of the republic." Earlier that day, a handbill had been spread throughout Chicago mocking Roosevelt and announcing that he would be walking on the waters of Lake Michigan that evening. One historian has commented that, with his rousing speech at the Auditorium on the eve of the convention, Roosevelt's performance had surpassed the advertised miracle.[12]

Two women, Mrs. Francis Collins and Mrs. Charles Blaney, were delegates to the convention. Both were from California and were the first women to attend a Republican convention as full delegates. A few women had attended prior conventions as alternate delegates. By 1912, women could vote under the state constitutions of six western states. A week before the convention, Roosevelt announced his support for an amendment to the United States Constitution providing for nationwide women's suffrage, something that he had opposed when he was president. Some suffragette leaders criticized the timing of his switch on the issue, arguing that he was pandering to try to win the votes of women in those western states where they could already cast a ballot. In 1912, Taft remained opposed to national women's suffrage and held the view that it was a decision for each state.[13]

A nervous forty-one-year-old Victor Rosewater opened the fifteenth Republican National Convention shortly after noon on Tuesday, June 18. His job as RNC chairman was to preside over the gathering until a temporary chairman was named, a perfunctory role that normally lasted only a few minutes. With Roosevelt having announced that his supporters would be challenging the RNC's temporary roll of delegates at the convention's outset, Rosewater knew this convention would be different. A Taft supporter, it would fall to him to deny the challenge. With the rumors of possible violence at the convention circulating for days, a colleague warned Rosewater as he took the stage, "Victor, as soon as you've made that decision, jump off the platform, for someone is going to take a shot at you for sure."[14] As soon as the gavel was pounded, TR's floor leader, Governor Herbert Hadley of Missouri, was on his feet moving to substitute his own list of temporary delegates for that of the RNC. Taft's man in charge on the floor, James Watson, a former congressman from Indiana, quickly objected. Rosewater gave Hadley twenty minutes to state his case. The RNC, argued Hadley, did not have "absolute power" to name the convention's temporary delegates and seventy-two names on the committee's list were delegates "not honestly elected." Any standard-bearer for the party emerging from the convention with those delegates participating, he said, "will bear a tainted nomination." Having let Hadley have his say, Rosewater then ruled that Hadley's motion was out of order. Determining the credentials of delegates would not happen now, but later, once the convention formed its standard committees, which would include a credentials committee. Rosewater concluded that "The proper time for this investigation is after the temporary and before the permanent organization" of the convention . . . . It is not within the province of this unorganized assemblage to pass upon credentials." As most expected, the opening battle of the convention had gone to Taft. The next one would have more suspense.[15]

Rosewater then nominated Senator Elihu Root of New York as his committee's choice for temporary chairman. It was a wise choice for the Taft team. Root was well-respected and had been a prominent member of Roosevelt's cabinet, having served as secretary of war during his first term and as secretary of state in the second. Root had broken with his old boss when Roosevelt announced his support for recall of judicial decisions. His past ties, it was hoped, would bring crossover votes from some of Roosevelt's delegates. As soon as Root's name left Rosewater's lips, Henry Cochems, a Wisconsin delegate, was on his feet and announced "as an individual La Follette delegate" that he was nominating Francis McGovern, the governor of La Follette's home state of Wisconsin, for temporary chairman. There were no other nominations. This was a surprise, and a concern, for many Taft supporters in the hall. It had been thought that the Roosevelt campaign would be nominating Senator William Borah of Idaho, a strong supporter of the former president, for temporary chairman. Had a deal been struck between the TR and La Follette campaigns to unite on this issue to get the votes needed to defeat Root for temporary chairman? If successful, the Roosevelt team could then renew, before a sympathetic temporary chairman, their motion to purge the temporary roll of seventy-two Taft delegates and replace them with Roosevelt supporters before the convention was formally organized.[16]

The usual custom was for the national committee's choice for temporary chairman to be approved by the convention on a voice vote without any discussion. In the fourteen prior Republican conventions, there had been only one contest, in 1884, for temporary chairman. That year, Senator James Blaine of Maine and the incumbent president, Chester Arthur, were the frontrunners for the nomination. A small group of delegates disdained both Blaine and Arthur, viewing them as tainted by corruption, and decided to shake things up at the convention's opening session by contesting the national committee's choice for temporary chairman, who was a Blaine supporter. In a first, they nominated a Black delegate, John Lynch of Mississippi, for the largely ceremonial position. In the debate that followed, a young assemblyman from

New York made his debut on the national political stage, denouncing the RNC's power, and proclaiming, "I hold it to be derogatory to our honor, to our capacity for self-government [as a convention], to say that we must accept the nomination of a presiding officer by another body; and that our hands are tied, and we dare not reverse its action." This group of renegades, with the help of the Arthur delegates, was successful. Lynch won the vote for temporary chairman, although Blaine emerged as the convention's nominee. The young New Yorker who helped lead this charge, who was then only twenty-four years old, was Theodore Roosevelt.[17] Now, almost three decades later, Roosevelt was again embroiled in a contest to defeat the national committee's choice for temporary chairman at a convention. Both times, he was fighting against the party's establishment. But this time, he had much more at stake. His own nomination as the party's presidential candidate hinged on the outcome of the contest.

The convention then heard several seconding speeches supporting Root and McGovern for temporary chairman. The Taft team was confident, but worried. An alliance between the Roosevelt and La Follette delegates in voting for McGovern would make it a close race. A New York delegate spoke in favor of Root and quoted TR's lavish praise of Root just a few years earlier when Root was in his cabinet. Said Roosevelt then, "Elihu Root . . . is the ablest man that has appeared in public life of any country in any position in my time." During these speeches, heckling and disorder, which would come to characterize the convention, began. Shouts of "Steam Roller!" were directed at the Taft speakers. Any momentum for McGovern was halted when a Wisconsin delegate, Walter Houser, announced that the delegate from his state who had placed McGovern's name in nomination had done so without the approval of La Follette, nor from the majority of the Wisconsin delegation. Claiming to speak for La Follette, Houser advised that the senator had refused "from the beginning of the campaign . . . to enter into any combination or alliance with any candidate or set of men, [and] he refuses now to be forced into such an alliance." The Taft men breathed sighs of relief—there was no secret deal between Roosevelt and La Follette. Chairman Rosewater ruled that the voting on temporary chairman would not be by states, but by individual delegates, based on the precedent of the 1884 convention, the only time that there has been such a contest. This made for a long afternoon, for each time one of the seventy-two delegates that Roosevelt was contesting stood up to cast his vote, there was another mini-battle over his right to do so, requiring a ruling by the chairman. Finally, after three hours, the tally was announced and Root emerged the victor with 558 votes, compared to 501 for McGovern, and eighteen votes for others or not cast. The margin was eighteen more than the 540 votes needed to win the presidential nomination and seemed to foreshadow a Taft victory in that contest. There was much commentary in newspapers the next morning over interpretation of this vote, with Roosevelt's supporters arguing that their man would get votes from several delegates who had voted for Root, and with Taft's managers predicting that it was Taft who would pick up some of the delegates who had voted for McGovern. Regardless of the spin that the Roosevelt campaign tried to place on the outcome, with Root's election as temporary chairman, the odds of their man winning the nomination had significantly diminished.[18]

Newspapers contained rumors that the TR campaign was planning violence at the convention if things did not go their way. Years later, the recollections of some of Roosevelt's key players in Chicago confirmed that a plan had been agreed upon. On the opening day of the convention, they placed hundreds of "rough-and-ready supporters with strong lungs and strong arms" in the galleries. When the anticipated ruling from Rosewater denying a challenge to the temporary roll of delegates was announced, on an agreed-upon signal, the plan was to use "roughhouse tactics" to provoke a brutal response from the thousand Chicago police officers stationed in and around the Coliseum. Feigning outrage over such an attack, Roosevelt's delegates and supporters would then walk out of the convention, claim the moral high ground, and set up their own convention. There had been tension in the days before the convention among TR's closest advisers as to their strategy if the initial rulings at the convention were not in their favor. Some, led by Governor Hiram Johnson of California, wanted to bolt the convention and declare a new third party at the first opportunity. He favored provoking a confrontation on the opening day and then walking out. Others favored staying at the convention as long as possible, to build a public record of the "steamroller" tactics expected from the Taft men, and thereby creating sympathy among the public for patience in the face of adversity. The man who was had discretion to give the signal for disruption on the opening day, Hadley, Roosevelt's floor leader, decided not to do so, concerned over the blood that would likely be shed. Later, Johnson fumed at "the timid and shrinking men" who opposed starting a riot in the convention hall and using it as justification for an early walkout by TR's supporters.[19]

At eleven a.m. on Wednesday, June 19, Elihu Root pounded his gavel to open the convention's second day. Immediately, Governor Hadley renewed his motion to substitute his list of seventy-two Roosevelt delegates for the names of the contested seventy-two Taft delegates on the RNC's temporary roll. Root announced that he would allow three hours of debate on the motion, which followed, and which was heated at times. Hadley further proposed that the contested delegates not be permitted to vote on this issue and that it "be determined by the uncontested delegates of this convention." Watson, Taft's floor leader, argued that the matter had to be referred to the Committee on Credentials, once it was formed, and that no votes on delegate seating were proper until the permanent organization of the convention was established. A TR supporter, Governor Deneen of Illinois, agreed to a referral to the Committee on Credentials, but moved that none of the contested delegates be permitted to vote on the makeup of that committee, nor on its report. Deneen's motion was defeated by a vote of 567 to 507, giving the Taft forces another key victory. Root then announced his ruling on Hadley's underlying motion to exclude contested delegates from voting on disputed delegate contests. He held that a delegate could not vote in a contest involving his *own* seat, but that he could vote in the contests involving *other* delegates' seats. He noted that to rule otherwise would take away a convention's ability to function. Said Root, "To hold that a member whose seat is contested may take no part in the proceedings of this body would lead to the conclusion that if every seat were contested, there could be no Convention at all, as nobody would be entitled to participate." This was the fatal flaw of the Roosevelt argument—if adopted, it would permit a minority at *any* convention to contest enough delegate seats held by the majority, to exclude those contested delegates from voting, and the minority would then become the majority and control the convention. The convention then formed the four standard committees established at all Republican conventions (for permanent organization, for credentials, for rules, and to draft the party's platform), with the traditional one member on each committee from each state and territory. Taft men would hold the majority on all the committees and, with their appointment, the convention adjourned for the day.[20]

Rumors circulated on Wednesday that Hadley could emerge from the convention as a compromise nominee for president. As Roosevelt's floor leader, he had acquitted himself well on the opening day and had been positively portrayed in many newspaper articles around the nation that morning. For this reason, some of TR's ardent supporters viewed Hadley with suspicion and doubted the extent of his loyalty. Taft's managers, whose main goal was to see Roosevelt defeated, were willing to sacrifice Taft, if necessary. Watson, Taft's floor leader, decided to orchestrate a rally for Hadley. During debate on the disputed delegates, he intentionally called on Hadley, with complimentary language, to make a response and went over to Hadley's seat, gave him a friendly hug, and escorted him to the podium. As Hadley took the stage, in an orchestrated move, a Pennsylvania delegate rushed to the podium and, through a megaphone, shouted "Three cheers for Governor Hadley, the next president." The crowd went wild. In fact, Hadley was loyal to TR and would not have accepted the nomination, if it had come his way. Unknown except to a few close associates, Hadley had been diagnosed with tuberculosis shortly before the convention and was experiencing a very high fever when in Chicago. Uncertain over his health, Hadley would never have let himself become the nominee. Reportedly, Roosevelt was brought to tears when told during the convention of Hadley's diagnosis. On any possible compromise nominee, Roosevelt was adamant. He would not even consider one unless and until the convention first purged its roll of the seventy-two delegates he was contesting. It was a demand he knew the Taft men would never accept. The Rough Rider would not be dismounting.[21]

The Hadley demonstration was short-lived and was soon superseded by a more boisterous one for Roosevelt, during which talk of Hadley as an alternative nominee seemed to lessen. TR's ardent supporters were not about to let any momentum for Hadley linger. Roosevelt's delegates began to march around the floor shouting "Thou shall not steal!" (with the alleged "theft" of delegates by the RNC, the Eighth Commandment had become a favorite rallying cry in Chicago) and "We want Teddy!" Men held their canes aloft, topped with Rough Rider hats. Taft supporters in the New York delegation sat silent amid the tumult and, a reporter noted, "looked as if they regarded themselves as a body of visitors to an insane asylum." Mrs. W. A. Davis, the wife of a Chicago contractor, came to the convention that morning with a ticket designated for an alternate delegate. She was refused admission to the area reserved for alternate delegates, but a friendly police officer let her take a seat high in the galleries. As the Roosevelt demonstration began, Davis grabbed a large lithograph portrait of TR from the lap of a man sitting near her and, jumping and shouting, held it aloft. Within a couple of minutes, all eyes in the Coliseum were focused on her. The California delegation sent up to her a teddy bear on a pole, and she was then led down to the convention floor, where she led the Roosevelt demonstration to the front of the stage. Davis was hoisted up onto the area where reporters were seated, near the podium, until being escorted down by security. Newspapers the next day were filled with the story of the "wonderfully pretty young woman" with an "infectious smile" who had been the highlight of the convention's second day. The scene was reminiscent of the 1896 Democratic convention. Then, Minnie Murray, a young woman from Iowa and a supporter of the presidential hopes of her home state's governor, Horace Boies, energetically waved her arms and a flag, shouting out for Boies. She became the center of attention in the hall, was brought to the convention floor to lead a demonstration, and was featured in newspapers the following morning. The similar antics of Davis won her a brief audience with Roosevelt that evening at the Congress Hotel. "[A] bully piece of work," he told her. Both Davis and Murray had their fleeting moments of fame and have gone down in history as part of the lore of presidential nominating conventions.[22]

Nothing was accomplished on Thursday, June 20, the third day of the convention. Root called the gathering to order at noon, received an update that the Committee on Credentials was still meeting and had no report yet, and then recessed until the late afternoon. When Root reappeared hours later, the galleries were packed with thousands of Roosevelt supporters. There had been rumors (untrue) that their hero was going to show up in person at the convention, make remarks, and perhaps lead a walkout of his delegates. However, the credentials report was still not ready, Roosevelt was not present and Root gaveled the convention closed until the next day. Shouting "We want Teddy!," the crowd refused to leave and became boisterous. Extra police were called to the podium to protect it in the event of a rush. The barbed wire under the bunting may prove useful after all. It was more than an hour after the brief session ended, and after an announcement that the lights would be turned off, before the crowd began to file out and Root felt comfortable leaving the podium.[23]

On Friday, June 21, the report of the Committee on Credentials was finally ready and, not surprisingly, the Taft-controlled committee recommended affirming the RNC's decision and seating as permanent delegates the seventy-two Taft delegates that Roosevelt was contesting. The long process began of going through these contests, alphabetically by states, and Root restated his prior ruling that the contested delegates could not vote in contests over their own seat, but could vote in the contests over other disputed seats. Nonetheless, Root permitted a vote on his ruling and the convention affirmed him by a vote of 605 to 464. On the votes concerning contested delegates in specific states, the first roll call concerned Arizona and the Taft forces prevailed by a vote of 564 to 497, a difference of sixty-seven. The effect of Root's ruling, and the convention's affirmation of it, was obvious—if all of the contested delegates had been excluded from voting, the outcome would have been different. With the handwriting on the wall, the Roosevelt forces then permitted several of the contests to be decided by voice votes, on which Root ruled in favor of seating the Taft delegates. When the vote as to each state's contest was decided, Roosevelt's supporters loudly expressed their view that the convention was a steamroller, flattening them without giving a fair hearing, shouting, "Toot, toot!," "All aboard!," and blowing whistles. Of the roll call votes, the closest contest involved California. There, a primary had been held, which Roosevelt has won handily, and the state's primary law had a winner-take-all format. Taft had prevailed, however, in one congressional district and the RNC had awarded two delegates to him from that district. This was in conformity with the RNC's call for the national convention, which stated that delegates were to be selected by congressional district. The legal issue was whether the call for the convention trumped the state's primary law. The Taft forces prevailed by a 542 to 429 vote. There was ample legal precedent for the decision. As a private entity, courts had held that a political party could make its own rules and was not bound by conflicting rules imposed by state law. As one author has noted, the California loss, which many considered to be TR's strongest case, "took the remaining air out of the Roosevelt balloon." Roosevelt's wife, Edith, who had been watching from the galleries all afternoon, got up and left after the California vote was announced. By the time the convention adjourned in the early evening, half of the seventy-two contested delegate seats had been decided, and, in each one, the convention had voted to accept the majority report of the Committee on Credentials and seated all of the disputed Taft delegates that had come before it.[24]

At the opening of the convention's fifth day, a Saturday, the report of the Committee on Credentials concerning the remaining states was debated, with the same results as the previous day. At one point, amid the endless shouts of "Toot, Toot!," of whistles being blown from the galleries, and repeated interruptions, a Roosevelt delegate shouted out to Root to request a ruling on a point of order: "The point of order," he yelled, "is that the steam roller is exceeding the speed limit." Root, with a wry smile on his face, and in one of the few moments of levity during a contentious convention, responded, "The Chair is ready is ready to rule on the point of order. The point of order is sustained. The justification is that we have some hope of getting home for Sunday." The steamroller rolled on. Ultimately, the convention approved the committee's entire report and the permanent roll of delegates was complete, unchanged from the temporary roll that had been presented by the RNC on Tuesday. The Committee on Permanent Organization then reported and recommended that Elihu Root continue his role and serve as the convention's permanent chairman. Roosevelt's managers, knowing that any fight would be futile, did not oppose this and, according to the convention's transcript, Root "assumed the chair amidst a great demonstration." There had been rumors overnight, as there had been the previous night, that Roosevelt was going to appear personally at the convention that day and lead his delegates out of the hall. Instead, Root recognized delegate Henry Allen of Kansas, who asked to read a statement from the former president. It was Roosevelt's appeal to his delegates, *not* to walk out of the convention, but to no longer actively participate:

> The Convention has now declined to purge the roll of the fraudulent delegates placed thereon by the defunct National Committee, and the majority which thus indorsed [sic] fraud was made a majority only because it included the fraudulent delegates themselves, who all sat as judges on one another's cases . . . . This action makes the Convention in no proper sense any longer a Republican Convention representing the real Republican party. Therefore, I hope the men elected as Roosevelt delegates will now decline to vote on any matter before the Convention. I do not release any

delegate from his honorable obligation to vote for me if he votes at all, but under the actual conditions I hope he will not vote at all.

Any man nominated by the Convention as now constituted would be merely the beneficiary of the successful fraud . . . and any man thus accepting the Convention's nomination under these circumstances . . . would have forfeited the right to ask the support of any honest man of any party on moral grounds.

After reading the statement, Allen defiantly addressed the Taft forces that controlled the convention: "We do not bolt. . . . We have pleaded with you for ten days. We have fought with you for five days for a square deal. We fight no more, we plead no longer. We shall sit in protest, and the people who sent us here shall judge us." Any hope of party unity after the convention, if there ever was any, was now gone.[25]

Hours earlier, at two o'clock in the morning, Roosevelt, in his suite of rooms at the Congress Hotel, after receiving assurance from two key financial backers, Frank Muncey and George Perkins, that they would continue to support him, made a final decision that many of his closest advisers had been urging him to make for weeks. He would form a third party and would be its nominee for president. What happened at the Chicago Coliseum was no longer important to them. TR and his team began planning the formation of the Progressive Party.[26]

During the afternoon session, a Pennsylvania delegate, who was a Roosevelt supporter, grabbed a megaphone and announced that the convention's agenda for the rest of the day would be the funeral of its victim, the Republican Party, with Watson (Taft's floor leader) serving as the coroner, Root as the undertaker, and the man who would place Taft's name in nomination as the funeral orator. Before the "funeral," however, the party had to adopt its platform. The report of the Committee on Resolutions was read by its chairman, Charles Fairbanks of Indiana, a conservative Republican who had served as Roosevelt's vice president. There was no love lost between the two men and the platform generally reflected the conservative views of Taft and his supporters who controlled the convention. It praised the history of the Republican Party, going back to Lincoln, and supported a continued tariff to protect American industry and jobs, but agreed that some import duties were too high and should be adjusted. It affirmed support for the civil service, supported full disclosure of campaign contributions, and called for "fair and reasonable rules and regulations" for conservation of the nation's natural resources. It invited the "intelligent judgment" of the people on the peace and prosperity of the country under the Taft administration. While it supported the recall of judges "found to be derelict" in their duties, it opposed the recall of judicial decisions, which had been one of the most prominent issues during the campaign for the nomination. Rather, the platform reaffirmed that the Republican Party will "ever insist" that the power of the courts "to enforce their process and to protect life, liberty and property shall be preserved inviolate." As the platform was being read, a loud ovation began in the hall, unrelated to Fairbanks' rather dry presentation. He looked up and saw what was causing the commotion. William Jennings Bryan, the former Democratic nominee for president, who had been attending the convention all week as a reporter, had left his seat in the press section near the podium and was making his way out of the hall. It was not a sign of disrespect. Bryan had a train to catch. He was on his way to Baltimore, where the Democratic convention would be starting in a couple of days, and where he would play a prominent role. Fairbanks departed from the reading of the platform to acknowledge Bryan, noting "We have been greatly honored with the presence of some of our friends in political opposition, some of whom have business now in Baltimore." Republicans seemed to enjoy having Bryan, who had twice lost to McKinley and once to Taft, in their midst, perhaps as a living reminder of their past electoral successes in a year in which their prospects were looking bleak. One delegate, in a backhanded compliment, told a reporter that the Nebraskan was "One of the finest men ever beaten for President three times." After Fairbanks completed his task, an alternative platform from a minority of the Committee on Credentials was presented by a La Follette delegate, which was quickly laid on the table, and the report of the Committee on Resolutions was approved by a vote of 666 yeas, to 54 nays, and with 343 Roosevelt delegates not voting.[27]

The convention then moved, at the dinner hour, to the nomination of candidates for president. Taft personally chose Warren Harding, a small-town newspaper publisher from Marion, Ohio, to make his primary nominating speech. It was a reward to the forty-six-year-old Harding for his support of Taft during the primary battle in Taft's home state of Ohio, which Roosevelt had won handily. Harding had been the GOP's losing candidate for governor of Ohio in 1910. As a non-officeholder with no national political stature, the selection was an honor for Harding and was his debut on the national political stage. His remarks attacked Roosevelt, although not by name. If the word progressive meant making progress, proclaimed Harding, then it was Taft, not his predecessor in the White House, who best fit the definition:

> Progression is not proclamation nor palaver. It is not pretense nor play on prejudice. It is not personal pronouns, nor perennial pronouncement. It is not the perturbation of a people passion-wrought, not a promise proposed. Progression is everlastingly lifting the standards that marked the end of the world's march yesterday and planting them on new and advanced heights to-day. Tested by such a standard, President Taft is the greatest progressive of the age.

Harding's point, perhaps lost in the alliteration, was to call out Roosevelt as a publicity-seeking, self-centered egotist, who had stirred the people with words, while Taft, by his actions as president, without fanfare, had done the real work of a progressive and had moved the nation forward. The statement that Taft was the "greatest progressive of the age" was too much for Roosevelt's supporters, who began to boo and hiss Harding, behavior that continued throughout the rest of his speech. The noise became so great at one point that Root had to step in to gavel down TR's supporters who, per Roosevelt's wishes, were supposedly no longer going to actively participate in the convention. Said Root, "I beg the delegates who have announced their intention to sit mute in this assemblage, to preserve their self-respect for whatever cause the future has for them." Their lack of dignity, he said, reflected poorly on the people who had sent them to Chicago as their representatives. Harding then resumed, praising Taft's leadership and denouncing those in the party who had opposed him: "Opposition to his renomination is as nearly without precedent as it is without reason or excuse. This opposition was born of expediency and fostered in mendacity." The Republican Party, he said, had governed the nation for most of the past half-century by "holding measures above men, and principles above personalities, and aims above animosities." When the Republican voter in November decides how to cast his ballot, Harding predicted:

> I can foresee his plain and simple reasoning now, with one inevitable conclusion. Is my country at peace? Yes, honorable peace. Is my country prosperous? Yes, like no other on the earth. Is the law held supreme? Yes, as never before. Has my party kept the faith? Yes, and more, for its Chief Executive wrought reformations and advancement the party could not pledge. Is my government honestly and economically administered? Yes, the honesty is unquestioned and the economies set a new standard of national administration.

In the middle of the speech, when Taft's name was first mentioned, there was cheering and parading by the Taft supporters on the floor and in the galleries, lasting about fifteen minutes, the first real pro-Taft demonstration of the convention. However, the hostile reaction to Harding's speech from the TR supporters in the arena was so extreme that a planned seconding speech from Kentucky's William Bradley was not given. Watson, Taft's floor leader, told Bradley "I am afraid for you to try. I think you had better quietly slip away and go down the back stairway and over to your hotel." Bradley complied, although two other speakers did step up and gave brief seconding speeches for Taft. The 1912 Republican convention was not the only time that Warren Harding would nominate William Howard Taft to head a branch of the federal government. Eleven years later, in 1921, as president, Harding nominated Taft for chief justice of the Supreme Court, a position that Taft had coveted for most of his adult life. The nomination was affirmed by the Senate and Taft spent his later years leading the nation's highest court, serving with distinction and with personal satisfaction and happiness, unlike his turbulent years in the White House.[28]

Robert La Follette was then placed in nomination by a Wisconsin delegate, Michael Olbrich, who praised "Fighting Bob" as the one candidate who "furnishes your one salvation from defeat in dishonor and disgrace." He praised La Follette's record as governor of Wisconsin and then as its senator, and traced his rise to the leadership of the progressive movement: "They who scoffed have come to listen when he speaks. He is no mere jingler of euphonious words, no conjurer of fantastic phrases . . . . Step by step, no inch uncontested, undeterred by slander, ridicule, abuse, he fought along the way of dauntless self-reliance, till there came first one recruit and then another, and then they came by scores, and to-day a mighty army is assembled whose camp is filled with sounds of preparation for offensive warfare with all in readiness to march forth upon the morrow to retake the land of our inheritance, too long the spoilers' prey." According the *Chicago Tribune*, Olbrich's speech was an "impressive address, enunciating advanced progressive policies" and, unlike Harding, he was listened to attentively and with few interruptions. Taft and La Follette were the only two candidates formally nominated. Roosevelt, having asked his supporters to no longer participate in the proceedings, forbade his name from being placed before the convention. In a surprise, the Iowa delegation chose not to formally nominate its favorite-son candidate, Albert Cummins, although he was still in the race.[29]

The roll call of the states for the presidential nomination began around half past seven in the evening and lasted two hours. As it proceeded, the votes of most of Roosevelt's delegates were announced as "Present, but not voting." Although the outcome was certain, there was still more controversy. When a poll was requested of individual delegates from Massachusetts, where eighteen had been recorded as not voting, Chairman Root called for the votes of alternate delegates to be cast whenever the name of a delegate who had refused to vote was called. This prompted catcalls and angry fists being shaken at Root from TR's supporters, but did not change the outcome. The alternates also refused to vote. The finally tally was 561 votes for Taft, 107 for Roosevelt, 41 for La Follette, 17 for Cummins, 8 for others or absent, and 344 present but not voting. Those TR delegates who voted did so because they believed that instructions from their state primary to cast their ballots for him overrode the candidate's wish. It was a narrow victory for Taft, only twenty-one over the majority vote of 540 required for the nomination. As a Taft biographer has commented, "Taft's renomination came as an empty honor, for there was no enthusiasm for him at Chicago. The fight was not for him but against Roosevelt."[30]

The remaining agenda item for the convention was to nominate a running mate for Taft, which was done quickly and, noted the *Chicago Tribune*, "was admittedly the most uninteresting event of the entire five-day program." The incumbent vice president, James Sherman of New York, was nominated in a speech that only lasted a few seconds, given "the lateness of the hour." There were no other formal nominations and Sherman won with 595 votes (thirty-four more than Taft had received), with fifty-eight votes scattered among others, seventy-two absent, and 352 present but not voting. Unfortunately for Sherman, he would not live until election day. He died in late October from a kidney ailment and, after the election but before the Electoral College votes were cast, was replaced on the Republican ticket by Nicholas Murray Butler, who was the president of Columbia University.[31]

Taft received the news of his re-nomination on a Saturday evening at the White House, after a leisurely day that had included a round of golf. Unlike Roosevelt, he had not personally been setting strategy or directing his campaign team. Earlier in the week, he had gone to a baseball game during one of the convention's sessions. His managers had told him that he would likely win and he was relieved, but not surprised. The president promptly issued a statement, calling the nomination contest an attempt to "seize the Republican party and make it the instrument of reckless ambition and the unsettling of the fundamental principles of our government." He praised the outcome, which he stated had affirmed the "wise and valuable tradition" of no third presidential term for any man, and he was pleased that "a most serious menace to our republican institutions has been averted."[32]

Within hours of Taft's nomination, plans for a new political party were formed. That evening, while the Republican convention was still winding down at the Coliseum, Roosevelt's delegates and supporters began to gather at nearby Orchestra Hall. The room started filling up around nine o'clock and, shortly before midnight, TR appeared to a thunderous welcome. In remarks lasting for forty minutes, he advised that he was not prepared to accept their nomination that night, as some had expected. Rather, he told them to go home, listen to the people who had sent them to Chicago, and to return to the city in August. If they still wanted to nominate him at that time as their presidential candidate, he added, he would then gladly accept.[33]

Over a month later, on August 5, Roosevelt and his followers returned to the Chicago Coliseum for the first convention of the new Progressive Party, which was soon to be nicknamed the Bull Moose Party. The event had the feel of a revival meeting, with "Onward, Christian Solders" being the most frequently played song and becoming the unofficial anthem of the new third party. Roosevelt addressed the gathering as it began, stating, "both the old parties are controlled by professional politicians in the interests of the privileged classes," but that this new party would be founded on "the right of the people to rule." He spoke for two hours and ended with the same words that he had uttered in the same city several weeks earlier. "We stand at Armageddon," he again proclaimed, "and we battle for the Lord." He was unanimously nominated as the party's presidential candidate, Governor Hiram Johnson of California was named his running mate, and a thoroughly progressive platform was adopted.[34]

At the 1912 Republican convention in Chicago, Theodore Roosevelt was beaten by a party nominating system that he had supported, used, and strengthened when in office, and which he had passed on to Taft, his successor. As noted earlier, William Jennings Bryan, the thrice-defeated Democratic nominee, attended the convention as a reporter. As the convention reached its final day and Roosevelt's defeat was imminent, Bryan wrote of the irony of TR's situation: "It is no pleasant situation in which the ex-president finds himself . . . . Twice chief executive of the nation, the second time by the largest majority that a president ever achieved . . . he now finds the man whom he nominated and elected pitted against him in the most bitter contest that our country has ever seen, and he sees that opponent operating with a skill of a past master the very machinery which the tutor constructed and taught him to use."[35]

Post-mortems on nomination contests are always speculative but, with other strategies, could Roosevelt had won? Different choices on two decisions may have changed the outcome. What if TR had spent more time during the primaries and while in Chicago courting the votes of the like-minded progressive delegates supporting La Follette and Cummins? If successful, this could have picked up almost sixty votes. Would a narrower challenge to the credentials of Taft delegates have given Roosevelt's arguments more credibility? If he had focused only on those twenty or thirty contests where there was substantial evidence of irregularity, instead of the overbroad approach that was used, would it have resulted in some changes to the RNC's temporary roll and given his forces momentum during the convention? Or, was the whole convention just a show, with Roosevelt and his supporters having determined to start a third party before they arrived in Chicago and their actions there designed as merely a prelude to that strategy?

As the *New York Times* noted at the end of the Republican convention, "The Grand Old Party is for the moment smashed to pieces."[36] For only the second time in history, a major American political party had split in two at its presidential nominating convention. The other occasion was in 1860, on the eve of the Civil War, when Democrats had fractured at their convention in Baltimore, with the party's northern faction nominating Stephen Douglas and its southern faction nominating John Breckinridge. That split led to the election of the first Republican president, Abraham Lincoln. In 1912, the roles of the parties were reversed. As the Republicans left Chicago, it was hard to see how their division would not result in handing the election to the nominee of the Democratic Party which, ironically, would be returning the next week to Baltimore for its convention, the site of its own debacle in 1860.

Democratic Convention

From their invention during the campaign of 1832 and through the Civil War, Baltimore had been the city of choice for hosting presidential nominating conventions. Over the next generation, that title passed to Chicago. In 1912, however, Maryland's largest city had another turn in the nation's political spotlight. Only three days after the Republican convention in Chicago ended in chaos, the Democrats met in Baltimore to nominate their candidate. With the GOP schism between Taft and Roosevelt, for the first time in two decades, the man nominated by the Democrats would likely be the favorite to win the White House.

On Tuesday, June 25, 1912, a crowd of more than 15,000 gathered in Baltimore's Fifth Regiment Armory, a massive fortress-like gray granite structure that had opened in 1903 and which was used primarily for the training of national guard troops. Over the next week, on the concrete floor of the armory, political tactics, strategy, and maneuvers would replace military ones, as an intense battle for the Democratic presidential nomination played out, rivaling the fireworks and contentiousness that had marked the Republican gathering the previous week. For the first time, women were full delegates to a Democratic convention. Mary Arkwright Hutton of Washington State and Anna Hamilton Pitzer of Colorado were among the 1,088 delegates, and hundreds of alternates, present in the armory for the quadrennial spectacle of the nation's oldest political party selecting its presidential nominee. Another woman, Nellie Taft, the wife of the sitting Republican president, was among the honored guests at the convention.[37]

There were four major contenders for the nomination, two acceptable to the liberal faction of the party and two supported by the party's conservatives. Going into the convention, the man considered the frontrunner was sixty-two-year-old Champ Clark, a longtime member of Congress from Missouri and speaker of the House of Representatives. An expert and leader on tariff reform, which had been a mainstay Democratic issue for years, Clark had built a solid record over the years and was considered a regular party man, trustworthy, and more of a moderate than a liberal. He had a campaign song, an old tune from the Ozarks, entitled "They Gotta Quit Kickin' My Dog Around," which told the story of a man's hound dog getting picked on and the dog and its owner exacting their revenge. During the convention, the "houn' dawg song" was loudly sung in hotel lobbies by Clark supporters and leashed hound dogs on the streets of Baltimore were a frequent site, one man claiming to have walked his long-eared friend all the way from Oklahoma. Whatever advantage Clark gained with the masses from the folksy song was offset by the aversion to it by the progressive eastern elites in the party, who viewed the song, and the candidate associated with it, as "seedy and provincial."[38]

The man favored by those eastern elites, Woodrow Wilson, was a newcomer to the political arena. Fifty-five years old, he had become governor of New Jersey less than two years earlier, in 1910, his first elected position. Born in Virginia and raised in Georgia, Wilson had spent most of his career as a college professor in the northeast, with a focus on political science, eventually rising to become president of Princeton University. Throughout most of his life, he held conservative political views, having written disparagingly about liberalism over the years and not voting for his party's liberal icon, William Jennings Bryan, in 1896. Wilson had been elected governor with the help of New Jersey's conservative political boss, James Smith, but once in office, he turned on Smith and moved rapidly to the progressive wing of the party. In his first year as governor, he successfully guided through the state legislature several laws that were tenets of progressivism, including workers' compensation for injured employees, greater regulation of public utilities, and revised and more open election procedures.[39]

The other two major contenders for the nomination were from the party's conservative faction and were considered "second-tier" candidates, below Clark and Wilson. Alabaman Oscar Underwood was, like Clark, a powerful Democratic member of the House of Representatives, serving as chairman of the Ways and Means Committee and as majority leader of that body. He was the first southerner living in the South to make a serious run for the presidency since the Civil War. At best, Underwood was viewed as a regional candidate and was unable to make a breakthrough in any states outside his home region. The other conservative in the race was Judson Harmon, the governor of Ohio, who had served as attorney general in Grover Cleveland's cabinet. In addition to Ohio, he was rumored to be the choice of New York, which had come to the convention uncommitted. Without a candidate of their own in 1912, the New York delegation, which included Wall Street financier Augustus Belmont, was united under the leadership of Charles Murphy, the boss of Tammany Hall. As the largest state, with 90 of the 726 votes needed for the presidential nomination, New York was guaranteed to be in the thick of the fight in Baltimore.

One eager New York politician who supported Wilson had been denied a seat by Boss Murphy in the Empire State's delegation, as either a full or alternate delegate. Just thirty years old, he had recently been elected to the state senate and had already started to become a thorn in Tammany's side. Undeterred by being shut out of the official delegation, he organized a Woodrow Wilson Club of around one-hundred and fifty members and led them to Baltimore. There, he was a constant presence in hotel lobbies and restaurants, promoting Wilson and making acquaintances. The club secured seats in the galleries each day of the convention, where they led cheers for the New Jersey governor. It was the young man's first exposure to the national political scene. It would not be Franklin Roosevelt's last Democratic convention.[40]

A man who had vowed that he would not be a candidate in 1912 was William Jennings Bryan, the party's three-time nominee (in 1896, 1900, and 1908), losing the general election each time by large margins, twice to McKinley and once to Taft. Despite his defeats, Bryan remained the darling of the party's liberal faction and he would be in Baltimore as a delegate from his home state of Nebraska. He had publicly stated that either Champ Clark or Woodrow

Wilson would be acceptable to him as a nominee, but declined to personally endorse either one. Most of the Nebraska delegation, including Bryan himself, were pledged to vote for Clark, as Clark had won their state's primary. At the last convention in which he was not a candidate for the presidential nomination, held in St. Louis in 1904, Bryan was also a delegate and had been a dominant force in the proceedings. If anyone thought that the Great Commoner planned to be a wallflower in Baltimore, they were sorely wrong. The Nebraskan arrived in the city to a reception befitting a modern-day rock star, with his train met by hundreds of admirers. Dozens of taxis, filled with reporters, trailed him to his hotel, where another throng of supporters waited to greet him. Some thought that he coveted a fourth nomination, with the *Baltimore Sun* reporting on the eve of the convention, "[t]alk of Bryan for President is heard on all sides." One longtime Bryan supporter, sadly, had already given up hope. James Waite of California had vowed when Bryan was first nominated in 1896 to not shave his beard until the Nebraskan was in the White House. A few weeks before the 1912 convention, after reading Bryan's many declarations that he was not a candidate, Waite walked into a barber shop, and with half of his small town watching, unfolded his sixteen years of whiskers, and got a clean shave. As Waite read about Bryan's actions in Baltimore, he may have regretted his decision.[41]

The 1912 presidential campaign was the first to see the widespread use of state primary elections to select delegates to the national conventions of the two major parties. As noted earlier, Roosevelt, Taft, and La Follette battled it out in the Republican primaries, with Roosevelt winning the most primary votes and delegates. In the dozen states in which Democratic primaries were held over the first few months of 1912, Clark came away with the most delegates, his most impressive win being a decisive victory over Wilson in Illinois. As the convention opened, combining delegates selected in primaries with those chosen at state conventions, Clark held a commanding lead of around 425, with Wilson's total between 250 and 275. Underwood was in third place with 91 and Harmon in fourth with 57. More than a hundred delegates were pledged minor candidates (mostly favorite sons from various states) and over two hundred were uncommitted to any candidate, most of their votes controlled by party bosses. Newspapers reported that the betting odds were eight to five that Clark would emerge the victor. In keeping with tradition, none of the candidates came to Baltimore. Clark and Underwood monitored events from their offices in Washington, D. C., Harmon was in Ohio, and Wilson was at the summer home of the New Jersey governor in the coastal town of Sea Girt. All were in constant contact by telephone with their teams in Baltimore.[42]

The convention in the largely Catholic state of Maryland opened shortly after noon on Tuesday, June 25, with a prayer for harmony and divine wisdom from seventy-seven-year-old James Cardinal Gibbons, the patriarch of the Baltimore Archdiocese. While the last amen still echoed in the packed armory, William Jennings Bryan shouted for the attention of the party's chairman, Norman Mack, who had followed the prayer with the recommendation of the Democratic National Committee ("DNC") that Alton Parker of New York serve as the convention's temporary chairman. The choice required the full convention's approval. This was a largely ceremonial role, but it included giving the keynote speech. Parker, the party's 1904 presidential nominee (who lost in a landslide to Roosevelt) was strongly identified with the party's conservative faction, with which Bryan had been battling for years for control of the party. Bryan was furious at the choice, believing that it would be disastrous for Democrats to open their convention with a speech from a man put forward by, and identified with, "the reactionary element of the party," *i.e.,* Wall Street and Tammany Hall. Instead of Parker, he thought, a progressive Democrat needed to be the temporary chairman. When he learned of the choice of Parker a few days before the convention, Bryan immediately fired off telegrams to all of the progressive candidates for president, advising that he planned to challenge the selection and demanding to know whether they were of like mind. Clark waffled and advised that he wanted harmony in the party and urged more efforts at a compromise by all. Wilson's two managers in Baltimore, William McCombs and William McAdoo, were split over strategy. McCombs felt that a deal needed to be cut at some point with the bosses of key state delegations, like Murphy of New York, in order to win the nomination, while McAdoo felt that Wilson's only path to victory was in beating the bosses, not joining them. After initially taking a hands-off approach to the issue, Wilson was then convinced, some say by his wife, Ellen, to join Bryan in opposition to Parker. "You are quite right," his response telegram to Bryan read, "The Baltimore convention is to be a convention of progressives—of men who are progressives on principle and by conviction," and it ought not to begin with a featured address by one who did not share those values. "You are," continued Wilson, "entirely within your rights in doing everything within your power" to defeat Parker and "[n]o one will doubt where my sympathies lie."[43]

Bryan, the most famous Democrat in the country, marched to the podium to the sound of cheers. He reminded the delegates that he had been their nominee three times and spoke for the more than six million Democrats who had voted for him in each of those elections. He recited a quotation on a large banner in the upper reaches of the arched roof of the armory—"He never sold the truth to serve the hour"—and pointed to a nearby portrait, stating that the words "were the language of the hero of Monticello" and that he, Bryan, would not be worthy of the Democrats who had voted for him if, in Baltimore, he "were willing to sell the truth to serve the present hour." The crowd roared its approval. Hats were lifted and tossed around the armory like frisbees. As one author has observed, "these were the days when a man was willing to sacrifice his hat to a cause." No one seemed to notice that Bryan had not pointed to a portrait of Thomas Jefferson, but instead, erroneously, to one of Andrew Jackson, or that the quoted phrase had not been written by Jefferson, but by the English post, Alfred Lord Tennyson, in honor of the Duke of Wellington. It was an era before the internet and instant fact-checking. Bryan then began a verbal lashing of Parker, who sat only feet away, as a tool of big money and corrupt politicians. "Let the commencement of this convention be such" he proclaimed, "that the Democrats of this country may raise their heads among their fellows and say, 'The Democratic party is true to the people. You cannot frighten it with your Ryans nor buy it with your Belmonts.'" The references were to Thomas Ryan, a wealthy financier from Virginia and August Belmont, a Wall Street mogul, both of whom were delegates to the convention. The crowd roared. But Bryan went on, and on, for too long. He began to lose his audience. Cries of

"Parker! Parker!" started to predominate. Cardinal Gibbons, his plea for harmony abandoned in the convention's first few minutes, gathered his red robes and quietly left the podium. Bryan then proposed Senator John Kern of Indiana as his alternative to Parker as temporary chairman. Kern, who was a longtime friend of Bryan and his running mate on the party's 1908 ticket, after pleading in vain for Parker to withdraw, stated that this was "so great a cause" that he was "not fit to be its leader." He declined to run himself and, instead (apparently to the surprise of his friend) nominated Bryan for the position. The Nebraskan could hardly refuse and a roll call of the states began. Bryan lost. The tally was 579 for Parker and 508 for Bryan. Over half of the delegates pledged to Champ Clark voted for Parker, while most of the Woodrow Wilson delegates sided with Bryan. As expected, delegates who supported the two conservative candidates, Underwood and Harmon, voted for Parker.[44]

Although Bryan lost this first skirmish in Baltimore, the contest revealed who was with him and who was against him, information that would factor into his strategy over the next few days. As one delegate shouted during the contest for temporary chairman, "The fight is on and Bryan is on one side and Wall Street is on the other." Editorials in pro-Bryan newspapers all over the country urged their readers to send telegrams to their delegates in Baltimore, demanding that a progressive candidate be the party's nominee. More than a hundred thousand were sent, much to the delight of Bryan.[45]

Bryan's actions at the convention, viewed by some as those of a troublemaker and by others as the gathering's moral conscience, continued on the third day of the proceedings. The second day had been taken up mostly with credential debates over the seating of contested delegates. Bryan's brother Charles, a close confidant who was with him in Baltimore, heard a rumor that a deal had been struck between the Clark managers and New York. The uncommitted Empire State delegation, headed by Tammany's Boss Murphy, had initially announced after arriving in Baltimore that it would be voting for Governor Harmon of Ohio, one of the conservatives in the race. However, at some point on later ballots, Charles told his brother, he heard that New York had agreed to switch its votes to Champ Clark, with the intention of starting a bandwagon effect that would propel Clark to the two-thirds figure needed for victory. Charles believed this is why most of Clark's delegates had not supported his brother in the fight to prevent conservative New Yorker Parker from becoming the convention's temporary chairman. The votes of Clark delegates had led to Parker's victory. It was a tit for tat, the Bryan brothers were now convinced—Clark's men gave New York the votes needed for Parker to win and, in exchange, New York would switch its massive block of delegates to Clark at some point during the convention. Outraged, and convinced that Wall Street interests were behind all of this, they devised a plan that would once again put brother William in the headlines from Baltimore.[46]

Shortly after the convention's Thursday evening session opened, Bryan rose and requested recognition from Ollie James, a progressive Kentuckian who had been named the permanent chairman. Bryan, the "Great Commoner," came to the podium and read a resolution that he was offering for approval by the convention: "As proof of our fidelity to the people," Bryan stated, "we declare ourselves opposed to the nomination of any candidate for president who is the representative of or under obligation to J. Pierpont Morgan, Thomas F. Ryan, August Belmont, or any other member of the privilege-hunting and favor-seeking class." Further, Bryan's resolution provided, "That we demand the withdrawal from this convention of any delegate or delegates constituting or representing the above-named interests." Morgan, the richest man in the country, was not in Baltimore, but Ryan and Belmont were present as delegates. Bryan was demanding that the convention boot them out onto the street. Both men had been seated as delegates without objection from their states (Virginia and New York), or from the credentials committee. Even some of Bryan's supporters thought he had overreached. Chairman James muttered, "What is the matter with Bryan? Does he want to destroy the Democratic Party?" One man was heard to shout an offer of $25,000 to any man who would kill the Nebraskan. Another, a Virginia delegate, stood directly in front of Bryan, ranted about his "insolent proposition," and became so enraged that he began frothing at the mouth and had to be led away. After heated discussions, Bryan agreed to withdraw the second portion of his resolution, the part that would evict Ryan and Belmont as delegates. What remained was a statement that the party opposed nominating any man who represented or owed anything to "the privilege-hunting and favor-seeking class." Opponents of Bryan, even those in the New York delegation, anxious to move on the nomination of candidates for president, decided that voting for the watered-down resolution was the best way to move forward, reasoning that it would not look good if the convention *rejected* a resolution opposing the nomination a candidate beholden to the rich and powerful. The vote was 883 in favor and only 201 against.[47]

In many ways, the resolution was meaningless, but once again, as on the convention's first day with his challenge to Parker as temporary chairman, Bryan had succeeded in making himself the focus of attention in Baltimore. The headline in the next morning's *Baltimore Sun* proclaimed "Bryan's Thunderbolt at Night Session Stuns All."[48] No one doubted that Bryan wanted his stated goal—for the convention to name a progressive as its nominee—but many now openly speculated that his ultimate plan was for the name of that nominee to once again be William Jennings Bryan.

After Bryan's theatrics, the convention then moved, at eleven o'clock on Thursday evening, to the nomination of candidates for president. The nominations began with a speech by Senator William Bankhead for his fellow Alabaman, Congressman Oscar Underwood.[49]

Senator James Reed then spoke on behalf of his fellow Missourian, Speaker Champ Clark. He traced Clark's life, from being born into poverty in Kentucky, to working since the age of twelve, to putting himself through law school, to moving to Missouri and becoming a successful attorney and public servant. "He loves the common people," Reed declared, "because he is the common people." To contrast Clark with his main opponent, Wilson, who was a political newcomer and who was known to have not voted for the party's nominee in 1896 (the very same William Jennings Bryan who had dominated the convention that evening), Reed stated that Clark "does not come with promises upon his lips, but with achievements in his hands." He pointed out that Clark had been working in Congress for almost two decades for progressive causes—for antitrust laws, against corrupt corporations, for lower tariffs, and for election reforms such as primaries, the referendum, and the direct election of senators. Clark was a loyal party man, declared Reed, "He has not been an occasional Democrat. He does not belong to that class of Democrats who steal out o' nights, sleep in strange political beds, and then come trailing home" when conditions were more favorable to the party. "I nominate this man," Reed concluded, "who has fought a thousand battles for Democracy and not one against her . . . who does not know how to quit a friend or betray a party; whose back the enemy has never seen, but whose breast is covered with the scars of honor; who leads today, and who should lead tomorrow—the Lion of Democracy, Champ Clark of Missouri." The demonstration for Clark at the conclusion of the speech lasted for an hour and five minutes, a respectable showing in the eyes of reporters, who always placed great value on such things. More speeches followed, placing in nomination the names of a handful of minor candidates, as well as Governor Harmon of Ohio.[50]

Shortly after two o'clock in the morning, the name of the other main contender, Woodrow Wilson, was placed in nomination. By this time, given the hour, there had been a steady stream of departures from the now half-empty galleries. John Wescott, a lawyer and judge from Camden, who had initially opposed Wilson for governor two years earlier, but had since become one of his most ardent admirers, strode to the podium. Before he could get started, a demonstration for Wilson broke out in the armory, lasting for an hour and fifteen minutes. Wilson's managers gleefully noted that the hoopla lasted a few minutes longer than the earlier one for Clark. Wescott finally got the crowd quieted and spoke of Wilson having moved his state away from boss rule during his first days in the governor's chair. "New Jersey is free," he declared, and on "the wreck and ruin of a bi-partisan machine a master hand has erected an ideal Commonwealth in less than two years." New Jersey proudly offered its "militant and triumphant leader" to the nation, a man who is:

> a scholar, not a charlatan; a statesman, not a doctrinaire; a profound lawyer, not a splitter of legal hairs; a political economist, not an egotistical theorist; a practical politician . . . a resistless debater and consummate master of statement, not a mere phrase-maker; a humanitarian, not a defamer of characters and lives; a man whose mind is at once cosmopolitan and composite of all America; a gentleman of unpretentious habits, with the fear of God in his heart and the love of mankind exhibited in every act of his life; above all a public servant who has been tried to the uttermost and never found wanting . . . the ultimate Democrat, the genius of liberty and the very incarnation of progress.[51]

The main issue before the country, Wescott proclaimed, was fighting against corporate greed, and only Wilson could lead the charge:

> This convention stands between ninety millions of people and a thousand monopolies. It stands between ninety millions of people who need a free and fair opportunity and a thousand trusts that have special privileges. The great issue is to restore to the people equal opportunity, and, at the same time, to compel monopolies and trusts to proceed upon the same principle. This issue cannot be solved by a platform. Thousands of platforms will not solve it. The man on the platform alone can solve it . . . . If Providence could spare us a Washington to lay deep in the granite of human need the

foundations of the United States; if Providence could spare us a Jefferson to give form and vitality to the most splendid democracy the sun ever shone upon; if Providence could spare us a Lincoln to unite these states in impregnable unity and brotherhood, New Jersey appeals to the patriotism and good sense of this convention to give to the country the services of the distinguished governor of New Jersey, that the doors of opportunity may again be opened wide to every man, woman and child under the Stars and Stripes . . . .

New Jersey appreciates . . . the honor which she now has . . . of placing before this convention as a candidate for the presidency of the United States the seer and philosopher of Princeton, the Princeton schoolmaster, Woodrow Wilson.[52]

Having exerted most of their energy before Wescott began speaking, there was little left in the Wilson supporters on the convention floor and in the galleries when he had finished. When the judge left the podium, only a few minutes of bedlam could be summoned. It was four in the morning and those who remained had been in the hot and steamy hall for more than eight hours, their clothes soaked with sweat. Yet, there was more oratory to come—more nominating speeches for minor candidates and seconding speeches for all whose names had been placed in nomination. For three more hours, it continued, to the dismay and anger of the tired and exhausted crowd. The speeches were a "tidal wave of talk," the *Baltimore Sun* noted, "All of them were good—any other time, but the sleep-paralyzed delegates, reporters, and spectators cried, 'Enough,' and turned thumbs down as each fresh arrival reached the stand, threw up his hand and started in to declaim." After all had their say, convention officials were determined to have at least one ballot completed before adjourning. A roll call of the states was done and the results announced. There were few surprises. As expected, Speaker Clark was in the lead with 440½ votes, Governor Wilson was second with 324, Governor Harmon was third with 148 (including New York's 90 votes), and Congressman Underwood was fourth with 117½. Approximately sixty votes were scattered among five minor candidates. No candidate had a majority, much less the 726 two-thirds vote needed to win the nomination. It was not until after the sun had cleared the Baltimore horizon, at 7:36 am on Friday morning, that the gavel fell to end the nearly twelve-hour session and the weary souls who remained began to leave the armory, to get some rest before returning in the afternoon.[53]

At the Friday afternoon and evening sessions, from one ballot to the next, there were mostly incremental changes. The first major shift occurred when Boss Murphy rose during the tenth ballot and cast all of New York's ninety votes for Clark. Previously, New York had been casting its votes for Harmon. The shift seemed to confirm the rumors that Murphy and the Clark managers had cut a deal, with Clark delegates providing sufficient votes for New Yorker Alton Parker to win the job of temporary chairman on the convention's first day, and with Murphy agreeing to switch the Empire State's votes to Clark for the presidential nomination at an appropriate point. With this shift, Clark had 556 votes, giving him a majority of the delegates. Wilson, at 350½, trailed by more than two hundred, Underwood had 117½, and Harmon dropped to only 31. If history was any guide, the contest was over. Once a candidate at a Democratic convention got over the hurdle of getting a majority, the usual pattern was for him to see steady increases and soon reach the two-thirds threshold and win the nomination. Only once in the history of the party had a candidate who had attained a majority of votes *not* become the nominee. That had occurred seven decades earlier, in 1844, when former President Martin Van Buren's bid for a comeback was unexpectedly ended by the nomination of a dark horse candidate, James Polk. Interestingly, Van Buren's downfall had occurred at a convention in Baltimore, held only a few blocks away from the Fifth Regiment Armory where Champ Clark now also seemed to be on the threshold of victory. Clark, in his congressional office in nearby Washington, getting regular updates by telephone, began to draft a telegram accepting the nomination. His supporters in the armory began a celebratory demonstration, marching up and down the aisles, shouting and cheering for more than an hour.[54]

As it turned out, the celebration was premature, and it may have been fatal. Instead of quickly moving to the next ballot and a bandwagon effect for Clark taking hold, the hour's delay gave the Wilson managers on the convention floor time to scurry around and urge others to continue to fight. Promises were made. If the Underwood team would keep their man in the battle, then, if Wilson did not pick up votes and surpass Clark, Wilson's men agreed that he would withdraw and shift his votes to Underwood. If Indiana, which had been voting for its favorite son candidate, Governor Thomas Marshall, stayed in for now and if Wilson were nominated, then it was promised that Marshall would be Wilson's first choice for vice president. It all seemed to work. When the eleventh ballot was finally held, there was little change. In fact, Clark *lost* a few votes. After one more ballot that was basically a repeat of the last one, the convention adjourned, shortly after three o'clock in the morning, to resume on Saturday afternoon.[55]

That morning, at the summer governor's mansion on the New Jersey shore where Wilson had been closely following the news from Baltimore, after being told of New York's shift to Clark, the governor weighed his options. In a breakfast telephone call with one of his managers, McCombs, who agreed the outlook was grim, Wilson advised that he would release the delegates pledged to him and he sent a telegram to McCombs confirming this. At mid-morning, when Wilson's other manager, McAdoo, came into the headquarters at the Emerson Hotel and McCombs told him of what had transpired, McAdoo was shocked and livid. He accused McCombs of selling out the governor and quickly got Wilson on the phone, told him that there was still hope for victory, and got him to reverse his position releasing his delegates. The withdrawal telegram that Wilson had sent was set aside and never used. It should be noted that McCombs, in his book, *Making Woodrow Wilson President*, gives a different version of these events. He alleges that *he* was the one who never wavered in thinking that Wilson would win and convinced Wilson and others to remain in the fight. It is a claim that should be viewed with some skepticism. After Wilson became president, McCombs believed his work for Wilson deserved a cabinet appointment, which he did not receive. In his book, McCombs takes all the credit for getting Wilson nominated and portrays the president as ungrateful, narcissistic, and vindictive. Regardless of which version of the events in Baltimore is correct, both agree that Wilson was ready to withdraw, prepared a telegram to that effect, and someone on his team persuaded him to change his mind.[56]

When the convention resumed that afternoon, on the fourteenth ballot, Nebraska asked to be passed. After all the other votes were cast, the clerk returned to Nebraska and, for the third time during the convention, William Jennings Bryan rose and asked to be heard. Up until then, Bryan had been voting for Clark, as had most of the Nebraska delegation, as they were required to do because Clark had won their state's primary. Advising the chairman that he wanted to "explain my vote," the Great Commoner then read a lengthy prepared statement. Clark had declared himself a progressive, Bryan said, and it was on that basis that Nebraskans had supported him. He reminded the convention of the resolution that had been approved the previous day, at his instigation, stating that the party would not nominate any man beholden to "the privilege-hunting and favor-seeking class." By accepting New York's ninety votes, Bryan strongly implied that Clark was corrupt, that he had made a deal with the devil, could no longer be considered a progressive, and was not worthy of nomination. "I shall withhold my vote from Mr. Clark as long as New York's vote is recorded for him," Bryan declared, to the shock of most in the armory. Further, he advised, he would also withhold his vote from "any other candidate" whom New York may later support in the balloting. In effect, Bryan stated that receiving the votes of New York should be a kiss of death to *any* candidate and disqualify him from the nomination. Delegates rose to angrily confront Bryan, one arguing that there "are a thousand delegates here, and we have something else to do beside listening to Mr. Bryan make his fourth or fifth speech." Bryan was asked if he would pledge to support the eventual nominee, if the outcome was not to his liking. He responded that he did not expect that someone would be nominated whom he could not support, but that he did not wish to answer hypothetical questions. He then announced that he was casting his vote for Woodrow Wilson. Importantly, he did not *endorse* Wilson, and from his words, it was clear that if New York should decide later to shift its votes to Wilson, then he would move on from Wilson, just as he had deserted Clark. A poll of the Nebraska delegation revealed that eight other delegates from that state sided with Bryan and were violating their instructions and switching their votes to Wilson. Over the next several ballots, there were no dramatic changes, but there was a steady trend of gradual increases for Wilson, sometimes by only a vote or two. The small Wilson gains were usually accompanied by small losses for Clark. Keeping tabs on the results from the New Jersey shore, Wilson joked, "at the present rate of gain I will be nominated in 175 more ballots."[57]

What was Bryan up to? No one really knew. One thing was certain—before Bryan spoke, Clark was the likely nominee and, when he had finished, Clark was not. Bryan's failure to endorse Wilson at this crucial point, when he had all eyes in the armory on him, raised more questions. If he had wanted to make Wilson the nominee, he could have given a ringing speech and started a stampede for the New Jersey governor. Instead, it seemed his only goal was to halt Clark's progress toward the nomination. Was he trying to make sure that the convention remained deadlocked, so that it would eventually turn to him as its nominee?

Clark's team quickly reported, by telephone, Bryan's maneuver to their candidate, who was livid. Bryan, Clark fumed, had accused him of being corrupt, of being beholden to Wall Street and Tammany Hall, simply because New York had decided to switch its votes to him. In past campaigns, Clark well knew, Bryan had personally courted the support of, and had touted his endorsements from, the same men—Tammany's Murphy and Wall Street's Belmont—who Bryan now condemned Clark for having an association with, by having their votes cast for him. Only forty miles away in Washington, Clark immediately got on a train to Baltimore. It was late on Saturday evening, but the convention had been meeting through most of the night on previous days. His intent was to go to the convention hall and, from the podium, refute what he viewed as lies that Bryan had spread about him, to deny any deal with New York. To his dismay, upon his arrival, he observed people leaving the armory. He was too late. The convention had adjourned fifteen minutes earlier. Clark later wrote that one of Bryan's "henchmen" had spotted him at the train station in Washington and that he was certain that the man had telephoned Baltimore with the news that he was on his way, leading the Bryan men at the convention, in cahoots with Wilson's, to request and obtain an adjournment before Clark could arrive. On the last ballot taken that evening, the twenty-sixth, Clark still led Wilson by almost sixty votes. The next day was Sunday, on which the convention would not be meeting, and a disgusted Clark went back to Washington.[58]

Sunday, June 30, was not a day of rest for the politicians in Baltimore. As one author has observed, "There was never a Sabbath more shattered by deals, plots, bargains and intrigues." Despite all the meetings, by Monday morning, there was no indication that a deal had been struck. The major players were holding firm, or so they said. The *Baltimore Sun* reported that the general feeling was that Clark could not now win, that Wilson had a fighting chance, but that Clark's men would keep him in the race to block Wilson. If there was a stalemate, some thought that Congressman Underwood of Alabama, who was in third place on the last ballot, could emerge as the nominee. Bryan's name continued to be mentioned as a possible nominee. Norman Mack, the DNC chairman, told reporters he did not believe that either Clark or Wilson could be nominated and that the convention would likely turn to a dark horse.[59]

The early voting on Monday saw no significant changes. On the twenty-ninth ballot, however, Indiana, with the promise from Wilson's team that their man would name the Hoosier State's Marshall as vice president, switched its votes from Clark to Wilson. On the next ballot, Wilson surpassed Clark in total votes. On the final ballot of the day, the forty-second, taken well after midnight, Wilson, with 494 votes, maintained his lead, but was short of a majority and nowhere near the 726 two-thirds required for victory. Still, the New Jersey governor had momentum. He had started the day 56 votes behind Clark and had ended it 64 votes ahead of him.[60]

On the convention's seventh and final day, Tuesday, July 2, the logjam finally broke. Two key states, Illinois and Alabama, determined the outcome. Illinois, whose 58 votes were controlled by Chicago party boss Roger Sullivan, had been voting for Clark since the first ballot. Alabama had been casting its 24 votes for its own candidate, Underwood. Sullivan, who detested Bryan, was rumored to prefer Underwood of all the contenders. Concerned that the convention would deadlock and that Bryan would be the beneficiary of this, he agreed to switch the votes of Illinois to Wilson for a time, telling Senator Bankhead of Alabama, Underwood's manager at the convention, that he then planned to move his state to Underwood after a few ballots. On the first ballot of the day, the forty-third, the 58 votes of Illinois went to Wilson. This shift was followed by Virginia, with 24 votes, and West Virginia, with 16 votes, also going to Wilson. After two more ballots, Wilson had 633 votes, within a hundred votes of victory. Sullivan then reneged on his promise to move Illinois to Underwood and, instead, told Bankhead that he was going to go back to Clark on the next ballot. Years later, a report surfaced that Clark had come back to Baltimore on Monday, had met personally with Sullivan, and allegedly made various promises. Feeling betrayed by Sullivan, and knowing that Underwood could not win without Illinois, Bankhead rose on the forty-six ballot and withdrew Underwood from the contest and released all the Alabaman's delegates. This was the final straw. Sullivan never got the opportunity to switch back to Clark. State after state broke for Wilson and he won the nomination with 990 votes.[61]

The Democratic platform adopted in Baltimore contained many of the key progressive ideas of the era, many of which had been included in prior platforms—tariffs for revenue only, for laws that would make it impossible for monopolies to exist, for greater enforcement of antitrust laws, for primary elections in each state to select delegates to future Democratic nominating conventions, forbidding corporate campaign contributions, against the establishment of a central banking system, limiting use of judicial injunctions in labor disputes, for workers' compensation for federal employees, and for independence of the Philippines. It congratulated the country on two longstanding progressive reforms that had recently become law by constitutional amendments—a federal income tax and the direct election of senators. There was no plank supporting women's suffrage. One interesting plank called for only one term in office for a president, something that would require a constitutional amendment and would never be pursued by the Democrats once in power. It would be conveniently forgotten four years later when the party nominated Wilson again for a second term.[62]

The convention's final act was for the party to complete the bottom half of its ticket. Wilson, who preferred Underwood and was unaware that, to secure Indiana's votes, his team in Baltimore had promised the vice-presidential slot to that state, required that feelers be placed out to Underwood. The Alabama congressman responded that he had no interest. Wilson's much relieved managers then advised their boss that the convention seemed to favor Governor Thomas Marshall of Indiana. Wilson was reluctant, advising that he considered Marshall "a small-calibre man," a viewpoint that the often-arrogant Wilson had of most men. The choice made good political sense. It gave regional balance to the ticket. Moreover, Indiana was one of the few swing states of that era and putting a Hoosier on the ticket was a proven path to victory in the Electoral College. Two recent vice presidents, Thomas Hendricks (who served under Grover Cleveland) and Charles Fairbanks (under Theodore Roosevelt) had been from Indiana. Wilson relented and Marshall's name was placed in nomination, although there was competition. Georgia's attempt to nominate Champ Clark by acclamation was quickly shot down by Clark's home state of Missouri, which advised that he absolutely declined and would not accept. Clark, still fuming about how the top half of the ticket had been taken from him, was in no mood to be on the bottom. In addition to Marshall, North Dakota nominated its governor, John Burke, with many westerners wanting one of their own paired with Wilson. Three other names were placed in nomination. On the first ballot, Marshall led, but had fewer than 400 votes, with Burke not far behind. By the end of the second ballot, Marshall shot up to almost 650 votes, following which Burke's name was withdrawn and the Indianan was nominated by acclamation.[63]

It has been said that the gate of history turns on small hinges. Small things can make big differences. Woodrow Wilson became one of the most consequential presidents of the twentieth century. If any number of things in Baltimore had turned out differently, he would not have been nominated. Instead, Champ Clark would have been the Democratic standard-bearer and likely elected president. What would a Clark administration have been like? Clark remained in Congress as speaker until his death in 1921. He did not blame Wilson, but Bryan, for his loss and he generally supported Wilson's progressive domestic agenda. In foreign affairs, however, Clark was only one of sixteen Democrats in the House of Representatives to oppose Wilson's declaration of war on Germany in 1917, which brought the United States into World War I. If Clark's train from Washington to Baltimore that Saturday evening in July 1912 had arrived fifteen minutes earlier, or if word of Wilson's decision to withdraw had leaked out, or if Underwood had stayed in the race for one more ballot, how would the history of the world have changed?

There is one unknown from the 1912 convention—what was Bryan's ultimate goal in Baltimore? Was it, as he claimed until his death, that he was just trying to ensure that the most progressive candidate was nominated, whom he believed would be the best man to win the fall election against the divided Republicans? Or did he act out of a personal grudge against Clark? Or did he have a secret deal with Wilson, who would later name Bryan his secretary of state? Or was the Great Commoner acting out of self-interest, trying to stir dissension and slow the momentum of both Clark and Wilson, hoping that a deadlocked convention would turn to him as its nominee? Henry Watterson, a noted Kentucky journalist, wrote while the convention was still going on that "[e]very inference" points to Bryan "playing an artful but perfidious game to secure the nomination for himself by the attempt to hold a balance between Clark and Wilson" and that he "must be forever regarded as one given over to vanity and revenges—loving nobody except himself—casting to the winds all that exalts self-sacrifice." Years later, Senator Carter Glass of Virginia, who was at the convention, left no doubt where he stood. "Mr. Bryan had not the slightest idea," wrote Glass, "when he changed the vote of Nebraska, of contributing to the nomination of Wilson. He merely desired to defeat Champ Clark, with the concealed hope and expectation of prolonging the contest and receiving the nomination himself." Others have sided with Bryan, calling his actions in Baltimore his "finest hour," his "greatest achievement," and argue that he was "[f]ighting not for himself but for the rank and file of his party." One thing is certain. Without Bryan, Wilson would not have been nominated.[64]

Champ Clark never forgave Bryan, writing years later in his memoirs that he "lost the nomination solely through the vile and malicious slanders" of the Nebraskan. Of Bryan, Clark asserted, "There can be not even the shadow of a doubt that he not only eagerly but voraciously desired the nomination at Baltimore, which accounts for his outrageous conduct." Clark denied that he or any member of his team ever entered into any "deal" with the New Yorkers during the convention and pointed out that Bryan had sought and accepted their support in all of his own prior campaigns. "His theory seems to have been," Clark charged, "that Tammany is a great and beneficent institution when for Bryan, but a lot of scoundrels when for anyone else."[65]

The Campaign and Election

Taft chose to not actively campaign in the general election. He believed that his main goal had been achieved by defeating Roosevelt for the Republican nomination and appeared resigned to losing the presidency. He gave only two major speeches, one at the White House in early August, when he formally accepted his nomination, and another in Massachusetts, where he had a summer home. In the latter speech, made before local Republican clubs, he lashed out at those Republicans who left the party to follow Roosevelt as misguided followers of a cult of personality. They split from the Republican Party, charged Taft, "not for any one principle, or indeed on any principle at all, but merely to gratify personal ambition and vengeance."[66]

Wilson traveled widely and spoke often, although he was not a natural politician and glad-handing did not come naturally to him. He made attacks on monopolies his major issue, arguing that government should keep them from forming in the first place, not simply regulate them once they existed. Those in business who sought and obtained special advantages from government, he argued, must be stopped. "Every form of special privilege and private control must cease," he proclaimed, "Private interests, special favors, must not be encouraged by the government."[67]

Roosevelt also campaigned extensively, sometimes making up to twenty speeches a day. He sensed early on that it was a race between himself and Wilson. The most memorable event of his campaign occurred in Milwaukee on October 14. As he was leaving his hotel and getting into his car to go to a nearby auditorium for a speech, Roosevelt waved his right arm to acknowledge onlookers and a shot rang out and struck him. He sank onto the car's seat. The assailant, John Schrank of New York City, who had been stalking Roosevelt for days, was wrestled to the ground. Roosevelt, not knowing the extent of his injury, urged the angry crowd not to harm the man. It was soon discovered that the bullet had entered the right side of his chest, luckily slowed and deflected by a metal case for his eyeglasses and a thick folded copy of the speech he was about to deliver, which were in the right breast pocket of his suit coat. His shirt had a large bloodstain, but the bleeding seemed to have stopped. Overruling the advice of three doctors, who urged that he immediately go to a hospital, Roosevelt insisted on being driven to the auditorium and delivering his speech. His wife, Edith, perhaps the only one who could have countermanded his demand, was in New York. No doubt realizing the dramatic effect this event could have on his campaign, Roosevelt opened his remarks by stating, "Friends, I shall have to ask you to be as quiet as possible. I do not know whether you fully understand that I have just been shot. But it takes more than that to kill a Bull Moose." Amazingly, he went on for more than an hour, after which he finally went to a hospital. It was determined that the bullet ended up in tissue near a rib, did not affect any organs, and it was decided to leave it there. The attempted assassin, Schrank, claimed that he had shot Roosevelt over opposition to a third term for any president and alleged that he had been told to do so by none other than the ghost of President McKinley, who had appeared to him in a dream. Roosevelt had been McKinley's vice president and had assumed the presidency in 1901 when McKinley had also been shot, and killed, by a gunman.[68]

There was another candidate of note in the 1912 election, Eugene Debs of the Socialist Party. It was the fourth time that Debs had run on the Socialist ticket. Support for the party and its philosophy had been growing, it was more organized than ever before, and Debs had become a better candidate and orator. Without the corporate financing of the other parties, the Socialists charged admission to their campaign rallies. Thousands paid a quarter to hear Debs compare the plight of American workers to that of Blacks, whose enslavement had led to the Civil War. "The issue then was chattel slavery; it is now wage slavery," Debs declared, arguing that the situation existing in 1912 was larger than the "liberty of three million wealth producers of the black race." Instead, he proclaimed, "The question of wage slavery involves the complete liberty of every producer of wealth without reference to race or color" and whether the issue "shall be settled without another terrible physical conflict will depend largely upon the action of the workers in the present campaign."[69]

The attempted assassination on Roosevelt, occurring just three weeks before the election, essentially froze the campaigns of all the candidates in place until he recuperated, which was around the end of October. Then, the nation was further rocked by the death of Taft's sitting vice president and running mate, James Sherman, on October 30. The fifty-seven-year-old Sherman had been suffering from a kidney disease. He was replaced on the Republican ticket by the RNC with Nicholas Murray Butler of New York.[70]

On election day, November 5, the voters gave Woodrow Wilson and the Democrats a significant victory. With the split of the Republican vote between Taft and Roosevelt, Wilson won an Electoral College landslide, carrying forty of the forty-eight states, compared to only six for Roosevelt, two for Taft, and none for Debs. The tally was 435 electoral votes for Wilson, 88 for Roosevelt, and only 8 for Taft. In the popular vote, Wilson's margin was comfortable, but was less than a majority. He received 6,293,454 votes (42%), while Roosevelt was second with 4,119,538 (27%), Taft third with 3,484,980 (23%), and Debs last with 901,873 (6%). It was the most embarrassing loss by an incumbent president seeking re-election in American history. It was also an impressive showing for Debs and the Socialist Party, who doubled their vote count from the 1908 election. Democrats also maintained and strengthened their majority in the House of Representatives and, for the first time in twenty years, narrowly won control of the Senate. But their victories were largely due to the Republican schism, not to a surge of additional votes to Democrats. While Wilson had won the presidency, it was with 100,000 fewer votes than had been cast for Bryan and the Democrats in a losing effort in 1908.[71]

Analysis of the returns shows, that if Roosevelt had won the Republican nomination, he would likely have won the election. He and Taft carried over half of the popular vote. While some Taft supporters would likely have stayed home on election day with Roosevelt as the Republican nominee, if most had fallen in line with their party, the outcome would have been different. The 1912 election proved, once again, that the drama, twists, and turns at presidential nominating conventions mattered. Had things gone differently in Baltimore, Champ Clark would have been the Democratic nominee. If things had gone differently in Chicago, Theodore Roosevelt may well have been the first man to serve a third term in the White House, a feat that would finally be achieved by his distant cousin, Franklin Roosevelt, twenty-eight years later.

CHAPTER 4

1916: Too Proud to Fight

*Wilson knows the sorrows of a war
And he's trying to spare us the pain.
But even he may have to call on you,
And so prepare to play your part.
Polish your gun while you pray for peace
And say to him with all your heart:*

*Go right along, Mister Wilson,
We're all for you strong.
You speak for us as a nation
And we're for the nation right or wrong.*
–Democratic campaign song, 1916

After taking office in 1913, with Democratic majorities in both houses of Congress, President Woodrow Wilson succeeded in having much of his "New Freedom" progressive agenda enacted into law. Tariffs were lowered and, to offset the loss of revenue, the nation's first income tax was passed, made possible under the recently enacted Sixteenth Amendment to the Constitution. To regulate banking, the Federal Reserve System was created. Anti-trust laws were strengthened and the federal government obtained greater oversight over business with the creation of the Federal Trade Commission. Various laws supported by labor unions were passed. Wilson's progressive views did not extend to race relations. Although offices of the federal government had been integrated since the Grant Administration, he permitted his cabinet officers, many of whom were southerners, to institute segregation of white and Black employees in their departments.[1]

Wilson's record in foreign affairs was mixed. He took sides in a revolution in Mexico, which led to Mexican rebels crossing into New Mexico and killing several Americans. The president responded by sending troops into Mexico in search of the rebels. Some argued for a more aggressive response, other than just seeking out those who had killed Americans. In response to the outbreak of war in Europe in 1914, Wilson's official position was neutrality, but he vacillated. At first, he urged strict neutrality, but after a German submarine sank the British passenger liner *Lusitania* in 1915 (killing more than a hundred Americans), he took a more aggressive approach against Germany, threatening to break off diplomatic relations. Although some were outraged and believed that this violated his neutrality pledge, it did result in Germany temporarily suspending unrestricted submarine warfare in the Atlantic, promising to not target passenger ships, and to sink merchant ships only after searching them first for weapons. Others charged that Wilson had not been aggressive enough against Germany (he had said in a speech after the *Lusitania* sinking that there was such a thing as a nation being "too proud to fight"), that he projected American weakness, and that he had failed to prepare the nation's defenses if entry into the war became necessary.[2]

On a personal level, Wilson experienced tragedy after taking office. In 1914, his wife, Ellen, died of kidney disease. A little more than a year later, the fifty-eight-year-old president married again, to Edith Bolling Galt, a wealthy Washington, D.C., widow who was sixteen years younger than he.[3]

Republican Convention

The last time a political party split apart at its convention, it took twenty-four years to reclaim the White House. The Republicans hoped that their debacle in 1912 would not leave them in the political wilderness as long as the Democrats had been after that party had divided at its 1860 convention. The nemesis of the Republicans in 1912, the breakaway Progressive Party, was still a functioning entity in 1916, but its influence was waning. After getting four million votes in 1912 with Theodore Roosevelt at the head of its ticket, the Progressives got only half that in the 1914 midterm elections, winning only six seats in Congress. Many Progressives had already returned to their Republican roots, but some remained die-hard loyalists to the new third-party, and passionately devoted to Roosevelt. As the 1916 election year began, political conversations focused on whether the Republicans and the Progressives could heal their rift. If so, it was felt that they had a decent chance to defeat President Wilson and the Democrats. If not, most believed a second term for Wilson was guaranteed.

The 1912 loss did not end Theodore Roosevelt's time in the public arena, nor his desire to return to the White House. After the outbreak of war in Europe in 1914 and Woodrow Wilson's declaration of neutrality in that conflict, Roosevelt gave speeches and wrote extensively criticizing the president. Wilson, he proclaimed, projected weakness, was not doing enough militarily to strengthen the nation's defenses, and was allowing Americans with divided loyalties to shape his foreign policy. These two issues of "preparedness" and "Americanism" became the focal points of his castigation of Wilson. Roosevelt proclaimed, "I am not for war . . . [but] you don't in the long run avoid war by making other people believe that you are afraid to fight for your own rights." The question of whether Roosevelt would actively seek the presidency in 1916—and if he would do so as a Progressive, a Republican, or both—was clarified by him, somewhat, early in the year when he stated that he would not actively seek the Republican nomination, but would accept it *if* he was convinced that the party and the country were determined to "put honor and duty ahead of safety," *i.e.*, if his two key issues predominated. It was a foregone conclusion that the diminished Progressive Party would nominate him, although he would not actively seek their nomination either.[4]

It is said that an elephant never forgets and the Republican Party, whose symbol was then and remains that massive animal, was in no way ready to accept Roosevelt back into its good graces and make him its nominee in 1916. The party's leadership fell into three main groups in 1916. The conservative "Old Guard" favored Elihu Root, a seventy-one-year-old New Yorker who had been Roosevelt's secretary of state and a senator. Root had also been the permanent chairman of the party's 1912 convention and had presided over and facilitated Taft's defeat of Roosevelt. Other Republicans supported favorite son candidates, mostly conservatives, the most prominent of whom were Senator Theodore Burton of Ohio, Senator John Weeks of Massachusetts, Senator Albert Cummins of Iowa, and Charles Fairbanks of Indiana, who had been vice president under Roosevelt. Their goal was to keep as many names in the mix as possible, lessening the chance that any candidate would enter the convention as a prohibitive favorite, and hoping that the convention would move to one of them after several ballots. A third group promoted an unlikely choice, a man who had been removed from the political arena for several years.[5]

Charles Evans Hughes, fifty-four years old, was an associate justice on the Supreme Court. On the bench since his 1910 nomination by Taft and approval by the Senate, Hughes had the good fortune of not having had to take sides in the party's 1912 rift. As a judge, he had not stated his opinions on any political issues for the past six years. Born in the upper Hudson Valley area of New York, Hughes showed intellectual promise as a child, entered college at the age of fourteen, and ultimately graduated from Brown University and earned a law degree from Columbia. After several years working at a prominent law firm in New York City, and a brief stint as a law school professor, he reluctantly accepted positions as legal counsel for state legislative committees investigating New York's gas utilities and its insurance companies. Both investigations uncovered extensive graft and corruption, earning Hughes a reputation for honesty and integrity, and as a reformer. Some leaders of the state Republican Party were ensnared in the insurance investigation. In 1906, the party was looking for a candidate for governor who was a fresh face and untainted by scandal. With support from President Theodore Roosevelt, who had begun his own political career as a reformer in New York politics, Hughes was nominated as the Republican candidate for governor. Although the Democrats won all other statewide offices in the 1906 election, Hughes beat his Democratic opponent, publisher William Randolph Hearst, and became the Empire State's governor. Several progressive reforms were passed under Hughes, including setting limits on campaign contributions by corporations, civil service reform, restrictions on child labor, and workers' compensation for injured employees. Reelected in 1908 to a second two-year term as governor, Hughes resigned from the position in 1910 upon confirmation by the Senate of his appointment by Taft to the Supreme Court.[6]

During his governorship, a rift developed between Hughes and Roosevelt. It started with the president's firing of a minor patronage official in New York, of which the governor let his disapproval be known. Roosevelt, who viewed himself as a mentor of Hughes, began to feel that the governor was ungrateful and acted too independently. In 1907, after Roosevelt had settled on Taft as the man whom he would support to succeed him in the White House, some began to push Hughes as an alternative. Although Hughes did not endorse their actions, he did not renounce them, and his name was put before the 1908 Republican convention as New York's favorite son candidate against Taft. Although Taft won overwhelmingly, the episode exacerbated Roosevelt's growing distaste for Hughes, despite the fact that they agreed on most political issues. In 1916, when talk of Hughes for president began again, Roosevelt, noting the bearded Hughes' aloofness and concerned that he would not take a stronger stance against Germany in the European War, privately dismissed him as "Wilson in whiskers."[7]

In early 1916, Hughes had let it be known that he was not a candidate for the presidency. "I am totally opposed," he wrote, "to the use of my name in connection with the nomination . . . either directly or remotely." His promoters, led by Frank Hitchcock, who had headed Taft's 1912 campaign, were not deterred and noted that he had not given a Shermanesque statement that he would decline the nomination, or refuse to serve if elected. There is some evidence that President Wilson feared Hughes as an opponent and made him a tempting offer to stay out of the contest. Shortly before the convention, Chief Justice Edward White met with Hughes and advised that he planned to resign from the Court and that the president wanted it known that he would be willing to elevate Hughes from associate justice to chief justice. Hughes advised that he would make his decision whether to accept the Republican nomination, if he won it, without being influenced by this roundabout offer from the president.[8]

The 1916 election was the second one in which the use of statewide primary elections to select convention delegates was widespread, there being twenty such contests, all in northern and western states. As declared non-candidates, Hughes and Roosevelt succeeded in keeping their names off of most, but not all, of the primary ballots. Supporters were able to enter them in a few primaries without their permission. Hughes won primaries in Oregon and Vermont. Roosevelt won in New Jersey. The primaries in most of the other states were won by favorite son candidates, or their results were mixed and inclusive. Some of the largest states—New York, Pennsylvania, and Massachusetts—were split among various candidates. When the primary results were combined with those in states that used statewide conventions to select delegates, Hughes entered the national convention with around 225 delegates, more than double the number pledged to any other candidate, but well short of the 495 needed for the nomination.[9]

The fate of the Republicans and the Progressives in 1916 became more closely intertwined when the Progressives decided to open their presidential nominating convention on the same day (June 7) and in the same city (Chicago) as the Republicans. The GOP met at the larger Coliseum and the Progressives at the smaller Auditorium. Along with the conventions in Chicago that week of two women's suffrage groups, the National American Woman Suffrage Association (NAWSA) and the Congressional Union (CU), up to 35,000 visitors flooded into the Windy City. There were three women as full delegates to the Republican convention, one of whom, Olive Cole of California, at the age of eighty-three, was the oldest delegate. The Republican gathering had fewer Black delegates than in past years. After 1912, the party adjusted its method of delegate allocation, which had traditionally been based upon twice the number of a state's electoral votes. Now, the strength of the Republican Party in each state was also a factor. A state's base allocation of delegates was reduced to a number roughly equal to its electoral votes, but it could gain a delegate for each congressional district where more than 7,500 votes had been cast for Republicans in the last election. Because the party was never competitive in the region's elections, the new formula reduced by almost eighty the number of delegates from southern states, and resulted in a diminished number of Black delegates. At all prior Republican conventions since the Civil War, Blacks had made up a significant percentage of the delegates from the South.[10]

In the days leading up to the Republican and Progressive conventions, it appeared as though the two parties were far apart in their positions and that any agreement was unlikely. The Progressives were hellbent on nominating Roosevelt and insisted that Republicans also nominate him. Republicans made it known that Roosevelt was absolutely not an option for them, but that they would consider alternative nominees that Progressives may offer. The most likely compromise candidate seemed to be Hughes, who had a reformist record when he was governor, but Progressives demanded that Hughes publicly state his views on all of the pending issues of the day before they would even consider him. As a sitting member of the Supreme Court, however, Hughes had refused all requests for his political stances, which made him a non-starter for the Progressives.[11]

The Chicago Coliseum was filled with more than twelve thousand people for the opening of the sixteenth Republican convention on Wednesday, June 7. A large picture of Abraham Lincoln loomed above the podium, which had seating for three hundred distinguished guests to its rear and for five hundred reporters on its wings. An immense triangular sounding board was suspended above the rostrum, to improve the projection of the voices of the speakers into the cavernous arena. After the singing of the song "America," and an opening prayer, everyone was asked to turn to one corner of the building and to "face the camera as well as they can and be very quiet" while an official photograph of the convention was taken. The chairman of the Republican National Committee, Charles Hilles of New York, then announced his committee's choice of Senator Warren Harding of Ohio to be the temporary chairman, which was quickly confirmed on a voice vote. The fifty-year old Harding was a newspaper publisher in a small Ohio town, had held state offices and, in 1914, had been elected to the United States Senate.[12]

Harding then began his keynote speech with an acknowledgment of the disaster that befell the party in 1912 and a plea for unity: "We did not do very well in making for harmony the last time we met," he said, which "the country has regretted . . . . We split over methods of party procedure and preferred personalities. Let us forget the differences, and find new inspiration and new compensation in an united endeavor to restore the country." He then launched into a long-winded address, lasting almost two hours, and which generated little enthusiasm from the crowd. In response to the European war, he called for a stronger navy and army and proclaimed that "Justice points the way through the safe channel of neutrality." He called for a restoration of protective tariffs that the Democrats had reduced. He derided Wilson's actions in Mexico as "humiliating" and "the greatest fiasco in our foreign relations." There had been some speculation that Harding could be a possible "dark horse" nominee and that a rousing opening speech could start a movement toward him. With the tepid response from the crowd, however, the *New York Times* commented that it was not even necessary to remember the Ohioan's name: "Harding could not stampede any convention . . . . His full name is Warren G. Harding and he is Senator in Congress from Ohio; but it is not necessary to burden one's memory with these statistics if one is merely trying to remember the names of persons likely to be nominated for President." Following Harding's speech, which ended in the early afternoon, the convention adjourned for the day.[13]

To the extent that Harding's speech is remembered today, it is for a nugget of historical linguistic trivia that it contained. In reviewing American ingenuity, Harding spoke the following sentence: "Mine is a deep conviction that the founding fathers were divinely inspired, and the wisdom of representative popular government is proven in the surpassing achievement." This was the first time that the title of "founding fathers" had been bestowed upon the core group of patriots (Washington, Jefferson, Franklin, Adams, Hamilton, and a few others) who led the American Revolution. Harding repeated the term in later speeches, including in his inaugural address when he became president in 1921. It began to be used by others and became the standard term used for the nation's first statesmen.[14]

A stretch of cold and rainy weather settled over Chicago as the convention began, which likely contributed to the lack of excitement. Reporters could not recall a convention at which the presidential nominee was uncertain that was so subdued. Part of it was that the two men whose names were on most lips—Hughes and Roosevelt—were not actively in the contest for the nomination. As one observer has noted, "Each was a candidate, and yet not a candidate." Cynics believed that the delegates were just biding time, waiting to be told how to vote by the bosses. Calling it "the most lifeless convention ever conceived," the *New York Times* opined that the identity of the party's nominee "is not being fought out, it is being settled. It is a convention of the tongue and brain behind the door, not of the fist and club in the ring."[15]

Despite this, the carnival atmosphere that was often on display at conventions of the era was still present in Chicago. Much of it came from Roosevelt supporters, who were noted to be "loud and everywhere." A group of young men carried an upright piano from hotel lobby to hotel lobby, with one playing it as the others belted out campaign songs about the Hero of San Juan Hill. In the bars, it was reported that "The Colonel is nominated on the average of once every ten minutes." A crowd at the Congress Hotel surrounded a Roosevelt lookalike, who gave "a rip-roaring campaign speech about preparedness with violent gesticulations that shook the walls." Some believed they were listening to the former president himself until the speaker smiled, revealing several missing teeth. Only then, when the famous Roosevelt toothy grin was not evident, "were they quite sure that it wasn't 'Teddy.'" Press photographers, and the attempts of the famous to evade them, are not just a modern phenomenon. Roosevelt's eldest daughter, Alice Roosevelt Longworth, who was married to a Republican member of Congress, Nicholas Longworth, was the subject of much press attention in Chicago. Upon arriving at her hotel for the first time, a gaggle of photographers waited outside. Congressman Longworth emerged from his vehicle, to the sounds of cameras clicking, holding hands with a smiling woman, as they both waved to the crowd and entered the building. Only later, when the photographs were developed, was it noticed that the mischievous Alice had played a trick. It was her maid by her husband's side who had attracted all of the attention, as Alice, several steps behind, had quietly entered the hotel unnoticed.[16]

The main subject of conversation the evening of the convention's rather boring first day was not the proceedings, but a parade that had been held in the late afternoon. The morning had started out rainy and cold in Chicago and the bad weather had only worsened as the day progressed. At four in the afternoon, when the delegates were safely back in their dry hotel lobbies and bars, many heard loud noises coming from the streets and rushed to the nearest windows. Outside, in a driving rainstorm, up to ten thousand women were marching and singing suffragist songs, accompanied by brass bands and an elephant borrowed from the nearby Lincoln Park Zoo. The parade was organized by NAWSA, the larger of the two suffragist organizations then meeting in the city. Wearing white dresses, straw hats with yellow bands, and yellow sashes with suffrage slogans on them, many of the women had fortunately been able to procure raincoats and umbrellas. Those carrying banners and holding flags struggled mightily in the wind and rain, but persevered, earning a grudging respect from the dry men watching from a distance. The "moving army of bobbing umbrellas" ended at the Coliseum, where NAWSA President Carrie Chapman Catt delivered her group's proposed suffrage platform plank to a prominent senator. It read: "The Republican Party, reaffirming its faith in government of the people, by the people, and for the people, favors the extension of the suffrage to women as a measure of justice to one-half the adult people of this country." Despite the nasty weather, Catt had insisted on going through with the parade, over the opposition of some who wanted to cancel it. One of Catt's supporters noted that, if women won the right to vote, they would surely be willing to go to the polls to cast ballots on rainy election days. Some called the parade the "wisest political move" made so far in Chicago that week. A headline in the *New York Times* proclaimed "Pluck Gains Them Friends," as many politicians and delegates were impressed by the devotion of the women to their cause under adverse circumstances.[17]

The convention's second day began with the report of the credentials committee. Unlike the last convention in 1912, there were few challenges to the proposed delegates and all 987 were seated. Most states also had full slates of alternate delegates. Senator Harding was nominated, and approved, as the permanent chairman, and would continue to wield the gavel. Perhaps because of the lackluster response to his speech the day before, he declined to deliver a new one as permanent chairman. When Harding was advised that the committee drafting the party's platform was not ready to report, in a move to fill time, politicians were called upon to give speeches. The most prominent was Chauncey Depew, a former senator from New York. Then in his eighties, Depew had a reputation over the years as one of the most entertaining speakers in the country. He criticized President Wilson for lack of preparedness of the nation's defenses. If the Germans were to land of the shores of the United States, he said, pacificists naively believed that a million Americans would drive their Model T's to the beaches and turn them away. Never one to resist a joke, Depew added, of the owners of those popular, but not stylish, automobiles: "a Ford machine is like a bathtub: Everyone wants one and nobody wants to be seen in it."[18]

The convention then adjourned until the late afternoon, at which time the proposed platform was ready and was presented to the convention by Senator Henry Cabot Lodge of Massachusetts, the chairman of the Committee of Resolutions. While supporting "strict and honest neutrality" in the European war, it criticized the Wilson administration for vacillating, for "shifty expedients" and "phrase-making" in an ever-changing "effort to secure groups of voters." It called for "not only adequate but thorough and complete national defenses," including a stronger army and navy. The platform called for increases in tariffs that the Democrats had reduced, to the extent that they were a "reasonable amount but sufficient to protect adequately American industries and American labor and so adjusted as to prevent undue exactions by monopolies or trusts." It included the draft language from NAWSA for a women's voting rights plank, but with the additional wording that the party "recognizes the right of each state to settle this question for itself." This was the first time that a major political party had included a suffrage plank in its platform. It rejected the more comprehensive proposal put forward by the CU, the other main suffragist group, for a federal constitutional amendment. In a weak criticism of those whose ethnic origins influenced their politics, the platform stated that "We appeal to all Americans, whether naturalized or native-born, to prove to the world that we are American in thought and in deed, with one loyalty, one hope, one aspiration." German-Americans thought that Wilson, although officially neutral, had come down too hard on Germany in the European war and Republicans did not want to offend this voting bloc. A delegate from Wisconsin then read a minority platform, which Senator Lodge noted had been supported in the committee by only that delegate, compared to forty-four votes for the majority platform that Lodge had put before the convention. The lone Wisconsinite's proposals were quickly voted down and the platform as proposed by Lodge was approved on a voice vote.[19]

Chairman Harding then read a message from the Progressive convention, then meeting elsewhere in Chicago, requesting that the Republicans "appoint a Committee on Conference to meet with a similar committee from this body." The message was greeted with "enthusiastic applause" and a five-member committee was appointed to meet with the breakaway party. The convention then, just before six o'clock, adjourned for the day. It was in no rush to select a presidential nominee that evening, if some sort of accommodation or agreement could be reached with the Progressives.[20]

The convention's third day began with an update from the conference committee appointed to meet with the Progressives. It was reported that the meeting was "frank, free and most friendly," that all agreed that "the complete defeat of the present Democratic Administration" was needed, but that Progressives were unanimous in the opinion that Theodore Roosevelt was "the most desirable candidate upon which to unite." Chairman Harding ordered the committee to continue its consultations, but all knew that Republicans were never going to nominate Roosevelt and, unless the Progressives changed their tune, there would be no agreement.[21]

Nominations of candidates for president were next on the agenda. The alphabetical roll call of the states began. Alabama passed, Arizona yielded to New York, and the name of Charles Evans Hughes was placed in nomination by Charles Whitman, the sitting governor of the Empire State. If there was any doubt that conservatives were predominant at the convention, it was dispelled when Whitman mentioned in passing the name of William Howard Taft, which caused the delegates to jump to their feet and wave flags and handkerchiefs, the longest and most vocal demonstration thus far. The nomination of Hughes was necessary, Whitman proclaimed, because:

> He, above all other men, can bring home to the people the fact that the Democratic party has failed and miserably failed, in its stewardship. He, above all other men, can bring to the people a conviction of the dangers which surround us. He, above all other men, can assure this country that the Republican Party, the Party of progress, of union, and of patriotic achievement, is once more united and capable of assuming the helm of the ship of State.... He, above all others, can bring to the country prosperity, security and honor. He above all other men embodies in himself and represents to all the world a great people's courage, ambition and character. He is the American spirit incarnate.[22]

The demonstration for Hughes following Whitman's speech came mostly from the delegates, not the galleries, and was not overly boisterous. It lasted twenty minutes, fairly short, by historical standards, for a frontrunner for the presidential nomination. Unlike Roosevelt, Hughes was not a man who inflamed one's passion, either for or against.[23]

Numerous other candidates were then placed in nomination—Elihu Root of New York, former Senator Theodore Burton of Ohio, Senator John Weeks of Massachusetts, T. Coleman duPont of Delaware, Senator Lawrence Sherman of Illinois, former Vice President Charles Fairbanks of Indiana, Senator Albert Cummins of Iowa, former President Theodore Roosevelt (whose supporters, mostly in the galleries, staged the longest demonstration of the day, clocking in at just over forty minutes), Senator Robert La Follette of Wisconsin, and Governor Martin Brumbaugh of Pennsylvania. In all, the names of eleven men were formally placed before the convention. Of the second-tier candidates—below Hughes, Roosevelt, and Root—the strongest were believed to be Fairbanks, Cummins, Weeks, and Burton. Of these four, all but Cummins were conservatives.[24]

The first ballot was held, resulting in Hughes in first place with 253½ votes, Weeks was second with 105, Root third with 103, and Cummins fourth with 85. Roosevelt received only 65 votes, putting him in eighth place. Governor Brumbaugh of Pennsylvania then withdrew his name, with the suggestion that Roosevelt be nominated. A second ballot quickly followed, which showed a significant gain of seventy-five votes for Hughes, and a few losses for Root and Weeks, a steady vote for Cummins, and only slight gains for Roosevelt. The tally was Hughes with 328½, Root with 98½, Fairbanks with 88½, Cummins with 85, and Roosevelt with 81. At that point, sensing that momentum had swung to Hughes, most of those opposing him wanted time to regroup and plot strategy. A motion to adjourn was made. It was objected to and a roll call vote was held, with most of the Hughes delegates opposing it. The motion carried by a margin of more than two to one and, shortly before ten o'clock in the evening, the convention's third day ended.[25]

That Friday night was a sleepless one for the key players. The Old Guard had won a double victory that day—keeping Hughes from being nominated and all but eliminating Roosevelt from the contest. Their continued grip on the convention depended on keeping all of the favorite sons in the race until a majority of the delegates became convinced that Hughes could not prevail. Frank Hitchcock, Hughes' primary organizer in Chicago, worked through the night. He persuaded Congressman William Vare of Philadelphia and Vare's brother, who controlled about twenty delegates, that a Hughes win was inevitable and to switch to him, which led to most of the large Pennsylvania delegation doing the same. Elsewhere overnight, the coalition of favorite sons began to break apart. At 2:30 a.m., Senator Sherman of Illinois was told that he had no path forward. He agreed to withdraw and most of his delegates favored Hughes. Word of this began to spread in the Chicago darkness. After trying and failing to get Roosevelt to endorse Fairbanks, the Indiana delegation decided to drop their man and move on. Iowa's delegates, most of whom wanted to vote for Hughes, convinced Senator Cummins that he would not pick up additional votes and he agreed to withdraw. The same thing happened with Wisconsin—Senator La Follette decided to withdraw and announced that Hughes was his personal choice. By dawn, it was apparent that the favorite son strategy that had seemed so strong hours earlier was now in tatters. The broader group was unwilling to unite behind a single candidate of their own as the alternative to Hughes and, one by one, they began to drop out and Hughes was the beneficiary.[26]

The conference committees of the Progressives and Republicans also met for hours overnight. At four in the morning, a call was placed to Roosevelt at his Long Island home. He was asked if he could support Root, Fairbanks (who had been his vice president) or Philander Knox (a conservative Pennsylvanian not in the race, but who had served in his, and Taft's, cabinet). He advised that he could not and proposed two other names, Senator Henry Cabot Lodge of Massachusetts (his longtime friend) and General Leonard Wood (who had led his Rough Rider cavalry unit in Cuba during the Spanish-American War and had recently become a leader in the preparedness movement). Neither of the committees was interested in Lodge or Wood and the call ended. There would be no agreement between the two parties on a nominee.[27]

By the time that the gavel fell for the convention's fourth day on the morning of Saturday, June 10, it had all been decided. Justice Charles Evans Hughes would be the first (and to date, the only) sitting member of the Supreme Court to be nominated by a major political party as its candidate for president of the United States. The inevitable would not happen, however, before a last-minute twist from Roosevelt.

Chairman Harding opened the proceedings with a request for a report from the committee negotiating with the Progressives. The chair of the committee advised that his group had suggested Hughes to the Progressives as a nominee that both parties could agree upon. In response, the Progressives revealed that Roosevelt had written a letter early that morning urging both conventions to make Senator Lodge their nominee, and they provided a copy of the former president's letter. The committee of Progressives further advised that Roosevelt's letter had already been presented to their convention, which had tabled it. (The Progressives went on to nominate Roosevelt). The Republicans ignored Roosevelt's letter and moved on with their third ballot. Before the voting began, Senator Weeks of Massachusetts rose and withdrew his name, stating that it was "quite apparent to me that the Convention prefers another candidate." The chairman of the Illinois delegation advised that Senator Sherman was withdrawing and releasing his delegates. An Illinois delegate, who had been one of Roosevelt's most ardent supporters at the convention, then announced that "following my conscience and my duty," he was voting for Hughes. The roll call proceeded quickly and it was a landslide for Hughes. He received 949½ of the 987 ballots cast, with Roosevelt, at fewer than twenty votes, finishing second. The rest of the states then withdrew their favorite son candidates and the nomination of Hughes was made unanimous.[28]

The convention then moved on to its vice-presidential nomination. Only two men, Charles Fairbanks of Indiana and Elmer Burkett, a former senator from Nebraska, were nominated. Fairbanks, who had already served four years in the office of vice president under Roosevelt, won easily, with 863 votes to only 108 for Burkett. It was not so much a vote of confidence in Fairbanks, but a recognition of the importance of Indiana in the election. Once again, men from the two major swing states of the era—New York and Indiana—would be paired by a major party on its ticket.[29]

In Hughes, the Republicans had nominated their most electable candidate, likely the only man who could both hold the party's conservative base and win back more Progressives than any of the other options. In modern terms, Hughes was seen as a "moderate," neither reactionary nor radical. As one author has noted, by gravitating to Hughes, the party had shown that it was confident that he could "carry his home state of New York, run well in the Middle West, and carry the traditionally Republican bastions in the West. He would make a campaign on the protective tariff, rouse the electorate, and oust the hated Wilson." The *New York Times* speculated that the sedate and rational atmosphere of the convention, with only a minimal amount of hoopla, was a sign of things to come. "It was," the paper noted, "a convention which had no enthusiasm, no life, but went to work at everything in a dogged and practical way . . . . [Perhaps] future conventions will be business-like mechanical affairs, with no more cheering and standard waving and stampeding . . . ." The editorial writer then realized that he was likely being too optimistic about the American political class. "It is, however, equally possible," he added, "that the strange spectacle seen this week will go into history as altogether solitary."[30]

Democratic Convention

"There is not a storm cloud in sight," Democratic National Committee Chairman William McCombs confidently proclaimed to reporters in the days before the opening of the 1916 Democratic convention. He was right. The nomination of Woodrow Wilson for a second term as president was as certain as anything in politics could be. It was a far cry from four years earlier when McCombs, one of Wilson's managers at the party's last convention, had been working hard in the trenches over forty-six ballots and cutting deals to make Wilson the nominee.[31]

McCombs's sunny weather prediction was correct for the nomination, but perhaps not for the general election. Recent news could cause rain to pour down on the Democratic parade. Their convention opened four days after the conclusion of the Republican and Progressive ("Bull Moose Party") conventions in Chicago, with Hughes having been named the Republican nominee and Roosevelt the Progressive nominee. Roosevelt, however, shocked the Bull Moosers by advising that he would not accept their nomination "at this time," while he awaited more information from the Republican nominee, Hughes, on his views on "the vital issues of the day." Most saw it as a sign that TR was done with the Progressives, likely deciding that he could not win on their ticket in 1916 and that the best path for him to get back to the White House in 1920 was by returning to the Republican fold. It was seen as the end of the Progressive Party, the existence of which was based mostly on Roosevelt's personality and popularity. "Moose Death Knell" proclaimed a headline in the *Washington Post*. At the Wilson White House, upon hearing the news from Chicago, it was reported that hopes for November "sank with a thud." The coming election would not be a repeat of 1912, when the split between the Taft-led Republicans and the Roosevelt-led Progressives had given Wilson and the Democrats an easy win in the general election.[32]

The Democrats selected St. Louis for their convention, the fourth time that the party would be meeting there to select its nominee. Some saw it as an ominous choice, as their three prior nominees chosen in St. Louis—Tilden in 1876, Cleveland in 1888, and Bryan in 1904—had all lost their elections. The convention was held in the St. Louis Coliseum at Washington and Jefferson Avenues, which had opened in 1909 and was said to be the largest arena in the country. With the lack of any contest over the presidential nomination, much of the usual excitement on the streets was lacking. One reporter called it "a dull and stupid gathering" and noted that the most heard question was whether the newly-named Republican nominee, Hughes, would be a strong opponent against Wilson. As delegates arrived over the weekend in advance of the Wednesday opening of the convention, some were disappointed to find that local laws prohibited the sale of alcohol in bars and restaurants on Sundays. Clever entrepreneurs found a way around this, hanging out in hotel lobbies and giving delegates membership cards to private "literary clubs" where they could go to "read" and also to find their favorite beverages being served. In keeping with tradition, Wilson did not go to St. Louis and followed the convention by telephone from the White House. He had personally prepared a draft of the party's platform and sent it to St. Louis with one of his cabinet members.[33]

One well-known Democrat was not scheduled to have any role at the convention. William Jennings Bryan, the party's three-time nominee, would be attending, but only as a reporter. He had lost in his attempt to win a seat as a delegate from his home state of Nebraska. For twenty years, since he had electrified the 1896 convention with his "Cross of Gold" speech, Bryan had been a dominant force at all the party's conventions, including the last one in 1912, where he had sabotaged Champ Clark's likely nomination, resulting in Woodrow Wilson becoming the party's standard bearer. Bryan had gone on to be Wilson's secretary of state, but had only lasted a couple of years. He was a pacifist, favored strict neutrality in the European war, and had resigned his cabinet position in 1915 to protest the president's stern words to Germany after the sinking of the *Lusitania*. Byran arrived at his hotel in St. Louis almost unnoticed. Prominent politicians looked the other way, wanting nothing to do with him. A reporter observing the scene commented, "His magic has waned. His influence is dissipated. His fighting spirit seems to be dulled. He has come to be a looker-on, a commentator of other men's acts and words. There is something of tragedy in all this . . . ."[34]

Suffragettes had been attending the conventions of both major parties for more than a generation, since 1868, seeking, in vain, support in platforms for voting rights for women. In 1880, Susan B. Anthony had personally appeared before the Democratic convention and had been rudely received. Suffragettes were optimistic that the 1916 conventions would finally act on their requests. At the recently concluded Republican convention in Chicago, they finally succeeded in having the GOP include a plank in its platform supporting women's suffrage, but with the caveat that it should be decided by each state. The suffrage movement was itself split over strategy—some favored a state-by-state approach, while others pushed for an amendment to the Constitution that would apply nationwide. The former approach was working, albeit slowly. By 1916, a dozen states had full voting rights for women, and several more had partial voting, limited to local elections. Some suffrage leaders hoped that the Democrats would not only match what the Republicans had done, but would also endorse a federal constitutional amendment. Vocal protests and marches for voting rights by women over the past few years had alienated some to their cause. They had something different planned for St. Louis.[35]

As delegates walked the ten or so blocks down Locust Street from the main hotels to the Coliseum for the convention's opening session on the morning of Wednesday, June 14, they passed through, lining each side of the street, a row of women, dressed in white, with yellow and gold "Votes for Women" sashes and carrying parasols of the same colors. Billed as a "walkless, talkless demonstration," the women, numbering between six and eight thousand, stood four feet apart and stared silently at the men as they walked by. As one author described the scene, "The men emerged from breakfast in marching ranks, wearing snappy suits, straw hats, and medals announcing their status in their [political] clubs, and then found themselves embarrassed by a row of staring women. Their swaggers gone, the men faced a mile of mothers, grandmothers, aunts and sisters . . . . There was no break where they might dive out and escape down a side street." On the steps of a museum along the route, the men passed a visual depiction of the status of women's suffrage in the country. Some fifty women were arranged on the steps in the formation of a pyramid. At its top, on a pedestal, stood a robed woman representing the goddess Liberty. Directly beneath her were thirteen women, dressed in white, representing the states and territories where women had full voting rights. The right side of the pyramid consisted of a diagonal line of women dressed in gray, representing states and territories where women had only partial voting rights. On the left side was a similar line, but with the women dressed in black, wearing black veils and with their heads bowed, representing states and territories where no voting rights existed for women. Called the "Up to Liberty" tableau, the scene caused some sympathetic delegates to raise their hats and cheer as they walked by. The entire event, known to history as the "Golden Lane" protest, is one of the most-remembered events from the convention.[36]

As they approached the Coliseum, the delegates passed by a relatively new innovation, as a "moving picture machine" captured their movements. Once inside, Texas delegates tossed miniature bales of cotton as souvenirs to the packed galleries. It was a hot day and, before long, many had removed their coats. Chairman McCombs called the convention to order at 12:30 p.m. and announced his committee's selection of Martin Glynn, the former governor of New York, to be the convention's temporary chairman and keynote speaker. Unlike four years earlier in Baltimore, when the nomination of Alton Parker for this position had led to a divisive opening battle between the party's liberal and conservative factions, there was no objection and Glynn was unanimously confirmed as the initial presiding officer.[37]

Glynn's keynote speech began with a rousing defense of Wilson's strategy of neutrality in the war then raging in Europe. It was thought by many to be the best speech of the convention. Neutrality, Glynn asserted, had been an American tradition since the founding of the republic and he cited several prior incidents when European powers had provoked America, including some with loss of American lives, after which prior presidents had been watchful, restrained, and did not take the country to war:

> For supporting this policy of neutrality, George Washington was hooted by a howling mob of 10,000 war fanatics who threatened to pull him from the presidential chair and start a revolution. But half a century later Charles Sumner said that 'Washington upholding the peaceful neutrality of this country, while he met unmoved the clamor of the people wickedly crying for war, is a greater man than Washington crossing the Delaware or taking Cornwallis's sword at Yorktown . . . .'
>
> For supporting this policy of neutrality, Thomas Jefferson was called a spineless poltroon, and yet to-day Jefferson is hailed as one of the wise men of the world and for millions his opinions are a political bible.
>
> For supporting this policy of neutrality, Abraham Lincoln was pictured as a craven, and yet to-day Lincoln is enshrined in the heart of Americans and canonized . . . .
>
> When Grant was President . . . a Spanish gunboat seized the vessel 'Virginius,' flying the American flag, and a Spanish commandant in cold blood shot the captain . . . thirty-six of the crew and sixteen of the passengers.
>
> But we didn't go to war. Grant settled our troubles by negotiation . . . .
>
> When Benjamin Harrison was President the people of Chili conceived a violent dislike to the United States . . . . When this feeling was at its height one junior officer from the United States warship 'Baltimore' was killed outright in the streets of Valparaiso and sixteen of our sailors wounded, of whom one afterward died . . . .
>
> But we didn't go to war. Harrison settled our troubles by negotiation . . . .[38]

At one point, Glynn stated that he did not want to take the time to go through each prior example of neutrality and why the current war advocates were out of step with American history, but the crowd urged him to continue. "Go on, go on . . . . Give it to them," they shouted. "All right," he responded, "I'll hit them again, and I'll hit them fair, and I'll hit them hard." Glynn continued and he went on a roll. With each recitation of an insult to American honor under a prior president, the crowd in the Coliseum shouted, "What did we do?," followed by Glynn's response of "We didn't go to war!" and that the crisis was settled by negotiation.[39]

Of Wilson's neutrality in response to the ongoing European war, Glynn, in moving words, contrasted it with the heartbreak that war brings:

> This policy does not satisfy those who revel in destruction and find pleasure in despair. It may not satisfy the fire-eater or the swashbuckler. But it does satisfy those who worship at the altar of the God of Peace. It does satisfy the mothers of the land, at whose hearth and fireside no jingoistic war has placed an empty chair. It does satisfy the daughters of this land, from whom brag and bluster have sent no husband, no sweetheart and no brother to the mouldering dissolution of the grave. It does satisfy the fathers of this land, and the sons of this land, who will fight for our flag, and die for our flag, when Reason primes the rifle.[40]

Glynn went on to discuss the laws passed in Wilson's first term and the domestic agenda for a second, but the crucial moment had passed. The audience was uninterested, or exhausted. His speech would be remembered for its beginning, not for its end. Prior to the convention, Democrats had thought that the progressive legislation passed during Wilson's first term, and the promise of more, would be their primary pitch to voters in the quest for another four years. With his electrifying words on the president's neutrality in response to the European war, however, Glynn had given the Democrats a different theme for the upcoming campaign. "He kept us out of war!" would become their rallying cry.[41]

A couple of items remained on the June 14 opening day of the convention. June 14 was the day in 1777 when Congress adopted a flag of stars and stripes as the emblem of the new country. Two weeks before the convention, President Wilson had issued a proclamation urging celebration of the day each year as Flag Day. A New York delegate, Alfred Smith (who would become the party's presidential nominee in 1924) rose and read Wilson's words. Decrying recent influences "which have seemed to threaten to divide us" and of "forces within and forces without that seemed likely to draw us away from the happy traditions of united purpose and action of which we have been so proud," Wilson had declared, "I therefore suggest and request that throughout the nation and if possible in every community the fourteenth of June be observed as Flag Day with special patriotic exercises." The convention approved a resolution adopting the president's words and from that day to the present, the United States has celebrated June 14 as Flag Day. The convention then appointed its various committees and, in mid-afternoon, adjourned for the day.[42]

The convention's second day began with the receipt of two committee reports. The Committee on Credentials advised there were no controversies over the proposed delegates and all 1,093, as well as hundreds of alternates, were seated. Among them were thirteen women as full delegates and eight as alternates. As at all prior Democratic conventions, there were no Black delegates. The Committee on Permanent Organization recommended Senator Ollie James of Kentucky as permanent chairman, the same position he had held at the last convention. Both committee reports were quickly approved on a voice vote.[43]

Senator James gave the traditional speech of the permanent chairman, going through Wilson's domestic legislative accomplishments and defending his Mexico policy. He then moved on to the war in Europe. As with Glynn's speech the previous day, it was this topic that drew the greatest response from the crowd. Noting Germany's agreement to suspend unconditional submarine warfare in response to Wilson's threat to end diplomatic relations, James proclaimed, "Without orphaning a single American child, without widowing a single American mother, without firing a single gun, without the shedding of a single drop of blood, he wrung from the most militant spirit that ever brooded above a battlefield an acknowledgment of American rights and an agreement to American demands." The crowd erupted for almost twenty minutes, with delegates marching in the aisles and bands playing, while the senator, catching his breath and trying to get some relief from the heat, fanned his face and waited for the opportunity to continue his remarks.[44]

Although it was still early in the afternoon, the convention adjourned until the evening. The time for meeting again was moved from eight to nine o'clock, at the request of a Missouri senator, who advised that the citizens of St. Louis had "arranged for more than fifty banquets, dinners, and other entertainments" for the delegates and that the extra hour would give the locals more time to show their appreciation for the convention coming to their city.[45]

The convention moved to the nomination of candidates for president and a roll call of the states began. Alabama yielded to New Jersey and John Wescott, the same man who had given the nomination speech for Woodrow Wilson at the last convention in Baltimore, placed the incumbent president's name before the delegates for a second term. With rhetorical flourishes, Wescott reviewed the legislation enacted in the past four years, praised Wilson's restraint in Mexico and in the European war, and argued that all of humanity demanded a second term: "Therefore, my fellow-countrymen, not I, but his deeds and achievements; not I, but the spirit and purposes of America; not I, but the prayers of just men and women; not I, but civilization itself, nominate to succeed himself to the Presidency of the United States, to the Presidency of one hundred million free people, bound in impregnable union, the scholar, the statesman, the financier, the emancipator, the pacificator, the moral leader of Democracy, Woodrow Wilson." A lively demonstration lasting forty-five minutes followed Wescott's speech.[46]

There were no other nominations and, before a roll call vote began, a motion was made to suspend the rules and nominate Wilson by acclamation. One delegate, Robert Burke of Illinois, objected and requested a full vote. He was shouted down and the vote for Wilson was recorded as 1,092 in favor and Burke's lone vote in dissent. Burke, who was an uncommitted delegate from Illinois, had said before the convention that he would never vote for Wilson, in protest against what he perceived to be Wilson's hostility to Germany, and favoritism to Great Britain and France, in the European conflict.[47]

The nomination of a running mate for Wilson then followed and was completed in a matter of minutes, which was somewhat of a surprise. Although the Wilson men had made it known that they did not want to see any shakeup of the 1916 ticket, in the days leading up to the convention, newspapers had been filled with stories of possible alternatives to Vice President Thomas Marshall of Indiana. Chicago party boss Roger Sullivan had hoped to make a serious run and opened a headquarters in St. Louis and hundreds of his supporters from Illinois paraded around the streets of St. Louis on his behalf. Other states were rumored to be offering their own favorite son candidates. When, however, the New York delegation, led by Boss Charles Murphy of Tammany, failed to endorse Sullivan's bid and let it be known that his state would be supporting a little-known New Yorker, the air went out of all of the vice-presidential trial balloons and no alternative candidates were placed before the convention. Marshall was renominated by acclamation.[48]

Wilson, had, as did most presidents before him, frozen his vice president out of any influence in his administration. Marshall, an intelligent and competent man, was known for his wit and humor, something that was looked down upon by the intellectual Wilson and his advisors. Upon Marshall's renomination, the *Washington Post* reported that, since taking office in 1913, the vice president had generally remained out of the limelight, "except when one of his quaint stories had attracted the attention of the press." Like other vice presidents before and after him, Marshall joked about the powerlessness and obscurity of the job. On the frustration felt by all vice presidents, Marshall would later write: "He cannot speak; he cannot move; he suffers no pain; yet he is perfectly conscious of everything that is going on around him." He loved to tell a story about a woman who had two sons, one of whom was lost at sea. The other had become vice president of the United States. Sadly, Marshall would deadpan, neither was ever heard from again. He is most famous for a comment that he made in 1914 when presiding over the Senate. A long-winded senator was going on and on in a speech about his solutions to the nation's problems, beginning each sentence with the phrase, "What this country needs is . . . ." Marshall leaned over to a clerk sitting near him on the rostrum and declared, "What this country needs is a really good five-cent cigar."[49]

With its ticket nominated, the only item that remained for the convention's third day was the approval of the party's platform. The committee working on the platform had met for more than twenty hours. As expected, the platform endorsed the "record of achievement" of the legislation concerning domestic issues passed over the past four years and pledged to "now remove, as far as possible, every remaining element" of special privilege and unfair discrimination in the economy to secure "a continued period of quiet, assured and confident prosperity." The proposed plank that had been most discussed in the press during the convention was one entitled "Americanism," which President Wilson had personally drafted. It concerned (without directly saying so) the ongoing European war and criticized Americans who promoted a foreign policy aligned with the interest of the country of their family origin. The intended targets were German-Americans, who wanted Wilson to be softer on Germany, and Irish-Americans, who wanted him to be tougher on Great Britain. The president was adamant about this plank. There were reports that, if the convention changed his words in any significant way, he intended to come to St. Louis himself and argue for his original language. Given this, the committee made only minor revisions. The key language stated, "Whoever, actuated by the purpose to promote the interest of a foreign power in disregard of our own country's welfare or to injure this government in its foreign relations . . . is faithless to the trust which the privileges of citizenship repose in him and is disloyal to his country." Such actions were deemed to be "subversive" and "destructive" of the nation's welfare and all individuals, alliances, and political parties promoting such actions were condemned. One newspaper called it "a bold defiance of the German vote" and of those who play for its support.[50]

The other plank that attracted attention concerned women's suffrage, which had consumed much of the committee's time. The committee did not support a federal constitutional suffrage amendment that would apply to all states. Rather, what resulted from its meetings was the following: "We recommend the extension of the franchise to the women of the country by the States upon the same terms as to men." This was the only plank of the platform challenged before the convention, contested by anti-suffragists because they felt that it went *too far*. A minority report on suffrage, presented by Governor James Ferguson of Texas, stated that the Democratic party had always "stood for the sovereignty of the several States in the control and regulation of elections and in "the power to prescribe the qualifications" of their voters, and urged reaffirmation of this "historic position of our party." In other words, under the doctrine of states' rights, the minority report held that the party had no business recommending to the states that they permit women to vote. Ferguson stated that he knew that many of the men who favored the majority position adopted by the committee did so, not because they believed in the principle of women's suffrage but, rather, out of "political expediency," as they were fearful that the party "might lose the votes of three or four Western States" if the party said nothing. After a heated debate, the minority report was rejected by a vote of 888½ to 181½, following which the full platform was approved on a voice vote and the convention adjourned. Although it was the first time that the Democrats had endorsed any form of voting by women, suffrage leaders were not happy, after hearing in the debate that the party did so only because they felt that they needed to do something, or else lose the election. The Democrats, said suffrage leaders, "thought to hoodwink the women by a jumble of words that were designed to meet the situation, but in no sense succeeded." The language adopted, they said, "may be interpreted in as many ways as there are people." They vowed to take their fight to the president and to Congress.[51]

Democrats ended their convention united, hopeful of making Woodrow Wilson the first president of their party to be elected to a second consecutive term since Andrew Jackson. The general view in the country was that the campaign—with the Democratic nominee having been a professor and the Republican nominee a judge—would be civil. An editorial in the *Washington Post* was optimistic: "With all the rubbish of the conventions cleared way, the real contest will begin. Two clean and courteous men are rivals for the presidency. From them may be expected light rather than heat and always a decent respect for the opinions of mankind."[52]

The Campaign and Election

As the incumbent president, Wilson followed tradition and did not actively campaign. "Don't worry" he told his campaign manager, "this is exactly what the people want. They want the President at a time like this to stay on the job." Hughes did travel extensively throughout the country, as did former President Theodore Roosevelt, both attacking Wilson. Hughes, with his judicial mindset, proved to be a mediocre campaigner, unable to stir up passion in crowds. One observer of his rallies in Colorado commented that they had "none of the old time rousing enthusiasm. The whole thing was rather flat." Much of the campaign concerned foreign policy and how to deal with the European war. Wilson's slogan was "He Kept Us Out of War." Hughes and Roosevelt attacked Wilson from opposite positions—with Hughes courting German-Americans by criticizing British interference with American commerce on the seas, and with Roosevelt taking an aggressive stance against Germany, stating that, if he had been president when the *Lusitania* was sunk, he would have seized all German vessels in American waters. Both argued that Wilson had not adequately prepared the nation's defenses, in the event it was drawn into war.[53]

One incident in California during the campaign, seemingly minor at the time, may have determined the outcome of the election. That state's governor, Hiram Johnson, a Republican who had left the party in 1912 to be Roosevelt's running mate on the Progressive Party ticket, had rejoined the party and was running as a Republican for the Senate in 1916. During a western campaign trip in August, Hughes met with leaders of the conservative faction of the California Republican Party that opposed Johnson. One night, both Hughes and Johnson stayed in the same hotel in Long Beach, but never crossed paths. Although it is unclear if Hughes ever knew that Johnson and he were at the same hotel, Johnson viewed the failure of Hughes to meet with him as a snub, and he did nothing to support Hughes for the rest of the campaign.[54]

The 1916 presidential election was one of the closest of its era. Wilson won the popular vote by more than a half million, with 9,129,606 (49.4%), compared to 8,532,221 (46.2%) for Hughes. Of the several third-parties that fielded candidates, the Socialist Party and its nominee, Allan Benson of Michigan, led with 585,113 (3%) votes. In the Electoral College, where presidential races are decided, it was much closer. Wilson won thirty states and 277 electoral votes, compared to eighteen states for Hughes and 254 electoral votes. Hughes won most of the Northeast and Midwest, while Wilson won the entire South and most of the West. Wilson won California's thirteen electoral votes by a narrow margin of only 4,000 popular votes. If Hughes had won California, he would have won the election. Johnson won his Senate race there, leading many to conclude that his feud with Hughes had cost Republicans both California and the presidency. In congressional elections, there was little change in the Senate and Democrats kept their sizeable majority there. They lost several seats in the House, but narrowly retained control of that body.[55]

Woodrow Wilson became the first Democratic president to be reelected to a consecutive second term since Andrew Jackson had accomplished that feat in 1832.

Chapter 5

1920: Best of the Second Raters

We need a man to guide us
Who'll always stand beside us,
One who is a fighter through and through.
A man who'll make the White House
Shine out just like a light-house,
And Mister Harding we've selected you.

Harding, lead the G. O. P.
Harding, on to victory!
We're here to make a fuss!
Mister Harding, you're the man for us!
—**Republican Campaign song, 1920**

The three years from Woodrow Wilson taking the oath of office for a second term in March 1917 until the beginning of the 1920 election year were more eventful than most. After running in 1916 on having kept the United States out of the European war, in April 1917 Wilson asked for, and received from Congress, a declaration of war against Germany. Only a few months after the election, circumstances changed. Germany resumed unrestricted submarine warfare against American ships, including passenger ships, and a secret German message (the Zimmerman telegram) to Mexico was intercepted, in which Germany urged Mexico to become its ally, with a promise of helping Mexico take back from the United States the lands it had lost in the 1840s to its northern neighbor, including Texas, New Mexico, and Arizona. The United States entered World War I on the side of the Allies (Great Britain, France, and Russia). American weapons and troops broke the stalemate on the battlefields of Europe and, by November 1918, Germany was defeated. The victory was costly, with more than 115,000 American deaths and more than 200,000 wounded.[1]

Those three years also saw President Wilson go from triumph to tragedy, both politically and personally. He went to Europe to negotiate a peace treaty between the Allies and Germany. Hailed on the world stage, Wilson, ever the professor and intellectual, envisioned a new world order, with future conflicts debated and resolved in an international organization, to be called the League of Nations. And then, all of his grand plans fell apart. Most Americans, isolationists at heart, wanted none of it. They had intervened and won World War I, at great sacrifice, and that, they felt, was enough. Republicans in the Senate opposed Wilson's treaty, especially its League of Nations. They proposed changes. A stubborn Wilson refused and headed out on a cross country speaking tour to try to sell the treaty. In September 1919, while in Colorado, the president suffered a stroke. He returned to Washington and had another, more serious, stroke a few days later. His true condition (he was virtually an invalid) was kept from the country. For more than a year, until the end of his term, the country was run by First Lady Edith Wilson, assisted by the president's physician, Dr. Cary Grayson, who issued optimistic (and false) medical reports on the president's health. Wilson's treaty was defeated in the Senate. His agenda, and his health, were in shambles. Despite this, Wilson entertained thoughts of running for a third term. Even his most loyal supporters knew that was not possible. Democrats would be looking for new leadership in 1920.[2]

Theodore Roosevelt, still only in his fifties, eyed a return to the White House in 1920. The Old Guard that still ran the Republican Party, and which had successfully blocked him from the 1916 nomination, seemed to have warmed up to him, or at least accepted the inevitable. In 1918, in March, a convention of Maine Republicans endorsed him. In May, at a chance meeting in a Chicago hotel, Roosevelt and William Howard Taft, who had fiercely battled each other in 1912, exchanged pleasantries and made a first step to heal the rift between them. That autumn, Senator Boies Penrose, Pennsylvania's conservative Republican boss and the unofficial head of the party's establishment, met with Roosevelt. Advising that he still did not "like" the former president, Penrose stated that he no longer "despised" him and that "Theodore Roosevelt is now the one and only possible Republican candidate in 1920. He will surely receive the nomination." TR began gearing up for his last campaign. And then he died. In January 1919, at his home on Long Island, the nation's twenty-sixth president passed away in his sleep at the age of sixty, of what was believed by his doctors to have been a coronary embolism. Teddy was gone and the nation mourned.[3]

As the 1920 campaign season began, both parties would be focusing on a large field of politicians from which to select their nominees. It would be a political year of twists and turns. It was anybody's guess who would lead each party into the November election and, as the year began, few would have bet money on the two men who emerged as the Democratic and Republican nominees for president, nor on the two nominees for vice president.

Republican Convention

As the 1920 campaign season opened, with Roosevelt deceased, four men were considered top-tier candidates for the Republican nomination, followed by a host of lesser candidates and favorite sons who were likely to enter the contest.

If anyone could legitimately claim to be TR's political heir, it was General Leonard Wood. A doctor, Wood attended medical school at Harvard, joined the Army, and served as the personal physician to two presidents, Cleveland and McKinley. When Roosevelt came to Washington as McKinley's assistant secretary of the Navy, he and Wood became good friends. At the outbreak of the Spanish-American War in 1898 (which Roosevelt had a hand in instigating), both men formed a volunteer cavalry brigade, called the Rough Riders, with Wood becoming the group's leader and Roosevelt his second in command. Their unit was sent to Cuba, where it fought bravely, and both became war heroes. While Roosevelt soon left the military to run for governor of New York, Wood stayed in the Army and held a series of increasingly important jobs over the years, from military governor of Cuba, to commanding general in the Philippines (where there was an insurrection against American occupation of the islands), to chief of staff of the Army under President Taft. When war in Europe broke out in 1914 on President Wilson's watch, Wood, along with his old friend Roosevelt, were two of the loudest voices urging upgrades in military preparedness, with the clear implication that Wilson's efforts (or lack thereof) had left the country at risk. Upon America's entry into the war in 1917, a miffed Wilson kept Wood stateside, refusing to let him see action in France. When Roosevelt, who had been making plans to run for president again in 1920, died unexpectedly in early 1919, Wood was seen by many as the man to carry on TR's torch. The Roosevelt family came out in support of the general, as did many of the former president's supporters. Although considered the topmost candidate among the frontrunners, Wood was vulnerable. His views on, and comprehension of, the domestic political issues of the day were largely unknown. H. L. Mencken of the *Baltimore Sun* was no fan, writing of Wood, "No one knows precisely what he is in favor of—least of all himself . . . the gallant old bloodletter is intrinsically a hollow and stupid fellow." Also, though Wood was an attractive militaristic "man on horseback," Americans in 1920 had just come out of World War I, with many having opposed entry into the conflict. In a nation weary of war, a military man, many thought, was not right for the times.[4]

Wood's campaign was led by William Procter, the president of Procter & Gamble and a grandson of one of that company's founders. A political novice, Procter donated huge sums of his own money, and got other wealthy industrialists to do the same, in a national publicity effort to sell Wood (who always appeared at campaign events in his military uniform) to the country, much as Procter sold Ivory soap and other consumer products to Americans. He set up the non-partisan "Leonard Wood League" throughout the country, which bypassed, and caused resentment from, the regular Republican organizations in the states. Procter also entered Wood in state primaries where favorite sons were on the ballot, antagonizing local party leaders and making it unlikely that they would later make deals or negotiate with him for delegates at the convention. It was an aggressive, in-your-face strategy that offended many and made enemies in the party.[5]

The candidate considered second to Wood as the 1920 campaign began was Governor Frank Lowden of Illinois. The son of a Minnesota blacksmith, Lowden was raised in Iowa and ended up in Chicago, where he became a prominent attorney, a wealthy man, and a gentleman farmer. His riches increased when he married Florence Pullman, the daughter of the founder of the Pullman railroad coach company. Lowden entered politics at the turn of the century as a supporter of McKinley and sided with Taft in the Roosevelt/Taft schism of 1912. After a couple of terms in Congress, he won the governorship of Illinois in 1916. As governor, he walked a path between the progressive and conservative wings of the Republican Party and had a record of competence and accomplishment. He built roads, supported education, made government more efficient, and cut taxes. Lowden had a record of being honest and independent. Journalist Walter Lippman thought that Lowden, who, like General Wood, was fifty-nine years old, might be the right man for the country in 1920. "There is logic to Lowden," Lippman wrote, "once you grant the premises. He comes from the middle of the country, he stands in the middle of the road, in the middle of the party . . . . He had risen from a farm to an estate, from obscurity to moderate fame . . . . The people are tired, tired of noise, tired of politics . . . and longing for a place where the world is quiet . . . . Lowden is the noiseless candidate in this campaign. I have watched his appeal to the voters . . . . He assures them that he will not bother them much and he will not."[6]

In contrast to Lowden, another candidate, if his past was any indication, promised to make a lot of noise. Hiram Johnson was a Republican progressive with a brash style that offended many. A Californian, Johnson first made a name for himself as a prosecutor in San Francisco, taking on political bosses and railroads. He favored the liberal causes of the era—greater regulation of business, pure food and drug laws, workers' compensation, recall of public officials, an eight-hour work day for women, etc. When governor of California, in 1912, he left the party with Roosevelt and had been TR's vice-presidential running mate on the Progressive Party ticket. He returned to the Republican fold in 1916 and ran for a seat in the Senate. During that campaign, he publicly feuded with Charles Evans Hughes, the party's presidential nominee, over an alleged personal snub. While Johnson won his Senate race, Hughes narrowly lost California in his fight to deny Woodrow Wilson a second term. Had Hughes won California, he would have beaten Wilson in the Electoral College and been president. Many Republicans in 1920 were not about to forgive Johnson for his actions in 1916, which they believed cost their party the White House. As an ideologue, Johnson took everything personally. "When a man opposes Johnson," his progressive ally Senator Borah of Idaho once said, "he hates him." When giving speeches, Johnson harangued his audiences. A reporter noted that the senator "is utterly lacking in charm" and that he "does not talk at his crowd but through them." Johnson was also an ardent isolationist. He was what was called an "irreconcilable," opposed to *any* entry of the United States into the League of Nations. Most of the party, known as "reservationists," and led by Senator Henry Cabot Lodge, did not oppose America's entry into the League entirely, but wanted substantial changes to the League provisions in the peace treaty negotiated by President Wilson. They had successfully defeated the treaty in the Senate. While Johnson attracted the pure ideological progressives who had supported Roosevelt, many political observers thought his gruff personality and uncompromising stance on issues would make it difficult for him to expand his support beyond that base.⁷

The fourth and final of the top-tier contenders was Senator Warren Harding. The son of a doctor, Harding was an Ohio native who settled in Marion, a small town in the central part of the state. As a young man, he bought a bankrupt local newspaper, rechristened it the *Marion Star*, and lived the comfortable life of a small-time publisher and editor. He married Florence Kling, the ambitious daughter of a wealthy merchant. Her father did not approve, in part, due to rumors that Harding had a grandparent, or great-grandparent, who had been Black. Harding became a community leader, entered politics, was elected to the Ohio Senate, and then the state's lieutenant governor. Despite losing a race for governor, he was chosen to give the main nominating speech for President Taft at the 1912 Republican convention, which received national attention. Harding was elected to the United States Senate in 1914 and, two years later, was the temporary chairman and keynote speaker at the party's 1916 convention. He developed a reputation as an amiable man, a decent orator, a conservative, but by no means an intellectual. Mencken called him "a second rate provincial." Harding's personal life, unknown to the public, was messy. In 1905, he began an affair with Carrie Phillips, the wife of a friend that he and Florence socialized with from time to time. In 1917, when he was a senator, Harding became involved in another extramarital relationship, this one with Nan Britton, an eighteen-year-old secretary from Marion. Harding's marriage to Florence produced no children. Nan gave birth in October 1919 to a daughter, Elizabeth Ann Britton. Harding was the child's father. Although he refused to publicly acknowledge Elizabeth and avoided even meeting her, he did provide Nan with support payments. The extent to which Florence knew of her husband's relationships is unknown.⁸

The second-tier candidates included Calvin Coolidge, the governor of Massachusetts. A Vermont native, the shy and taciturn Coolidge had gotten national attention in 1919 with his aggressive handling of a strike by Boston police. Supporting the city's mayor, Coolidge sent the state's national guard troops to quell violence that had erupted in the absence of police authority. After the strike was over, he refused to consider a request from labor union leaders that the striking police officers be rehired. Coolidge responded, in words that would make him famous, "There is no right to strike against the public safety by anybody, anywhere, any time." Coolidge's run for the nomination was a low budget and somewhat half-hearted, although his campaign did mail a book of his speeches, entitled *Have Faith in Massachusetts*, to all of the delegates.⁹

Herbert Hoover, another long shot in the race, had perhaps the best-known name in the entire field of contenders. He was an engineer who had made a fortune in the mining industry across the world. As a private citizen, Hoover had, before the United States entered World War I, led charitable efforts to provide food and other relief to Belgium, which had been invaded by Germany. After America became a combatant in the war, President Wilson, impressed by Hoover's competency and efficiency in Europe, named him the nation's food administrator. Again, Hoover was successful, overseeing food conservation efforts during the conflict and earning praise throughout the country. Hoover, who had never been openly political, was mentioned by prominent Democrats, as well as by Republicans, as their party's potential nominee in 1920. His name was entered, without his consent, in a couple of Democratic primaries. When he finally declared that he was a Republican and actively entered the GOP race, many in the party were suspicious of a man who had served so prominently in a Democratic administration, and who had worked so closely with President Wilson, who they despised.[10]

Between March and early June, primaries were held in twenty states. Wood and Johnson competed in most of them, while the others were more selective. Then, as now, New Hampshire was the first primary and Wood prevailed there. Johnson won handily over Wood and Lowden in Michigan, while Lowden took his home state of Illinois, despite heavy spending by Wood's campaign. Wood narrowly beat Johnson in New Jersey. Harding won in his home state of Ohio, but Wood also spent heavily there, came in a close second, and picked up a few delegates. In his home region of the Midwest, Harding sustained an embarrassing fourth place loss in Indiana, with Wood the victor. Johnson and Hoover, both Californians, fought it out in their home state and Johnson easily won, dooming Hoover's chances for the nomination. In Coolidge's home state of Massachusetts, the delegates were officially unpledged, but were actually for their governor. Primaries in the two large states of New York and Pennsylvania went to favorite sons, with Nicholas Murray Butler (the president of Columbia University) winning the Empire State and Governor William Sproul carrying the Keystone State. The bosses in those states had no illusion of their man winning the nomination, but would trade their delegates for the best deal they could get at the convention. The outcome of the primaries was inconclusive. Wood and Johnson had won the most delegates, with over one hundred each, followed by Lowden with around seventy, and Harding with about forty. Johnson, however, had won the popular vote, with a count of 965,651, compared to 710,863 for Wood. Lowden and Harding, who only competed in a few primaries, had much lower vote totals, with 389,127 for Lowden and 144,762 for Harding. With no delegates pledged to him outside of Ohio and failing to win the entire delegation from his home state, Harding was portrayed in the press as the big loser in the primaries.[11]

It was what happened in Washington while the primaries were winding down that did more than the actual primary results to shake up the race. Beginning in March, newspapers criticized the enormous amount of money that was being spent in the campaign for the Republican nomination. Senator Borah of Idaho, a friend of Johnson, demanded an investigation of campaign expenses and a Senate subcommittee was formed. Shortly before the convention, the results of the investigation were revealed. Wood had spent more than $2,000,000, an unheard-of sum in that era for a race for a party's nomination, with most of it coming from his campaign manager, Procter, and his wealthy friends. Lowden was the second highest spender, with around $400,000, much of it coming from his own pocket. Johnson spent just under $200,000, while Harding's expenditures were just over $100,000. But it was what was in the details that severely damaged one candidate. Lowden's campaign had deposited checks of $2,500 each into the personal bank accounts of two Missouri court clerks who had become delegates for Lowden. The clear implication was that their votes had been bought. Lowden was not aware of it, but he was held responsible. The outcome of the Senate investigation wounded all three of the top contenders. Wood was viewed as a man whose rich friends were trying to buy him the presidency. Lowden was seen as a rich man who was seeking to buy the White House for himself and, more devastating, one whose campaign had bribed delegates for their support. Johnson was seen as a sore loser, who had gotten one of his Senate pals to launch an investigation that had uncovered dirty laundry that the party would have preferred to have been kept hidden. Most Republicans already could not stomach Johnson for what he had done by abandoning the party in 1912 and feuding with Hughes in 1916. As author David Pietrusza has noted of the California senator, "the fact was that his camp had triggered an investigation that embarrassed [the party] . . . infuriated everyone." Now, "[t]hey *despised* Hiram Johnson." All of a sudden, Harding, who had underperformed in the primaries, but who was untouched by the financial revelations, seemed to have gained ground on his opponents.[12]

Harding's campaign was headed by Harry Daugherty, an Ohio politician who had failed in many of his own attempts to win public office. Although he had a somewhat unsavory reputation, Daugherty knew how politics worked, and the weaknesses of the other contenders. In a biography of Coolidge, author Robert Sobel retold a story of Daugherty's, as relayed years later, of a pre-convention conversation with a doubtful Harding (who was unsure of himself and had at times thought of dropping out of the race), wherein Daugherty handicapped the main contenders and why he thought Harding would win. Said the campaign manager to his candidate:

> "Neither one of the leading candidates can win. General Wood is backed by a powerful group of rich men who wish a military man in the White House. They are nervous over the social disorders following the World War . . . . They wish to entrench themselves behind the invisible force of the bayonet and the machine gun. The scheme won't work. The people are sick of war . . . . [Veterans] hate war to a man. They'll not vote for a general. The women will vote in the next election. It would be suicide on that account to name a general. The Republican convention will not do it . . . ."

"Lowden's a power to be reckoned with," Harding suggested.

"Sure. The best man on the list, too. I like him. He'd make a fine president. But he'll never have the prize or the nomination."

"Why?"

"Because he's too rich."

"Nonsense."

"[H]e married Pullman's daughter. No party will name a railroad magnate for the office of president . . . . He'll never win. He and Wood will fight each other to a finish and deadlock the convention."

"Then Johnson may slip in."

"Never. They'll say he defeated Hughes in California, and the real Republicans will not forgive him."

"Come down to brass tacks," Harding ordered. "Am I a big enough man for the race?"

"Don't make me laugh! The day of giants in the presidential chair is passed. Our so-called great Presidents were all made by the conditions of war under which they administered the office. Greatness in the presidential chair is largely an illusion of the people."[13]

The convention opened on Tuesday, June 8, at Chicago Coliseum, during a heat wave that had settled over the city. Throughout the week, during the convention's sessions, temperatures inside the arena (which had no air conditioning system) hovered at ninety degrees or above. It was the fifth straight time that Republicans met under the Coliseum's arched roof. Roosevelt had been nominated there in 1904, Taft in 1908 and 1912, and Hughes in 1916. There had been technical innovations since the last convention. Although radio broadcasts would not come to conventions until 1924, a telephone company installed a "newfangled" voice amplifying device above the podium. Instead of shouting at the top of their lungs, as all prior convention orators had to do to be heard in massive arenas like the Coliseum, a white circle had been painted on a bridge that extended forward from the rostrum. Above it, a huge sounding board curved upward, on which speakers, described as "black trumpets," had been installed. Those addressing the convention were told to "stand within the circle and speak slowly."[14]

As the convention began, the contest for the party's presidential nomination was viewed as wide open. Newspapers reported that there was "no more certainty as to its nominee" than there had been six months earlier. Most of the candidates, from the frontrunners to the wannabes, were in the Windy City to press flesh, woo delegates, and to negotiate deals. Several of the party's conservative senators were also in Chicago and it was believed that they would have a great deal of influence over the outcome. Of the 984 delegates, twenty-seven were women and fifty-five were Black. The youngest delegate was twenty-four-year-old Anna Anderson of Montana. During the convention, another woman, sixty-year-old Margaret Hill McCarter of Kansas, would become the first of her gender to address a Republican convention, in remarks pledging the loyalty of women to the party. "We are organized," she proclaimed, "we are trained, we are ready for the duties of citizenship." Slightly over half of the delegates, 506, were uncommitted to any candidate. Of the 478 who were committed, 125 were for Wood, 112 for Johnson, 76 for Sproul (Pennsylvania's governor and its favorite son), 72 for Lowden, and 39 for Harding. Although Wood was in the lead, it was felt by many that his "pyramid will cave in" and that the real battle would be the conservatives uniting to first deny the nomination to Hiram Johnson and his progressive followers, and then nominate one of their own. The conservatives would first rally, it was thought, behind Lowden and, if he could not be nominated, move on to someone else. For months, the party's last nominee in 1916, Charles Evans Hughes, had been mentioned as a compromise candidate whom most could unite behind. Hughes, however, who was grieving the death of his daughter from tuberculosis in April, forbade his name from being brought into the mix.[15]

The major candidates set up their headquarters in the Congress Hotel. Visitors to Wood's were met by a "grotesquely large" bust of Roosevelt on a table in the middle of the room, while young ladies pinned colored feathers (Wood's campaign symbol) on lapels. The general himself, in his green field uniform, with a chest full of medals and ribbons, was on hand for a greeting. Lowden's room was smaller and his supporters gave out badges of the candidate. Harding was in the elaborate Florentine Room (which Roosevelt had occupied in 1912 when he battled Taft for the nomination), with portraits of distinguished-looking senator covering the walls. Daugherty, Harding's manager, had arranged an extensive presence for his man's campaign in Chicago. He initially brought in five hundred campaign volunteers, with the number growing throughout the week. Smiling Harding supporters met each train of arriving delegates, and staked out the hotels, restaurants, and other sites, to pick up on any rumors. The seventy-five-member Glee Club of Columbus was sent around each day, in dress suits, to hotel lobbies and the headquarters of the other candidates, to serenade all, not with Harding campaign ditties, but with popular tunes that all would enjoy. The Harding strategy was to offend no one and to have the Ohioan considered favorably by all as their second, third, or even fourth choice for the nomination. Senator Johnson's campaign set up shop in the Auditorium, adjacent to the Congress, where a large photo of the candidate, his son, and the family dog was on display, flanked by photos of Roosevelt. Perhaps pushing his Teddy connection to excess, Johnson wore a Rough Rider hat as he pressed the flesh of those who entered. If the crowds on the streets seemed subdued, it was not just due to the uncertainty over the outcome of the convention. This was the first presidential nominating convention to be held since Prohibition went into effect. It did not mean that alcohol was not available, just that conventioneers had to rely on their own supply, or would have to seek it out in speakeasies, at inflated prices. Many of the delegations brought their own stock of libations with them. Unfortunately for the Massachusetts delegates, their train was raided by federal agents in Detroit and, much to their dismay, it was "relieved of all the wet goods that were aboard."[16]

The convention met at a time when the movement for a constitutional amendment for nationwide voting rights for women, which women had been seeking support for at conventions of both parties for decades, was in its final stage. Prior to the convention, thirty-five states had ratified what would become the Nineteenth Amendment. Only one more was needed. Hundreds of women stood outside of the arena and picketed, holding banners urging that Republicans put pressure on the Republican governors of Connecticut and Vermont to call special sessions of their legislatures to vote on the amendment. Of the states that had not yet acted, it was believed that those two offered the best hope for ratification. The amendment would ultimately pass two months after the convention, in August, but with Tennessee being the thirty-sixth and deciding state.[17]

At the opening session, RNC Chairman Will Hays of Indiana presented Senator Henry Cabot Lodge of Massachusetts as the nominee for temporary chairman, who was unanimously confirmed. Hays handed over to Lodge the official gavel of the convention, which had been carved from a rafter in Independence Hall. Lodge, the head of the Senate Foreign Relations Committee, was best known for his role in the Senate's defeat of ratification of the Treaty of Paris that President Wilson had negotiated to end World War I. The rejection was primarily over objections to the United States entering the proposed League of Nations. Lodge had drafted reservations to the League provisions of the treaty, which he believed were required for constitutional purposes and to protect American sovereignty. Wilson stubbornly refused to consider any changes and the entire treaty had been defeated. Lodge minced no words about Wilson in his keynote speech. Accusing the president of being an autocrat, he declared: "Mr. Wilson and his dynasty, his heroes and assigns . . . anybody who with bent knee has served his purposes, must be driven from all control, from all influence of the Government of the United States." At the conclusion of Lodge's speech, the convention appointed its various committees and adjourned for the day.[18]

There was one man who arrived in Chicago that week on a personal crusade, and with a warning. Tall, middle-aged, with spectacles and bushy eyebrows, he visited the headquarters of various candidates, leaving behind crudely-printed flyers. He was William Estabrook Chancellor, a professor at Wooster College in Ohio who had, as Warren Harding's biographer Francis Russell described him, "the soft-spoken manner of a teacher and the glare of a fanatic." Chancellor was a white supremacist, in the extreme, and was convinced, based on his research (mainly oral interviews with dozens of Ohioans, or so he claimed), that Harding had Black blood flowing in his veins and was, therefore, unqualified for the presidency. Chancellor, who was well-educated and had written several academic books, was active in Democratic politics in Ohio. He claimed that Harding's great-grandmother had been Black and that his father had been considered a mulatto by many who knew him. With Harding considered unlikely to win the nomination, few paid attention to, or cared about, Chancellor and his handouts.[19]

The convention's second day, Wednesday, June 9, consisted of a brief morning session. The reports of the Committee on Credentials, the Committee on Permanent Organization, and the Committee on Rules and Order of Business were received, which included the recommendation that Senator Lodge continue to preside over the convention as its permanent chairman. The three committee reports were approved on voice votes without any controversy. Lodge expressed his thanks and, jokingly, advised the convention that "the most practical way to show my gratitude is to tell you there will be no speech by the Permanent Chairman." When the report from the Committee on Resolutions was called for, it was advised that the committee was still meeting.[20]

To fill time, requests were made for a speech by Chauncey Depew, a former New York senator and a noted speaker, known for his humor, who had addressed numerous Republican conventions. Depew, who was eighty-six years old, had attended his first convention, also held in Chicago, sixty years earlier, in 1860, when Abraham Lincoln was nominated. The aged New Yorker did not disappoint, standing in the designated white circle, with the "black trumpets" above him, which "worked their magic on his ancient voice." Depew criticized and mocked President Wilson for personally going to Europe to negotiate a treaty to end World War I. He noted that prior presidents had sent subordinates to successfully negotiate agreements with Europe. Washington's emissary had prevented war with Great Britain, Jefferson's had purchased the Louisiana Territory, Polk's had secured Oregon, and McKinley's had brought back the Philippines and Puerto Rico, as well as independence of Cuba from Spain. Yet, Depew asserted, the naive Wilson, in his arrogance, had gone to Europe himself and, in his desire for his cherished League of Nations, had been outwitted by more experienced negotiators:

> When we came to the settlement of the recent world war our President said: Nobody understands this question but myself. Nobody can properly represent the people of the United States but myself. I will go abroad . . . .
> He was dealing with the ablest men in the political game, in the diplomatic game, in the international game, [that] there are in the world. And he was a babe confident in himself . . . . He said: I want a League of Nations which will put us like a heaven on earth . . . of which I will be the recording angel . . . .
> Those astute old players said to him: All right, Mr. President, that is the most magnificent proposition ever offered since Calvary . . . . Said Lloyd George [of Great Britain], I would like to have the German possessions in Africa . . . . 'All right,' said the President . . . . Australia [said its prime minister, Hughes] wants Guinea, belonging to Germany, but close to us. And Wilson said, 'Take it.' And then came forward Clemenceau [of France] and he said: 'We need coal; we need iron; we need the Saar Valley and we need the Ruhr Valley. The President said, 'Take them.'

The "situation" of the League, and of Republican "needs and of our conditions" concerning it, DePew concluded, had been fully discussed by Lodge in his keynote speech and "no man, either by tongue or pen, is big enough, no man is eloquent enough," to improve on the senator's words.[21]

With the committee report on the platform still not ready, Lodge requested that the convention be in order while lights and movie cameras were turned on to record a brief video of the convention. After a singing of the "Battle Hymn of the Republic," the convention, just over an hour after it had been gaveled to order, adjourned for the day.[22]

When the convention met for its third day on the morning of Thursday, June 10, a progress report on the status of the platform was presented. Newspapers were reporting that the delay was over a plank dealing with the League of Nations. The party, and the committee, was badly split over the issue, with the "reservationists," led by Senator Lodge (who were willing to enter the League with conditions) on one side and the "irreconcilables," led by Senator Johnson (who were isolationists and objected to American entry into the League under any conditions) on the other. The convention was advised that a subcommittee, after meeting throughout the night, had worked out appropriate language to address the League, but that several more hours of work was needed before it would be finalized. Given that, the convention adjourned until the late afternoon.[23]

When the convention resumed around 4:30 p.m., it was kept occupied with various housekeeping measures for an hour and a half until, finally, Senator James Watson of Indiana went to the podium and began reading the long-awaited—and very lengthy—report from the Committee on Resolutions. Hearing how the committee addressed the League of Nations was the most eagerly awaited issue among the press and the delegates. As one author has noted, it was "the hidden reef threatening to wreck the Republican ship." If the plank favored joining the League, even with reservations, Johnson and his isolationist friends had threatened to bolt the party. If it rejected the League entirely, those who supported joining the League with conditions may do the same, or sit out the election. The final product, said to be primarily the work of Elihu Root, was a masterpiece in obfuscation. Root, a veteran conservative voice in the party, had been McKinley's secretary of war and Roosevelt's secretary of state. The plank read as follows:

> The Republican party stands for agreement among nations to preserve the peace of the world. We believe that such international association must be based upon international justice . . . and . . . shall secure instant and general international conference, whenever peace shall be threatened by political action . . . .
>
> We believe that all this can be done without the compromise of national independence, without depriving the people of the United States in advance of the right to determine for themselves what is just and fair when the occasion arises, and without involving them as participants and not as peacemakers in a multitude of quarrels, the merits of which they are unable to judge.[24]

No one knew exactly what the language meant, but none of the key players found it offensive enough to not accept it. Some newspapers called it a surrender to the isolationists; others concluded that ratification of the League, in some form, was not precluded. Otherwise, the platform criticized the Wilson administration for its "[i]nexcusable failure to make timely preparations" for the recent war, which "resulted in unnecessary losses to our gallant troops, in the imperilment of victory itself." It called for an end to "executive autocracy" and the restoration of "constitutional government." The platform endorsed protective tariffs, a "more business-like" government, and supported arbitration in labor disputes. It favored women's suffrage and passage of the Nineteenth Amendment, urging those Republican state legislatures that had not yet acted on the amendment to do so before the election. It urged Congress to consider "the most effective means to end lynching," which it called "a terrible blot on our American civilization." There were some progressive measures—for extension of the civil service in government hiring, for equal pay for women, against child labor, for federal aid in construction of highways, and for "conservation of human resources through an enlightened measure of social and industrial justice." On immigration, the platform favored continuation of existing laws excluding Asiatic immigrants and limits on the overall number of immigrants, so as to "not exceed that which can be assimilated with reasonable rapidity, and to favor immigrants whose standards are similar to ours." After an attempt by a Wisconsin delegate to substitute several more progressive planks on various issues, (which, according to the official transcript was "greeted with a volley of hisses and cries of 'Sit down,' 'Put him out,' 'That is enough,' and 'This is a Republican Convention, not a Socialist gathering'"), the entire platform was approved on a voice vote. Following the platform's adoption, the convention's third day ended.[25]

On the morning of Friday, June 11, the convention began its fourth day with a resolution mourning the loss of Theodore Roosevelt. The former president was honored more in death by this Republican convention than he had been in life at the last two. His name had been anathema to party leaders at the 1912 and 1916 conventions. Now, his voice silenced, the convention, with "inexpressible loss," remembered a "great leader, wise in counsel, far-seeing, valiant . . . to be loved as long as our nation cherishes its ablest and noblest patriots."[26]

Nominating speeches for president then began with General Wood the first to be placed before the convention, in remarks by Governor Henry Allen of Kansas. The speech focused on Wood's military career, both as a soldier and an administrator. Noting that some had criticized the fact that the general had campaigned in uniform, Allen asked, "Since when has this uniform become a symbol of disqualification? Washington wore this uniform; so did Jackson and Harrison . . . . Grant wore it; so did Garfield and McKinley and Roosevelt." Maybe not *while* campaigning for president, but Allen made his point—that Wood was proud to be a military man. A seconding speech for Wood by Roosevelt's sister, Corinne Roosevelt Robinson, was well-received by the convention. "I want Leonard Wood for President," she declared, "not because he was [my brother's] . . . friend, but because he is his type." There are, she said, three "types" of men. One uses "only words," while another uses "the brawn and blood of another man by saying "Go!" The third, she said, which included Wood and her brother, "is the kind of man who says "Come!," and those are the only true leaders who people will follow. The demonstration following Wood's nomination lasted more than forty minutes, as red, green, and blue feathers were released from the upper portions of the arena and floated about the crowd.[27]

Lowden was nominated by Congressman William Rodenberg, who compared the Illinois governor to Lincoln and to Roosevelt, and praised him as "a manly man of courage and conviction, endowed with the genius of common sense, faithful and fearless, whose every heart beat is in full sympathy with the noblest aspirations of his fellowmen." As with Wood, the demonstration following Lowden's nomination lasted just over forty minutes. The speech was better received in the arena than in the newspapers. It was chocked full of cliches, one reporter commenting that Rodenberg must have prepared his remarks by "memorizing all of the platitudes that have been employed in political oratory since Demosthenes."[28]

Hiram Johnson's nominating speech came from a fellow Californian, attorney Charles Wheeler, who cast Johnson as Roosevelt's true heir. "Of all the public men in the country today," Wheeler quoted TR as having said in 1917, Senator Johnson "is the one with whom I find myself most in sympathy." Like his candidate, Wheeler was defiant of the Republican establishment. The presidency, he said, was not "to be treated as the bauble of rich men . . . . You men of honest big business; take just once from your stubborn ears the plugs of prejudice, so that you may permit yourselves to learn what this man's creed really is." He continued, "My fellow Americans, the hour has struck, the time has come to scourge the last of the bosses from this great temple of the Republican party." At a convention dominated by conservative Republicans, it was not a speech designed to win converts to Johnson and it was met with jeers at times. Instead of wooing the delegates, Wheeler antagonized them. In doing so, a reporter noted, he "made every mistake known to public speaking except that of falling off the platform." Despite this, Johnson's supporters were vocal when he finished, with the shouting and cheering lasting almost as long as the demonstrations for Wood and Lowden.[29]

There followed several seconding speeches for those already nominated, as well as nominating speeches for additional candidates—Calvin Coolidge of Massachusetts, Jeter Pritchard of North Carolina, Nicholas Murray Butler of New York, and Herbert Hoover, who was not nominated as being tied to any state or region.[30]

In mid-afternoon, Harding was placed in nomination by Frank Willis, a former Ohio governor. Harding was praised as "Ohio's second McKinley." While speakers for other candidates had stressed their personal and philosophical relationship with Theodore Roosevelt, Harding had been critical of the former president, so Willis made the best of it, arguing that TR had no political heirs. "Ohio bids me mention this," he said, "not because she acclaims our candidate the successor of Theodore Roosevelt, for that great leader is gone and he left no successor, his mantle fell upon no earthly shoulders, no chieftain remains to bend the bow of Ulysses, but the fragrant memory of his great life abides." He asserted that Harding was electable and reminded his audience that no Republican had ever won the White House without carrying Ohio. Harding was presented as a "safe and sane" choice, as a president who understood and would cooperate with Congress, and as a "great stalwart American-thinking Republican; not a professing progressive but a performing progressive." At times, Willis was folksy, drawing laughter from the crowd. Noting that women were now among the delegates, he leaned over the railing of the platform and inquired, "Say, boys—and girls, too—why not name as the party's candidate" the man whose nomination would not require any "explanations or apologies," but whose record "has been coincident and synonymous with the record of the party." While Wood had feathers raining down from above, Harding's campaign had staffers stationed near the roof with stacks of postcard-size pictures of their man, who tossed them into the air at the conclusion of Willis's remarks and watched as they floated down to the convention floor. The demonstration for Harding was not long, lasting only ten minutes, but observers noted that it appeared to be spontaneous, a good sign. Among those cheering in the crowd was Nan Britton, Harding's secret mistress and the mother of his child, who was then living in Chicago with her sister. Harding had snuck away a few times during the week of the convention to privately meet with her and he had provided her with a ticket to watch the nominations. He refused, however, her pleas to meet with their daughter, who was then less than a year old.[31]

The long afternoon of oratory continued with three more names, all favorite sons, placed in nomination—Governor William Sproul of Pennsylvania, Senator Miles Poindexter of Washington, and Senator Howard Sutherland of West Virginia. When it finally ended, the total number of candidates in the race was eleven.[32]

The first ballot began, at the dinner hour, without any break. It confirmed that no candidate was anywhere near victory and that many more ballots would follow. With 493 votes needed for the nomination, Wood led with 287½, followed by Lowden with 211½, and Johnson with 133½. Harding, with 65½ votes, was in sixth place, behind Sproul, who had 84, and Butler, who had 69½. The tally slightly overstated Lowden's strength and understated Harding's. Daugherty, Harding's manager, in a deal with his Lowden counterpart, had agreed to have some of his delegates vote for Lowden on the first few ballots, in an effort to defeat Wood. He warned, however, "the minute you pass Wood, the minute Wood is out of the race, all friendship between us on the floor of this convention ceases."[33]

Three more ballots quickly followed. Wood remained in the lead, but Lowden gained strength on each. Harding's votes barely changed. At the end of the fourth ballot, the results were Wood at 314½, Lowden at 289, Johnson at 140½, Sproul at 79½, and Harding at 61½. A voice vote on a motion for adjournment was then held and, despite the fact that the nays were much louder than the yeas (the Wood and Lowden forces wanted to continue), Chairman Lodge ruled that the motion had passed, quickly gaveled the session closed, and left the podium before anyone could request a roll call. The convention was in recess until Saturday morning. When one of Lodge's senatorial cronies was asked why Lodge had disregarded the voice vote, which had clearly been to go forward with the balloting, he responded, "Oh, there's going to be a deadlock, and we'll have to work out some solution; and we wanted the night to think it over."[34]

The convention's fifth day, a Saturday, began in the morning with the fifth ballot, on which Lowden, with 303 votes, moved into first place, with Wood at 299. Harding picked up 16½ and stood at 78. On the sixth ballot, Wood and Lowden tied at 311½ and Harding gained 11, moving up to 89. On the seventh, Harding moved into third place, adding another 16, and was in triple digits at 105. On the eighth ballot, Lowden was in the lead with 307. Wood dropped to 299 and Johnson to 87. Harding picked up another 28½ and had 133½. At the end of the eighth, a voice vote was held on another motion to adjourn. Just as had occurred the prior evening, despite the noise for going forward being louder than that wanting to take a break, Lodge again ruled that the convention was in recess until the late afternoon.[35]

When the convention resumed shortly before five in the afternoon, there was a buzz in the air. Word was circulating that Lowden had just bowed out of the race and had released his delegates. The vote-buying by his subordinates during the primaries had done him in, one newspaper observing that "the Governor would have been nominated as certainly as the sun shines," but for the taint of bribery against his campaign. Many of Lowden's delegates were expected to shift to Harding and, indeed, once the voting began, a stampede for Harding was evident. On the ninth ballot, he jumped into first place with 374½ votes, a gain of 241, a large portion of which came from those who had been voting for Lowden. Wood was in second, with 249, while Lowden dropped to 121½, and Johnson held steady at 82. Kansas, formerly for Wood, went over to Harding. So did Oklahoma and several other delegates from the southwest. Most of New York went for Harding. Pennsylvania, however, held firm for its favorite son, Governor Sproul. Although Harding still needed more than a hundred votes to clinch the nomination, the outcome was now evident. Daugherty was prepared for the moment. Streamers and banners for Harding popped up everywhere around the arena. From the upper reaches of the arena, hundreds more postcard-size photos of Harding were released and filtered down on the crowd, which began chanting "Harding! Harding!" While the voting was going on, Daugherty went up to the gallery to sit briefly with Harding's wife, Florence, telling her, "I want you to be prepared . . . . We have the votes. Your husband is going to be nominated on the next ballot." Due to the extreme heat in the hall, she had removed her hat and was sitting with it and two large hat pins in her lap. When she heard the word "nominated," she leapt up from her seat and, in her excitement, inadvertently plunged the two hat pins deep into Daugherty's side. He felt faint, thinking that one of his lungs had been punctured. A trickle of blood, he sensed, began to run down a leg into his shoe. Not wanting to upset Florence, he said nothing, steadied himself, and moved back to the convention floor. He would deal with the wound later. He had work to do.[36]

Daugherty was correct. On the tenth ballot, the floodgates broke open for Harding. When Pennsylvania was called, 61 of its votes were cast for the Ohio senator, putting him over the top, and he won the nomination with almost two hundred more votes than needed. The final count was 692.2 for Harding, 156 for Wood, 80.8 for Johnson, 11 for Lowden, and the rest scattered. Harding was in a back room of the arena, with Lowden and Nicholas Murray Butler (who had been New York's favorite son candidate), when he received word of his nomination. As he reached out to shake their hands, he appeared humble, yet confident. "If the great honor of the Presidency is to come to me," he said, "I shall need all the help that you two friends can give me." Still, there were those who refused to join the Harding bandwagon. When a motion to make the nomination unanimous was made, there were several loud shouts of "No!" Despite this, Lodge ruled that the motion had passed. Daugherty, still in pain in his hour of triumph, finally found a seat and pulled off one of his shoes, convinced that his sock would be soaked with blood from the wound from Florence's hat pins. He was much relieved to find that moisture was only perspiration. It was, indeed, a good day.[37]

The preceding paragraphs recount the ballot-by-ballot vote tallies on the convention floor, but what *really* happened from the time the convention adjourned early Friday evening that led to Warren Harding being nominated for president almost twenty-four hours later? The 1920 Republican convention is viewed in history as the classic example of party leaders meeting in secret, selecting a nominee, and imposing him on a convention. A new term, the "smoke-filled room," was coined to describe the precipitating event that led to Harding's nomination. The story is that a group of the party's Old Guard leaders, mostly senators and former senators, met in Room 404 of the Blackstone Hotel in the wee hours of the morning, took a vote anointing Harding as the nominee, and then forced their will on the convention. Like many so-called historical facts, this one is part truth and part myth. There were multiple meetings, phone calls, and actions taken during those hours that led to Harding's unexpected nomination.

There was a meeting in Room 404 of the Blackstone Hotel. It was the parlor room in the suite of Colonel George Harvey, a conservative New Jersey Democrat who had owned several publications over the years, including *Harper's Weekly*. Harvey had been instrumental in getting Woodrow Wilson elected governor of New Jersey in 1910. Once in office, however, Wilson governed as a progressive and renounced his prior association with conservatives such as Harvey, making Harvey his enemy for life. Although Harvey provided the room, Senator Henry Cabot Lodge (the convention's chairman) seemed to be in charge. A dozen or more party leaders, many current senators, wandered in and out of the room during the late evening and early morning hours. There was no formal agenda. The various candidates were discussed, with the focus on who would be the strongest nominee in the general election. Most saw Wood as too militaristic and objected to him because he had bypassed the party organization in setting up and running his campaign. Johnson was a non-starter—was seen as too progressive and he had been disloyal to the party in the past. Lowden was liked, but the revelation of his campaign buying delegates (although done without his knowledge) was viewed as fatal. Senator Borah confirmed this, stopping by to say that his friend Johnson had told him that he would leave the party again if Lowden was nominated. Hoover was out because of his Wilson connection and no one knew if he was really a Republican or a Democrat. Coolidge of Massachusetts and Sproul of Pennsylvania were rejected, because their states were solidly Republican and the party would not gain electoral votes by nominating them. When Lodge's name was suggested, he took himself out of consideration for being too old. "Seventy, a month ago!," he barked. Other candidates in the mix were too conservative, or had something else that was seized upon as disqualifying them.[38]

When all of the names had been discussed and eliminated for one reason or the other, Lodge observed, the only one left was Warren Harding of Ohio. As Senator Frank Brandegee of Connecticut commented, "There ain't any first-raters this year.... We've got a lot of second-raters and Warren Harding is the best of the second-raters." At about one o'clock in the morning, the half dozen or so men left in the room took a vote, agreeing that "it would be the wise course to nominate Harding just as soon as this could be brought about." No one was precluded from later changing his mind and, in fact, some explored other options the next day. Harding was sent for and was found wandering the hallways of the hotel. He was taken into a bedroom of the suite by Colonel Harvey, who brought him up to date and requested information. "We think," Harvey told the Ohio senator, "you may be nominated tomorrow." He advised that before any final decisions are made, "we think you should tell us, on your conscience and before God, whether there is anything that might be brought up against you that would embarrass the party, any impediment that might disqualify you or make you inexpedient, either as a candidate or as President." Harding asked for some time to think about the question and Harvey left the bedroom. Ten minutes later, the senator opened the door and assured Harvey that, no, there was nothing in his life that would preclude him from being the nominee or serving in the presidency. Unmentioned by him were the facts that he had, in the past, a lengthy affair with the wife of a close friend, his other romantic dalliances, or that he had recently had a young mistress, whom he had seen that very week in Chicago and who had borne his daughter less than a year earlier. He also failed to mention the rumors concerning his racial heritage.[39]

Word of the meeting and its outcome appeared in the Saturday morning newspapers. The *New York Times* reported that an overnight meeting of conservative Republican leaders had been held and "a sort of tentative understanding existed among its members that Senator Harding fitted into the complex situation better than any other candidate." An Associated Press article in several papers reported on the meeting and that "Delicate relationships were involved . . . but most of the leaders . . . appeared agreeable to trying Harding first among the large field of dark horses."[40]

Hours earlier, Harding had been certain that he was out of the race. He faced a deadline of midnight that Friday to file papers in Ohio to run for another term in the Senate. Concerned that filing to keep his Senate seat would be viewed as his own lack of confidence in his chances for the presidential nomination, he had delayed a decision as long as he could. That Friday evening, he sent word to a friend in Ohio to get the Senate papers filed. They were, with only hours to spare. A reporter saw Harding coming out of a hotel elevator earlier that night and described him as looking like a shipwreck. He had, the reporter noted, "two days' beard and was disheveled. His eyes were bloodshot. He evidently had been drinking . . . . He was discouraged."[41]

The meeting in Room 404 was not the only one going on that night to try to steer the nomination one way or the other. Jake Hamon, wealthy Oklahoma oilman, had spent a lot of money to control the delegates from his own state, as well as some from neighboring southwestern states, about fifty delegates altogether. "Big Jake" made it known in Chicago that he was willing to spend more, in exchange for a nominee that would permit him to name the next secretary of the interior and the ambassador to Mexico. He wanted oil rights to federal lands, as well as the inside track to rights on oil fields south of the border. He walked into General Wood's headquarters Friday evening and stated his terms. An enraged Wood charged at Hamon, shouting, "I'll be damned if I betray my country! Get the hell out of here." Earlier, Wood had rejected a similar offer, made by telephone, from Pennsylvania's Republican boss, Senator Boies Penrose (who was ill and unable to travel to Chicago), to shift the majority of the Keystone State's delegation to Wood in exchange for Penrose being able to name three cabinet members. One author, Laton McCartney, asserts that both Hamon and Penrose then approached Harding's manager, Daugherty, who, unlike Wood, agreed to cut a deal with both of them, which included Hamon paying $250,000 to Penrose for the right to have himself, or a crony, named to one of the three promised cabinet posts as secretary of the interior. According to McCartney, by the time the senatorial meeting at the Blackstone had settled upon Harding, his "selection was already a fait accompli." Harding's nomination, the author opines, had far less to do with what happened at the Blackstone "than it did with Jake Hamon's checkbook."[42]

Whatever the factors that led to the decision, Warren Harding was the party's nominee and the final act of the convention was to name his running mate. It was Saturday afternoon and the decision needed to be made quickly. There was no way that party leaders, or the delegates, wanted to extend the convention over until Monday to fill the bottom spot on the ticket. The convention took no break and moved forward. Harding himself expressed no preference as to who would join him. Party leaders, many of the same men who had been at the Blackstone hours earlier, met in a room underneath the platform and quickly settled on Senator Irvine Lenroot of Wisconsin. Lenroot had previously been a progressive ally of his fellow Badger State senator, Robert La Follette. In recent years, their relationship had cooled and Lenroot had become more conservative, but he was still viewed as more progressive than Harding and provided an ideological balance. When Chairman Lodge asked for nominations for vice president, Senator McCormick of Illinois rose and, in a two-paragraph speech, nominated Lenroot, followed by four quick seconding speeches for the Wisconsin senator. There was little reaction from the delegates, who appeared indifferent and unenthused as to what was going on. It was all a formality, most thought, including an exhausted Lodge, who had been up most of the night at the Blackstone meeting, and who took a break and handed the gavel over to Frank Willis, the man who had made the nominating speech for Harding.[43]

An Oregon delegate, Wallace McCamant, jumped to his feet and sought recognition. Willis, presumably thinking that McCamant also wanted to second Lenroot's nomination, called upon him. McCamant began by explaining that the Oregon delegation had come to Chicago intending to nominate Senator Lodge of Massachusetts for vice president, but that Lodge had asked them not to present his name. In a surprise to everyone in the arena, McCamant then continued: "But there is another son of Massachusetts who has been much in the public eye in the last year, a man who is sterling in his Americanism and stands for all that the Republican party holds dear, and on behalf of the Oregon delegation I name for the exalted office of Vice-President Governor Calvin Coolidge of Massachusetts." According to the convention's official transcript, the Oregonian's words were met with "an outburst of applause of short duration but of great power, being joined in by the Massachusetts and a number of other delegations." Many on the floor of the convention began to stir, suddenly energized. The delegates, who had seen Harding forced down their throats by the party's leaders, and who were being told that Lenroot was to be his anointed running mate, were in a mood to revolt. And they did. One by one, delegates from various states—Michigan, Maryland, North Dakota, Arkansas, Kansas, Connecticut, Pennsylvania—rose and seconded Coolidge's nomination. Although a couple of other names were brought forward (Henry Allen of Kansas and Henry Anderson of Virginia), no one seemed to care. Delegates from five more states rose and seconded Coolidge. The first ballot was taken, amid chants of "We want Coolidge!," and it was a landslide for the Massachusetts governor, who received 674½ votes, compared to only 146½ for Lenroot, and with the rest scattered among a handful of other candidates. The nomination of was then made unanimous and, after some final housekeeping matters were taken care of, the seventeenth convention of the Republican Party adjourned at 7:30 p.m. on a Saturday.[44]

In a matter of minutes, the delegates had seized control of the convention from the party's leaders and bosses and had put Calvin Coolidge, a man who was more conservative than Harding, on the ticket. The elder statesman of the party, Chauncey Depew, who had addressed the convention on its second day, fired off a telegram of congratulations to Coolidge: "I have been at every Republican convention since 1856," Depew wrote, "and I have never seen such a spontaneous and enthusiastic tribute to a man as the vote for you for vice president." As author David Pietrusza has observed, "The 'bossed' convention had proven to be un-bossed. It had stampeded, done its own will, shaped the ticket in its own image . . . . *Everyone* was for Silent Cal." McCamant later explained that he had read, before coming to Chicago, the book of Coolidge's speeches, *Have Faith in Massachusetts*, that had been sent to all the delegates by Coolidge's lackadaisical campaign for the presidential nomination, and that he had been impressed with "the soundness of his thinking and the conservative trend of his thoughts." His fellow Oregon delegates agreed. "No one," he said "was pleased by the Lenroot suggestion," so they decided to act on their own.[45]

Coolidge was with his wife, Grace, in a hotel suite in Boston where they had been following the convention all week. He was notified of McCamant's speech nominating him for vice president. A short time later, the telephone rang again. Coolidge picked up the receiver, said a few words, hung up, and turned to Grace. "Nominated," he said. Shocked, she responded, "You aren't going to take it, are you?" He looked at her and replied, "Well—I suppose I'll have to." Within a few minutes, Coolidge wrote out a statement and handed it to reporters who had gathered outside his room. "The nomination for the vice-presidency, coming to me unsought and unexpectedly, I accept as an honor and a duty."[46]

The Republicans left Chicago with unexpected nominees at both the top and bottom of their ticket, but they had avoided pitfalls that could have led to a repeat of 1912. No one, not even the cantankerous Hiram Johnson, was threatening to bolt the party. They were relatively united and turned their eyes westward, to San Francisco, where the Democrats would soon be meeting to select their nominees.

Democratic Convention

In the days leading up to its 1920 convention, there was no more certainty as to who the Democratic Party's nominee would be than there had been as to the identity of the Republican nominee before their convention began. There were three frontrunners for Democratic presidential nomination, a host of minor candidates, and one wild card.

The latter was President Woodrow Wilson. Although virtually an invalid since sustaining a stroke in October 1919 (with First Lady Edith Wilson thereafter controlling access to him and making key presidential decisions), Wilson still had dreams of breaking the two-term precedent that had existed since George Washington and serving a third term. In March, he told his personal physician, Dr. Cary Grayson, "The convention may come to a deadlock as to candidates, and there may be practically a universal demand for the selection of someone to lead them out of the wilderness. The members of the Convention may feel that I am the logical one to lead . . . . In such circumstances I would feel obligated to accept the nomination." In this wish, he was almost alone. Most party officials were ready to move on. Since the end of World War I in late 1918, the president's popularity had plummeted. Throughout the country, many questioned whether the cost of the war in blood and treasure had been worth it. There was opposition to America remaining a leader on the world stage, especially as envisioned by Wilson with his cherished League of Nations, which had been twice rejected by the Senate. Domestically, inflation was out of control. Prices had more than doubled from 1914 to 1920. Labor strikes were rampant. The president had been out of the limelight, largely unseen by the public for the better part of a year. Many of those close to Wilson did not want to see him seek another term, knowing that he was not up to it physically nor mentally, and that continuing in office would likely kill him. His top aide, Joseph Tumulty, wanted Wilson to issue a definitive statement before the convention that he would not accept the nomination and, to get the word out, he made arrangements with a reporter from the *New York World* for an interview. His plan backfired. The "interview" turned out to be responses to written questions, to which Mrs. Wilson had revised Tumulty's suggested answers and, when published on June 18, just over a week before the convention, had rosy (and false) descriptions of a president who had recovered his health, who was hard at work, and not a word about him *not* seeking a third term. In an unusual move, Secretary of State Bainbridge Colby, a close friend and ally of Wilson, was named as a late addition to the District of Columbia's delegation. This had been arranged by Wilson and it was publicly announced that Colby would be the president's official representative at the convention. Some suspected that Colby was being sent by the president to the convention to organize a stampede of it for him, if and when the opportunity arose.[47]

The man considered most likely to walk away with the Democratic nomination was William McAdoo. Tall and lanky (Lincolnesque, some said), the fifty-six-year-old McAdoo was a native Georgian who had moved to Tennessee in his youth and, there, had become a lawyer and businessman. After financial setbacks from investments in streetcar systems in Chattanooga and Knoxville, he moved on to New York City where he led an effort to construct railroad tunnels under the Hudson River connecting Manhattan with New Jersey. When opened in 1908, the Hudson and Manhattan Railroad (nicknamed the "McAdoo Tubes") made McAdoo wealthy and famous. His business success attracted the attention of Wilson, who named McAdoo his secretary of the treasury when he took office in 1913. A year later, McAdoo, a widower, married one of Wilson's daughters, Eleanor (who was twenty-five years younger), becoming not only a member of the president's cabinet, but also his son-in-law. McAdoo won praise for his actions as the head of the nation's finances, including for implementation of the new Federal Reserve System and, when war broke out in Europe in 1914, for forcing a lengthy closure of the stock market to prevent a selloff by foreign interests and a depletion of American gold reserves. When the United States entered the war in 1917, Wilson nationalized the nation's railroads and gave McAdoo a second job as the federal director overseeing them. Again, he earned respect for his fair-minded policies in this position. With the war's end in late 1918, McAdoo resigned, resumed practicing law in New York, and began exploring options for seeking the presidency in 1920.[48]

McAdoo's relationship with Wilson was a two-edged sword. Politically, like Wilson, he was a progressive and was viewed by many in the Democratic establishment as the president's heir apparent. Personally, however, so long as Wilson refused to rule himself out as the nominee, as his son-in-law, McAdoo could not actively seek the nomination. In early 1920, McAdoo called for states to send uncommitted delegates to the upcoming convention and advised that he would be willing to accept a draft, if nominated. His friends set up a campaign organization, although, per McAdoo's wishes, they kept him out of the primaries. A *Literary Digest* poll in the spring had McAdoo leading all others for the nomination, with more than half of the respondents favoring him. An endorsement from Wilson at any point before, or during, the convention would likely have made McAdoo the nominee, but it never came. Shortly after Wilson's so-called "interview" in the *New York World* was published (which many thought increased the odds that the convention would turn to Wilson), McAdoo issued a written statement that he had reached an "irrevocable" decision to not have his name put before the convention. He urged his followers to support Senator Carter Glass of Virginia, who had succeeded him as treasury secretary. McAdoo's campaign managers, who had been dealing for months with a candidate who had publicly professed that he was not actively seeking the nomination, ignored his statement and kept on working, noting that their man had never said he would not accept the nomination, if it were offered to him by the convention.[49]

A sitting member of Wilson's cabinet, Attorney General A. Mitchell Palmer, had no qualms about offending his boss and made a full out run for the nomination. Before joining the administration, Palmer had been a prominent Democratic member of Congress from Pennsylvania. He had been much in the news in the year prior to the convention for coordinating the administration's response to the "Red Scare," a series of bombs sent to law enforcement and government officials, believed to have been inspired by communists and supporters of the recent revolution in Russia. Palmer was one of the officials targeted for assassination. An anarchist blew himself up—along with the front of Palmer's Washington, D. C. home—while setting off a bomb intended for the attorney general. To combat real and perceived threats to the nation by Bolsheviks, the attorney general ordered massive arrests, deemed "Palmer Raids" by the press. Many of those arrested were then deported. Some felt that Palmer's response was too aggressive. Mencken wrote, while Americans generally "enjoy the public pursuit of criminals," that Palmer "carried the farce to such lengths that the plain people began to sympathize with his victims, nine-tenths of whom were palpably innocent of any worse crime than folly." Palmer's presidential campaign never gained steam. He underperformed in primaries in two states that he had deemed crucial—Michigan and Georgia—and administration officials tended to favor McAdoo over him.[50]

The largely unknown governor of Ohio, James Cox, was the third major contender for the nomination. The seventh child of a poor Ohio farm family, Cox was a self-made man. A school teacher in his teens, he also worked part time doing odd jobs at a small newspaper owned by a relative and developed a love of the news business. He landed a job as a reporter in Cincinnati and, in his late-twenties, with financial help, purchased a fledgling paper in Dayton and renamed it the *Dayton Daily News*. Through hard work and long hours (he hustled for advertisers, wrote editorials, kept the accounting books, and rolled up his sleeves and set type at times), Cox made the *Daily News* a success and himself a wealthy man. He was elected to Congress in 1908 and served two terms. In 1912, he won the Ohio governorship, was turned out of office by the voters in 1914, but came back and won elections for governor in 1916 and 1918. Only one other man, Republican Rutherford B. Hayes, had won three elections as Ohio's governor, but Cox's wins were more impressive because he had won as a Democrat in a mostly Republican state. He governed as a progressive, getting the legislature to pass Ohio's first workers' compensation law, laws reforming schools and prisons, and concerning the state's budgeting process.[51]

In personality, Cox was tenacious, described as having "a downright and decisive character . . . restless, dynamic, a hustler." These traits were belied by his unassuming appearance. He was of medium build and height, had brown hair and eyes, and wore glasses. Cox was divorced, something considered taboo for politicians in that era. His first marriage, which produced three children, ended in 1910 with a charge of "cruelty" by his then wife. Cox's friends later termed the parting an "incompatibility of temperament." Two of the children stayed with him. He married for a second time in 1917 and had another child, who was an infant at the time of the 1920 campaign. Surprisingly, Cox's divorce was never made an issue in his Ohio elections. He chose to not run a national race for the 1920 presidential nomination, seeking and winning delegates only in his home state of Ohio and neighboring Kentucky. He explained his strategy: "My friends are urging me to open up a vigorous campaign. But I prefer to wait. If, when the convention opens, they finally turn to Ohio, all right. We either have an ace in the hole, or we haven't . . . [and] no amount of bluffing and advertising can do much good."[52]

Each of the three main contenders had strengths and weaknesses. McAdoo, as a Wilson man, was supported by many of those who still stood by the president. Organized labor found him acceptable. He supported Prohibition, which was favored in the South and West. Big city bosses, however, detested him over patronage issues when he ran the treasury department and for his association with Wilson. Palmer had support from many DNC officials, but little from those in the Wilson administration. Labor opposed him, as did progressives and civil libertarians, who thought that his crackdown in response to the "Red Scare" had been too harsh. Cox, as an administration outsider, drew support from those who did not care for the president, as well as from those opposed to the Eighteenth Amendment. He was a "wet," at least moderately so, favoring legalization of beer and wine only. Most believed that Tammany's boss, Charles Murphy, and the other big city bosses, all of whom bitterly opposed Prohibition, would end up in Cox's camp. Just before the convention, however, Cox issued a statement that he favored keeping Prohibition out of the party's platform, either for or against. This angered his "wet" supporters. As one newspaper commented, "Cox is too wet for the drys and too dry for the wets."[53]

Among the dark horse candidates, one of the most talked about was John W. Davis of West Virginia, who was thousands of miles away, serving as Wilson's ambassador to Great Britain. A prominent and respected attorney, Davis had been solicitor general before assuming his post in London. He had, to his surprise, received the endorsement of the *New York Times* in an editorial in May, the paper lauding him as "a great man, a great American, a great Democrat." Davis had the strong support of his home state delegation and they would open a headquarters for him at the convention. Another dark horse was Alfred ("Al") Smith, who was in his first term as governor of New York. Smith was a Tammany man and, as such, had the votes of the majority of his home state's delegation. He was also an opponent of Prohibition and would attract "wet" votes from other states. But opposing the alcohol ban in 1920 was not a likely formula to winning the nomination. The Eighteenth Amendment had only been in effect for a few months and most Democrats were willing to give it a chance, or at least unwilling to insist on its repeal so soon. Even Smith's most ardent supporters knew that he had no realistic chance of winning the nomination.[54]

There would be 1,092 delegate *votes* at the convention, with 728 required to reach the two-thirds threshold needed to win the nomination. There were actually far more than 1,092 *persons* present as delegates. Some states, to allow more party loyalists to participate as delegates, sent twice as many people as their delegate allotment, with each casting half a vote. State primaries and conventions, most of which were held between March to June, did little to settle the race. Most states sent uncommitted delegations to the convention, or ones that were pledged to a favorite son. Only 336 delegates were pledged to anyone. Palmer had his home state of Pennsylvania, as well as Georgia; Cox had his home state of Ohio and nearby Kentucky; McAdoo had avoided actively seeking delegates, but several uncommitted delegations were said to be for him. Palmer was the only major candidate who attended the convention in person to try to sway delegates to him. McAdoo was in New York and Cox in Ohio, the latter issuing a statement that he believed it was inappropriate for "presidential candidates extending personalities into the deliberations" of the convention by being on the scene themselves. There were more than three hundred women delegates and alternates at the convention. The battle for nationwide suffrage for women was in its final stages. At the time the convention met, approval of only one more state was needed for the Nineteenth Amendment to become part of the Constitution. At this convention, as at all prior Democratic conventions, there were no Black delegates. Three groups would battle for control of the convention—the Wilsonites, the bosses of northern big cities, and the remnants of the old William Jennings Bryan coalition, which had an agrarian base at its core. Bryan himself, a three-time nominee of the party, was present as a delegate and had advised that his primary effort would be to work for a plank in the platform firmly endorsing Prohibition. He also dropped hints that he was available to be the nominee again, if needed. Bryan had a history of working his way onto the podium at conventions, and into the headlines. Although most felt that Bryan's time had passed long ago, he did not. Observed one reporter, "Bryan is positively satisfied that only one platform and one candidate has a chance, the same being himself."[55]

Democrats chose San Francisco as the host city for their 1920 convention, the first major party convention held on the west coast. Denver had been the previous westernmost convention outpost. With a population of just over 500,000, San Francisco was the nation's twelfth largest city in 1920 and had mostly recovered from the massive earthquake that had devastated the city fourteen years earlier. The convention was held in the Civic Auditorium, a fairly new facility that was smaller (seating fewer than 10,000) than the often-used and rundown Chicago Coliseum (where the Republicans had met three weeks earlier). The San Francisco arena was modern and inviting, described as "a fine picture of neatness and polish unusual in convention halls." For better acoustics, the walls were covered with padded canvas and an attractive canopy draped from the domed roof. Above the platform, an array of telephonic speakers hung from the ceiling, to carry voices throughout the hall. A huge pipe organ was behind the platform. American flags were placed "in artistic groupings" and "without a touch of gaudiness." The seats were roomy, the public areas were clean, and local residents serving as attendants, mostly young women, were friendly and hospitable. San Francisco's summer weather, with its cool days and chilly nights, required wardrobe adjustments from the usual convention attire in hot and muggy East and Midwest cities. A spring overcoat was needed and, it was observed, only "a tenderfoot from the East" would sport "a Palm Beach suit or white flannel trousers." Despite the coolness, it did not get cold, and palm trees swayed in the breeze and tropical flowers bloomed in the plaza outside the arena. On nearby sidewalks, a tall, thin man wearing a top hat, frock coat, and gray trousers caused "gasps, gulps, arm clutches, excited finger pointing and general excitement" as he walked along, frequently bowing to his left and his right. Ralph Faulkner was a "dead ringer" for Woodrow Wilson and, as a part-time actor, had portrayed the president in a few movies during the war.[56]

Six months into Prohibition, alcohol flowed freely for conventioneers and it was the good stuff—quality bourbon and gin—much of it said to have been taken from bonded warehouses, with Republican Mayor James ("Sunny Jim") Rolph's approval. Moreover, the libations, which were intended for medicinal use at hospitals, were available free of charge. A request at one's hotel for a bottle, a reporter noted, "was met within half an hour by a committee of pretty women, with no bill attached." Some felt that local residents would later regret their generosity, as liquor that had been "stored away as if it were fine gold" was being "brought out and literally squandered on the city's guests." The gruff and cynical reporter H. L. Mencken, a veteran of many conventions and a strong opponent of Prohibition, thought he had died and gone to heaven. "There is an air here," Mencken wrote of San Francisco, "that is simply unmatchable in the East and it is social as well as atmospheric. One notes at once a touch of spaciousness and freedom. The town is genuinely gay. There is a touch of the exotic in its life, almost a touch of the Asiatic. Once gets a sense of deliverance from the oppressive Puritanism of the East." After frequently imbibing during the convention, Mencken suffered from a bout of "alcohol gastritis" on the long train ride back to Baltimore. Despite his illness, he would later write to a friend, "I must see San Francisco [again] before they put the formaldehyde in my veins. And maybe twice more. You can't imagine what a gorgeous impression I took away."[57]

The twenty-third convention of the Democratic Party was called to order shortly after noon on Monday, June 28, by Bruce Kremer of Montana, the vice-chairman of the Democratic National Committee. He held in his hand a gavel made from California redwood trees. A color guard of Marines stood at attention on the platform as a huge American flag was lowered from above, followed by the singing of "The Star-Spangled Banner." At the song's conclusion, the flag was raised, revealing a large oil painting of President Wilson. A demonstration for Wilson gradually took shape, with delegates parading in the aisles and waving their state's signs in support of the commander-in-chief. Reporters described the scene as appearing to be somewhat forced, with the participants (many of whom were federal officeholders who owed their jobs to Wilson) acting more out of a sense of duty than affection. Notably absent from the parade was the large New York delegation and a burly Tammany delegate gripped the New York standard tightly in his hands. Tammany controlled the majority of the Empire State's delegation and was strongly opposed to Wilson. One of the few pro-Wilson New York delegates, thirty-eight-year-old Franklin Roosevelt, who had been serving the past eight years as the president's assistant secretary of the Navy, walked over to the New York sign and, after a brief struggle, wrested it from the Tammany man's hands. Followed by a few other New York delegates, Roosevelt hoisted the sign and joined the parade. The Tammany men remained in their seats and silent. The demonstration went on for half an hour. The near fistfight by the "aristocratic and handsome" young Roosevelt, in order to participate in honoring the president, drew favorable headlines the next day in newspapers across the country. Little did anyone then know how the convention would end for this relatively unknown New Yorker.[58]

After an opening prayer and brief remarks, Kremer advised that his boss, DNC Chairman Homer Cummings, was being proposed to be the convention's temporary chairman, which was quickly confirmed on a voice vote. Cummings then launched into his keynote speech, lengthy remarks full of praise for the sitting Democratic president and denouncing the recent political battle over the League of Nations in the treaty that Wilson had negotiated. Cummings was as uncompromising as the president on the issue. "We will not submit," he declared, "to the repudiation of the Peace Treaty or to any process by which it is whittled down to the vanishing point. We decline to compromise our principles or pawn our immortal souls for selfish proposes . . . . We seek no avenue of retreat. We insist that the forward course is the only righteous course."[59]

The accolades to Wilson continued. When Cummings finished, a Missouri delegate rose and proposed a long resolution of praise to be sent by the convention to the president, hailing his achievements, rejoicing "in the recovery of your health and strength after months of suffering and affliction," and resentful of "the malignant onset which you have most undeservedly been called upon to sustain from partisan foes." The resolution was unanimously adopted and, after the convention moved on to the appointment of its various committees, it adjourned for the day.[60]

The convention's second day began with receipt of the reports from various committees. Wilson's portrait remained above the podium, affixed to the longest shaft of the pipe organ, the stern-looking president appearing to gaze at the Alaska delegation. The recommendations of the Committee on Credentials for the seating of permanent delegates were approved on a voice vote. The report from the Committee on Rules and Order of Business was adopted, which provided that the platform be approved before any voting on nominees began, that nominating speeches be limited to twenty minutes, and that there be a maximum of three seconding speeches for each nominee lasting no more than five minutes each. The choice by the Committee on Permanent Organization of Senator Joseph Robinson of Arkansas to be the permanent chairman was approved. Robinson was a compromise choice. Wilson had wanted Secretary of State Colby (whom he had sent as his personal representative at the convention) in the role, but some on the committee objected and wanted Senator Thomas Walsh of Montana. Wilson objected to Walsh (who was a League opponent) and all then agreed on Robinson. As permanent chairman, Robinson delivered a speech criticizing the recent Republican convention in Chicago and, like Cummings the day before, focused on the Republican policy of "harassment and embarrassment" of Wilson over the League of Nations. After debate over unimportant resolutions, the convention adjourned for the day.[61]

When the convention began its third day, the report from the platform committee was still not ready. Although the rules precluded any voting on nominations before the platform was adopted, nominating speeches could be heard. Thus began a seemingly endless array of speeches for multiple candidates that would last all day and carry over to the next. Most were favorite son candidates of various states and had no chance of being the nominee. Those placed in nomination included Senator Robert Owen of Oklahoma, former Ambassador James Gerard of New York, Homer Cummings (who had been the convention's temporary chairman) of Connecticut, Senator Gilbert Hitchcock of Nebraska, Secretary of Agriculture Edwin Meredith of Iowa, Governor Al Smith of New York, and Governor Edward Edwards of New Jersey. Each candidate had seconding speeches, several of which were given by women, and had demonstrations of support that varied in intensity and length.[62]

Interspersed among this daylong volley of oratory were the nominating speeches of the three main contenders. Palmer was the first of these to be placed before the convention. The speaker, John Bigelow from Pennsylvania, praised Palmer's stern actions as attorney general during the recent "Red Scare." His remarks left no doubt that Palmer was running as the "law and order" candidate. Proclaimed Bigelow, "When the insidious evils of anarchy and her lawless litter arose, it was he that stood valiantly against the protests of parlor Bolshevists, against the trusts of venal pen and slanderous tongue, and deported and imprisoned the defamers of the nation—aye, even at the threat of the terrorists' bombs." Palmer's enemies, he declared, were the nation's enemies. He had defeated them and "Pennsylvania's noblest product" should be rewarded with the presidency.[63]

Cox was nominated by James Johnson of Ohio. The nomination of Ohioan Warren Harding by Republicans at their convention two weeks earlier was seen as a boost to Cox. Some speculated that, if Democrats wanted any hope of carrying the Buckeye State, choosing Cox, who had won three elections as its governor, was the best option. Johnson emphasized this in his speech, stating that his candidate was not being offered as "a better Democrat or a better statesman" than the others, but as the one "who can carry in the election the great and necessary state, the industrial center of Ohio." Johnson reviewed Cox's stint in Congress and his multiple terms as governor, praising his "real genius for executive duty and his record of accomplishment," as one who is "a splendid example of what America can do" and as the man who "meets the needs of the hour."[64]

McAdoo's off-again campaign was given a boost when a Missouri delegate, Burris Jenkins, the editor of the *Kansas City Post*, rose and advised that he had "intended" to give a speech nominating McAdoo but, "on account of insistent and persistent request from him that his name should not be presented in a speech, I have decided not to do so." Instead, he simply placed McAdoo's name in nomination, without any accompanying words of praise, adding that "any rumor of telegrams supposed to have been received . . . denying that he will accept the nomination, are falsehoods perpetrated by the enemies of our party." Historians have debated whether McAdoo's "irrevocable" refusal days before the convention to have his name put in nomination was real, or part of a well-planned strategy. Most likely, it was the latter, a "possum policy" of pretending to be dead when actually very much alive. It was necessitated to take into account Wilson's coldness to his son-in-law seeking the nomination when he coveted it for himself and, conversely, to prevent it from looking like Wilson was imposing McAdoo, as his crown prince, on the convention. "McAdoo's peculiar campaign was devised," one contemporaneous writer was told by someone with inside knowledge, "to the double end of getting rid of the President's opposition and of dispelling the idea that Wilson was forcing his nomination." The plot was required to "keep peace within the Wilson family" and to make it appear that "the convention was forcing the nomination" on McAdoo, rather than him being forced upon the convention.[65]

The strategy appeared to have worked. During the whole day of speeches, the cheering that followed the brief statement from Jenkins placing McAdoo's name in nomination was judged by most observers to have been the loudest. Palmer's supporters were the most organized, with cheerleaders stationed around the arena and leading their supporters in a campaign song, "Palmer, Palmer, Pennsylvania!," written to the tune of the "Battle Hymn of the Republic." Cox was the only candidate to have his own band in the hall. But, a reporter observed, it was the McAdoo demonstration that won the day. It was "not only longer and louder than either that for Palmer or for Cox, it was also incomparably more hearty and spontaneous. All that is needed," it was thought, to clinch the nomination for McAdoo, was "a single wink from the White House."[66]

Of the nominations of the lesser contenders, only that of Governor Smith, the favorite son of New York, attracted much attention. Smith was nominated by Bourke Cochran, an aging former congressman and Tammany leader, who had once been one of the nation's best orators. At the party's 1892 convention, he had given a famous speech opposing the nomination of Grover Cleveland. Winston Churchill, who became acquainted with Cochran on a visit to New York, would later call Cochran one of his mentors, largely due to admiration of his speaking skills. Cochran traced Smith's rise from poverty, noting that anarchists and socialists of the day preached that it was "impossible for a poor man" to succeed in America. Smith's life, Cochran proclaimed, refuted their lies, as Smith "had himself risen from conditions humbler and harsher than any anarchist or socialist have ever known." Smith, he said, had not forgotten his roots, still called "Al" by all, from "those who played with him on an east-side sidewalk . . . [to] the wisest statesmen and the greatest leaders." It was a remarkable moment, something unheard of in that era, nor at any time in the nation's past—Smith, a Catholic son of immigrants, was being nominated by the biggest state in the Union for the highest office in the land. The crowd in the arena seemed to have sensed the significance. After Cochran finished, the band in the hall began playing "sentimental songs of a yesteryear," including "The Sidewalks of New York," "A Bicycle Built for Two," and "Sweet Rosie O'Grady." A genuine demonstration for Smith developed and, unlike those for other candidates, it was not organized or led, but spontaneous. Even the gruff reporter Mencken was emotional over the scene, calling it "the most charming episode" of the convention, with ten thousand people, who, "carried away by the homely music of those bedraggled old songs, sang with the band, danced around the hall and yielded themselves unashamed to a debauch of sentiment."[67]

The magic ended when Franklin Roosevelt rose to give a brief seconding speech for Smith. A rival of Smith's in New York Democratic politics, Roosevelt had come to the convention a McAdoo supporter. His speech was not one of the future president's best efforts. Although he said of Smith, "I love him as a friend; I look up to him as a man," he ended by mentioning his own service as assistant secretary of the Navy, saying, "In the Navy we shoot fast and straight. Governor Smith, in that respect, is a Navy man." Mencken thought that Roosevelt killed any chance of a boom for Smith. "What was demanded by that golden opportunity," he wrote, "was a flash of genuine eloquence, a ringing appeal to the delegates . . . . But all that Roosevelt had on tap was a line of puerile and ineffective bosh about the great achievements of the navy. As the delegates listened all their enthusiasms oozed out of them. Thus the Smith boom died in the hour of its birth."[68]

The convention's fourth day, a Thursday, began in the morning with more candidates being placed in nomination for president. Added to the ten candidates nominated the day before were Senator Furnifold Simmons of North Carolina, Senator Carter Glass of Virginia, Ambassador John W. Davis of West Virginia, and Governor General of the Philippines Francis Harrison, making it a field of fourteen formally in the race. When word was received that the committee writing the party's platform was still working, and with the rules providing that the platform must be approved before any voting for president could begin, the convention adjourned shortly after noon and did not resume until the evening.[69]

In its evening session, the convention, still waiting for the platform committee to finish its work, took up housekeeping measures, including the appointment of members for the Democratic National Committee to serve for the next four years. In a change to the rules, each state and territory would now have two members on the committee, one of which would be a man and the other a woman. When it was learned that the platform would not be ready until the morning, the convention adjourned for the day.[70]

Friday, July 2, began with receipt of the long-awaited report from the Committee on Resolutions, with the proposed platform read by Senator Carter Glass of Virginia, the committee's chairman. The document, more than eight thousand words, was the longest platform in the history of the party and it took Glass more than two hours to get through it. It was full of praise for President Wilson and hailed "with patriotic pride the great achievements for country and the world wrought by a Democratic administration under his leadership." It reaffirmed the longstanding Democratic position of tariffs for revenue only, expressed "sympathy" for Irish independence, opposed compulsory arbitration in labor disputes, opposed child labor, and favored free speech and a free press, but with "no toleration of enemy propaganda or the advocacy of the overthrow of the government." The platform endorsed women's suffrage under the proposed Nineteenth Amendment (then only one state away from ratification) and urged the Democratic governors and legislatures of Tennessee, North Carolina, and Florida to take up the amendment and secure its approval in time for women throughout the country to participate in the fall election. Tennessee did act in August and approved the amendment, making it part of the Constitution.[71]

There were two issues—Prohibition and the League of Nations—that had consumed much of the committee's long hours of meetings and on which those in the arena eagerly awaited to hear how they were handled. Prohibition opponents, the "drys," led by William Jennings Bryan, wanted a statement of support for the recently enacted Eighteenth Amendment and for its strict enforcement. The "wets" wanted revision of the Volstead Act, the enabling legislation for the amendment, to permit beer and wine. Both sides were disappointed, as the committee decided that the platform should be silent on the alcohol issue. Regarding the League of Nations, the question was whether the platform would call for ratification of the peace treaty negotiated by Wilson, including its League provisions without any reservations, as was the president's position. The committee generally favored Wilson's position, but compromised a bit. It called for "immediate ratification of the treaty without reservations which would impair its essential integrity." It added, however, that the party does "not oppose the acceptance of any reservations making clearer or more specific the obligations of the United States to the league associates."[72]

After Senator Glass offered the platform for approval, Bryan, as expected, rose and proposed five changes, the two most important of which involved the hot issues of alcohol and the League. On Prohibition, Bryan offered a plank pledging the party "to the effective enforcement of the present enforcement law, honestly and in good faith, without any increase in the alcoholic content of permitted beverages, and without any weakening of any other of its provisions." On the League, Bryan (a pacifist who had resigned as Wilson's secretary of state in protest before the United States entered World War I) opposed the president's position and called for ratification of the treaty "with such reservations as a majority of the Senators may agree upon." He also called for amending the Constitution to permit approval of treaties by a majority of the Senate, rather than two-thirds, so that it would be "as easy to end a war as to declare a war." On Prohibition, New Yorker Bourke Cochran, who had given the main nominating speech for Al Smith, offered, in response, a plank acknowledging the Eighteenth Amendment, but "allowing the manufacture and sale, for home consumption only, of cider, light wine, and beer reserving to the various states power to fix any alcoholic content thereof."[73]

After much debate, both of the proposed alcohol amendments went to a roll call vote and both were defeated. Bryan's pro-Prohibition plank was rejected with only 133½ in favor and 929½ against. Cochran's plank calling for home use of cider, light wine, and beer was also voted down, by a margin of 356 for and 726½ opposed. Bryan's League of Nations plank, as well as all of his other proposals were rejected on voice votes. The entire platform, as written by the committee, was then also approved on a voice vote. The Democrats would enter the fall campaign officially silent on Prohibition and supporting (mostly) Wilson's hardline stance on the League of Nations.[74]

With the platform finally adopted, the convention began voting, on Friday evening, for its presidential nominee. A two-thirds vote of 729 was needed for victory. The first ballot confirmed that no candidate was even close. McAdoo had a slight lead with 266 votes, Palmer a close second place with 254, trailed by Cox with 134, and Smith with 109. None of the others had more than 45 votes. Delegates cast their ballots for twenty-three different men, some receiving only a single vote. A second ballot quickly followed, with McAdoo and Cox picking up around twenty votes each and Palmer ten. With the battle lines drawn and with the clock approaching midnight, the convention adjourned for the day.[75]

The convention's sixth day, Saturday, July 3, began with the third ballot. With 323½ votes, McAdoo increased his lead to almost seventy-five, with Palmer at 251½ and Cox at 177. Smith was holding at around 90 votes, almost all of which came from his home state. There was little change until the seventh ballot, when New York abandoned Smith as a favorite son and he dropped to only four votes. Cox (as long rumored, because of his more "wet" stance on Prohibition than the other main contenders), was the main beneficiary of New York's shift, with 68 of that state's vote going to him and only 16 to McAdoo. New Jersey, following New York's lead, moved 25 of its votes to Cox. The tally on the seventh ballot showed McAdoo still leading with 384, but with Cox moving up to second with 295½, and with Palmer falling to third with 267½. More shifting came on the twelfth ballot, when Illinois (another state controlled by an anti-Prohibition boss, as were New York and New Jersey) moved 30 of its votes from Palmer to Cox, and with Iowa also casting 26 votes for the Ohio governor. Cox's supporters filled the aisles for a ten-minute demonstration. For the first time, with 404 votes, Cox had moved into the lead. McAdoo dropped to second with 375, while Palmer was losing support and was more than two hundred votes behind McAdoo, with 201. Over the next few ballots, Cox's lead gradually increased, fueled by more states dropping their favorite son candidates and by the continued dwindling of Palmer's support. After the sixteenth ballot, with the clock approaching the dinner hour, the convention agreed, by a vote of 619 to 455, to recess until the evening. With momentum on their side, most of Cox's supporters had objected, wanting to continue.[76]

During the break, McAdoo's managers met personally with Palmer (the only one of the three major candidates in San Francisco) and requested that he withdraw and endorse McAdoo, so that all Wilson administration supporters could unite and defeat Cox. An angry Palmer refused and left the meeting "in high dudgeon." He told reporters that he was staying in the race. He had a path to the nomination, he said, but if he fell short, he vowed, "you can be assured that the nominee for President will be someone other than McAdoo or Cox." With Palmer refusing to bow out, McAdoo's team focused on bringing Cox down, criticizing him as a pawn of the big city bosses, as a "wet," and an opponent of the Wilson administration.[77]

During Saturday's evening session, five additional ballots were taken with no significant movement. On the last ballot of the night, the twenty-second, Cox still led with 430, McAdoo second with 372½ and Palmer third with 111½. Among the dark horses, John W. Davis had 52, leading the rest of the pack. Around midnight, the convention adjourned for the day. It would not meet on Sunday and the campaigns would have a full day to plot their strategies.[78]

Sunday's and Monday's newspapers were at a loss to predict the convention's outcome. Some compared it to the party's 1912 convention, which had also adjourned on a Saturday after more than twenty ballots, with Woodrow Wilson and Champ Clark battling for the nomination and neither able to shake off the other. "Not even the prophet Jeremiah," an exasperated Secretary of the Navy Josephus Daniels told a reporter, "could tell how the voting will end." Unlike most delegates, at least he and his top assistant, Franklin Roosevelt, would not incur extra expenses by the convention carrying over into a second week. They were both staying free of charge and entertaining guests on battleships of the Pacific Fleet anchored in the harbor. Being a Navy man had its privileges. "This is a genuinely deadlocked convention," declared the *Washington Post*, "There is nothing fake about it." The campaigns of the three leading contenders—McAdoo, Palmer, and Cox—all professed confidence and vehemently denied that there was any thought of their man withdrawing. "We are ready to ballot till doomsday," proclaimed McAdoo's manager. One of Palmer's friends declared that the attorney general was the logical compromise choice and "holds the whip hand." The Cox team, viewing McAdoo as their main obstacle to victory, began handing out business cards that they had hastily arranged to be printed. There was only one word—"McAdieu"—on the cards. The *New York Times* opined that the logjam required that a dark horse be nominated and renewed its prior call in May for Ambassador Davis. "The opportunity is clear for a calm and considered choice," the paper reasoned, and "unless the convention can find a better man than Mr. Davis, it will be blameworthy if it does not take him."[79]

Meanwhile, at the White House, President Wilson remained silent. The official word was that he did not want to be seen as dictating the convention's choice. In fact, he liked what he was hearing from San Francisco, hoping that the deadlock meant that the convention would turn to him. It was later revealed how close the convention had come to an attempt to stampede it for Wilson. Friday evening, after the first two ballots showed no consensus, Secretary of State Colby fired off a telegram to the president telling him of the division at the convention. He advised that, unless the president forbade it, he intended, at the appropriate opportunity, to put the president's name before the convention and felt with "certainty" that all would fall in line and that Wilson would be drafted as the nominee. When others close to Wilson learned of this, they were shocked—and angry. Some were certain that any such effort would fail, embarrass the president, and stain his legacy. Others believed that if it succeeded, given Wilson's poor health, it would be his death sentence. Still others felt the convention needed to play out to its end without any interference. On Saturday morning, a handful of party leaders (including Temporary Chairman Cummings and Permanent Chairman Robinson) descended upon Colby's hotel room and berated him. "I never saw more indignation and resentment in any small gathering," one of the participants later wrote. Colby reluctantly dropped his plan and the group agreed to send periodic messages to Wilson telling him that they believed the convention would work through its divisions and that it would not be necessary to turn to him to unite the party. Saturday evening, on the twenty-second ballot, two Missouri delegates switched their votes to Wilson. There was little reaction in the arena to votes being recorded for the sitting Democratic president. They would be the only votes cast for him during the convention. Any attempt by Colby to formally bring Wilson's name before the convention would likely have not succeeded and been embarrassing to the president.[80]

The first ballot (the twenty-third overall) taken on the convention's seventh day, Monday, July 5, showed little change from the last one on Saturday. Cox led with 425 votes, McAdoo was second with 364½ and Palmer third with 181½. There was no movement until the twenty-ninth ballot when Indiana, which had previously been casting two-thirds of its votes for Cox, deserted the Ohioan and cast 29 of its 30 votes for McAdoo. Indiana's boss, Tom Taggart, who had been in cahoots with his counterparts in New York, New Jersey, and Illinois in favoring Cox, saw an opportunity to be a kingmaker for McAdoo and, for a while, it appeared that he had guessed correctly. On the next ballot, McAdoo retook the lead, with 403½ votes, compared to 400½ for Cox and 165 for Palmer. Then, surprisingly, Palmer began to gain ground, increasing his total to 241 over the next few ballots. There seemed to be no rhyme nor reason to many of the shifts. As one longtime convention participant observed, "I have never seen such a grasshopper convention as this. With the exception of six or seven states, the delegates are jumping around," seemingly at random. Concerned about the Palmer surge, the McAdoo and Cox teams agreed on one thing—the need for an adjournment to stop the attorney general's momentum. Shortly after 5:00 p.m., the convention voted to recess for more than three hours, until the evening.[81]

The delay succeeded in dooming Palmer. During the break, many of the delegates who had switched to him decided that he could not win and moved on. On the thirty-eighth ballot (the first one taken after the break), Palmer dropped to 211. After the results of that ballot were announced, Palmer's manager, Charles Carlin of Virginia, went to the podium and was granted permission to address the convention. "I am requested by the Honorable A. Mitchell Palmer," Carlin declared, "to express to those Democrats who have so faithfully and long supported him in this Convention his sincere gratitude, and to advise the Convention that he is unwilling to delay its deliberations longer . . . . I am authorized by him to unconditionally, absolutely and finally release his delegates." On the next ballot, although a third of Palmer's delegates stuck with him despite his withdrawal, 85 switched to Cox, putting him in the lead again. Only 35 of Palmer's delegates went to McAdoo. The tally on that thirty-ninth ballot was 468½ for Cox, 440 for McAdoo and 74 for Palmer. The end was finally in sight. Cox continued to gradually gain delegates and, on the forty-second ballot, with 540½ votes, he gained a majority of the overall votes cast. Only twice in the party's history (in 1844 and 1912) had a candidate who received the majority of votes failed to go on to get the two-thirds necessary to win the nomination. Fortunately for Cox, he would not join Martin Van Buren and Champ Clark as the third name on this ill-starred list. Near the end of the forty-fourth ballot, with Cox closing in on the two-thirds needed, one of McAdoo's managers, Samuel Amidon of Kansas, made a motion, which was quickly approved on a voice vote, to suspend the rules and make the nomination of Cox unanimous. The weary delegates made an attempt at a demonstration for Cox and, at nearly two o'clock in the morning and after three days of voting, walked out of the arena with the identity of their presidential nominee finally known.[82]

The convention met for its final day on Tuesday, July 6, to select a running mate for Cox. The night before, Cox had decided that Franklin Roosevelt was the best option. Roosevelt made good political sense. He balanced the ticket geographically, he came from a big state that was needed in the election, he was a Wilson administrator insider, and he had one of the most famous last names in the country. Knowing the tense relationship that Roosevelt had with the Tammany organization that controlled the New York delegation (it was Roosevelt who had ripped New York's state sign out of a Tammany man's hands on the convention's opening day), Cox asked that Tammany boss Charles Murphy be consulted for his consent. It was a smart move. "I don't like Roosevelt," Murphy told Cox's manager, "but this is the first time a Democratic nominee for the Presidency has shown me courtesy. That's why I would vote for the devil himself if Cox wanted me to. Tell him we will nominate Roosevelt on the first ballot as soon as we assemble."[83]

Something other than just pleasing Cox likely played in Murphy's decision. New York would be electing both a governor and a senator in November. Roosevelt, who would soon be out of his job in the Wilson administration, was interested in both races. What better way to keep him from challenging Tammany's man, Al Smith, who would be running for reelection as governor, or to oppose a Tammany man for the Senate seat, than having him go on the national ticket as the party's vice-presidential nominee? Roosevelt would be out of Murphy's hair. It was reminiscent of the strategy used by another New York political boss, Republican Thomas Platt, twenty years earlier, concerning another eager and aggressive young politician with the last name of Roosevelt. Platt wanted the reform-minded Theodore Roosevelt out of the Empire State's governorship and pushed him onto the Republican ticket in 1900 as President McKinley's running mate, where (he thought and hoped) Roosevelt would be in the powerless job of vice president and forgotten. Platt never imagined that McKinley would be assassinated only months into his new term.[84]

Conventions, even ones that have been in session for more than a week, rarely seem to move as quickly as they should. Although Franklin Roosevelt's nomination as vice president was assured before the delegates began their Tuesday session, five other candidates were placed in nomination for the second spot on the ticket. After several speeches for the others had been given, Timothy Ansberry, a delegate from the District of Columbia, placed the thirty-eight-year-old Roosevelt before the convention, praising him as an "able experienced campaigner, full of the virility and optimism of youth, yet sobered by service as Assistant Secretary of the Navy during the period of the war . . . . His is a name to conjure with in American politics." Several speakers later, Al Smith gave a brief seconding speech for his fellow New Yorker. It lacked any personal affection, but noted that Roosevelt was "one of our best-known Democrats, a man who has been active in the affairs of our state . . . [and] a man who, during the present administration, has held positions of great power and importance." As a Tammany man, Smith's speech revealed to all that Tammany was on board with Roosevelt and, in quick succession, the names of all of the other candidates were withdrawn. State after state then seconded Roosevelt's nomination and he was unanimously selected for vice president on a voice vote. Within minutes, after sessions that had lasted for more than a week, the first presidential nominating convention held on the West Coast adjourned.[85]

Cox received the news of his nomination shortly before dawn at the plant of his newspaper in Dayton, where he, his wife, and friends had been throughout the night. He went into a nearby room and was congratulated by his employees, who had also been waiting for the final word from San Francisco, so that they could put out a special edition of the paper. Later that morning, Cox visited the grave of his mother, who had predicted great things for her son. A quarter of a century earlier, in 1895, Eliza Cox had attended a New Year's Day reception at the White House. As she greeted President Grover Cleveland, she confidently told him that her son "will be here where you are now, some day." There are conflicting reports as to Franklin Roosevelt's location at the time of his nomination for vice president. Some indicate that he was sitting in the New York delegation, others state that he had heeded advice to leave the hall, the thought being that it would be inappropriate to be present. All agree that, if he was present in the arena as the voting occurred, he quickly left once his nomination was official. Calls by the crowd for him to address the convention went unanswered. Roosevelt would follow tradition and receive, several days hence, formal notification of his nomination at his home by a committee appointed by the convention.[86]

Historians generally credit Cox's nomination to the support of big city bosses from New York, New Jersey, and Illinois. Reporters at the time noted the contrast with the recent Republican convention, one writing, "While it is true that Cox was named by the bosses, they did it in the open. There were no conferences in closed rooms." Cox fit the needs of the Democratic Party in several ways. As author Irving Stone has commented, although Cox "had backed the Wilson administration, he had not been identified with it and could not be held responsible for its conduct; he had played no part in the quarrels over the League of Nations, and hence he accumulated no enemies on that score; he was wet enough to assure the anti-prohibition forces but not sufficiently wet enough to antagonize the drys . . . [and] he had a progressive record." Add the fact that he was likely the only Democrat who had any hope of beating his fellow Ohioan, Warren Harding, in their key home state and Cox was clearly the logical choice for the party.[87]

The Campaign and Election

The 1920 election was the third in American history in which the presidential nominees of the two major parties came from the same state, the others being Lincoln and Douglas from Illinois in 1860 and Theodore Roosevelt and Parker from New York in 1904. Republicans began the campaign as the clear favorites. Although he was not on the ballot, the election was largely a referendum on Woodrow Wilson, especially his internationalism. Cox and the Democrats embraced Wilson's policies, while Harding and the Republicans denounced them. Harding succinctly stated his philosophy, in what would become his most famous words: "America's present need is not heroics but healing; not nostrums but normalcy; not revolution but restoration." The press picked up on "normalcy," some thinking that Harding had made up the word, or had misspoken and had intended to say "normality." Neither was the case. It was an existing word and its use was intended. A "return to normalcy" became the slogan of the Republican campaign. In keeping with that theme, they ran a folksy "front porch" campaign, as they had done with McKinley in 1896. Hundreds, sometimes thousands, of supporters came most days from across the country to Harding's hometown of Marion, Ohio, where he addressed them in well-rehearsed speeches from the porch of his modest home. In his remarks, he favored high tariffs, restrictions on immigration, lower taxes, and opposed entry into the League of Nations. Professor Chancellor, with his racist allegations that Harding was part Black, resurfaced late in the campaign and there was some evidence that Democrats helped spread his charges. Harding never issued a formal denial, his campaign deciding that to do so would give the issue more credence and attention. Harding himself did not know where the truth lay, confiding privately to a reporter, "How do I know, Jim?"[88]

While Harding stayed mostly at home, Cox campaigned across the country, traveling more than twenty-two thousand miles and giving more than four hundred speeches. He and his young running mate, Franklin Roosevelt, ran as liberal Democrats, urging a continuation and expansion of Wilson's domestic progressive policies, as well as support for the League of Nations and active American involvement on the world stage.[89]

With the passage of the Nineteenth Amendment in August, the 1920 presidential election was the first in history in which women across the country were eligible to vote. As a result, the total number of ballots cast was almost 27,000,000, an increase of more than 8,000,000 over 1916. The overall turnout rate, however, was fairly low, at just over half of eligible voters. The outcome of the election was a Republican landslide. In the Electoral College, Harding won thirty-seven states and 404 electoral votes, including every state in the North, Midwest, and West. Cox won only eleven states and 127 electoral votes, all of which were in the South. Even there, he lost Tennessee, the first time that a Democrat had lost that state since 1868. In the popular vote, Harding received 16,153,115 (60.3%) votes, compared to Cox's total of 9,133,092 (34.1%), a margin of more than seven million. The only significant third-party candidate was Eugene Debs, of the Socialist Party, who was in prison during the campaign for a conviction of sedition during the war. Debs received almost 900,000 votes, a little more than three percent of the total. The Democratic strategy of nominating an Ohioan and a New Yorker for their ticket did not work. Republicans won Ohio with more than 58% of the vote and New York with almost 65%. The Republicans also won heavily in the congressional races, increasing their majorities and gaining almost sixty seats in the House and ten in the Senate.[90]

The nation had turned inward and had elected Warren Harding as its president, an unexpected compromise choice at the Republican convention, and a man who was the antithesis of his predecessor, Woodrow Wilson, in personality, in perspective, and in policies. In the new decade of the 1920s, there would be changes. As the years unfolded, some were predictable, some not.

Chapter 6

1924: Keeping Cool

In a quaint New England farmhouse on an early summer day,
A farmer's boy became our Chief in a homely simple way.
With neither pomp nor pageantry, he firmly met the task,
To keep him on that job of his, is all the people ask.

So "Keep Cool and Keep Coolidge" in the White House four years more,
We have a chance to do it in this year of twenty-four,
He's been tried, he's never wanting,
He is giving of his best,
So "Keep Cool and Keep Coolidge" in our country's mighty test.
—**Republican campaign song, 1924**

On August 2, 1923, Calvin Coolidge became the sixth vice president to assume the presidency upon the death of his predecessor. Warren Harding had left Washington in July on an extended cross-country trip to Alaska and died (likely of a heart attack) in a San Francisco hotel while en route back to the capital. The genial Harding had been a popular president, but too trusting of greedy friends whom he had appointed to high offices. Only after his death would the corruption that occurred on his watch, including the Teapot Dome scandal, come fully to light.

While Harding was in office, the stoic Coolidge had been an outsider in Washington, even more so than most vice presidents of that era. On days that he presided over the Senate, he often ate lunch alone in that body's dining room, ignored by its members. There were rumors that Harding had plans to replace Coolidge as vice president when he ran for reelection in 1924. "Fate made him president," one reporter noted, "at the very moment it was planned to drop him overboard."

When he got word of Harding's death, Coolidge was visiting his father in the small community of Plymouth Notch, Vermont. In the modest home where Coolidge had grown up, by candlelight in the middle of the night, his father, who was a notary, administered the constitutional oath of office and swore his son in as the thirtieth President of the United States.[1]

Americans liked the modest man who, through death, came to occupy the White House. Known as "Silent Cal," he was indeed a man of few words, but he had a sense of humor and a sharp wit. He cultivated his stoic image and found it was an effective way of conducting business. He later gave his successor, Herbert Hoover, some advice on strategy to use in meetings. Every day, he said, you have "three or four hours of visitors. Nine-tenths of them want something they ought not to have. If you keep dead-still they will run down in three or four minutes. If you even cough or smile they will start up all over again."[2]

Coolidge continued Harding's conservative policies, with an emphasis on reducing government expenditures and cutting taxes. He vetoed bills that he thought were too expensive (including bigger pensions for veterans and higher wages for postal workers), earning the ire of some Republicans in Congress. He had only been in office for a few months when he announced, in December 1923, that he would seek a term of his own in 1924. If they could have, the Old Guard of the party would have tried to defeat him, but they lacked the power to do so. Coolidge was popular with the party's rank-and-file, as had been seen at the 1920 convention, when delegates rejected the choice of party bosses and had nominated him for vice president. As more evidence of the Harding scandals came out in early 1924, Coolidge successfully distanced himself from them by appointing two special counsels (a Republican and a Democrat) to investigate the matters and he accepted the resignation of Attorney General Harry Daugherty, who had been Harding's campaign manager and close confidant, and about whom rumors of corruption had been swirling.[3]

Republican Convention

No serious challengers arose to Coolidge for the nomination. Governor Gifford Pinchot of Pennsylvania (an old TR ally) made noises about trying to replace Coolidge on the GOP ticket, but never entered the contest. A man many thought to be a likely contender, former Governor Frank Lowden of Illinois, who had been one of the frontrunners in 1920 before the convention unexpectedly turned to Harding, also stayed out of the 1924 race. Two candidates from the progressive faction of the party, Hiram Johnson and Robert La Follette, did actively campaign against Coolidge, but with little success. Republican primaries were held in seventeen states and Coolidge won fifteen of them, including in Johnson's home state of California. Johnson did, however, narrowly beat Coolidge in South Dakota and La Follette won in his home state of Wisconsin. In the rest of the states, where delegates were selected at state conventions, Coolidge ran the table with solid support in the South, the Northeast, the Mid-Atlantic, and the West. Well before the convention began, Silent Cal's nomination was conceded and the only mystery was who would emerge as his running mate.[4]

After holding their past five conventions in Chicago, Republicans selected Cleveland as the location of their 1924 gathering, the first time that either major party had met there to select their presidential nominee. With a population of almost 800,000, Cleveland was, at that time, the fifth largest city in the United States. The convention was held in the still-standing Public Auditorium, a large rectangular neoclassical structure that had opened in 1922, with an arched roof and seating for more than thirteen thousand. For several reasons, the party atmosphere of past conventions was not present. In terms of entertainment options, Cleveland was not a Chicago nor a New York. The nation was in its fourth year of Prohibition and extra federal agents were sent to the city to step up enforcement of the alcohol ban. Newspapers reported that "hunting for hooch" would require some effort. One could quench a thirst, however, by going to a lunch counter at one of the city's drug stores and, for a quarter, enjoy a "Coolidge Highball," consisting of ice, pineapple juice, grape juice, and an egg. The less than festive attitude was reflective of the man being nominated, who promoted an image of lacking emotion. Posters of a dour-looking Coolidge were in many storefront windows and plastered on walls throughout the city. Even his campaign slogan, "Keep Cool With Coolidge," referred to self-control. "Cool" in that era was a word used more to describe having a dispassionate calmness, rather than its modern usage of being fashionable or hip.[5]

In the ten months from the time that he assumed the presidency until the convention, Coolidge had successfully taken over the Republican Party. Most of the members of the party's Old Guard either died off or had been shoved aside. The most obvious among the latter was Senator Henry Cabot Lodge of Massachusetts. Lodge had been the chairman of past conventions, or had written their platforms. Four years earlier, he had presided over the "smoke-filled room" meeting in Chicago that decided to nominate Harding. In his rise in Massachusetts Republican politics, Coolidge had been aligned with a faction of the party then led by Murray Crane, which had often opposed Lodge. With that group controlling the Bay State's delegation to the 1924 convention, Lodge was a mere delegate and not given any prominent role or committee assignment. As author Herbert Eaton has observed, the seventy-four-year-old Lodge "wandered about the convention a pathetic old man shorn of all power and influence. Coolidge was the boss of the party now." Lodge was not the only one of his breed to be out of favor. Much of Coolidge's popularity came at the expense of Republicans in Congress. Commented the *Washington Post*, "Coolidge has gained strength as his party has lost it in Congress." Will Rogers agreed. "The People said," he observed, "If he [Coolidge] is against Congress he must be right."[6]

Coolidge installed his own team to run the convention. The man at the top was William Butler, a lawyer and industrialist who had taken over the Crane faction of the party in Massachusetts after Crane's death in 1920. Butler was the president's choice to become chairman of the RNC at the end of the convention and to direct the general election campaign. Reporters detested Butler, describing him as "dictatorial," the "Massachusetts iceberg," and a "cold and uncommunicative person." Also present in Cleveland to help oversee the president's nomination were Frank Stearns (a Boston department store merchant who had been a longtime Coolidge supporter and who had largely financed Coolidge's run for the 1920 nomination) and Bascom Slemp (a former Virginia congressman and Washington insider whom Coolidge had appointed as his personal secretary shortly after he became president).[7]

With Coolidge's nomination a certainty, reporters did little of their usual hanging out in hotel lobbies for the latest in tips or gossip, and, with Prohibition in effect, doing so in bars was not an option. Before the convention opened, with little to do after arriving in Cleveland, several of them hit the local golf courses. A few later admitted to having already written, before they arrived, some of the stories they would post from the convention. The cynical H. L. Mencken of the *Baltimore Sun*, a veteran observer of conventions (who both loathed and loved them), and who was no fan of Coolidge, wrote a few days before the convention: "[A] half dozen windjammers will hymn good Cal as a combination of Pericles, Frederick the Great, Washington, Lincoln, Roosevelt and John the Baptist; and then there will be an hour or two of whooping.... A stupid business indeed.... Here will be assembled all the great heroes and masterminds of the majority party in the greatest free nation ever seen on earth, and ... after three or four days of bombarding the welkin and calling upon God for help, they will choose unanimously a man whom they regard unanimously as a cheap and puerile fellow!" Humorist Rogers, who wrote a daily newspaper column from the convention, wondered why go through all the trouble of having everyone come to Cleveland. Republicans always "preach economy," he noted. With the outcome certain, Coolidge, he joked, "could have been nominated by postcard."[8]

The 1924 Republican convention was the first presidential nominating convention to be heard over radio. Twenty radio stations from New York to Kansas City broadcast the proceedings live to owners of the new-fangled device, an audience estimated to be more than three million. A glass-enclosed booth to the right of the stage was staffed by a commentator, who filled the radio audience in on what was happening during lulls in the proceedings. The reception of voices from the convention by radios throughout the country was reported to be "well-nigh perfect," with little or no static. Coolidge listened in from the White House. His seventy-nine-year-old, twice-widowed father, John, also tuned in, dressed in coat and tie, from his home in Vermont. He sat in the same room in which he had administered to his son the presidential oath of office less than a year earlier. John had hoped to make the trip to Cleveland, but poor weather had delayed his planting. Getting his potatoes in the ground had to take priority over seeing his son nominated for president.[9]

The eighteenth convention of the Republican Party began on Tuesday, June 10, a cold and rainy day in Cleveland. The huge arena was devoid of the plethora of American flags and bunting that usually adorned such gatherings. A sole large flag hung from above the stage, in front of which were three large portraits of Harding, Roosevelt, and Lincoln, the latter of which had been transported "at great risk and expense" from the Union League Club of New York. As the crowd wandered in, they were entertained by tunes from John Philip Sousa and his band. At the appointed opening time of 11 a.m., red, white, and blue lights flooded the arena and Sousa's band launched into "The Star Spangled Banner," followed by Sousa's own famous patriotic march, "The Stars and Stripes Forever." Of the former song, Will Rogers joked, "by the way, the Republicans don't know [the lyrics] any better than the plain people. It will take the American people two more wars to learn the words of our national hymn."[10]

There were 1,109 delegates and a simple majority of 555 was required for nomination. Of the delegates, 120 were women, a substantial increase over the last Republican convention. Another 277 women were present as alternates. This was the first convention held since the ratification of the Nineteenth Amendment giving women nationwide voting rights. Women had prominent roles at the convention, with several making speeches. Elizabeth Martin of Pennsylvania was named chair of the Committee on Permanent Organization, the first woman to head a standing committee at a convention of either major party. Moreover, the party amended its rules during the convention to double the membership of the RNC, with two representatives from each state and territory, one man and one woman. While women made advances, Blacks regressed. New rules for each state's delegate allocation resulted in a loss of delegates from the South, and a corresponding decrease in the number of Black delegates. Under the new procedures, each state got one delegate (instead of the prior rule of two) per congressional district, and was awarded three extra delegates if that state's Electoral College votes were cast for the Republican nominee in the last election, and one extra delegate for each 10,000 votes cast for Republican candidates in each congressional district. Almost no southern states qualified for the extra delegates. In addition to being reduced in number, Black delegates were treated with little respect. The *Baltimore Sun* reported (using racist terms that were then acceptable) that Blacks were upset, seeming "about as happy as Eskimos in a Turkish bath." They were provided lodging at a hotel in the area of Cleveland where Blacks resided, which was three miles from the convention hall and the main hotels. Fraternizing with their white counterparts was discouraged. There were several noted political figures at the convention. Theodore Roosevelt, Jr. was a New York delegate. He was the assistant secretary of the Navy, a job in which both his father and his distant cousin, Franklin, had served. Roosevelt was planning a run in the fall for the governorship of New York, a position also previously held by his father, and aspired to by his cousin. His older sister, Alice, the wife of Ohio Congressman Nicholas Longworth, was present as an observer. The sitting Chief Justice of the Supreme Court, William Howard Taft, watched parts of the convention. The former president had been appointed to the nation's top judicial job, which he had long coveted, by Harding in 1921. One of the country's most prominent Democrats, William Jennings Bryan, a three-time nominee of his party for president, attended the convention as a reporter and was seated next to Will Rogers in the press section. Rogers wrote that he and Bryan had a deal—he would feed any serious tips or rumors that he heard to Bryan and Bryan, in turn, agreed to pass on to him any funny ones.[11]

At the convention's outset, the extra dimension that radio coverage added to the proceedings was evident. RNC Chairman John Adams introduced his committee's choice of Theodore Burton of Ohio as temporary chairman, which required a routine confirmatory vote from the delegates. As an escort committee began walking Burton to the podium, a voice was clearly heard by the radio audience. "But John," someone advised, "you've got to ask them if there's any objection or any other nominations," to which Adams responded, "Are you sure?" "Dead sure," came the response. Adams then followed the correct parliamentary procedure and Burton was officially handed the gavel.[12]

The keynote speech from the seventy-two-year-old Burton, a former Ohio congressman and senator, began with a tribute to the seven Ohio-born presidents, including Warren Harding, who had been the party's nominee at its last convention and in his grave less than a year. With news of Teapot Dome and other scandals dominating headlines over the past several months, Burton attempted to distance Harding from any blame. "If ever he made those mistakes which mortals make," he said, "it was because of the kindness of his heart, because of a noble mind which thought no ill of friend or foe but reposed trust in everyone." After reviewing the prosperity of the country under Harding and then Coolidge, Burton then moved to the investigations of the recent scandals, arguing that it was time to reign them in. The guilty, he said, must "suffer the severest punishment," but, he added: "It is time to call a halt upon indiscriminate scandal mongering, which is largely designed to insult the intelligence and undermine the patriotism of the American people." Burton then criticized Republicans in Congress (some sitting before him) who had not supported Coolidge in his vetoes of spending legislation. "The strength and usefulness of the Republican Party," he proclaimed, "must depend on party solidarity and an organization whose members unite in closed formation to do battle to every foe." He called for the election of Republicans to Congress who are "tried and true, who will stand united," and he left no doubt about whom they should stand behind. "[B]y far," Burton stated, "the greater share of our citizenship looks to President Coolidge rather than to Congress for leadership . . . . The people—and all of the people—have confidence in Calvin Coolidge."[13]

Newspaper reviews of Burton's speech focused on his rebuke of Republicans in Congress, and on the reaction of the newly powerless Senator Lodge, who sat in the first row of the Massachusetts delegation, with a forced smile on his face, as he endured his "public reprimand." There had been a loud shout of "Put Lodge out!" from the galleries in response to Burton's call to elect "tried and true" Republicans to Congress. Through it all, the dignified Lodge tapped his cane on the floor a few times at the appropriate applause lines and "gave his foes no sign of his pain."[14]

The convention's second day saw Frank Mondell, a former congressman from Wyoming, take the gavel from Burton as permanent chairman. Mondell lambasted Democrats as a party "devoid of a single redeeming feature" and for an "utter lack of fixed and definite principle or policy, save that of muck-raking and obstruction." He praised Republicans for a "marvelous record of legislative and administrative accomplishment . . . without parallel in all the annals of government." Mondell's hyperbole was a bit too much for the *New York Times*, which criticized him for his "magnificent disregard of facts" and "pre-Adamite views."[15]

The platform was presented by Charles Warren of Michigan, who had recently been appointed by Coolidge as the American ambassador to Mexico. Warren noted that all of the members of his committee, "save one," voted for the document that he was about to read. The platform lamented the departed Harding as "a public servant unswerving in his devotion to duty" and noted the economic prosperity of the country under Republican rule since 1921.

Conservative in nature, it contained virtually all of the major planks that Coolidge had wanted. It demanded "rigid economy in government," praised the tax reductions enacted in the past three years, and called for "the progressive reduction of the taxes of all the people as rapidly as may be done." It reaffirmed long standing Republican support for protective tariffs. On civil rights, it called for enactment of "a Federal anti-lynching law, so that the full influence of the Federal Government may be wielded to exterminate this hideous crime." It praised the passage of the Nineteenth Amendment and welcomed women delegates to the convention "not as assistants or as auxiliary representatives but as co-partners." One plank was "firmly opposed to the nationalization or Government ownership of public utilities." Another supported the eight-hour workday, opposed child labor, and called for "high standards" for working women in "wages, working, and living conditions." In foreign affairs, the platform reaffirmed the party's opposition to the United States joining the League of Nations, but favored joining the World Court, with reservations that had been stated by Coolidge. Two items that had been the subject of speculation in newspapers before and during the convention—planks supporting Prohibition and opposing the Ku Klux Klan—did not get majority support from the platform committee. The Klan had become resurgent in the country over the past few years, especially in the Midwest, and there were proposals for a firm condemnation of the organization. Republicans chose to be silent. On Prohibition, lax enforcement of the alcohol ban was already evident in parts of the country. The platform did not mention Prohibition specifically, but called, in general, for "respect for law" and "enforcement of law," which the "very existence of the Government depends upon."[16]

The lone holdout on the Committee on Resolutions who refused to sign on to the proposed platform was Henry Cooper, the member from La Follette's Wisconsin. When Warren mentioned Coolidge's name in reading the platform, almost all in the arena stood and cheered. The Wisconsin delegation remained firmly planted in their seats with determined looks on their faces. Boos and hisses rained down on them, along with shouts of "Stand up Wisconsin!" After Warren finished, Cooper took the podium to present Wisconsin's minority report, seeking to add or substitute numerous progressive planks to the platform. At first, the jeering continued. Cooper pointed out that Wisconsin had also presented its own progressive platform at the party's 1908 convention, and had also then been shouted down. Most of the causes then urged by Wisconsin, he pointed out, had become the law of the land. He quoted from Whitelaw Reid, a noted New York Republican from a generation earlier and the party's 1892 vice-presidential nominee, about the need to be tolerant of differing opinions. "The great curse of our present politics," Cooper quoted Reid as warning, "is that your heated partisan never knows the other side. It seems to him that it is disloyal to be on the other side. The element now so sadly needed in our politics is consideration of every question on its individual merits and willingness to hear the other side." As Cooper read the progressive items in his proposed platform (which included a call for election of all federal judges, public ownership of railroads, a rejection of Coolidge's tax policies, and a drastic reduction in tariffs) he gradually won the respect of many in the crowd. The hostility subsided and he was heard out. Respect, however, did not mean agreement. The

Wisconsin minority platform was overwhelmingly rejected, and the majority platform from the committee was overwhelmingly adopted, on voice votes.[17]

On the convention's third day, Coolidge was nominated by Marion Burton, the president of the University of Michigan. A decade earlier, Burton had been president of Smith College in Massachusetts and had become friends with Coolidge, then a rising politician in the Bay State. Largely absent from Burton's speech were references to politics or to pending domestic or foreign issues. Rather, he stated, "my function is to present the man." The entire speech, which was lengthy, was devoted to touting the personal qualities of Calvin Coolidge, characteristics that are still today associated with him:

> He is not a superman and would be the last to think so. There is not a trace of ostentation about him . . . . He personifies the plain simple virtues of our citizens at their best . . . .
> He has moral fibre . . . . He aims to do what he knows he ought to do. There is a rigor and vigor in his life which suggests sternness and discipline . . . . From his youth up he learned that self restraint is a necessity for useful living . . . .
> Frugality is a part of his being . . . To him waste is a vicious betrayal of our country, while thrift is the constructive force which assures a stronger future. He seems to personify this philosophy . . . . He believes there is urgent necessity the world over for actual retrenchment in the use of public funds. His insistence upon tax reduction and tax reform illustrates emphatically the practical application of his sense of thrift . . . .
> Has he a sense of humor? Emphatically yes. It is not the type that wastes time in recounting incidents of ever increasing triteness . . . . He is not given to hilarity. His humor is dry and delightful and its expression as a rule is just as sententious as his more serious utterances . . . .
> He knows that progress will require hard unrelenting toil. To him a better future means continuous struggle and presents a constant challenge. He is no day dreamer for he knows the stern realities of a work-a-day world. We cannot legislate mankind into a state of perfection . . . .
> To the national convention of the greatest party in American history, I have the distinction to present as candidate to succeed himself as President of the United States of America, the virile man,—the staunch American—the real human being—CALVIN COOLIDGE."[18]

The *New York Times* was impressed with Burton, noting that fiery oratory and flowery sentiment were not needed for a successful speech, and were no longer in style. What was needed to win over an audience of the 1920s, the paper opined, was to be "brisk and snappy, but the old sentiment must be there underneath. Burton had it all, and more important still, he knew just what was wanted at any given moment. He could sell building lots in the Saragossa [sic] Sea and put over hell as a Summer resort." The demonstration for Coolidge following Burton's speech lasted only eighteen minutes, short for the hoopla usually displayed for presidential nominees in that era, and ended with a singing of "The Battle Hymn of the Republic." Like the man it had nominated, this convention was not noted for its emotion. There followed nine seconding speeches for the president, three of which were made by women. No other names were placed in nomination. La Follette had instructed his Wisconsin delegates to vote for him, but to not formally nominate him. There was already rampant speculation that, shortly after the convention, La Follette would bolt the party, form his own third party, and run for president on that party's ticket. As expected, the first ballot resulted in an overwhelming victory for Coolidge, who got 1,065 of the 1,109 votes cast. La Follette received 34 votes (28 from Wisconsin and 6 from North Dakota) and Hiram Johnson received ten votes from South Dakota. Calvin Coolidge became only the second vice president in American history (Theodore Roosevelt in 1904 being the first) who had assumed the presidency on the death of his predecessor to be nominated by his party for a term of his own.[19]

After a two-hour afternoon recess, the convention then moved to its only unknown—the nomination of Coolidge's running mate. The president's public position was that he would leave the matter up to the delegates. For weeks, newspapers had been full of speculation. The man considered the favorite, former Governor Frank Lowden of Illinois, had issued several statements advising that he did not wish to be considered. Privately, Coolidge did have a preference. He wanted someone from the progressive wing of the party and, a few months before the convention, had asked Senator William Borah of Idaho to be on the ticket with him. Borah's alleged response, probably apocryphal, was "At which end?" Coolidge persisted and called Borah to the White House during the convention, telling him that he was going to be nominated, whether he liked it or not. Borah again refused. William Butler, Coolidge's manager at the convention, continued to tell insiders in Cleveland that Borah was the one, apparently in an effort to create pressure on him to accept. An angry Borah was having none of it and fired off a telegram to a friend at the convention, Senator Albert Beveridge of Indiana, with a firm statement withdrawing his name, if it were placed in nomination. Butler then proposed William Kenyon of Iowa, a former senator with progressive leanings who had been appointed as a federal appellate judge by Harding. Conservatives in Congress opposed Kenyon and countered with Senator Charles Curtis of Kansas, who was one of their own. Butler then pushed Herbert Hoover, who was then viewed as aligned with the progressive wing of the party, and who had been serving as secretary of commerce under both Harding and Coolidge. Hoover was objected to by the conservatives, who then suggested Charles Dawes, an Illinois banker who had served as a top administrative aide to General Pershing during World War I and who had been named director of the Bureau of the Budget by Harding. Dawes, fifty-nine years old (a few years older than Coolidge), had never held elective office, but was generally respected. Coolidge biographer Robert Sobel described Dawes as "a talented executive with an ability to get things done" and who was "a maverick, hard to pin down or place in any category. The progressives considered him conservative, the conservatives, progressive." Other names were tossed out and discussed, including Theodore Burton of Ohio, who had been the convention's temporary chairman.[20]

All of the back and forth of proposed candidates produced no consensus. When the time came for vice-presidential candidates to be placed before the convention, eight were formally nominated. Among them was Lowden, who, despite his prior statements, was nominated by an Arizona delegate. A delegate from Lowden's home state of Illinois interrupted, advising that Lowden had made it clear that he was not to be a candidate, had avowed that he "can not accept the nomination," and that his decision "is final and irrevocable." Despite this, Lowden's name was not withdrawn. When the votes on the first ballot were tallied, Lowden led with 222, Kenyon was second with 172, Dawes third with 149, and Burton fourth with 139. Votes were cast for sixteen different men. A second ballot quickly followed and there was a bandwagon effect for Lowden, who got 766 votes and was nominated. His nomination was made unanimous on a voice vote.[21]

But there was a problem—Lowden *really* meant it. He did not want to be nominated and would not accept. Only once in American history, in 1844, had a major party candidate refused to accept a nomination for vice president. Then, Silas Wright of New York, a close friend of Martin Van Buren, declined the Democratic nomination for vice president after Van Buren had lost the presidential nomination to a dark horse candidate, James K. Polk. Wright had been nominated to appease Van Buren's disappointed supporters. History was about to repeat itself. After the vote nominating him, a letter written by Lowden a few days earlier declining any nomination was read to the convention, but was not taken seriously. Once again, as on the convention's first day, radio microphones picked up chatter from the podium. "What are we going to do?," someone asked, followed by, "Why not get him on the phone?" Another voice suggested, "Adjourn the convention for an hour." Then, Chairman Mondell was handed two fresh dispatches from the Associated Press, which he had the convention's secretary read aloud. One of the news reports stated "Frank O. Lowden, at his home, formally announced that he would refuse to accept the Republican nomination for Vice President a few moments after having been notified of the same." The other, issued minutes after the first one, repeated the same thing. The convention then recessed, just after the dinner hour, with instructions for Mondell to personally contact Lowden and ascertain his final answer.[22]

When the convention resumed in the evening, a fresh telegram from Lowden to Mondell was read. It was blunt, all but calling the convention a bunch of idiots for having nominated him. "I have said a thousand times, I think," Lowden asserted, "that I would decline if nominated. I must keep my word. To yield now would mean the loss of my self-respect." Voting for vice-president was then reopened and a third ballot was taken. Dawes was easily nominated with 682½ votes, Hoover was second with 234½, and Kenyon was third with 75. The outcome was a resounding defeat for William Butler, Coolidge's manager, who had failed in his attempt to force Borah onto the ticket, and who had then recommended Kenyon, Burton, and, lastly, Hoover. It was interpreted as payback for the high-handed and dictatorial manner in which Butler acted at the convention, and as revenge by the party's conservatives in Congress, who had been shoved aside by Coolidge and his team.[23]

What a difference four years, and an unexpected death, had made. Calvin Coolidge, the man whom delegates at the 1920 convention had named their vice-presidential nominee as a way to thumb their noses at the party's establishment for secretly plotting and forcing Warren Harding on them as their presidential nominee, was now president, in charge of the Republican Party, and had been nominated for a term of his own by a united, if not enthusiastic, convention.

Democratic Convention

While Republicans had entered their 1924 convention certain of their nominee, Democrats faced the opposite outlook. The party had no dominant leader. After leaving office in 1921, Woodrow Wilson remained a virtual invalid and died in early February 1924, just as the campaign season was beginning. He had no true political heir. James Cox of Ohio, the party's 1920 nominee, who had lost in a landslide to Harding, retained no significant following. Cox's young vice-presidential running mate, Franklin Roosevelt, contracted polio in 1921 and lost the use of his legs, necessitating a hiatus from politics to recover, and pushing back his timetable for seeking the top spot on his party's ticket. Sixty-four-year-old William Jennings Bryan, a three-time Democratic nominee, who had been a potent force in the party for almost a generation, finally realized that time had passed him by and that he would never be president. Bryan moved from his native Nebraska to Florida and focused on his religion, and fighting any attempt to weaken Prohibition.

Most Democrats thought it would take several ballots to agree upon a nominee at their 1924 convention. That was nothing new. They were, after all, Democrats. They had done it before. In 1912 and just four years earlier, in 1920, it had taken them over forty ballots to reach a consensus. Despite their spirited history, however, Democrats had no idea what was in store for them as they gathered for their twenty-fourth national convention. As author Robert Murray has observed, the 1924 Democratic convention "was certainly the most acrimonious and bitterly fought event in the Democratic party's modern history. It involved more arguments, aroused more passion, left more wounds, and shed more political blood than any other single incident . . . . [T]he party virtually committed suicide."[24]

Two candidates emerged as the frontrunners for the nomination, both of whom had been contenders in 1920. The strongest was William McAdoo, the Georgia native turned New York lawyer and businessman, who had been secretary of the treasury under Wilson, and was also Wilson's son-in-law. McAdoo, sixty years old in 1924, had led for several ballots in 1920 before that convention nominated Cox. Never accepted by New York City's politicos (neither on Wall Street nor at Tammany Hall), McAdoo moved after the 1920 election across the country to California, where he pursued his legal career and became a leader among Democrats in the Golden State. On economic and social issues, McAdoo was, like his mentor Wilson, a progressive. He held anti-Wall Street and anti-Tammany views, and was a strong proponent of Prohibition. His positions lined up with those of agrarians and southerners who had supported Bryan over the years. It was to them, and to westerners, that McAdoo looked to for the support needed to win the nomination. At first, he made good progress, but all presidential campaigns have unexpected setbacks. Some survive them; some do not. In early 1924, the McAdoo campaign ran into two obstacles that made his path to the nomination much more difficult.

In Washington, a Senate investigation spearheaded by Senator Thomas Walsh of Montana was looking into corruption under the late President Harding, primarily involving the leasing, on favorable terms, of oil fields owned by the Navy to oil companies. The leases were made in exchange for bribes and kickbacks. The ensuing scandal came to be known as "Teapot Dome" (the name of an oil field in Wyoming), but it also involved the leasing of another field in California. Harding's secretary of the interior, Albert Fall, resigned in disgrace and was convicted of accepting bribes from the presidents of two oil companies, one of whom was Edward Doheny of the Pan American Petroleum and Transport Company. Doheny's company had interests in Mexico, as well as in the United States. While the scandal ensnared mostly Republicans, in testimony before a Senate committee in early February 1924, Doheny named McAdoo as a lawyer to whom he had paid two annual retainers of $25,000 in the early 1920s. He also admitted having paid a larger legal fee of $100,000 to McAdoo's law firm. The revelations struck the McAdoo campaign like a bombshell. The leading candidate for the Democratic presidential nomination appeared to be as tarred by oil as the corrupt Republican cronies of Harding. No wrongdoing on McAdoo's part was ever proven. He requested and was granted the opportunity to appear before the Senate committee to respond to Doheny's testimony. Yes, McAdoo admitted, he had received the retainers, but it was for honest and legitimate legal work involving litigation that Doheny's company had in Mexico, and had nothing to do with the scandalous leases of American oil fields. He had not lobbied, McAdoo said, any government officials over the American leases and had no knowledge of them. Despite McAdoo's pleas of innocence, there were calls in the press for him to withdraw from the presidential contest. His own campaign team was divided, with a majority believing that he had been mortally wounded and could not survive. McAdoo resisted and vowed to stay in the race. Unfairly charged or not, he never fully overcame his ties to Doheny's oil company and suspicions that he had acted improperly.[25]

The second setback for McAdoo was largely of his own doing. In the years prior to 1924, there had been a revival of the Ku Klux Klan. The original KKK, active in the South after the end of the Civil War, had been mostly anti-Black, and disbanded after several years. The new Klan (which, like the former one, featured cross-burning members who wore white robes and hoods) was broader, both in its hatred and its territory. It opposed not only Blacks, but also Catholics, Jews, and immigrants of all kinds, and was strong not only in the South, but also in the Midwest and West. By 1924, it was estimated that the KKK had more than three million members. Support for, or opposition from, the Klan determined the outcome of many local and statewide elections. The organization was strongest in the states where McAdoo needed delegates. Despite calls that he denounce the Klan, McAdoo refused to do so, even after it became known that the organization was publicly supporting him in several states. His silence would have major ramifications at convention time.[26]

The other frontrunner of the nomination was Governor Alfred Smith of New York. The fifty-two-year-old Smith was in his second term as governor and had made a half-hearted run for the party's top prize in 1920, but never got much support outside of his home state He was used as a stalking horse by party bosses until they shifted to their favorite candidate, Cox, the eventual nominee. Smith was in a stronger position in 1924, having been elected again in 1922 as governor of the nation's largest state by a margin of almost 400,000 votes. He was New York City to his core. The Catholic son of an Irish-American mother and an Italian-American father, he was born and raised in the Lower East Side of Manhattan. Lacking much of a formal education (he dropped out of school at age fourteen), he was outgoing, friendly, and called "Al" by most people, which he encouraged. He had risen in politics as a Tammany man, although he maintained a reputation as a reformer. When he signed a law repealing the New York enforcement law for Prohibition, Smith became the leader of the anti-Prohibition movement in the country.[27]

Smith's campaign for the 1924 nomination was spearheaded by Tammany's boss, Charles Murphy. A second-generation New Yorker of Irish heritage, "Silent Charlie" had started his career as a saloon keeper and became the head of the Tammany organization in 1901. Unlike its past corrupt leaders, Boss Tweed and Richard Croker, Murphy worked to bring respectability to Tammany and met with some success. Over time, he came to control not only New York City's politics, but also Democratic politics throughout the state. Al Smith was Murphy's prize pupil, the symbol of the "new" Tammany. Murphy's dream was to put Smith in the White House and he met with two other political bosses, George Brennan of Illinois and Thomas Taggart of Indiana, to plot strategy. Smith campaign organizations were started in several states. Murphy also recommended to Smith that he bring on Franklin Roosevelt as his campaign manager. Roosevelt, sidelined by polio and out of the public's eye since 1921, had been a frequent Tammany critic when he was in the state legislature years earlier. Reluctantly, Smith agreed and Roosevelt eagerly accepted. It was good for both—Smith got an establishment and Protestant upstater with the most famous last name in American politics to lead his campaign team, while Roosevelt got back into active politics and was able to connect with and expand the nationwide party contacts that he had made in his 1920 run for vice president. Then, with all of Murphy's plans in place, tragedy struck. On April 25, 1924, two months before the convention was set to begin, Murphy unexpectedly died at the age of sixty-five. Smith was heartbroken, shedding tears and telling reporters, "No one had a better friend." His campaign for the nomination would go on, but without its key strategist.[28]

McAdoo and Smith were embodiments of the divergent factions of the Democratic Party in the 1920s—rural versus urban, dry versus wet, Protestant versus Catholic, North versus South and West, and established Americans versus recent immigrants. With so many differences among the varied constituencies of the two men, it did not bode well for an agreement on either one of them emerging as the presidential nominee at the convention. With the party's two-thirds rule, only a third of the delegates could block any candidate from being nominated.

There were several other candidates in the race, favorite sons from various states, who hoped, if the convention became deadlocked between McAdoo and Smith, that it may turn to them. Among them was Oscar Underwood of Alabama. Underwood had been an "also ran" for the nomination at the 1912 convention, when Woodrow Wilson won over Champ Clark after more than forty ballots. At that time, Underwood was a Democratic leader in the House of Representatives. By 1924, he had moved to the Senate and hoped to be a regional candidate from the South. Perhaps as a way to attract support outside of the South, Underwood seized upon one issue for his campaign. He became an outspoken critic of the Ku Klux Klan and vowed to fight at the convention for a plank in the party's platform denouncing the Klan.[29]

Another second-time candidate was John W. Davis. A West Virginian, Davis's friends had put his name before the last convention in 1920, when he had been serving as President Wilson's ambassador to Great Britain. A prominent lawyer, Davis had previously served one term in Congress, and as Solicitor General. After Wilson left office in 1921, Davis moved to New York City and accepted a lucrative position with one of its leading law firms, the clients of which included J. P. Morgan and Company, railroads, and insurance companies. In 1923, he became president of the American Bar Association. Davis was again promoted for president in 1924 by his West Virginia friends. He did not actively campaign, but did not try to stop their efforts and kept in close contact with them. Compared to 1920, he had warmed up to the idea of being president. Davis kept his views on the issues of the day mostly to himself, but was thought to be more conservative than progressive. After the revelations came out in February of McAdoo's connections as a lawyer to an oil company, many of Davis's supporters urged him to cut ties with his corporate clients, particularly to the Morgan financial empire, and to come back to West Virginia to practice law there. Davis adamantly refused, penning a lengthy letter to a key supporter explaining his reasons. It is a duty of a lawyer to, he wrote, to represent the interests of his clients and "to serve them without the slightest thought of the effect such a service may have upon his personal popularity or his political fortunes." Any lawyer who fails to do so, Davis asserted, in order to "fit the gusts of popular opinion in my judgment not only dishonors himself but disparages and degrades the great profession to which he should be proud to belong . . . . I tell you in candor that I would not pay this price for any honor in the gift of man." Davis's campaign, unable to get him to cut and run from his clients, recognized that his honest and eloquent defense of his position could be a political asset. They requested, and received from him, permission to publish the letter and parts of it appeared in numerous newspapers across the country. Davis had, many thought, turned a potential liability into an asset. Editorial writers sang his praises, one congratulating him "for his forceful rebuke of the suggestion that a lawyer cannot service a rich client without injury to his character or without sacrificing his claim to public confidence and trust." It was an argument that McAdoo was likely jealous of, and perhaps wished he had thought of, to defend himself in the oil scandal involving his own work as a lawyer.[30]

In addition to Underwood and Davis, other favorite-son candidates included Senator Carter Glass of Virginia, Governor George Silzer of New Jersey, Senator Samuel Ralston of Indiana, and Senator Pat Harrison of Mississippi. Also put forward by their states were James Cox of Ohio (the party's last nominee) and Charles Bryan, then serving as governor of Nebraska, and who was the younger brother of Williams Jennings Bryan.[31]

Democratic primaries were held in a dozen states in 1924. McAdoo entered most of them. Underwood entered only a few in the South, while Smith and Davis mostly chose not to compete. McAdoo came away the winner in many, but not without costs. Several states had favorite sons. In that era, there were two strategies that frontrunners could follow for primaries—one was to compete one-on-one with a favorite son in his own state, while the other was to cede that state and concentrate on states that did not have their own candidate in the field. The former antagonized state party officials, while the latter allowed for later cooperation with them and deal making. McAdoo took the aggressive, in-your-face approach and it hurt him in three key states. In Missouri, he challenged that state's longtime senator, James Reed, who was running as a favorite son. McAdoo received active support from the Ku Klux Klan and beat Reed in the popular vote, although the formula used to allocate the delegates made the contest closer. McAdoo also took on Chicago's Democratic boss, George Brennan, in the Illinois primary. By a large margin, Brennan's slate of uncommitted delegates defeated a slate of delegates for McAdoo. Not only had McAdoo made Brennan his enemy, he lost and had nothing but scars to show for the fight. Similarly, in Ohio, he took on James Cox, that state's former governor and the party's last standard-bearer for president. Cox was running as a favorite son and, while he knew he had virtually no chance of repeating as the nominee, he hoped to be a power broker at the convention. It was thought by many that Cox would ultimately line Ohio up behind Smith. Cox beat McAdoo by more than a two-to-one margin in the Ohio primary and won all of that state's delegates. McAdoo had better success against Underwood, beating him in Georgia, again with support from the Klan. Elsewhere in the South, where most of the delegates were chosen at state conventions instead of primaries, McAdoo did very well, winning most or all of the delegates in Florida, Texas, Kentucky, Tennessee, and both Carolinas. Underwood's hope to be the regional southern candidate was not to be. His anti-KKK stance doomed him and the Klan's leaders in several states made no secret that McAdoo was their choice for president. McAdoo came to be viewed by many as the KKK's candidate for president. As one author has noted, "He never spoke out in favor of the Klan; he never spoke against it." His silence, many thought, sent signals of support. Smith won delegates from his own state of New York, in most of the northeast, and also in Wisconsin, where his anti-Prohibition stance was popular. Davis had only his home state of West Virginia pledged to him.[32]

There would be 1,098 delegates at the convention, with a two-thirds vote of 732 needed to win the nomination. In what had become a more acceptable practice over the past few elections, all of the major candidates chose to go to the convention city to direct their forces and woo delegates. On the eve of the convention, newspapers estimated that McAdoo had around 300 delegates, that Smith had around 150, that the favorite sons combined had more than 200, and that the rest were uncommitted. No one was anywhere near the magic number. McAdoo and his team thought they could get votes from a majority (550 delegates) after several ballots, but that getting two-thirds would be almost impossible. They developed, according to author William Harbaugh (a John W. Davis biographer), a "bold, yet uniquely devious plan." Once they got a slim majority and the convention appeared deadlocked, at the appropriate "psychological moment," they would "denounce 'the obstructive minority' and move to drop the two-thirds rule . . . and drive through his nomination."[33]

Democrats selected New York City to host their 1924 convention. With an agreement to contribute $255,000 to the cash-starved party and to provide an arena rent-free, New York beat out San Francisco and Chicago. Surprisingly, it was only the second time that either major party had gathered in the nation's largest city to select its nominees. Democrats had met there in 1868 and nominated a reluctant Horatio Seymour, who lost the election to General Ulysses Grant. The location was a decided advantage to Al Smith. The convention would be in his hometown, and Tammany members, who always packed the galleries at Democratic conventions and could be counted on to be vocal, would show up in force for their local hero. The convention was held in Madison Square Garden, the second arena in New York to hold that name (the current one is the fourth). It was a Beaux-Arts brick structure located at Madison Avenue and 26th Street and designed by the famous architect Stanford White. Its most distinguishing feature was a tower in one corner that rose more than ten stories. Opened in 1890, the arena was, by 1924, run down and scheduled for demolition. The city gave "the Garden" a facelift for the convention, increasing its seating capacity to 14,000, adding refreshment stands, loudspeakers, and wiring it (as the arena in Cleveland had been wired a couple of weeks earlier for the Republican convention) for broadcast of the convention's sessions by radio over a national network of stations. Elsewhere in the city, delegates and guests could walk down an illuminated Fifth Avenue, which was transformed into the "Avenue of States," featuring golden lights and colored searchlights, with each block dedicated to a specific state or territory. The sheer size of, and the mass of people and the bustle of the city, overwhelmed many of the delegates and made them uncomfortable, especially those from outside of the Northeast, a large number of whom were supporters of McAdoo, or of a favorite son from their own state. As author Robert Murray has observed, "New York represented everything that was alien to [them] . . . . Here more than three-quarters of the white population were either foreign-born or the children of foreign-born. Here was the largest concentration of Jews and Catholics in the country. Here was the home of Wall Street . . . of Tammany Hall . . . . And here was the Sodom of the prohibitionists . . . where liquor was easier to get than water."[34]

The convention was called to order by DNC Chairman Cordell Hull, a Tennessean, on Tuesday, June 24, in the midst of a New York City heat wave. Senator Pat Harrison of Mississippi was named temporary chairman and delivered the keynote speech. In denouncing Republican rule since 1921 under Harding and Coolidge, Harrison mentioned the name of the last Democratic president, Woodrow Wilson, who had died a few months earlier, which caused a tribute demonstration for Wilson that lasted twenty minutes. Focusing on the Teapot Dome scandal, Harrison charged that, under Republicans, "Oil has become the Open Sesame of power," gaining "admittance to the robbers' cave and participation in the plunder . . . . It has been the inspiration of this Administration's foreign, as well as domestic policy." Harrison's hard-hitting speech was well-received and was a brief moment of Democratic unity that would soon be absent from Madison Square Garden. He would later turn over the gavel to Senator Thomas Walsh of Montana, the convention's permanent chairman.[35]

Nomination speeches for president began on the second day. They would extend for two and a half days, with forty-three speeches delivered (there were no time limits) for sixteen candidates. McAdoo was the first of the leading candidates to be placed before the convention, in remarks by James Phelan, a former California senator. He was chosen largely because he was Catholic. With it known that the KKK was for McAdoo and with the Catholic Smith as his main opponent, it was hoped that Phelan could blunt some of the hostility of Catholics toward McAdoo. It did not work. The speech was too long, was poorly written, and poorly delivered. He portrayed McAdoo (who had lived his entire life in the East before having recently moved to California) as having "the pioneer spirit of the West." McAdoo "is a human being," said Phelan, "He speaks out like a man. He talks," as if that distinguished him from any of the other candidates. The speech was so bad, one critic wrote, it "would have stopped the nomination in a Democratic convention of Thomas Jefferson running on a ticket with Andrew Jackson." The galleries, packed with hometown supporters of Al Smith, were not kind, interrupting Phelan and necessitating Chairman Walsh to intercede more than once and call for order. "We have received much kindness from New York," a frustrated Phelan pleaded, "but we also ask for a share of its intellectual hospitality." He managed to finish and there followed a well-organized demonstration in support of McAdoo, with delegates from more than half of the states participating. There were altercations between some McAdoo and Smith delegates during the parading through the aisles while, above, a torrent of pro-Smith and anti-McAdoo chants were shouted down, including "Smith, Smith, Alfred E. Smith!" and "Ku, Ku, McAdoo!"[36]

The next day, Smith was nominated by Franklin Roosevelt. When one of Smith's key advisors, Judge Joseph Proskauer, suggested Roosevelt for the task, the governor at first resisted, asking, "For God's sake, why?" When Proskauer responded, "Because you're a Bowery mick and he's a Protestant patrician," Smith saw the political wisdom in the move and relented. As McAdoo had chosen a Catholic to nominate him the day before, the Episcopalian Roosevelt would nominate Smith. Proskauer had written a speech, but Roosevelt also prepared his own draft and insisted on using it. After the two argued, a newspaper publisher who supported Smith reviewed both speeches (without knowing who wrote which one) and pronounced that Proskauer's was by far the better. Roosevelt backed down and agreed to go before the convention speaking Proskauer's words.[37]

It could be a moment of triumph, or tragedy, for the polio-stricken Roosevelt. Appearing in public in his wheelchair was *never* an option. He would *walk* to the podium. But if he fell while getting there, or during the speech, with the whole convention watching and a nationwide radio audience listening in, it would be a disaster and likely end his hopes for a political comeback. After he was wheeled, out of sight, to the back of the stage, he had a friend go to the podium to shake it and test its sturdiness, as he would need to grip it firmly to remain upright while delivering his remarks. Then, in a process that would be repeated endless times over the next twenty years, Roosevelt, with heavy leg braces concealed under his pants, gripped the arm of his son, James, and slowly maneuvered the six or so steps to the podium. His top aide, Louie Howe, who had carefully planned Roosevelt's entrance, watched anxiously from the first row of the galleries and breathed a sigh of relief, muttering "Spunky damn Dutchman" as his boss successfully made it to the podium. Roosevelt grasped it tightly, tossed back his head, flashed a smile, and the crowd went wild.[38]

He began with a plea to the galleries, asking that New Yorkers "render the same fair play to all candidates and their friends as we would expect to receive in any other city." The passion displayed at the convention for Al Smith, he suggested, merely showed "the profound love" of the people for the man. "When you leave this session," Roosevelt proposed, "ask the woman who serves you in the shop, the banker who cashes your check, the man who runs your elevator, the clerk in your hotel, men, women and children, rich or poor, high or low, and you will be told with convincing unanimity that the first in the affections of the people of the State, first, far above all others . . . is the man who has been twice honored with election to the Governorship of the State of New York." People liked, he said, and got along with his candidate. "Save for those whose enmity is a badge of honor," Roosevelt asserted, "he has no enemies." Smith had risen from humble beginnings, "not with the art of a demagogue, not with the wiles of a trickster, but with a dignity, a knowledge and a wisdom that demonstrate him a statesman." Toward the end of his remarks, Roosevelt uttered the two words for which the speech is remembered, bestowing upon Al Smith a nickname by which he would forever be known. "He has a personality that carries to every hearer," Roosevelt proclaimed, "not only the sincerity but the righteousness of what he says. He is the 'Happy Warrior' of the political battlefield." It was a term that Proskauer had pulled from a poem, "Character of the Happy Warrior," by the English poet William Wordsworth. Roosevelt had objected to including it in the speech, thinking the language too flowery and telling Proskauer, "you can't get across Wordsworth's poem to a gang of delegates." It was staying in, Proskauer insisted. As it turned out, the words did as much for Roosevelt's career as for Smith's.[39]

Roosevelt's speech, which ended in the early afternoon, was followed by a demonstration for Smith that was one of the loudest and rowdiest in the history of American political conventions. Smith's hometown supporters were packed like sardines into Madison Square Garden, thousands more than its seating capacity of 14,000. Author Robert Murray vividly described the scene: "The bedlam was indescribable. The Garden turned into a cauldron of sound and movement . . . . In from the street marched an entire procession, fully organized, carrying huge Smith pictures and banners. The aisles were jammed not only by a parade of states but by Al's New York City friends." And then, the galleries got in on the action. Several fire sirens, connected to dry batteries, were set off, unleashing "a nerve-racking tidal wave of sound." Bands played, but could not be heard. It was an hour and a half before the convention could be called to order. Roosevelt finally made it back to his hotel room, where a visitor found him exhausted, but elated. "I did it!," he exclaimed.[40]

The seemingly endless nominating and seconding speeches for multiple candidates went on and on. It was not until the end of the next day's session, more than twenty-four hours after Roosevelt had spoken, that the alphabetical roll call of the states finally reached West Virginia and John W. Davis was nominated. John Holt, a judge from the Mountain State, advised, in a short speech, that it "behooves us to consider well the character of the man we name." Davis, he said, "has the calm courage of a Cleveland and the progressiveness of a Wilson." He is, Holt argued, a man who can "stand the test of the violet ray of pitiless publicity without the disclosure of a single unhealthy spot," a man who, if nominated, "will become a platform in himself." Compared to the loud and lengthy demonstrations for several of the other candidates, the showing for Davis was paltry. The West Virginia delegates stood on their chairs, waved portraits of their distinguished-looking candidate, and it was all over in six minutes.[41]

On Saturday, its fifth day, the convention moved to discussion of its proposed platform from its Committee on Resolutions, which had been in heated meetings all week. The highlight of the platform debate, and the most written about and remembered scene of the entire convention, was a contest over whether the party would condemn the Ku Klux Klan by name. For months, Oscar Underwood of Alabama and his supporters had been vowing to bring the issue before the convention. It was reported in the press during the convention that more than 300 of the 1,100 delegates were Klan members. The majority of the platform committee, in what was called the "Religious Liberty Plank," proposed that the party generally reaffirm its devotion to the free exercise of religion and speech and proclaim "these principles we pledge ourselves ever to defend and maintain. We insist at all time upon obedience to the orderly processes of the law, and deplore and condemn any effort to arouse religious or racial dissention." A minority plank, supported by fourteen members of the committee, proposed adding the following language: "We condemn political secret societies of all kinds as opposed to the exercise of free government and contrary to the spirit of the Declaration of Independence and the Constitution of the United States. We pledge the Democratic Party to oppose any effort on the part of the Ku Klux Klan or any organization to interfere with the religious liberty or political freedom of any citizen, or to limit the civic rights of any citizen or body of citizens because of religion, birthplace or racial origin."[42]

The debate over the minority plank was acrimonious and lasted for hours. There were threats of violence and a thousand New York police officers patrolled throughout Madison Square Garden, one author noting that "every delegate was within reach of a nightstick." A speaker for the anti-Klan plank wondered, "If 343 members of the Klan who are members of this Convention can control the action of the other eight hundred . . . . The thing for us to determine here tonight is whether the tail wags the dog, or the dog wags the tail." The most effective speech for the proposal to condemn the Klan came from Andrew Erwin, a Georgia delegate, who described it as "the most vital" issue before the party. "You have two courses that you may follow," said Erwin, "You can, by adopting the report of the majority, evade the issue, which would, in effect, give your approval to the activities of this organization." That path, he said, will lead to "an ignominious defeat at the polls in November." Or, he argued, the convention could "[m]eet the issue squarely, as the people of this Country expect you to meet it, and a glorious victory will be yours." He continued, in eloquent words:

> The Ku Klux Klan makes a direct attack on these vital principles of our fundamental law. Its insidious activities have spread discord and distrust through this land of peace and harmony . . . . [I]t constitutes the most destructive element in America today. The time has passed to temporize with these misguided people. They have challenged every citizen who cherishes and respects the Constitution. I, for one, am ready to accept that challenge . . . . I say that those Georgians who do not take a stand against this hooded menace, which prowls in the darkness, that dares not show its face, is not worthy of his

ancestry.... I call upon you, my fellow-delegates from the South... to purge from your hearts this senseless prejudice. To my fellow-delegates from the entire Country I invoke the memory of those Americans of other races than your own who died with your own kindred on the fields of France.... Let us show the world that no American worthy of the name will bend his knee to this un-American and un-Christian thing."[43]

At the end of Erwin's speech, there was, according to the convention's official transcript, a ten-minute demonstration, with delegates rushing to him and "cheering him wildly." Then, the anti-Klan delegates raised the standards of half of the states and carried them through the aisles, with Erwin "lifted upon their shoulders and paraded around the hall."[44]

The most famous of those who spoke *against* condemning the KKK was William Jennings Bryan, a delegate from his new state of Florida and a member of the platform committee. It was not the finest hour for the man whose words had electrified several prior Democratic conventions. He argued that the platform contained many progressive causes which were, unfortunately in his view, being overshadowed by the issue of the Klan. "Strike out three words," he said he had argued to his opponents on the committee, "and there will be no objection." But nothing, he said, "stirred the hearts of these men like the words, 'Ku Klux Klan.'" His criticism of those on the committee who wanted to condemn the Klan was met with "[l]ong and continued hisses, boos and jeers." Byran then shifted his attention to the galleries, attacking those above the convention floor who were booing him. "Citizens of New York," he shouted, "show your appreciation of the honor we did you in holding our Convention here." As would be expected, his comment only caused the jeering to increase and Chairman Walsh threatened to clear the galleries. Bryan argued that the minority plank was not needed because the nation had laws upon which "anybody whose rights are denied" can rely upon "and find redress." The Democratic Party, he said, did not need to speak out for Catholics and Jews, because "both the Catholic Church and the Jewish Faith have their great characters today who plead for respect for them." The best way to handle the Klan, he said, was to ignore it, alleging that it "does not deserve the advertisement that you give them." His main argument was that Democrats should focus on the real enemy—big business, monopolies, and Republicans—and not, as Christians, fight among themselves. "I am not willing to divide the Christian Church," he proclaimed, "when we ought to stand together." The party should focus on "recognizing their [the Klan's] honesty and teaching them that they are wrong," said Bryan, rather than publicly condemning them.[45]

Bryan's speech was criticized in newspapers at the time and has been denounced ever since then by historians. Author Herbert Eaton described it as "the saddest of all the speeches" in the debate and commented that Bryan was "[o]ld and tired, bewildered and out of step with a world that had passed him by." Journalist William Allen White wrote that Bryan's remarks were "an apology for expediency in the name of party solidarity." The thrust of his argument, accused White, was "that the members of the Ku Klux Klan are poor misguided creatures, but none the less fellow followers of the Christian faith who should be treated as honest men and taught their error. Also they should not be rebuked by the Democratic convention because the Ku Klux Klan had more than a million votes!"[46]

The vote on the minority plank to condemn the KKK was just as contentious as the debate, with several states called upon to poll their delegates individually and with fistfights breaking out. The outcome was the closest recorded vote in the history of conventions, with 542 and 7/20 votes for it and 543 and 3/20 votes against. It failed by less than one vote. Under pressure, three delegates from Georgia (having one-half vote each) switched to voting against the minority plank after initially voting for it, which made the difference in the outcome. By the time the vote was final, it was two o'clock on a Sunday morning. The Democratic Party had gone on the record as unwilling to denounce the Ku Klux Klan, with millions of Americans listening in by radio.[47]

The rest of the platform contained standard Democratic dogma of the era—for lower tariffs, against monopolies, and for state's rights. It highlighted the Republican scandals of the past three years, proclaiming, "Never before in our history has the Government been so tainted by corruption, and never has an Administration so utterly failed." Other than the proposed anti-Klan plank, the only other item of controversy concerned a longstanding issue from the Wilson years—should the United States join the League of Nations, on what terms, and how? The majority of the committee called for an election, a national referendum, to address solely whether America should join the League "upon such reservations . . . as the President and the Senate of the United States may agree upon." A minority plank, favored by many of the party's Wilsonites, proposed that the party state, as its policy, that it favored joining the League. Newton Baker, who had been Wilson's secretary of war, gave an eloquent speech for the minority position, invoking Wilson's memory. "The man who ought to be pleading this cause," he solemnly declared, "is dead and lies in consecrated ground!" Baker called the majority position for a national vote on whether to join the League "a fanciful, irregular, unconstitutional, revolutionary referendum" that had no basis under any existing law. It was all impractical and nonsense, he argued. The Democratic Party should take stances, not throw up its hands. "What becomes of men when they are afraid to say what they think?," Baker asked, "What becomes of parties when they abandon their ideals?" He asked the convention to imagine the late president, looking over his shoulder and reading the majority proposal on the League of Nations, and his facial reactions to it. Anyone who ever knew Wilson, or who ever saw him, Baker declared "would know from the length of his face and the set of his chin" that he would disapprove of it, that it was "not the kind of leadership that Woodrow Wilson gave to a great political party." Despite Baker's pleas, the convention rejected, by a vote of only 353 for and 742½ against, the minority League plank that he had spoken for and, instead, voted to accept the national referendum proposal, along with the rest of the proposed platform.[48]

Voting on the presidential nomination began on Monday, June 30. It would continue for well over a week and 103 ballots, making the 1924 Democratic convention the longest in American history. Analyzing each up and down movement or shift of delegates is beyond the scope of this book. A brief summarization of the initial ballot and where each day's voting ended provides an understanding of the trends and how the final outcome was reached.

As expected, McAdoo was the leader on the first ballot, with 431½ votes, but leaving him almost three hundred votes short of the two thirds needed to win the nomination. Smith was second with 241 and Cox third with 59, followed by Harrison with 43½, Underwood with 42½, Silzer with 38, Davis with 31, and the rest scattered. The last ballot of the day, the fifteenth, ended around midnight and had McAdoo rising to 479 and Smith up to 305. Davis stood in third place with 61, followed by Cox with 60.[49]

On Tuesday, the second day of voting, an additional fifteen ballots were taken, bringing the total to thirty. At the end of the day, McAdoo was still leading, but had dropped to 415½. Smith was second, increasing his count of 323½, and Davis had the biggest gains of the day, moving up to 126½ and solidly in third place. Each alphabetical roll call of the states started with Alabama, which consistently cast all of its votes for its favorite son, Senator Underwood. During the second day, many in the crowd, mimicking the drawn-out southern cadence of the head of the Alabama delegation, shouted along with him, "Al-a-bam-ah—twenty-foah votes foah Un-da-wood!"[50]

Another twelve ballots were held on Wednesday, ending with the forty-second overall. McAdoo still led with 503.4 votes, Smith with 318.6, and Davis dropping to 67½. The most dramatic event of the day occurred on the thirty-eighth ballot, when William Jennings Bryan rose to, as he said, "explain my vote." As with his earlier remarks during the Klan debate, it was not the Great Commoner's best outing. He rattled off the names of seven men who were acceptable nominees to him, including his own brother, Charles. He finally advised that he was voting for McAdoo, which was met with shouts of "Oil, Oil, Oil," from the crowd, references to McAdoo's legal fees from an oil company as revealed during the Teapot Dome hearings. After pointing out that McAdoo's fees dealt with Mexican oil fields, not American ones, Bryan advised that it didn't really matter, because Wall Street did not like McAdoo and that trumped any questions over oil money that he received. "If any oil has ever touched William G. McAdoo," Bryan proclaimed, "the intense, persistent, virulent opposition of Wall Street washes all the oil away . . . . No man who allows Wall Street to influence his action has any right to criticize McAdoo, who cannot be controlled by Wall Street." Most knew that Bryan was referencing Al Smith, who had the support of the overwhelming majority of the large New York delegation. It was reminiscent of Bryan's actions at the 1912 convention in Baltimore, when he withdrew his support from Champ Clark because New York (representing what he then called "the privilege-seeking, favor-hunting class") had switched its votes to Clark. Bryan's theatrics went over better in Baltimore than in a New York arena packed with Smith's supporters. He continued to be booed and hissed, someone shouting out, "Who is paying you for this?" It was all, commented *TIME*, an "inglorious" effort from the party's three-time nominee.[51]

The fourth day of balloting on Thursday saw another eighteen ballots taken, ending with the sixty-first, which had McAdoo still in the lead with 469½, Smith second with 335½, and Davis in third with 60. McAdoo had met overnight with representatives of some of the favorite sons, urging them to withdraw their candidates and endorse him, but was unsuccessful. After the first couple of days, it was clear that Smith had no path to winning the nomination, but stayed in the contest to block McAdoo from getting to two-thirds. If Smith withdrew, he suspected that many of the favorite son candidates would also get out and jump on a McAdoo bandwagon.[52]

On Friday, which was the Fourth of July, the convention slogged on, with no commemoration of the patriotic day. Another nine ballots were taken, ending with the seventieth overall. McAdoo still led with 528½ votes. He reached a peak of 530 during the day, only twenty votes short of a majority, although still well short of the two-thirds that was needed. Only twice in the party's history (in 1844 and in 1912) had a candidate who won a majority vote of the delegates failed to go on and win the nomination. McAdoo came *so* close, but then he stalled. Without ever getting a majority, the plan of the McAdoo team to accuse an "obstructive minority" of deadlocking the convention and then moving to abolish the two-thirds rule could never be put in motion. Smith picked up a handful of votes during the day, reaching 334. Davis was in third place with 67. During the day, various motions were made to try to expedite the proceedings—to have the convention meet without spectators, to have all of the candidates address the delegates in person, to have both McAdoo and Smith withdraw—and all were defeated on voice votes. Delegates were frustrated and running out of money. Said the head of the Massachusetts delegation (which voted mostly for Smith) to his colleagues, "Gentlemen, we are faced with a choice—either we have to move to a more modest hotel or to a more liberal candidate."[53]

It was more of the same on Saturday, the sixth day of voting. More proposals were made—to drop the candidate with the lowest vote on each ballot and continue until only two were left, to do the same thing until only five candidates were left, to get rid of the two-thirds rule, to adjourn and reconvene in two weeks in Kansas City—and all were rejected. Seven more ballots were taken, ending with the seventy-seventh, and McAdoo still led with 513, Smith second with 367, and Davis third with 76½. At the end of the day, a resolution was approved to have representatives of all the candidates meet that evening "for the purpose of reaching an understanding so as to hasten the conclusion of this Convention." The meeting was held and nothing was resolved. A proposal that all candidates release their delegates was rejected, with McAdoo's team holding firm and refusing to do so. The convention did not meet on Sunday.[54]

The voting continued Monday, with McAdoo gradually losing support. Unfortunately for Smith, the former McAdoo delegates did not shift to him, but went to various favorite sons, which did nothing to break the deadlock. The last ballot of the day was the eighty-seventh, by which time Smith had taken the lead with 361½ and McAdoo was in second with 335½. A candidate who had dropped out and then reentered, Senator Samuel Ralston of Indiana, was in third with 98 votes, while Davis, holding steady at 66½, dropped to fourth.[55]

On Tuesday, an attempt to push through Ralston as a compromise choice failed. He picked up strength and climbed to almost two hundred votes, but then lost steam and dropped out for the second time. Hours more of balloting continued. On the ninety-ninth ballot, which concluded at three o'clock in the morning, McAdoo, with 353½, and Smith, with 353, were virtually tied, with Davis having gained votes and standing at 210. Then, the breakthrough finally came. Days after it became clear that he had no path to reaching two-thirds and winning the nomination, McAdoo's closest advisers finally convinced him, for the good of the party, to give up the contest. Reluctantly, he drafted a letter that was read to the convention. Advising that he was "unwilling to contribute to a continuation of a hopeless deadlock," he did not withdraw, but released his delegates "to take such action as, in their judgment, may best serve the interests of the party." He got in one last dig at Smith, stating that his campaign had been to fight for progressive causes, but also for "the defeat of the reactionary and wet elements in the party which threaten to dominate it." After one more ballot, the convention adjourned.[56]

The presidential nomination was finally settled on Wednesday, as the convention began its third week. Both McAdoo and Smith lost support, with many of McAdoo's supporters going to Davis and many of Smith's to Underwood. On the one-hundred-and-first ballot, Davis led with 216 votes, with Underwood in second at 229½, Smith in third and dropping to 121, and McAdoo in fourth and falling to only 52 votes. Underwood then faded and John W. Davis of West Virginia, whose team had been biding their time in third place with around sixty votes over most of the ballots, won the nomination with 844 votes on the one-hundred-and-third ballot. His nomination was then made unanimous.[57]

For vice president, there was a movement to nominate the convention's chairman, Senator Walsh of Montana, who had received high marks for the manner in which he had presided over the long and unruly gathering. But Walsh was adamant that he did not want to be considered and would not accept. He drafted a letter stating this and had it read to the convention. This led to a wide-open field, with thirteen names placed in nomination to be Davis's running mate. (Nothing was done quickly at this convention.) Among those nominated was Lena Springs of South Carolina, who had chaired one of the committees. It was the first time that a woman was placed in nomination by a major party for the second spot on its ticket. In the nominating speech for her, Springs was praised as one "who expresses in her life the best of the traditions of the old South, the vision and the hopes of the new; one queenly in bearing, yet Democratic in faith and life." A native of Tennessee, the forty-one-year-old Springs had college and post-graduate degrees and had been the head of the English department at a North Carolina college before marrying and moving to South Carolina. Active in the suffragist cause, she knew that she had no chance of winning, but viewed her nomination as another first step for women in politics. One of the men nominated was Charles Bryan, the governor of Nebraska and the younger brother of William Jennings Bryan. With Davis's ties to Wall Street through his legal work, and with elder Bryan's anathema to anything or anybody associated with Wall Street, some party leaders felt that the best way to attach William and his followers to the ticket was to put Charles in the second spot. After Davis sounded out a couple of alternative candidates whom he preferred, who advised that they were not interested, he grudgingly agreed to Brother Charlie and the word was sent out. With 740 votes, eight more than the two-thirds needed, Charles Bryan was nominated on the first ballot. In the final tally, Lena Springs received only South Carolina's eighteen votes, although some other delegates had initially cast votes for her before shifting and jumping on the bandwagon for Bryan.[58]

Before final adjournment, Davis appeared before the convention and made brief remarks, but advised that he would keep with tradition and not accept his nomination until formally notified in the coming days. The country was no doubt happy, he joked, that the delegates had "acted in haste and without deliberation." Acknowledging the "conflict of opinion" at the convention, he tried to put the best face on it, stating that the divisive deliberations "were but the thunder storm that has cleared the clouds away and left shining on us the sun of coming victory and success." Before Davis spoke, Smith also addressed the delegates. They did not appear together. The victorious and vanquished candidates appearing onstage at a convention, with hands clasped and arms raised for a photo opportunity, was, in 1924, still a thing of the future. For ten minutes, Smith touted his own record as governor of New York and thanked his supporters. Vowing that he had "nothing in my heart but real gratitude, and entertain no harsh or ill feeling," only as he finished did Smith briefly refer to Davis, calling the convention's decision "a wonderful nomination," and describing Davis as "a man of brains and of capacity." Because he talked mostly about himself, Davis biographer Harbaugh called Smith's remarks "one of the most tasteless performances of the entire convention" and "the first round of the campaign of 1928." At least Smith took some small step to try to unite the party. McAdoo, still sulking, refused to appear before the convention and it was announced that he would be leaving soon for a vacation to Europe. He sent a brief telegram to Davis with his congratulations, but not with his endorsement. A day later, before his ship sailed from New York, he met briefly with Davis and came away with a belief that Davis was far more conservative than progressive. He issued a statement that the party had hope for the future, but only "if [its] . . . progressive influence is wisely and vigorously used."[59]

Democrats could have saved themselves a lot of time and suspense, and achieved the same result, had they agreed upon their arrival at Madison Square Garden to simply ratify the decision reached at a mock convention, held two months earlier, by students at Washington and Lee College in Lexington, Virginia. A tradition since William Jennings Bryan visited the campus during the 1908 campaign, the school's mock conventions (which are still held every four years) follow the rules and procedures of the real conventions. Of the 1924 mock convention, a reporter observed, "It was not lacking in a single detail when compared to the real convention." In Lexington, as would later occur in New York, the supporters of McAdoo and Smith battled each other, with neither able to gain an advantage, and most of the favorite son candidates refused to withdraw. After more than twenty ballots, the convention was deadlocked. At the end of the twenty-second ballot, delegates from three states (Texas, Ohio, and Connecticut) withdrew for a caucus. When they returned, it was announced that they were switching their support to John W. Davis. This started a stampede for Davis and he was nominated on the twenty-third ballot. It should be noted that Davis may have had an advantage at Lexington, as he was a graduate of Washington and Lee.[60]

As Democrats left New York City after sixteen days and the longest convention in American history, the consensus of most editorials in the nation's newspapers was that the party had, after a notoriously divisive convention, made the best of a bad situation by nominating Davis. A "redeeming climax... the antidote for all the passion brewed," opined the *Atlanta Constitution*. It was, considered the *Denver Post*, "the best possible selection that could have been." The *New York Times* wrote, with "party animosities to be soothed... [and] personal difference to be adjusted," that Davis has "a heavy burden laid upon him." Others praised Davis, but held out little hope for optimism. It was "too bad that such a man," wrote the *Des Moines Register*, "should be handicapped by such a convention." After the "chaos" of the convention, reckoned the *New York Herald-Tribune*, even "the benign dignified figure of Mr. Davis will hardly assuage the doubts of the voters." Perhaps the bluntest assessment came from the *Lincoln State Journal*, which concluded, "It looks like another Alton B. Parker episode in Democratic history," a reference to the party's 1904 nominee who had lost in a landslide to Theodore Roosevelt.[61]

It was another Roosevelt, Franklin, who perhaps came away with the biggest gains from the convention. In virtual seclusion for three years after his onset of polio, Roosevelt, with great physical effort and careful planning, proved that he was able to appear in public as having little or no disability. He was, wrote the *New York Times*, "the most popular man in the convention," receiving great applause from the galleries whenever he took his seat in the New York delegation. His rousing nomination speech for Al Smith as the "Happy Warrior" was well received and would go down in history. He was back in the game.[62]

The Campaign and Election

There was a significant third-party candidate in 1924. Senator Robert La Follette, a progressive Republican who had first run for president in 1908, broke away from his party and was nominated, at a convention held in Cleveland, by a labor and farm organization called the Conference for Progressive Political Action (CPPA). This group had close ties with left-wing parties and, after socialist leader Eugene Debs endorsed La Follette, so did the Socialist Party. Senator Burton Wheeler of Montana, a progressive Democrat who thought Davis too conservative, was named La Follette's running mate. The party adopted an extremely liberal platform, written mostly by La Follette, calling for government ownership of railroads, aid to farmers, low tariffs, election of federal judges, and a constitutional amendment permitting Congress to reinstate laws declared unconstitutional by the courts. At the age of sixty-nine, it was to be La Follette's last hurrah. He campaigned extensively throughout the country and drew large crowds. Many speculated that he could carry enough states to prevent any candidate from getting a majority of the Electoral College and that the election, under the Constitution, would be decided by the House of Representatives.[63]

Coolidge, the clear favorite in the race, ran on the prosperous economy and did little campaigning. "I don't recall any candidate for President," he said in typical Coolidge fashion, "that ever injured himself very much by not talking." Beyond his own inclination to not campaign, he and his wife were in mourning. In July, during the Democratic convention, their teenage son, Calvin, Jr., died of blood poisoning after injuring a toe when playing tennis at the White House. When Coolidge did give speeches, they were usually on broad topics such as education and citizenship, rather than traditional campaign stump speeches. He also used the new medium of radio effectively to get out his message.[64]

Davis and the Democrats never really settled on an overall strategy. Coolidge had the conservative vote locked up, La Follette had the progressives, and they were stuck in the middle. The divisions in the Democratic Party from the convention never fully healed. As a St. Louis newspaper commented, "On the Democratic side there was only John W. Davis, making an able, eloquent but lonely campaign, with little money, a poor organization and not much support from the leaders of the party." Davis campaigned extensively, but became frustrated, especially at his inability to draw Coolidge into the fray. "What I wanted," he later said, "was for Coolidge to say something. I didn't care what it was, just so I had someone to debate with." He focused on Republican corruption and Progressive radicalism. In August, Davis did forcibly speak out against the Ku Klux Klan, something that his party was unwilling to do at its convention. His campaign canceled a planned trip to the West Coast, where La Follette was thought to be strong, the thought being that going there and drawing support away from La Follette would only strengthen Coolidge.[65]

On election, day, the voters kept Coolidge in the White House in a landslide. In the Electoral College, the count was 382 for Coolidge, 136 for Davis, and 13 for La Follette, who carried only his home state of Wisconsin. It was a poor showing for Davis and the Democrats, who finished third in a dozen northern states. Davis won the South, but lost three border states—Missouri, Kentucky, and Maryland. He also lost his home state of West Virginia. In the popular vote, Coolidge received 15,775,003 (54%) votes, compared to 8,385,586 (29%) for Davis, and 4,826,471 (17%) for La Follette. At fifty-one percent, voter turnout was low. La Follette clearly drew more votes from Democrats than from Republicans. In the congressional elections, Republicans maintained a comfortable majority in the House, but only a narrow one in the Senate.[66]

The outcome of the 1924 election hastened the coming transformation of the Democratic Party into a liberal party. As Franklin Roosevelt wrote shortly after the results were known, "it is hopeless for the Democrats to try and wear the livery of the conservative."[67] For the time being, however, the country would "Keep Cool with Coolidge."

CHAPTER 7

1928: I Do Not Choose to Run

Charles Lindbergh flew his plane to France to see what he could see.
Now that he's back he's looking at our old country
And what he has to say stands out in bold relief,
Herbert Hoover is the only man to be our nation's chief.

Now you all remember Hoover, back in the war
He saved us from the Kaiser, now he'll give us something more.
He'll serve as the President of the land of the free
If he's good enough for Lindy, he's good enough for me.
—**Republican campaign song, 1928**

It was classic Calvin Coolidge. The popular president was on an extended vacation in the Black Hills of South Dakota in the summer of 1927. Most of the American economy was prospering. The nation was at peace. The Republican Party had survived the scandals of the Harding years and was united under Coolidge as it had not been since the days of McKinley. The incumbent president appeared to be a certain bet to win reelection to another term in 1928. On August 2, four years to the day after he became president upon the death of Warren Harding, Coolidge called an impromptu press conference at a high school in South Dakota for the thirty or so reporters who were covering him on vacation. As they entered a classroom, the president handed each a slip of paper with a single twelve-word sentence on it, written in his own handwriting. The reporters glanced down at the words and were shocked. "I do not choose to run," Coolidge had scribbled, "for President in nineteen twenty eight." He took no questions and gave no explanation. The brief event was Silent Cal at his best. Reporters rushed from the room to spread the news to a startled nation.[1]

Coolidge's decision set off a firestorm of political speculation and maneuvering. Most accepted him at his word, but some did not. What did he intend by "I do not choose to run?" Did he mean that he would not be an active candidate, but that he would accept a draft, if the Republican Party nominated him at its convention the following year? If not, who would the Republicans nominate in his place? Would the Democrats, who had been thought to have little chance against Coolidge, now have an opportunity to win back the White House?

Republican Convention

In the whole span of American history, very few men, if any, who aspired to the presidency have possessed as compelling a life story and as impressive a résumé as Herbert Hoover. Born in Iowa in 1874, his father a blacksmith and his mother a seamstress, Hoover was orphaned before the age of ten and was sent off to Oregon to live with an uncle. He became one of the first students at Stanford University and earned a degree in geological engineering. In his twenties, he traveled the world, overseeing mining operations in obscure places, including western Australia and northern China, and became a leader in the mining industry. By the time he was forty, he had earned a fortune, was based in London, and had turned his efforts to philanthropic causes. With the outbreak of World War I in 1914, years before the United States entered the conflict, he helped organize, and headed, a private group that provided relief to more than a hundred thousand American citizens trapped in the war zone, including assistance and loans to help many of them return home. When a severe food shortage broke out in German-occupied Belgium, Hoover headed a commission that bought and shipped food supplies into the country and he negotiated with the opposing Allied and German governments to make sure that the relief would not be blocked or confiscated and would reach the needy civilian population. During the war, Hoover's efforts helped save more than ten million Belgians from starvation. When the United States entered the war in 1917, President Wilson tapped Hoover to head a federal agency that oversaw the production, distribution, and conservation of food to Americans. After the war, Hoover's focus returned to a desolate Europe and he led a public/private American organization that fed millions in Poland, Russia, and other countries. It has been said that Hoover's combined relief efforts saved more lives than the actions of any other single person in the history of the world.[2]

In 1920, Hoover was so admired by Americans of all political persuasions that both Democrats and Republicans sought to recruit him as their nominee for president. Franklin Roosevelt lavished praise on him, writing to a friend that Hoover is "a wonder" and "I wish we could make him president of the United States." Hoover declared himself a Republican and made a feeble attempt at that party's presidential nomination, but was never really in the mix when that year's brokered convention made Senator Warren Harding of Ohio its nominee. After Harding became president, he named Hoover his secretary of commerce, a position that Hoover remained in after Harding's death in 1923 and through the Coolidge administration. Hoover turned the relatively obscure Department of Commerce into a powerful agency affecting the entire economy, from regulation of radio airwaves, to airplanes and air travel, to organizing relief assistance to victims of an extensive Mississippi River flood. He oversaw a pact among western states for water rights on the Colorado River, leading to the construction of a massive dam that bears his name. *TIME* magazine called Hoover, mostly with admiration, the "Beaver Man," because he was physically "chunky, round-faced" and had a "peculiar slant" of his teeth, but also for his "well-earned reputation for patient industry and . . . his familiarity with rivers and dams and husbanding food through lean seasons." With his activist views on what government could accomplish, Hoover was popular among rank-and-file Republicans, but he also ruffled the feathers of the eastern establishment that still had great influence over the party.[3]

When President Coolidge made his surprising announcement that he would not run again in 1928, Hoover became the favorite to win the Republican nomination. The opposition to him fell into two groups. The party's Old Guard, led by Secretary of the Treasury Andrew Mellon of Pennsylvania, hoped to get Coolidge to reconsider, or to get the convention to draft the President as its nominee for another term and convince him to accept it. Mellon controlled most of the Keystone State's large delegation. The other group against Hoover was led by Republican senators from the farm states of the Midwest, who did not like his opposition to farm subsidies. A bill to grant such subsidies, the McNary-Haugen Act, had twice passed Congress, but had been vetoed both times by Coolidge, with Hoover having strongly urged the President to reject the legislation. The strategy of this group was one used previously in both parties—to enter several favorite son candidates in the race, have them control their state's delegations, try to block the frontrunner from getting the nomination on the early ballots, and hope that one of them would emerge from a deadlocked convention as the nominee. The press called this group "the Allies." The favorite son candidates in 1928 included Senators Charles Curtis of Kansas, James Watson of Indiana, George Norris of Nebraska, Guy Goff of West Virginia, as well as Frank Lowden, a former governor of Illinois. Of this group, Lowden was viewed as the one with the most support.[4]

State primary elections to express preferences for president, a progressive reform of the early twentieth century, had, after peaking in 1920, begun to decline in number. In 1928, there were only fourteen such contests, all in northern and western states. The rules varied from state to state as to whether the primary results were just a popularity contest, or whether they bound delegates to support the winning candidate at the party's convention. Hoover, who had settled in central California near the Stanford University campus where he had been a student, ran a national campaign for the nomination, spending more than $400,000 in the process. He was the only candidate to win primaries in different regions of the country, including his home state of California, as well as in Oregon, Ohio, Michigan, New Jersey, Maryland, Massachusetts, and New Hampshire. Four favorite son candidates won their home states—Lowden in Illinois, Curtis in Kansas, Watson in Indiana, and Goff in West Virginia. Lowden also won in South Dakota and Curtis in Wisconsin, the only candidates besides Hoover to win more than one primary. Combining the primary results with delegates selected at state conventions, by May, Hoover had more than four hundred delegates pledged to him, with all of the other candidates trailing far behind. Two of the largest states, New York and Pennsylvania, remained uncommitted. In the days before the convention opened, most of the talk was still over whether Coolidge was *really* out of the race. It was speculated that the president would send some word to Kansas City, via a cabinet member or a senator, as to his true wishes. Secretary Mellon, who was close with Coolidge, was thought to be the most likely messenger.[5]

After the primaries ended, Hoover, as a member of Coolidge's cabinet and having heard rumors that the President may still desire the nomination, despite his statement in 1927, went to see Coolidge at the White House. He offered his delegates to the president, if he wanted to run. Otherwise, he was hoping to get an endorsement, or at least a firm disavowal from Coolidge that he would not accept a draft nomination from the convention. Silent Cal was as enigmatic as ever. "If you have 400 delegates," he told his secretary of commerce, "you better keep them."[6]

The Republicans selected Kansas City to host their nineteenth nominating convention. It was the second time the city had such an honor. The aging Convention Hall, which had been new when the Democrats had nominated William Jennings Bryan there in 1900, was given a facelift for the occasion. More than 50,000 people were expected in the city for the convention, including caravans of farmers from several Midwest states, who were opposed to Hoover because of his position on agriculture policy. Newspapers reported that the convention's planning committee went to excess in decorating the downtown area, with seemingly miles of bunting on display. Signs with GOP printed on them were everywhere, with each of the three letters formed by a drawing of a twisted elephant, the party's symbol. Hoover supporters walked around sporting yellow California poppies in their lapels, and pinning them on anyone who would accept them. Outside the main entrance to the arena, a huge electrified eagle attracted the attention of pedestrians. The night before the convention opened, the city held an old-fashioned torchlight political parade, with more than five thousand participants and floats honoring each of the nine past Republican presidents. The Lincoln portrayer "caught all eyes" and the one depicting Roosevelt had "the famous grin going strong." With the nation in its eighth year of Prohibition, many visitors to the city sought out local speakeasies, as did government agents. Several "soft drink" merchants near the main hotels were raided and closed just before the convention, it being reported "that 'soft' applies only to the tone of voice employed in the transaction," not to the beverages being served. Conventions were known to attract gangs of professional pickpockets. Kansas City police brought in detectives from seventeen cities, and security officers from several railroads, to keep a sharp eye out for the "nimble-fingered ones" and to assist in patrolling the convention area. In keeping with tradition, Hoover, as the frontrunner, did not attend the convention and was at his office and home in Washington. He tapped one of his fellow cabinet members, Secretary of the Interior Hubert Work of Colorado, to lead his team in Kansas City. Improved and expanded radio technology since 1924 meant, for the first time, most of the country could listen to the convention. Both NBC and CBS broadcast the proceedings live over radio networks. It was estimated that up to fifty million people, almost half of the population of the United States, listened to parts of the convention over radio. Easterners awoke each morning with photographs from the convention on the front pages of their newspapers. This was achieved by snapshots taken by Associated Press photographers being flown two hours on a small plane to St. Louis, where they were telephonically transferred to the offices of major eastern papers.[7]

Humorist Will Rogers was in Kansas City and wrote, "The convention opens Tuesday and closes when Coolidge makes up his mind." Rogers speculated that he was one of the few arrivals in the city who "wasn't bringing a letter from Coolidge" revealing the president's true intentions. Of the group of favorite son candidates seeking to deny Hoover the nomination, Rogers imagined a conversation among them in which they admitted that there "don't seem to be" a demand for any one of them to be president, but agreeing that they will stick together to "stop the fellow that the majority wants" and that "we won't start killing each other off till after we have all killed" off Hoover first. A few days before the convention, the *New York Times* estimated the delegate count at 477 for Hoover, 230 for Lowden, 81 for others, and 300 uncommitted. Of the latter group, 200 were believed to favor drafting Coolidge. A total of 545 delegates was needed to win the nomination.[8]

Any lingering doubt as to the nominee was resolved in the hours before the convention's scheduled opening on Tuesday, June 12. Secretary Mellon arrived in Kansas City at midday on Monday, having spoken with Coolidge in Washington before beginning his trip. He asked the president to reconsider his decision and was met with a firm "no." Working with New York's Charles Hilles and a party boss from Connecticut, Mellon had also tried to get Charles Evans Hughes, the party's 1916 nominee, to agree to enter the race, or to accept a draft from the convention. Like Coolidge, Hughes declined. Mellon had no interest in joining forces with the Midwest anti-Hoover farm interests, whom he considered too radical, and they had no desire to ally with conservative easterners like him. A divided opposition made Hoover's path to victory much easier. Privately, Mellon had written to a friend days before the convention advising that they would reluctantly have to accept Hoover, but he did not yet want to make it public. With Hoover believed to be about fifty votes short of the 545 delegates needed to win, Pennsylvania's seventy-nine votes would put him over the top and Mellon wanted to be the kingmaker in Kansas City. However, William Vare, a Pennsylvania delegate and the boss of the Philadelphia Republican machine, stole Mellon's thunder. Vare announced late Monday afternoon that he and fifteen delegates from the Philadelphia area would be voting for Hoover. Vare was a controversial figure who owned garbage businesses, was known as the "Ash Can King," and had a seedy political reputation. He had won an election to the United States Senate in 1926, but the Senate had refused to seat him, due to questions of fraud during his campaign. A Senate investigation of the matter was ongoing. Soon after Vare's announcement, word spread that Vermont and Massachusetts were going with Hoover. By the time the Pennsylvania delegation caucused on Tuesday morning and Mellon announced that he and the rest of Pennsylvania's delegates would also be supporting Hoover, the news was anticlimactic. Vare was portrayed in the press as the one who started the Hoover stampede and Mellon as someone who jumped onto the moving bandwagon. The optics were not what party leaders had wanted. Given the Harding scandals only five years earlier, the less news made at the convention by tainted machine politicians, the better. As the *Washington Post* noted, "Thus, the Republican nominee was named, not by the august Mellon, but by Vare, the hem of whose garment the righteous fear that they may not touch without contamination." Another newspaper commented that "the notorious Vare" had "provided a denouement which neither Mr. Coolidge nor his party can view with anything but intense dissatisfaction."[9]

The convention opened at eleven on Tuesday morning with the party's chairman, William Butler of Massachusetts, introducing the temporary chairman, Senator Simeon Fess from Ohio, who gave the traditional keynote speech to a hall with less than full galleries. Fess's remarks were lengthy, lasting well over an hour, and drew little response from the crowd. The only times they stood and cheered were twice at the mention of Coolidge's name, and then for only a few seconds. Fess went through the achievements of Coolidge, focusing on lower taxes and cost cutting by the government. He ended with high praise for the president: "Few are his words, decisive his judgments. His comprehension of problems is broad, his vision clear, and his action dauntless. His conception of public duty forstalls the employment of mere political expediency . . . . [H]e leaves office by his own fiat . . . in spite of the fact that his nomination and election would be a foregone conclusion . . . . [He] is the greatest personal and political force in the world today."[10]

The goal of a keynote speech is to rouse the crowd at the convention's outset and, in this, Fess failed. One newspaper noted there was "little attempt at oratory" and others commented on the lack of enthusiasm not only for the speech, but at the convention in general, one calling it "more depressing than a funeral." Will Rogers found some amusement in the speech. Of Fess's lengthy recitation of how much money the federal government had saved under Coolidge, the Oklahoma humorist commented, "I think if he had talked another hour he would have paid us a dividend." When Fess closed with his tribute to Coolidge, Rogers joked that he turned and asked the man next to him if the speaker was talking about "Our Savior." He then added, of Fess, "The way he rated 'em was Coolidge, The Lord, and then Lincoln."[11]

After the appointment of the standard committees, the convention adjourned in mid-afternoon, with no evening session scheduled. Notable among the heads of the committees was Mabel Walker Willebrandt, a California delegate and Hoover supporter, who was also an assistant attorney general in the Department of Justice and known for her prohibition enforcement. She was one of sixty-nine voting female delegates at the convention and she was named as chair of the Committee on Credentials, making her the first of her gender to lead a committee at a major party convention. It was rumored, if Hoover won the election, that Willebrandt was on his short list to be attorney general and the first female cabinet member.[12]

The farmers' protest, dubbed the "cornbelt army" by the press, was a bust. Organizers had promised up to a hundred thousand marching against Hoover's nomination. Although numerous farmers came to Kansas City, arriving in muddy cars adorned with signs of "Listen, or Lose the West," when the time came for a march on the convention hall, fewer than a thousand were present. Reporters questioned how many of those were really farmers. "People dressed up as agriculturists have been parading the streets," the *New York Times* observed, "the majority of them in brand new overalls, the majority of which probably will never see a corn stalk, or a potato furrow." Several were noted through "thin disguises" to bear a "striking resemblance" to men who had been handing out pamphlets at Lowden's headquarters over the past few days. As the second day of the convention began, the group attempted to enter the hall, but, as they had no tickets, they were blocked by doorkeepers and security officials. One of their leaders, who had a pass to enter, went to the podium and pleaded with the sergeant-at-arms to permit the group to come in, make one loop around the floor, and then leave. The request was denied. The frustrated protesters marched around the outside of the building a few times, listened to some speeches from their leaders, milled about for a while, and then left. The Hoover floor leaders at the convention had to have been looking on with smiles.[13]

While the farmer protest was going on outside, the convention proceeded with its second day's agenda. Temporary Chairman Fess called the gathering to order in mid-morning. The galleries were only half filled. He was presented with a gavel made of copper, mined in Utah. (Special gavels such as this, made from the wood of trees at the homes of past presidents, or of mineral deposits in a state, had been presented to chairmen of past conventions over the years.) The first item of business was receipt of the report from the Committee on Credentials, which was not ready when first called. The convention's official band, located in the upper portion of the galleries, played songs to pass the time. The committee was finishing up hours of meetings to decide on competing delegate slates in several states, most in the South. The disputes were primarily over whether to seat pro-Hoover or anti-Hoover delegates, but they also had an underlying racial context. Although Black delegates had attended Republican conventions since the Civil War, the 1920s was an era when Jim Crow laws and the Ku Klux Klan were strong, and white Republicans in some southern states saw an opportunity to exclude Blacks from official state party organizations. Several all-white slates of delegates, called "lily-whites," competed with mixed-race slates, referred to as "black-and-tans." Most of the credentials committee members were Hoover supporters and they were not concerned about the ramifications of their decisions on racial policy in the South. Their goal was to seat the pro-Hoover delegations, be they "lily-white" or "black-and-tan." The committee voted to seat "black-and-tan" delegations from Tennessee, Mississippi, and Georgia, but also "lily-white" delegations from Texas, Louisiana, and Florida. In the latter three states, such an action by the national convention in effect transferred control of the Republican Party there to whites, and excluded Blacks from the leadership. The only thing the six delegate slates that the committee voted to seat had in common was that they were all for Hoover. Prominent Blacks in those states where the "black-and-tans" lost out denounced the committee's decision as racist, and as a pullback from the party's commitment to their race since the days of Lincoln.[14]

After about an hour of waiting, Mabel Walker Willebrandt, the chair of the Committee on Credentials, walked down the arena's center aisle, "looking fresh as a daisy" and presented the report of her committee in a voice "as clear as any yet heard in the big hall." Normally, drab credentials battles were not of much interest to those in the galleries, but reporters noted that "the novelty of feminine participation" caused most in the hall to pay attention. Willebrandt was poised and professional. At prior conventions, a woman being in a position of power and addressing the gathering on a matter of such substance would have been unheard of. The main credentials dispute taken to the full convention concerned Texas. Willebrandt advised that the majority of her committee, by a vote of thirty-four to fifteen, recommended seating a delegate slate headed by a R. B. Creager, which was "lily-white" and pro-Hoover. A minority report presented by a delegate from Delaware argued for seating a "black-and-tan" delegate slate from Texas that was uncommitted to any candidate. On a roll call vote, the pro-Hoover and white Texas delegates were seated by a vote of 659½ in favor and 399½ against. For the first time since the Civil War, an all-white delegation would represent the Lone Star State at a Republican convention. This was the first vote to test the strength of the Hoover forces at the convention and it showed that they easily had more than the 545 votes needed to win the nomination. But the vote is also remembered for its racial implications. About sixty Blacks were seated as delegates at the 1928 convention, a number that was half what it had been at the 1904 convention. As one commentator has noted, "There was also at stake the historic if long-neglected commitment of the party to protect and defend the black people of the South. For decades black-and-tan leaders had fought off lily-white challengers, but during the 1920s their enemies had gained more and more recognition at the national conventions . . . . With lily-whites again triumphant in three states formerly controlled by black and tans, angry black leaders could not help believing that the Hoover majority cared little or nothing for black leaders in the South."[15]

The credentials battle was the highlight of the convention's second day. Following it, the Committee on Permanent Organization presented its report and named Senator George Moses of New Hampshire as the permanent chairman. After an uneventful speech from Moses, the convention adjourned until the evening. However, the evening session lasted less than a minute. Moses was advised that the committee drafting the platform was still not ready to report and, given this, the convention adjourned before most of the delegates and most of those who had planned to watch from the galleries had even entered the hall. Still, it had been a memorable day in the history of presidential nominating conventions, a day that saw one step forward for women, but also a significant step back for Blacks.[16]

The convention's third day began with receipt of the party's proposed platform. Prohibition was one of two issues that dominated the deliberations of the Committee on Resolutions. By 1928, it was well known that enforcement of Prohibition was lax, especially in certain parts of the country. William Borah, a longtime progressive Republican senator from Idaho, was the leader of the "dry" forces in the party, *i.e.*, those who strongly supported Prohibition and its enforcement. In his speeches and writings in the months leading up to the convention, Borah argued that the country could not select which laws it wanted to enforce, and those it did not. In an opinion piece published in the *New York Times* just before the convention, entitled "Away With Political Cowardice," he wrote, "But for a great political party to be lukewarm is to be indifferent, or to adopt a course of equivocation upon a subject which involves the maintenance and support of the law of the land would be an exhibition of shameful treachery of the fundamental principles of constitutional government." If people did not like Prohibition, Borah argued, then it should be repealed, rather than turning away from its strict enforcement. Hoover, who had been a social drinker before Prohibition, abstained after its enactment and supported Borah's call for strict enforcement. With the Democratic Party expected to nominate New Yorker Al Smith, a "wet" who opposed Prohibition, alcohol was an issue on which the parties would likely present strong differences for the voters in the fall campaign. The Committee on Resolutions adopted Borah's strong enforcement position in a plank entitled "Law Enforcement," which stated, "The people through the method provided by the Constitution have written the Eighteenth Amendment into the Constitution. The Republican Party pledges itself and its nominees to the observance and vigorous enforcement of this provision of the Constitution."[17]

The second main issue of contention during the drafting of the platform concerned agriculture policy. Farming interests wanted some endorsement of subsidies to be paid to farmers when crop surpluses led to low prices, which had been a key provision of the McNary-Haugen farm bill that Coolidge had vetoed. The committee rejected this and, instead, called for a policy that both Hoover and Coolidge favored, which was the creation of a federal farm board that would establish farmer-owned cooperatives to set up a system to prevent, or have an orderly distribution of, crop surpluses. A minority plank offered by the anti-Hoover farmers was debated by the full convention and was overwhelmingly rejected, with a vote of only 267 favoring it and 817 opposed. The full platform as written by the committee—which also included a continuation of Coolidge's foreign policy, tax reductions, support for protective tariffs, a federal anti-lynching law, and other provisions—was then adopted on a voice vote.[18]

The convention then adjourned for several hours and resumed in the early evening with its next agenda item the naming of a nominee for president. With Chairman Moses presiding, the arena was packed for the occasion, although there was no suspense over the outcome. All knew from the events of the past few days that Herbert Hoover would be nominated by a comfortable margin. Despite this, the names of several other candidates were placed before the delegates. The nominating speeches, seconding speeches, the roll call of the states for voting, and a couple of unexpected surprises, took several hours and Hoover's nomination would not be final until the midnight hour.

The frontrunner was the first to be placed in nomination in a speech delivered by John McNab, a California attorney and one of Hoover's personal friends. McNab committed a blunder by mentioning Hoover's name in his first couple of sentences, which set off a demonstration. Convention audiences over the years had been conditioned to erupt in a frenzy whenever a candidate's name was first mentioned in a nominating speech, which is why most seasoned orators saved the name until the very end of their remarks. Most of the delegates (except for those from some farm states, who sat on their hands) paraded around the hall and most in the galleries joined in, while the band played "California, Here I Come." For twenty-three minutes, "[c]owbells, rattlers, tambourines and tin pans were brought into play," until Chairman Moses finally restored order. This was unfortunate for McNab, and for Hoover, since the audience in the hall (and likely the millions listening on the radio) paid less attention to the rest of his remarks than they would have otherwise. The speech reviewed Hoover's humble origins as an orphan and his Quaker upbringing ("The story of his life is an epic of modern achievement"), his start as a low-level worker in the mining industry and his rise to the top of it ("one of the most dramatic careers in history"), his leadership in feeding Belgium during the First World War ("He heard the cry and answered . . . . To him, hunger knew no nationality"), his direction of food conservation efforts at home once American troops were deployed ("a unison of patriotic effort"), and his prominent role and achievements as secretary of commerce under Harding and Coolidge ("What a beneficence he's made that department to the business and industrial world"). All of these experiences, McNab stated, uniquely qualified Hoover to be the nation's chief executive:

> If the American people a quarter of a century ago had set about the task of preparing a man for the Presidency, how could they have done more to equip him for those vast responsibilities than through the experiences which have made up the romance of this man's life?

He then proclaimed that California offered Hoover to the nation:

> I name him who rose from poverty to feed more hungry people than any man in the history of the world.
> I nominate him because he has labored with his hands and knows the problem of the toiler.
> I name him as a great engineer who understands the problems of our inland waterways and the vast resources of river and lake and soil.
> I name him as a great humanitarian who, in the midst of a woe of war, gave his best that human beings might live and live abundantly . . . .
> I name him as statesman and executive whose unfaltering courage, inflexible Americanism and understanding of nations and peoples have given him a grasp on national and international affairs that commands respect throughout the world . . . .
> Engineer, practical scientist, minister of mercy to the hungry, administrator, executive, statesman, beneficent American, kindly neighbor, wholesome human being, I give you the name of Herbert Hoover.[19]

There followed another demonstration for Hoover, less intense and shorter than the one that had taken place at the outset of McNab's remarks.[20]

An Illinois senator then came to the podium for what was thought to be a nomination speech for former Governor Lowden, who was from the same state. Instead, he read a terse statement from Lowden, who had been the most prominent of the farm state candidates opposing Hoover. Lowden declined to have his name placed in nomination. He stated that his decision was to protest the rejection of the farm subsidy plank that he had wanted in the platform, which he said was a clear sign that the party was not prepared "to meet fully and thoroughly the agricultural problem." The announcement was met mostly with silence. Lowden's supporters were dejected. As one author has noted, "Many delegates who would have preferred to fight to the finish felt that Lowden had let them down." There followed nominating speeches for Senator Watson of

Indiana, Senator Curtis of Kansas, and Senator Goff of West Virginia. Only the speech for Curtis sparked any lengthy demonstration, likely because many Kansans were in the galleries, that state being just across the Missouri River from Kansas City. A second unexpected event then occurred when an Ohio delegate rose and nominated President Coolidge. This was done without any authority from Coolidge or the Old Guard of the party that supported him. The speech was reported as mostly "a shaft directed at Mr. Hoover," as every sentence seemed to criticize the likely nominee, including a rumor that Hoover in 1920 had flirted with running for president as a Democrat. "Cannot we nominate a Republican?," the speaker asked. There was little positive response to the speech and Hoover's floor leaders were outraged by it. The *Baltimore Sun* reported that, taken together, the nomination speeches "were far below par" when compared to prior conventions and none "reached the emotions of the audience."[21]

The first ballot for president then followed and, with Lowden's withdrawal, the results were even more of a landslide for Hoover than had been expected. The Californian received 837 votes, almost three hundred more than the number needed for victory. Lowden, despite not being placed in nomination, was second with 74 and Curtis third with 64. The rest of the tally was 45 for Watson, 34 for Norris, 18 for Goff, 17 for Coolidge, and a handful scattered among others. The nomination was then made unanimous and, around midnight, the convention adjourned, to meet again in the morning to select a vice presidential nominee.[22]

Meetings were held throughout the night to select a running mate. One name, the current vice president, Charles Dawes of Illinois, was not on the list of those considered. Dawes had sided with the farming interests in supporting the McNary-Haugen bill and he was a good friend of Lowden, who had been, before his sudden withdrawal that evening, Hoover's leading opponent. Hoover did not want Dawes, and Coolidge had also let it be known that he would be displeased if Dawes were placed on the ticket again. Most agreed on the need for someone from the farm states. Senator Borah of Idaho, who had influence and respect in the party, favored his colleague, Senator Curtis of Kansas, who had been one of the also-rans for the presidential nomination. The Hoover men did not want to oppose Borah and conceded to Curtis as the selection. The sixty-eight-year-old Curtis was the majority leader in the Senate and was viewed as a conservative. He was of mixed race, being part Native American and part white, and was from the farm state of Kansas. Perhaps more importantly, he could appeal to those on both sides of the McNary-Haugen Act. He had initially voted for the bill in the Senate, but as the Republican leader in that body, he had also voted to sustain Coolidge's veto of it.[23]

Despite the overnight consensus for Curtis, when the convention met for its final day, six names were placed in nomination for vice president, with most of those withdrawn before the voting began. Curtis won with 1,052 votes, compared to less than forty scattered among others. A few minutes after the voting ended, the nominee was ushered into the hall and gave brief remarks praising Hoover as "an able, experienced man" who would lead the party to victory in November. It was quite a change of opinion from when Curtis had arrived in Kansas City a week earlier. Then, he had confidently predicted that he would be the presidential nominee and said of Hoover, that Republicans could not afford to nominate "one for whom the party will be on the defensive from the day he is named." Charles Curtis was not the first, and certainly not the last, vice-presidential nominee to quickly change his tune about the candidate at the top of the ticket after being placed on its bottom. In addition to Curtis's mixed race, the pairing was also historic from a geographic standpoint. It was the first time that both candidates on a major party ticket had been born west of the Mississippi River.[24]

Republicans left Kansas City, if not enthusiastic about Hoover, at least relatively united behind him. It was unknown if the discontented farmers were sufficient in number to be a factor in the election, or what impact the strong position that the party had taken on Prohibition enforcement would have on voters. The party hoped that Hoover's impressive résumé, combined with the economic prosperity under Coolidge, would be sufficient to carry them to victory, as they waited for the upcoming Democratic convention and the naming of Hoover's opponent.

Democratic Convention

By the time the 1928 campaign season began, most Democrats had coalesced behind, or resigned themselves to, one candidate as their presidential nominee. It was to be Al Smith's year. Reelected easily to a fourth two-year term as New York's governor in 1926, Smith became the most prominent Democrat in the country. One of his biggest foes in the party, ardent-Prohibitionist William Jennings Bryan, died in 1925. The last two standard-bearers of the party, James Cox and John W. Davis, had both lost their general elections in landslides and had no desire to be candidates again. Smith's main opponent in the 1924 contest, William McAdoo, announced in September 1927 that he would not seek the Democratic nomination in 1928. The downsides to Smith as the nominee had not changed since 1924—he was still a Tammany-backed New Yorker, Catholic, and anti-Prohibition in a country where most still favored the alcohol ban—but his opponents in the party failed to unite behind a single candidate. The most promising alternative was thought to be Senator Thomas Walsh of Montana, who had an anti-corruption reputation for having led the investigation into the Teapot Dome scandals, and who had presided as a dignified chairman over the undignified 1924 convention. Walsh was also Catholic and many felt that he was the only one who could take on Smith without causing a religious rift in the party. Walsh entered primaries in South Dakota, where he and Smith fought to a stalemate, and in California, where Smith beat him badly. After the California loss, which was in early May, Walsh withdrew from the contest. The field was cleared for Smith.[25]

In the weeks leading up to the convention, there was little doubt that Al Smith would emerge as the nominee, likely on the second or third ballot. There were 1,100 delegates. A two-thirds vote of 734 was needed and most conceded that Smith would have in excess of 600 on the first ballot. Still, there were some states that just could not accept, without registering their objection, the party's nominee being a cigar-chomping Tammany man, an alcohol lover, a Catholic, and one who spoke with a heavy New York City accent. These states, mostly southern, put forth favorite son candidates (including Missouri's Senator James Reed, Georgia's Senator Walter George, and Tennessee's Representative Cordell Hull), but none had any chance of winning the nomination. One ardent Smith opponent, the virulent anti-Catholic Senator Thomas Heflin of Alabama, vowed he would not even attend the convention. "If Smith is going to be nominated," Heflin told a gathering of the Ku Klux Klan, "I don't want to be there."[26]

In a surprising move, Democrats selected Houston as the host city for their convention. With a population of only 300,000 (barely one of the nation's thirty largest cities), Houston was, in the 1920s, a mostly unknown and overlooked shipping center. One local civic leader, Jesse H. Jones, dreamed of making Houston the talk of the country and almost single-handedly brought the convention to his city. A banker, businessman, builder, and owner of the city's largest newspaper, Jones was also the head of the finance committee of the Democratic National Committee. At meetings held in Washington in January 1928, Jones aggressively lobbied his DNC colleagues to bring the convention to Houston, presenting his personal check for $200,000 to the party, if they chose Houston, and making a promise to construct a new arena, built to their specifications. "Houston's hospitality will be a blank check," he told them, "You can fill it in yourself for what you want." The city's weather in June, when the convention would be held, he assured them, would be "very comfortable" with cool "gulf breezes." Houston offered the most money and was selected over five other cities (San Francisco, Detroit, Cleveland, Miami, and Chicago). Jones had not told Houston's leaders, not even the mayor, of his plan to bring the convention there until it was a done deal. For Democrats, the choice made not only financial sense, but also political sense. With Smith their likely nominee, the decision to go to Houston was a peace offering to the South, which was largely opposed to the New Yorker. It would be the first time that the party held its convention in a southern city since before the Civil War, when they had met in Charleston in 1860.[27]

Jones, with the support of thousands of Houstonians, kept his promises to the party. With a construction time of just over two months, Sam Houston Hall rose on the edge of the city's downtown. A temporary structure made mostly of yellow pine, it had 80,000 square feet of open meeting space (a third larger than the rundown Madison Square Garden, where the party had last met), seating for 16,000, an open ventilation and fan system near its three-arched roof, and state-of-the-art facilities for the press, telegraphs, telephones, and radio. "Vast and gay and graceful," a reporter for the *Washington Post* wrote of the building, marveling that it had "risen as by magic almost overnight." The arena was dedicated by former First Lady Edith Wilson the weekend before the convention opened. Houston's seventeen-story Rice Hotel (owned by Jesse Jones) was the main convention hotel. If there was one thing that Jones had misled the DNC about, it concerned the city's June weather, which was always hot and humid. During the convention, temperatures exceeded ninety degrees most days. A reporter noted that one of the first stops for arriving delegates was a haberdashery, in search of cooler clothing, where they purchased "ill-fitting, hastily-chosen seersucker suits." By the convention's end, he noted, the city's merchants will "have reclothed the Democratic party." Will Rogers, in town to write a daily newspaper column from the convention, also wrote of the hot and humid weather. "If perspiration was a marketable commodity," Rogers joked, "the party could pay off the national debt."[28]

The convention, as would have been expected, had uniquely Texas touches. For fifteen cents, visitors could view a Texas horny toad, said to have survived without water for thirty-five years in the cornerstone of a local courthouse. At a convention where Prohibition was going to be one of the key issues, the creature gave new meaning to being a "dry." For a dollar, one could purchase a less famous horny toad to take back home, complete with its own box and a red, white, and blue ribbon tied in around its neck. Texans showed off for visitors. Katie Myrl Parks, described as a "blonde Texas cowgirl beauty," clad in chaps and a ten-gallon hat, rode her horse through hotel lobbies, followed by her red-shirted Old Gray Mare Band. Horses were not the only large animals to greet folks indoors. The Texas delegates to the convention made the rounds of the hotel lobbies accompanied by their donkey, the symbol of the Democratic Party. With hotels packed (more than 25,000 guests were in Houston for the convention), the wait time for elevators was lengthy, sometimes half an hour or more. Will Rogers wrote that he and a group of ladies were invited to a breakfast on the rooftop restaurant of the Rice Hotel, but "on account of the elevator we all arrived for a lovely luncheon." One hotel guest was not so patient for a ride to the upper floors. After having to wait several minutes, he pulled out a revolver and fired several shots through an elevator door. Fortunately, the car of the elevator was elsewhere at the time.[29]

George Van Namee, a Smith aide and former clerk of the New York State Assembly, was named by Smith to oversee his campaign team at the convention. After the often-outrageous antics of Smith's Tammany supporters at the 1924 convention, the watchwords for the New Yorkers in Houston were harmony and dignity. Journalist Frank Kent of the *Baltimore Sun*, in an article headlined "Refined Tammany on Display," noted that, at past conventions, the typical Tammany delegates were "heavy, wide-walking, red-faced, pot-bellied boys . . . [who] swaggered about the lobbies, puffed on long and expensive cigars and peeled ten-dollar bills off plethoric rolls with offensive and inimitable nonchalance." With one of their own about to be nominated for president, a new and different image for Tammany was being shown in Houston. "There never was such a delegation," an amazed Kent observed, "Literally it reeks with class. It is overpoweringly overloaded with representatives of fashion, finance, literature, law and art. One of its members diverts himself by reading in the original Greek. Another wrote a satirical poem last night . . . ." As the prohibitive favorite for the nomination, Smith stayed in Albany, went about mundane gubernatorial tasks during the day, and listened in by radio at night. Katie Smith, his wife, insisted on going to the convention. She was joined in Houston by three of their five adult children.[30]

Houston, like all southern cities in that era, was racially segregated—in hotels, in restaurants, in public transportation. And in its conventions. Sam Houston Hall had a "Colored Section," which was separated from adjacent seating by chicken wire walls, where any Blacks watching the convention were required to sit. It was noted that attendance by Blacks was sparse, and who could blame them for their lack of interest. Democratic regimes throughout the South had not only imposed segregation, but had also enacted Jim Crow laws to keep most Blacks from voting. Those who did manage to cast ballots voted Republican, the party of Lincoln. There were no Black delegates to the 1924 convention, just as there had *never* been a Black delegate to *any* Democratic convention. One prominent northern Democrat vented his anger in a letter to a fellow party member: "When one reads the story of the wire cage in . . . Houston . . . it makes me feel that it is almost impossible for me to ask a Negro to vote the Democratic ticket this year." The racism against Blacks in Houston took forms that were worse than segregation. A week before the convention, newspapers reported that an injured Black man had been forcibly taken from a local hospital by a group of whites and lynched, hanged from a tree just outside the city.[31]

The convention was called to order at noon on Tuesday, June 26, by DNC Chairman Clem Shaver, who used a gavel made of hickory, from a tree that Andrew Jackson ("Old Hickory") had planted at his Hermitage home near Nashville. It was noted that 1928 was the centennial of the year that Jackson, the first Democratic president, had been elected. The gavel, described as "a small, graceful thing, but useless to quell the din," was soon discarded and replaced by a much larger mallet that could be heard when pounded. Shaver announced that his committee recommended Claude Bowers as temporary chairman, a job that came with the task of delivering the keynote speech. It was a departure from tradition. Bowers was not a politician, but a historian and an editorial writer for the *New York World*. He had come to the attention of party leaders for his fiery speech lambasting Republicans at a dinner in Washington a few months earlier. The opening midday session was short. With the Texas daytime heat, and with a much larger radio audience available in the evening, the convention adjourned for several hours, when it would hear from Bowers.[32]

Jesse Jones was not a happy man that Tuesday afternoon. A couple of hours before the convention's first evening session was to begin, a violent Texas thunderstorm roared through Houston, causing leaks in the roof of his new showcase arena. Water poured down in the section for reporters and also on the first rows of seating for delegates. With one of the major issues at the convention the division between pro-Prohibition "drys" and anti-Prohibition "wets," headline writers could not resist the humor in the situation. "Democrats Become Real Wets When Convention Roof Leaks," proclaimed the next morning's *Baltimore Sun*. Fortunately, the worst of the storm had passed by the time that Bowers, described as a "short, slim, dark, studious, scholarly, quiet man," belted out a speech that had the crowd roaring. After eight years of Republican rule and scandals, he began, "We battle for the honor of the nation besmirched and bedraggled by the most brazen and shameless carnival of corruption that ever blackened the reputation of a decent and self-respecting people." A few minutes later, discussing farm policy, he proclaimed, "Now we do not ask paternalistic privilege for the farmer, but we do demand that the hand of privilege shall be taken out of the farmers' pockets and off the farmers' throats." The words started a demonstration around the floor of the convention, led by delegates from the farm states and lasting several minutes, during which a Kansan went to the podium and pinned a Kansas sunflower on the speaker's lapel. Democrats, Bowers said, stood for "restoration of the government to the people," while continuation of Republicans in power would only add to "the fortunes they have legislated into their coffers." It was, the *New York Times* thought, "the most shrill 'keynote' ever sounded," delivered in "a delightful style of oratory which we feared had vanished." Flaying the opposition party had long been a theme of keynote speeches and, in this, most thought, Bowers succeeded. "This is not a convention," one columnist quipped, "It's an elephant roast." After the speech ended, crews of workers, carrying rolls of tarpaulins, were seen headed toward the roof of the arena. Fortunately for Jesse Jones and the Democrats, it did not rain for the rest of the convention.[33]

On the second day, Senator Joseph Robinson of Arkansas was named permanent chairman. While the most openly discussed issue between the factions of the party at the convention was Prohibition—whether one favored a "dry" or a "wet" policy on alcohol—an underlying and often unspoken division was over religion. Democrats, for the first time by any major party, were about to nominate a Catholic for president, and many of them wanted to celebrate that fact. They found an opening in Robinson's speech. "Jefferson gloried in the Virginia statute of religious liberty," the senator proclaimed, "He rejoiced in the provision of the Constitution that declares that no religious test shall ever be required as a qualification for any office of trust in the United States." The lines, which had not been in the printed version of the speech that had been circulated to reporters beforehand, set off a spontaneous demonstration from many of Smith's delegates. Most states joined in the cheering, with the notable exception of a handful of southern states, whose delegates remained quiet and seated. Interestingly, the New York delegation, under strict instructions not to make any scenes in Houston, looked on with approval, but did not participate.[34]

The nominating speeches were highlighted by Franklin Roosevelt's speech for Smith. The governor had named Roosevelt his floor manager at the convention and also chose him to place his name in nomination. It was the third time that Roosevelt had addressed a Democratic convention on behalf of Al Smith. At the 1920 convention, he had given a brief seconding speech and, in 1924, had made the rousing "Happy Warrior" speech that had become famous. Will Rogers had a lot of fun with this "three-peat" performance. Roosevelt is "a fine and wonderful man," joked Rogers, "who has devoted his life to nominating Al Smith . . . . He could have gotten far in the Democratic Party himself, but he has this act all perfected . . . just seems satisfied going through life nominating Al Smith." Roosevelt's 1928 speech matched, and perhaps exceeded, his 1924 performance. He had prepared the speech with an emphasis on a delivery style that would attract the ear more than the eye. An estimated fifteen million people would be listening to him on radios. Focusing on the personal qualities that he believed would make Smith a "great president," he stated that Smith possessed "that quality of soul which makes him a strong help to all those in sorrow or in trouble, that quality which makes him not merely admired but loved by all the people—the quality of sympathetic understanding of the human heart, of real interest in one's fellow man." The people loved Smith because "he himself has lived through the hardship, the labor and the sacrifice which must be endured by every man of heroic mold who struggles up to eminence from obscurity and low estate." Roosevelt, in his conclusion, proclaimed that Smith was not only a fighter, but a winner: "To stand upon the ramparts and die for one's principles is heroic. To sally forth to battle and win for one's principles is more than heroic. We offer one who has the will to win—who not only deserves success, but commands it. Victory is his habit—the happy warrior—Alfred E. Smith." The usual demonstration followed, but it was more subdued and shorter than at past conventions for the frontrunner. Party leaders wanted no fire sirens blaring and no comparisons to the excesses they remembered all too well from 1924.[35]

The speech was a triumph, not only for the man nominated, but also for the man who nominated him. The well-planned efforts of Roosevelt and his team to mask his disability while on the stage were successful. With leg braces on and holding on to the arm of one of his sons, he slowly maneuvered to the podium. Eight years earlier, when he had first spoken at a convention for Smith, a reporter for *TIME* wrote, he "had been crippled by, but now had almost recovered from, infantile paralysis." Roosevelt, the article continued, spoke in a reasoned voice that was "more persuasive than any Bryanesque blaring could have been." It was an effort that "all critics agreed was the most intelligently well-bred speech" delivered at either one of the major party conventions that summer.[36]

Eight other names were placed in nomination for president, all favorite sons who had no chance. Some were put forward by their state as a protest against Smith, while others were nominated as a courtesy, to recognize one of their own. The clearest example of the latter was businessman Jesse Jones, the man who had brought the convention to Houston, who was nominated by a unanimous Texas delegation.[37]

The platform was presented by Senator Key Pittman of Nevada, the chairman of the Committee on Resolutions. Most of the debate in the committee had been over how to handle Prohibition. At one extreme were the "ultra-drys," who called for endorsement of, and a vow to strictly enforce, the Eighteenth Amendment, as well as the Volstead Act, which was the federal law implementing it. At the other extreme were the "ultra-wets," who favored support for a repeal of the alcohol ban. The committee straddled the issue, as Republicans had done, and focused on enforcement of existing laws, rather than taking a position, one way or the other, on the underlying issue. It criticized Republicans, who had been in power for eight years, for having "to apologize" in their platform for their "failure to enforce laws enacted" relating to Prohibition. The Democratic convention, it said, "pledges the party and its nominees to an honest effort to enforce the eighteenth amendment and all other provisions of the federal constitution and all laws enacted pursuant thereto." (The Republicans had pledged "vigorous enforcement.") In Albany, Al Smith, listening by radio, was not happy, telling his daughter, "That isn't on the level . . . . It doesn't say anything. It only dodges and ducks." On other issues, the platform promised relief for farmers "on the basis of an economic equality of agriculture with other industries," but did not call for direct relief payments. It supported public works jobs in times of high unemployment. There was no civil rights plank, nor any reaction to the support in the Republican platform for federal anti-lynching legislation. On two key issues, the document differed from prior Democratic platforms. There was no call for the United States to join the League of Nations, which had been a priority of the past two platforms. Also, there was no blanket denunciation of protective tariffs, a longstanding Democratic issue. Rather, the party now favored tariffs "that will permit effective competition, insure against monopoly and at the same time produce a fair revenue for the support of the government." Frank Kent of the *Baltimore Sun* wrote that the Democratic platform was "ludicrously and significantly" like the Republican one. "There is," he complained, "not a single fundamental difference between them." A man who had been a key member of Woodrow Wilson's cabinet, Newton Baker, agreed. "McKinley could have run on the tariff plank," Baker said with disgust, "and Lodge on the international relations."[38]

Voting on the presidential nomination went smoothly and as expected. When all votes had been cast on the first ballot, Al Smith had 724⅔, only ten short of the two-thirds needed for the nomination. None of the other candidates received more than fifty-three votes. Before the results were finalized, a delegate from Ohio, a state which had voted for its favorite son, rose and announced his state's shift of its forty-five votes to Smith, which put the New Yorker over the top. Other states quickly jumped on the bandwagon and moved their votes to Smith. By the time the first ballot was officially recorded, Smith had 849⅔ votes and became the first Catholic in American history to have been nominated for president by a major party. A motion to make the nomination unanimous failed, as delegates from several southern states refused to join in.[39]

At the executive mansion in Albany, around midnight, Smith's eyes moistened as he heard by radio the official announcement of his nomination. "My heart," he told a small group of friends and reporters in the room, "is where my palate ought to be." Within minutes, he stepped out onto a balcony and briefly addressed a cheering crowd that had gathered. While Smith was elated at his victory, something was bothering him. On the one issue about which he felt strongest, Prohibition, the convention had not taken a stand. Its platform contained only a weak statement about making an "honest effort" to enforce existing laws. He wanted to make it clear that the convention, and the country, knew the position he would be taking on Prohibition in the coming campaign.[40]

Early the next afternoon, Senator Pat Harrison of Mississippi, who was presiding over the convention in place of Chairman Robinson, was shocked when he read a six-hundred-word telegram that Smith had sent to Robinson that morning. "My God," he muttered, "This will cause a riot." In his message, Smith accepted the nomination, but also advised, in blunt terms, what he believed should be done with respect to Prohibition:

> It is well known that I believe there should be fundamental changes in the present provisions for national prohibition. . . . While I fully appreciate that these changes can only be made by the people themselves through their elected legislative representatives, I feel it to be the duty of the chosen leader of the people to point the way which, in his opinion, leads to a sane sensible solution. . . .
> Common honesty compels us to admit that corruption of law-enforcement officials, bootlegging and lawlessness are now prevalent throughout this country. I am satisfied that without returning to the old evils that grew from the saloon . . . by the application of the Democratic principles of local self-government and States' rights, we can secure real temperance, respect for law and eradication of the existing evils.[41]

Smith was calling for repeal of the Eighteenth Amendment and for letting each state decide its own policy on alcohol, something that the convention had rejected. It was reminiscent of a telegram sent by the party's 1904 nominee, Alton Parker, shortly after his nomination, advising that year's convention that he favored the gold standard for currency, and that he intended to campaign for it, despite the silence on that issue in the party's platform. Concerned about how Smith's telegram would be received, Harrison delayed reading it from the podium until the hall was mostly empty. Importantly, Smith did not repudiate the law enforcement plank in the platform and he vowed, if elected, that he would execute and enforce all laws, "without reservation or evasion." When the telegram was read to the convention, the reaction was not the condemnation of Smith that Harrison had feared. According to the *Washington Post*, "Delegates were not outraged or even shocked . . . . Most of them had expected the nominee sooner or later to amplify his stand on prohibition in line with his previous utterances." While many ardent "drys" were outraged, they were already opposed to Smith and the telegram likely changed few opinions of him. Smith did receive credit in much of the press for his honesty.[42]

The final act of the convention was to nominate a vice-presidential candidate. It had long been rumored that Smith wanted a southerner, to provide regional balance to the ticket. Shortly after the convention began, it was decided that the man who had presided as permanent chairman, Senator Joseph Robinson of Arkansas, was the best choice. Robinson, the party's minority leader in the Senate, had drawn the attention of Smith and his team months earlier. During a Senate debate, bigoted Alabama Senator Thomas Heflin denounced the Catholic church for sending out an edict, in supposedly "secret articles," that Smith was to be president, that Catholics had pledged their allegiance "first to Romanism and second to Americanism," and that, if Heflin had his way, Smith, because of his religion, would never be nominated, much less elected president. An angry Robinson immediately took to the Senate floor and denounced Heflin. "No man who is a Democrat in the finest sense of the word," he declared, "would ever proscribe another man because of that man's religion." Although a handful of vice-presidential candidates other than Robinson were placed in nomination, some of them withdrew before the voting began. Robinson was easily nominated on the first ballot with more than a thousand votes. It was the first time since the Civil War that a candidate who lived in the South was nominated by a major party to be on its national ticket.[43]

Despite a relatively united convention, Democrats faced an uphill battle in the coming election. They were the minority party in the country. The economy was prospering under Republicans, and their nominee, Herbert Hoover, had an impressive résumé. Moreover, as the *Baltimore Sun* noted, Democrats would be facing a factor "the weight of which it is impossible to determine." The effect on the election of nominating Al Smith, a Catholic, for president, the newspaper wondered, is "the one thing uppermost in the minds of every politician."[44]

The Campaign and Election

Hoover, who was viewed as the favorite in the race, did not extensively campaign. He gave only six major speeches, calling for continuation of most of Coolidge's policies, for protective tariffs, mediation of labor disputes, cooperative marketing for farmers, and opposing government ownership of utilities. He was not a natural politician and had never before run for political office. His speeches were full of excessive details, were delivered in monotone, and with few gestures. One supporter wrote to Lou Hoover, the candidate's wife, with a suggestion. Regarding her husband's speeches, it was asked, "Could he possibly put more 'pep' in his delivery?" Prohibition became a major issue, one on which the two candidates had significant differences. It was, said Hoover, "a great social and economic experiment, noble in motive and far-reaching in purpose." He was for enforcement and argued that those who opposed it should work for repeal, rather than skirting the laws. Hoover was a Quaker and was attacked by some for that religion's pacifism. His opponent, Smith, faced far more criticism for his Catholicism, and Hoover strongly denounced, when any defamatory religious propaganda against Smith was brought to his attention, religious bigotry in any form. "There are important and vital reasons for the return of the Republican administration," he declared, "but that is not one of them."[45]

Smith campaigned much more than Hoover, traveling by train around the country and wearing his trademark brown derby. On economic issues, he was generally pro-business, certainly much more so than prior Democratic candidates, such as Bryan, Wilson, and Cox. As he had indicated in his telegram to the Democratic convention, he called for major changes to Prohibition and letting each state decide the issue. While his campaign persona came off well to crowds, it did not work on radio, which played an increased role in the 1928 election. While Hoover's voice was generally well-received over the airwaves, Smith's was not. His New York accent was difficult to understand at times, he fidgeted at the microphone, causing his voice to fade in and out, and his stage presence and gesturing, so much a part of his effectiveness when seen in person, was of no use when sitting behind a radio microphone. Smith was attacked for his association with Tammany, seen by many as the epitome of corruption, and for his opposition to Prohibition, which was still popular in much of the country. But the most bitter attacks on him, by far, were due to his religion. The Ku Klux Klan worked all across the South and the Midwest for his defeat. On a campaign trip through Oklahoma, Smith's train passed through fields with burning crosses. As Smith biographer Robert Slayton has written, Smith's campaign "got drowned in a sea of hate."[46]

On election day, the Republicans won in a landslide. In the Electoral College, the margin for Hoover was overwhelming. He carried forty states and won 444 electoral votes, with Smith winning only eight states and 87 electoral votes. Smith lost his home state of New York and carried only two northeastern states, Massachusetts and Rhode Island. His only other wins came in the South, but there, he lost four traditionally Democratic states (Texas, Florida, North Carolina, and Florida). In the popular vote, Hoover received 21,437,277 (58.2%) votes, compared to 15,007,698 (40.8%) for Smith, a margin of over six million. There were no significant vote totals for any third parties. Republicans increased their majorities in both houses of Congress, picking up more than thirty seats in the House and seven in the Senate. Most historians have attributed the loss of some states, especially those in the South, to Smith's Catholicism, but have concluded that Hoover would still have won the election, even if Smith's religion had not been a factor. Under Republican rule, the nation's economy was prospering and voters rewarded the party in power and its candidate.[47]

But the economic climate in the country would soon change and, much to the dismay of Hoover and the Republicans, change drastically.

Chapter 8

1932: Cloudy Gray Times

So long sad times
Go along bad times
We are rid of you at last.
Howdy gay times,
Cloudy gray times
You are now a thing of the past.

Happy days are here again
The skies above are clear again,
So let's sing a song of cheer again
Happy days are here again!
—**Democratic campaign song, 1932**

In his speech in August 1928 accepting the Republican nomination, Herbert Hoover spoke words that he would live to regret. "We in America today," the would-be president proclaimed, "are nearer to the final triumph over poverty than ever before in the history of any land. The poor-house is vanishing among us."[1] Eight months into his presidency, the stock market collapsed and the Great Depression began. Hoover acted more forcefully than any prior president who had been confronted with an economic downturn. He convened business leaders and convinced them to not lay off workers nor cut wages. He persuaded labor leaders to not call strikes nor make increased wage demands. But Hoover rejected calls for direct federal relief to the poor, believing that solution to be inefficient and ill-advised. Instead, he coordinated and promoted the efforts of the states and private charities to provide such relief. He cut taxes and created jobs through public works projects. Nothing, however, seemed to have any lasting positive impact. By the fall of 1930, when midterm elections were held, the unemployment rate had risen to almost ten percent, or five million people. In those elections, the Republicans lost more than fifty seats in the House and the Democrats took control of that body. Republicans also had losses in the Senate, but retained control by one vote.[2]

By the time that the 1932 campaign season began, Hoover looked hapless. None of his efforts had revived the sinking economy. Although the seeds for the calamity had been planted before he took office, it happened on his watch and most Americans held him responsible. Encampments of the homeless were called "Hoovervilles" and newspapers that the destitute pulled over their bodies at night for some warmth were dubbed "Hoover blankets." Despite this, Republican leaders were relatively united behind their president and no serious opponent rose to challenge him. To have replaced Hoover would have been an admission by the party that he had been a failure. By endorsing a "hard times" president for a second term, one commentator noted, the Republicans had to "find a goat on which to lay the burden of the depression, and he cannot be a Republican goat . . . He must be part Democrat, part cosmic."[3] Republicans were still the majority party in the country and believed they could best weather the storm with Hoover at the helm. Democrats saw their best opportunity in twenty years to reclaim the White House.

Republican Convention

The early twentieth century progressive reform of state presidential primary elections had declined in importance by 1932. Republicans held only fourteen such contests that year, all in the north and west. Almost all were merely popularity contests, with only one state requiring its delegates to the party's national convention to support the primary winner. With virtually no delegates at stake, Hoover's reelection team kept him out of most primaries, not wanting to give rank-and-file voters an opportunity to express their displeasure over his handling of the Depression. Most delegates were selected at state and local conventions, many of which were controlled by party bosses. Although never enamored with Hoover, the bosses stood by him.

The only candidate to openly challenge Hoover for the nomination and to stay in the race until the national convention, Joseph France, was never considered a serious contender. A physician, he was a former one-term senator from Maryland, losing a bid for reelection in 1922. France's voting record in Congress was erratic. He supported some conservative fiscal policies but opposed others, and was considered a liberal on free speech and foreign policy. Campaigning against Hoover in 1932, he proclaimed that the people were "thoroughly disgusted and completely despairing" of the president. France's intent was to be a conduit for Republicans opposed to Hoover, with his ultimate goal having Coolidge come out of retirement and be the nominee. Although he won several primaries in states where Hoover was not on the ballot, he only won delegates in Oregon, the sole state that bound delegates to the outcome of its primary. Any hope of France being a credible candidate was dashed in his home state of Maryland. It was one of the few primaries in which he went head-to-head with Hoover, and the president prevailed by a large margin. By the time of the convention, France's candidacy was ignored by most political observers and Hoover's renomination was considered a certainty.[4]

For the first time since 1920, Republicans returned to Chicago in 1932 for their national convention. With a population of more than three million, Chicago was then the nation's second largest city, less than half that of New York, but with a million more residents than third place Philadelphia. Centrally located and a rail hub with more than twenty railroads servicing it, the city had long been a favorite choice for conventions of all kinds. Its major hotels (the Drake, the Palmer House, the Blackstone, the Congress, and the Sherman House), struggling since the onset of the Depression, were finally full, at least for a few days. Those in town for the convention could get a preview of the upcoming 1933 Chicago World's Fair. Entitled a "Century of Progress," the fair had several structures that were already completed and could be visited. One of these, part of a section containing replicas of key structures in the life of Abraham Lincoln, included a scaled-down version of the Wigwam, the famous wooden arena in Chicago where the relatively new Republican Party held its convention in 1860, at which Lincoln emerged the unexpected winner of its presidential nomination. Although the United States was into its second decade of Prohibition in 1932, those in town for the convention and wanting a drink would not have to go far to find one. There were more than six hundred speakeasies in the downtown area. Bootleggers raised their prices and anticipated a fourfold increase in business during the week of the convention. With its tall buildings, bright lights, elevated trains, and spectacular views of Lake Michigan, the glitz of Chicago was on display for all to see. "There is something like the spirit of carnival throughout Chicago," one visitor in town for the convention noted. But the city also had its dark underside. Gang violence had been rampant for years, much of it related to the illegal alcohol trade. Those who looked could easily find abundant signs of the Depression. Soup kitchens were everywhere. Near Union Station, one of the city's main train stations, thousands of homeless people lived in crude shacks, made of scrap wood, cardboard, and tar paper. Thousands more slept on the grass in Grant Park.[5]

The 1932 Republican convention was held in a new arena, the Chicago Stadium, which had opened in 1929. Located on Madison Street, on the city's west side, it could seat more than twenty thousand and was used mainly for professional hockey and basketball games. The proceedings would be held in relative comfort for the participants. Unlike prior convention halls, the Chicago Stadium had an air conditioning system, although primitive by modern standards. The days of convention speakers shouting to be heard in cavernous arenas were over. State-of-the-art microphones and loudspeakers gave even "the feeblest human tones earth-shaking volume." The building's most interesting feature was a huge pipe organ, said to be the largest in the world, with six keyboards and more than three thousand pipes. The 1932 Republican convention was the first of a total of five presidential nominating conventions of both parties that the Chicago Stadium would host, the last being in 1944. The building continued to be the home of the Chicago Blackhawks and the Chicago Bulls until the mid-1990s, when it was torn down and a new sports arena, the United Center, was built across the street. Chicago had pledged $150,000 to the RNC for the right to host the convention and locals who made a donation of $100 were given a ticket for a mezzanine seat to all of the sessions. Low demand led to a price drop to $40 just before the convention. Most Chicagoans were not interested in, or could not afford, to watch Hoover be renominated. Millions of Americans, however, would listen in over the radio. NBC and CBS broadcast all of the proceedings, with their hosts near the podium in glass enclosed booths (to keep the surrounding noise at a minimum) and providing commentary. A generation before Walter Cronkite brought conventions to television viewers, Lowell Thomas, the "News Voice of the Air," broadcast his popular nightly radio news show from the convention.[6]

Women were present at the convention in official roles as never before. There were 92 women full delegates and 291 alternates, an increase of more than fifty from 1928. In contrast, there were fewer Black delegates, only about forty, a decline of one-third since the last convention, as "lily-white" Republicans continued to gain control of the party organization in more southern states. Only Mississippi had a majority Black delegation. Of the 1,157 delegates, around 400, almost a third, were federal officeholders. In a departure from precedent, Congress, at Hoover's request, remained in session during the week of the convention, resulting in few Republican lawmakers traveling to Chicago. The president remained in Washington and sent his personal secretary, Lawrence Richey, to oversee his team in Chicago and communicate with him by telephone.[7]

With Hoover's nomination a certainty, there was some talk of changing bottom of the ticket. Vice President Charles Curtis, from Kansas, was generally well liked in Washington and had not been an embarrassment to the administration. Like all vice presidents of the era, he had no significant role or influence over policy. Opposition to Curtis focused mainly on his age. He was seventy-three in 1932. Former Vice President Charles Dawes (who had served in the office under Coolidge) was the alternative most mentioned. Dawes was in the process of stepping down as president of the Reconstruction Finance Corporation, a federal agency Congress had created, at Hoover's request, which made loans to distressed banks. Although Dawes issued a statement a few days before the convention advising that he had no interest in being vice president again and urging his friends to not "embarrass me" by pursuing his nomination, several state delegations, including Texas, Illinois, and Iowa, announced their support. Only when Dawes, after the convention began, issued a firmer statement declaring that he would not accept a nomination, did it appear that Curtis's position on the ticket was safe.[8]

With the nation mired in the Depression, one would think that the economy would have been the focus of newspaper headlines and public discussion concerning the convention. Surprisingly, it was not. Instead, one issue—Prohibition—was the talk of Chicago. In their 1928 platform, Republicans had affirmed their support for the Eighteenth Amendment and called for its strict enforcement. In the four years since then, opposition to the national ban on alcohol had significantly grown. A *Literary Digest* poll found almost three-quarters of Americans wanted an end to Prohibition. Republicans were divided. There were three camps—one favored immediate implementation of the constitutional process for a total repeal, one demanded retention and enforcement, and a third middle position favored a national referendum on whether to retain, modify, or repeal the amendment. Hoover, who had supported Prohibition in the past, was in a quandary. Any movement away from his position would upset his "dry" supporters. It was rumored that he would disavow any plank in the party's platform for outright appeal, but the extent to which he was willing to compromise was unknown. At a meeting in Chicago the weekend before the convention, the keynote speaker at a large meeting of the Woman's National Committee for Law Enforcement had a stern warning for the president. "If President Hoover," she proclaimed, "stands firm for Prohibition, God bless him. If he wobbles, God pity him." The "wets," those seeking repeal, were the most visible and loudest in Chicago, hiring buses and trucks to go up and down Michigan Avenue, and in front of the main hotels, with loudspeakers blaring out for repeal. "Vote Wet" buttons were handed out on the streets. A "wet parade" of ships and planes was held on Lake Michigan, with a large crowd watching from the Navy Pier, as a dummy labeled "Old Man Prohibition" was dropped from a plane and symbolically drowned in the water.[9]

The convention opened on Tuesday, June 14, under the flag-draped roof of Chicago Stadium. George Washington's portrait hung above the podium. No portraits of Hoover, or of prior Republican presidents, were on display. When RNC Chairman Simeon Fess, a senator from Ohio, brought down his gavel, the galleries were only half full. Thousands of the arena's red-painted seats remained empty. When movie producers turned on the banks of floodlights near the roof to film an opening ceremony in honor of Flag Day, Fess, angered by the glare and the heat from the lights, ordered them turned off. "I'm running this show!," he yelled. He soon found out that he was not, as the lights remained on until the ceremony ended. He then introduced his committee's choice for temporary chairman, Senator Lester Dickinson of Iowa, whose nomination was approved on a voice vote.[10]

Dickinson then delivered the traditional keynote speech, drawing upon Lincoln's Gettysburg Address and comparing the nation's current "most perilous economic crisis" with the breakup of the Union that Lincoln had faced. "Three score and twelve years ago," he proclaimed, "our nation was at grips with its most perilous political crisis . . . . In that dark hour, the Republican party gave to the country its first Republican president, Abraham Lincoln." He then compared Hoover to Lincoln. "In this grave hour," he continued, "the Republican party meets in national convention to nominate another stalwart American, Herbert Hoover." This mention of Hoover's name produced some applause and cheering from the crowd, but it lasted only two minutes, far shorter than the demonstrations at prior conventions for an incumbent president and the man who was sure to be nominated again. A later reference to Hoover produced an even shorter response. Dickinson touched on themes that the party would rely on in the coming campaign, namely that Hoover did not cause the Depression and that it was international in scope. The president, he said, "had scarcely taken the oath of office before economic storm clouds had begun to cast their sinister shadow over the nations of the world." He reviewed Hoover's actions to fight the crisis and stated that all would have been much worse without his leadership. The speech was criticized by journalist Walter Lippman for its high praise of Hoover. Even Lincoln made mistakes, Lippman wrote, "but if the Senator's story is to be believed Herbert Hoover has been invincibly right from start to finish," which "is nonsense or that the office of the President of the United States is a paltry thing for one who has such cosmic genius." Prohibition, the issue that had attracted the most attention in the days before the convention, was not mentioned by Dickinson. After his speech, the traditional routine of appointing the various committees was completed and the convention adjourned for the day in the early afternoon, after a session of only two hours. Reporters were not impressed, one calling the opening day "a continual procession of dull moments" and another "a somewhat dreary event." The delegates were likely, a reporter speculated, "a little ashamed" for not having been more vocal in support of Hoover when his name had been spoken by Dickinson.[11]

The convention's second day began with receipt of the reports from the various committees. Congressman Bertrand Snell of New York was named the permanent chairman and delivered his own speech. He praised the president as a "genius" who had "met the storms of depression and weathered every gale." Snell declared that "No man living or dead has fought world-wide economic adversity with so stout a heart and so deep an understanding." In his speech, he also mentioned Hoover by name, which, unlike the previous day, ignited a demonstration of applause and cheering, as a parade of delegates marched up and down the aisles, carrying the signs of various states. A glee club from Ohio sang and bands played. It lasted seventeen minutes and it was not as spontaneous as it seemed. The evening before, Snell sent word to most of the delegations that he did not want a repeat of the "disgraceful lack of enthusiasm" for Hoover that had been shown on the opening day. When *he* mentioned Hoover's name, Snell demanded, he wanted a *real* demonstration. The delegates complied. Partway through, the permanent chairman stood at the podium, rapped his gavel a few times for order, and smiled when the delegates ignored him. Following Snell's speech, the convention adjourned until the evening.[12]

When the convention resumed for its night session, the agenda was receipt and approval of the party's proposed platform. There was only one plank in the platform that most cared about and that was the one dealing with Prohibition. The galleries filled early, with many spectators wearing "Vote Dry" badges. The delegates from the home state of Illinois left no doubt where they stood, walking onto the convention floor in unison and holding beer steins. The New York delegation marched in behind a large "We Want Repeal" banner. The organist operating the huge pipe organ in Chicago Stadium, also making his views apparent, began playing "How Dry I Am." Hoover had made it clear that he did not favor an outright repeal of the nationwide alcohol ban. His team was on edge. All week, they had been trying to work out some compromise that would avoid a fight over Prohibition going to the floor of the convention. They had failed. Now, with that moment at hand, they went from delegation to delegation demanding loyalty from the bosses and delegates who supported Hoover. "Stand by the President" was their battle cry. If the convention defied Hoover and endorsed repeal, they knew that they could lose control over the proceedings and that the president's nomination could be in jeopardy.[13]

The chairman of the Committee on Resolutions, sixty-six-year-old James R. Garfield, who had served in Theodore Roosevelt's cabinet, had followed Roosevelt to the Progressive Party in 1912 and, like Roosevelt, had then returned to the GOP. A half century earlier, in 1880,

Garfield's father, then a relatively unknown congressman from Ohio, had risen at another Republican convention in Chicago to give a presidential nominating speech for a senator from his home state. The speech was so impressive that, when that convention deadlocked, it turned to Garfield, on the thirty-sixth ballot, as its nominee. The younger Garfield would not have as successful an experience as his father in addressing a Republican convention. The platform that his committee had drafted was long, almost eight thousand words, and it took some time for him to read the entire document to the convention. Mostly, the delegates and the crowd in the packed galleries sat in silence. All were waiting to hear how the committee handled Prohibition. When Garfield said "Eighteenth Amendment," they perked up. After he read his committee's proposal, a chorus of boos filled the hall, coming mostly from the galleries. The verbose and confusing language was difficult to understand, but all knew that it did not call for repeal. A defiant Garfield stared at the delegates before him and shouted, "I take it those who sit as delegates will determine what we will do, not those in the galleries." More jeers rained down on him. Chairman Snell gaveled for order, with little success. When Garfield finished reading the entire document, Senator Hiram Bingham of Connecticut rose and announced that he and others on the committee were offering a minority report on Prohibition to the convention, one that called for its outright repeal. It was as if "thunder roared," as Bingham's words were met with cheers and shouts of approval. Two hours of debate were agreed upon, with Garfield and Secretary of the Treasury Ogden Mills arguing for the majority position of the committee, and with Bingham and Dr. Nicholas Murray Butler, the president of Columbia University, arguing for the minority. Murray, a longtime opponent of the Eighteenth Amendment, had almost been laughed out of the party's 1928 convention when he had proposed repeal at that time. What a difference four years had made. During the debate, the hall was "a madhouse." Reporters noted "[f]istfights on the floor and uproarious hoodlum demonstrations in the galleries." Garfield continued to be booed whenever he spoke, but Mills was treated with a bit more respect. The remarks of Bingham and Murray were wildly cheered. Bingham concluded by arguing that the end of Prohibition would increase grain sales and provide the government with tax revenues. "Let the people get their good beer," he declared, "It would turn the corner of the depression."[14]

Under Article V of the Constitution, any action on Prohibition would have to first be passed by two-thirds of both houses of Congress, and then ratified by three-quarters of the states, either by their state legislatures or by special conventions called for that purpose. The Prohibition plank of the majority of the platform committee called for each state to be allowed to vote, through a state convention, up or down on Prohibition, that the federal government would continue to enforce Prohibition in states that choose to keep the alcohol ban, and that it would also have a role in how alcohol was sold in states where it was reinstated. The pertinent language of the majority plank was as follows: "We therefore believe that the people should have an opportunity to pass upon a proposed amendment the provision of which, while retaining in the Federal Government power to preserve the gains already made in dealing with evils inherent in the liquor traffic, shall allow States to deal with the problem as their citizens may determine, but subject always to the power of the Federal Government to protect those states where prohibition may exist and safeguard our citizens everywhere from the return of the saloon and attendant abuses." It was clearly an attempt to straddle the issue, not wanting to totally offend those who held extreme views on both sides. The president had signed on to the language, but it was so wordy and convoluted that few understood what it really meant. Will Rogers joked that the members of the "resolutions committee just got a dictionary . . . and found all the possible phrases and words that didn't mean anything, then got 'em together and called it a resolution. Its dry in the morning and becomes wetter in the afternoon." He added that there could only be two arguments about Prohibition going forward, with "one fellow denouncing the Hoover plank and the other trying to explain it." The minority plank offered by Senator Bingham was more direct and provided that Congress shall "immediately propose an amendment to the Federal Constitution repealing the 18th Amendment thereto, to be submitted in conventions of the people of the several States called for that sole purpose."[15]

When the roll call of the states was completed, the Hoover team breathed sighs of relief. The minority repeal plank received 420 votes, but 690 votes were cast against it, and it failed. The full platform, as proposed by Garfield's committee, was then approved on a voice vote. Other than its Prohibition stand, the platform reinforced Hoover's policy of federal support for state and local governments and private charities to provide relief from the Depression, without direct federal payments to those suffering. The federal government's job was only to assist. "The people themselves," Republicans declared, "by their own courage, their own patient and resolute effort in the readjustments of their own affairs, can and will work out the cure." The heated debate and voting over the Prohibition part of the platform had lasted most of the evening, with the convention not adjourning until after midnight.[16]

The convention's third and final day started around noon with nominating speeches for president. Joseph Scott, a prominent Los Angeles attorney, placed Hoover's name before the convention. Interestingly, the speech was totally devoid of any discussion of policy. Others, said Scott, could speak of the president's actions with respect to finance, agriculture, and commerce. He wanted to talk, instead, of a man whom he called a master of "human engineering," one who "has given his life to service of his fellow-man." Scott's strategy was to personalize a president who was often viewed as aloof and unfeeling:

> I want you to think of him as I think of him in his study in the White House, in the room where Lincoln signed the Emancipation Proclamation, working through ceaseless hours over the problems that are your problems, seeking solutions that will aid mankind . . . .

For the past four years, Scott proclaimed, Hoover had stood courageously at the helm of the ship of state and guided it through turbulent waters:

> At times upon the ship's bridge he has stood alone with his thoughts—alone with his conscience. He has never lost faith. He has never relinquished his soul for the applause of the moment. He stands today serene and confident in the knowledge that he has kept the faith . . . .

To those who had called for massive intervention by the federal government to cure the Depression, Scott declared that Hoover had rightly resisted the temptation:

> He has come back to us with his shield untarnished and his head unbowed. He has taught us to strain our individual selves to the limit rather than cowardly to lie down under a paternal government because he knows that rewards come to those who bear the burden of the heat of the day....
>
> I nominate him and I give to you as your candidate our great Californian, Herbert Hoover.[17]

The demonstration following Scott's nomination speech for Hoover was a first in the history of conventions—a carefully choreographed display of bedlam, led by a "director" standing on the platform. Upon entry to the session that day, each delegate had been given a noisemaker and a small American flag. As at prior conventions, once the frontrunner's name was placed in nomination, bands played and signs designating each state and territory were pulled up and delegates paraded with them up and down the aisles, cheering and making noise. But the Hoover team had much more planned. Just as the first wave of emotion began to wane, Snell, the permanent chairman, held aloft a portrait of Hoover, whose image had not been seen before in the arena, and the noise intensified. Reporters noticed that a man standing near the podium, Charles Hutson, a California delegate from Los Angeles, was periodically holding up large pasteboard signs, each with a number written on it. The numbers designated the minutes since the start of the demonstration and were a signal for something new to begin. When Hutson held up a sign with "1" on it, a band began playing "California, Here I Come" and marched onto the convention floor, with the governor of Hoover's adopted state, James Rolph, marching at its head. Several minutes later, when Hutson displayed a "12" sign, hundreds of red, white, and blue balloons were released from fishnet baskets at the roof of the arena. It was the first significant balloon drop in convention history. When the noise began to die down again, Hutson held up another numbered sign, calling for "something fresh from his bag of tricks." Other portraits of Hoover suddenly appeared, one of the other bands in the hall started a new song, or some other preplanned effort to keep the rally going. The *New York Times* was impressed, calling Hutson a "clever Californian whose art makes up for in effectiveness what it lacks in subtlety." Two large printed banners appeared with the words "PRESS ON WITH HOOVER" and joined the parade. A few minutes later, somewhere around Hutson's "15" placard, the voice of Hoover could be heard in the hall, although few could make out his words over all the noise. Some noticed the president's talking image on white sheets that had been placed on walls at opposite ends of the arena. When Hutson held up "22," the bands stopped playing and the huge organ in the arena launched into "Onward Christian Soldiers." Five minutes later, on cue, Chairman Snell began to bang his gavel and, thirty minutes after it began, the delegates were back in their seats.

It was later revealed that the man behind it all was Louis B. Mayer (he of the second "M" in MGM Studios), a California delegate and a longtime Hoover supporter. For the first time, Mayer had brought Hollywood stagecraft and "organized pandemonium" to political conventions. Some of it worked, some not. The first video presentation of a president addressing a convention was not effective, as it was too light in the hall for Hoover's image to be clearly seen, and the crowd was too loud to hear his words. Noisemakers and flags, while given to the delegates, had not been provided to the thousands seated in the galleries and, "[u]nable to play, they sat and sulked." Cynics noted that "PRESS ON WITH HOOVER," if intended to be the slogan of the coming campaign, was "a dangerous battle cry." By adding the letters "DE" before the first word and putting an "I" after it, the slogan could easily be made to read "DEPRESSION WITH HOOVER." Still, these were problems that could and would be corrected over the years. Any television viewer who has seen the carefully staged demonstrations at modern conventions, with slick videos and thousands of falling balloons, can appreciate how far this craft has come since 1932.[18]

Amid several seconding speeches for Hoover (including some by female and Black delegates), an Oregon delegate, Lawritz Sandblast, was recognized and began a nominating speech for Hoover's only expected opponent, Dr. Joseph France, the former Maryland senator. Just as Sandblast began, however, the sound system in the arena failed. It has never been determined whether it was intentional. It was certainly timely. Sandblast continued talking and, from those who could hear him, drew some applause when he said that his nominee, as a senator, had voted against the Eighteenth Amendment. He stated that France had, at times, "been called too radical, at others too conservative," but that he was a loyal Republican who "belongs neither to the right wing of greed nor to the left wing of license." The Maryland delegation, who opposed their native son, stood as one, booed, and waved their Hoover signs. After Sandblast finished, the most dramatic moment of the convention occurred. A man was seen walking toward the center of the stage, agitated and with his arms raised. Quickly intercepted by Chairman Snell and others, it turned out that this was none other than Dr. France himself, who advised that he wanted to address the convention, to withdraw his own name and to nominate Calvin Coolidge. Hoover's team had managed to limit any references to Coolidge from the podium to a minimum, and only in passing. There were no portraits of Silent Cal in the arena and there were none of the oral tributes that a party usually made to its past presidents who had left office in good standing. Given the right circumstances, it was feared that the convention could be stampeded against Hoover and for the still-revered former president. France was not a delegate and, as such, without approval, he had no right to address the convention. Snell was determined that the Marylander would not speak, called in nearby security guards and Chicago police, and the still shouting Dr. France was led away. Humorist Will Rogers observed the scene and wrote that, by keeping Coolidge's name from going before the convention, Snell and his "strong-arm men" would likely be rewarded by Hoover and "no possible Cabinet job can ever be too high for them."[19]

After more seconding speeches, with the sound system restored, the roll call of the states began and, around 2:30 p.m., Herbert Hoover was nominated for a second term. He received 1126½ votes, with only 23½ votes scattered among others. France had only four votes. The nomination was quickly made unanimous.[20]

The convention then moved to the selection of a running mate for Hoover. Although the renomination of Vice President Charles Curtis seemed assured after Dawes issued a definitive statement that he would not accept a nomination, those opposed to him did not quietly submit to the inevitable. Perhaps their ire was more directly aimed at Hoover, whose team had successfully controlled the convention. Other than Curtis, five men—James Harbord of New York, Hanford MacNider of Iowa, Edward Martin of Pennsylvania, Alvin Fuller of Massachusetts, and J. Leonard Replogle of Florida—were formally nominated. Three of them (Harbord, MacNider, and Martin) had distinguished military records from service in the First World War. A sixth name, that of Senator Snell, the convention's permanent chairman, was placed in nomination by a Texas delegate, but Snell quickly advised that he would not consent and withdrew his name. The opposition to Curtis became more scattered when the formal roll call began and votes were cast for six additional men. When all of the states and territories had been called, Curtis had 559½ votes, less than twenty votes short of the number needed for nomination. Pennsylvania then withdrew Martin's name, switched its 75 votes to Curtis, and the incumbent vice president was declared the victor.[21]

Renomination of the same ticket was somewhat of an anomaly for Republicans. Lincoln, Grant, Benjamin Harrison, and McKinley (whose first term vice president had died in office), all had different running mates when nominated for their second terms. Only in 1912, the year of the Roosevelt defection to the Progressive Party, had a Republican president and vice president been renominated together for a second term. That election did not turn out well for President William Howard Taft and Vice President James Sherman, who finished third behind both the Democrats and the Progressives, and with Sherman dying a week before the voting. With the Great Depression ongoing and no end in sight, things did not look much better for Hoover and Curtis.[22]

Democratic Convention

The 1932 Democratic convention is one of the most written about political conventions in American history. Because of what Franklin Roosevelt and his administration became, the convention has been studied extensively and is rightly viewed as a turning point for the country. With the Depression having devastated the nation's economy since 1929, Democrats were confident that their nominee would succeed President Hoover in the White House. The convention was full of twists and turns, had colorful personalities, and more than its share of intrigue. One thing is certain—the nomination of FDR was not inevitable.

Franklin Roosevelt was one of his nation's most consequential leaders. In polls by historians ranking America's chief executives, he is usually in the top three, along with Washington and Lincoln. The only man to serve more than two terms in the presidency, he led the United States through most of the Great Depression and most of the Second World War. While his predecessor, Herbert Hoover, entered the White House with a stellar reputation, Roosevelt did not. Many questioned his intellect, his character, and believed he lacked true political convictions.

In his teens, classmates derisively referred to him, in a play on his initials, as "Feather Duster Roosevelt," someone considered a lightweight and lacking in substance. The nickname stuck well into adulthood. Once in politics, he was accused of being a flip-flopper who changed his positions when politically advantageous to do so. The often-caustic *Baltimore Sun* commentator, H. L. Mencken, wrote a month before the 1932 Democratic convention, "No one, in fact, really likes Roosevelt, not even his own ostensible friends, and no one quite trusts him. He is a pleasant enough fellow, but . . . [lacks] visible conscience." Walter Lippman, one of the most influential journalists of the era, also wrote of Roosevelt on the eve of the 1932 convention, that he "is a highly impressionable person, without a firm grasp of public affairs, and without very strong convictions . . . . He is a pleasant man who, without any important qualifications for the office, would very much like to be President."[23]

Born in 1882 into a New York family of wealth and privilege, young Franklin grew up in a mansion at Hyde Park, along the Hudson River. The only child of an older father and a domineering mother, he was educated at home by tutors until his teens, when he was sent to the Groton School, a prestigious academy in Massachusetts. College at Harvard followed, where he was a "C" student and was viewed by professors and classmates as "pleasant, energetic, and ambitious but also lacking in depth and strength of character." He then attended law school at Columbia University, where he was again an average student. He practiced law for a while in New York City, but always had an eye on politics and, in 1910, ran as a Democrat and won a seat in the state senate from the Hyde Park district. In Albany, he sided with reformists who opposed Tammany Hall, the powerful New York City organization that controlled much of the Democratic politics in the state.[24]

In 1905, he married a distant cousin, Eleanor Roosevelt, whom he had known since childhood. Eleanor's uncle, Theodore, then president of the United States, was also Franklin's fifth cousin. Eleanor's branch of the Roosevelt family, from New York City and Long Island, were Republicans, while Franklin's branch, from the Hudson Valley, were Democrats. The couple had six children, five surviving to adulthood. The marriage was rocked in 1918 when Eleanor discovered that Franklin was having an affair with her former secretary, Lucy Mercer. Upon his promise to end all contact with his paramour, Eleanor stayed in the marriage, but it was thereafter "more of a political partnership." Franklin had high goals and publicly-exposed infidelity and divorce in that era would have been a death knell to a political career.[25]

Roosevelt was an early supporter of Woodrow Wilson in the 1912 election, campaigned for him, and was rewarded with a job in Wilson's administration as assistant secretary of the Navy. He became a strong proponent of Wilson's internationalist views. Seen as a rising star in the progressive wing of the party, he was placed on the national ticket for vice president in 1920, paired with the governor of Ohio, James Cox. They lost in a landslide to the Republican ticket of Warren Harding and Calvin Coolidge. Despite the loss, Roosevelt was in position to make a run for the party's presidential nomination in four or eight years. Then, tragedy struck. In 1921, he contracted polio and lost the use of both of his legs. Years of rehabilitation followed, with Eleanor loyally by his side, and politics were mostly put on hold. He found that therapy in heated pools at a spa in Warm Springs, Georgia, helped his condition, so much so that he purchased the facility. Despite this, his legs never regained any strength and he used a wheelchair for the rest of his life. Due to the prejudices in that era toward those with disabilities, Roosevelt, with dedication and strenuous physical effort, sought to appear in public as having overcome his disease. With heavy metal braces on his legs, he could stand, and with someone by his side supporting him, could swing his hips and give the illusion of walking for a few steps. Using his braces, he gave speeches at the 1924 and 1928 Democratic conventions, both nominating a fellow New Yorker, Governor Al Smith, for the presidency. When Smith vacated the governorship of the Empire State in 1928, FDR ran for that office, with Smith's encouragement, and won narrowly. Two years later, he was reelected in a landslide, with a margin of 725,000 votes. After years of delay due to his health, as 1931 began, Roosevelt was ready to pursue the presidency.[26]

Roosevelt named two men, James Farley and Louis Howe, to lead his campaign for the 1932 Democratic nomination. Their strategy focused on the South and the West. Farley, in his early forties, was chairman of the New York Democratic Party and had headed the 1930 gubernatorial campaign. Born in the Hudson Valley area, he was a part owner of a building materials company and over the years had worked his way up in the ranks of the party. An outgoing and amiable man, Farley made a cross-country trek in mid-1931, visiting eighteen states and meeting with state and local Democratic officials to sell them on Roosevelt. The trip was very successful. Howe, then almost sixty years old, had been working for Roosevelt as his top aide for almost twenty years. A former reporter, Howe's personality contrasted sharply with that of the gregarious Farley. Small in size and often in poor health, Howe was a gruff man whose talents were in planning and organization and, if need be, threats. Farley and Howe opened a Roosevelt campaign office on Madison Avenue in New York City, from which they made thousands of phone calls and sent thousands of letters to important Democrats across the country. Their work throughout 1931 was successful and, by the time the official campaign season began in early 1932, Roosevelt was touted in the press as the favorite for the nomination. But frontrunner status did not mean that other Democrats were ready to accept defeat and various factions in the party, acting independently, became a "Stop Roosevelt" movement. During this era, Mencken wrote that the Democratic Party "is no party at all, but simply an illogical and uncomfortable compound of irreconcilable factions [among whom] . . . there is no more possibility of peace than there is between cats and rats." This had been evident at the party's marathon convention in 1924 and was again on display in the candidates who rose to try to deny Roosevelt the 1932 nomination.[27]

The Democratic urban north, with its base of recent immigrants, largely Catholic, and controlled mostly by party bosses in large cities, lined up behind Al Smith. Although Smith had vowed that he was through with politics after his 1928 loss to Hoover, friction that later developed with Roosevelt led him to reconsider. Smith thought that Roosevelt was ungrateful and disrespectful to him, as he was the one who had given FDR national prominence. He had chosen Roosevelt to give his nominating speeches at the 1924 and 1928 conventions, and had encouraged Roosevelt to make the 1928 run for governor. Once in office, however, Roosevelt did not call on Smith for advice on policy or appointments. Feeling slighted, Smith entered the 1932 contest, likely initially only to stop Roosevelt, but then convinced himself that he could again win the nomination. As the party's last presidential nominee and still its titular leader, Smith announced that would not personally campaign in 1932, but made it known that he wanted the nomination and felt that he deserved it. Smith could count on most of the large New York delegation, keeping it from Roosevelt.[28]

The party's Jeffersonian conservative faction was represented in the 1932 contest by Albert Ritchie of Maryland. In his fourth term as governor of the Old Line State, Ritchie was a pro-business Democrat with a record of making government more efficient and accountable, reducing taxes, and improving education and public health. He was against Prohibition, which was a popular position to have in the northeast. Called "the handsomest man in American public life," Ritchie entered the 1932 race as a favorite son candidate of Maryland but, if the convention deadlocked, many political observers saw him as a man the party could turn to and unite behind.[29]

The Wilson internationalist faction of the party favored Newton Baker in 1932. Baker, a former progressive mayor of Cleveland, had served in President Wilson's cabinet as secretary of war during World War I. After Wilson left office, he developed a lucrative law practice in Cleveland and was viewed by Democratic liberals and intellectuals as Wilson's political heir. He gave a moving speech honoring Wilson at the 1924 convention. Baker's strategy in 1932 was to work behind the scenes and not be an active candidate, but as one to whom the convention would turn in the event of a deadlock. His supporters did not enter him in any primaries. Roosevelt, who had also served under Wilson, admired Baker's intellect and wrote a friend that Baker would likely be a better president than he, but he did not think Baker could win the election because, as a corporate lawyer and one closely tied to the British during his years as secretary of war, he would be opposed by organized labor, as well as by German and Irish Americans.[30]

The Democrats of the southwest were represented in the 1932 race by sixty-three-year-old John Nance Garner. "Cactus Jack," as he was known in his home state of Texas, was a crusty self-made man with white hair and a ruddy complexion who enjoyed smoking cigars, playing cards, and drinking whiskey. He was also intelligent, shrewd, and competitive. A thirty-year member of Congress who had just become speaker of the House in late 1931, Garner was seriously considered as a nominee for president only after publisher William Randolph Hearst pushed him into the race. Hearst, then almost seventy, was a liberal who had briefly served in Congress with Garner, and had run for president himself earlier in life. He became more conservative as he aged and became a bitter foe of President Wilson and his internationalist agenda during and after World War I, including Wilson's defeated plan for the United States to enter the League of Nations. When Hearst surveyed the field of potential nominees for 1932, he decided upon Garner, who shared his isolationist views. In a nationwide radio address in January, Hearst threw his support to Garner. The other potential nominees, he said, were all "internationalists," disciples of Wilson "fatuously following his visionary policies of intermeddling in European conflicts and complications." With a nationwide chain of newspapers, radio stations, and magazines, Hearst's endorsement made Garner a contender. Garner did not know of Hearst's intentions in advance of the radio address and was surprised by it. He did not actively enter the nomination contest, but did not prevent Hearst and others from promoting him. Texans lined up behind Garner and Hearst set up a campaign organization for Garner in his own state of California.[31]

In addition to Roosevelt, Smith, Baker, Ritchie, and Garner, there were several others in the race, who were favorite son candidates with the support of their home state delegations. They had little or no hope of winning the nomination, but their presence in the contest could help to keep Roosevelt from gaining the two-thirds vote needed for victory. One of these was William Murray, the governor of Oklahoma. Known as "Alfalfa Bill" (for being one of the first to grow the crop in his state), Murray was a colorful, plain-spoken, and openly racist politician who fancied himself as a champion of the downtrodden, especially farmers suffering from the Depression. Other favorite sons were former Governor Harry Byrd of Virginia, former Senator James Reed of Missouri, George White of Ohio, and banker Melvin Traylor of Illinois.[32]

Democrats held primaries in fifteen states in 1932, in all regions of the country. Neither Roosevelt nor Smith, or most of the other contenders, personally campaigned in these elections. The only candidate to actively campaign in multiple states was Murray. His biggest head-to-head contest with Roosevelt was in North Dakota, which Roosevelt won handily. Other than in Ohio (a state that did not bind its delegates to its primary winner and where Roosevelt was not on the ballot), Murray did not win any primaries, although he did obtain the delegates from his home state of Oklahoma, who were chosen at a convention. Four primary states—New Hampshire, Wisconsin, Massachusetts, and California—attracted the most attention. In early March, Roosevelt won New Hampshire over Smith with more than sixty percent of the vote. In April, he again beat Smith in Wisconsin. A couple of weeks later, Smith rebounded with a resounding win in Massachusetts, getting more than seventy percent of the vote. Garner stayed out of the primaries, except in California, where he had the support of Hearst and of William McAdoo, a Californian who had been prominent figure in the Wilson administration. McAdoo had also been a major contender for the party's 1924 nomination. In a three-way race, Garner beat both Roosevelt and Smith in the Golden State's primary. Combined with delegates from his home state of Texas, who were selected at a convention, the California win made Garner a force to be dealt with. Roosevelt, however, was the clear winner of the primaries. He won eleven of the thirteen contests that he entered, with victories in all regions of the country, and got almost forty-five percent of the overall primary vote.[33]

But primaries were only part of the hunt for delegates. Most states still selected delegates at state conventions, often controlled by party bosses. Smith had the support of Tammany's boss, John Curry, who could bring the majority of the New York delegation with him, and of Mayor Frank Hague of Jersey City. Two-thirds of the 1,154 delegates, or 770, were needed for the nomination. By the time all were selected, the Roosevelt camp claimed 588 delegates, a majority, but well short of two-thirds. Smith was second with 94 and Garner third with 90. A handful of favorite sons trailed behind, each with fewer than sixty delegates. There were about two hundred uncommitted delegates, almost half of whom were from New York, and it was believed that most of them would end up in Smith's column. The strategy of the "Stop Roosevelt" forces was to keep all candidates in the race for several ballots, prevent Roosevelt from reaching two-thirds, and hope that the convention would then deadlock and move to an alternative nominee. It had been done before. At seven prior Democratic conventions, the leader on the first ballot had failed to win the nomination. Of the first ballot leaders who had won, only two of them (Buchanan in 1856 and Douglas in 1860) had survived if the voting extended past four ballots.[34]

The convention began on Monday, June 27, in Chicago, at Chicago Stadium, which had been vacated a week earlier by Republicans, who had renominated President Hoover under its roof. In the interim, microphones and speakers in the arena had been upgraded after complaints of spotty radio reception at the prior convention. In keeping with tradition, Roosevelt, as the frontrunner, remained in Albany, at the governor's mansion, but was in constant contact by a direct phone line to Louis Howe's suite at the Congress Hotel. At times, undecided delegates, or Roosevelt delegates who were suspected of wavering, were brought into the suite for a telephonic pep talk from the candidate. Speaker Garner stayed in Washington and monitored events from his office in the Capitol. Newton Baker, officially a non-candidate, was in Cleveland. Otherwise, most of the candidates were on the scene in Chicago. Smith arrived days before the convention and held a much-publicized meeting with his old rival McAdoo, a Garner supporter. The two had battled for the presidential nomination at the 1924 convention. McAdoo blamed Smith for his defeat. Now, they were allies in stopping Roosevelt. Although they smiled and shook hands after their meeting, they made no comments and few believed that the rift between them had been healed. Mayor Anton Cermak of the host city of Chicago arranged a huge welcoming parade for Governor Ritchie of Maryland, with a hundred thousand people lining the streets from the train station to the governor's hotel. Cermak was officially supporting a favorite-son candidate, Traylor, from Illinois, but was really for Smith. The mayor knew that enthusiasm on the streets of Chicago for Ritchie or, for that matter, anyone other than Roosevelt, aided Smith's cause.[35]

In the lead-up to the convention, two matters—the choice of a permanent chairman and whether to abolish the longstanding two-thirds rule for nomination—were poorly handled by the Roosevelt team. As discussed below, their actions on these opened them up to charges of duplicity and unfairness, and emboldened the opposition.

Other than the choices for president and vice president, the selection of a permanent chairman is one of the most important decisions made by a convention. In a disputed contest, the rulings of the chairman can determine the outcome. The election of Elihu Root, a Taft supporter, as permanent chairman of the 1912 Republican convention doomed any chance that Theodore Roosevelt had of winning the nomination that year and led to his bolt from the party. At an April 1932 meeting of the DNC's arrangements committee in Chicago, an agreement was thought to have been reached concerning the permanent chairman. The party's chairman, John Raskob, favored his right-hand man, Jouett Shouse, for the position. Shouse headed the DNC's executive committee and, like Raskob, had been a prior supporter of Al Smith. As party officials, both were now supposed to be neutral as to a nominee. After negotiations, with Roosevelt participating by phone and tweaking the final language, the committee agreed in writing to "commend" Shouse for permanent chairman. A few weeks later, Farley issued a statement that Roosevelt would be supporting Senator Thomas Walsh of Montana for the position. Walsh, in his early seventies, was a respected figure in the Senate, having led the investigation into the Teapot Dome scandal under President Harding. He also had experience in the role, having served as permanent chairman of the 1924 convention. The opposition cried foul and alleged that Roosevelt had broken a promise to back Shouse. It was an example of alleged deception that would be charged against Roosevelt throughout his career. The Roosevelt team responded that the governor had agreed only to "commend" Shouse (meaning, they said, that he was qualified) for the position, not to "recommend" him (meaning that Shouse had Roosevelt's full support). After the April meeting, they had received word that Shouse had encouraged some states to send uncommitted delegations to Chicago, which they felt violated his neutrality as a DNC official. The Roosevelt team was concerned that Shouse's rulings would not be favorable to them if he wielded the gavel at the convention and decided to support Walsh. The issue would be taken before the full convention and the outcome would be an early test of the strength of both Roosevelt and his opposition.[36]

The Democratic Party's two-thirds rule for nominations had been in existence for a full century, ever since its first convention in 1832, when President Andrew Jackson had it imposed. Jackson wanted a new vice president for his second term, replacing John Calhoun with Martin Van Buren. He believed that a win for Van Buren by a two-thirds vote at the convention would be more impressive and make voters more accepting of the change. Over the years, many saw the rule as an undemocratic albatross around the party's neck, but prior attempts to do away with it had gone nowhere. In practice, the rule gave the southern states, which had just over one-third of the overall delegates, a veto over the party's nominations. As recently as 1924, the rule had led to disaster, with the 103-ballot debacle at Madison Square Garden. At a strategy meeting in early June, Roosevelt and his team agreed to try to abolish the rule, but did not want it known until after the convention began, so that opponents would be taken by surprise and not have time to organize. A change to a majority vote rule would lower by almost two hundred, from 770 to 578, the number of delegates needed to win the nomination. Roosevelt supporters would control the Committee on Rules and getting rid of the two-thirds rule would require a majority vote by that committee and by the full convention. But trying to change the rule was risky. Much of Roosevelt's support came from the South, the region where the rule had its strongest proponents. At a meeting the Thursday night before the convention began, a group of sixty-five key Roosevelt supporters voted unanimously to do away with the rule. They issued a statement pledging "to do all within our power to bring about the abolition of the two-thirds rule and the adoption of the majority rule for this Democratic convention." This was a few days before Roosevelt's top advisors had wanted it known. It set off a firestorm of criticism and gave the "Stop Roosevelt" movement a new rallying cry. It was, Al Smith charged, an "eleventh-hour, unsportsmanlike attempt to change the rules after the game has been started." The party's 1924 nominee, John W. Davis, and its 1920 nominee, James Cox, denounced any rule change. Within a couple of days, more than a hundred Roosevelt delegates publicly disagreed with their candidate, with more likely to do so. Stung by the strong reaction, Roosevelt retreated. He issued a statement advising that, since the delegates had been selected before the proposed rule change was announced, "I decline to permit either myself or my friends to be open to the accusation of poor sportsmanship" and "I am accordingly asking my friends in Chicago to cease their activities to secure the adoption of the majority nominating rule." He added, however, that he hoped something could be done "to insure against the catastrophe of a deadlock or prolonged balloting." The Committee on Rules then adopted a proposal that the two-thirds rule be in effect for the first six ballots and, if there was no winner by then, a majority vote would suffice. When news of this leaked out, there was renewed outrage and Roosevelt caved again and persuaded the committee chairman to drop any change to the two-thirds rule in 1932, but with a suggestion that it be reviewed in 1936. The whole episode played into the hands of Roosevelt's opponents, who argued that he was not to be trusted. Later, a top advisor to Roosevelt wrote that trying to change the two-thirds rule was "the major mistake" made at the convention.[37]

Roosevelt's health and stamina had been whispered about since he announced for the nomination in early 1931. His campaign tried to put concerns over this to rest with a favorable article published in *Liberty* magazine in July of that year. A writer from the magazine followed Roosevelt around for days as he performed his job as New York's governor, and interviewed more than forty of Roosevelt's associates, as well as his doctors. Roosevelt's medical team gave him a clean bill of health, which included an exaggeration of his ability to "maintain a standing position without fatigue" and a falsehood that his legs were "getting stronger." The author of the *Liberty* article concluded, based on his personal observations and interviews, that Roosevelt "seemed able to take more punishment than many men ten years younger. Merely his legs are not much good to him." That was the general public impression—that Roosevelt had had a bout with polio and lost some, but not all, use of his legs. It was not known that he used a wheelchair to get around and it was made known to the press by Roosevelt's staff that photographs of him in a wheelchair were not to be taken. In that era, there was a belief that a physical disability was associated with a mental disability. Some speculated that Roosevelt suffered not from polio, but from syphilis, which could have a mental component. As the convention neared, what had been whispered was spoken openly. Mayor Frank Hague of Jersey City, one of Al Smith's key supporters, was the bluntest, stating that Roosevelt "is crippled both mentally and physically." Smith himself wrote on the eve of the convention, without mentioning Roosevelt by name, that leading a nationwide campaign for president, lasting four months, "requires a man of great vigor and bodily strength . . . to make no mention whatever of the tax he has to put upon his mental qualities." Despite these attacks, there is no evidence that the open talk in Chicago of Roosevelt's polio changed any minds on his fitness to be president and his health was not a factor at the convention.[38]

The convention opened almost an hour late, at 12:50 p.m. on Monday, June 27, with DNC Chairman Raskob presiding. The galleries, which had been almost empty, quickly filled once the gavel was pounded. A reporter noted that many had been in speakeasies surrounding the arena, sipping beer and munching on meatball sandwiches. They listened by radio until hearing that the convention was about to start and then headed to their seats. The opening prayer was given by Commander Evangeline Booth of the Salvation Army, the first time that a woman led a convention of either major party in its religious ritual. There followed a speech from Raskob, a welcoming speech from Chicago Mayor Anton Cermak, and a reading of Thomas Jefferson's first inaugural address. Raskob then introduced his committee's choice of Senator Alben Barkley of Kentucky as temporary chairman, which was quickly approved on a voice vote. Barkley, dressed in a white linen suit, then performed the primary job of the temporary presiding officer—delivering the keynote speech. The speech was long, lasting two hours, and was mainly an attack on Republicans, accompanied by waved arms and pounded fists. The loudest response from the crowd came when Barkley, formerly a Prohibition proponent, called for repeal of the Eighteenth Amendment. For seven minutes, delegates paraded up and down the aisles and the galleries cheered. Other than being criticized for its length, the speech was generally well-received. Humorist Will Rogers, at the convention as a reporter, said of Barkley's keynote, "This was no note. This was in three volumes." Still, he said, it had to be long, because with Republicans in charge for twelve years, "when you jot down our ills you got to have a lot of paper." He noted that, despite all the pre-convention talk in the press of a "gigantic struggle" over the nomination, the proceedings began with seeming unity and lack of controversy. They "met, talked, agreed and adjourned," acting too much, he thought, like Republicans. "Cheered everything; hissed nothing—why it almost made me," lamented Rogers, "ashamed I was a Democrat."[39]

Rogers would not have to wait long for things to change. In his column reviewing the convention's next day, Tuesday, June 28, he gleefully noted, "Ah! They was Democrats today, and we was all proud of 'em. They fought, they fit, they split, and adjourned in a dandy wave of dissension." The second day's proceedings began with the report of the Committee on Credentials and the main contest was over Louisiana, which had three competing delegate slates. In the days since his arrival in Chicago, newspapers had been full of articles about the antics of Senator Huey "The Kingfish" Long of Louisiana. Long was a populist whose slogans were "Share Our Wealth" and "Every Man a King." Not yet forty, he was by 1932 the virtual dictator of Louisiana, known for doling out benefits to the poor, but also for enriching himself, and stifling his opposition, in the process. As governor in 1930, he ran and won a seat in the Senate, but refused to resign as governor and kept his federal legislative seat vacant until his term as the state's chief executive expired in early 1932. He then had a crony succeed him as governor. Long was backing Roosevelt, although he had told a fellow senator and FDR supporter, "I don't like your son of a bitch." A flamboyant dresser, Long arrived in Chicago with new double-breasted suits, flashy ties, and two-toned shoes. He headed a slate of pro-Roosevelt Louisiana delegates selected by the party's state central committee, which he controlled. Long was opposed by a delegation led by a former governor, Jared Sanders, which had been chosen at a state convention (the traditional method used in that state). There was also a third slate of Louisiana delegates, headed by a former lieutenant governor, Fernand Mouton. Long was behind this third group, which had made ridiculous claims and were considered a joke (pledging, among other things, to move the nation's capital to a small Louisiana town), apparently thinking his group had a better chance if there was a more outlandish slate of delegates in the contest. Farley and the rest of the Roosevelt team were wary of Long and found him hard to control. It was Long who had led the move for abolition of the two-thirds rule at the meeting a few days before the convention, publicizing the issue before Roosevelt's men had intended. But, if seated, Long would have Louisiana's twenty delegate votes in his pocket, and Roosevelt's team had to strongly support his delegate slate. They needed him on the convention floor.

At a meeting before the DNC addressing the competing Louisiana delegations, the Kingfish "screeched himself into a frenzy that left him with popping eyes and a frothing mouth." With the backing of pro-Roosevelt members on the committee, Long won that battle, as he did a later hearing before the Committee on Credentials, where he put on a similar, but slightly less boisterous, show. When the fight went before the full convention, Farley and the Roosevelt team had to be concerned and worried as Long strode to the podium to argue his case. Surprisingly, Long presented a logical argument, even reading from Louisiana law books at times. After being jeered at the start of his remarks, he managed to win over the crowd, both among delegates and those in the galleries. By a vote of 638 to 514, the convention voted to seat Long's slate of delegates. Another delegate dispute involving Minnesota was then taken before the full convention and pro-Roosevelt delegates from that state were also seated by a margin similar to that of the Louisiana contest. With these two victories, the Roosevelt team solidified forty-four delegate votes that they had been counting on, and sorely needed.[40]

One interesting disputed delegate contest before the credentials committee was not challenged before the full convention. The committee voted to seat six pro-Roosevelt delegates from Puerto Rico. Among these was one with the curious name of Alcalde Jaime Miguel Curleo. It turned out that Alcalde (the Spanish word for mayor) was none other than James Michael Curley, the mayor of Boston. Curley, like Long, was one of the many colorful (and corrupt) Democratic politicians of the era. Early in his political career, while serving a jail sentence for having taken a civil service examination for a constituent, he won election as an alderman, running on a slogan of "He Did It For a Friend." As mayor, Curley was "as crooked as a pretzel," taking kickbacks from companies that he awarded city contracts to, including having them build, at virtually no cost to him, a twenty-one-room mansion. An Irish Catholic who had been an early supporter of Roosevelt, Curley had been denied a seat in the Massachusetts delegation over what other Boston Democrats viewed as his betrayal of Al Smith, a fellow Irish Catholic. Not to be denied a role at the convention, Curley showed up in Chicago and, reportedly after several drinks, got a Puerto Rican delegate to agree to hand over his credentials. During the convention, he grinned and "did a small jigstep" whenever he walked by the glowering Massachusetts delegation.[41]

The convention next took up the dispute over permanent chairman, with Roosevelt supporting Senator Thomas Walsh of Montana and the "Stop Roosevelt" forces lining up behind Jouett

Shouse, a DNC official. Walsh had won the vote before the Roosevelt-controlled Committee on Permanent Organization by a three-to-one margin. The speakers on behalf of Shouse accused Roosevelt of "bad faith" after having agreed to "commend" Shouse for the job at a meeting in April. Roosevelt's men argued that a commendation was not a commitment, meant nothing, and that the overwhelming vote of the Committee on Permanent Organization should control. In what was the second key test vote of the day, Roosevelt won by a vote of 626 to 528 and Walsh became the permanent chairman. Similar to the earlier Louisiana and Minnesota credentials battles, the vote showed that Roosevelt could muster a majority of the delegates, but that he was well short of the 770 votes required to win the nomination. Still, it was a win and FDR's chosen man would be the presiding officer. As one author has noted of the dumping of Shouse for Walsh, "It may have been bad faith, but it was good politics." With the nomination in doubt, the Roosevelt team could not risk having someone hostile wielding the gavel.[42]

The first agenda item on the convention's third day, Wednesday, June 29, was to receive the proposed platform. At the time the afternoon session began, however, the committee was still meeting, with heated arguments over the Prohibition and farm policy planks. Instead of the platform, the delegates and those in the galleries were presented with what amounted to an impromptu vaudeville show. Chairman Walsh introduced Eddie Dowling, a "song and dance man" who was active in the party and who served as emcee. Dowling introduced well known radio personalities, a glee club, boxer Gene Tunney, and famed trial attorney Clarence Darrow (who joked that, as a lawyer, he "usually got a fee" before speaking). The highlight of the performers was Will Rogers, who was at the convention to write a daily column for a syndicated newspaper chain. One of Rogers' best-known lines was "I don't belong to any organized political party. I'm a Democrat." He did not disappoint the crowd at Chicago Stadium, putting in "a good word" for each of the major candidates and predicting that, before long, the delegates could probably move forward with approval of the platform. "As soon as enough members of the committee get sober," he joked, "we will probably hear the Prohibition plank." With the nation having been in the Depression for three years, Rogers told the delegates to not worry about nominating one of the weaker candidates to run against Hoover, because, "If he lives until November, he'll be in." After a couple of hours and having run out of acts, the show ended and the convention adjourned until the evening.[43]

While the first couple of days of the convention played out in Chicago Stadium, the Roosevelt team was desperately trying to round up additional votes. Farley was pressing flesh and Howe, confined to his hotel rooms with asthma attacks (while still chain smoking), was making calls and consulting with FDR on all developments. As at many conventions, the vice-presidential slot on the ticket was used for horse trading. In exchange for their state's votes, Farley offered the spot to two favorite son candidates, Byrd of Virginia and Ritchie of Maryland. Both declined. Ritchie still held out hope that he could be a compromise nominee, thinking that Smith would drop out after a couple of ballots and then support him. Meanwhile, in Washington, two pro-FDR senators, Harry Hawes of Missouri and Key Pittman of Nevada, thought that offering the vice-presidential position to Speaker Garner, in exchange for his

Texas and California delegates, was the best path forward. They called Roosevelt on Monday night, got his consent, and he told them to reach out to Farley, which they did. Hawes also immediately sent telegrams to hundreds of key Democrats urging a Roosevelt-Garner ticket. Early the next morning, an angry Garner telephoned Hawes and gave him a tongue-lashing, saying that he was committed to the race for the top spot on the ticket and had not authorized anyone to consider him for the bottom.

Late on Tuesday evening, Farley met in his room at the Congress Hotel with Congressman Sam Rayburn of Texas, Garner's campaign manager. The New Yorker argued that FDR, with the clear majority of the delegates, deserved the nomination and pledged to do what he could, if Rayburn helped, to put Garner on the ticket. The Texan was non-committal, but stated that he and Garner "don't intend to make it another Madison Square Garden," a reference to the 1924 deadlocked convention. They agreed to speak again and a second meeting was set for Thursday night. Farley made a firm offer for vice president and proposed that Texas vote for Garner on the first ballot, and then switch to Roosevelt before the votes were tallied at the end of that ballot. Rayburn declined, advising that the Texas delegates had come a long way to Chicago, at great expense to them, and they deserved to see if Garner could pick up more support after the initial ballot. The were a *lot* of Texans in Chicago. Following a common practice, that state had more people acting as delegates than it had delegate votes, with each person casting only a partial vote. That is why many of the vote totals cast at conventions of the era are in fractions. It was a way to reward more party activists and let them participate in the process. In 1932, Texas had four bodies for each of its forty-six delegate votes, meaning that each person cast only one-quarter of a vote. Additional Texans were present as alternate delegates. Rayburn asked Farley how long he could hold FDR's delegates in line. "Three ballots," Farley replied, "four ballots, and maybe five." Rayburn was again vague, saying that they needed to "let the convention go on for a while" and see what happened.[44]

Getting more votes for FDR would be of no help if he could not hold on to those he already had. The campaigns of the other candidates were constantly probing, trying to peel off some of the frontrunner's delegates. Mississippi was a prime target. The Magnolia State, along with several others, voted under the unit rule, with all of its twenty votes going to the candidate favored by a majority of the delegation. Roosevelt held Mississippi by a hair's breadth, with 10½ votes. A single vote could flip the state. Senator Pat Harrison, the FDR leader in Mississippi, was under constant pressure. A breaking away from Roosevelt by Mississippi could lead to defections in other states, including Alabama, Arkansas, Iowa, Maine, and Michigan, and a collapse of the coalition that the Roosevelt team had worked so hard to assemble over the past year and a half.[45]

By the time of the evening session on June 29, the platform was ready. The galleries were full, but many who had paid for tickets stood outside and fumed, unable to get in. Their seats had been taken by thousands of Mayor Cermak's supporters, who had been let in by showing fake copies of "courtesy cards" issued by the mayor. Cermak's goal was to pack the arena for Al Smith, whom he was unofficially supporting, and drown out the Roosevelt supporters in the crowd. The platform was read by Senator Gilbert Hitchcock of Nebraska, the head of the

Committee on Resolutions. Only two thousand words, it was short for platforms of that era, and only a quarter of the length of the Republican platform that had been read from the same podium a couple of weeks earlier. Although its introduction decried the "unprecedented economic and social distress" caused by the Depression and pledged "a drastic change in economic governmental policies," the platform was actually fairly conservative, especially when compared to policies that would later be enacted under FDR's administration. As one author has commented, "On the whole, there was little in the platform that had not appeared in previous Democratic platforms." It called for a balanced federal budget and a twenty-five percent reduction in federal expenditures, as well as "a competitive tariff for revenue," a longstanding Democratic issue. The platform advocated unemployment relief and old-age insurance, but under state law, not federal law. It favored the "removal of government from all fields of private enterprise except where necessary to develop public works and natural resources." The crowd sat mostly in silence as the platform was read, with only occasional applause. As at the Republican convention, it was the proposed plank on one issue—Prohibition—that all eagerly waited to hear.[46]

Roosevelt's position on Prohibition since its enactment in 1920 mirrored that of much of the country. He had started out as a strong "dry" favoring the alcohol ban, but gradually moved to what was referred to as a "moist" stance, between the extremes. His attempt to straddle the issue put him at odds with fellow New Yorker Al Smith, the most prominent "wet" politician in the country, who had for years been calling for the immediate repeal of the Eighteenth Amendment and for soft enforcement of existing laws on alcohol. Eventually, FDR came out for a nationwide referendum that would give states the option of having alcohol or not. As he moved more to the "wet" position, however, he risked alienating his base of support for the 1932 presidential nomination in the South and West, where Prohibition still remained popular. The fact that Smith emerged as his main opponent for the nomination made him look even more like a fence-sitter. By the time of the convention, most felt that the Democratic Party would take one of three options: the platform could declare that the party favored full repeal and support a constitutional amendment to that effect; it could call for a repeal process to begin but not take a position on it; or it could endorse permitting each state to decide if it wanted to keep the ban on alcohol or not. The latter position was essentially the one that the Republicans had taken, although with convoluted language, in their platform. After hours of heated debate, the platform committee voted, by thirty-five to seventeen, to endorse full repeal. The plank read, "We advocate the repeal of the Eighteenth Amendment. To effect such repeal we demand that the Congress immediately propose a Constitutional Amendment" and for conventions to be held in each state "called to act solely on that proposal." A minority plank also emerged from the committee, which provided "that the Congress immediately propose to truly representative conventions in the states, called to meet solely on the proposal, a repeal of the Eighteenth Amendment." The two options differed on whether the party itself endorsed repeal, or just called for a constitutional process to be set in motion to determine the issue. Roosevelt sent word that his team was to be "hands off," meaning that his delegates were released to vote as they wanted, with FDR's team not wanting to take a stand and risk offending one side or the other.[47]

When Hitchcock read the words of the majority plank, the convention, especially those in the galleries, went wild. Eight years ago, even four years ago, a major political party endorsing repeal would have been unheard of. A debate followed over whether to substitute the minority plank. The main speakers were Senator Cordell Hull of Tennessee for the minority and Al Smith for the majority. Hull was jeered and booed by the crowd, while Smith was treated as a hero, getting a ten-minute demonstration as he arrived at the podium. Twice before (with Republican Garfield in 1880 and Democrat Bryan in 1896), rousing speeches given at a convention had propelled the speaker to their party's nomination. Could Smith ignite a spark that would do the same for him? In a not-so-veiled reference to Roosevelt, he proclaimed, "If there is anything in the world today that the American people dislike it is a dodger . . . . The time has thoroughly passed when you can carry water on both shoulders, when you can be wet when you are among the wets, and dry when you are among the drys." When the votes were counted, Smith's side won overwhelmingly by a vote of 934¾ to 213¾. Democrats would enter the 1932 campaign as a "wet" party endorsing immediate repeal of the Eighteenth Amendment.[48]

On the convention's fourth day, nominating speeches for president were on the agenda. It would be a long day. The afternoon session began with the most prominent contenders—Roosevelt, Garner, and Smith—being put before the delegates. FDR was nominated by John Mack, an attorney from the Hyde Park area who had, in 1910, been the first to urge his neighbor to run for the New York state legislature. Mack praised FDR's character ("His reputation is unsullied, his character spotless"), but focused on the broad base of the governor's support. He read the names of the thirty-four states and six territories in which Roosevelt had won delegates, proclaiming, "There never was a candidate who appealed to the whole country as this man has." Mack concluded with the demand that "the candidate of this convention shall be, must be and will be Franklin Delano Roosevelt!" There followed a forty-three-minute demonstration, led by two of FDR's sons, who grabbed one of the signs of the New York delegation and led a parade around the convention floor. The organist played "Anchors Away," a nautical tune that FDR had requested as his campaign's theme song. He considered himself "a Navy man," based on his prior job as assistant secretary of the Navy. Back in Louis Howe's suite in the Congress Hotel, listening over the radio, someone complained to Howe that the song "Sounds like a funeral march." Garner was then nominated by Senator Tom Connally of Texas, who noted his candidate's humble birth and traced his rise to power. Aware that no one from the South had won the party's nomination since the Civil War, Connally proclaimed of Garner, "He is more than a Southerner . . . . His statesmanship is bigger than his geography." There was a twenty-two-minute demonstration for Garner, led by the Texas and California delegations. Al Smith was nominated by Joseph Ely, the governor of Massachusetts. "Fifteen million people," said Ely, "were drawn to him in 1928, unswerving in their devotion in spite of all the political propaganda and personal attack directed against him . . . . He has come through still the 'happy warrior.'" He confronted Smith's Catholicism head on, declaring that the New Yorker's creed would preclude any interference by his church on his duties as president. Ely compared Smith to Thomas Jefferson, the party's founder, noting that Jefferson "also ran once and lost" and that his political opponents had questioned his fitness for office, due to unorthodox religious beliefs. "Has any man ever questioned," Ely asked, "the devotion of Thomas Jefferson to American principles?" With Mayor Cermak having once again packed the galleries with Smith supporters, the demonstration following Ely's speech was the longest of the day, lasting a full hour. At its conclusion, the convention adjourned until the evening.[49]

When the convention resumed shortly after 9:00 p.m., more nominating speeches were given. Farley, on the floor and listening to it all, called it "a merciless and unholy flood of oratory." Six more candidates were nominated—Byrd of Virginia, Traylor of Illinois, Ritchie of Maryland, Reed of Missouri, White of Ohio, and Murray of Oklahoma. Each had his own demonstration, his own songs played, and an array of seemingly endless seconding speeches. There were also more seconding speeches for the three candidates nominated during the afternoon. After midnight, the FDR team caucused and agreed to go forward with voting before an adjournment, concerned that a delay would give the opposition an opportunity to steal away some of their delegates. When Farley asked some who had been lined up to give seconding speeches for FDR to forgo their speeches, in order to speed things up, they refused. Later, he noted that he learned something important that night: "a thorough-going Democrat will give you his support, his loyalty, his vote, and his money—but never his radio time." The politicians wanted to be heard by the folks at home who were tuning in.[50]

The Roosevelt forces survived an adjournment motion from the opposition and, around 4:30 a.m., the first ballot began. By this time, the galleries were mostly empty. The weary delegates remained on the convention floor. One author vividly described the scene: "Amid the clutter of abandoned banners, old newspapers, crumpled coffee cartons, and stale, half-eaten sandwiches and hot dogs, the weary, rumpled delegates sat slumped in their seats or stretched out asleep on the chairs. Some had to be awakened to cast their votes."[51] The results of the first ballot were about what had been expected. Roosevelt had a huge lead with 666¼ votes, but was 104 short of the two-thirds needed for victory. Smith was second with 201¾ and Garner third with 90¼. The favorite son candidates trailed far behind. Smith's well-received speech on the Prohibition plank the day before had not increased his vote total, as his level of support was what had been expected, and was mostly from the northeast. FDR had commanding leads in the other regions, and had also eaten into Smith's base, getting just over half of Pennsylvania's delegates and a third of those from New York.[52]

The second ballot immediately followed. The tally was 677¾ for Roosevelt (a gain of 11½), 194¼ for Smith (a drop of 7½), Garner held steady at 90½, and with only minor changes among the others. It was not what the FDR team had wanted. Some of their increase had come from Roosevelt delegates that Farley had held back on the first ballot, hoping to generate momentum, which had not come. Now, it was the Roosevelt brain trust that wanted a break to reassess and negotiate. The opposition, sensing that things were breaking their way, objected. FDR's team made a motion to adjourn, but when it appeared on a voice vote that it would lose on a full roll call, they agreed to go on. The third ballot was taken and, again, there were few changes. Roosevelt had a gain of about five, to 682.79, Smith dropped four to 190¼, and Garner was at 101¼, an increase of eleven. Later, it was learned that FDR had narrowly averted disaster. His key man in Mississippi, Senator Harrison, knowing of the plan to adjourn after the second ballot and, assuming that it would pass, left the convention and went back to his hotel. As he was starting to undress for bed, he turned on a radio and heard that the third ballot was about to begin. Shocked, and not bothering to fully dress again, he rushed out of his hotel, hailed a taxi, and made it back to the arena just in time to hold his state for FDR. Without this, the almost evenly split Mississippi delegation, which voted under the unit rule, would likely have slipped away from Roosevelt, which may well have led to defections in other states. By the end of the third ballot, the convention had been in session for twelve hours and, at 9:15 a.m., all agreed it was time to take a break and adjourn. Many of FDR's opponents left Chicago Stadium that morning thinking that they had accomplished what they came to do—stop Roosevelt. History showed they had reason to be optimistic. At past Democratic conventions, if the frontrunner on the first ballot did not win by the fifth ballot, more often than not, his support started to peel away. Chicago bookies switched their betting odds to five to one *against* Roosevelt.[53]

The convention would meet again in ten hours. It was crunch time for all concerned. Attempts to change votes, both to and from FDR, had already been made while the balloting had been going on. A lawyer for New York City Mayor Jimmy Walker, who had corruption charges pending against him, approached a Roosevelt floor leader and advised that Walker could shift the Tammany delegates in New York from Smith to Roosevelt, if FDR, as that state's governor, would make the charges against Walker go away. Not wanting to win by making promises to such a tainted politician as Walker, the offer was rejected. Farley cornered Chicago's Mayor Cermak on the convention floor and argued that the mayor could be the kingmaker if he moved the forty votes of Illinois from that state's favorite son to FDR. Cermak refused. As noted earlier, before the voting began, Farley and Howe had already made overtures to Garner's managers, knowing that Garner's ninety delegate votes in Texas and California were the easiest path to victory. The vice presidency for Garner had already been dangled. Multiple additional avenues to sway Garner were made after the voting began. Joseph Kennedy of Massachusetts (the father of a future president), a FDR supporter, called publisher William Randolph Hearst, who was at his home in California. It was Hearst's endorsement of Garner back in January that had gotten the Texan into the race. Hearst's motivation had been that Garner, unlike the other major contenders, was not a Wilson internationalist. Kennedy told Hearst that the convention was likely to deadlock and, if it did, Newton Baker, a Wilson acolyte, would be the nominee. A concerned Hearst ordered one of his editors in Washington to meet with Garner and find out if he would withdraw and support FDR, to keep Baker from being nominated. The fear of Baker was legitimate, as those behind his shadow candidacy had sprung into action. Thousands of telegrams promoting Baker were sent that Friday morning to delegates. Columnist Walter Lippman also sent a petition to influential Democrats arguing that the failure of FDR to win on the first three ballots was a blessing, as it gave the party an opportunity to "unite on a man who is stronger than any of the leading contenders." Lippman stated "[t]hat man is Newton

Baker of Ohio," whom he called "an acceptable second choice to every one." FDR was aware of the surge in activity for Baker. In the afternoon, he placed a curious telephone call to Baker, telling him that it looked like the convention would deadlock and turn to Baker, and offering to assist, if needed. Baker, likely not up to date on the latest rumors, professed ignorance of any such swing to him and advised FDR to hold firm. Most likely, FDR was just probing Baker for information, since he was not about to quit, having, just before he placed the call to Baker, sent a telegram to his delegates advising "I am in this fight to stay" and "Stick to your guns."[54]

Roosevelt's team put out additional feelers to Garner's two top Texans in Chicago, Congressman Rayburn and Senator Connally, as well as to William McAdoo, who headed the California delegation, also committed to Garner. Friday morning, shortly after adjournment, Farley and Mississippi's Harrison met with Rayburn and another Garner manager and begged that they move Texas into FDR's column. Rayburn's response of "We'll see what can be done" was not definitive, but Farley was optimistic. Farley then met with two Californians who had McAdoo's ear, with the vice presidency for Garner again being mentioned. Things then moved quickly. Some time on Friday (exactly when is disputed), Garner agreed to release his delegates and placed calls to Rayburn and McAdoo. Caucuses of the Texas and California delegations were then scheduled around dinner time. Both meetings were raucous and there was strong resistance by many of the delegates to dropping Garner and going with FDR. By a narrow margin, a vote of the Texans endorsed the move. The Californians appointed a subcommittee of four, with McAdoo on it, to decide how to proceed. McAdoo got promises that FDR would support Garner as his running mate and that he, McAdoo, would control FDR's federal patronage appointments in California and have a veto over certain cabinet appointments. His subcommittee then agreed to move the Golden State to FDR. It was decided, since California came before Texas on the roll call, that McAdoo would announce to the convention that evening that the two states were shifting to FDR. Meanwhile, the "Stop Roosevelt" group, most of whom were unaware of what was going on with Garner, had finally broken through in Mississippi and gotten assurances that that state would drop FDR and move on, likely to Baker. There were rumors that other states would break away from FDR on the next ballot.[55]

The climax of the convention—McAdoo's announcement of the shift of California and Texas to FDR—almost did not happen. The story is almost comical and includes a possible political dirty trick. McAdoo left his hotel in a limousine (provided by Mayor Cermak's host committee) to head for Chicago Stadium. On the way, in heavy traffic, the car ran out of gas. A Chicago police officer offered McAdoo (who was very tall) a ride on the back of his motorcycle. After a short distance, McAdoo's long legs kept dragging on the pavement and they could not continue. The officer then hailed a cab, put McAdoo in it, turned on his motorcycle's siren, and escorted the cab to the arena. McAdoo arrived late. The evening session had already started and the fourth ballot was in process. Alabama had already voted and Arkansas was casting its vote when McAdoo came rushing down the aisle to his seat in the California delegation, which would cast its vote fourth in the alphabetical list of states. McAdoo always believed that Cermak had gotten word that he was going to announce the shift of the two key states of California and Texas to FDR and that the mayor had ordered the gas siphoned out of his limousine.[56]

When California was called, McAdoo rose and asked to come forward to "explain California's vote." As he stood at the podium, covered by a spotlight, those in the galleries, who again this night were mostly Smith supporters, stood and cheered, thinking that he was going to announce a shift by California to Smith. "California came here," McAdoo proudly proclaimed, "to nominate a President of the United States. She did not come here to deadlock this convention or to engage in another disastrous contest like that of 1924." The reference was to his own loss of the presidential nomination that year to a dark horse nominee, after leading for many of the 103 ballots. McAdoo blamed his loss on Al Smith, who had been his main opponent that year, who had far fewer votes, and who had refused to drop out of the contest. It is said that revenge is a dish that is best served cold. Now, eight years later, McAdoo got his retribution against Smith. California, he said, was taking a stand that would bring a "swift" conclusion that would "promote party harmony," a move "prompted by our belief that when any man comes into a Democratic National Convention with the popular will behind him to the extent of almost seven hundred votes . . . ." Before he could get out Roosevelt's name, the cheers from the galleries turned into jeers. Chairman Walsh had to call Mayor Cermak to the podium for an attempt to calm his hometown crowd, which was only partially successful. McAdoo then continued, "The great state of Texas and the great state of California are acting in accordance with what we believe to be best for, first for America and next for the Democratic Party . . . . California casts forty-four votes for Franklin D. Roosevelt." With those words, advising that Texas would also be shifting, all knew that the contest was over. The dam had been broken. The roll call continued and, when Illinois was called, Cermak went to the podium and announced that his state, as well as neighboring Indiana, were shifting all of their eighty-eight votes to FDR. State after state then withdrew their favorite sons and jumped on the Roosevelt bandwagon. The main holdouts were Smith and his delegates, who refused to budge. The final tally of the fourth ballot was 945 for Roosevelt, 190½ for Smith, and a few votes scattered for others. When a DNC official approached Smith, who was sitting in the New York delegation, and asked if he would come to the podium to make the traditional motion for the victor's nomination to be unanimous, he refused. "I won't do it," he sternly replied, with his arms crossed, "I won't do it. I won't do it." The man America knew as the "Happy Warrior" sulked out of Chicago an angry and bitter man.[57]

Later, Farley, Kennedy, Hearst, Rayburn, Connally, McAdoo, and others, would all take credit for being the key player in the final shift to FDR. All had a role, but it was ultimately Garner who made the decision to get out of the contest before the fourth ballot began. Although he accepted the vice-presidential spot on the ticket, the best evidence is that he did not act for that reason, but out of a sincere belief that preventing a deadlocked convention was in the best interest of the party. Interestingly, almost all of these men would end up opposing FDR at some point during his presidency and some later regretted the role that they had taken at the 1932 convention. Among historians, there has been much speculation that, if Garner had waited one more ballot to release his delegates, whether some states would have broken away from FDR on the fourth, dooming his chances, and whether Baker would have been nominated. Kennedy later told friends that "few people know what a close shave Roosevelt had or how near Baker came to winning the nomination." Others have blamed Smith for handing the nomination to FDR. It was clear after three ballots that Smith could not win, yet his ego kept him in the race. Some believe if he had thrown his support to Ritchie, or someone similar, the convention would have deadlocked and Roosevelt would have been beaten. Mencken, a longtime admirer of Smith, placed FDR's nomination squarely on Smith's shoulders: "The failure of the opposition was the failure of Al Smith," the Sage of Baltimore later wrote, "From the moment he arrived on the ground it was apparent that he had no plan, and was animated only by his fierce hatred of Roosevelt, the cuckoo who had seized his nest [as governor of New York]."[58]

Weeks before the convention, FDR and his advisors decided on a secret and dramatic move if he prevailed. He would go to Chicago and accept the nomination with a speech to the convention. This had never been done at any major party convention. Since the mid-1800s, a traditional ritual had been followed by the major parties after a presidential nomination was made. The convention would appoint a committee of distinguished party leaders to formally call upon the nominee at his home, usually two to four weeks after the convention ended. The nominee would then stand on his porch or in his front yard and accept the nomination, and read from prepared remarks, usually very lengthy and often delivered in monotone. Roosevelt resolved to end this staid ceremony. Given the distance from Albany to Chicago and the need to reach the convention as soon after his nomination as possible, the Roosevelt team ruled out travel by train and decided that FDR would fly. The plan had an added benefit. In the early 1930s, travel by air was still relatively new and was rightfully considered risky and dangerous. There was no better way, it was felt, to address concerns over FDR's health and stamina than to have him take a daring flight halfway across the country to Chicago to address the convention in person. After receiving news of his nomination on Friday, Roosevelt sent a telegram, which was read to the delegates, announcing to them, and to the country, his intent to fly to Chicago the next day.[59]

Arrangements were made with American Airways to charter a fifteen-seat Ford Tri-Motor airplane, which had been brought to Albany during the convention and hidden in a locked hangar. There, modifications were made, including removing the seat in front of Roosevelt's to fashion a makeshift desk and installing a typewriter table in front of a nearby seat for use by a secretary. A special ramp was made, up which FDR was carried backward onto the plane. In addition to the governor, there were twelve passengers and crew, including Eleanor, two of their sons, a few aides, two New York state troopers, two pilots, and Max Pollet, an official with American Airways, who served as the steward. Newsreel crews, reporters, and a small crowd gathered at Albany Airport on an overcast morning to see the plane lift off around 8:30 a.m. and head westward on the eight-hundred-mile trip to Chicago. The pilots used short-wave radio to provide constant updates on their progress. The flight, which took place on a Saturday, excited the nation and captured its attention. Two refueling stops were made along the way, at Buffalo around 11:00 a.m. and at

Cleveland around 2:00 p.m., with large crowds having gathered at both airports. Headwinds and bad weather made the flight slower than expected, and turbulent, at times. One of Roosevelt's sons had severe air sickness most of the way, and a few of the others on board had milder symptoms for portions of the flight. Shortly after leaving Buffalo, Pollet served a full lunch, including dessert, which he reported that the passengers "did full justice" in consuming. Roosevelt then worked on his speech, which had been prepared in Albany, making edits and deleting some paragraphs as they fell further behind schedule. Nine hours after leaving Albany, the Ford Tri-Motor touched down at Chicago's airport at 4:30 p.m. local time, where more than ten thousand people waited, and with millions listening over national radio networks.[60]

While Roosevelt's plane made its way westward, the convention met at two in the afternoon to select a nominee for vice president. The arena was packed. Overnight and throughout the morning hours, word had spread that Speaker John Nance Garner was to be the choice and that he had Roosevelt's backing. Garner had confirmed that he would go on the ticket. There was never a specific *quid pro quo* of Garner releasing his Texas and California delegates in exchange for the vice-presidential slot. It was in many ways a step down for him, as the job of speaker of the House had far more power and influence than that of vice president. As a strong party man, Garner's primary motivation in withdrawing was to avoid a deadlock, with the debacle of the 1924 convention on his mind. The Texan was nominated by Congressman John McDuffie of Alabama, who praised him as a man of "sturdy and rugged character" and as a "real, red-blooded he-man." As the roll call of the states proceeded, only Iowa offered an alternative choice, Matthew Tinley, a career Army officer who had served with distinction during World War I. The nomination was a gesture of respect for Tinley, who was a member of the Iowa delegation, and he withdrew his name at the end of the roll call. At 3:40 p.m., Garner was unanimously nominated as vice president. A perfunctory demonstration lasting only five minutes followed. The crowd had not come to see Garner nominated; they had come to see and hear Roosevelt accept his nomination.[61]

In late afternoon at Chicago's airport, the city's mayor, Anton Cermak, who until a day earlier had been working against Roosevelt's nomination, welcomed the man he now proudly introduced to the crowd as "the next President of the United States." Jim Farley and Louis Howe were there to greet their boss. It was the first time that Howe had left his rooms in the Congress Hotel in over a week. He had received a copy of the speech prepared in Albany, which he did not like, and had stayed up most of the night preparing his own draft. As FDR and a few key aides, including Howe, sped away toward Chicago Stadium in a huge white Cadillac convertible provided by Cermak (and trailed by a motorcade of sixty cars), Howe thrust his version of the speech in front of the governor and almost demanded that it be delivered. Roosevelt read a few pages and liked the original speech better. When Howe persisted, Roosevelt shouted, "Dammit, Louie, I'm the nominee!" To appease Howe somewhat, he decided to take the first page of Howe's speech and to use the rest of the Albany speech.[62]

With its vice president selected and bad weather having delayed Roosevelt's plane by two hours, the convention had time to fill. For a while, the live radio broadcast of Roosevelt's arrival at the airport, twenty-five miles away, was played over the stadium's speakers. Chairman Walsh then introduced the widows of Woodrow Wilson and Thomas Marshall, the last Democratic president and vice president, who were applauded. The crowd began chanting "We want Rogers!," but Will Rogers rose from his seat in the press section near the podium, quieted them, and declined the invitation. A young woman took the stage and sang a few songs. Walsh then moved to an agenda item that had been intended for after Roosevelt's speech, calling the roll for each state's nomination for members of the Democratic National Committee over the next four years. It was a dreary process, but it served its purpose of passing time and of keeping the convention occupied.[63]

Finally, the big moment arrived. Roosevelt, dressed in a blue suit with a red rose in his lapel, with his heavy leg braces on and using two canes, walked slowly, with a New York state trooper at his side, to the steps leading up to the podium. He placed his arms around the shoulders of two men on each of his sides and was hoisted up the stairs as the organ in the stadium blared out "Onward Christian Soldiers." The New York governor listened as Walsh formally advised him of his nomination and, escorted by one of his sons, slowly moved to the podium and gripped it to maintain his balance. Opening with an apology to the crowd for his delay ("I have no control over the winds of Heaven"), he acknowledged with pride that his appearance before the convention was a first and declared that he did not intend for it to be his last departure from orthodoxy:

> The appearance before a National Convention of its nominee for President, to be formally notified of his selection, is unprecedented and unusual, but these are unprecedented and unusual times. I have started out on the tasks that lie ahead by breaking the absurd traditions that the candidate should remain in professed ignorance of what has happened for weeks until he is formally notified of that event many weeks later. . . .
>
> Let it also be symbolic that in so doing I broke traditions. Let it be from now on the task of our Party to break foolish traditions. We will break foolish traditions and leave it to the Republican leadership, far more skilled in that art, to break promises.

As he went through his speech, which lasted an hour, the crowd hung on every word. The *New York Times* reported that he was "in splendid form" and that he "rarely has spoken with such vigor." He made it clear that, under his leadership, he intended the Democratic Party to be the party of liberalism, which he held out as the correct path forward, between the extremes of radicalism and reaction. "To meet by reaction that danger of radicalism," he proclaimed, "is to invite disaster. Reaction is no barrier to the radical. It is a challenge, a provocation. The way to meet that danger is to offer a workable program of reconstruction." The Republican view of government's role in the economy, he declared, "sees to it that the favored few are helped and hopes that some of their prosperity will leak through, sift through, to labor, to the farmer, to the small business man." That view, he declared "is not and never will be the theory of the Democratic Party . . . . Ours must be a party of liberal thought, of planned action, of enlightened international outlook, and of the greatest good for the greatest number of our citizens." He called for economy in government, for public works projects to stimulate employment, for reforestation of unused land, for a reconstruction of agricultural policy, and for tariffs that will lead to "the restoration of the trade of the world." He praised the delegates for their "courage" to call for the outright repeal of Prohibition. "This convention wants repeal," he declared, "Your candidate wants repeal. And I am confident that the United States of America wants repeal." In his closing paragraph, Roosevelt uttered two words that would become synonymous with his administration:

> I pledge you, I pledge myself, to a new deal for the American people. Let us all here assembled constitute ourselves prophets of a new order of competence and of courage. This is more than a political campaign. It is a call to arms. Give me your help, not to win votes alone, but to win in this crusade to restore America to its own people.[64]

The inclusion of the words "new deal" in the conclusion of the speech had not been intended as a campaign slogan. They had been used before by others in conjunction with calls for political change. The speech, and the flight that FDR took to deliver it, were the talk of the nation. The day after the convention, a cartoon in the *New York World* depicted a farmer gazing up from his field at an airplane (Roosevelt's plane on its way to Chicago) with the words "New Deal" written on its underside. Others in the press quickly adopted the term and it became a catchy slogan for FDR's campaign and, later, his administration.[65]

When FDR ended his speech, the organist in the arena played "Happy Days Are Here Again," a peppy tune that he had performed at times earlier during the convention. The song had been around since 1929 and was sung in *Chasing Rainbows*, a popular movie musical. As noted earlier, Roosevelt had asked that "Anchors Away" be his theme song, but when it had been played, it had failed to generate a positive reaction from the crowd. Some on the FDR team thought it too somber. There is a story that, during the convention, Louis Howe's secretary sang and danced to "Happy Days" in Howe's gloomy and smoke-filled hotel suite, to convince him to switch to it as FDR's theme song. The upbeat tune, with lyrics ushering away "cloudy gray times" and welcoming "gay times" again, meshed well with Roosevelt's theme of hope to bring the country out of the Depression. It became synonymous with Roosevelt for the rest of his career.[66]

The 1932 Democratic convention was the last convention for several of the key participants. Senator Walsh, the permanent chairman, was named by FDR to be his attorney general, but died in March 1933 on a train en route to the inauguration. His death was ruled at the time to have been from a heart attack, although there have been rumors over the years that he was murdered by poison, for various alleged reasons. Chicago Mayor Cermak, who had opposed FDR until the end of the convention, went to visit the president-elect in Miami in February 1933 to mend fences. While standing next to Roosevelt, who was seated in a car, Cermak was struck by one of five bullets fired by an assailant, shots that were intended for Roosevelt, who was uninjured. The mayor died three weeks later. Will Rogers, the comedian turned columnist who reported from the convention, died in a plane crash in Alaska in August 1935. Less than a month later, Senator Huey Long was assassinated in the Louisiana State Capitol in Baton

Rouge by a relative of a political enemy. The Kingfish was forty-two years old. Governor Albert Ritchie of Maryland, one of FDR's opponents for the nomination, died in early 1936, at the age of fifty-nine, of a cerebral hemorrhage.[67]

The Campaign and Election

The ongoing Depression was the overriding issue in the fall campaign. Roosevelt blamed its cause on years of Republican mismanagement and greed, while Hoover argued that its origins were global in scope. Roosevelt was the clear favorite, exuding confidence, while Hoover was dour and defensive at times. Any hope Hoover had lay in some sudden economic upturn during the campaign, which did not happen. FDR traveled throughout the country by railroad and delivered twenty-seven major speeches, and more than thirty shorter ones. In his remarks, he made it clear that he intended the federal government to have an expansive role in reviving the economy, but he was less than specific on the details. If there was a secondary issue, it was Prohibition, and Roosevelt's calls for its outright repeal were cheered. Hoover adhered to the position in the Republican platform for a national referendum on alcohol, which would let each state to decide its own course. Also, typical of incumbent presidents, he continued to work in the White House and campaigned less than his opponent, making only ten major speeches. When he traveled, he sometimes faced hostile audiences. If Roosevelt was vague about exactly what his "New Deal" would involve, Hoover claimed to know. He charged that Roosevelt was a radical, that his program would be an assault on the Constitution, that electing him would do away with American individualism and replace it with collectivism and regimentation, making government the "master of people's souls and thoughts." A *Literary Digest* poll on the eve of the election showed Roosevelt with a significant lead, with more than a third of those who had voted Republican in 1928 switching to the Democrats.[68]

The voters delivered a landslide for Roosevelt and the Democrats. FDR carried forty-two states and Hoover only six (Connecticut, Delaware, Maine, New Hampshire, Vermont, and Pennsylvania). The electoral count was a lopsided 472 to 59. In the popular vote, Roosevelt got seven million more votes than Hoover, 22,829,501 (57.4%) to 15,760,684 (39.7%). The only third party of any significance in 1932 was the Socialist Party, which had Norman Thomas as its nominee. With 884,649 votes, Thomas received almost two-percent of the overall votes cast, but his candidacy did not change the outcome in any states. Hoover became the seventh president seeking reelection to be voted out of office. Democrats also won huge majorities in both houses of Congress.[69]

As 1932 turned into 1933, the nation eagerly awaited to see if Franklin Roosevelt could deliver on his promises.

CHAPTER 9

1936: Rendezvous with Destiny

Herbert Hoover promised us two chickens in each pot,
But breadlines and Depression were the only things we got.
I lost my job, the banks blew up, and I was on the spot.
So, that's why I'm voting for Roosevelt.

Hurray, hurray! Herb Hoover's gone away,
Hurray, hurray! I hope he's gone to stay.
O' now I'm back to work, I get my three squares every day
And that's why I'm voting for Roosevelt.
—**Democratic campaign song, 1936**

There was no question that Franklin Roosevelt would be renominated by the Democratic Party for a second term in 1936. His New Deal reforms—including programs for public works jobs, relief for the unemployed, assistance to farmers, greater regulation over the stock market, protection of bank deposits, social security for the elderly, as well as other programs—were popular with the public. Roosevelt's periodic fireside chats by radio were listened to by millions and transformed the way a president communicated with the people. By the time the 1936 election season began, the United States was not out of the Great Depression, but many saw progress under Roosevelt's leadership. Still, there was significant opposition to the president and his administration. A Gallup poll released in June 1936 found that 55% of the country thought that the New Deal was helping the economic recovery, but that 45% believed that it was hindering it.[1] As usually occurs when an incumbent president seeks reelection, the 1936 election would be a referendum on Roosevelt and his policies.

Republican Convention

To say that the Republican tide in the country seemed to be at its low ebb in 1936 would be an understatement. In a landslide, the party's incumbent president, Herbert Hoover, had been turned out of office in 1932 and it had lost control of Congress. In 1934, Democrats padded their solid majorities in Congress by *gaining* nine seats in both the House and the Senate, a reversal of the usual losses in midterm elections by the party holding the White House. As of 1935, the GOP held only 103 seats out of 435 in the House, only 25 of 96 in the Senate, and only 7 of 48 governorships.

One of the few bright spots for the GOP in 1934 had been in Kansas, where Alfred ("Alf") Landon was the only one of the party's governors to win reelection. Born in Pennsylvania in 1887, Landon had moved with his family to Kansas as a teenager. His father was an oil speculator. Landon studied law at the University of Kansas, but never practiced. Instead, he took an accounting job at a bank in his hometown of Independence and began investing his extra money in new oil wells. After four years, he had made enough money to follow in his father's footsteps. He entered the oil business full time and began traveling around Kansas looking for the next gusher. By the time he was forty, he was a millionaire. Always interested in politics, and a Republican, Landon, while in his mid-twenties, left the party in the 1912 schism and organized his county for Theodore Roosevelt, who ran on the third-party Progressive ticket for president that year. Like Roosevelt, he soon rejoined the Republicans. He worked on the staff of one Republican governor of Kansas and became the campaign manager for another. In 1932, he ran for governor himself and emerged the victor in a close three-way race. Two years later, he won the governorship again, one of only a small number of Republicans in the country to survive Democratic waves in two elections.[2]

Landon was no orator, but what he lacked in inspiration when before a crowd he made up for by staying around afterward and listening and talking with them in his natural, folksy manner. A sandy-haired man of average height and build, who wore rimless eyeglasses, the Kansan was not an intellectual, but he was intelligent. One author has noted, as governor, he "gave the people of Kansas the kind of administration they had asked for: sound, economical, mildly progressive, tolerant, businesslike." He balanced his state's budget, a feat that few other governors were able to do during the Depression, and in stark contrast to the massive deficit spending going on at the federal level under the New Deal. His financial conservatism led some to call him the "Kansas Coolidge," a term he disliked because he was generally progressive on non-fiscal issues. "I believe a man can be a liberal," he once said, "without being a spendthrift!" His criticism of the New Deal was not a frontal assault, but focused more on its excessive scope, cost, and inefficiency. With his reelection and his budget balancing prowess, Landon began to attract attention for president in 1936. Publisher William Randolph Hearst sent reporters to Kansas, who turned out favorable stories. Talk of a presidential run was also promoted by a prominent non-Hearst local newspaper, the *Kansas City Star*, running articles "with quiet talk and sage advice." In the fall of 1935, friends of the forty-eight-year-old Landon set up a small campaign headquarters in a Kansas City hotel.[3]

Over the next few months, four other GOP contenders joined the Kansas governor in the race for the 1936 nomination. To the left of Landon, and of most of his party, was seventy-one-year-old Senator William Borah. In office for a generation, the "Lion of Idaho" was one of those politicians who cultivated the image of being a maverick, of bucking the leadership of his party. In the mid-1920s, President Coolidge once saw Borah in a park in Washington, on horseback, moving swiftly along. "Must bother the Senator," Silent Cal deadpanned to a friend, "to be going in the same direction as the horse." Over the years, Borah supported many progressive policies, ranting against monopolies and supporting a federal income tax and the direct election of senators. He avoided committee meetings in the Senate, more interested in grabbing headlines than in doing the mundane work of a legislator. In Washington, he was also known for his after-hours activities. A married man, he had several affairs, including one with Theodore Roosevelt's daughter, Alice, who was wed to Congressman Nicholas Longworth at the time. Alice gave birth in 1925 to a daughter, Paulina, a product of the relationship with Borah, and who was raised as Longworth's child. Borah was no party man. If he didn't like the GOP's nominee for president in a given year, he sat out the election. His politics were hard to pigeonhole. Although a progressive, he was an ardent isolationist, had been one of Prohibition's most vocal proponents, opposed women's suffrage on the national level, and opposed a federal anti-lynching law. After FDR took office, Borah voted for several key pieces of New Deal legislation and was known to have had several private meetings and lunches with the president, all of which increased the suspicions that his fellow Republicans had long held about him.[4]

One of Borah's more traditional Republican colleagues in the Senate, Arthur Vandenberg of Michigan, also saw himself as the man who could take on FDR. Vandenberg began his career as a journalist in Grand Rapids and was active in Republican politics. He authored biographies of Alexander Hamilton, his political idol. When a vacancy in one of Michigan's seats in the Senate opened in 1928, Vandenberg was appointed to fill it and soon won it on his own. Vandenberg became a leading critic in the Senate of FDR and his New Deal policies. Like Landon in Kansas, he survived the Democratic surge in 1934 and won reelection. He was generally viewed as an effective senator, although was not well liked because of his arrogance. A colleague observed that Vandenberg was "the only Senator who can strut sitting down," while a journalist wrote of the Michigan senator, "Politicians as a class are vain but he was vain beyond most of the tribe." Such men often see themselves as sitting in the Oval Office. With GOP ranks thinned in 1936, as author David Pietrusza has noted, "with few other Republican hopefuls rating a first look, let alone a second, bloviating show horse Arthur Vandenberg entered 1936 as a dark horse . . . in the race."[5]

Another candidate was Frank Knox, the sixty-two-year-old publisher of the *Chicago Daily News*. A self-made man who was raised in Michigan, he left college to fight in the Spanish-American War, serving in TR's famous Rough Rider unit. Like Vandenberg, Knox started his career in the newspaper business in Michigan. He began as a reporter and, within a few years, owned several upstate newspapers and became active in Republican politics. In 1917, he founded a newspaper in New Hampshire that would become the *Manchester Union Leader*, a leading conservative voice in the Granite State for generations. When the United States entered World War I, Knox, then in his forties, rejoined the military, served in an Army artillery unit in France, and rose to the rank of colonel. In the 1920s, he worked for Hearst, first in Boston and then supervising all of the magnate's newspaper empire, becoming a wealthy man in the process. He then parted ways with Hearst, and, in 1931, moved back to the Midwest, where he had started, and became the part owner and publisher of the *Chicago Daily News*. Soon, Knox's newspaper, and Knox himself, became leading critics of the New Deal. Despite not having never been elected to any public office previously, Knox threw his hat into the ring for the 1936 GOP nomination for president.[6]

The final contender in the 1936 GOP field was the most well-known of them all—former President Herbert Hoover. After leaving office in March 1933, Hoover mostly stayed out of the public eye for a couple of years. After he reemerged in early 1935 with hard-hitting speeches criticizing the New Deal, he began to dream of vindication, of beating FDR in 1936. His preference was to not openly seek his party's nomination, but to have his friends and supporters make the case for him. Most were not interested, viewing him as permanently damaged goods. Neither were the eastern elites who still held much sway in the GOP, and who had been forced to accept the Californian in 1928, when he rode a crest of popularity to the nomination. A Hoover/Roosevelt rematch was the last thing party leaders wanted. As author Glen Jeansonne commented, in 1936, "the Republican Old Guard would have built a wall around the White House to keep Hoover out." Hoover did not actively participate in the primaries held during the first few months of 1936 and had no committed delegates, although the California delegation, pledged to a favorite son (future Chief Justice Earl Warren), could have been swung to him if needed. After a half-hearted campaign that consisted mainly of giving speeches around the country and mailing copies of them to influential Republicans, Hoover finally faced up to reality and made a statement in May, only a month before the convention, that he was not, and (so he said) had never been, a candidate, and that his only interest had been to get "critical issues before the country."[7]

GOP leaders decided early on that Landon, perceived as the moderate in the race (with Borah to his left and the rest of the field to his right), was the only candidate who had any chance of beating FDR. He seemed to be the perfect contrast to the president. As author Herbert Eaton has observed, "Reckless spending could be countered with Kansas thrift, a mellifluous, almost hypnotic orator offset by a halting, labored midwestern twang, and eastern worldliness contrasted to homespun simplicity." Landon also seemed to be the first choice of Republican voters, becoming more popular over the first few months of the election season. The 1936 campaign was the first during which Gallup Polls were taken. George Gallup had pioneered a new method of polling by obtaining the opinions of a demographically-based small sample of random voters. Prior polls, such as the ones done by the *Literary Digest*, relied on responses to questionnaires sent out to millions of voters. Gallup's polling in December 1935 found Landon had 33% support from Republican voters, increasing to 43% in February 1936, and to 56% in May. During the same time frame, support for Borah, the second-place contender, dropped from 26% to 19%. Hoover, in third place, stayed around 14%, with Knox and Vandenberg hovering around 5% each.[8]

From March to May, primaries were held in a dozen states. As the frontrunner, Landon's team kept him out of most of them, as losses would lessen his momentum. Still, his name went on the ballot in a few, without his consent, and he won in New Jersey and Massachusetts. Knox won in New Hampshire, where he had previously lived, and also in his then home state of Illinois, but Borah made a surprisingly strong showing there, carrying most of the state outside of Chicago. Favorite sons won in Ohio, California, and South Dakota. Borah won five states—Wisconsin, Oregon, Nebraska, West Virginia, and Pennsylvania—but the laws in some of them (including delegate-rich Pennsylvania) did not award delegates to the winner of the popular vote in a primary. Borah would have done better in the primaries, but for the strong opposition of northern Blacks. His vocal stand against a federal anti-lynching law led the NAACP to boycott his candidacy and send protesters to many of his speeches, especially in Ohio and Illinois. While the primaries attracted attention, and were heavily covered in the press, their actual impact on the race was less important than they seemed. Most states still chose their delegates at state conventions and Landon racked up wins in many of those, while, in several states, the delegates were uncommitted.[9]

As the convention opened in Cleveland, John Hamilton, Landon's campaign manager, claimed to have at least 400 votes for the Kansan, up about 60 from his estimate a few days earlier. Newspapers estimated the rest of the field as 240 for Knox, 120 for Borah, 38 for Vandenberg, and the remainder scattered among a handful of favorite sons. No credible "Stop Landon" movement emerged. It was speculated that blocking Landon would require the placing of at least ten names in nomination, including Hoover, with all pledging to work together for several ballots. No one took the lead, or seemed interested. Of the major contenders, most seemed resigned to losing. Only Borah continued to put up a fight, likely not thinking he could win, but to bolster his image as a maverick and to be viewed as going down fighting. His campaign manager, Carl Bachmann of West Virginia, charged just before the convention that Landon was really a New Dealer in disguise. It looked like a desperate move as, a few weeks earlier, Borah's team had alleged that Landon was a tool of Wall Street. The latest charge, the *Washington Post* commented was a "really ridiculous change of tactics," noting that, based on his voting record in the Senate, it was Borah who "stands closer to the New Deal in the public mind than any other major candidate." There were rumors that most of the delegates from two large states, New York and Pennsylvania, would be coming out for Landon once they arrived in Cleveland and held a caucus. If true, the contest was over.[10]

There were 1,003 delegates at the convention, with a majority of 502 needed to win the nomination. The Ohio delegation included Alice Roosevelt Longworth, who had attended several prior conventions as an observer, but never as a participant. There was irony in her position. She was pledged to support Ohio's favorite son candidate, Robert Taft, the son of former president William Howard Taft, whom her father had battled and lost to at the party's 1912 convention. Also, as a Taft delegate, Alice would *not* be voting for Senator Borah, the father of her daughter. There was talk among a few women delegates of putting Alice's name in nomination for president or vice president, to "consolidate the women's vote against the New Deal." The caustic-tongued Alice declined, stating that she "could guarantee to antagonize" everyone, and did not want to be "the worst-defeated candidate who ever ran for office." The reduction in the number of Black Republican delegates, which was evident at the 1928 convention, continued in 1936. At RNC meetings in Cleveland to decide disputes in southern states between mixed race "Black and Tan" and "Lily White" delegate slates, newspapers reported that Black delegates "have been going down like tenpins." When all was said and done, only Mississippi had a majority Black delegation, and only five other southern states had any Black delegates at all. The takeover of state Republican organizations in the South by whites was almost completed. Women fared somewhat better than Blacks, with around sixty serving as full delegates, and a greater number as alternates. Landon delegates and supporters were not hard to spot walking around Cleveland. Many sported a sunflower, the state flower of Kansas, pinned to their jacket or dress. Bands moved through hotel lobbies playing "Oh! Suzanna," which the Landon team had selected as their campaign song. As in current times, rumors of election fraud and of dead people voting then existed. The press noted with interest the address listed for an Indiana delegate. The man, according to the records, resided in "Highland Lawn Cemetery" in Terre Haute. Landon remained in Topeka during the convention, showing up in the governor's office daily and performing routine tasks. His seventy-nine-year-old father, John, and nineteen-year-old daughter, Peggy, attended the convention as representatives of the family. A widower who had remarried, Landon also had two young children, ages two and three, from his second marriage. Most of the other contenders for the nomination came to Cleveland.[11]

With Landon in the driver's seat for the presidential nod, talk began to shift to a vice presidential nominee, with Vandenberg and Knox considered the top contenders. Vandenberg, officially still in the race for president, issued a statement that he would not accept the vice-presidential slot. Some noted that almost every prior nominee for vice president said the same thing. Until he accepted. No politician would ever admit to *wanting* to be vice president. One name floated was Governor Styles Bridges of New Hampshire, but there were second thoughts about his pairing with Landon when a columnist for the *Cleveland Plain Dealer* observed that such a ticket would give the Democrats "a prize ready-made slogan of the century." Being confronted with an opposition cry of "Landon Bridges Falling Down" was likely not a risk that Republicans wanted to take in 1936.[12]

By the 1930s, both major parties recognized that conventions, in addition to performing their official functions, were propaganda tools, to be used to promote the party to the country. Image was everything. Interesting photographs and favorable articles in newspapers were prized. A memorandum from Bruce Barton, a New York advertising executive, to RNC Chairman Harry Fletcher suggested "publicity stories" for the party in Cleveland. Find "the oldest Republican in the United States," Barton proposed, and have him come to the convention. Or, perhaps, seek out young Republicans who will turn twenty-one (the minimum voting age at that time) on the day the convention opens and bring five of them to Cleveland. Potential speakers at the convention, he advised, should include a dirt farmer, a young Republican, a woman, and a "Constitutional Democrat." Further, Barton recommended that Fletcher wire each state chairman to "bring the prettiest young Republican" to the convention and have her "seated on the platform." It is not known how many, if any, of Barton's suggestions were used in 1936, but any observer of modern conventions can verify that publicity and advertising techniques continue to play a prominent role. New convention strategies were needed not just for the eyes, but also for the ears. Radio had changed the way conventions worked. Tighter schedules and shorter, crisper speeches were needed to hold a radio audience. In 1936, there were twenty-three million radios in homes and businesses in the United States, plus an additional three million in automobiles. Major convention speeches and key events were moved to the evenings, when more people would be tuning in. CBS had sixty-eight microphones and more than seven miles of wires in the convention hall. Hans von Kaltenborn was that network's lead host and its coverage featured a new innovation, a "pause interpreter," who was a political analyst stationed on the podium to explain to the audience the reasons for any gaps or delays in the proceedings. NBC's coverage featured Lowell Thomas and Graham McNamee, with commentary by journalist Walter Lippman.[13]

Republicans opened their twenty-first national convention in Cleveland's Municipal Auditorium on Tuesday, June 9, 1936. The building was familiar to many of them, the party having met there twelve years earlier to nominate Calvin Coolidge. Then, with a popular GOP incumbent president seeking renomination, an air of confidence had pervaded over the convention. In contrast, in 1936, there was apprehension and doubt. While delegates and visitors from Kansas and from a few other Midwest states openly expressed confidence in a November victory over the Democrats, many others had a "defeatist complex" and questioned reporters whether there was *any* chance that FDR could be beaten. It was the beginning of a big summer for Cleveland. Adjacent to the auditorium, along the shoreline of Lake Erie, the Great Lakes Exposition was set to open shortly after the convention ended. An unofficial world's fair marking the centennial of Cleveland's founding, it featured exhibits showcasing the region's iron and steel industry (including replicas of a mine shaft and a blast furnace), rides on the Goodyear Blimp, food and culture from forty countries, as well as a copy of Shakespeare's Globe Theater. Visitors walked through the Court of Presidents, a bridge connecting the two main sections of the grounds, which had sixteen pillars, topped by huge gilded eagles, each dedicated to one of the sixteen presidents (including Lincoln of Illinois and New York's two Roosevelts) who were born or lived in the eight states bordering the Great Lakes.[14]

The convention was called to order at midday on Tuesday, June 9, by RNC Chairman Fletcher, who wielded a gavel made of ivory and Brazilian rosewood, selected out of a dozen that had been submitted by people across the country. It was a short opening session, with a few welcoming speeches, the approval by delegates of the RNC's choice of Senator Frederick Steiwer of Oregon to be the temporary chairman, and the selection of the various committees. The convention then adjourned until the evening, at which time Steiwer gave the keynote speech, the traditional role of the temporary presiding officer.[15]

Radio had changed the way convention speeches were delivered. Gone were the days of orators shouting at the top of their lungs, waving their arms and strutting around the podium like a fire-and-brimstone preacher. For consistent pickup of their words by microphones, speakers were told where to plant their feet and not to move them, to not flail their arms, to keep head movements at a minimum, and to keep their voices at a consistent pitch. Steiwer, a second-term senator, was supposedly selected by the RNC because he had "a magnificent radio voice." His speech was a "sharp indictment" of the New Deal, criticizing what he called make-work government projects, no help to private business, and its massive costs and deficit spending. "The only business fostered by this administration," proclaimed Steiwer, "is the debt business." It had, he lamented, been "three long years" since Roosevelt had been in office. At one point, he got on a roll by posing rhetorical questions to the audience, to which they enthusiastically responded with his suggested answer. One such exchange went as follows: "For how long," he asked, "have we lived under the evil trinity of increased deficits, increased debt and increased taxes?" The shouted reply of "FOR THREE LONG YEARS!" rang throughout the hot and muggy arena. Overnight, the chant became a slogan for Republicans and was converted into a song, sung to the tune of the nursery rhyme "Three Blind Mice." One version of it went:

Three long years, Three long years,
Full of Grief and Tears, Full of Grief and Tears,
Roosevelt gave us to understand,
If we would lend a helping hand,
He'd lead us to the promised land.
For three long years,
When we got to the promised land,
We found it nothing but shifting sand,
For three long years!"

In the next day's newspapers, Steiwer's speech received good, but not great, reviews. There had been some talk of him as a potential vice-presidential nominee, but reporters concluded that the speech was not the stemwinder that would have been needed to propel him onto the ticket.[16]

At its daytime session on Wednesday, June 10, the convention received and acted on the reports from its committees on credentials and permanent organization. It was recommended that Bertrand Snell, a longtime congressman from New York, be the permanent chairman, which was approved by the delegates. Snell then gave a speech, hitting on the same anti-New Deal themes that Steiwer had emphasized the night before. There never seemed to be much interest at conventions in speeches from permanent chairmen, which were usually seen as an afterthought to the keynote speech. Snell's was no exception. It was the speech scheduled for that evening that most of the delegates, those in the galleries, and reporters were most anticipating.[17]

The Wednesday evening session featured a speech from Herbert Hoover, the first time a former president had addressed a convention. Convention officials had first offered him a morning or afternoon time slot, when the radio audience would be much smaller. Hoover rejected these, argued that he deserved better, and held out for a prime-time evening speech. It was a good move on his part, as he rose to the occasion. Although most Republicans did not want to see Hoover a candidate again, they still respected him, as shown in their welcome for the man who was still the titular leader of their party. He was greeted with a fifteen-minute ovation that was reported as "genuine and joyous." After arriving in Cleveland that morning, he had avoided any one-on-one meetings with representatives of any of the candidates, not wanting to stir up "rumors of intrigue" of any alleged plotting with them to try to stop Landon, nor of some last-ditch effort to claim the nomination for himself. Although he had previously referred to Landon in private as "wishy-washy," he made it known to party officials that he would not oppose him or any of the other contenders, except for Borah. The former president spoke with the pages of his manuscript on a metal stand atop the podium, blocking his face from much of the audience. This was not a concern to him, since the millions listening on the radio were his primary target. When in office, Hoover's speeches tended to be delivered in monotone, and were stuffy and boring. In this one, he injected emotion and pep. It was, without doubt, the best speech of the convention, and perhaps the best of his career. Hoover detested the New Deal, sincerely believed it endangered the country, and wanted everyone to know it. "In this room," he began, "rests the greatest responsibility that has come to a body of Americans in three generations. In the lesser sense this is a convention of a great political party. But in the larger sense it is a convention of Americans to determine the fate of those ideals for which this nation was founded. That far transcends all partisanship." Referring to the decisions of the Supreme Court striking down key parts of the New Deal as unconstitutional, Hoover proclaimed, "The American people should thank Almighty God for the Constitution and the Supreme Court." He was interrupted again and again by cheers and applause. Noting the explosion of government bureaucracy under Roosevelt, and its intrusion into trivial matters, he stated, "I noticed recently that they spent three hundred words on how to choose a hat. It is slightly more important," he joked, "to know the fate of a nation." American history, he noted, was replete with the struggle for freedom over tyranny. Now, he stated, the battle was between economic freedom, or centralization of government and collectivism. "Let this convention proclaim without shrinking," Hoover asserted, "the source of economic prosperity is freedom. Man must be free to use his own powers in his own way. Free to think, to speak, to worship. Free to plan his own life. Free to use his own initiative. Free to dare in his own adventure." In a call to arms, Hoover concluded his remarks: "Republicans and Americans! . . . . Stop the retreat, and turning the eyes of your fellow Americans to the sunlight of freedom, lead the attack to retake, recapture, and retain the citadel of liberty . . . . Thus can the opportunity, the inheritance, and the spiritual future of your children be guaranteed. And thus you will win the gratitude of posterity, and the blessing of Almighty God."[18]

The demonstration at the end of Hoover's speech exceeded that at the beginning, lasting for more than a half hour. Delegates paraded around the floor, the band played, and those in the galleries cheered and waved their hats and flags. The *Baltimore Sun* reported that the former president had "laid a merciless lash upon the New Deal," noting that much of what he said had been in prior speeches, but on the convention's stage and with the entire nation listening, "he said it better than ever before and under infinitely more inspiring auspices." When Chairman Snell tried to restore some order by introducing the widow of a former Republican president, Mrs. Benjamin Harrison, no one cared and the hoopla continued. It was some vindication for the man once hailed as the Great Engineer and a national hero, but who had turned into a national pariah after the onset of the Depression and who had been removed from office in a landslide. Those who hoped that the speech might start a stampede for Hoover's nomination were disappointed. After leaving the stage, and with the cheers continuing, he refused requests to return, saying that it would be "a cheap thing to do." Hoover was resigned to his fate. He was no great fan of Alf Landon but, he told friends, for him to try to inject himself into the nomination contest at this time "would have torn the party to shreds." Within hours, he was on a train to New York.[19]

The next day, Thursday, June 11, the proposed platform was read to the convention by Herman Langworthy of Missouri, the chairman of the Committee on Resolutions. "America is in peril," the document began, and it criticized FDR and the New Deal for usurping the powers of Congress, flouting the integrity and authority of the Supreme Court, and violating the rights and liberties of the people. The Democratic administration was, it charged, "guilty of frightful waste and extravagance, using public funds for partisan political purposes" and had "destroyed the morale of our people and made them dependent upon government." Despite this, the platform was not against the use of governmental tools to fight the Depression. Rather, it called for "a return of responsibility for relief administration" to community charities and to states, with the federal government providing grants to them. The platform called for a balanced federal budget, not by raising taxes, but by cutting expenditures "drastically and immediately." It supported social security, but called for "a pay-as-you-go policy." It called for vigorous enforcement of all existing laws against monopolies and for new laws to make it impossible for private monopolies to exist. It charged that the civil service system for obtaining federal jobs had, under FDR, been "virtually destroyed by New Deal spoilsmen" and called for restoration and extension of merit, not political patronage, in federal employment. A couple of weeks before the convention, in a five-to-four decision that even some Republicans denounced, the Supreme Court (in the case of *Morehead v. New York ex rel Tipaldo*) had struck down as unconstitutional a New York minimum wage law for women. The platform supported laws to protect women and children with respect to maximum hours, minimum wages, and working conditions, and stated (inexplicably, given the *Tipaldo* decision) that we "believe that this can be done within the Constitution as it now stands." It advocated "a sound currency" and opposed "further devaluation of the dollar." The platform retained the party's traditional isolationism, opposing membership in the League of Nations and the World Court, and any "entangling alliances." The platform favored "equal opportunity for our colored citizens. We pledge," it vowed, "our protection of their economic status and personal safety." In its entirety, the document was seen as "a compromise . . . with a New Deal flavor . . . but with enough of the traditional Republican conservatism." There was little audience reaction as the planks of the platform were read and the entire document was quickly approved on a voice vote.[20]

Nominations for president were next. John Hamilton, Landon's campaign manager, went to the podium to deliver the main nomination speech for the frontrunner. Before he launched into his speech, however, Hamilton advised that while Landon supported the platform in "word and spirit," the governor felt "compelled" to make his views on three points known before voting on the nomination began. Hamilton pulled out of his pocket what he said was a telegram from Landon stating that he interpreted the support for a "sound currency" in the platform to mean "a currency expressed in terms of gold and convertible into gold." Reportedly, Hoover had threatened to not support the platform unless there was a specific reference to the gold standard, which FDR had taken the country off of in 1933. Landon did not want Hoover publicly denouncing the platform. Landon's telegram also stated, regarding minimum wage laws for women and children, that, if necessary, he would support a constitutional amendment specifically giving the states the ability to pass such laws. Finally, on civil service, he stated that he would go further than the plank had stated and favored requiring federal jobs to be acquired by merit for all positions "below the rank of assistant secretary," including post offices. The delegates cheered as Hamilton read what were, in effect, Landon's amendments to the platform. There were no objections raised and, as Hamilton began his formal nomination speech, these supplements were considered to be a quasi-official part of the platform. This strategy of informal amendment to the platform was conceived by Landon's team in a successful attempt to avoid a floor fight over these items, which had been heatedly debated before the committee drafting the platform. They were confident that they could have won any battles over the platform, but it would have been divisive and would have delayed Landon's nomination until the next day.[21]

Any person who has ever had a bad shaving cut can empathize with John Hamilton. It was the biggest day of his professional life—standing before thousands at a national convention, his face to be photographed and to appear in newspapers all across the country, and with newsreel cameras focused on him. He addressed the convention with a huge white bandage covering his chin and jaw, said to be from an accident during a shave. Hamilton was, *TIME* magazine wrote, the unfortunate victim of "a virulent attack of a barber's itch." He began by contrasting Landon's life with that of the patrician Roosevelt, without mentioning the president by name. The party's nominee, he said, must be one who has "a sympathetic understanding of the problems at hand" from personal experience, who had labored himself, who had run a business, and met a payroll. One is more likely to be a watchdog over public expenditures, proclaimed Hamilton, "if his own property has not been bestowed upon him, but has been gained through his own efforts." On policy, Hamilton declared that Landon agreed with those "who want the Government to play its proper part in meeting the problems of our times, but who wish it to do so without wasting the substance of the people or endangering their future." About a quarter way through his remarks, Hamilton mentioned Landon's name, which resulted in the usual demonstration from the convention crowd whenever the likely nominee's name is first mentioned. After several minutes, he resumed his speech, followed by another long demonstration when he finished.[22]

That morning, all of Landon's opponents, faced with the Kansan's inevitable nomination, had issued statements releasing their delegates. As the roll call of the states for nominations continued, no other names were added and most of the other candidates, including Vandenberg and Knox, rose and urged support for Landon. Only Borah failed to participate in this show of unity on the convention floor. When the voting was completed, Landon won an overwhelming first ballot victory with 982 votes. Nineteen votes were cast for Borah. Of those, eighteen were from the progressive stronghold of Wisconsin. One was from West Virginia, cast by Borah's campaign manager. Wisconsin then moved to make the nomination of Landon unanimous, which was approved on a voice vote without opposition.[23]

Upon hearing the news from Cleveland, a crowd of thousands that had gathered on the grounds of the Kansas State Capitol in Topeka paraded eight blocks to the Executive Mansion, where Landon and his wife greeted them from the porch. "Nothing is more worthwhile than the regard of one's neighbors," the governor said in his folksy manner, "Nothing tugs more strongly at one's heart strings than their good wishes." He vowed to "wage one of the most aggressive campaigns the Republican party has seen in years and lead the party to victory in November." The campaign would not begin, as Roosevelt had started his in 1932, by flying to the convention city and addressing the convention in person. Landon had declined an offer from a famous pilot, Clarence Chamberlin of Iowa (the second man, after Charles Lindbergh, to fly nonstop across the Atlantic) to take him from Topeka to Cleveland. Landon likely knew that he could not compete with FDR in firing up a packed convention hall with his oratory. He would, instead, follow tradition and wait a couple of weeks for a committee from the convention to come to Topeka, at which time he would formally accept his nomination.[24]

When the convention met for its final day on Friday, June 11, a vice presidential nominee was selected. Senator Vandenberg of Michigan was Landon's first choice. Despite prior statements that he would not accept, Vandenberg advised, on the night that Landon was nominated, that he *would* agree to the second spot on the ticket *if* it came to him by acclamation. Hamilton and others worked through the night and, around 2:30 a.m., cleared the field for Vandenberg. However, early the next morning, having not gotten word of this, Vandenberg sent a telegram to Hamilton, again declining. Knox, early that same morning, who had advised that he would accept the vice-presidential slot, but having heard that all had been worked out with Vandenberg, got into his car and headed home in Chicago. With its overnight work wrecked by Vandenberg's telegram, the Landon team moved on to Knox as their choice and the Pennsylvania delegation met that morning and voted to endorse him. That afternoon, Knox's name, along with three others, were placed into nomination, but the others were quickly withdrawn before any vote was taken, and the publisher from Illinois, Frank Knox, was nominated for vice president by acclamation. Somewhere on the road in Indiana, Knox, accompanied by his wife and an aide, stopped at a restaurant and heard over the radio that he was being nominated for vice president.[25]

In nominating the down-to-earth and moderate Alf Landon, the Republicans had nominated the man among their potential nominees who would likely run the strongest in the election. Whether the Kansan could remove a popular incumbent president from office remained to be seen.

Democratic Convention

To renominate Franklin Roosevelt for a second term in 1936, the Democratic Party chose the city of Philadelphia as the site for its convention. Although Republicans had met there three times for their conventions (in 1856, 1892, and 1900), it was the first time that the City of Brotherly Love hosted the Democrats. For years, a city's right to host a convention had come with a price tag, in the form of a contribution to the national committee of the party. In 1936, Philadelphia agreed to pay $200,000 to the Democratic National Committee. At the close of the party's 1932 convention, Roosevelt's top political strategist, Jim Farley, had been made chairman of the DNC and, after the election that year, Farley had also been named by FDR to his cabinet as postmaster general, a key federal position for dispensing patronage. Farley, who remained in both of his jobs in 1936, worked closely with the president in planning every detail of the Philadelphia convention. Roosevelt's other key political strategist, Louis Howe, had died in 1935, after a lengthy respiratory illness. It was Howe, FDR's longest serving aide, who had helped see Roosevelt through the onset of polio in 1921, who planned out his political rise, and who had been instrumental in making him president.[26]

With no contest over the 1936 nominations (Vice President Garner was also unopposed for a second term), to keep the delegates and visitors occupied, a variety of activities in the city were planned, including a Mardi Gras festival, a prize fight, parades, and concerts. There was even a ringing of the Liberty Bell (then housed in Independence Hall), by striking it several times with a rubber hammer. Despite three microphones placed in its inside, this produced "barely audible tones from the hallowed bell." The bell's curator had advised those who organized the event that strong thrusts with an elbow against the bell's side usually got the loudest response, but, with the national press watching and a radio audience listening, poking the bell with an arm was rejected as undignified.[27]

The convention was held in Municipal Auditorium, an art deco structure with an arched roof that could seat more than 12,000, located just west of the Schuylkill River near the campus of the University of Pennsylvania. After several later nominating conventions of both parties were held there, its name was officially changed to Convention Hall. The structure was torn down in 2005. The main convention hotel was the still standing Bellevue-Stratford, where Farley set up FDR's headquarters and many delegates stayed. The convention, commented Frank Kent of the *Baltimore Sun*, would be the "greatest propaganda effort ever made by a political party." Although its business could have been completed in two days, to maximize media coverage, it was scheduled to last five, beginning on Tuesday and ending with a grand finale on Saturday.

Most of its important sessions were held in the evenings, when the radio audience would be the largest. Advance copies of all major speeches were made available by the DNC to reporters, to appear in newspapers the next day. Large black and white lithographs of Roosevelt and Garner were passed out on the city's street corners. In the city's Commercial Museum, located next to the auditorium, a large government-funded display, erected by a hundred WPA workers, touted the accomplishments of each of the New Deal's "alphabet agencies." Newspapers noted that FDR's administration had "offered" to set up the exhibit in Cleveland for the recent Republican convention, but that the GOP had "declined with thanks." In keeping with tradition, the certain nominee, President Roosevelt, was not in Philadelphia. He remained at the White House, but was in constant contact with Farley and others on his team.[28]

In the days leading up to the convention, two issues dominated the headlines. The feud between Roosevelt and Al Smith, the party's 1928 nominee and FDR's predecessor as governor of New York, had intensified. Smith, who had been beaten by Roosevelt for the nomination at the 1932 convention and who left Chicago in a huff, did eventually endorse the party's ticket and even made a few campaign speeches. However, once Roosevelt was in office and his New Deal agenda was implemented, Smith denounced the administration. He joined and became a leader of the American Liberty League, an anti-New Deal organization funded largely by the du Pont family and other wealthy Democrats. At a glitzy meeting of the league at the Mayflower Hotel in Washington in January 1936, Smith was the featured speaker and made a scathing denunciation of the takeover of the Democratic Party by FDR and his New Dealers, accusing them of being socialists and communists. "It is all right with me if they want to disguise themselves as," Smith proclaimed, "Karl Marx, or Lenin, or any of the rest of that bunch, but what I won't stand for is allowing them to march under the banner of Jefferson, Jackson or Cleveland." Days before the Philadelphia convention, Smith and four other leaders of the Liberty League sent a telegram to all the delegates, urging them to "put aside Franklin D. Roosevelt and substitute some genuine Democrat." But they knew, as did everyone else, that FDR was going to be renominated by acclamation and that the party would turn a deaf ear to their rantings against him.[29]

The other main topic of discussion in the days before the convention was the fate of the two-thirds rule that Democrats had used for their nominations for more than a century. Roosevelt and his team had tried to get rid of the rule at the 1932 convention, but backed down after being accused of being unfair and unsportsmanlike by raising the issue after the delegates to that convention had been selected. Opposition to any change was strongest in the South, because the rule gave that region a veto over the party's presidential nominee. The 1932 convention had gone on the record with a recommendation that the rule be reviewed for possible change at the next convention, so all were on notice for 1936. FDR and his team decided, with his renomination assured and his dominance over the convention, that 1936 was the time to do away with the rule and replace it with one providing that a simple majority vote of delegates sufficed for nominations for president and vice president. There was speculation at the time that Roosevelt was already looking ahead to running for a third term in 1940 and, knowing that there would be strong opposition to breaking the two-term tradition that had existed since George Washington, viewed the two-thirds rule as a barrier to his continuing in office after eight years.[30]

Of the 1,100 delegates who descended on Philadelphia, two-thirds were Democratic officeholders or party workers. There were 1,500 people to fill 1,100 delegate seats. As at past conventions, to allow more to participate, some states allowed the casting of only a partial vote by an individual delegate. More than two hundred of the delegates were women, who also made up a substantial percentage of the alternate delegates. These were increases over 1928 and 1932. Despite their numbers, women had never had a significant role at the party's prior conventions. In an effort to remedy this, a resolution was proposed at the 1936 convention that each state and territory name a woman delegate to serve as an alternate member of the Committee on Resolutions, with the power to vote if the male committee member were absent from any meetings. This was described as the "biggest coup in years" for women and was "adopted without a ripple." In reality, it gave little actual power to women (the 1936 platform had been drafted at the White House and there were few changes), but was viewed as a small step forward. There were also, for the first time in 1936, Blacks serving as full delegates from a state at a Democratic convention. (There had been one Black alternate from New York in 1924 and two Black delegates from the Virgin Islands in 1932). In Philadelphia, there were twelve Blacks as full delegates and twenty-two as alternates. This was symbolic of the dramatic shift of the party allegiance of Black voters that was occurring. Before FDR, most Blacks supported the Republicans, the party of Lincoln. Under Roosevelt, Blacks became a key part of the New Deal coalition, alongside southern whites, northern urban ethnic groups, farmers, and organized labor. By the time of Roosevelt's death in 1945, most Blacks had become loyal Democrats. Regardless of the gender or race of the delegates in Philadelphia in 1936, there was little of substance for them to do. As the party's nomination was uncontested for the first time in twenty years, and with no disputes over the platform or other issues, there was no need for anyone to court or plead with them, to try to sway them one way or the other. They soon found out, with no decisions to make, "they were there for their lungs, not their heads." In a rarity at conventions of both parties, not a single roll call vote was held during the entire Philadelphia convention. Everything was decided by consensus, or by a voice vote. As author David Pietrusza had commented, the delegates were "the Stepford Wives of Modern Democracy, ready, willing . . . and able to cast their votes for Franklin Delano Roosevelt and the New Deal for which he stood."[31]

It was not the presence of Blacks as delegates, but on the podium, that caused one of the most controversial scenes at the convention. On the second day, the traditional opening prayer was given, for the first time, by a Black man, Marshall Shepherd, a clergyman from Philadelphia and also a member of the Pennsylvania legislature. When Senator Ellison Smith of South Carolina saw Shepherd standing before the convention and leading it in prayer, he was outraged. He bolted from his seat on the convention floor and shouted, "By God, he's as black as melted midnight!" Smith stormed toward an exit, trailed by a handful of other South Carolina delegates. "Get outta my way," he blared, "This mongrel meeting ain't no place for a white man!" Smith did return, but not for long. The next day, Arthur Mitchell of Chicago (the first Black Democratic member of Congress), gave a speech to the convention, again enraging the racist Smith, who stormed out one more time, not to return. A photograph of Smith in several newspapers shows him seated with several torn pieces of paper floating about his head—his delegate credentials that he had ripped apart and tossed into the air. Speaking later to the press, Smith was unapologetic: "[P]olitical equality means social equality and social equality means intermarriage and that means mongrelization of the American race." He could never support, he continued, "any political organization that looks upon the Negro and caters to him as a political and social equal." Congressman Mitchell was equally angry. "I fear," he said, "the Senator is ignorant and steeped in prejudice . . . . [T]he sooner we get rid of his type the better. He is a disgrace to his state and to our party." The tension between southern whites and Blacks as part of the new Democratic coalition would increase over the years, culminating at the 1948 convention, when, after a strong civil rights plank was included in the party's platform, there was another and larger walkout by southern delegates. They went on that year to form a third party, the Dixiecrat Party, with Governor Strom Thurmond of South Carolina as their presidential nominee.[32]

The 1936 Democratic convention opened at midday on Tuesday, June 23, to half-filled galleries, with a rap of the gavel by DNC Chairman Jim Farley, who stood behind a podium adorned with a profile portrait of Thomas Jefferson, the party's founder. It was to be a short session, with the traditional main attraction of the first day—the keynote speech by the temporary chairman—moved to the evening, so that a larger radio audience could tune in. Farley gave an opening speech that set the tone. "[S]tripped of all camouflage," he declared, the main issue before the convention was, "Shall we continue the New Deal . . . or shall the Government be turned back to the Old Dealers who wrecked it?" The grab for headlines by Al Smith and his anti-FDR Democratic colleagues days before the convention provided fodder for a Farley attack. "The crew of the du Pont Liberty League and their allies," he declared, have "disgraced American politics with their appeals to race prejudice, religious intolerance, and personalities so gross they had to be repudiated," even by Republicans. It was clear from the outset, *Baltimore Sun* columnist H. L. Mencken commented, that Al Smith, the party's former nominee, was to be "the anti-Christ of this convention."[33]

At the evening session, Senator Alben Barkley of Kentucky, who had been selected by the DNC as temporary chairman, delivered the keynote address to a packed auditorium. The role was a reprise for Barkley, considered one of the party's best orators, having done the same at the 1932 convention. At the Republican convention in Cleveland a couple of weeks earlier, speakers had bemoaned the "three long years" since Roosevelt had taken office. In a take-off of that theme, Barkley declared, "For twelve long years . . . the leaders of the Republican party [under Harding, Coolidge, and Hoover] dwelt in a fool's paradise," with policies that led to the Depression and which, once it began, did little to arrest its effects. Bigger government, he said, was now a necessity: "In this age of infinite complexity . . . all responsible governments must enlarge their field of activity and supervision to the end that the weak may be protected against the strong and the rapacious, and that the approximation of justice may be obtained among all classes of our people." The Supreme Court, which had struck down two key New Deal pieces of legislation (the National Industrial Recovery Act and the Agricultural Adjustment Act) as unconstitutional by violating, among other things, the founding document's commerce clause, was treated by Barkley with "soft rhetoric." Noting that some of the Court's decisions were made by a five to four vote, he asked, if those "nine eminent men" could not agree on what is constitutional and what is not, who is to say that the five in the majority "are not infallible?" (Barkley did not mention that the Court's opinion in the NIRA case had been unanimous, nor that the AAA case had been decided by a six to three margin). Stating that FDR would "abide by" the Court's decisions, Barkley then asked, "Is the Supreme Court beyond criticism? May it be regarded as too sacred to be disagreed with?" He noted that prior presidents, including Jefferson, Jackson, Lincoln, and Theodore Roosevelt, had all raised objections to decisions of the Court during their administrations. Barkley's keynote was "a hard hitting, fighting speech" that received a fifteen-minute demonstration at its end. The main criticism of it was, as with his speech to the 1932 convention, that it was "a very long harangue," lasting an hour and a half, not ending until around midnight. By then, many who had crowded into the galleries had already headed home and, likely, many more in the radio audience had tuned out.[34]

On the convention's second day, Senator Joseph Robinson of Arkansas, the Democratic majority leader in the Senate and the party's vice-presidential nominee in 1928, delivered a speech, but not in the official capacity that had been expected. Even in a convention as micromanaged as this one, things did not always go as planned. Robinson, who had led the passage of New Deal legislation through the Senate, was FDR's choice to be the convention's permanent chairman. The vote on his appointment could not occur until after the Committee on Credentials had reported, but that committee was still deliberating when, with a national radio audience tuned in, the allotted 10 p.m. time for his speech arrived. The speech went on but, because of the delay of the committee, Barkley, still presiding as temporary chairman, was unable to pass the gavel to Robinson and was forced to introduce his fellow senator as "a delegate from Arkansas." Like Barkley's speech the night before, Robinson's was full of praise for FDR and attacks on Republicans and the Supreme Court. According to Mencken, the speech "turned out to be pretty dull" and, as with Barkley's, many in the galleries began to leave long before he was finished. Those who were left by the end applauded and cheered for only four minutes, brief for a major convention speech in that era. The demonstration was, the caustic Mencken observed, "born of hookworm, and died swiftly."[35]

On the convention's third day, at a brief afternoon session, two committee reports were received and approved on a voice vote. There were three jurisdictions with competing delegate slates (Minnesota, Puerto Rico, and the Canal Zone) and the Committee on Credentials, apparently not wanting to offend anyone at a feel-good convention, decided to seat both slates from each, but to allow each delegate only half a vote. Also, with the final list of delegates determined, the Committee on Permanent Organization finally reported and bestowed the title of permanent chairman on Senator Robinson, who was then able to officially take the gavel from Senator Barkley.

The evening session began with the report from the Committee on Rules and the much-anticipated decision to abolish the two-thirds rule for nominations. The chair of the committee, Senator Bennett Clark of Missouri, had a vested interest in presiding over the rule's demise. His father, former Speaker Champ Clark, would likely have been president, but for the rule. At the party's 1912 convention, Speaker Clark had the majority of delegate votes for several ballots, but ultimately lost the nomination to Woodrow Wilson. The Committee on Rules voted, by a margin of 36 to 13, that all questions before the convention, including nominations for president and vice president, "shall be determined by a majority vote of the delegates to the convention, and the rule heretofore existing in Democratic conventions requiring a two thirds vote in such cases is hereby specifically abrogated." To appease the South for its perceived loss of influence without the two-thirds rule, the committee's report also included an instruction to the DNC to develop "a plan for improving" the system of allocation of delegates at future conventions, which "shall take into account the Democratic strength within each State, District of Columbia, and Territory, etc., in making said apportionment." Under this, states with large Democratic majorities in elections, such as in the South, would be allotted more delegates at future conventions. When a voice vote on the committee's report was called, Chairman Robinson quickly ruled that it was passed, despite many in the arena thinking that the nays had outweighed the yeas. No request for a roll call vote was made and the two-thirds voting rule that had governed Democratic conventions for more than a century was abolished with hardly a whimper, a testament to the power that Franklin Roosevelt held over the party.[36]

The evening session concluded with the presentation of the party's platform which, like everything else at this convention, was approved without debate and on a voice vote. Presented by the committee's chair, Senator Robert Wagner of New York, the document was "all New Deal" and had been written mostly by two of Roosevelt's speechwriters. The president's input included a request (likely because the convention was in Philadelphia) that one of the most famous phrases from the Declaration of Independence, "We hold these truths to be self-evident," be used repetitively as an introduction to some of the platform's planks. Among these "self-evident" truths were that government was to "promote the safety and happiness of the people," that three years of Democratic rule had put the country "back on the road to restored health and prosperity," and that this had been done by "humanizing the policies of the Federal Government." The platform demanded that the issue of unemployment be dealt with "in a national way," favored continued cash payments to farmers, and, as a way to outmaneuver the Supreme Court (which had struck down several New Deal laws as unconstitutional), resolved, if needed, to "seek such clarifying amendment [to the Constitution] as will assure" to Congress "the power to enact those laws which [it] . . . shall find necessary, in order adequately to regulate commerce, protect public health and safety, and safeguard economic security." Gone were the pledges in the 1932 platform to reduce the spending of the federal government by twenty-five percent, and for a balanced budget. Journalist Walter Lippman noted the platform's fundamental shift in the role of government. It accepts, he wrote, "the thesis of a paternalistic government and to believe that the responsibility of the citizen to earn his own living has been superseded by the philosophy that the government owes the citizen a living and financial support."[37]

If there was a lack of drama on the convention floor that evening, it was present briefly in the galleries. As a speaker was touting how America's youth were head over heels for the New Deal, about thirty young men seated in the upper seats near the roof of the arena stood and began shouting "We want Smith!" They unfurled two banners proclaiming "Al Smith Democrats" and "We Want Al Smith." They were booed lustily by the crowd and several men rushed up to their section. Fists flew, canes were wielded, and the banners were ripped away. The interlopers were, according to a nearby reporter, "beaten up . . . with obvious brutality." Soon, Philadelphia's finest arrived and hauled the Smithites to the basement and, after some questioning, they were ushered out a side door with a warning not to return. No arrests were made. Sometime later, it was announced from the podium that the young men were not Smith supporters at all but, rather, were "merely hoodlums" that had been recruited by Republicans in the city's second ward to disrupt the convention.[38]

New technology in 1936 confirmed what reporters and others had believed for years—that Democrats, at their conventions, "always yell louder, boo more shrilly, and whoop it up more frantically than Republicans." The CBS radio network installed "roar machines" to measure the noise levels at both of that year's conventions. These "scientifically proven" devices revealed that the noise during demonstrations by the Democrats in Philadelphia frequently exceeded 100 decibels, while a high of 85 was the best that the Republicans in Cleveland could muster.[39]

Like all conventions, this one was part carnival and part sideshow. Those entering the arena passed by four young Mississippians who displayed their take on the cry at the recent Republican convention bemoaning "three long years" under Roosevelt. Two lean, dirty, and dour-looking lads, dressed in rags, held signs reading "Three Hard Years With Hoover" and, next to them, two rather plump young ladies, smiling and scantily clad in blue rompers, held aloft "Three Years With Roosevelt" signs. The message was clear—life was better under Roosevelt. In the convention hall, the Iowa delegation stood on their chairs and sang the Iowa Corn Song ("We're from I-o-way, I-o-way, That's where the tall corn grows!"), raising fresh ears of corn and corn stalks above their heads as they belted out the chorus. Philadelphia put on a Mardi Gras parade one night, featuring the city's colorfully-dressed Mummers, with a half million people lining the streets. At the conclusion of the parade, the results of the "Queen of the Convention" beauty contest were announced, with twenty-year-old Marion Fore of Texas named the winner and presented with a crown and trophy. Alice Roosevelt Longworth, the oldest daughter of the *other* President Roosevelt and a Washington socialite, attended the convention and always had a good quote. She was no fan of her distant cousin who now resided in the White House. "Franklin," Alice once deadpanned, "is two-thirds mush and one-third Eleanor."[40]

At noon on Friday, June 26, the convention proceeded with nominations for president. Only one name, Franklin Roosevelt, was placed before the convention. The president was nominated by John Mack, a longtime friend and neighbor from Hyde Park, who had also given the main nomination speech at the 1932 convention. Mack, who spoke in "a simple and straightforward manner and without effort at oratorical effect," reviewed FDR's life since childhood and then focused on his actions as president. His nominee came to the White House, Mack declared, "filled with relentless determination to rejuvenate the Nation, to break down special privilege and to place this country on permanently sound and stable footing." Roosevelt did not, he asserted, simply "wait for prosperity to come around the corner." Rather, "he proceeded to place this country on its feet . . . blazing a path to prosperity and security." There was a demonstration of more than an hour at the end of Mack's remarks, by far the longest of the week. The post-nomination demonstration, Mencken had observed, was the most important one at any convention. It must be carefully planned, but also appear to be spontaneous. There had to be, he said, a sufficient number of "Uncle Sams carrying American flags, of girl drum corps . . . of fair blonde creatures to be tossed in the air, and of well-liquored patriots trained to toss them." Without all of the hoopla over the speech and the candidate, Mencken observed, the radio audience will start to tune out and "the whisper will spread that all is not well" with the party or its nominee.[41]

In what must have seemed like a good idea at the time, Farley and the rest of FDR's team decided that the best way to showcase the unanimity of the convention for Roosevelt was to have a speaker from *every* state and territory—all fifty-seven of them—deliver a seconding speech for the president. Although the rules limited such speeches to five minutes, the long-winded speakers, who included governors, senators, and members of Congress, did not comply and there was no enforcement. By late afternoon, the half-way point had not been reached and the convention adjourned for a couple of hours until the evening. When it resumed, there were several more hours of speechifying to endure. "All of the whoopers said substantially the same thing," a reporter noted, "and none of them said it well." Finally, at 12:42 a.m. on Saturday morning, after most of the galleries had emptied, Franklin Roosevelt was nominated by acclamation by his party for a second term. The weary delegates mustered whatever energy they had left to cheer for a few minutes and then headed to their hotels for some needed sleep.[42]

On Saturday afternoon, the convention met to nominate its vice-presidential candidate. After the "political talkathon" the previous evening that "took all of the pep out of the convention," reporters noted that this session was "brief, listless and sparsely attended" by both delegates and those in the galleries. Vice President John Nance Garner of Texas, sixty-seven years old, was the only candidate put before the convention and, like Roosevelt, was nominated by acclamation. Mercifully, there were only a few seconding speeches and they were brief. The recently crowned convention queen, Marion Fore of Texas, led the listless delegates around the floor in a thirteen-minute demonstration for Garner. The convention then quickly adjourned, in anticipation of what was promised to be a much more dramatic evening meeting.[43]

FDR had broken with tradition in 1932 by making a risky and daring trip by airplane to Chicago to deliver his acceptance speech at the convention. In 1936, his team continued this change of tradition, but added a new twist. Instead of speaking indoors in the convention hall, to a crowd of 20,000, he would deliver his speech outdoors to an audience five times that size, at a football stadium. Careful planning went into the event, which was announced well in advance. It was held on the evening of the convention's last day, Saturday, June 27, at Franklin Field, located on the campus of the University of Pennsylvania and a few blocks from the arena where the rest of the convention had been held. Built in 1895 and still in use today, Franklin Field is the oldest football stadium in the United States. The DNC used the event as a fundraiser, hoping to raise a million dollars for the campaign by encouraging people to donate a dollar to the party and then attend a "nominator" meeting near their home, where they could listen to the speech with fellow FDR supporters.

At the stadium, the seats for the delegates were arranged on the field by states, as they had been in the convention hall. The stands were packed with 100,000 thousand people, with thousands more outside and unable to get in. Concerned about potential no shows, Farley had ordered 200,000 free tickets for the event. It was the largest crowd ever assembled to see and hear a candidate for the presidency. An afternoon drizzle turned, after most of the crowd had arrived, into a brief downpour in the early evening, leaving the crowd "wet by showers but undampened in spirit." Then, the skies began to clear. Many had traveled hours for the event. Some wore dinner jackets and evening gowns, while others were in tattered clothes. All were entertained by opera singer Lily Pons and the Philadelphia Symphony Orchestra. There were several warnings over loudspeakers that, due to safety concerns with such a large crowd, marching and parading were prohibited. Shortly after 9:30 p.m., the speakers throughout the stadium blared "Your president has arrived!," the symphony began playing "Hail to the Chief," and Roosevelt's open convertible was seen pulling up to one of the end zones, where a platform had been erected. Within a few seconds, triumph almost turned into tragedy in what FDR would later call "the most frightful five minutes of my life."[44]

The illusion of Roosevelt appearing to walk a few steps (accomplished by strapping on heavy leg braces and swinging his hips while clutching onto the arm of someone beside him) was central to the president's public persona. At Franklin Field, with son James by his side and after he was on the platform crowded with dignitaries, FDR recognized an old friend, the elderly Edwin Markham, a famous poet. As Markham reached out to shake the president's hand, someone pushed him from behind, resulting in him jostling James, and causing James to lean against his father. FDR went sprawling toward the ground and the pages of his speech, which James had been holding, were strewn everywhere. The tumult had caused a lock on one of the president's leg braces to become dislodged. Although he was unhurt, he was lucky, as his leg could easily have been broken. It is the only known incident of Roosevelt falling in public during his presidency. His security team had practiced what to do in such an emergency. They closed in on him, formed a tight circle, blocked the public's view, and avoided what could have been a public relations disaster. As one author has noted, "To the casual observer it appeared the President had been momentarily engulfed by the welcome he was receiving. Even on the platform itself only a very few were aware of what had transpired." Although witnessed by reporters, the incident was not mentioned in the press. As a secret service agent helped him up, FDR was furious, barking, "Clean me up" and "Pick up those damned sheets." Fortunately, the brace was not broken and its lock was able to be put back into position. Markham was mortified by the scene and his unwitting role in it. Within a minute or so, the president regained his composure and reached out and shook the poet's hand. A spotlight soon found FDR and he smiled and waved to the crowd as he made his way, with James, to the podium. The retrieved pages of his speech had been jumbled, but the presidential son got them back in their correct order. It is a testament to Roosevelt's unflappability that he delivered that night what many historians consider one of the most memorable speeches of his presidency.[45]

The official notifications to Roosevelt and Garner of their nominations, along with speeches praising both men, were cut short, due to time constraints. There was a schedule to be followed, as the radio audience had been told the president's speech would begin promptly at 10 p.m. Garner's acceptance remarks were, a reporter noted, "beautifully brief." They were also dutifully subservient, the vice president stating, "I am a soldier and my duty is to follow where the commander leads." Even so, Garner earned the ire of the watching Roosevelt by mangling the president's middle name, pronouncing it once as "Delaney" and another time as "Deluno."[46]

In a method he had used before, FDR had assigned two separate teams of two speechwriters to work on the speech, with each pair initially unaware of the other. One pair was told to write a conciliatory speech, while the other was told to write a defiant one. After reviewing both drafts, he had the writers combine the best parts of both, although it is the defiant tone that predominates. The final product is known to history as the "Rendezvous with Destiny" speech. It has been called one of the most radical speeches ever delivered by a president—a frontal assault on the wealthy and their attacks on his administration. He did not mention his Republican opponent, nor the leaders of the Liberty League of conservative Democrats by name, nor did he make attacks against any individual. The speech contained no references to specific New Deal policies, of those enacted in the first term or those to be proposed in a second. Rather, FDR presented the coming campaign, in lofty terms, as a struggle for the survival of democracy. Noting that, "Philadelphia is a good city in which to write American history," he recalled the royalists that patriots fought during the American Revolution. After the industrial revolution, he said, those royalists and oppressors of 1776 had been replaced by "economic royalists," who had, until his election, succeeded in controlling the federal government. Now, he proclaimed, the government had a new role:

> It was natural and perhaps human that the privileged princes of these new economic dynasties, thirsting for power, reached out for control over Government itself. They created a new despotism and wrapped it in the robes of legal sanction . . . .
> The collapse of 1929 showed up the despotism for what it was. The election of 1932 was the people's mandate to end it. Under that mandate it is being ended.
> The royalists of the economic order . . . granted that the Government could protect the citizen in his right to vote, but they denied that the Government could do anything to protect the citizen in his right to work and his right to live.
> Today we stand committed to the proposition that freedom is no half-and-half affair. If the average citizen is guaranteed equal opportunity in the polling place, he must have equal opportunity in the market place.

Roosevelt noted the stifling of democracy and the rise of dictatorships "in other lands," where people have "grown too weary to carry on the fight." The challenge to Americans in 1936—the opportunity to Americans—he declared, was to resist and rise to the occasion:

> There is a mysterious cycle in human events. To some generations much is given. Of other generations, much is expected. This generation of Americans has a rendezvous with destiny....
> [H]ere in America we are waging a great and successful war. It is not alone a war against want and destitution and economic demoralization. It is more than that; it is a war for the survival of democracy. We are fighting to save a great and precious form of government for ourselves and for the world.
> I accept the commission you have tendered to me. I join with you. I am enlisted for the duration of the war.

Audio of the entire speech, and video of portions of it, exist and confirm that it was a masterful performance. The *Washington Post* called it a "scathing" denunciation of the nation's elite. After finishing, Roosevelt got back in his convertible and, escorted by a half-dozen mounted police officers, his car made two laps of the track around the perimeter of the field. As the crowd cheered, the president smiled, waved, and soaked it all in.[47]

As the presidential vehicle headed toward the exit of the stadium, the twenty-seventh national convention of the Democratic Party came to an end. It had been a good week for Franklin Roosevelt—from the speeches since the convention's first day, to the demise of the two-thirds rule, to the New Deal platform adopted, to his own closing oration before a massive audience. It had all, as FDR biographer Frank Freidel commented, "effectively set the theme of his campaign. It was to be a war upon entrenched privilege." The president was ready, and was confident, to take his case for re-election to the American people.[48]

The Campaign and Election

Landon proved to be a lackluster campaigner. Being down-to-earth was one thing; being colorless and boring was quite another. He started out with a moderate tone, mainly criticizing the New Deal for its excesses and inefficiencies. As the campaign wore on, however, with polls showing him falling farther behind FDR, his attacks, and those of other Republican speakers, became more critical, accusing Democrats of putting the nation on the road to socialism and communism. Leading newspapers across the country, most of which were against FDR, chimed in. "Moscow in the White House," proclaimed a headline in the *Chicago Tribune*.[49]

In contrast with the strategy that had been used by most prior incumbent presidents, Roosevelt often took to the road and campaigned. He knew that the election was a referendum on him and he wanted an even more decisive victory than he had won in 1932. In his speeches, he often used the "economic royalists" term he had coined for his opponents in his acceptance speech at Franklin Field. After a Republican attack, late in the campaign, on social security (which the overwhelming majority of Republicans in Congress had voted for and which was going into effect in 1937), he unleashed on those who opposed him. "They are unanimous," the president proclaimed, "in their hate for me—and I welcome their hatred. I should like to have it said of my first administration that in it the forces of selfishness and of lust for power met their match. I should like to have it said of my second administration that in it these forces met their master."[50]

There were two third parties of note in 1936. Senator Huey Long of Louisiana, a Roosevelt supporter in 1932, unveiled in 1934 his "Share Our Wealth" program, which was far more radical than Roosevelt's New Deal and which called for, among other things, annual payments of thousands of dollars to each household, to be funded by limits on inheritances and incomes, and massive taxes on the rich. Some historians believe that Long planned to run as a third-party candidate to the left of FDR in 1936, throwing the election to the Republicans, and then, with FDR out of the way, run and win as a Democrat in 1940. It is unknown how this would have played out, as Long was assassinated by the relative of a political opponent in Louisiana in May 1935. The remnants of his movement joined with two other far left opponents of FDR, Father Charles Coughlin and Dr. Francis Townsend, to form the liberal Union Party. That party ran William Lemke, a congressman from North Dakota, as its presidential nominee. The Socialist Party chose Norman Thomas, a Presbyterian minister from New York as its nominee, the third time that he had headed that party's ticket.[51]

As the election approached, almost all signs pointed to a significant Democratic victory. The only outlier was the poll of the *Literary Digest* (which had accurately called past election results, but was not scientifically based), that predicted a comfortable win for Republicans. That poll could not have been more wrong. Roosevelt was re-elected in a landslide of historic proportions. The Electoral College tally was overwhelming, with FDR winning forty-six states and 523 electoral votes, compared to only two states (Maine and Vermont) and eight electoral votes for Landon. Not since James Monroe had run unopposed in 1820 had a presidential candidate won so decisive a victory. In the popular vote, Roosevelt received 27,747,636 (60.8%) votes, over eleven million more than Landon, who had 16,679,543 (36.5%). The Union Party candidate, Lemke, received almost 900,000 (2%) votes, while Thomas of the Socialist Party received less than 200,000 (0.5%). In addition to keeping the White House, Democrats increased the size of their huge majorities in both the House and the Senate.[52]

The 1936 election solidified the New Deal coalition that had formed in 1932, making it the majority force in American politics for a generation. Franklin Roosevelt won huge majorities from voters of low incomes, of union members, of Blacks, of Jews, and of Catholics while, at the same time, keeping conservative southern Democrats on board. Barring unforeseen circumstances or self-inflicted wounds, little could be done to stop Roosevelt from getting what he wanted during his second term.

Chapter 10

1940: No Ordinary Time

We all are just awaitin' for a bright November day
The New Deal will be movin' far from Washington away,
And so we are a shoutin' and we're happy and we're gay
For we have Willkie now!

We're for Willkie and McNary,
Every state they're going to carry.
So, we're singing and we're merry
For we have Willkie now!
—Republican campaign song, 1940

For a century and a half of government under the United States Constitution, the unwritten rule in American politics was that no man should serve more than two terms as president. The precedent had been set by George Washington, who voluntarily stepped down after eight years, and had been followed by all subsequent two-term presidents, including Thomas Jefferson, James Madison, and Andrew Jackson. Wariness of too much power in the nation's chief executive, and fear of the presidency becoming something akin to a monarchy or dictatorship, was ingrained in the American spirit. If these giants of American history thought that two terms were enough for them, how could any subsequent president think he was entitled to more?

As of 1940, this tradition of no third term had been challenged only twice, albeit indirectly. Washington and his two-term successors had declined a third *consecutive* term in office, but should their precedent apply to a two-term president who sought a non-consecutive third term? In 1880, supporters of Ulysses Grant, who had been a two-term president, thought it should not. Four years after leaving office, Grant, who remained personally popular, despite the corruption that occurred during his administration, was the choice for the Republican nomination by party bosses in three large states, New York, Pennsylvania, and Illinois. Grant supported their efforts and was eager to return to the White House. Going into the 1880 Republican convention, Grant and James Blaine of Maine were the two frontrunners. Opposition to Grant was based largely on anti-third term sentiment. Grant's supporters argued that disapproving him on that basis was misplaced, since he had stepped aside in 1876 and, in seeking a non-consecutive third term, was not disturbing the spirits of Washington, Jefferson, Jackson and others. At a bitter and divisive convention, neither Grant nor Blaine was able to win a majority of the delegates and the convention, on the thirty-sixth ballot, turned to a dark horse candidate, James Garfield, a congressman from Ohio, as its nominee.[1]

A generation later, in 1912, the third term taboo was also raised against Theodore Roosevelt when, after four years out of office, he challenged the incumbent president of his own party, William Howard Taft, for the Republican nomination. Like Grant, Roosevelt argued that he was not violating the tradition of no third terms, since he was seeking a third non-consecutive term. Moreover, his supporters noted that he had not served two *full* terms, having, as vice president, assumed the presidency in 1901 when President McKinley was assassinated six months into his second term. While opposition to Roosevelt within the Republican Party in 1912 was based more on the political issues of the day, anti-third term sentiment was a factor in the contest, and was an issue raised by Taft and his supporters. With support from the party's establishment, Taft narrowly defeated Roosevelt for the nomination, leading to the formation of a third party, the Progressive Party, by Roosevelt and his supporters.[2]

As the 1940 campaign season approached, the no-third-term tradition was alive and well. Another Roosevelt, Franklin, was in the White House, ending his second term. Unlike the campaigns of 1880 and 1912, any attempt by Franklin Roosevelt to seek the White House again in 1940 would be a direct challenge to precedent, since he would be seeking a third consecutive term. Would he, or wouldn't he? The nation eagerly waited to find out.

Republican Convention

Before the country would find out Roosevelt's plans, its attention focused on the Republicans, who would be holding their 1940 nominating convention three weeks before the Democrats held theirs. After what many felt had been a lackluster second term for FDR, Republicans were optimistic that they could win back the White House in 1940. They had a strong showing in the 1938 midterm elections, in which they picked up almost eighty seats in the House, eight in the Senate, and more than ten governorships.

Unlike the past few elections, foreign policy would play an important role in 1940. How could it not? One had only to read the headlines. Geographically separated from most of the world by two vast oceans, Americans were traditionally isolationists and most held the view that events in far-off lands were of little or no concern to them. The First World War, in which the nation had sent its soldiers to fight on European battlefields against Germany, had, if anything, reinforced this sentiment. More than 115,000 Americans had lost their lives. Never again, many vowed. But, as the 1930s ended and the 1940s began, it was hard for Americans to ignore what was going on, once again, in Europe. In March 1939, German leader Adolph Hitler's army invaded Czechoslovakia and, six months later, in September, his troops invaded Poland. The latter led to declarations of war against Germany by Great Britain and France. In 1940, the Germans continued their march westward across Europe, with April invasions of Denmark and Norway, and, in May, of France, Belgium, Luxembourg, and the Netherlands. By mid-June, all had fallen. Hitler toured Paris and the Nazi flag flew from the Eiffel Tower. Of all the democracies in Europe, only Great Britain remained beyond Hitler's grasp, and it was his next target. Against this backdrop of world events, only a couple of weeks after the Nazis took France, Republicans met to select their nominee for president.[3]

The leading candidate for the Republican nomination going into the campaign season was Thomas Dewey of New York. Born in 1902 in Michigan and raised there, Dewey attended the University of Michigan, had an excellent baritone singing voice, and had originally considered becoming an opera singer. Instead, he decided on a more stable employment as a lawyer and moved east to attend Columbia Law School, from which he graduated in 1925. He stayed in New York City and began a highly successful legal career. By the mid-1930s, Dewey made headlines as a special prosecutor in Manhattan, investigating racketeering, prostitution, organized crime, and political corruption, winning convictions of the notorious Charles "Lucky" Luciano, and other mobsters. He then was elected district attorney in Manhattan, where he continued his crime fighting crusade. "Gangbuster" Dewey's career became the basis of depression-era radio shows and movies and he gained a national reputation as a champion of justice. An effective public speaker and a lifelong Republican, the popular Dewey won the 1938 nomination of his party for governor of New York, but narrowly lost the general election to the incumbent Democrat, Herbert Lehman. His prosecutorial career, and his strong showing in the governor's race, made Dewey the favorite among eastern, younger, and moderate Republicans for their party's 1940 presidential nomination. Only thirty-eight years old in 1940, Dewey was a fresh face on the national political scene. Harold Ickes, an often-witty Roosevelt advisor, commented, when Dewey formally entered the race, that he had "thrown his diaper in the ring." In the spring of 1939, a Gallup poll found him the choice for president of slightly more than half of Republicans, a level of support almost four times that of his closest competitor. The downsides to Dewey were his personality and his cautious nature. Short in stature and sporting a mustache, he was vain, nattily attired, and yet colorless. In a later campaign, Washington socialite and gossip Alice Roosevelt Longworth would mock Dewey as looking like "the little man on the wedding cake," a comparison that seemed to stick. Always calculating, Dewey often hedged his comments on the issues of the day, tailoring them to opinion polls.[4]

If Dewey was the newcomer and Washington outsider among Republican candidates in the 1940 nomination contest, the leading veteran insider was fifty-six-year-old Senator Arthur Vandenberg of Michigan. Originally a journalist, Vandenberg had been in the Senate for a dozen years and had developed a reputation as a moderate Republican voice in opposition to

Roosevelt and the New Deal, endorsing some of FDR's reforms. He had been in the mix for the nomination in 1936 and had turned down an offer from that year's nominee, Alf Landon, to be on the ticket with him as vice president. Vandenberg wrote books about his hero, Alexander Hamilton, and considered himself a constitutional scholar. A pompous man, Vandenberg let it be known that he wanted to be president and would accept his party's nomination in 1940, but that he did not feel that he should have to actively campaign for it. He felt that primaries were little more than popularity contests. "Imagine killing yourself," he said, "to carry Vermont!"[5]

The third name most mentioned for the 1940 Republican nomination was Senator Robert Taft of Ohio. The son of former president William Howard Taft, he had attended college at Yale and law school at Harvard, was first in his class at both, and had been active in Republican politics in Cincinnati since the 1920s. Taft served more than a decade in the Ohio legislature before his election as a United States senator as part of the strong Republican showing in the 1938 midterm elections. Although having just begun his first term in the Senate, the fifty-year-old Taft aimed for the presidency in 1940. Taft was, in many ways, like his father. He had a strong intellect, was a favorite among conservatives in his party, but lacked the speaking and people skills often expected of politicians. As one observer noted, Taft spoke to audiences "as if he were submitting a brief in a probate case." Taft did not shy away from definitive stands on the issues. He detested the New Deal, rejecting even partial support for it that the last Republican nominee, Alf Landon, had espoused during the 1936 campaign.[6]

These three top contenders had different approaches as to how to win the nomination. In 1940, in about a third of the states, delegates to the Republican convention would be chosen in state primary elections, with the rest selected by the more traditional method of local and state conventions. Dewey, the most popular candidate, focused on winning primaries. Taft, other than the primary in his home state of Ohio, concentrated on getting the support of party leaders in states where conventions would select delegates. Vandenberg did not actively campaign, but did not discourage those working on his behalf, and his supporters did enter him in a couple of primaries. He hoped that the party would anoint him as its nominee, perhaps as a compromise choice if Dewey and Taft fought each other to a standstill.[7]

Notably absent from the political chatter about the Republican presidential contest during 1939 and early 1940 was any mention of Wendell Willkie. And with good reason. Willkie was not a politician, had never run for or held elective office, and had been a lifelong Democrat. Born and raised in Indiana, Willkie's life gave no indication of any interest in Republican politics. His father had been a strong Democrat, hosting William Jennings Bryan in the family home when Wendell was a child. As a student at Indiana University for both college and law school, Willkie was a vocal student leader supporting liberal causes. In foreign affairs, he favored internationalism. In the early 1920s, Willkie began his legal career in Akron, Ohio, was active in Democratic politics, and was a delegate to both the 1924 and 1932 Democratic conventions. By 1930, he moved to New York City and, within a few years, became chief executive officer of the Commonwealth and Southern Utilities Corporation, one of the nation's leading utility holding companies. In that position, he became a spokesman for the utilities industry. Initially a supporter of many of FDR's New Deal policies, Willkie opposed the creation of the Tennessee Valley Authority, a publicly-owned utility, and the passage in 1935 of the Public Utility Holding Company Act, which required his company and several others like it to sell some of their assets. By 1936, he had begun to criticize the Roosevelt administration for its regulatory and anti-business policies. Standing six feet tall and weighing well over two hundred pounds, Willkie was a bear of a man, but had a charismatic boyish charm about him that captivated those he met. Smart, inquisitive, and a voracious reader, he loved history, and stimulating conversation. In New York, although he remained married to his Indiana-born wife, Edith, Willkie had a mistress, Irita Van Doren, a divorcee, who was the book editor of the *New York Herald Tribune*. Van Doren was influential in New York literary and media circles. Willkie and Van Doren did nothing to hide their relationship and became part of New York's intellectual and social societies.[8]

In New York, Willkie attracted the attention of Henry Luce, the publisher of three of the most influential magazines of the era—*TIME, LIFE,* and *Fortune*—and became good friends with one of Luce's key deputies, Russell Davenport, who was the editor of *Fortune*. Davenport and Willkie had extensive discussions on politics and found much agreement in their views. Luce's publications began to run favorable articles on Willkie and, during the last few months of 1939, Willkie and Davenport plotted a strategy for Willkie to seek the 1940 Republican presidential nomination. First, Willkie had to become a Republican, which he did by quietly changing his party affiliation. As a non-politician and a political outsider, the plan was for Willkie to eschew running in primaries, or seeking delegates by courting party leaders at state conventions. Rather, the strategy was for him to give speeches and write articles on the issues of the day, and to use favorable coverage in the press, led by Luce's publications, to build momentum for his campaign. Soon, some Wall Street financiers and Madison Avenue advertising executives came on board, the latter of which created a media blitz that downplayed Willkie's life as a utilities executive and corporate lawyer and, instead, focused on his Midwest upbringing and portrayed him as a homespun and friendly self-made man. There was also grassroots support for Willkie across the country. In April 1940, Oren Root, Jr. (a nephew of former Secretary of State Elihu Root) formed the first of what would eventually be five hundred "Willkie for President" clubs. Author Herbert Eaton has written of these clubs and those who joined them: "Eager amateurs from . . . the 'station wagon set' flocked to the call, and thousands of young, middle-class Republicans, whose previous experience with grass roots had been limited to crab grass, found themselves in the vanguard of a great, spontaneous movement."[9]

Primary elections were held in a dozen states from March to May, with delegates selected at state conventions in the rest. As noted earlier, Dewey focused on the primaries and Taft on the conventions. Vandenberg competed in only a few of either. Willkie competed in none. Dewey won the Wisconsin and Nebraska primaries over Vandenberg, which was seen as the death knell of Vandenberg's hopes, as they were defeats in his home region of the Midwest. Dewey also won primaries in Illinois, New Jersey, and Maryland. In the rest of the primary states, uncommitted delegate slates were selected, or ones that supported favorite sons. The most prominent of the latter were Representative Joseph Martin of Massachusetts and Senator Charles McNary of Oregon. An upstate New York newspaper publisher, Frank Gannett, also entered the race. And there was one more possible nominee. Former President Herbert Hoover, eight years after his landslide loss to Roosevelt, still held out hope for a political comeback. With 1,000 delegates at the convention, a majority vote of 501 was needed to win. By June, Dewey was the frontrunner, with around 300 delegates, but well short of the number needed. Taft was second, with around 200 pledged delegates. Vandenberg had about seventy delegates, more than half of whom were from his home state of Michigan. Willkie had no publicly pledged delegates, but he had something else—momentum from the people. By 1940, public opinion polls, especially those from respected pollster George Gallup, had become influential. In early May, a Gallup poll showed Dewey with a commanding lead of 67% among Republican voters, with Vandenberg at 14%, Taft at 12%, and Willkie with only 3%. Two weeks before the convention, Willkie jumped up to 12%. The week before the convention, Gallup released a new poll showing that Dewey had dropped to 47%, and that Willkie had surged to 29%, moving into second place, well ahead of both Taft and Vandenberg, who had 8% each.[10]

With the German takeover of most of Europe, the positions of the candidates on American assistance to the fallen democracies there, and to the last surviving one, Great Britain, became more important. Taft remained the most isolationist of the major contenders, calling the Democrats the "war party" and stating that Republicans needed to be the "peace party." He accused Roosevelt of trying to distract attention from his domestic failures by "ballyhooing the foreign situation." In mid-May, Taft told a Kansas audience, "This is no time for the people to be wholly absorbed in foreign battles" and to ignore the "screaming headlines" in the newspapers. Dewey was only slightly less isolationist, initially saying the United States must "keep its hands wholly out of the European war." He later amended his position to call for "all proper" aid to the Allies, by which he meant the sale of surplus military supplies, but nothing more. Influential columnist Walter Lippman blamed Taft and Dewey for feeding Nazi aggression. They had, Lippman wrote, assured "Hitler that he could safely disregard America and go to war." Vandenberg also focused on the home front, declaring that America should "cling relentlessly" to a policy of neutrality in the European war. He was for increased defenses to any possible invasion, a policy he dubbed "insulationism." He argued that, with vast oceans protecting both of its coasts, "the United States need fear no other nation, if we mind our own business." Willkie held a more internationalist view, stating he favored "all possible aid to the Allies," short of providing troops. He later wrote that the isolationist position of the leading candidates was one of the main reasons that he decided to enter the contest.[11]

The 1940 Republican convention was held in Convention Hall in Philadelphia, the same building in which Franklin Roosevelt had been nominated for a second term in 1936. The arena, exposed to the sun during daytime, had a modest air conditioning system, but that provided little relief from outside temperatures that rose to ninety degrees on most days that the convention met, especially with more than 16,000 people packed inside. One observer called it "a filthy, sweaty hell of sealed-in heat." As at most political conventions, the arena was decorated with

American flags and red, white, and blue bunting. A large bronze spread-winged eagle adorned the front of the podium. The coats of arms of each of the forty-eight states hung from the balconies. On the convention floor, the signs designating each state's delegation were topped by a figure of an elephant holding a flag in its trunk. Distinguished guests included the widows of two former presidents, Mrs. Benjamin Harrison and Mrs. William Howard Taft. The latter, Helen "Nellie" Taft, was there hoping to see her eldest son, Robert, nominated for the job once held by her husband. Some of the "Republican Roosevelts" of Oyster Bay (as opposed to the "Democratic Roosevelts" of Hyde Park) were present. Three of Theodore Roosevelt's children, each supporting different candidates, attended the convention. Son Ted, Jr. was a New York delegate supporting Dewey. Another son, Archie, favored Willkie. Daughter Alice, the widow of an Ohio congressman, Nicholas Longworth, supported the Ohioan Taft. A future president, Gerald Ford, then a twenty-six-year-old law student at Yale, watched from the galleries and was a Willkie supporter.[12]

Radio coverage of conventions had begun in 1924 and, ever since then, millions of Americans listened in as Democrats and Republicans went about the process of selecting their nominees for president and vice president. In 1940, a new medium—television—came to the Republican convention. Using technology that was then in its infancy, NBC installed four television cameras in Convention Hall, along with special cables that ran over a hundred miles to New York City and to a RCA exhibit at what had been the 1939 World's Fair. The range of coverage was mostly limited to the Northeast and few at that time owned televisions, but it is estimated that some fifty thousand people watched some of the convention. The quality of the black and white images varied and background noises sometimes overcame the voices of the speakers. Still, it was a beginning. It would not be many more years before television would drastically change the way in which conventions were covered by the media, and the way in which the parties presented themselves to the nation.[13]

All of the major candidates came to the convention city to be visible, to participate in campaign strategy, and to assist in attracting more delegates. Following the custom of candidates in prior years, Dewey, Taft, and Vandenberg arrived by rail and were greeted by crowds at the train station. They then motorcaded, with police escorts, to their hotels, where they were greeted by, and made brief remarks to, their supporters. They then huddled in private with their advisors. Willkie's arrival was different. Wearing a rumbled suit and a straw hat, he told reporters on the train platform that he had no grand strategy, but predicted it would be a "wide-open convention" and that he would win the nomination. "Ask me any damn thing in the world," he told them, "and I'll answer it. Nothing is off the record." He ended up walking most of the way to his hotel, followed by a throng of people that increased in number with each passing block. He smiled, shook hands, and bantered with the crowd. When he got to the Bellevue-Stratford Hotel, he strolled into the bar and ordered a scotch and soda, trailed by reporters and onlookers. After a while, he said, "Let's have another," and began shaking hands with the new arrivals. He moved on to the lobby of the Benjamin Franklin Hotel, where he saw James Watson, a conservative former Republican senator from his home state of Indiana.

When Willkie asked Watson, who was supporting Dewey for president, to consider switching to him, Watson responded that Willkie wasn't his "type of Republican." Alluding to Willkie's recent conversion to the party, Watson added, "Well, Wendell, you know that back home in Indiana it's all right if the town whore joins the church, but they don't let her lead the choir the first night." Unscripted encounters, as Willkie found out with Watson, sometime had their downside.[14]

How many of Willkie's actions that day were planned, and how many were spontaneous, is not known. But, mostly, they worked. A reporter for the *New York Times* was impressed, writing of Willkie, "he is at once a novelty, a sparkling political prism and a thrilling entertainment." With a down-to-earth, folksy manner, Wendell Willkie that day revolutionized the way in which future politicians would present themselves to the people. Modern era politicians who have carried their suit bags on their shoulders, who have played saxophones on late-night television, who have flipped pancakes in diners, or who have competed in axe throwing contests, owe a debt to Willkie.[15]

The convention was called to order around noon on Monday, June 24, by RNC Chairman John Hamilton, the man who had led Alf Landon's campaign for the nomination in 1936, and who had been rewarded by Landon with the party's top job. After Landon's landslide defeat, Hamilton became an effective leader of the party, guiding it to gains in the 1938 midterm elections. Although Hamilton, in his role as party chairman, had to be officially neutral in the 1940 nomination contest, he was known to personally favor Willkie and had agreed to do what he could, behind-the-scenes, for Willkie during the convention. Hamilton introduced the youthful governor of Minnesota, Harold Stassen, as the convention's temporary chairman, and the man who would, at the Monday evening session, deliver the convention's keynote speech.[16]

Harold Stassen would become, years later, a joke in presidential politics. He was a perennial candidate for the Republican nomination, running *nine* times between 1944 and 1992. Only in 1948 was he a serious contender. In 1940, however, at just thirty-three-years-old, Stassen was a fresh face and an up-and-coming star in the party. His keynote speech was well-received. He attacked the Roosevelt administration for seeking to cling to power too long. "Instead of keeping its eyes statesmanlike on the welfare of the nation," he declared, "[it] has turned its political eye upon a third term." A few days before the convention, FDR had named two prominent Republicans, Frank Knox (who had been Landon's vice-presidential running mate in 1936) and Henry Stimson (who had served as secretary of state under President Hoover) to national defense posts in his cabinet. Pending Senate approval, Knox would be the secretary of the Navy and Stimson the secretary of war. The nominations were portrayed in the press as a masterful stroke by Roosevelt, a way for him to deflect GOP criticism of his defense policy. Many Republicans denounced Knox and Stimson as traitors to their party for their willingness to serve under FDR. Stassen, in his speech, portrayed the actions as weakness by the president, and as a "confession of failure" of the Democrats who had held those posts. It was good, he said, that a couple of "New Deal incompetents" in the cabinet were being replaced. Stassen then proclaimed, "it is only regrettable that we cannot change the entire Cabinet."[17]

While he was temporary chairman, Stassen was required to be neutral in the battle for the nomination. Two days after his speech, however, when his official role as temporary chairman had ended, Stassen held a press conference and announced his support for Willkie. In a new role that Stassen had requested, he was named by Willkie to be his floor leader for the rest of the convention. The recruitment of Stassen was a big coup for the Willkie team. Not only did the Minnesota governor appeal to the young members of the party that they were trying to attract, he was from the Midwest, where Willkie sorely needed additional support.[18]

The highlight of the convention's second day was a speech at the evening session by former President Herbert Hoover. Earlier that day, Stassen had turned the gavel over to Congressman Joseph Martin of Massachusetts, who had been named the permanent chairman and who would preside over the rest of the convention. At the 1936 convention, Hoover had delivered a spirited and scathing denunciation of Roosevelt's first term. After four more years of rule under the man who had tossed him out of office in 1932, Hoover had become even more strident in his criticism of his successor. Although his political views aligned most closely with the conversative Taft, Hoover had not endorsed anyone in the 1940 race. He was not a formal candidate, but he held onto some hope, as he had in 1936, that the party might somehow again turn to him as its nominee. The former president made a dramatic entrance to the convention, walking down the center aisle toward the platform, as those in the hall rose to their feet and cheered, and as a band played "California, Here I Come." It was seven minutes before Chairman Martin was able to quiet the crowd and Hoover began his remarks. He proclaimed that the Depression, if he had won a second term, would have ended sooner, and that the survival of American democracy was at stake if Roosevelt continued in office. "We are here," Hoover proclaimed, "faced with the task of saving America for free men." But it was Hoover's isolationist views for which his speech is mostly remembered. Although he acknowledged the aggression of the Nazi regime, he urged caution in confronting Germany. Americans should not, he said, "exaggerate our immediate dangers. Every whale that spouts is not a submarine. The 3,000 miles of ocean is still a protection." Hitler's war machine, he argued, was "useless to attack us," unless it could "first pass our Navy," which he held that it could not do.[19]

There was a curious lack of applause during Hoover's speech, especially given the ovation with which he had been greeted. The audience listening on radios could hear him clearly, but those in the arena could not. When he began, there were shouts of "Louder!," but the delegates and those in the galleries soon lost interest in what he was saying. It was later believed that the microphone connected to the hall's sound system (as opposed to the separate microphone for radio) had been defective. An angry Hoover later claimed that it had been an intentional act—that those in charge of the convention had literally silenced him, so that no movement by the convention to draft him as its nominee could develop. Years later, Hoover obtained an affidavit from an electrician, who claimed that he had been told by a Willkie supporter to switch out the microphone earlier that day. There had been some problems with microphones on the convention's first day and the change could have been to fix that problem. Whether that was the case, or whether Hoover had been the victim of a political dirty trick, was never definitively determined.[20]

In the second decade of the twenty-first century, efforts by foreign nations, particularly Russia, to influence American elections were in the headlines and much discussed. Such attempted interference was nothing new. It had been done before—by Nazi Germany in 1940. President Roosevelt, Hitler's government thought, was too interventionist, was likely to bring the United States into the European war on the side of the Allies, and needed to be defeated. It was, the Nazis decided, in the interest of Germany that the Republican Party adopt an isolationist platform, that its nominee be an isolationist, and that he be elected as Roosevelt's successor. Hans Thomsen, the German charge d'affaires in Washington, directed his nation's efforts to achieve this result. On the second day of the convention, a full-page advertisement appeared in the *New York Times* and several other major newspapers around the country. Directed primarily to delegates to the convention, the ad proclaimed, in bold headlines, "STOP THE MARCH TO WAR! Stop the Interventionists and Warmongers!" The first signature at the bottom of the ad was that of Congressman Hamilton Fish of New York, who was listed as the chairman of "The National Committee to Keep America Out of Foreign Wars." Fish was one of the most prominent of the many Republican isolationists in Congress. When hearings began in Philadelphia on the foreign policy plank in the Republican platform, Fish and his committee arranged for fifty isolationist Republican congressmen to go to Philadelphia and to testify against American support for the Allies. Years later, in 1956, it was revealed that the newspaper advertisement and the travel expenses of the congressmen were mostly paid for by the German government, in what Thomson bragged to his superiors in Berlin was "a well-camouflaged blitz propaganda campaign."[21]

Packing the galleries at conventions with supporters of a particular candidate, in an effort to have the noise and emotion of a crowd to sway the outcome of a presidential nomination, was a strategy that had been around almost as long as conventions had existed. Lincoln's team at the 1860 Republican convention in Chicago had done it. At Democratic conventions, New York's Tammany organization was notorious for skirting the rules and getting hundreds, sometimes thousands, of their boisterous members into arenas during crucial speeches and votes. Counterfeit tickets, bribed doorkeepers, or just crashing through gates, were tactics that had previously been used. In Philadelphia in 1940, the Willkie team had an "inside man" who did the job for them. Samuel Pryor, a RNC committee member from Connecticut and an early Willkie supporter, was head of the Committee on Arrangements for the convention, a position that oversaw ticket allocation. Pryor cut by half the normal ticket allotments to states in which Dewey and Taft controlled the delegations, and he reduced the number of tickets given out to party officials and to financial contributors to the party. He also created a new category of "special admission" standing room tickets, good at only one gate, and had them handed out on the streets of Philadelphia to those who favored Willkie. As a result of Pryor's actions, and as the nation would soon see, the galleries in Convention Hall would be decidedly pro-Willkie.[22]

On the convention's third day, the party's platform was presented by Herbert Hyde of Oklahoma, the chairman of the Committee on Resolutions. Most of the debate in the committee's meetings had centered on the foreign policy plank and how isolationist or interventionist it should be. As was often the case with the language of party platforms, the words of this plank could be subject to different interpretations. It declared, "The Republican Party is firmly opposed to involving this nation in foreign war," but added, "[w]e favor the extension of aid to all people fighting for liberty or whose liberty is threatened as long as such aid is not in violation of international law or inconsistent with the requirements of our national defense." The platform was approved on a voice vote without any proposed amendments. The often-cynical H. L. Mencken of the *Baltimore Sun* was not impressed with the foreign policy straddle, writing that the plank was "so written that it will fit both the triumph of democracy and the collapse of democracy, and approve both the sending of arms to England and sending only flowers."[23]

After the platform was adopted, the convention moved to nominations for president. Dewey was the first of the major contenders to be placed in nomination. The speaker, John O'Brian, a noted New York lawyer, reviewed Dewey's well-known work as a gangster-busting prosecutor in New York City, proclaiming, "To the citizens of the greatest city in the world he brought safety and confidence." Dewey was praised for his "integrity, dynamic energy and boundless courage" and, it was noted, "above all, he can be trusted to keep us out of war." O'Brian declared that Dewey was "a lifelong Republican," an obvious criticism of Willkie, who had been a Democrat for most of his life. The New Yorker was offered by O'Brian as "the nation's favorite son." In a new rule adopted for this convention, bands in the arena were prohibited from playing during demonstrations for candidates, a change intended to speed up the nominating process. As a result, the show of support for Dewey, after O'Brian concluded, as well as for other candidates who would later be nominated, "lacked much of the expected color" of past conventions. Still, there were parades of delegates up and down the aisles, carrying signs and banners, and shouting. The Dewey hoopla lasted for twenty-five minutes.[24]

Taft was nominated by Grove Patterson, a newspaper editor from Toledo, who confronted the Ohio senator's reputation for having a cold personality. "If our candidate is not the best back-slapper," said Patterson, "he has the best back-bone. He has the courage to be himself." As president, it was asserted, Taft would rescind the New Deal and end "the million-dollar-per-hour spending of your money, the primeless pump of the bottomless well, quack remedies for chronic ills, the concentration of power in a bureaucracy, the tank attack on business, and the experiment with a Russianized economic system." Patterson, as the speaker for Dewey had done, proclaimed that his candidate was "a real Republican," another clear shot at Willkie. When the speech ended, the demonstration for Taft included balloons dropped from the rafters and a sea of Taft banners, proclaiming, among other things, "Trust in Taft" and "Statesmanship Not Showmanship." Reporters noted that there had been more intensity in the Taft demonstration than in the one for Dewey, but that Dewey's had lasted a few minutes longer.[25]

Willkie was nominated by Charles Halleck, a young congressman from Indiana. Knowing that Willkie was not the choice of party leaders, and that any chance his candidate had of winning would come not from the top down, but from the bottom up, Halleck declared, "This is a free and independent convention . . . in which the delegates are going to choose the candidate." To rebut the charge that Willkie had only recently become a Republican, Halleck asked,

"[I]s the Republican party a closed corporation? Do you have to be born into it?" Early in his speech, he mentioned Willkie by name. On cue, it seemed, the Dewey and Taft supporters among the delegates, who together were in the majority, launched into a chorus of boos and catcalls. Halleck had anticipated this, as his congressional office had been flooded with hate mail from the party's isolationists and conservatives after it had been announced that he would nominate Willkie. But the boos on the floor were soon drowned out by shouts of "We Want Willkie!," coming mostly from the galleries. The impact of Sam Pryor's ticket-scheming was now on display for all to see. Halleck continued his remarks, declaring that Willkie would unite the country and would be "the strongest campaigner that the people of this country have seen in a generation." When he finished, with 15,000 people in the galleries shouting "We Want Willkie!," the Willkie delegates went into action. A scuffle broke out in the New York delegation, which ended when one of that state's Willkie supporters grabbed, after a good bit of resistance from a Dewey delegate, the state's standard and led a train of Willkie supporters around the convention floor. The next day's newspapers noted the apparent spontaneity and intensity of the demonstration for Willkie. Some called it a "riot." It seemed to confirm what opinion polls in the weeks before the convention had indicated—that Willkie had momentum and was the choice of rank-and-file Republicans. At one point, while pandemonium was occurring above the convention floor, Chairman Martin banged his gavel and reminded those in the galleries that they were guests of the convention and should mind their manners. A voice shouted back, heard by most in the arena, "Guests hell! We're the people!" With some stacking of the deck by Sam Pryor, Wendell Willkie—a political novice and a man who had belonged to, and been actively involved in, the opposing political party for most of his life—was on his way to accomplishing one of the most dramatic feats in American political history.[26]

Nominating speeches continued on the convention's fourth day. Senator Vandenberg was nominated, as well as five favorite son candidates—Hanford MacNider of Iowa, Senator Styles Bridges of New Hampshire, Senator Charles McNary of Oregon, Governor Arthur James of Pennsylvania, and Governor Harlan Bushfield of South Dakota.[27]

After a recess, the voting began. On the first ballot, Dewey was in first place with 360 votes, Taft in second with 189, and Willkie in third with 105. Vandenberg had 74 and James (Pennsylvania's favorite son) had 74. The rest of the field had fewer than 50 votes each. Dewey was strongest in his home state of New York (61 of 92 votes), in Illinois (52 of 58 votes), and in Wisconsin (all 24 votes). Taft won all 52 votes from his home state of Ohio, and all 26 votes from Texas. Willkie won all of Connecticut's 16 votes, but only 9 of 28 from his home state of Indiana. The majority of the states split their votes among two or more candidates, an indication that many delegates were voting on their own and not being controlled by party bosses.[28]

On the second ballot, Dewey had 338 votes (a loss of 22) and Taft had 203 (a gain of 14). But it was Willkie who had the biggest shift in votes, picking up 66, for a total of 171. There was a recess for dinner after the second ballot. Many reporters focused on the Kansas delegation, which was headed by Alf Landon, the party's nominee in 1936 and still its titular leader. The majority of Kansas's 18 votes, including that of Landon, had been cast for Dewey. Landon told his fellow Kansans during the break that he was sticking with Dewey, but that he could not recall a prior convention where the leader on the first ballot had lost votes on the second and had still won the nomination. He was not optimistic and told a reporter that he did not think Dewey could win. Stassen, Willkie's floor manager, conferred with Landon during the recess, but no public announcement was made after their meeting.[29]

At the evening session, the third ballot saw further losses for Dewey, who dropped another 23 votes, and stood at 315. Willkie had another big gain, of 88 votes, and moved into second place with 259. Half of his gains came from three northeastern states—New York, Massachusetts, and Pennsylvania. Taft had a small gain of 9 votes, but still dropped to third place, with 212 votes.[30]

On the fourth ballot, Willkie, with a pickup of another 47 votes, moved into first place with 306. Taft was close behind with 254, and a gain of 47. Dewey lost another 65 votes and stood at 250. Vandenberg held fairly steady at 61, James of Pennsylvania had 56, and former President Hoover (who was not officially a candidate) had 31.[31]

Prior to the fifth ballot, Alf Landon went to the platform to confer with Joe Martin, the permanent chairman. They knew that, unless there was a recess and party leaders met and decided on a strategy, Willkie would soon be nominated. Neither wanted another "smoked-filled room" scenario. "Alf," said Martin, "we agreed before the convention that for the sake of the party we ought to make a nomination from the floor. I think we should stick to it." Landon agreed and decided to shift his vote, and the rest of the votes of Kansas, to Willkie, a man who had not even been a Republican until a year or so earlier. As author Herbert Eaton has written, Landon's decision was crucial for acceptance of Willkie by party leaders: "Although this decision meant only 13 more votes, it had an importance beyond the delegate strength. That the 1936 standard-bearer would come out for the man so recently a Democrat was of psychological importance and gave Willkie, as it were, his official membership card in the Republican Party."[32]

On the fifth ballot, Dewey's collapse became almost total. He lost 193 votes, dropping to only 57. It was now clearly a two-man race between Willkie and Taft. Each of them gained, coincidentally, 123 votes, with Willkie in first place with 429 and Taft in second with 377. Willkie's gain included the votes of Landon and twelve other Kansas delegates, who mostly had been voting for Dewey. When Landon announced the shift, a huge roar went up for the pro-Willkie crowd in the galleries.[33]

The contest was decided on the sixth ballot. An attempt by Taft's managers to call for an adjournment until the morning was rejected by Chairman Martin, who had already ordered that the sixth ballot begin. It was, by then, after midnight. Michigan was finally ready to abandon Vandenberg, but one of its leaders, RNC committee member Frank McKay, wanted something in return—the right to select federal judges from Michigan, if Willkie were elected president. Willkie, who had refused all prior offers of deals during the convention, was presented with the demand from McKay and consented to it. "To hell with the judges," he said, "get the delegates." When Michigan was reached during the roll call, it was announced that Vandenberg was withdrawing and that thirty-five of Michigan's thirty-eight votes were being cast for Willkie. That put Willkie only two votes short of the 501 needed. The race was over.

State after state, including Oregon, Pennsylvania, and Virginia, cast most or all of their votes for the political newcomer and newly-minted Republican. At the conclusion of the sixth ballot, it was announced that Willkie had been nominated with all of the 998 votes that had been cast. As author Herbert Eaton has observed, referring to the remark that James Watson, the former Indiana senator, had made to Willkie several days earlier: "The convert was going to lead the choir after all."[34]

On the convention's fifth and final day, a running mate for Willkie was selected. The weekend before the convention, after his arrival in Philadelphia, Willkie met with Connecticut's governor, Raymond Baldwin. Connecticut was the first state to announce its support for Willkie and Willkie had promised, if he won the nomination, to name Baldwin as his running mate. On the morning after his victory, however, Willkie was besieged with recommendations that Senator Charles McNary of Oregon be chosen for vice president. McNary, who had been Oregon's favorite son candidate, made more political sense than Baldwin did. McNary provided geographic balance, as he was from the West. Although born in Indiana, Willkie had not lived there for years and had been a longtime resident of New York. McNary was a horticulturist and popular with farmers. He was also respected by isolationists in the party, who were wary of Willkie because of his statements favoring limited American aid to the Allies in the European war. Willkie was persuaded that McNary was the wisest choice and met with Baldwin, who graciously agreed to step aside. A reluctant McNary, who was no fan of Willkie, agreed, for the good of the party, to join the ticket. Another candidate, Representative Dewey Short of Missouri, was placed in nomination by the party's conservatives, but it was never a contest. Willkie wanted McNary and the delegates obliged, by a vote of 890 for McNary and 108 for Short.[35]

Late afternoon on a Friday, after the vice-presidential voting was completed and as the final gavel on the convention was about to be pounded, a buzz of excitement spread around the arena. Willkie, in a first for a Republican presidential nominee, was going to address the convention. Roosevelt had broken with tradition in 1932 and 1936 and had personally appeared before Democratic conventions in those years to accept his nominations and deliver speeches. Alf Landon, the 1936 GOP nominee, had declined an offer to fly him from his home in Kansas to Cleveland to address the convention that had nominated him. Willkie's appearance, unlike the two from Roosevelt, was not a formal acceptance speech. He would follow tradition and deliver such a speech in the coming weeks at his hometown in Indiana. Still, it was a break with precedent, when Willkie, with his wife, Edith, by his side, walked down the center aisle of Convention Hall, to a deafening roar from the crowd, as a band played the popular song "Heigh-Ho, Heigh-Ho, It's Off to Work We Go." The tune, from the 1937 Disney movie, *Snow White and the Seven Dwarfs*, was to become the Willkie campaign song, with the substitution of the word "back" for "off," as in *back to work* the country would go with Willkie as president. In remarks that lasted only a few minutes, Willkie thanked the delegates for their trust in him. "I stand before you," he declared, "without a single pledge or promise or understanding of any kind . . . ." Alluding to the dangerous world situation, he said, "Democracy and our way of life is facing the most crucial test that it has ever faced in all its long history, and we . . . dedicate ourselves to the preservation of the democratic way of life in the United States, because here stands the last firm, untouched foothold of freedom in all the world." He continued, "The cause is great, we must win." After the singing of "God Bless America," as balloons and confetti wafted down from the arena's rafters, the new Republican nominee returned to the microphone and advised the crowd, "And now, I'm going to sleep for a week." With that impromptu and classic Willkie remark, the twenty-second national convention of the Republican Party came to a close.[36]

The nationwide reaction in the press to Willkie's nomination was overwhelmingly positive. Underneath a headline of "What Happened?," an article in the *Washington Post* concluded that staid Philadelphia had been hit by "a tornado that blew in from Indiana." It quoted a delegate, who said of Willkie's nomination: "You can't analyze a miracle. That guy is Joan of Arc with pants on." Much of the focus was on the fact that the convention had not been controlled by party leaders, and that it had bowed to the will of the people. The convention was "bossed," thought the *Boston Herald*, but it "had the right boss. The boss was public opinion. If the American people ever had their own way, they had it at this Philadelphia convention." Mencken wrote that Willkie's "nomination is a triumph of the amateur over the professional. Virtually all the professionals were against him when the convention assembled, and up to the moment of his nomination tonight nine-tenths of the applause for him came from the galleries, not the floor." Figuring out how and why it happened, the Sage of Baltimore thought, would require a few weeks of "extensive autopsy" by "the political pathologists." The *Kansas City Star* praised the Republican Party for being bold and cutting loose "from the moorings of political regularity." It portrayed Willkie as a savior for the nation: "If ever the people of America prayed, 'God send us a man,' it has been in the last six weeks, and if ever such a prayer was answered, it has come in the nomination of Wendell Willkie." Another writer for the *Baltimore Sun* opined that Dewey had failed because he had "leaped onto the band wagon" of isolationism, causing him to appear insincere, given reports that his own personal views were to the contrary. Taft was unable to take advantage of Dewey's collapse because "he was without imagination." Willkie won, the *Sun* concluded, "when he offered intelligence and bold sincerity in contrast to Mr. Dewey's trimming and when he offered imagination in contrast with Mr. Taft's dull, routine calculations. There are times when this American democracy seems to be an inert thing, placid under manipulations of second-rate men, lacking spirit, lacking purpose. There are other times when it is a torrent of feeling and conviction. Today is such a time."[37]

Strongly suspecting, but not certain, that he would be facing FDR in the general election, Willkie left Philadelphia a confident man. When asked by a reporter, if invited by Roosevelt, whether he would attend an upcoming White House conference on foreign policy, he responded that, yes, indeed, he would love to go. "I think," Willkie said with a grin, "one should always be courteous to his predecessor."[38]

Democratic Convention

After a successful first term, during which his popular New Deal agenda had been enacted to combat the Great Depression, Franklin Roosevelt's second term had decidedly more mixed results. His proposal in 1937 to pack the Supreme Court with justices favorable to his policies (by allowing an additional justice for each one over the age of seventy) was seen as an overreaching grab for power and was soundly defeated in Congress. The economy went into another downturn in 1937, with unemployment rising to alarming levels. In 1938, FDR attempted to purge Congress of conservative Democrats who did not support his policies, by intervening in primary elections and supporting the liberal opponents of several Democratic congressmen and senators. He was mostly unsuccessful. In this effort, he was seen as vindictive and he created bitter enemies in the party. In the 1938 midterm elections, for the first time since 1930, Democrats lost seats in Congress. Although the party still controlled both the House and the Senate, for all practical purposes, after 1938, with conservative Democrats siding with Republicans on key issues, Roosevelt no longer had a working majority to pass additional New Deal legislation.[39]

The evidence suggests that Roosevelt initially decided to step aside in 1940. He then changed his mind, likely sooner than he wanted people to believe. Outwardly, he gave every sign that he would retire. In 1939, construction began on the Franklin D. Roosevelt Presidential Library, located on the grounds of his family's Hyde Park estate, where he would have all of his papers during his years of public service stored, and where he would maintain an office to work out of in retirement. To help rebuild his depleted finances, in early 1940, he signed a three-year contract with *Collier's* magazine to write a column every two weeks once he left office. It would pay him $75,000 a year, the same as his salary as president. In meetings with his closest advisors, Roosevelt clearly implied that he would not run, even suggesting to some that they should pursue the Democratic nomination. With others, however, Roosevelt was equivocal. He told them that he did not personally desire to seek a third term in 1940, but mentioned two caveats. First, he said, the deteriorating situation in Europe, with Hitler and Nazism on the march, could cause him to change his mind. Second, he wanted to make sure that the Democratic Party would nominate someone whom he viewed as a worthy successor, *i.e.*, a liberal who would not dismantle his New Deal policies, and who would seek to expand them.[40]

At a meeting in Washington, D. C., in early February, the Democratic National Committee, in what was reported as "an exciting and spirited contest," selected Chicago, over Philadelphia, Houston, and San Francisco, as the site for the party's 1940 convention. For years, cities had been offering large contributions to political parties for the right to host their conventions. Philadelphia's backers advised the committee that they were offering $150,000, Houston's $200,000, and San Francisco's $200,000. Initially, those lobbying for Chicago offered no money but, when it looked like the committee would award the convention to Philadelphia, Mayor Ed Kelly of Chicago "rushed to the rostrum" and guaranteed $150,000 from his city. Kelly's action changed several votes and Chicago prevailed. The battle over the convention city was seen as an early test of strength between those Democrats who favored a third term for Roosevelt and those who did not. Kelly was a strong Roosevelt supporter and an outspoken advocate of another four years for the president. Third-termers tended to favor Chicago, where FDR had first been nominated in 1932, and where the support of Kelly's local organization during the convention could be crucial. Those opposed to a third term generally favored Philadelphia. Kelly had no authority to guarantee $150,000 from Chicago and had to raise the money afterward. His successful bluff and the resulting choice of Chicago as the host city would prove to be crucial to Roosevelt during the convention.[41]

One key Roosevelt advisor who opposed a third term, on the basis of tradition, was James "Jim" Farley. An Irish-Catholic from upstate New York, who had never held elective office beyond the local level, Farley had been instrumental in all of Roosevelt's elections. As chairman of the Empire State's Democratic Party, he had helped FDR win his two gubernatorial elections. Then, as chairman of the national Democratic Party, had done the same in Roosevelt's presidential races in 1932 and 1936. Roosevelt rewarded Farley by making him postmaster general, a cabinet post that was a key dispenser of patronage jobs by the federal government. A genial and likable man, Farley, who continued to serve as national chairman of the party, began to see himself as FDR's heir. In a July 1939 meeting with Farley at Springwood, Roosevelt's Hyde Park home, the president flatly stated that he would not run again in 1940. Farley advised of his own interest in the nomination and that he planned to set up a campaign organization. He went away from this meeting with permission to do so, and with an assurance from the president that an announcement of retirement would be forthcoming in early 1940. The first few months of 1940 came and went, and FDR's announcement never came.[42]

Roosevelt devised a strategy for pursuing a third term, the details of which he was unwilling to fully share with anyone. By the spring of 1940, and possibly much earlier, he had decided that he wanted to be nominated again but, because of the no-third-term tradition, did not want to be seen as doing anything to encourage that outcome. His preference was to be drafted by the convention, hopefully by a unanimous vote. A week before the convention, he once again met with Farley at Hyde Park. It was an awkward meeting. A year earlier, in the same room, the president had told Farley that he absolutely would not run in 1940. Since then, Farley had become a candidate for the nomination himself. FDR now backtracked, telling Farley that, personally, he still did not want to run, but might have to accept the party's nomination. He advised that he had decided to write out a statement expressing his wishes and would have it read to the delegates. Farley suggested that this be a Shermanesque statement, containing refusals to run if nominated, or to serve if elected. FDR demurred, citing the situation in Europe. If the convention chose to draft him, in such perilous times, he told Farley, he had a duty to accept. The president declined to reveal to Farley, the chairman of the Democratic Party, the content of his statement to the convention. An angry Farley vowed that he was not going to drop his own bid for the nomination, despite what Roosevelt now said.[43]

The convention was held at Chicago Stadium, which was located near the present-day United Center. The facility had opened in 1929 and was the home of the city's hockey team, the Blackhawks. It had also been the site of the 1932 Democratic convention, when FDR had first been nominated for president, and could seat more than 20,000 people. The hall was decorated with hundreds of American flags, giving it, a reporter noted, the appearance of "a high-toned county fair in the hog-and-hominy belt." The seats for the delegates were painted bright red. A large spread-winged gilded eagle was mounted just below the podium. A portrait of FDR dominated one end of the hall. Hanging from the ceiling above the podium, in what was described as a "beehive," was a compilation of sixteen loudspeakers, containing the latest in amplification technology, which had been installed by Mayor Kelly's crew. The old days of convention orators not being heard from more than a few feet away where they stood were long gone.[44]

There were 1,094 delegates to the convention. With the 1936 repeal of the party's long standing two-thirds rule, a simple majority vote of 548 delegates was needed to win the nomination. Many of the delegates were pledged to vote for Roosevelt *if* he were a candidate and would accept the nomination. The weekend before the convention, there was still no formal word from the White House, one way or the other. H. L. Mencken of the *Baltimore Sun* wrote that Roosevelt's shadow hung so heavily over the convention that all Democrats could do was "stagger around in the dark" while waiting for some sign from the president. The FDR strategy of not actively seeking the nomination, but to have the convention draft him, precluded him from having any official campaign organization in Chicago. He asked Harry Hopkins, who had become one of his closest advisers and was the secretary of commerce, to be in charge of his interests in Chicago, but gave no specific instructions as to how to proceed. James Byrnes, a senator from South Carolina and a delegate, was asked by Roosevelt to be his manager on the floor of the convention, but was likewise given little direction. From his suite in the Blackstone Hotel, Hopkins met with numerous Democratic leaders to orchestrate a draft of Roosevelt. Some viewed Hopkins' tactics as overbearing and complaints filtered back to the White House about feathers that had been ruffled. But Hopkins was given free rein by the president, who was in contact with him through a direct telephone line, installed, to ensure privacy, in the bathroom of Hopkins' hotel room.[45]

The president's wish to be drafted for a third term by a unanimous call from the convention was not going to happen. In addition to Jim Farley, a few others decided to pursue the nomination. The most prominent among these was the sitting vice president, John Nance Garner of Texas. The seventy-one-year-old Garner was a conservative Democrat who had never been part of FDR's inner circle and who had opposed many of the president's policies during the second term. Garner's frustration with his role in the Roosevelt administration can be seen from his most famous statement. Years later, when fellow Texan Lyndon Johnson called him in 1960 asking for advice on whether to accept John Kennedy's offer to be his running mate, Garner told Johnson that the vice presidency was an office that was "not worth a bucket of warm piss." The quote was later softened to refer to spit. A traditionalist, Garner was adamantly opposed to Roosevelt seeking a third term. If FDR was not a candidate in 1940, polls of Democrats showed that Garner was the frontrunner for the nomination and, in late 1939, he formally announced his candidacy.

Other than Garner and Farley, the remaining candidates were not well known. Burton Wheeler, a senator from Montana, was being put forward by the isolationist wing of the party. Millard Tydings, an anti-New Deal senator from Maryland (one whom FDR had tried and failed to defeat in his 1938 "purge" of conservative Democrats), was running as a favorite son candidate of his state. There were also a few other favorite son candidates. Another potential nominee was Cordell Hull, a sixty-eight-year-old Tennessean who had been serving for eight years as Roosevelt's secretary of state. On those occasions when FDR discussed with others that he might not run, Hull was usually someone he mentioned who could be, in his opinion, a worthy successor. But Hull had little interest in being president, would not actively seek the office, and his age was a concern for FDR and others.[46]

The convention opened shortly after noon on Monday, July 15, with Farley, in his role as party chairman, gaveling it to order. By 1940, daytime sessions at conventions were unimportant and routine. Key speeches and events were scheduled for evenings, when a much larger national radio audience would be listening. Farley introduced Mayor Kelly of Chicago to give a speech welcoming all to his city. Kelly, an outspoken Roosevelt supporter and the man most responsible for bringing the convention to Chicago, launched into a draft Roosevelt diatribe. Proclaimed Kelly, "The human family of democracy everywhere will be forever grateful, or forever saddened, by the final verdict of this convention . . . . We are praying and hoping that a man who can keep the White House as the lighthouse of humanity will accept the crushing load the next four years are sure to bring." The convention, he said, *had* to nominate Roosevelt again, regardless of the president's personal preferences. Shouted Kelly, "The salvation of the nation rests in one man!" His remarks, delivered to a mostly empty hall in the early afternoon, did not generate the enthusiasm for the president that he and others working for a draft of Roosevelt had hoped.[47]

After a break lasting several hours, the convention resumed in the evening, to a packed house. On the agenda were speeches from Farley and the man who had been named the convention's temporary chairman, Speaker of the House William Bankhead of Alabama. In contrast to Kelly's earlier pro-Roosevelt rant, neither Farley nor Bankhead mentioned the president by name. Farley, a candidate himself, and miffed over FDR's reneging on his earlier no-third-term promise, was not about to let Roosevelt's name pass his lips, which he knew would start a pro-Roosevelt demonstration in the arena. Farley was well-received by the delegates and the galleries. He had been a popular and successful chairman of the party, and had announced that he would be stepping down. This was his valedictory address as chairman to a Democratic convention. A diehard baseball fan, Farley was, at the time of the convention, involved with a group of investors attempting to purchase the New York Yankees and, if successful, he would be the club's president. A band played "Take Me Out to the Ballgame" as he walked to the podium. Farley lauded the New Deal and "the Democratic administration." His biggest applause, however, came from a statement on foreign policy, proclaiming, "This administration has given its solemn pledge that no American boy will be sent to die in the battlefields of Europe and this compact will be kept." Farley then handed the convention's gavel, adorned with a red, white and blue ribbon, to Bankhead, the temporary chairman. Although an accomplished politician, Bankhead was perhaps more known to the American public as the father of Tallulah Bankhead, a flamboyant actress in that era of the stage and screen. In his slow, southern drawl, Bankhead praised the accomplishments of the New Deal and lambasted Republicans but, like Farley, never referred to Roosevelt by name. His speech received mediocre reviews in the press and the response in the hall was not overwhelming.[48]

According to newspaper reports, the convention's opening day met with a largely apathetic response. Many delegates, sporting "Just Roosevelt" buttons, were angry over the lack of any definitive word from the president. The *Chicago Tribune* reported that the failure of the third term effort to "strike fire" was the most noticeable feature of the first day. Opined the newspaper, "Unless the Roosevelt leaders succeed in evoking a greater display of enthusiasm for the renomination of the President in subsequent sessions than materialized on the first day he might decline to run." Some of Roosevelt's closest advisors who were in Chicago, including Secretary of the Interior Harold Ickes and Secretary of Labor Frances Perkins, were concerned about the lack of direction of the convention and urged FDR to personally come to Chicago to take charge. He declined, but suggested that his wife, Eleanor, may be willing to come to shore up his support at the convention. Characteristic of the strange ways of the Roosevelt marriage, Franklin did not personally ask Eleanor to go to Chicago, but asked Perkins to talk to her. Reluctantly, Eleanor agreed.[49]

On the convention's second day, the afternoon session was again perfunctory. The convention's four standard committees (for credentials of delegates, for permanent organization, for rules, and to draft the party's platform) were announced, and there were a couple of minor speeches, following which there was an adjournment until the evening. The highlight of the evening was to be a speech from Senator Ablen Barkley of Kentucky, who had been named the convention's permanent chairman. The sixty-two-year-old Barkley was a longtime senator and had risen to the post of majority leader, where he had helped guide Roosevelt's legislative agenda through Congress. That afternoon, at a press conference in the White House, Roosevelt revealed that he had asked Barkley to read a personal message from him to the convention. This was the statement that FDR had told Farley about at their meeting a week earlier, but the contents of which he had refused to reveal. Mayor Kelly and other key Roosevelt supporters in Chicago likewise did not know the substance of the message that Barkley would be reading from the president. About fifteen minutes into his speech, Barkley mentioned Roosevelt's name in passing, which set off a pro-Roosevelt demonstration in the hall, lasting about twenty minutes. When the crowd quieted, Barkley resumed, finished his remarks, and closed by noting that he had a statement from the president, which he wished to read. Paraphrasing the words that he had been given from the White House that afternoon, he continued, "The President has never had, and has not today, any desire or purpose to continue in the office of President, to be a candidate for that office, or to be nominated by the convention for that office. He wishes in all earnestness and sincerity to make it clear that all of the delegates to this Convention are free to vote for any candidate." Barkley concluded, "That is the message I bear to you from the President of the United States."[50]

Many in the arena were dumbfounded. As one author has observed, the reading of Barkley's statement from FDR "was followed by a moment of stunned silence as the delegates tried to digest its meaning." Roosevelt had released his delegates, but what did his words mean? Had he taken himself out of the race? As the delegates mulled the words over in their minds (he had said they were free to vote for *any* candidate, and had not said he would refuse a draft), a deep voice came from the "beehive" accumulation of loudspeakers located above the podium, proclaiming "We want Roosevelt!," over and over again. It continued with "The party wants Roosevelt!" and "The world wants Roosevelt!" Reporters looked at the podium and there was no one there. Where, they wondered, was this voice coming from? As if by magic, all around the hall, in the galleries and on the floor, a full-fledged Roosevelt demonstration came to life, with people marching in the aisles, blowing horns, and waving flags and banners. The delegates, after being in Chicago for days, not knowing for sure if Roosevelt was in or out, now heard this voice—emanating from somewhere—calling out for Roosevelt. As author Herbert Eaton has observed, "the delegates were cheering from relief. They were no longer in any doubt. They knew what was expected of them." Bands played "Happy Days Are Here Again," the Roosevelt theme song from past campaigns. The voice continued to repeat the words "We want Roosevelt!" Microphones throughout the convention floor, one located in each state's delegation, were then turned on, and the chairmen of various delegations chimed in with "New York wants Roosevelt!," "Illinois wants Roosevelt!," and so on. Veterans of conventions looked on and realized what they were seeing—this is what a stampede of a convention looked like.[51]

Taking it all in, with a broad smile on his face, was Mayor Kelly. And with good reason. He had organized the whole thing. Uncertain of exactly what Roosevelt's statement to the convention would contain, Kelly was determined that it would be followed by a monstrous demonstration of support for the president's nomination. According to newspaper reports, "The city organization called in the boys for the big moment and packed the balconies" with ward and precinct workers. "We could not take a chance on a lull," Kelly later said, "for fear Roosevelt's message would be damaging." The mayor's cronies were admitted to the galleries without having tickets and were told to break into a Roosevelt demonstration on cue. The signal to begin was the "We Want Roosevelt!" chant coming from the "beehive" of speakers, the wires of which led to a small room in the basement of Chicago Stadium. There sat Thomas D. Garry, Kelly's superintendent of sewers, and the man whom he had placed in charge of the convention hall. It was Garry who had shouted into the microphone and ignited the demonstration above him. His middle initial, "D," he would later tell reporters, was "for Democrat." When the full story became known, Garry became famous in his own right and would go down in history as the "Voice from the Sewers" and part of the lore of presidential nominating conventions. The decision to hold the convention in Chicago, which Mayor Kelly had engineered at the meeting of the DNC months earlier, had proved to be crucial to Roosevelt's strategy for a third term. The Kelly-inspired demonstration lasted an hour, ending around midnight. If there had ever been any doubt, FDR's nomination for a third term, with the help of Chicago's mayor, was now certain. The next morning, newspaper articles contained confirmation from the White House of what most had suspected for months. Yes, if nominated, FDR would accept.[52]

On the convention's third day, the first item on the evening session's agenda was approval of the party's platform. The lengthy document was read by Senator Robert Wagner of New

York, the chairman of the Committee on Resolutions. The platform pledged to "strengthen democracy by defensive preparedness against aggression . . . by increasing our efficiency . . . [and] by improving the welfare of the people." It called for continuation and expansion of New Deal programs, including aid to farmers, protective legislation for organized labor, federal unemployment relief, and expansion of social security benefits. As the platform was being presented, there was little interest in it in the arena. The only significant applause came in response to the anti-war plank, which vowed that America would not send its troops to fight in the ongoing European war, "except in case of attack." Mencken of the *Baltimore Sun* noted the disinterest of the delegates in the platform, which he attributed to their belief that it "was not their business and they didn't give a damn. If it had repudiated liberty, equality and fraternity, and come out for cannibalism, they would have been for it, in all probability, just as heartily." They resented, he thought, the strings being pulled by the president and his team, who controlled everything that was going on in Chicago, but who did not want to appear to be doing so. Mencken added, "They learned the moment they got to town that their opinions were not solicited on any known subject, whether political, economic or epistemological. They were here to indorse and continue the New Deal, and for no other purpose, and it was intimated plainly that the terms in which the job was to be done would be chosen and determined by competent authority." The only amendment to the platform offered from the floor came from a Minnesota delegate, who proposed adding a plank opposing a third term for presidents. The convention, on the verge of being the first convention in history to nominate a sitting president for a third term, rejected the amendment on a voice vote. The entire platform was then quickly approved.[53]

The convention then moved to roll call of the states for nominations of candidates for president. When the first state, Alabama, was called, one of its senators, Lister Hill, went to the podium to nominate Roosevelt. Wearing a white summer suit and speaking with words that were "crooned rather than spoken," Hill declared, "This is no time for untried hands to pilot the ship of state." The crisis in Europe, he said, demanded an experienced American president. He proclaimed there is "no choice left to us" but to renominate Roosevelt, for "If peace is possible . . . he can preserve it for us and he will. If war is inevitable, he can win it for us and he will." The words "third term" were not spoken. The speech was followed by a demonstration lasting a little more than twenty minutes, much shorter and less enthusiastic than that in the loudspeaker-driven show for FDR that Mayor Kelly had orchestrated the previous evening.[54]

Speeches for the rest of the candidates followed. Farley was nominated by Senator Carter Glass of Virginia, a respected conservative in the party, who was in his early eighties and in frail health. Glass had received pressure from FDR's supporters not to trouble himself with a long trip to the convention to help lead what was sure to be a losing cause for Farley. The Virginia senator told Farley he was coming to Chicago. "Nothing can stop me," he vowed, "and I mean nothing." After a slow start and being booed by the pro-Roosevelt crowd, Glass's voice then "surged into a fighting roar." He praised Farley "as a man whose word every human being can always rely, a man who never in his lifetime violated a pledge once given." His intended contrast with Roosevelt was unspoken, but obvious. Glass proclaimed that Farley was "a man who believes in the unwritten law of the Democratic Party, as advocated ever since before the days of Thomas Jefferson . . . never to nominate a man to the third term for the presidency." There followed a five-minute demonstration for Farley, joined in by delegates from only a handful of states. Two more candidates, Vice President Garner and Senator Tydings of Maryland, were formally nominated, with no significant interest or reaction in the arena.[55]

The voting for president immediately followed the speeches and there was no drama, no doubt as to the outcome. Roosevelt received 946 and 13/30 votes, Farley received 72 and 9/10, Garner 61, and Tydings 9½. A handful of votes were cast for Secretary of State Hull, who had not been nominated. The tallying ended at two o'clock in the morning and the tired delegates filed out of the arena, to return in a few hours for the selection of a new running mate for Roosevelt. Vice President Garner, estranged from FDR and having openly challenged him for the presidential nomination, was obviously not an option.[56]

History was made that night. Americans had fought a revolution to rid themselves of the British monarchy and had always been wary of giving too much power to the executive branch of their government. For better or for worse, for the first time, a major American political party had nominated a sitting president for a third term. Mark Sullivan, a noted columnist of the era, and a critic of the action taken, wrote that Democrats were in denial of the reason why the no-third-term tradition had stood since the founding of the republic. In a column entitled, "We Are Not Afraid," Sullivan wrote that Democrats comforted each other in Chicago by saying to one another, "'It is not true we must keep a limit upon the power of the men we set over us—that is just an old wives' tale.' It was like men saying, 'Fire does not burn.' Or 'Water does not drown' . . . . [T]hey hope that by saying it all together, they would believe it . . . [yet] in their hearts they were a little afraid."[57]

Even before the voting for president had begun, word was circulating around Chicago that FDR had made a controversial choice for vice president. He wanted Henry Wallace, who had been serving in his cabinet the past eight years as secretary of agriculture. Wallace was, in the words of one author, an "oddly calibrated bird," especially for a politician. Born into a prominent Iowa farm family (his father, a Republican, had also been secretary of agriculture, under Harding and Coolidge), Wallace was a plant geneticist who had developed a type of hybrid corn that made him a millionaire. Politically, he was liberal, much more so than Roosevelt. He was fascinated by, and saw little to be critical of, the communist regime of Joseph Stalin in the Soviet Union. In religion, Wallace's interests and beliefs were unconventional. For most of his adult life, he was a follower of various religious spiritualists. He studied Theosophy, a movement begun in the late nineteenth century that focuses on mystical insight and has some beliefs in common with Buddhism and Brahmanism. The most prominent spiritualist with whom Wallace associated himself was a Russian named Nicholas Roerich. Among other things, Roerich was a noted artist, a student of several religions, an advocate of hypnosis, and of various spiritual practices. In letters between the two, Wallace sometimes addressed Roerich as "guru." More about Wallace's ties to Roerich would come out in later years, but by 1940, enough was already known for Democratic Party leaders to view him with great suspicion.

He was described by them as "mystical" and "starry-eyed," certainly not someone whom they wanted a heartbeat away from the presidency.[58]

Few of FDR's advisors supported Wallace. Hopkins, the president's main man in Chicago, urged him to reconsider, as did Byrnes, his floor leader, and Bankhead, who had given the keynote speech. Some objected to Wallace because, as recently as the late 1920s, he had been a Republican. Governor Leon Phillips of Oklahoma, when asked by another governor if he supported Wallace, left no doubt where he stood. "Henry's my second choice," Phillips replied, "After anyone else—black, white, or yellow—who can get the nomination." Despite all of the resistance, a stubborn Roosevelt would not budge. He instructed his team to spread the word that, if the convention did not nominate Wallace for vice president, then he would decline his own nomination for president.[59]

On Thursday, the convention's fourth day, Eleanor Roosevelt arrived in Chicago, heeding the roundabout request that had been made to her. Farley, despite his differences with the president, still maintained a good relationship with the first lady. He met her at the airport and accompanied her to her hotel. According to Farley, Eleanor told him she agreed that Wallace was not a good choice, and she and Farley placed a telephone call to the president. Roosevelt was defiant, telling Farley, "I've given my word to Wallace, Jim." And that, he implied, was the way it was going to be, like it or not.[60]

Before FDR made his choice of Wallace known, several men had been seeking the vice-presidential nomination. Under pressure from the Roosevelt team in Chicago, however, most bowed out. Senator Byrnes of South Carolina, FDR's floor leader, had gone around to the various state delegations, spreading Roosevelt's threat that he would not accept his nomination unless Wallace was on the ticket with him. "Do you want a vice president," Byrnes kept asking, "or a president?" Only three candidates were put before the convention. William Bankhead, the speaker of the House and the man who had delivered the convention's keynote speech, was nominated by his home state of Alabama. Although the demonstration for him started slowly, it gradually spread throughout the hall, included most of the southern states, and lasted for twenty minutes. Paul McNutt, a former governor of Indiana, was also nominated, but went to the podium before the voting began and withdrew his name, stating, Roosevelt "is my leader and I am here to support his choice for vice president." He was booed by the crowd for withdrawing. Wallace was then nominated. The reaction in the arena to the nominating speech for him could not have been reassuring for Roosevelt and his brain trust at the convention. There were more jeers than cheers. Wallace's wife, Ilo, who was seated next to Eleanor Roosevelt in the VIP seats behind the podium, tried to hold back tears as her husband was booed by the crowd. The first lady reached out and grasped her hand, trying to comfort her.[61]

When all of the nominating and seconding speeches were done, Farley escorted Eleanor to the podium. Never before had a first lady given a speech to a nominating convention. She had a typed outline, but her remarks, which were brief, were mostly extemporaneous. She began by praising Farley's service as DNC chairman, expressing her "thanks and devotion" to him.

Without specifically saying so, she recognized that, by nominating her husband for a third term, the convention had broken with tradition, in her opinion, justifiably so: "You cannot treat it as an ordinary nomination, in an ordinary time. We people in the United States have got to realize today that we face now a grave, a serious situation." Her husband, she said, due to the dire world situation, "cannot make a campaign in the usual sense of the word. He must be on his job." She urged the delegates to support him and "to rise above considerations that are narrow and partisan." Caution and responsibility, she warned, were needed: "We cannot tell from day to day what will come. This is no ordinary time. No time for weighing anything, except what we can best do for the country as a whole. And that rests, that responsibility on each and every one of us as individuals."[62]

The crowd in the stadium rose to their feet and cheered the first lady. She did not linger at the podium, but turned and walked toward the rear of the stage. Someone placed a large garland of flowers around her neck. She was then escorted by one of her sons, Franklin, Jr., back to her seat next to Mrs. Wallace to observe the voting for vice president.[63]

The roll call of the states began at 10:40 p.m. in a hot and stuffy Chicago Stadium. According to the *Baltimore Sun*, when states declared their votes for Bankhead, "there was deafening applause," but when votes were announced for Wallace, "the boos shook the rafters." Bankhead took an early lead. At the White House, in the Oval Study, surrounded by a few aides, Roosevelt, with a grim look on his face, listened on the radio as he played solitaire. Becoming angry as Bankhead maintained his lead over Wallace, he picked up pencil and paper and scratched out a five-page letter confirming his threat to not accept his own nomination, if Wallace were not nominated. He gave instructions for his notes to be quickly edited and typed, saying, "I may have to deliver it very soon so please hurry up." As events turned out, it was not needed. Shortly thereafter, several large states, including New York, Ohio, and Pennsylvania, announced their votes for Wallace and he went over the majority threshold that was needed and won the nomination for vice president. The final tally was 626 and 11/30 for Wallace, 329⅗ for Bankhead, and (although he had withdrawn) 68⅘ for McNutt. Interestingly, had the party's two thirds rule for nomination not been abolished (at Roosevelt's instigation) at the last convention in 1936, Wallace would not have won on the first ballot and later ballots may well have resulted in another nominee. Some historians have credited the first lady's remarks, urging unity and support for her husband, and which had been delivered just before the voting began, as having pushed Wallace over the top.[64]

Wallace, who was in the arena and had prepared an acceptance speech, started toward the podium to deliver it. He was intercepted by Byrnes, the FDR floor leader, who warned him that the convention would boo him off the stage. "[D]on't go out there," Byrnes pleaded, "You'll ruin the party if you do." Reluctantly, Wallace gave in and went back to his seat.[65]

The convention did hear from Roosevelt that night, who delivered his acceptance speech shortly after the voting for vice president ended. It was a far different mood and setting than his two prior acceptance speeches. In 1932, he had electrified the nation by shattering tradition and flying to Chicago to accept his nomination in person, the first nominee of a major party to do so. In 1936, he addressed a cheering crowd of more than 100,000 packed into a football stadium in Philadelphia. But in 1940, with Hitler having recently marched through most of Europe and the American people in a somber mood, Roosevelt was in a basement room in the White House, in his shirtsleeves, surrounded by only a few aides, speaking into a microphone and on a telephone link to Chicago Stadium. His words were received by the huge crowd in silence. Although the nation was still at peace, the events of the last several weeks had made it likely that war was on the horizon. He explained his willingness to serve a third term as a call to duty. Despite his "deep personal desire of retirement," he said he had experienced many sleepless nights, asking himself "whether I have the right as Commander in Chief of the Army and Navy to call on men and women to serve their country . . . and at the same time decline to serve" himself. He starkly outlined the decisions to be made in the coming months:

> We face one of the great choices of history. It is not alone a choice of government of the people versus dictatorship. It is not alone a choice between freedom and slavery. It is not alone a choice between moving forward and falling back. It is all of these rolled into one. It is the continuance of civilization as we know it versus the ultimate destruction of all that we have held dear, religion versus godlessness, the ideal of justice against the practice of force, moral decency versus the firing squad, courage to speak out and to act versus the false lullaby of appeasement. But it has been well said that a selfish and greedy people cannot be free. The American people must decide whether these things are worth making sacrifices of money, energy, and of self.[66]

The president spoke for just over half an hour. When he finished, at almost one o'clock in the morning, the historic twenty-eighth national convention of the Democratic Party came to a close.[67]

The convention had not been the resounding success that Roosevelt and party leaders had hoped. By not stating in advance that he would serve a third term, while at the same time covertly working for the convention to draft him, by forcing an unpopular choice for vice president on the party, by threatening to decline his nomination (despite all he had said about his duty to serve), Roosevelt's actions left a sour taste in many mouths. As Mencken observed, "The steam-roller had worked, but certainly not smoothly. It heaved and pitched . . . and more than once it appeared to be on the verge of disaster." A reporter for *LIFE* perhaps best summarized the country's view of the convention. Many who believed that they were "completely reconciled to the idea of a third term came away shocked and sick at heart." They had witnessed not a true, up-from-the-people draft of the president, but "the shabby pretense" of one, which was pulled off by a "cynical ends-justifies-the means alliance of New Deal reformers and self-seeking big-city bosses."[68]

One question about the 1940 Democratic convention remains—if war in Europe had not been raging, would Franklin Roosevelt have sought a third term? Was Adolph Hitler the reason for breaking with the no-third-term precedent, or was he the excuse for doing so? Roosevelt's supporters thought the former; his opponents the latter. Only he knew for sure.

The Campaign and Election

As the challenger and the perceived underdog, Willkie hit the rails and campaigned extensively, traveling to thirty-four states and making more than five hundred speeches. On domestic policy, he supported many New Deal programs, but argued that they would be administered more efficiently under the rule of Republicans. Much to the dismay of conservative Republicans, it was similar to the approach that Landon had taken in 1936. They had wanted from Willkie a sharp denunciation of the expansion of government under FDR. Instead, Willkie focused on two issues—opposition to a third term and the war in Europe. As to the former, he denounced the perpetuation of "one man rule" and argued that, if Roosevelt is indispensable as president, "then none of us is free." On the war, Willkie supported the enactment in September of the Selective Training and Service Act, the first peacetime military draft in American history. As the campaign wore on, however, he became critical of Roosevelt's handling of matters concerning the overseas war. He opposed a deal that Roosevelt made (in which the president bypassed Congress) to provide fifty old warships to Great Britain in exchange for American leases on some British naval bases in the Western Hemisphere. He implied that Roosevelt was likely to send American soldiers into combat in Europe. In a speech in October, Willkie declared, if elected, "We shall not undertake to fight anybody else's war. Our boys shall stay out of European wars." He did see an uptick in his poll numbers as he focused more on opposition to America joining the war, but he never overtook Roosevelt in opinion surveys.[69]

Roosevelt did not actively campaign until mid-October, when he began the first of five major speeches, mostly delivered to large audiences in northeastern cities. To charges that the nation was not prepared for war, he pointed out that it had been Republicans in Congress who had opposed many of his efforts in 1938 and 1939 to put the country on a firmer war footing. He refuted Willkie's allegation that he was going to send American troops to Europe. "I have said this before," he declared in a speech in Boston, "but I shall say it again and again and again: 'Your boys are not going to be sent into foreign wars.'" In his final speech on the eve of the election, the president closed his campaign with a moving speech focusing on domestic issues and his vision for the future. "I see an America," he declared, "where factory workers are not discarded after they reach their prime, where there is no endless chain of poverty from generation to generation . . . where small business really has a chance to flourish and grow . . . [and] where those who have reached the evening of life shall live out their years in peace and security."[70]

Two matters were never publicly discussed during the general election, possibly as the result of a secret deal between the Roosevelt and Willkie campaigns. Letters that Henry Wallace had written years earlier to his onetime Russian spiritual advisor, Nicholas Roerich, had been obtained by Republicans and were locked away in a vault. Some of the letters began "Dear Guru" and were described as "imprudent" and containing "mystic nonsense." The Republican plan was, late in the campaign, to release the letters to a GOP-friendly newspaper in Pittsburgh and have them published, a 1940s version of an "October surprise" that would be used in later elections. But the Democrats had a response. It was known to insiders in Washington and New York that

Willkie was involved in a longstanding and ongoing extra-marital affair with Irita Van Doren, a prominent New York journalist. Democrats threatened to publicize Willkie's affair, if the Wallace "guru letters" became public. In a recording from an Oval Office taping system that was briefly in use in 1940, FDR is heard saying, "[W]e can't have any of our principal speakers refer to [Willkie's affair] but the people down the line can get it out . . . . [I]f they want to play dirty politics [with the Wallace letters] in the end, we've got our own people . . . . Awful nice gal [Van Doren], but there is the fact." Neither the affair nor the letters became public knowledge during the fall of 1940. Although no definitive evidence exists of a *tit-for-tat* agreement, some historians strongly suspect that one was reached.[71]

On election day, Roosevelt became the first American president to be elected to a third term. In the Electoral College, he won thirty-eight states and 449 electoral votes, compared to ten states and 82 electoral votes for Willkie. Roosevelt won all of the South, all of the West, all of the Mid-Atlantic, and the Northeast (except for Maine and Vermont). Most of Willkie's wins were in the Midwest. Although the popular vote was closer than in his landslide wins over Hoover in 1932 and Landon in 1936, Roosevelt still had a comfortable margin of five million votes over his opponent. He received 27,243,466 (54.7%) votes, compared to 22,304,755 (44.8%) for Willkie. The only third party of note was the Socialist Party and its nominee, Norman Thomas, received around 100,000 votes. In the congressional races, Democrats maintained their solid majorities, but there was little change in the margins. They gained five seats in the House, but lost three seats in the Senate.[72]

Franklin Roosevelt would soon become the nation's longest-serving president. As had been feared and predicted by some during the campaign, his third term would also make him a wartime president, although not in the manner that had been anticipated.

CHAPTER 11

1944: Clear It with Sidney

Let's make each one of our blows felt
For the causes of humanity and war.
With world peace just around the corner,
His leadership is necessary still.

So, Let's Re-Re-Re-Elect Roosevelt.
—**Democratic Campaign Song, 1944**

On December 7, 1941, with the attack by Japan on the American naval base at Pearl Harbor in Hawaii, Franklin Roosevelt officially became a wartime president. For the prior two years, the United States had inched closer to involvement in the European war against Germany. FDR pursued policies (often opposed by isolationists in the Republican Party) to provide military equipment and other supplies to Great Britain and to Russia. A year before Pearl Harbor, the president, in a fireside chat, called on Americans to be "the great arsenal of democracy." The economy hummed with the manufacture of weapons of all types—of military aircraft, of tanks, of trucks, and of other war materials. After the attack on American territory, production of these items greatly increased. The nation rallied behind Roosevelt. A massive Army and Navy were raised, trained, and deployed. At times in 1942 and 1943, it appeared that the war was a stalemate, or that little progress was being made. By the time the election year of 1944 began, however, plans were being made for an Allied invasion of Europe, likely to begin in France, to take the continent back from Hitler. It seemed as though a corner had been turned, and that the end of the war, while not imminent, was at least visible.[1]

As the 1944 campaign season began, Democratic Party leaders were certain that Franklin Roosevelt would seek a fourth term and there was strong support for him within the party.

The nation was at war and Roosevelt would be, by far, the best Democratic candidate. After the political ruckus in 1940 over nominating and electing him to a third term, and thus abandoning a century-and-a-half tradition of only two terms for presidents, there was surprisingly little opposition in the country in 1944, as a matter of principle, to a fourth term. Once the red line of a third term had been crossed, taking another step was much easier.

Despite the support that Roosevelt enjoyed as a wartime president, Republicans had reason to be optimistic as they looked toward the 1944 presidential election. In the 1942 midterms, they had gained more than forty-five seats in the House, seven in the Senate, and several governorships. Although still in the minority in both houses of Congress, with conservative Democrats joining them on many issues, they could block any significant additional New Deal legislation proposed by FDR. Polls showed that if the war was still being fought at the time of the election, Roosevelt was the clear favorite of the people. If the war was over, however, Americans were ready to move on and a Republican was favored for president. The open question was, which Republican would it be?[2]

Republican Convention

There were three main contenders for the 1944 Republican nomination—Thomas Dewey, John Bricker, and Wendell Willkie. Bricker was a newcomer to presidential politics. Dewey and Willkie had battled it out before, in 1940, with Willkie emerging as the surprise nominee, and Dewey, who had been the frontrunner going into that year's convention, performing poorly. The other two major candidates from 1940, Senator Robert Taft and Senator Arthur Vandenberg, announced that they would not be seeking the 1944 nomination.

Dewey, at forty-two-years old, was still young for a presidential candidate. He had, however, significantly upgraded his résumé since he had last run in 1940. Then, although he had a significant national reputation as a crime-busting prosecutor, the only elective office he had ever held was as district attorney in Manhattan. He had lost a close race in 1938 for the New York governorship. In 1942, he ran again for governor, and won. Thus, in 1944, he was the chief executive of the nation's most populous state, an office that had, in both parties, been a springboard to presidential nominations. Since 1900, four major party nominees—Republicans Theodore Roosevelt and Charles Evans Hughes and Democrats Al Smith and Franklin Roosevelt—had served as governor of the Empire State. Although he was a good administrator and a successful governor, Dewey still had a downside that no elective office could cure. He was not a likable man, a characteristic that is often a kiss of death for a politician. As journalist David Brinkley has written, "In public Dewey came across as pompous and cold. And for good reason. He was both." Dewey also had another problem in running for president in 1944. When campaigning for governor in 1942, he had vowed that, if elected, he would devote the next four years "exclusively to the service of the people of New York State." That pledge meant that he could not publicly announce his candidacy for president in 1944, nor take steps himself to seek the nomination. It did not mean, however, that his friends and supporters throughout the country (with his consent and collaboration) could not actively line up support for him, and they did so. Being a stealth candidate was a strategy that others had used before. Democrat Alton Parker in 1904 and Republican Charles Evans Hughes in 1916 had both won their party's nomination without being active candidates. Appearing to be uneager and uninterested in the presidency was sometimes appealing to voters.[3]

Wendell Willkie, the political newcomer who had unexpectedly won the party's last nomination, was again a candidate in 1944. He had lost the general election in 1940 (rather badly) to Roosevelt and, in the process, had made few friends among the party's establishment. They had strongly opposed his prior nomination and certainly did not want to see him as their nominee again. In his ideology, Willkie was a liberal, much more attuned to the New Deal beliefs of President Roosevelt than the beliefs held by most Republicans. Although the GOP, after the attack on Pearl Harbor, was supportive of American entry into World War II and mostly cooperated with Roosevelt as a wartime president, Willkie, many Republicans thought, went to the extreme. In early 1941, he endorsed Roosevelt's lend-lease proposal to the Allies (which mainly benefitted the United Kingdom and the Soviet Union), despite opposition from much of the leadership of the Republican Party. Willkie's support helped secure the passage of the program by Congress. In August 1942, Willkie embarked on a two-month world tour, as Roosevelt's personal representative, meeting with Allied military and civilian leaders in Africa, the Middle East, the Soviet Union, and China. Upon his return, he wrote a best-selling book about his trip, entitled *One World*, promoting his vision of a post-war international organization to preserve the peace, as well as denouncing colonization and racism. His philosophy, Willkie declared, was to "unify the peoples of the earth in the human quest for freedom and justice." With his ardent internationalism, to many Republicans, Wendell Willkie had become another Woodrow Wilson. By early 1943, Willkie had decided to again seek his party's presidential nomination and he began touring the country. In August, he formally announced his candidacy.[4]

John Bricker, the fifty-year-old governor of Ohio, was the most conservative of the major Republican contenders in 1944. An Ohio native, Bricker was tall, athletic, and had a likable and outgoing personality. A self-made man, he was born in a log cabin on a farm near Columbus. After attending college at Ohio State University, where he played on the baseball team, he also earned his law degree there. During World War I, Bricker tried to enlist in various military branches, but was rejected due to a congenital heart condition. Determined to serve, he became ordained as a minister and managed to get a commission as a chaplain in the Army. He began his political career in the early 1920s as a lawyer for Ohio's Public Utilities Commission, where he became an advocate for consumers against utility companies. In 1932, a year when Democrats across the country were elected in landslides, Bricker was one of the few Republican victors, winning election as attorney general of Ohio. After losing a race for governor in 1936, he succeeded on his second attempt in 1938. As governor, he reduced state expenditures, decreased the state payroll, and demanded that state relief payments for the unemployed be matched by contributions from local governments. Bricker had considered making a run for president in 1940, but he and Senator Robert Taft of Ohio reached an agreement. Bricker agreed to support Taft for the nomination in 1940 and, if Taft lost, he agreed to support Bricker in 1944. Thus, Taft sat out the 1944 race and endorsed his fellow Ohioan. The silver-haired and distinguished-looking Bricker was reelected as governor in 1942, setting the stage for his presidential run. There were whispers in Republican circles about Bricker's intelligence. One prominent Republican-leaning journalist referred to him as "[a]n honest Harding," a not so flattering comparison to another Ohioan whose gray matter had also been questioned. As author David Jordan has written of Bricker's 1944 candidacy for the Republican nomination, "Certainly no one considered Bricker an intellectual giant, but the people of Ohio were comfortable with him, and he hoped the American people would be in the mood, after twelve years of Franklin Roosevelt and excitement, for a calm and conservative presidency." Bricker's campaign got off to a slow start, due to lack of organization, lack of direction, and lackluster speeches by the candidate.[5]

Beyond Dewey, Willkie, and Bricker, there were a few second-tier candidates for the 1940 Republican nomination. Harold Stassen, the youthful former governor of Minnesota, who had given the keynote speech at the 1940 convention and then became a floor manager for Willkie, was in the mix. Reelected in 1942 as governor, he resigned in 1943, joined the Navy, and was assigned to the Pacific theater of the war, where he worked under Admiral William Halsey. As an active sailor, Stassen could not actively seek the 1944 nomination, but his friends and supporters worked on his behalf. A much more prominent military man, General Douglas MacArthur, was also frequently mentioned as a possible Republican nominee in 1944. MacArthur had served with distinction in Europe during the First World War, had been superintendent of West Point, as well as the Army's chief of staff. Early in the Second World War, he was assigned to the Philippines and was forced by the advancing Japanese to retreat to Australia. His famous vow of "I shall return" inspired the nation and, as the 1944 presidential campaign was unfolding, he was planning an island-by-island strategy of returning to the Philippines, with the ultimate goal of advancing to the mainland of Japan. At times vain and sanctimonious, MacArthur was a favorite among conservative Republicans and was supported in 1944 by Senator Arthur Vandenberg, who had been a contender for the 1940 nomination. MacArthur was aware of the political activities on his behalf and did not discourage them. Two other names, Representative Everett Dirksen of Illinois and Governor Earl Warren of California, were also put forward by their supporters for the 1944 GOP nomination.[6]

A "Stop Willkie" movement was formed by key party leaders, led by John Hamilton (a former RNC chairman), Alf Landon (the party's 1936 nominee), and Robert McCormick (the conservative publisher of the *Chicago Tribune*). Hamilton traveled to seventeen states in late 1943, urging party leaders to recruit and support favorite son candidates, or to send uncommitted delegations to the convention, to keep their states from falling into Willkie's hands. The strategy largely succeeded. Party leaders in Pennsylvania announced their delegation would endorse no one. Favorite sons did emerge in South Dakota, Massachusetts, Nebraska, Kentucky, and West Virginia. New York was for Dewey and Ohio was for Bricker. In California, an agreement was reached with Willkie. Governor Warren would head the Golden State's delegation as a favorite son, with half of the delegates pledged to him and half to Willkie.[7]

Willkie was brash and outspoken, believing, as he had in 1940, that he could get more votes by denouncing the Republican establishment than by trying to reach compromises with it. At a meeting early in 1943 with the party's freshmen congressmen, he declared, "I know you people are opposed to me. You don't like me. But I am going to be nominated whether you like it or not. Better get right with me." He was equally outspoken in remarks made in St. Louis in October, telling a group of industrialists who supported the party, "I don't know whether you're going to support me or not, and I don't give a damn. You're a bunch of political liabilities who don't know what's going on anyway." At times during 1943, Willkie led in opinion polls for the nomination, with Dewey usually closely behind. By the beginning of 1944, however, Willkie was fading. A January poll found Dewey nineteen points ahead of him among Republican voters. In the first primary of the 1944 election season, held in New Hampshire in March, Willkie had been favored. He won, but not by much, getting only six of the state's eleven delegates.[8]

A few days after the New Hampshire primary, Willkie made a bold decision. The next primary was set for early April, in Wisconsin, and he announced that he would travel there and personally campaign across the state for two weeks. It was a gamble. As Willkie biographer Steve Neal has written, "Never before had a national political figure of his stature invested so much energy and time in a single primary." Although Wisconsin Republicans, led years earlier by Senator Robert La Follette, and been among the most progressive in the party during the Theodore Roosevelt era, the state had also historically been a bastion of isolationism and it had a large German-American population. Neither boded well for Willkie, who was an internationalist and strongly favored the Allies in the war. In Wisconsin, Willkie had the field to himself. Bricker did not campaign there. Dewey, officially a non-candidate, did not actively campaign in any of the primary states, nor did Stassen and MacArthur, who were on active military duty in the Pacific. Willkie campaigned all across Wisconsin, making more than forty speeches, and he drew large crowds. He denounced his opponents and his critics. He criticized Dewey for his shadow campaign. "I almost despise those who remain silent," he said, "more than those who speak out in open opposition." Of his conservative opponents in the party, he told one Wisconsin audience, "I am entitled to at least some of your support for the enemies I have made. I have the most valuable list of enemies of any public or quasi-public figure in America."[9]

When the results were tallied, the voters of Wisconsin handed Willkie a crushing and embarrassing defeat. Twenty-four delegates were at stake and he won *none* of them. He finished in fourth place, behind Dewey, who won seventeen delegates, behind Stassen, who won four, and behind MacArthur, who won three. By the time the results were known, Willkie had moved on to Nebraska, which was the next state to hold a primary. In a speech in Omaha a day later, he criticized the voters, saying that he feared that Republicans "may be the party of negation," that perhaps their "conscience . . . is dulled," and that "the people are not willing to bear the sacrifices" that were needed. He ended his remarks with a shocking announcement—he was withdrawing from the contest. "It is obvious now," he stated, "that I cannot be nominated. Therefore, I am asking my friends to desist from any activity toward that end and not to present my name at the convention." He expressed his hope that the party would "nominate a candidate and write a platform which really represents the views . . . for which I have fought during the last five years."[10]

With Willkie's abrupt departure from the race, state after state moved toward Dewey. Bricker was unable to make any significant gains. In May, MacArthur announced that, if nominated, his war duties would prevent him from accepting. There would be 1,059 delegates at the convention, with a majority of 530 needed to win the nomination. After all of the delegates were chosen, Dewey had 385 pledged to him and the delegations from several large states, including Pennsylvania and Illinois, were known to be leaning toward him. Bricker had around 225 pledged delegates, with few prospects for gaining more. The day before the convention opened, the *New York Times* reported that it would be "one of the most cut-and-dried conventions" in the history of the Republican Party and that the country should expect "the virtually certain nomination" of Thomas Dewey.[11]

After having met in Cleveland in 1936 and in Philadelphia in 1940, Republicans returned to Chicago for their 1944 convention. The site was Chicago Stadium, the same arena in which they had nominated Herbert Hoover for a second term in 1932. It was the first presidential nominating convention since 1864 to be held when the nation was at war. The war, and the lack of suspense over the nominee, made for a subdued atmosphere in the city. One could hardly walk more than a block without spotting uniformed soldiers and sailors. Anti-aircraft balloons hung in the air over Lake Michigan. Wartime rationing made many items scarce. Lumber to construct the platform in the arena had been hard to get and, to obtain it, the city had to agree it would be salvaged for additional uses. Fewer campaign buttons were manufactured in 1944, as there were many more important needs for metal. Photographs and posters of candidates, which usually were abundantly on display in convention city storefronts and street corners, were in short supply, as was campaign literature. Bricker's team seemed to have the most paraphernalia on display, including the most creative campaign slogans, which included "Let's Not Bicker, It's Bricker" and "Get the Boys Home Quicker With Bricker." The arena also had far fewer decorations than did past conventions. Lincoln's portrait was the only one that hung from the rafters, a reporter commenting that Abe's gaze, in the midst of the bloodiest American war since the one over which he had presided, "seem[ed] somehow, sadder than usual." In the arena's basement, the odor of elephants from a recent circus lingered. With the elephant being the symbol of the Republican Party, a city worker in charge of the facilities, referring to the smell, jokingly asked a reporter, "but can you figure a Republican convention squawking about that?" Americans would listen to the convention over almost seven hundred radio stations. The radio networks—CBS, NBC, Blue (a predecessor to ABC), and Mutual—employed between eight and ten thousand engineers and workers to bring audio from the convention to millions. Several thousand owners of televisions, located mainly in New York City and Philadelphia, were able to watch video of portions of the proceedings, within a couple of hours of them taking place. With his nomination all but certain, Dewey did not go to the convention and remained in Albany. Bricker was an Ohio delegate and did travel to Chicago. Willkie was not a delegate, was not invited to speak at the convention, and chose not to attend.[12]

The convention began on the morning of Monday, June 26, with a call to order by RNC Chairman Harrison Spangler of Iowa. One of the more interesting of the speeches during the brief session was made by the winner of an essay contest sponsored by the RNC's Young Republican division. The topic for the young GOP writers was "Why the Republican Party Should Win." The contest's winner was Harry Reasoner, a twenty-one-year-old Army private from Minneapolis, who read his essay, entitled "A First Voter Looks at the Republican Party," to the crowd. Young Reasoner would go on to have a distinguished career as a television news journalist, including as an original correspondent on *60 Minutes* and as an anchor on *ABC Evening News*. After the committees were appointed and Spangler introduced the RNC's choice of California Governor Earl Warren to be the convention's temporary chairman, there was an adjournment until the evening, at which time Warren would deliver his keynote speech. Unfortunately for the thousands inside Chicago Stadium, a heat wave hit the city during the week of the convention, with outside temperatures reaching one hundred degrees, and higher inside. The arena's inefficient air conditioning system, which provided only minimal relief during much lower temperatures, did not have sufficient ice to function properly. One of the arena's workers said that it was just as well, for the system was "[n]o good, anyway," as the cooling it provided was only "a spit in the ocean."[13]

Fifty-three-year-old Earl Warren was elected governor of California in 1942, the same year that Tom Dewey had been elected governor of New York. More liberal than Dewey, he was often mentioned in newspapers as being at the top of Dewey's list for a vice-presidential running mate, as he would provide both ideological and regional balance to the ticket. In his keynote speech, delivered to crowd packed into a sweltering Chicago Stadium, Warren gave support to the Roosevelt Administration its handling of the war effort, but criticized it for its domestic policies and for its longevity in office. "What is our job?," he asked, and then answered, "To get our boys home again, victorious and with all speed. To open the door for all Americans; to open it, not just to jobs, but to opportunity! To make and guard the peace so wisely and so well that this time will be the last time that American homes are called to give their sons and daughters to the agony and tragedy of war." A quick conclusion to the war, he said, did not require keeping Roosevelt in office for a fourth term. "It is the purpose of this convention," he proclaimed, "to put the public welfare above private self-interest, to put the nation above the party . . . to put indispensable principles, once and for all, above indispensable men." Warren then launched a stinging attack on FDR and his core-group of New Deal advisers. "The New Deal is no longer the Democratic Party," he warned. "It is an incongruous clique within that party. It retains its power by patronizing and holding together incompatible groups. It talks of idealism and seeks its votes from the most corrupt political machines in the country." Holding onto power, Warren continued, was all that Roosevelt and his cronies wanted: "To perpetuate themselves in power the New Deal clique has always capitalized upon some crisis. It has always had the indispensable man—the same man—for each succeeding crisis. The first time it was the depression. The second time it was the recession. Last time it was to keep us out of war. This time it will be to achieve peace. The next time—who knows what the crisis will be? That there will be one and that the indispensable man will still be indispensable, we can rely upon the New Deal clique to assert." Warren's speech was popular in the hall and with the press. The "stalwart Westerner," opined the *Washington Post*, had kicked off the convention "on a high level" and had "heaped ridicule" on the notion that only FDR could lead the nation to the end of the war and beyond.[14]

On the convention's second day, Representative Joseph Martin of Massachusetts was named permanent chairman, the same post he had held at the last convention. In the late afternoon, Martin called on Senator Robert Taft of Ohio, the chairman of the Committee on Resolutions, to present the proposed platform. Taft read the five-thousand-word document almost without interruption by applause, the audience likely too busy using their hands to fan themselves in the heat than to clap. Much of the debate before the committee had been over the foreign policy plank—would it be isolationist, as the party's conservatives wanted, or internationalist, as the more moderate faction of the party wanted? As was usually done with platform planks on controversial issues, the final language could be interpreted by either side as supporting its position. Declaring the party's "relentless aim" to win the war and to secure a peace based on "justice and security," the platform favored "responsible participation by the United States in post-war cooperative organization among sovereign nations," but opposed "joining a World State." Any such participation must be under the Constitution, and with all agreements or treaties made only with the advice and consent of two-thirds of the Senate. On domestic policy, the platform denounced the centralization of power in the federal government under the New Deal. It warned that another four years with Roosevelt as president "would daily subject every act of every citizen to regulation by his henchmen; and this country would remain a Republic only in name." Stung by the party's staggering loss of Black voters to the Democrats since 1936, and hoping to gain some of them back, the platform contained the strongest civil rights plank that had ever been proposed for a major party platform. It called for immediate passage of a federal anti-lynching law, for abolition of poll taxes, for a congressional investigation into discrimination against Blacks in the armed forces, and for addressing employment discrimination against Blacks by creation of a Fair Employment Practice Commission. The platform favored amendments to the Constitution providing equal rights for women, as well as for limiting the president to only two terms in office. Once the war was over, it called for tax reductions and rejected "the theory of restoring prosperity through government spending and deficit financing." At the conclusion of Taft's reading of the platform, there were no proposed modifications or additions. It was approved on a voice vote and the convention adjourned until the evening.[15]

Two speeches highlighted the second day's evening session. The first was from Herbert Hoover. It was the third time since his landslide defeat in 1932 that the former president had addressed a Republican convention. In his prior two appearances, in 1936 and 1940, he had forcefully denounced the implementation of the New Deal by his successor, Roosevelt, and had then held out hope that his party would somehow turn again to him as its nominee. By 1944, although Hoover, as one historian has noted, spewed out "his usual warnings of imminent disaster" if FDR were given yet another term, he was finally willing to pass the torch of party leadership to the forty-two-year-old Tom Dewey and the next generation. "In every generation," Hoover proclaimed, "youth presses forward toward achievement. Each generation has the right to build its own world out of the materials of the past, cemented by the hopes of the future . . . . This Convention is handing the leadership of the Republican Party to a new generation . . . . I rejoice that this is to be." Hoover's speech was well-received by the convention. For the rest of his long life (he lived until 1964, to the age of ninety), he would continue, with some success, to rebuild his tarnished reputation, arising from the Great Depression having begun during his time as president.[16]

After Hoover, the convention heard from Representative Clare Boothe Luce in what was the most controversial speech of the convention. Forty-one-years-old, Luce was the wife of Henry Luce, the publisher of *TIME, LIFE*, and other influential magazines. In 1940, Henry had been one of the most prominent supporters of Wendell Willkie. Clare was more conservative than her husband. In her speech, Luce essentially accused Roosevelt of having the blood of deceased American soldiers on his hands, for not having told the country during the 1930s that America's entry into World War II was inevitable. She spoke of two fictional soldiers, "G. I. Joe," representative of those still serving and still on the battlefields, and of "G. I. Jim," representative of those who had lost their lives in combat:

> Do we here in this Convention dare ask if Jim's heroic death in battle was historically inevitable? If this war might not have been averted? . . . . Might not skillful and determined American statesmanship have helped to unmake it all through the '30s? Or, when it was clear to our government that it was too late to avert war, might not truthful and fearless leadership have prepared us better for it in material and in morale, in arms and in aims?

Luce then pointed her verbal dagger directly at Roosevelt:

> The last twelve years have not been Republican years . . . . [I]t was not a Republican president who dealt with the visibly rising menaces of Hitler and Mussolini and Hirohito. Ours was not the administration that promised young Jim's mother and father and neighbors and friends economic security and peace. Yes, peace. No Republican president gave these promises which were kept to their ears, but broken to their hearts. For this terrible truth cannot be denied: these promises, which were given by a government that was elected again and again and again because it made them, lie quite as dead as young Jim lies now. Jim was the heroic heir of the unheroic Roosevelt decade: a decade of confusion and conflict that ended in war.

She continued, imagining the deceased "G. I. Jim" observing from above the current convention, alongside the spirit of George Washington:

> [J]im always knew from the history books . . . that President Washington might have stayed in power all his days, the early days of our weak and infant republic . . . .

Then every man said that George Washington was the indispensable man . . . . Jim knew that Washington so loved his country and the institutions that he helped to author, that he refused more than two terms. That was a tradition Washington's spirit never saw broken at any president-making gathering until it was broken by the man who promised in this very city twelve years ago that 'happy days are here again,' who promised peace, yes, peace, to Jim's mother and father . . . .

Jim and his friend, the father of his country, want us to choose [as our nominee] . . . a man who would rather tell the truth than be president; to choose a man who loves his country and its institutions more than he loves power.

In raising the issue of whether Roosevelt had lied to the country in the years leading up to the war, the *New York Times* commented that Luce "touched on dangerous ground" and noted that she was the only speaker at the convention "who even hinted at such an explosive question." Her "G.I. Jim" speech has generated much discussion among historians, more so than it did in Chicago in 1944. Many have criticized her for her failure to acknowledge that isolationist Republicans in Congress had opposed many of Roosevelt's efforts in the late 1930s to provide more assistance to the Allies. One author thought it a "brilliantly vicious speech," but one of questionable "taste and morality."[17]

On the morning of its third day, the convention moved to nominations of candidates for president. "The serious part of the convention has arrived," said Chairman Martin, as he pounded his gavel. The first speaker was Governor Dwight Griswold of Nebraska, who nominated Dewey. Under Dewey, Griswold asserted, the nation would have a president with "youth instead of decadence, vigor instead of cynicism, integrity instead of doubledealing, seriousness of purpose instead of flippancy, faith instead of defeatism." In Roosevelt, Griswold stated, "[t]he past will have its spokesman in this campaign." With Dewey as its nominee, he proclaimed, the Republican Party would offer the people "the spokesman of the future." The demonstration at the conclusion of the speech featured the usual marching through the aisles by delegates, with the standards of most of the states being carried aloft, along with newly-printed placards with various campaign slogans, including "Dewey Will Win!," "Dewey, the People's Choice!," and "America Wants Dewey!" Annie Dewey, the candidate's sixty-six-year-old mother, who lived in Michigan, sat in a box seat and looked at the scene with pride, tears of joy running down her cheeks. Others had sweat running down theirs, as the extreme heat in the arena continued, which, a reporter noted, "quite evidently oppressed what would otherwise have been a more exciting show." The hoopla for Dewey was cut short by Chairman Martin after only seven minutes. Party leaders were on a tight schedule, having decided that this would be the last day of the convention. Things had run so smoothly that a planned fourth day would not be needed.[18]

Shortly before noon, when Ohio was reached in the roll call of the states for nominations, Bricker's supporters were surprised to see their candidate go to the podium. A deal had been worked out overnight. In exchange for being named Dewey's running mate, Bricker had agreed to withdraw from the contest for president before the voting began. Dewey's first choice for vice president had been Governor Warren of California, who had delivered the keynote speech. Warren had declined, giving as his reason that he had promised the voters of California when running for governor in 1942 that, if elected, he would serve out his full term. The reason seemed to the Dewey team to be a criticism of their man, since Governor Dewey had made the same pledge to the voters of New York in 1942. (Later, it was rumored that Warren did not believe FDR could be defeated in 1944 and did not want to be on what he was almost certain would be a losing ticket.) With Warren out, Dewey turned to Bricker, which made sense politically. Bricker was more conservative than Dewey and putting him on the ticket was an olive branch to the conservative wing of the party. He also gave geographic balance to the ticket, and all knew that Ohio was going to be a key state for Republicans, if they were to win back the White House.[19]

Bricker's supporters sensed what his appearance at the podium meant, initially shouting "No, no!," and then breaking into a genuine show of support for the Ohio governor that lasted for twenty-five minutes. Bricker graciously withdrew from consideration for president and endorsed Dewey. "Mindful as I am," he said in a firm voice, "to the devotion to the cause which I have tried to represent . . . I understand as you do, the overwhelming desire of this convention to nominate a great, a grand, a vigorous fighting young American, the noble, the dramatic, and appealing governor of the great State of New York, Thomas E. Dewey." Bricker had been the only significant candidate who stood between Dewey and the nomination. After Bricker's remarks, the names of former Governor Stassen of Minnesota and Representative Dirksen of Illinois were also withdrawn.[20]

Dewey was the only candidate nominated and the voting was a formality. The New York governor, four years after having been the frontrunner at the 1940 convention and enduring there an embarrassing loss to Wendell Willkie, was finally the nominee of the Republican Party for president. He received 1,056 votes. The only vote against him came from a cantankerous Wisconsin delegate, who voted for General MacArthur and who shouted out, "I am a man, not a jellyfish."[21]

Without breaking for lunch, the convention quickly moved to selection of a vice-presidential nominee. Bricker was the only one nominated. He received all 1,057 votes cast. The lone Wisconsin delegate who had opposed Dewey was apparently satisfied that his earlier protest vote had been sufficient. The 1944 Republican ticket was formally in place by mid-afternoon.[22]

Dewey and his team, recognizing the excitement that Roosevelt had generated at the 1932 and 1936 Democratic conventions by appearing before them in person and giving dramatic acceptance speeches, decided to copy that campaign tactic. Alf Landon had declined to address the 1936 Republican convention in Cleveland that had nominated him. Wendell Willkie in 1940 had only spoken a few words to the Philadelphia convention that had named him as the party's standard-bearer, and had later given his formal acceptance speech at his hometown, which had been the tradition for both parties prior to 1932. Dewey's travel to the convention followed Roosevelt's path from 1932. Both were New York governors and flew from Albany, the state capital, to Chicago. With advances in aviation since 1932, Dewey's flight took only five hours, about half the time that it had taken Roosevelt's plane to go the same distance. He left in mid-afternoon and arrived in Chicago with time to spare before his scheduled speech at nine o'clock in the evening. During the flight, the often uptight Dewey joked with reporters, reviewed the text of his speech, and he and his wife enjoyed a steak dinner, with dessert from a cake decorated with an elephant and with "Dewey 1944!" written on it. After his arrival, led by a motorcycle police escort, Dewey's motorcade of eighty cars made its way into the city and to the Stevens Hotel, where the governor's campaign headquarters was located.[23]

Dewey began his speech by noting his pledge to New Yorkers in 1942 to serve out his term as governor, but advising that because the convention had "decided otherwise" and had honored him with "the highest duty to which an American can be called," he had no right to refuse the call. "I come to this great task a free man," he declared, "I have made no pledges, promises or commitments, express or implied, to any man or woman."[24]

Addressing the war first, he reassured the Allies that he and the Republican Party were "united with you to the limit of our resources and our manpower." To the nation's enemies, he had a warning: "To every member of the Axis Powers let us send this message from this convention: By this political campaign which you are unable to understand, our will to victory will be strengthened, and with every day you further delay surrender the consequences to you will be more severe."[25]

Moving on to domestic issues, he said that it was time for new leadership:

> The present Administration in Washington has been in office for more than eleven years.
> Today it is at war with Congress, and at war with itself. Squabbles between Cabinet members, feuds between rival bureaucrats and bitterness between the President and his own party . . . have become the order of the day . . . .
> [T]hey tell us . . . [of Roosevelt's administration] in its young days it did some good things. That we freely grant. But now it has grown old in office. It has become tired and quarrelsome. It seems that the great men who founded this nation really did know what they were talking about when they said that three terms were too many.[26]

In 1940, before America entered the war, Dewey pointed out, after "seven years of unequaled power and unparalleled spending" under Roosevelt and the New Deal, the nation still had ten million unemployed. "Do we have to have a war to get jobs?," he asked. He continued:

> The present Administration has never solved this fundamental problem of jobs and opportunity. It can never solve this problem. It has never even understood what makes a job. It has never been for full production. It has lived in chattering fear of abundance. It has specialized in curtailment and restriction. It had been consistently hostile to and abusive of American business and industry . . . .
> It is the New Deal that tells us that America has lost its capacity to grow . . . . Is America old and worn out, as the New Dealers tell us? Look to the beaches of Normandy for the answer. Look to the reaches of the wide Pacific—to the corners of the world where American men are fighting. Look to the marvels of production in the war plants in your own cities and towns. I say to you: Our country is just fighting its way through to new horizons. The future of America has no limit.[27]

Dewey spoke for less than a half hour. He did not linger in the arena after his remarks for the demonstration on his behalf, which was enthusiastic, but was whisked back to his hotel where thousands of other supporters waited. There, he mingled with the crowd and appeared happy and confident. Republicans finally had hope. "Here was a Republican," as authors Craig Sautter and Edward Burke have written, "who just might stop Roosevelt." Much of the press agreed. Of Dewey's speech, the *Cincinnati Enquirer* commented on "the force of his address . . . . There was meat as well as magnetism." *Newsweek* observed that Dewey had "snapped his party out of a twelve-year coma." Dewey had presented "himself and his cause both forcefully and attractively," wrote the *Louisville Courier Journal*.[28]

For the first time since the party had first nominated Herbert Hoover in 1928, Republicans left their convention with a realistic belief that victory in the general election could finally, once again, be theirs.

Democratic Convention

With Franklin Roosevelt's nomination for a fourth term a foregone conclusion, the focus of attention in the months leading up to the 1944 Democratic convention was the choice of his running mate. It seemed more important than in years past. The president was tired and ill. Those who met with him that winter and spring privately expressed concern over his appearance. He looked ashen, had bags under his eyes, his hands trembled at times, and he appeared mentally slower. Some suspected cancer. Few said it aloud, but most thought he would not live another four years. The whispering remained largely among Washington insiders and Democratic Party leaders. A consensus emerged among them that the party's upcoming convention would be nominating not one, but two, presidents.[29]

There was no investigation of the president's health by the Washington press corps, which reported only what it was told by the president's personal physician, Dr. Ross McIntyre. The sixty-two-year-old Roosevelt, said Dr. McIntyre, had recurring bouts of bronchitis, some sinus problems, and was overworked from managing the war. Nothing that a little rest would not cure. The real diagnosis, which came from a cardiologist who examined the president in late March, and which was kept from all but a few, was that Roosevelt had hypertension and congestive heart failure, and his condition was getting steadily worse. The president was whisked off in April to a private South Carolina estate owned by financier Bernard Baruch (an advisor and large donor to the Democratic Party) for rest and for treatment, including a new diet and medications. He stayed there for a month, but appeared to be no better when he returned to Washington in May.[30]

For almost four years, during the greatest war in the history of the world, Vice President Henry Wallace had been a heartbeat away from the presidency. The fifty-five-year-old Iowan had been handpicked by Roosevelt to be his running mate in 1940 and his nomination had been forced upon a reluctant convention that year by a petulant president, who had threatened to decline his own nomination if the party did not bow to his will. In 1944, however, Roosevelt decided (with some persuasion from others) to cast aside Wallace and run with a new vice president. He had done it before. That was how Wallace had gotten the job, because Roosevelt had tired of John Nance Garner, his vice president during his first two terms.

In the spring of 1944, party leaders decided that Wallace had to be replaced. They thought him too liberal, too kooky, too pro-Russian, and too independent. They conspired with Roosevelt's appointments secretary, Edwin "Pa" Watson, to only let people in to see the president who would put a bug in his ear questioning whether having Wallace continue in office would be good for the party, or for the country. Roosevelt came around to believing—or at least he seemed to—that Wallace needed to be replaced. But that was only part of the battle. Who would replace him? Several names were bandied about as potential new running mates.[31]

James "Jimmy" Byrnes was well known in the White House. A former member of both the House and Senate, the sixty-two-year-old South Carolinian had been a justice on the Supreme Court for a year, until Roosevelt asked him to resign in 1942 so that he could serve in an administrative capacity to help with the war effort. In 1944, he was Director of the Office of War Mobilization, a powerful position, based in the White House, that gave him constant contact with Roosevelt. Byrnes was competent and respected by FDR, who came to refer to him as the "assistant president." Politically, there were concerns about Byrnes as a potential vice president. He was a southerner, a region where Jim Crow laws, segregation, and discrimination against Blacks were facts of life. When in Congress, Byrnes had opposed a federal anti-lynching law. Blacks had become a key part of Roosevelt's New Deal coalition and it was thought they may not turn out in 1944 for Democrats if a southerner, particularly Byrnes, were on the party's ticket. Catholics were another part of the New Deal base. Byrnes had been born Catholic, but married an Episcopalian and had switched to her religion. Would Catholic voters hold that against the party if Byrnes were the vice-presidential nominee? Finally, in his White House job, Byrnes had opposed strikes and wartime wage increases for workers, which drew the ire of organized labor, another part of the New Deal coalition. Would labor leaders support a man for vice president who had worked against their interests?[32]

Two Democrats who held the top leadership positions in Congress were also in the mix as a replacement for Wallace. Speaker of the House Sam Rayburn of Texas, sixty-two-years-old, had been in the House of Representatives for more than thirty years. He was a Washington insider and, as vice president, could help move legislation through Congress. The fact that he was a Texan was a concern. Like Byrnes, he was a southerner and would likely face opposition from Blacks. Also, in Texas, as in many southern states, there was a faction of the Democratic Party that strongly opposed Roosevelt. It was known that two slates of delegates from Texas would be coming to the 1944 convention, one for Roosevelt and one against him. Although Rayburn backed the president, some thought that putting him on the ticket would be asking for trouble, since he would not have solid support from his own state. Kentucky Senator Alben Barkley, who was sixty-six-years-old, was the Democratic majority leader in the Senate and was well respected. Although mostly supportive of FDR's agenda, Barkley and the president had had a spat in early 1944 when a tax bill that the administration had asked for was passed, with Barkley's help, only to have Roosevelt veto it. An angry Barkley threatened to resign from his leadership position, but the president persuaded him to stay on and offered him the role of placing his name in nomination at the upcoming convention.[33]

Justice William Douglas of the Supreme Court, who was in his mid-forties, was a liberal and had numerous friends in Washington, including the president. He was a frequent poker player at the White House. Before his appointment to the Court by Roosevelt in 1939, Douglas had been chairman of the Securities and Exchange Commission. He was athletic and an outdoorsman, qualities that could offset Roosevelt's increasing frailty, and some thought he would be a good running mate. But he had never held political office and had no base of support within the party.[34]

Senator Harry Truman of Missouri was another contender to replace Wallace as vice president. Sixty years old, he was born into a farming family and, as a young man, worked on the farm and as a bank clerk. He never attended college. Truman served in the Missouri National Guard as an artillery officer and was in combat in France during World War I. After the war, he entered politics and was allied with the Democratic machine of Thomas Pendergast, a Kansas City party boss who had a reputation for corruption. Truman rose gradually in public office and was first elected to the Senate in 1934. Reelected in 1940, he gained prominence as the head of a special Senate committee that investigated wartime military spending, which came to be known as the Truman Committee. Truman had a record of supporting organized labor and, with Missouri being a border state (as opposed to a southern one), it was unlikely that he would face stiff opposition from Blacks. Although he was a loyal backer of Roosevelt, Truman had never been personally close to the president, nor was he part of FDR's wide circle of friends in Washington. Whenever talk of being vice president came up, Truman told colleagues that he had no interest in the position and that he enjoyed being a senator.[35]

Much has been written about the Democratic Party's vice-presidential selection process in 1944, with noted historian Robert Ferrell's book, *Choosing Truman: The Democratic Convention of 1944*, being the most detailed and insightful account. Recounting all of the players, the meetings, and the twists and turns that occurred, is beyond the scope of this account of the convention. Suffice it to say that Roosevelt gave commitments and then backed away from them. He made contradictory private statements expressing his support for different men. He wanted Wallace. He wanted Byrnes. He wanted Douglas. He wanted Truman. And then he didn't. Was he a sick old man who could not make a decision, or was he stringing everyone along, with the hope of doing the least political damage to himself? As journalist and author Michael Janeway has observed, "most of those who have written about the 1944 Democratic National convention have held back from the conclusion that Roosevelt was doing his cold-blooded best to manipulate the players and the fateful game—even as they contribute evidence that this is precisely what he was up to."[36]

The party leaders who had been working for months to keep Wallace off the ticket believed that they had the matter settled after a dinner with the president on July 11, eight days before the convention. They met that day for lunch at the Mayflower Hotel, a few blocks from the White House, to discuss strategy and to rehearse their pitch to the president. United in their disdain for Wallace, they were split on who should take his place on the ticket, Some preferred Byrnes, some Truman, some preferred others. The group that had dinner with Roosevelt that evening consisted of Robert Hannegan, the DNC chairman, Frank Walker, the postmaster general in FDR's cabinet and a former DNC chairman, Ed Flynn, the Democratic boss of the Bronx, Edwin Pauley, the DNC treasurer, Ed Kelly, the mayor of Chicago, and George Allen, the DNC secretary. After dinner, they retired to the Oval Study on the second floor, the president's favorite room in the mansion, and he mixed cocktails for all, as was his custom. The various contenders for the vice presidency were discussed. First to be eliminated were the two Democratic congressional leaders. Senator Barkley was rejected because of his age. At sixty-six, he was four years older than Roosevelt. With the president looking old, and with the Republicans having already nominated the forty-two-year-old Thomas Dewey, it was agreed that a younger man was needed. Speaker Rayburn was dismissed due to the party's political infighting in Texas. Byrnes was next on the chopping block. He was likely the most qualified to be vice president, having been a congressman, a senator, a justice on the Supreme Court, and then holding a top administrative job in the White House. But Flynn, the Bronx party boss, argued that putting a southerner like Byrnes on the ticket would cost the party hundreds of thousands of Black votes in New York and other northern cities. Although Byrnes's conversion from Catholicism was not thought to be of importance, his opposition to the interests of organized labor drew objections during the meeting. Byrnes was removed from the list. Roosevelt raised the name of Justice Douglas, but the group dismissed him as another starry-eyed liberal, much like Henry Wallace, and perhaps worse. When Truman was discussed, the group felt that he had more positives and fewer negatives than the rest. He had an advocate in DNC Chairman Hannegan, who was also from Missouri. The participants ultimately settled on Truman as the choice, and Roosevelt agreed. "If that's the case," the president said as he put a hand on Hannegan's knee, "it's Truman." Hannegan asked for, and received a handwritten note, scribbled on an envelope. It read, "Bob, I think Truman is the right man, FDR." Assignments were made to notify those not chosen, as well as to speak with Vice President Wallace, who had not yet been told that he was out of a job, as he had been on a two-month trip to Asia and would be returning to the United States the next day.[37]

Two days later, on July 13, Roosevelt and Wallace had lunch. After reviewing Wallace's trip, they discussed politics, with the president advising that key party leaders felt that Wallace would be a drag on the ticket and wanted him replaced. FDR said nothing about having held a meeting with them, that he had agreed with them, and that Truman had been selected as Wallace's replacement. Wallace disputed that he would cost the party votes, citing his support among delegates to the convention and advising that an upcoming Gallup poll (the results of which he had received advance notice) would show sixty-five percent of Democrats favored his renomination. Failing to get his vice president to voluntarily step aside, FDR then gave Wallace an endorsement, agreeing to write a letter stating that, if he were a delegate to the convention, he would vote for Wallace. The president concluded the meeting by telling Wallace, "I hope it will be the same old team."[38]

Just a couple of hours earlier, the president had met with Byrnes and expressed a preference for Byrnes as his running mate. FDR told Byrnes that he did not think Wallace could prevail at the convention and that Byrnes was the "best qualified" person to take his spot. He encouraged Byrnes to seek the nomination, assuring him, "If you stay in you are sure to win." The next day, July 14, an elated Byrnes relayed his conversation to Hannegan and Walker, who were incredulous at the duplicitous statements by the president. They advised Byrnes that, less than three days earlier, FDR had agreed that Truman was to be his running mate and had given them a note confirming it. A dismayed Byrnes phoned the president, who by then was at Hyde Park, and confronted him with this information. Oh no, said the president, Hannegan, Walker, and the others had expressed *their* preference for Truman; he had not. He had only agreed, he told Byrnes, that he would not oppose Senator Truman or, for that matter, Justice Douglas, if either one of them were chosen by the convention. Byrnes accepted the explanation. He decided to enter the race for vice president, thinking that he had FDR's support. Byrnes immediately called Truman, a friend from their days in the Senate and, after confirming with Truman that Truman was not interested in being vice president (but not saying that he knew party leaders had decided on Truman), Byrnes asked Truman to give the nominating speech for him at the convention. Truman readily agreed. In this, Byrnes was being as duplicitous as the president. By getting Truman to nominate him, Byrnes was trying to keep the man he knew would likely emerge as a strong opponent for the nomination from joining the contest.[39]

Chicago was, once again, the host city for the 1944 Democratic convention, set to open on Wednesday, July 19. Roosevelt would not be attending. Unknown to the public, he was scheduled to meet with General Douglas MacArthur in Hawaii to plot war strategy. On the Saturday afternoon before the convention, as FDR made his way westward to California, where he would board a Navy cruiser for Hawaii, his train stopped briefly at a railyard in Chicago. DNC Chairman Hannegan, along with Chicago Mayor Kelly, got on the presidential Pullman car, the *Ferdinand Magellan*, and met privately with Roosevelt for almost an hour. Reports differ as to exactly what transpired, but FDR apparently endorsed Byrnes for vice president, as Kelly phoned Byrnes shortly afterward and advised him that the president "has given us the green light to support you and he wants you in Chicago." Hannegan also got two letters from the president. The first was the one that FDR had promised to Wallace, advising that if he were a delegate, he would vote for Wallace. Language was added, however, weakening its impact. Of Wallace, the president wrote in the letter, "I like him and I respect him, and he is my personal friend. I personally would vote for his renomination if I were a delegate to the convention." But, FDR continued, "At the same time I do not wish to appear in any way as dictating to the convention. Obviously the convention must do the deciding. And it should—and I am sure it will—give great consideration to the pros and cons of its choice." The second letter, which Hannegan had requested, was a typed version of FDR's handwritten note supporting Truman. It turned out to be much different from what Hannegan had wanted and expected, in that it added Justice Douglas into the mix, and it was not an endorsement, but simply a statement of no opposition to the two men. Addressed to Hannegan, that letter read: "You have written to me about Harry Truman and Bill Douglas. I should, of course, be very glad to run with either of them and believe that either one of them would bring real strength to the ticket." Years later, FDR's secretary, Grace Tully, claimed that, as initially typed by her, the letter had Justice Douglas's name first, but that Hannegan requested that she retype it to put Senator Truman's name first. Hannegan always denied that he had asked that the order of the names be switched. Accounts of the railyard meeting all agree on one additional thing. After having agreed to Byrnes as his running mate, FDR added a caveat, saying to Hannegan, "Clear it with Sidney."[40]

"Sidney" was Sidney Hillman, one of the most powerful labor union officials in the country. In 1944, he was the vice president of the Congress of Industrial Organizations (the "CIO") and had been a strong supporter of Roosevelt for years. He ran the CIO's political action committee. Hillman had met separately with the president in the Oval Office the same day that FDR met with Byrnes, the meeting during which the president encouraged Byrnes to seek the vice-presidential nomination and advised that he was certain that Byrnes would win. Exactly what FDR and Hillman discussed during *their* meeting that day is not known. Some historians believe that Roosevelt ordered Hillman to veto any nomination of Byrnes in Chicago, so that he, Roosevelt, would not be seen as betraying one of his closest advisors. After events transpired over the next few days (Hillman opposed Byrnes strongly), Byrnes came to believe that that is what had happened. As author Robert Ferrell writes, Byrnes "became bitter about it, and indeed never forgot it for the rest of his long life. The president, he believed, slipped a knife into his back." Years later, the diary of Harold Ickes, a gossipy Roosevelt confidant, was made public and it provided support for the conclusion Byrnes had reached. Ickes wrote that another Roosevelt aide told him, "It had been necessary to rely upon Hillman to lay down the law as to Byrnes." Further, Ickes wrote that Hillman told him, when speaking of the possibility of Byrnes having been vice president, that "the President stopped that nomination" through him.[41]

From Sunday through Wednesday, who was up and who was down in the contest for vice president seemed to change hour by hour. Byrnes arrived in Chicago on Sunday, met with party bosses, and was confident of victory. Wallace arrived later, equally confident, vowing to a throng of two thousand supporters at his hotel, "I am in this fight to the finish." Truman arrived, telling all that he was not a candidate, and put the final touches on his speech nominating Byrnes. Hillman and his boss, CIO president Philip Murray, arrived and advised that labor was strongly supporting Wallace. Truman had breakfast with Hillman on Tuesday and asked him to reconsider labor's position and to support Byrnes. Hillman refused. The Bronx political boss, Flynn, arrived, still thinking that the president was for Truman, as had been decided at the meeting held at the White House a week earlier. When told that FDR had switched to Byrnes, Flynn objected, and again raised the issue that Byrnes being on the ticket would cost the party Black votes. Hillman joined the meeting and held firm against Byrnes because he had not supported labor's causes. A phone call was made to FDR, who was by then in San Diego. Each man spoke to him and, by the end of the conversation, Roosevelt flipped again, telling the group to "go all out for Truman." Byrnes was then told he was out. Angry, he issued a terse withdrawal statement: "In deference to the wishes of the President, I ask that my name note be placed before the convention." Truman was told he was in. Reluctantly, he accepted.[42]

By the time the convention opened on Wednesday, the battle lines were drawn. The contest for vice president would be between two men: Wallace, fighting to hold onto his job, and supported by the liberal faction of the party and organized labor; and Truman, favored by the conservative faction of the party, by most of the party bosses and party leaders and, unless he changed his mind again, by Roosevelt. Several states had announced that they would be putting forth favorite son candidates, but it was not thought that any of them had a chance and that their states would ultimately go with whoever looked to be the winner between Wallace and Truman.

DNC Chairman Robert Hannegan called the convention to order shortly after noon on Wednesday, July 19, in Chicago Stadium. In the coming days, under the stadium's arched roof, as it had in 1932 and 1940, the party would nominate Franklin Roosevelt as its standard-bearer for president. American flags hung from the rafters. Above one balcony section there was a long row of black-and-white images of the fourteen Democratic presidents. To the left and higher up, a large color image of Roosevelt had been hung. It was, a Chicago worker advised, the same one used at the 1940 convention but, having faded, had been touched up a bit. Committees were formed, Senator Robert Kerr from Oklahoma was named temporary chairman and, after a brief opening session, the convention adjourned for several hours.[43]

At its evening session, Kerr, a "strapping and eloquent orator of the old school," delivered the convention's keynote speech. He depicted Thomas Dewey, the Republican standard-bearer who had been nominated in the same building three weeks earlier, as a conservative "disciple" of former President Herbert Hoover. A dozen years out of office, Hoover was still the man Democrats loved to hate. In his acceptance speech at the same podium from which Kerr was speaking, Dewey had described President Roosevelt and his administration, after having been in office for eleven long years, as having grown "old and tired and quarrelsome." Kerr rolled off his lips the ages of some of the American military leaders who were fighting and winning the ongoing global war, including General MacArthur, General Marshall, Admiral Nimitz, and Admiral Halsey, most of whom were in their early to mid-sixties, and wondered what they would think upon hearing that Dewey looked upon them as a group of "tired old men." "No, Mr. Dewey," Kerr proclaimed, "We know we are winning this war with these 'tired old men,' including the 62-year-old Mr. Roosevelt as their Commander in Chief." The line was the highlight of the speech and resulted in a demonstration from the crowd that lasted for fifteen minutes.[44]

During the afternoon of the convention's second day, Senator Alben Barkley of Kentucky, the party's majority leader in the Senate, gave the main nominating speech for Roosevelt. A week earlier, Barkley had been on the short list for vice president, but had been eliminated because of his age. He was still miffed over this and there was some talk in Chicago that he might back out of giving the speech. Barkley was already upset with FDR for vetoing a piece of legislation a few months earlier. In his speech, he acknowledged that he had "on occasion found myself in disagreement" with the president, but portrayed it as a positive. "We both fight now and have all our lives fought," he said, "for the right to harbor our opinions, to express and defend them, and to change them when convinced of error." Describing Roosevelt as having "a leadership unsurpassed . . . in the annals of American history," Barkley concluded with, "I present to this assembly for the office of President of these United States the name of one who is endowed with the intellectual boldness of Thomas Jefferson, the faith and indomitable patience of Abraham Lincoln, the rugged integrity of Grover Cleveland, and the scholarly vision of Woodrow Wilson—Franklin Delano Roosevelt." Barkley's speech was followed by a forty-minute demonstration of cheers for the president and parading around the aisles by delegates, many holding aloft "Roosevelt and Victory" signs.[45]

The only other candidate placed in nomination for president was Senator Harry Byrd of Virginia, who was put forward by delegates from a handful of southern states that opposed Roosevelt for several reasons, especially the dramatic growth in the size and power of the federal government under the New Deal. As Ruth Nooney, a Florida delegate, took the podium to speak on behalf of Byrd, she was booed lustily by the pro-Roosevelt crowd. Senator Samuel Jackson, the permanent chairman, intervened, put his arm around Nooney's shoulders, and admonished the audience, "We will have no more of that." They quieted and Nooney praised Byrd as "a great legislator, farmer and businessman" who was a defender of "true democracy." Her remarks received only modest applause.[46]

In a surprise to many, Vice President Henry Wallace appeared on the stage to give a seconding speech for Roosevelt. It was a way for him to appear in front of the delegates before the battle for the vice-presidential nomination began. After the release of Roosevelt's lukewarm endorsement letter for Wallace a couple of days earlier, Wallace was thought to be the underdog in the contest against Truman. Of FDR's Wallace letter, an editorial in the *Washington Post* opined, "It is distant almost to the point of frigidity." It was written, the newspaper concluded, in a way to say, "Don't take this seriously, for I had to do it." Others called it "a death kiss." At past conventions, effective and dramatic speeches (most notably by James Garfield at the 1880 Republican convention and William Jennings Bryan at the 1896 Democratic convention) had swayed delegates and changed the outcome of nomination contests. Could Wallace do the same in his fight to hold onto his job? His backers hoped so, had planned for the moment, and packed the arena with Wallace supporters. Tickets for the convention were printed in booklets, with a separate ticket for each day and session, but each ticket was the same color, making it difficult to tell one from another. As author Robert Ferrell described the scene in Chicago Stadium that Thursday night, "Wallace supporters seem to have used every ticket in every book they had, knowing that in the rush at the gates the takers and ushers would not have time to check the tickets for the proper day and session." He continued, "Gaining entry to both the galleries and floor, Wallace supporters in the thousands packed the stadium to the highest seats under the eaves. The hall resembled a Wallace rally rather than a convention, backers spreading banners through the galleries and floor, displaying such slogans as 'We Want Wallace,' 'Keep the Winning Team, Roosevelt and Wallace,' and 'The People Want Wallace.'"[47]

The vice president rose to the occasion and made what many consider the best speech of his life. He praised Roosevelt for his liberalism, urged that the party continue on its liberal course, and clearly implied (without specifically stating so) that he was Roosevelt's liberal heir:

> The future belongs to those who go down the line unswervingly for the liberal principles of both political democracy and economic democracy regardless of race, color or religion . . . .

Roosevelt stands for all this. That is why certain people hate him so. That also is one of the outstanding reasons why Roosevelt will be elected for a fourth time....

Roosevelt is a greater liberal today than he has ever been. His soul is pure.... The only question ever in Roosevelt's mind is how best to serve the cause of liberalism in the long run. He thinks big. He sees far.

There is no question about the renomination of President Roosevelt by this convention. The only question is whether the convention and the party workers believe wholeheartedly in the liberal policies for which Roosevelt has always stood....

As head of the Iowa delegation, in the cause of liberalism, and with a prayer for prompt victory in this war, permanent peace, and full employment, I give you Franklin D. Roosevelt.[48]

Wallace's speech was, according to the *Baltimore Sun*, "Brief, militant, and well-delivered," overshadowed Barkley's primary nominating speech for FDR, and was "cheered to the rafters." Even one of the party bosses who opposed Wallace, and who watched from the stage, called it "the most inspiring talk" ever given by Wallace. The crowd enthusiastically demonstrated for the vice president, but Chairman Jackson put it to an early end. There was a schedule to keep. Roosevelt, on his presidential railcar in California, was scheduled to give his acceptance speech by an audio hookup to Chicago while the large nationwide radio audience was still tuned in. But first, the balloting had to take place. This was quickly done. With the party's two-thirds rule having been done away with at the 1936 convention, only a simple majority, 589 votes, was required. Roosevelt received 1,086 votes, compared to only 89 for Byrd, which came mostly from Virginia, Mississippi, and Louisiana. The only other vote cast was a single one from New York for Jim Farley, the man who had run FDR's 1932 and 1936 campaigns, but who had broken with him in 1940.[49]

After brief cheering following the vote, the crowd was quieted and the president's familiar voice, using the conversational tone of his fireside chats, came over the stadium's speakers. The audience had been told not to applaud until the end, so as to not miss any of the words. Before the speech, the public did not know FDR's whereabouts, only that he would be traveling for war meetings during the week of the convention. One report had him crossing the Atlantic, consulting with Churchill, and then delivering his acceptance speech from Normandy, in France, where Allied forces, only six weeks earlier, on D-Day, had begun the long-awaited Allied invasion to reclaim Europe from the Nazis.[50] Roosevelt began by revealing that he had not gone east, but west, had crossed the continent, and was speaking from an undisclosed naval base (later revealed to be Camp Pendleton, a base for the Marines near San Diego). He began by stating, as he had in his 1940 acceptance speech, that "in spite of my desire to return to the quiet of private life," he was running for another term as president out of a sense of duty to the people and to the country. He continued:

> I shall not campaign in the usual sense, for the office. In these days of tragic sorrow, I do not consider it fitting. Besides, in these days of global warfare, I shall not be able to find the time. I shall, however, feel free to report to the people the facts about matters of concern to them and especially to correct any misrepresentations....

The job before the country in 1944, he said, was to win the war, to form international organizations to make sure that another war was not possible in the foreseeable future, and to build a postwar economy that would provide employment to all and a decent standard of living. He then moved to criticism of Republicans:

> The people of the United States will decide this fall whether they wish to turn over this 1944 job—this worldwide job—to inexperienced and immature hands, to those who opposed lend-lease and international cooperation against the forces of aggression and tyranny, until they could read the polls of popular sentiment, or whether they wish to leave it to those who saw the danger from abroad, who met it head-on, and who now have seized the offensive and carried the war to its present stages of success....

He ended by comparing the condition of the nation in 1944 with its status near the end of another bitter war in its history, the Civil War, and focused on the words of Abraham Lincoln during his second inaugural address:

> The greatest wartime President in our history, after a wartime election which he called 'the most reliable indication of public purpose in this country' set the goal for the United States, in terms as applicable today as they were in 1865—terms which the human mind cannot improve:
> With firmness in the right, as God gives us to see the right, let us strive on to finish the work we are in; to bind up the nation's wounds; to care for him who shall have borne the battle, and for his widow, and his orphan—to do all which may achieve and cherish a just and lasting peace among ourselves, and with all nations.[51]

Roosevelt's speech ended around 10:30 p.m. and was followed by only three minutes of cheering and the playing of "The Star-Spangled Banner." The plan of party leaders was to get in a few of the nomination speeches for vice president (in addition to Truman and Wallace, there were several favorite son candidates who would be nominated), adjourn until the morning, finish the speeches, and then proceed with the balloting for a running mate. The Wallace team, with thousands of the vice president's supporters packed into the arena, had another plan—to stampede the convention that night and force the nomination of Wallace. Suddenly, chants of "We Want Wallace!" rang through Chicago Stadium. "Roosevelt and Wallace" signs and banners appeared everywhere. The organist at the arena's huge pipe organ began to play the state song of Wallace's home state, Iowa, over and over again ("I-o-way, I-o-way, that's where the tall corn grows!"). Party leaders, all Truman backers, huddled on the stage, with worried looks on their faces. The convention had gotten away from them. Senator Claude Pepper of Florida, a Wallace supporter, stood on his chair and waved and shouted for recognition. His intent was to make a motion to nominate Wallace by acclamation. "It was a moment," Robert Ferrell has written, "heavy with portent for the history of the American presidency, but it was a moment in which the tough leaders of the party confronted amateurs. They were not going to put up with nonsense." "Stop that organ!," one of them shouted, and a worker was dispatched with an axe, to search for the organ's cables and to cut them. Chicago's Mayor Kelly advised DNC Chairman Hannegan that the city's fire code allowed him, Kelly, to declare the overcrowded hall a fire hazard. Pepper, unable to get recognition, started wading slowly through the crowd toward the podium. Hannegan, determined to put an end to the pandemonium, took control.

He ordered Pittsburgh's mayor, David Lawrence, to make a motion to adjourn and turned to Senator Jackson, the convention's chairman, who was not at the podium, and shouted, "You get up there right now and I mean now, and recognize Dave Lawrence, or I'll do it for you." Pepper had made his way through the gate restricting access to the stage and was starting up the steps. Jackson, by then at the podium, stared at Lawrence, who shouted out his motion to adjourn. With Pepper walking toward him, Jackson quickly called for a voice vote, announced that it had passed, banged his gavel, and the convention was officially adjourned. The public explanation was that it had been a matter of public safety, with overcrowding in the hall and the need to enforce fire laws.[52]

The next morning, Jackson saw Pepper in a hotel lobby and offered "an apology of sorts," explaining that he was under strict orders from Hannegan to get the convention adjourned. "I hope you understand," he plaintively stated. Years later, Pepper would write, "What I understood was that, for better or worse, history was turned topsy-turvy that night in Chicago." As Wallace biographers John Culver and John Hyde have commented on what happened to Wallace's quest for renomination as vice president during those tumultuous moments, "It was over. Pepper had led the Pickett's Charge of the Wallace movement."[53]

Having fended off the Wallace surge of Thursday night, party leaders spent the next morning and most of the afternoon planning and implementing their strategy for a Truman victory. They encouraged states with favorite sons to stay in the race, at least through the first ballot, to lessen any chance of a quick Wallace victory. They met with delegates individually and in groups, as did Truman. Their argument was simple—Roosevelt preferred Truman over Wallace, and the party should defer to Roosevelt's wishes. They pointed to the lukewarm letter that FDR had written for Wallace and compared it to his letter for Truman, in which he said he would "be very glad to run" with Truman and that Truman would "bring real strength to the ticket." They explained away the fact that the letter also said the same things about Justice Douglas by arguing that he was not in the mix, and had really never been. Besides, they said, FDR had put Truman's name *first*, before that of Douglas, indicating a preference for Truman between the two. If the order of the two names had been switched from the original draft of the letter, as FDR's secretary later claimed, something so minor might have factored in the outcome and changed the course of history.[54]

By the time the convention resumed around noon, all was in place for a Truman victory on the second ballot. Mayor Kelly made sure that the gatekeepers at the entrances to the arena carefully checked all tickets to the galleries, so that there would be no repeat of the pro-Wallace crowd from the night before. Hollywood star power was added to the proceedings, as movie stars Spencer Tracy and Gloria Swanson were present and attracted attention. Nominating speeches took up most of the afternoon. Truman was nominated by Missouri's other senator, Bennett Clark, whose father, Champ Clark, had narrowly lost the party's 1912 nomination to Woodrow Wilson. Although a great orator, Clark had a drinking problem, had been out most of the night, and had to be sobered up in time for his turn at the podium. His speech was a disappointment. Historian David McCullough wrote that Clark "had none of his usual flair" and "moved the audience not at all." Wallace was placed in nomination by Richard Mitchell, an Iowa judge, who, according to McCullough, made a "vigorous speech," which was followed by a "moving" seconding speech for Wallace by Senator Pepper of Florida, the man who had come so close in his attempt to have Wallace nominated the night before. Speeches were also delivered for nine favorite sons, who were also formally placed in nomination. Fortunately for Truman and the party leaders backing him, the speeches would not decide the contest. They had the votes.[55]

The first ballot for vice president began in the late afternoon, with 589 votes required for victory. Wallace led with 429½ and Truman was second with 319½. The Truman team was not worried—394½ votes had been cast for the various favorite sons and they had secured enough pledges from those states to pick up a sufficient number of their votes on the second ballot to put Truman over the top. The second ballot began. Midway through the roll call of the states, Maryland switched its eighteen votes from its favorite son to Truman. Next, Oklahoma did the same, casting its twenty-two votes for Truman. As Ed Pauley, the DNC's treasurer and one of the Truman leaders, later wrote, "the rest was relatively easy." State after state switched to Truman. By the end of the second ballot, Truman easily won the nomination for vice president with 1031 votes, compared to 105 for Wallace, and forty-one scattered among a few others.[56]

Truman watched it all from the galleries, seated next to his wife, Bess, who had attended all of the convention's sessions. Wallace stayed at his hotel, perhaps knowing, or suspecting, the outcome. After his victory was declared, Truman briefly addressed the convention, noting the "great responsibility" of the office to which he had been nominated and vowing, "I am perfectly willing to assume it." Wallace sent his congratulations and pledged his support. With its new ticket in place, and with a vice-presidential nominee who was decidedly less liberal than the man whom had been defeated, the convention adjourned. The *Baltimore Sun* described the outcome as "a thumping defeat for the CIO Political Action Committee and other New Deal zealots," and a victory for "big-city bosses, new leadership of the party's national committee, and Southerners."[57]

Our opinions today about the outcome of the 1944 Democratic convention are colored by our knowledge of subsequent history. Roosevelt died less than three months into his fourth term, Truman became president, was elected on his own in 1948, and, in general, is viewed by historians as a good president. Henry Wallace went on to oppose Truman's aggressive stance against the Soviet Union as the Cold War began and became increasingly aligned with the left-fringe of American politics. Wallace ran for president on a liberal third-party ticket in 1948 and received only two percent of the national vote. Many view him as having been naïve about the Soviet Union. Truman's leading biographer, McCullough, has praised the party's boss system in the 1940s for bringing forth such a man as Truman. McCullough wrote, "There had been no popular boom for him [Truman] for Vice President. Nor had personal ambition figured . . . . [A]s time would tell, everything considered, the system, bosses and all, had produced an excellent choice."[58] Another historian, Robert Ferrell, in his account of the convention, focused not on praise for the boss system and Truman, but on criticism of Roosevelt for the way that he handled the whole vice-presidential selection process. "President Roosevelt," Ferrell wrote, "elevated untruthfulness to a high art. Roosevelt biographers have been tempted to excuse the president's lapses as half-truths necessary to all people . . . . The truth is that Roosevelt went well beyond the political pale. The president passed small untruths off as fibs, unworthy of attention; as for honest-to-goodness lies, he denied he made them."[59]

The Campaign and Election

Dewey traveled throughout the North, Midwest, and West. Instead of big campaign rallies, he focused on meetings with state and local party leaders, since they were the ones needed to get out the Republican vote. He used radio extensively, giving twenty-four national radio addresses. Dewey pledged no change in the handling of the war and argued that the country needed to look forward, asserting it would be at peace during most of the next four years. FDR, Dewey argued, had been in office too long and led an administration of "tired old men." Organized labor, Republicans charged, controlled the president. They derisively chanted "Clear it with Sidney" (the instruction that FDR had given that any choice for his vice president be approved by CIO union leader Sidney Hillman) as a campaign slogan. Dewey never received an endorsement from his Republican rival, Wendell Willkie, the man who had been the party's last nominee in 1940. In early October, Willkie died unexpectedly of a heart attack at the age of fifty-two. For the most part, Dewey avoided the lead up to the war as an issue. In response to a Democratic statement that the United States was fully prepared for the war, he did make a hard-hitting speech in Oklahoma City, citing quotes from others that the country had been unprepared. He declined, however, to use what could have been the most damaging allegation against Roosevelt, which had been circulating in Washington. The charge was that FDR knew in advance about the attack on Pearl Harbor. General George Marshall, the Army's chief of staff, sent Dewey a letter advising that, before December 1941, American codebreakers had, in fact, broken Japanese codes. Messages had revealed Japan's intent to attack the United States somewhere in the Pacific, but not specifically at Pearl Harbor. The information, Marshall assured Dewey, had not made its way up to the president before the attack. The general advised that Japan was still using in 1944 the same codes for its messages, that they were being decoded, and intelligence was still be gained. Any political charge about Pearl Harbor, Marshall told Dewey, would make the Japanese aware that their codes had been compromised, and they would change them, cutting off a valuable source of intelligence. In response to Marshall's request, Dewey instructed his aides to gather all information that had been obtained on the matter and "put it away securely and forget about it."[60]

Roosevelt's campaign is mostly remembered for two events, one of which showed his political skill and humor, and the other, his endurance. In a September speech to the Teamsters' Union, FDR recounted many of the Republican attacks against him. He could take it, he said, but "they now include my little dog Fala." He was referring to an allegation (ultimately proven to be false) made by a Republican congressman that, during a 1943 trip to Alaska for war planning, the president's black Scottish terrier dog, Fala, had been accidentally left behind on one of the Aleutian Islands, and that FDR had ordered a destroyer, at a cost of millions of dollars, to go back and fetch his pet. "Well, of course, I don't resent attacks," the president told the Teamsters, "but Fala does resent them. You know, Fala is Scotch, and being a Scottie . . . his Scotch soul was furious. He has not been the same dog since." The crowd loved the comments, and so did much of the country. *TIME* wrote that it was Roosevelt "at his best . . . like a veteran virtuoso . . . [with] perfection of tuning and tone . . . playing what he loves to play—politics." Later in the campaign, on October 21, FDR had a full day of campaigning in New York City. It was a miserably cold day, with heavy rain and high winds. He traveled more than fifty miles in an open car through Brooklyn, Queens, the Bronx, and Manhattan, with crowds, estimated to be well over two million, lining the streets and cheering on their rain-soaked president. That night, he gave a forceful speech to the Foreign Policy Association about post-war planning. The long day of campaigning, under adverse weather conditions, did much to rebut Republican charges about his frailty and poor health.[61]

On the eve of the election, several national polls predicted a close outcome. The final Gallup Poll had Roosevelt ahead, but with only 51.5%. *TIME* speculated that the results might not be known for weeks. The polls turned out to be wrong. The result was a significant Roosevelt victory. In the Electoral College, the president won thirty-six states and 432 electoral votes, compared to only twelve states and 99 electoral votes for Dewey. The South and West remained solidly Democratic. Dewey's wins were mostly in the Midwest. In the popular vote, it was the closest of FDR's four elections. He won by three-and-a-half million votes, with a total of 25,612,610 (53.5%), compared to 22,017,617 (46%) for Dewey. Roosevelt won New York, the home state of both men, by 300,000 votes. Democrats maintained their majorities in both houses of Congress. They gained twenty-two seats in the House, but lost one seat in the Senate.[62]

The ongoing war in Europe and in the Pacific, and a desire by voters to not change leaders until the conflict was won, has been viewed by most historians as the primary reason for the outcome of the 1944 election. In addition to electing Franklin Roosevelt to an unprecedented fourth term, the nation also elected a new vice president, Senator Harry Truman of Missouri. As analyzed in this chapter, Truman's addition to the ticket—and the booting of Vice President Henry Wallace from it—had been engineered by Democratic Party bosses, with Roosevelt's collusion, at the party's convention. It was a change that would have profound consequences for American history. Within six months of the election, Roosevelt would be dead and Truman would be president.

Conclusion

The modest white clapboard cottage still sits among towering Georgia pines. It is located on the grounds of the Warm Springs Spa that Franklin Roosevelt fell in love with in the 1920s, after polio caused him to lose the use of his legs. He found the waters of the springs to be soothing and medicinal for his legs and invested a good portion of his inheritance to purchase and upgrade the facility, and to ensure its availability to others who suffered from the same condition as he. Roosevelt had the cottage built for his own use during his stays at Warm Springs. Its only architectural flair is four columns that grace its front entrance. When it was completed in May 1932, Roosevelt was the governor of New York and, although running for president, had not yet been nominated by the Democratic Party. Residents of the town of Warm Springs were so confident of his nomination, and of his victory in the presidential election (which would not occur for another six months), that they dubbed the cottage the "Little White House."[1]

Roosevelt visited Warm Springs more than forty times to take comfort in its waters, and to rest and relax in its rural surroundings. He arrived for the final time on March 30, 1945, for what was to have been a two-week vacation. He was three months into his fourth term as president and victory against Germany in World War II was in sight. On April 12, he was at his cottage working on an upcoming speech and was having his portrait painted by artist Elizabeth Shoumatoff, who had previously done a portrait of him in 1943 at the White House. When Shoumatoff saw him at Warm Springs, she was shocked by the change in his appearance from two years earlier. He was much thinner, paler, and looked frail. The portrait session had been arranged by Lucy Mercer Rutherford, FDR's onetime mistress, who was also among those present at the cottage that day. When Eleanor Roosevelt learned in 1918 of her husband's affair with Lucy (who had been her secretary), she agreed to remain married to him on the condition that he sever all ties with Lucy. For a while, he did, but over the years, he provided Lucy with tickets to his inaugurations, had telephone calls with her and, eventually, clandestine meetings. Lucy had married a wealthy man, Winthrop Rutherford, who was almost thirty years older than she. After Winthrop died in March 1944, Lucy saw FDR more often. Shortly after one o'clock in the afternoon of April 12, as Roosevelt sat in his favorite leather chair in the cottage's living room, and as Shoumatoff put additional touches to her portrait of him, he raised an arm toward the back of his head, softly said "I have a terrific headache," and he slumped forward. A doctor arrived within a few minutes and FDR was taken to a bedroom. At 3:35 p.m., the president was pronounced dead. He was sixty-three years old and the cause of death was a massive cerebral hemorrhage.[2]

With the death of the president at Warm Springs in 1945, the era of the Roosevelts came to an end. During many of the preceding forty-five years, Theodore and Franklin Roosevelt, distant cousins, had dominated American politics and government. There had hardly been an election year since 1900 when the name of "Roosevelt!" was not shouted at a political convention or on the campaign trail. Since 1945, members of other political families have aspired to and attained the presidency—the Kennedys, the Bushes, and the Clintons—but none have had quite the success and the staying power of the Roosevelt cousins.

With the passing of the era of the two Roosevelts, there also came a waning of the significance of presidential nominating conventions. After the mid-1940s, conventions began to lose their importance as decision-making bodies in selecting nominees for president. As presidential primary elections became more widespread, more and more eventual nominees were able to secure the number of delegates needed to prevail through the primary process. Conventions became more a ratification of the outcome of the primaries, rather than deliberative bodies that determined who the parties would put forward to the country as their standard-bearers.

Despite the overall trend of their fading prominence, some conventions since 1944 had excitement and drama, and are worth noting.

At the 1948 Democratic convention, northern liberals proposed a strong civil rights plank for the party's platform. In a dramatic speech, Hubert Humphrey, then the mayor of Minneapolis, proclaimed, "To those who say that this civil rights program is an infringement on States' Rights, I say this, that the time has arrived in America for the Democratic Party to get out of the shadows of States' Rights and to walk forthrightly into the bright sunshine of human rights." The adoption of the plank for which Humphrey spoke led to a walkout of several southern delegates. They later formed the Dixiecrat Party, which nominated South Carolina Governor Strom Thurmond as its candidate for president that year.[3]

Four years later, the 1952 Democratic convention became the last major party convention (as of 2023) to require more than one ballot to select its presidential nominee. Senator Estes Kefauver of Tennessee led on the first and second ballots, but was overtaken by Governor Adlai Stevenson of Illinois, who was nominated on the third ballot. Before the convention, Stevenson had resisted pleas from the retiring President Harry Truman and others to enter the race, and he was drafted by the convention as its nominee.[4]

The 1968 Democratic convention in Chicago is one of the most written about conventions of the past several decades. It is remembered more for what happened outside the convention hall than what happened in it. It took place in August, only a few months after the assassination in April of Dr. Martin Luther King, Jr. and the assassination in June of Senator Robert

Kennedy. Thousands of demonstrators opposed to the Vietnam War went to Chicago to protest against the war policies of President Lyndon Johnson (who had withdrawn in March from the nomination contest) and of his heir apparent and the frontrunner for the nomination, Vice President Hubert Humphrey. Chicago Mayor Richard Daley ordered that the protesters be kept away from the vicinity of the convention hall and, over five days, with a national television audience watching, Chicago police clashed with the protesters, sometimes brutally, resulting in more than six hundred arrests and numerous injuries. Inside the convention hall, Vice President Humphrey easily won the presidential nomination.[5]

Two of the closest nomination battles since the 1940s occurred at the 1976 Republican convention in Kansas City and the 1980 Democratic convention in New York. Both were analogous to the 1912 Republican convention, in which an unpopular incumbent president narrowly won his party's nomination over a charismatic and more popular challenger. In 1912, the protagonists were President William Howard Taft and former President Theodore Roosevelt. In 1976, President Gerald Ford was challenged by the popular former California Governor Ronald Reagan for the Republican nomination. Ford held a small lead in delegates going into the convention. The Reagan team introduced a resolution at the convention requiring a candidate to name his running mate in advance of voting for the presidential nomination, hoping that Ford's choice, if known, might displease some of his delegates and that they would switch to Reagan. The resolution was seen as a test vote of the strength of the two candidates. Ford's supporters were successful in narrowly defeating the resolution and he went on to win the nomination by a margin of just over one hundred votes, out of more than twenty-two hundred delegates. Four years later, the Democrats had a close race. President Jimmy Carter and his challenger, Senator Edward Kennedy, battled each other in the primaries and Carter entered the convention with about three hundred more delegates (out of thirty-three hundred total) than were needed to win the nomination. A proposal by the Kennedy forces to permit delegates to be released from support for their pledged candidate on the first ballot failed by about five hundred votes. Carter went on to win the nomination with a margin of more than nine hundred votes. All three of these conventions—the Republicans in 1912 and 1976, and the Democrats in 1980—also have something else in common. A divisive convention led to the loss of the nominees, all incumbent presidents (Taft, Ford, and Carter), in the general election.[6]

Franklin Roosevelt's innovation at the 1932 Democratic convention of appearing in person before the convention and delivering a formal acceptance speech started a new tradition. It was adopted by the 1944 Republican nominee, Thomas Dewey, and, since then, for both parties, the speech of the presidential nominee accepting the nomination has become the highlight of most conventions. Three of the more memorable acceptance speeches were given by John Kennedy, Ronald Reagan, and Barack Obama. At the 1960 Democratic convention in Los Angeles, Kennedy delivered his remarks outside, at a football stadium, as Roosevelt had done in Philadelphia in 1936. JFK proclaimed to a crowd of more than 100,000 at the Los Angeles Memorial Coliseum, "[W]e stand today on the edge of a New Frontier—the frontier of the 1960's—a frontier of unknown opportunities and perils—a frontier of unfulfilled hopes and threats." At the 1980 Republican convention in Detroit, Ronald Reagan asserted, "Tonight, let us dedicate ourselves to renewing the American Compact.... I ask you to trust that American spirit... the spirit that burned with zeal in the hearts of millions of immigrants from every corner of the Earth who came here in search of freedom.... The American spirit is still there, ready to blaze into life if you and I are willing to do what has to be done." In 2008, Barack Obama also delivered, as Roosevelt and Kennedy had done, his acceptance speech outside, at a football stadium. The then Illinois senator declared at Invesco Field in Denver: "[O]ne of the things that we have to change in our politics is the idea that people cannot disagree without challenging each other's character and patriotism. The times are too serious, the stakes are too high for this same partisan playbook. So let us agree that patriotism has no party. I love this country, and so do you.... The men and women who serve in our battlefields may be Democrats and Republicans and Independents, but they have fought together and bled together and some died together under the same proud flag. They have not served a Red America or a Blue America—they have served the United States of America."[7]

One significant change in conventions since the 1940s has been in the racial, gender, and religious diversity of their nominees. Before then, all major party nominees for president and vice president were white (other than Charles Curtis, Coolidge's vice president, who was part Native American and part white), were men, and (except for Al Smith) were Protestant. Since then (as of 2023), Barack Obama, whose father was Black and whose mother was white, was nominated by Democrats and elected president in 2008 and 2012. Kamala Harris, whose father is Black and whose mother was South Asian, was nominated by Democrats and elected vice president in 2020. Besides Harris, there have been two other female nominees for vice president, Democrat Geraldine Ferraro in 1984 and Republican Sarah Palin in 2008. Democrat Hillary Clinton in 2016 has been the only female nominee for president to date. With respect to religious diversity in nominees, since the 1940s, three Catholics, all Democrats, have been nominated for president—John Kennedy in 1960, John Kerry in 2004, and Joe Biden in 2020, with both Kennedy and Biden elected. There have been five Catholic nominees for vice president, Republican William Miller in 1964, and Democrats Edward Muskie in 1968, Sargent Shriver in 1972, Ferraro in 1984, and Biden in 2008 and 2012.[8]

Conventions no longer need to debate, as they did concerning the Roosevelts in 1912, 1940, and 1944, the appropriateness of a president running for a third or a fourth term. Franklin Roosevelt will remain the only president in American history to have accomplished that feat. In 1947, a Republican-led effort in Congress endorsed what would become the Twenty-Second Amendment to the Constitution, providing, "No person shall be elected to the office of President more than twice...." The amendment was ratified by the required number of states and became law in 1951.

In recent years, with the declining importance of conventions, there have been proposals to drastically modify, or to abolish, them. Conventions will, no doubt, evolve over time. The 2020 conventions, held during the COVID pandemic, without crowds of thousands packed into huge arenas, showed that these national political gatherings can adapt and adjust to circumstances.

Conventions will likely continue to exist, if for nothing else, the reasons that Senator Henry Clay of Kentucky identified in 1830, before the first one was ever held. Conventions, Clay wrote, would be places where party leaders and rank-and-file members would meet and "form acquaintances, exchange opinions and sentiments, catch and infuse animation and enthusiasm, and return with a spirit of union and concert."[9]

Beyond the reasons cited by Clay, as professor and political scientist Gerald Pomper has argued, modern conventions are, in spite of their diminished status, still important as national political rituals. "Much of the convention's events exemplify ritual," writes Pomper, "They are laden with symbols, such as the flag. They recall the history of the group, as in the invocation of past leaders and triumphs . . . . They are staged events, using multimedia techniques to develop desired emotional responses, building to the dramatic climaxes of the presidential candidate's nomination and acceptance speech . . . . The convention itself is a ritualized form of representative democracy."[10] Rituals can be unifying events for a nation. Political junkies (like this author) will continue to get chills as convention clerks shout out "Alabama" to begin a roll call of the states to select a nominee who may well become the next president of the United States.

Selected Bibliography

Books

Anderson, Judith. *William Howard Taft: An Intimate History*. New York: W. W. Norton Company, 1981.

Bain, Richard and Parris, Judith. *Convention Decisions and Voting Records, Second Edition*. Washington, D.C.: Brookings Institution, 1960.

Baughman, James. *Henry R. Luce and the Rise of the American News Media*. Baltimore: The Johns Hopkins University Press, 2001.

Berg, A. Scott. *Wilson*. New York: G. P. Putnam Sons, 2013.

Brands, H. W. *T.R. The Last Romantic*. New York, Basic Books, 1997.

Brinkley, David. *Washington Goes to War*. New York: Alfred A. Knopf, 1988.

Burns, James MacGregor. *The Definitive FDR: The Lion and the Fox*. New York: Open Road Media, 1912.

Carlson, Oliver and Bates, Ernest. *Hearst: Lord of San Simeon*. New York: The Viking Press, 1936.

Chace, James. *1912: Wilson, Roosevelt, Taft & Debs—The Election That Changed the Country*. New York: Simon & Schuster, 2004.

Cherny, Robert. *A Righteous Cause: The Life of William Jennings Bryan*. Norman: University of Oklahoma Press, 1994.

Clark, Champ. *My Quarter Century in American Politics, Volume 2*. New York: Harper and Brothers Publishers, 1920.

Clements, Kendrick. *The Life of Herbert Hoover: Imperfect Visionary, 1918-1928*. New York: Palgrave McMillan, 2010.

Coletta, Paolo. *The Presidency of William Howard Taft*. Lawrence: The University Press of Kansas, 1973.

Congressional Quarterly, Inc. *National Party Conventions: 1831-1996*. Washington, D. C.: Congressional Quarterly, Inc. 1997.

Cowan, Geoffrey. *Let the People Rule: Theodore Roosevelt and the Birth of the Presidential Primary*. New York: W. W. Norton & Company, 2016.

Cramer, C. H. *Newton D. Baker: A Biography*. Cleveland: The World Publishing Company, 1961.

Critchlow, Donald. *When Hollywood Was Right: How Movie Stars, Hollywood Moguls, and Big Business Remade American Politics*. New York: Cambridge University Press, 2013.

Culver, John and Hyde, John. *American Dreamer: The Life and Times of Henry A. Wallace.* New York: W. W. Norton & Company, 2000.

Davis, Michael. *Politics as Usual: Thomas Dewey, Franklin Roosevelt, and the Wartime Presidential Campaign of 1944.* DeKalb, IL: Northern Illinois University Press, 2014.

Day, Frank and Knappen, Theodore. *Life of John Albert Johnson.* Chicago: Forbes & Company, 1910.

Dunn, Susan. *1940: FDR, Willkie, Lindbergh, Hitler—the Election Amid the Storm.* New Haven: Yale University Press, 2013.

Eaton, Herbert. *Presidential Timber: A History of Nominating Conventions, 1868-1960.* London: The Free Press of Glencoe, 1964.

Farley, James. *Jim Farley's Story: The Roosevelt Years.* New York: Whittlesey House, 1948.

Ferrell, Robert. *Choosing Truman: The Democratic Convention of 1944.* Columbia, MO: University of Missouri Press, 1994.

Ferrell, Robert. *The Presidency of Calvin Coolidge.* Lawrence: University Press of Kansas, 1998.

Freidel, Frank. *Franklin D. Roosevelt: A Rendezvous with Destiny.* Boston: Little, Brown and Company, 1990.

Gale, Albert and Kline, George. *Bryan the Man: The Great Commoner at Close Range.* St. Louis: Thompson Publishing Company, 1908.

Goodwin, Doris Kearns. *The Bully Pulpit: Theodore Roosevelt, William Howard Taft, and the Golden Age of Journalism.* New York: Simon & Schuster Paperbacks, 2013.

Gould, Louis. *Four Hats in the Ring: The 1912 Election and the Birth of Modern American Politics.* Lawrence: University Press of Kansas, 2008.

Harbaugh, William. *Lawyer's Lawyer: The Life of John W. Davis.* New York: Oxford University Press, 1973.

Haynes, Stan. *President-Making in the Gilded Age: The Nominating Conventions of 1876-1900.* Jefferson, NC: McFarland & Company, Inc., 2016.

Haynes, Stan. *The First American Political Conventions: Transforming Presidential Nominations, 1832-1872.* Jefferson, NC: McFarland & Company, Inc., 2012.

Janeway, Michael. *The Fall of the House of Roosevelt: Brokers of Ideas and Power from FDR to LBJ.* New York: Columbia University Press, 2004.

Jeansonne, Glen. *Herbert Hoover: A Life.* New York: New American Library, 2016.

Jordan, David. *FDR, Dewey, and the Election of 1944.* Bloomington, IN: Indiana University Press, 2011.

Joshi, S. T., Editor. *From Baltimore to Bohemia: The Letters of H. L. Mencken and George Sterling.* Cranbury, NJ: Associated University Presses, 2001.

Jeffries, John. *A Third Term for FDR: The Election of 1940.* Lawrence: University of Kansas Press, 2017.

Kelter, Bill. *Veeps.* Atlanta: Top Shelf Productions, 2008.

King, David. *Herbert Hoover.* Tarrytown, NY: Marshall Cavendish Corp., 2010.

Link, Arthur. *Wilson: Campaigns for Progressivism and Peace, 1916-17, Volume 5.* Princeton: Princeton University Press, 1965.

Lisio, Donald. *Hoover, Blacks, and Lily-Whites: A Study of Southern Strategies.* Chapel Hill, NC: University of North Carolina Press, 1985.

Lorant, Stefan. *The Glorious Burden.* Lenox, MA: Authors Edition, Inc., 1976.

McCartney, Laton. *The Teapot Dome Scandal.* New York: Random House, 2008.

McCombs, William. *Making Woodrow Wilson President.* New York: Fairview Publishing Co., 1921.

McCullough, David, *Truman.* New York: Touchstone, 1992.

McMillen, Margot. *The Golden Lane: How Missouri Women Gained the Vote and Changed History*. Charleston, SC: The History Press, 2011.

Mencken, H. L. *On Politics: A Carnival of Buncombe*. New York: Vintage Books, 1960.

Merrill, Horace and Marion. *The Republican Command 1897-1913*. Lexington: The University Press of Kentucky, 1971.

Milkis, Sidney. *Theodore Roosevelt, the Progressive Party, and the Transformation of American Democracy*. Lawrence: The University Press of Kansas, 2009.

Moe, Richard. *Roosevelt's Second Act: The Election of 1940 and the Politics of War*. Oxford: Oxford University Press, 2013.

Morris, Charles and Ellis, Edward. *Men and Issues of 1904*. Philadelphia: J. C. Winston Co., 1904.

Morris, Edmund. *Colonel Roosevelt*. New York: Random House, 2010.

Morton, Richard. *Roger C. Sullivan and the Making of the Chicago Democratic Machine, 1881-1908*. Jefferson, NC: McFarland & Company, Inc., 2019.

Murphy, M. C. *Calvin Coolidge: The Presidency and Philosophy of a Progressive Conservative*. Jefferson, NC: McFarland & Company, Inc., 2023.

Murray, Robert. *The 103rd Ballot: Democrats and the Disaster in Madison Square Garden*. New York: Harper Collins, 1976.

Nasaw, David. *The Chief: The Life of William Randolph Hearst*. Boston, Houghton Mifflin Company, 2000.

Neal, Steve. *Dark Horse: A Biography of Wendell Willkie*. Lawrence: University of Kansas Press, 1989.

Neal, Steve. *Happy Days Are Here Again: The 1932 Democratic Convention, The Emergence of FDR—and How America was Changed Forever*. New York: William Morrow, 2004.

O'Sullivan, Christopher. *Harry Hopkins: FDR's Envoy to Churchill and Stalin*. Lanham, MD: Rowman & Littlefield, 2015.

Peters, Charles. *Five Days in Philadelphia*. New York: PublicAffairs, 2005.

Pietrusza, David. *1920: The Year of Six Presidents*. New York: Basic Books, 2007.

Pietrusza, David. *Roosevelt Sweeps Nation: FDR's 1936 Landslide & the Triumph of the Liberal Ideal*. New York: Diversion Books, 2022.

Procter, Ben. *William Randolph Hearst: The Early Years, 1863-1910*. New York: Oxford University Press, 1998.

Remey, Oliver, Cochems, Henry, and Bloodgood, Wheeler. *The Attempted Assassination of Ex-President Theodore Roosevelt*. Milwaukee: The Progressive Publishing Company, 1912.

Ritchie, Donald. *Electing FDR: The New Deal Campaign of 1932*. Lawrence: University Press of Kansas, 2007.

Rodgers, Marion. *Mencken: The American Iconoclast*. Oxford: Oxford University Press, 2005.

Russell, Francis. *The Shadow of Blooming Grove: Warren G. Harding in His Times*. New York: McGraw-Hill Book Company, 1968.

Sautter, R. Craig and Burke, Edward. *Inside the Wigwam: Chicago Presidential Conventions, 1860-1996*. Chicago: Wild Onion Books, 1996.

Sheppard, Si. *The Buying of the Presidency? Franklin D. Roosevelt, The New Deal, and The Election of 1936*. Santa Barbara, CA: Praeger, 2014.

Simon, James. *FDR and Chief Justice Hughes*. New York: Simon & Schuster, 2012.

Slayton, Robert. *Empire Statesman: The Rise and Redemption of Al Smith*. New York: The Free Press, 2001.

Smith, Jean Edward. *FDR*. New York: Random House, 2007.

Smith, Richard Norton. *An Uncommon Man: The Triumph of Herbert Hoover*. New York: Simon and Schuster, 1984.

Smith, Richard Norton. *Thomas E. Dewey and His Times*. New York: Simon and Schuster, 1982.

Sobel, Robert. *Coolidge: An American Enigma*. Washington, D. C.: Regnery Publishing, Inc., 1998.

Stone, Irving. *They Also Ran: The Story of the Men Who Were Defeated for the Presidency*. New York: Signet, 1968.

Thorburn, Wayne. *The Republican Party of Texas: A Political History*. Austin: University of Texas Press, 2021.

Tobin, James. *The Man He Became: How FDR Defied Polio to Win the Presidency*. New York: Simon & Schuster Paperbacks, 2013.

Tucker, III, Garland. *The High Tide of American Conservatism: Davis, Coolidge, and the 1924 Election*. Austin: Emerald Book Company, 2010.

Waldman, Michael. *My Fellow Americans*. Naperville, IL: Sourcebooks, 2010.

Wesser, Robert. *Charles Evans Hughes: Politics and Reform in New York 1905-1910*. Ithaca, NY: Cornell University Press, 1967.

White, William Allen. *A Puritan in Babylon: The Story of Calvin Coolidge*. London: Papamoa Press, 2018.

Wolraich, Michael. *Unreasonable Men: Theodore Roosevelt and the Republican Rebels Who Created Progressive Politics*. New York: St. Martin's Press LLC, 2014.

Newspapers and Periodicals

Baltimore Evening Sun, Baltimore Sun, Chicago Daily Tribune, Chicago Tribune, Herald Democrat, Houston History Magazine, LIFE, Literary Digest, Long Beach Post, Nebraska History, New York Times, Philadelphia Inquirer, Phylon, Presidential Studies Quarterly, Reedy's Mirror, Rocky Mountain News, Saturday Evening Post, The Annals of Iowa, The Atlantic, The Chronicles of Oklahoma, The Forum, The Journal of Southern History, The Pacific Northwest Quarterly, TIME, Topeka Daily Capital, Wall Street Journal, Washington Post

Convention Proceedings

Blumenberg, Milton. *Official Proceedings of the Thirteenth Republican National Convention, Held in the City of Chicago, June 21, 22, 23, 1904*. Minneapolis: Harrison & Smith Co., 1904.

Blumenberg, Milton. *Official Report of the Proceedings of the Democratic National Convention Held in St. Louis, Mo., July 6, 7, 8, and 9, 1904*. New York: The Publishers' Printing Company, 1904.

Blumenberg, Milton. *Official Report of the Proceedings of the Fourteenth Republican National Convention Held in Chicago, Illinois June 16, 17, 18 and 19, 1908*. Columbus, OH: Press of F. J. Heer, 1908.

Blumenberg, Milton. *Official Report of the Proceedings of the Democratic National Convention Held in Denver, Colorado, July 7, 8, 9 and 10, 1908*. Chicago: Press of Western Newspaper Union, 1908.

Blumenberg, Milton. *Official Report of the Proceedings of the Fifteenth Republican National Convention Held in Chicago, Illinois, June 18, 19, 20, 21 and 22, 1912*. New York: The Tenny Press, 1912.

Blumenberg, Milton. *Official Report of the Proceedings of the Democratic National Convention Held in Baltimore, Maryland, July 25, 26, 27, 28, 29 and July 1 and 2, 1912*. Chicago: The Linotyping Co., 1912.

Couch, Harry. *Official Report of the Proceedings of the Democratic National Convention Held in San Francisco, California June 28, 29, 30, July 1, 2, 3, 5, and 6, 1920*. Indianapolis: Bookwalter-Ball Printing Co., 1920.

Granat, Louis. *Official Report of the Proceedings of the Democratic National Convention Held in Saint Louis, Missouri June 14, 15 and 16th, 1916*.

Granat, Louis. *Official Report of the Proceedings of the Democratic National Convention held in Madison Square Garden New York City June 24, 25, 26, 27, 28, 30, July 1, 2, 3, 4, 5, 7, 8 and 9, 1924*. Indianapolis: Bookwalter-Ball-Greathouse Printing Co., 1924.

Hart, George. *Official Report of the Proceedings of the Sixteenth Republican National Convention Held in Chicago, Illinois June 7, 8, 9 and 10, 1916*. New York: The Tenny Press, 1916.

Hart, George. *Official Report of the Proceedings of the Seventeenth Republican National Convention Held in Chicago, Illinois June 8, 9, 10, 11 and 12, 1920*. New York: The Tenny Press, 1920.

Hart, George. *Official Report of the Proceedings of the Eighteenth Republican National Convention Held in Cleveland, Ohio June 10, 11 and 12, 1924*. New York: The Tenny Press, 1924

Index

Baker, Newton, 167, 191, 208-10, 220-223
Baltimore, 1912 Democratic convention 76-89
Bankhead, William, 81, 86-87, 270, 275-76
Barkley, Alben, 213, 243, 244-45, 271, 293-95, 298-300
Barton, Bruce, 233-34
Baruch, Bernard, 292
Bell, Theodore, 47, 49
Biden, Joe, 309
Bimberg, Myer, 17
Bingham, Hiram, 201-02
Black, Frank, 13-15
Blaney, Mrs. Charles, 64
Borah, William, 65, 114, 116, 127, 155-56, 181-84, 230, 232, 236, 239
Bowers, Claude, 188-89
Bradford, Mary, 49
Bricker, John, 281-85, 289-90
Bryan, Charles, 80, 160, 170
Bryan, William Jennings, 18-29, 32-34, 46-55, 71-81, 85-90, 103-04, 134, 140, 151, 157, 160, 166, 168, 170-71, 177, 185, 255
Burrows, Julius, 41
Burton, Marion, 154
Burton, Theodore, 43, 94, 151-52, 155-56
Butler, Nicholas Murray, 74, 90, 116, 124, 201
Byrd, Harry, 209, 215, 219, 299-300

Byrnes, James, 269, 275-76, 293-87
campaigns and elections, of 1904 34; of 1908 54-56; of 1912 89-91; of 1916 110; of 1920 145-46; of 1924 172-73; of 1928 192-94; of 1932 227; of 1936 250-51; of 1940 278-79; of 1944 304-05
Cannon, Joseph, 11-16, 38, 40-45
Carter, Jimmy, 308
Cermak, Anton, 210, 213, 216, 219-226
Chancellor, William Estabrook, 120, 146
Chicago, 1932 Democratic convention 205-27; 1940 Democratic convention 267-78; 1944 Democratic convention 292-304; 1904 Republican convention 6-17; 1908 Republican convention 36-46; 1912 Republican convention 57-76; 1916 Republican convention 95-102; 1920 Republican convention 113-30; 1932 Republican convention 196-205; 1944 Republican convention 281-92
Clark, Bennett, 245, 303
Clark, Champ, 25, 30-31, 76-91, 194, 245
Cleveland, 1924 Republican convention 146-56; 1936

Republican convention 229-40
Cleveland, Grover, 1, 8, 17-24, 48-54, 138, 145
Clinton, Hillary, 309
Cochran, Bourke, 138, 140
Collins, Mrs. Francis, 64
Coolidge, Calvin, 115-117, 124-30, 147-56, 172-85, 196, 198, 204, 206, 230
Coolidge, Grace, 130
Cox, James, 132-38, 140-46, 157-61, 168, 185, 212
Cummings, Harry, 15
Cummings, Homer, 136-37, 142
Cummins, Albert, 61, 73-75, 94, 100-01
Curley, James Michael, 214
Curtis, Charles, 155, 176, 184-85, 198, 205
Daley, Richard, 308
Daugherty, Harry, 117, 119, 124-26, 128, 148
Davenport, Russell, 256
Davis, John W., 133, 139-42, 160-73, 185, 212
Dawes, Charles, 155-56, 184, 198, 205
Debs, Eugene, 34, 55, 90, 146, 172
Democratic Party, 1904 convention 17-34; 1908 convention 46-54; 1912 convention 76-89; 1916 convention 103-09; 1920 convention 130-45; 1924

convention 157-72; 1928
convention 185-92; 1932
convention 205-27; 1936
convention 240-250; 1940
convention 267-78; 1944
convention 292-304
Denver, 1908 Democratic convention 46-54
Depew, Chauncey, 17, 63, 99, 120-21, 129
Dewey, Thomas, 254-66, 281-91, 295, 298, 304-05, 308
Dolliver, Jonathan, 16, 45
Douglas, William, 294-96, 302
Dunn, Ignatius, 50-53
Erwin, Andrew, 165-66
Fairbanks, Charles, 16-17, 38, 43-44, 71-72, 87, 94, 100-02
Fall, Albert, 158
Farley, James, 207, 211, 215-16, 219-24, 240-43, 247-48, 268-75, 300.
Ferraro, Geraldine, 309
Fess, Simeon, 179-80, 199
Fish, Hamilton, 261
Flynn, Ed, 295, 297
Foraker, Joseph, 37, 40, 43-44
Ford, Gerald, 258, 308
France, Joseph, 196-87, 204
Gallup Polls, 228, 231, 254, 257, 275, 305
Garfield, James R., 200-02
Garner, John Nance, 208-24, 240-41, 247, 249, 269, 274
Garry, Thomas, 272
Glass, Carter, 88, 132, 139-40, 160, 273
Glynn, Martin, 105-06
Gore, Thomas, 51
Gray, George, 20-21, 28, 30, 48, 53-54
Griswold, Dwight, 289
Hadley, Herbert, 65, 67, 68
Halleck, Charles, 262-63
Hamon, Jake, 128
Hamilton, John, 232, 238-39, 259, 283
Hannegan, Robert, 295-98, 301-02
Harding, Florence, 115, 125-26

Harding, Warren, 72-73, 96-102, 115-29, 137, 145-158, 174-75
Harmon, Judson, 77-78, 80, 82-83
Harris, Kamala, 309
Harrison, Pat, 160, 162, 191-92, 216, 220-21
Harvey, George, 126-27
Hayward, Elizabeth, 49
Hearst, William Randolph, 18-31, 37, 55, 94, 208-09, 220, 222, 229, 231
Hill, Lister, 273
Hillman, Sidney, 297, 304
Hitler, Adolph, 254, 257, 260-61, 267
Hoover, Herbert, 115-16, 124, 127, 148, 155-56, 175-85, 192-205, 207, 215, 227-38, 243, 257-60, 264, 287-88, 292, 298
Hopkins, Harry, 265, 279
Houston, 1928 Democratic convention 185-92
Howe, Louis, 163, 207, 210, 215, 218, 224, 226, 240
Hughes, Charles Evans, 37, 43-45, 94-103, 110, 114, 117-18, 178, 281-82
Hull, Cordell, 162, 185, 218, 270, 274
Humphrey, Hubert, 307-08
Hutson, Charles, 203
Hutton, Mary Arkwright, 76
Ickes, Harold, 254, 271, 297
Jackson, Samuel, 299-302
James, Ollie, 80-81, 107
Johnson, Hiram, 67,75, 110, 114, 117-18, 123, 130, 148, 155
Johnson, John, 48, 53-54
Johnson, Lyndon, 308
Jones, Jesse, 186, 188-90
Kansas City, 1928 Republican convention 175-85
Kefauver, Estes, 307
Kelly, Ed, 267, 269-73, 295-96, 301-02
Kennedy, Edward, 308
Kennedy, John, 308-09
Kennedy, Joseph, 220-23
Kennedy, Robert, 307-08

Kent, Frank, 187, 191
Kerr, Robert, 298
King, Jr., Martin Luther, 307
Knox, Frank, 230-33, 239, 299
La Follette, Robert, 10, 38-39, 43-45, 57-61, 65-66, 73-78, 100-01, 128, 148, 153-55, 172-73
Landon, Alf, 229-33, 235-40, 250-51, 255, 259, 263-65
Lawrence, David, 302
Lemke, William, 251
Lenroot, Irvine, 128-30
Lippman, Walter, 114, 199, 206, 220, 234, 245, 257
Lodge, Henry Cabot, 8, 11, 41, 41-44, 99-102, 114, 119-29, 149, 152
Long, Huey, 213-14, 226-27, 251
Longworth, Alice Roosevelt, 40, 48, 98, 151, 230, 232-33, 246, 254, 258
Lowden, Frank, 114-19, 123-27, 148, 155-56, 176-84
Luce, Clare Boothe, 288-89
Luce, Henry, 256, 288
MacArthur, Douglas, 283-85, 290, 296, 298
Mack, John, 218, 246-47
Markham, Edwin, 248-49
Marshall, George, 298, 304
Marshall, Thomas, 84-88, 108
Martin, Joseph, 257, 260, 263-64, 287, 289
Mayer, Louis B., 203
McAdoo, William, 79, 84, 131-43, 157-71, 185, 209-10, 221-22
McCamant, Wallace, 129-30
McCombs, William, 79. 84, 103, 105
McKinley, William, 1, 5, 6-10, 16, 18, 34-39, 43, 48, 90, 113-14
McNab, John, 182-83
McNary, Charles, 257, 263, 265
Mellon, Andrew, 176-79
Mencken, H. L., 113, 115, 132, 135, 138-39, 150, 206-07, 223, 243-44, 247, 262, 266, 269, 273, 277

Mercer, Lucy, 206
Mitchell, Arthur, 243
Mondell, Frank, 152, 156
Moses, George, 181-82
Murphy, Charles, 22, 77-80, 83, 86, 108, 133, 144, 159
New York, 1924 Democratic convention 157-72
Nooney, Ruth, 299
O'Brian, John, 262
Obama, Barack, 309-09
Palin, Sarah, 309
Palmer, A. Mitchell, 132-43
Parker, Alton, 18-35, 46, 49-50, 55, 78-81, 105, 172, 192, 282
Patterson, Grove, 262
Pauley, Edwin, 295, 303
Pendergast, Thomas, 294
Pepper, Claude, 301-03
Perdicaris, Ion, 12-13
Perkins, Frances, 271
Philadelphia, 1936 Democratic convention 240-50; 1940 Republican convention 253-66
Pittman, Key, 190, 215
Pitzer, Anna Hamilton, 76
Progressive Party, 1912 convention 75, 1916 convention 95-102
Pryor, Samuel, 261, 263
Raisuni, Mulai Ahmed er ("Raisuli"), 12-13
Raskob, John, 210-13
Rayburn, Sam, 216, 221-22, 293, 295
Reagan, Ronald, 308-09
Reasoner, Harry, 286
Reed, James, 81-82, 161, 186, 209, 219
Republican Party, 1904 convention 6-17; 1908 convention 36-46; 1912 convention 57-76; 1916 convention 95-102; 1920 convention 113-20; 1924 convention 145-56; 1928 convention 175-85; 1932 convention 196-205; 1936 convention 229-40; 1940 convention 253-66; 1944 convention 281-92

Ritchie, Albert, 208-10, 215, 219, 223, 227
Robinson, Joseph, 136, 142, 189, 191-92, 244-45
Roerich, Nicholas, 274, 78
Rogers, Will, 149-51, 178-79, 186-89, 202, 204, 213, 215, 225-26
Roosevelt, Edith, 70, 89
Roosevelt, Eleanor, 206, 223, 246, 271, 275, 306
Roosevelt, Franklin, 2, 77, 139, 144-46, 163-64, 189-90, 203-28, 240-53, 267-81, 292-307
Roosevelt, Theodore, 1-2, 5-17, 34-45, 54-76, 89-102, 110-14, 124, 281, 307
Roosevelt, Theodore, Jr., 151, 258
Root, Elihu, 9-10, 65-74, 94, 100-01, 122
Rosewater, Victor, 60, 64-67
Rutherford, Lucy Mercer, 306
San Francisco, 1920 Democratic convention 130-45
Scott, Joseph, 202-03
Sherman, James, 45, 74, 90, 205
Shoumatoff, Elizabeth, 306-07
Shouse, Jouett, 210-11, 215
Smith, Alfred ("Al"), 133-44, 158-72, 185-93, 207-13, 243, 246, 281
Snell, Bertrand, 200-05, 235
Spangler, Harrison, 286
Springs, Lena, 170
St. Louis, 1904 Democratic convention 17-34; 1916 Democratic convention 103-09
Stassen, Harold, 259-60, 264, 283-84, 290
Steiwer, Frederick, 234-35
Stevenson, Adlai, 307
Stimson, Henry, 259
Sullivan, Mark, 274
Sullivan, Roger, 23-24, 86-87, 108
Taft, Nellie, 36, 38, 42, 44, 57, 96

Taft, Robert, 232, 255-66, 281-83, 287
Taft, William Howard, 133-44, 158-72, 185-93, 207-23, 243, 246, 281
Thomas, Norman, 227, 251, 279
Thomsen, Hans, 261
Truman, Harry, 294-305
Trump, Donald, 19
Tully, Grace, 296
Tydings, Millard, 269, 274
Underwood, Oscar, 77-88, 159-61, 165, 168, 170
Van Doren, Irita, 256, 279
Vandenberg, Arthur, 230, 232-33, 239, 254-58, 263-64, 281, 283
Vare, William, 101, 178-79
Wagner, Robert, 245, 272
Wallace, Henry, 274-79, 292-303, 305
Walsh, Thomas, 136, 157, 162-63, 166, 170, 185, 211, 214-15, 222, 225-26
Warren, Charles, 152-53
Warren, Earl, 231, 283, 286-90
Watson, James, 65-73, 121, 176, 183-84, 258-59, 265
Wescott, John, 82-83, 107
West, Mrs. J. B., 8
Wheeler, Burton, 172-269
White, William Allen, 166
Willebrandt, Mabel Walker, 179-81
Willkie, Wendell, 255-66, 278-79, 281-90, 304
Wilson, Edith, 112, 130, 186
Wilson, Woodrow, 77-90, 92-94, 103-46, 157-67, 175, 206-09
Wood, Leonard, 113-18, 123-28

Acknowledgments

I would like to thank the readers of my two previous books about 19th century presidential nominating conventions, who encouraged me to continue the series of books into the first half of the 20th century. My eternal gratitude goes out to my wife, Beth, who in addition to being my life partner and provider of moral support during the years that I have spent delving into American politics of the past, is also my much-appreciated editor and proofreader. One day, maybe, I will learn for myself about misplaced modifiers, subjunctive and conjunctive tenses, and other grammatical rules that I either never understood, or have forgotten. I would like to thank Dee Marley at White Rabbit Arts for the cover design of this book. Finally, for the campaign songs at the beginning of each chapter, I would like to acknowledge and thank Oscar Brand, *Presidential Campaign Songs: 1789-1996* (Washington: Smithsonian Folkways Recordings, 1999) and Orion Brey at www.youtube.com@presidentialcampaignmusic1018.

About the Author

Stan Haynes, an attorney and author, spent his legal career with a Baltimore law firm. A graduate of the College of William and Mary and of the University of Virginia School of Law, he has had a lifelong interest in American political history, particularly concerning the presidency. In addition to *Roosevelt to Roosevelt*, he is the author two other books on the history of presidential nominating conventions, *The First American Political Conventions* and *President-Making in the Gilded Age*. He has also written two historical fiction books set in the years before the Civil War, *And Tyler No More* and *And Union No More*. He resides in Maryland. Visit his website at *www.stanhaynes.com*.

Chapter Notes

Introduction

1. The Wilcox home has been a National Historic Site since 1966 and is open to the public; H. W. Brands, *T.R. The Last Romantic* (New York, Basic Books, 1997), pp. 411-16; Website of the Theodore Roosevelt Inaugural National Historic Site, *www.trsite.org,* viewed October 28, 2017.

2. Hanes Walton, Jr. and C. Vernon Gray, "Black Politics at the National Republican and Democratic Conventions, 1868-1972," *Phylon*, Vol. 36, No. 3 (3rd Quarter, 1975), pp. 269-70.

Chapter 1

1. Brands, pp. 450-62, 479-88, 490-92; *Baltimore Sun*, June 19, 1904.

2. *New York Times*, June 19, 1904.

3. *Baltimore Sun*, June 21, 1904; *New York Times*, June 21, 1904.

4. Boris Heersink and Jeffery Jenkins, *Black-and-Tans vs. Lily-Whites: Race and Republican Party Organization in the South after Reconstruction, 1868-1952,* presented at 2015 Annual Meeting of the Midwest Political Science Association.

5. *New York Times*, June 20, 1904.

6. *Baltimore Sun*, June 21 and 22, 1904; *New York Times*, June 21, 1904.

7. Brands, p. 503.

8. Horace Merrill and Marion Merrill, *The Republican Command 1897-1913* (Lexington: The University Press of Kentucky, 1971) p. 164, *Baltimore Sun*, June 22, 1904.

9. *New York Times*, June 20, 1904; *Baltimore Sun*, June 18, 19 and 22, 1904.

10. *Baltimore Sun*, June 22, 1904; *New York Times*, June 23, 1904.

11. Milton Blumenberg, *Official Proceedings of the Thirteenth Republican National Convention, Held in the City of Chicago, June 21, 22, 23, 1904*, (Minneapolis: Harrison & Smith Co., 1904), pp. 75-83 [hereafter, *Republican Proceedings of 1904*]; *New York Times*, June 23, 1904.

12. *Republican Proceedings of 1904*, pp. 110-20.

13. *Republican Proceedings of 1904*, pp. 120-32; *New York Times*, June 22, 1904; Michael Wolraich, *Unreasonable Men: Theodore Roosevelt and the Republican Rebels Who Created Progressive Politics* (New York: St. Martin's Press LLC, 2014), p. 8.

14. Stan Haynes, *President-Making in the Gilded Age*, (Jefferson, NC: McFarland & Company, Inc., 2016), pp. 91-93, 118.

15. *Republican Proceedings of 1904*, pp. 132-37.

16. U. S. Const. amend. XIV, section 2; *Republican Proceedings of 1904*, p. 135.

17. *Baltimore Sun*, June 25, 1904.

18. *Republican Proceedings of 1904*, pp. 132-37; *New York Times*, June 22 and 23, 1904.

19. *New York Times*, June 23, 1904.

20. Barbara Tuchman, "Perdicaris Alive or Raisuli Dead," *American Heritage*, Vol. 10, No. 5, (August, 1959), *see generally*.

21. *New York Times*, June 23, 1904.

22. John Milius (Director). (1975). *The Wind and the Lion*. MGM.

23. Tuchman, *see generally*.

24. *New York Times*, June 24, 1904.

25. *Republican Proceedings of 1904*, pp. 143-45.

26. *Republican Proceedings of 1904*, pp. 146-47.

27. *Republican Proceedings of 1904*, pp. 148-64; *Baltimore Sun*, June 24, 1904; *New York Times*, June 24, 1904.

28. *Republican Proceedings of 1904*, pp. 164-65.

29. *Baltimore Sun*, June 24, 1904.

30. Brands, pp. 504-05; *Baltimore Sun*, June 18, 21, and 24, 1904; *New York Times*, June 20, 21, and 23, 1904.

31. Haynes, *President-Making in the Gilded Age*, pp. 244, 256-57.

32. *Republican Proceedings of 1904*, pp. 165-80.

33. Haynes, *President-Making in the Gilded Age*, p. 257.

34. Wolraich, p. 10.

35. Haynes, *President-Making in the Gilded Age*, pp. 214-15; *New York Times*, June 19, 1904.

36. *Republican Proceedings of 1904*, p. 168.

37. Haynes, *President-Making in the Gilded Age*, pp. 221-32; 274.

38. Herbert Eaton, *Presidential Timber: A History of Nominating Conventions, 1868-1960* (London: The Free Press of Glencoe, 1964), p. 192.

39. Steve Neal, *Happy Days Are Here Again: The 1932 Democratic Convention, The Emergence of FDR—and How America was Changed Forever* (New York: William Morrow, 2004), p. 55.

40. David Nasaw, *The Chief: The Life of William Randolph Hearst* (Boston, Houghton Mifflin Company, 2000), pp. 145-85; Ben Procter, *William Randolph Hearst: The Early Years, 1863-1910*, (New York: Oxford University Press, 1998), pp. 179-83; *Public Opinion*, Vol. 36, March 10, 1904; Eaton, pp. 192-93.

41. Eaton, pp. 193-94.

42. Procter, pp. 186, p. 191.

43. Henry Phillips, "The Epic Food of the 1904 World's Fair, July 3, 2015, *www.gearpatrol.com*, viewed on August 27, 2023.

44. *Chicago Daily Tribune*, July 5 and 6, 1904.

45. *Baltimore Sun*, July 1 and 2, 1904.

46. *Chicago Daily Tribune*, July 4, 1904; *Baltimore Sun*, July 4 and 6, 1904.

47. *Baltimore Sun*, July 1, 1904; *Chicago Daily Tribune*, July 5, 1904; *New York Times*, July 4, 1904.

48. Oliver Carlson and Ernest Bates, *Hearst: Lord of San Simeon* (New York; The Viking Press, 1936), pp. 143-44.

49. *Baltimore Sun*, July 4, 1904.

50. Milton Blumenberg, *Official Report of the Proceedings of the Democratic National Convention Held in St. Louis, Mo., July 6, 7, 8, and 9, 1904*, (New York: The Publishers' Printing Company, 1904) [hereafter "*Democratic Proceedings of 1904*"], pp. 1-39, 40-46; Charles Morris and Edward S. Ellis, *Men and Issues of 1904* (Philadelphia: J. C. Winston Co. 1904), pp. 125-26; *Baltimore Sun*, July 7 and 8, 1904.

51. Richard Morton, *Roger C. Sullivan and the Making of the Chicago Democratic Machine, 1881-1908*. (Jefferson, NC: McFarland & Company, Inc., 2019), pp. 133-41.

52. *Baltimore Sun*, July 8, 1904; Morris and Ellis, pp. 129-30.

53. *Chicago Daily Tribune*, July 8, 1904.

54. *Democratic Proceedings of 1904*, pp. 103-08.

55. *Democratic Proceedings of 1904*, pp. 90-122; Eaton, p. 196; Richard Bain and Judith Parris, *Convention Decisions and Voting Records, Second Edition* (Washington, D.C.: Brookings Institution, 1960); *Chicago Daily Tribune*, July 8, 1904.

56. *Democratic Proceedings of 1904*, pp. 123-37; *Chicago Daily Tribune*, July 8, 1904.

57. *Democratic Proceedings of 1904*, pp. 138-44; *Baltimore Sun*, July 9, 1904.

58. Eaton pp. 196-97.

59. *Baltimore Sun*, July 9, 1904.

60. *Chicago Daily Tribune*, July 8, 1904; *Baltimore Sun*, July 9, 1904.

61. *Democratic Proceedings of 1904*, pp. 145-56; *Baltimore Sun*, July 9, 1904; Robert W. Cherny, *A Righteous Cause: The Life of William Jennings Bryan*, (Norman: University of Oklahoma Press, 1994), p. 100.

62. *Democratic Proceedings of 1904*, pp. 160-65.

63. Charles Erskine Scott Wood, "The Democratic Convention," *The Pacific Monthly*, Vol. 12, 1904, pp. 169-78; *Baltimore Sun*, July 9, 1904.

64. *Democratic Proceedings of 1904*, pp. 173-91; *Baltimore Sun*, July 9, 1904.

65. *Democratic Proceedings of 1904*, pp. 191-234; *Baltimore Sun*, July 9, 1904.

66. *Democratic Proceedings of 1904*, pp. 234-45.

67. *Democratic Proceedings of 1904*, pp. 246-51; Eaton, p. 198; Bain and Harris, p. 169.

68. *Baltimore Sun*, July 4 and 10, 1904; *New York Times*, July 12, 1904.

69. *Democratic Proceedings of 1904*, pp. 252-55.

70. Eaton, pp. 199-200.

71. *Democratic Proceedings of 1904*, p. 273; Carlson and Bates, p. 144.

72. Eaton, p. 199; *Democratic Proceedings of 1904*, pp. 273-77.

73. *Democratic Proceedings of 1904*, pp. 278-319; Eaton, p. 200; Bain and Parris, pp. 169-70; Cherny, p. 101.

74. *Democratic Proceedings of 1904*, pp. 319-29.

75. *New York Times*, July 11, 1904; *Baltimore Sun*, July 11,1904, *Washington Post*, July 11, 1904; *Wall Street Journal*, July 11, 1904.

76. Eaton, p. 197.

77. Wood, p. 170.

78. Albert Gale and George Kline, *Bryan the Man: The Great Commoner at Close Range* (St. Louis: Thompson Publishing Company, 1908), pp. 46-47.

79. Brands, pp. 506-13.

80. Brands, pp. 506-11; Stefan Lorant, *The Glorious Burden* (Lenox, MA: Authors Edition, Inc., 1976), pp. 486-88.

81. Brands, p. 513; Lorant, p. 488.
82. Lorant, p. 488.

Chapter 2

1. Doris Kearns Goodwin, *The Bully Pulpit: Theodore Roosevelt, William Howard Taft, and the Golden Age of Journalism* (New York: Simon & Schuster Paperbacks, 2013, p. 421; Brands, p. 514.

2. UVA Miller Center, "Theodore Roosevelt—Key Events," www.millercenter.org, viewed March 9, 2019; *see generally*, Brands, pp. 541-637.

3. Goodwin, pp. 517-20.

4. Goodwin, p. 518.

5. Haynes, *President-Making in the Gilded Age*, p. 152; Goodwin, pp. 519-20; *Washington Post*, February 12-15, 1908, *Baltimore Sun*, March 5, 1908.

6. Robert F. Wesser, *Charles Evans Hughes: Politics and Reform in New York 1905-1910* (Ithaca, NY: Cornell University Press, 1967), pp. 209-25; Goodwin, pp. 535-36.

7. Brands, p. 597; Eaton, p. 203.

8. Brands, pp. 625-26; *Chicago Daily Tribune*, June 14, 1908; Goodwin, pp. 522-33.

9. Haynes, *President-Making in the Gilded Age*, pp. 250-54; Cowan, pp. 80-84; Eaton, p. 203.

10. *Chicago Daily Tribune*, April 1, 1908; *New York Times*, May 14, 1908.

11. *New York Times*, June 17, 1908; *Washington Post*, May 10, 1908.

12. *New York Times*, June 13, 14, and 17, 1908; *Chicago Daily Tribune*, June 13, 1908.

13. *Chicago Daily Tribune*, June 14, 1908.

14. *Chicago Daily Tribune*, June 13 and 14, 1908; *New York Times*, June 13, 1908; *Saturday Evening Post*, June 19, 1908.

15. Milton Blumenberg, Official Reporter, *Official Report of the Proceedings of the Fourteenth Republican National Convention Held in Chicago, Illinois June 16, 17, 18 and 19, 1908* (Columbus, OH: Press of F. J. Heer, 1908) [hereafter *Republican Proceedings of 1908*], pp. 25–52; Eaton, pp. 203-04, Bain and Parris, p. 172.

16. *Republican Proceedings of 1908*, pp.53-81.

17. *Republican Proceedings of 1908*, pp. 81-87; *New York Times*, June 18, 1908; Goodwin, p. 544; Brands, pp. 626-27.

18. *Washington Post*, June 18, 1908; Goodwin, p. 544; Brands, pp. 626-27.

19. *Republican Proceedings of 1908*, pp. 87-88.

20. *Republican Proceedings of 1908*, pp. 81- 112; Cowan, pp. 83-84.

21. *Republican Proceedings of 1908*, pp. 156-60.

22. *Republican Proceedings of 1908*, pp. 142-77.

23. *Republican Proceedings of 1908*, pp. 179-83.

24. *Baltimore Sun*, June 19, 1908; *Washington Post*, June 19, 1908; Goodwin, p. 546.

25. *New York Times*, June, 19, 1908; Goodwin, p. 546.

26. *Republican Proceedings of 1908*, pp. 115-42; *Washington Post*, June 19, 1908.

27. *Republican Proceedings of 1908*, pp. 184-201; *New York Times*, June 19, 1908; Eaton, pp. 204-05; Wesser, pp. 224-25.

28. Haynes, *President-Making in the Gilded Age*, p. 44.

29. Cherny, pp. 91-107.

30. *Washington Post*, July 5, 1908; "1908 Democratic National Convention," *www.*

coloradoencyclopedia.org. viewed on June 5, 2023.

31. *Rocky Mountain News,* July 8, 1908; *New York Times,* July 7, 1908.

32. *Topeka Daily Capital,* July 11, 1908.

33. Frank Day and Theodore Knappen, *Life of John Albert Johnson* (Chicago: Forbes & Company, 1910), pp. 165-75.

34. *Washington Post,* July 5, 1908; *The Forum,* July, 1908, pp. 8-10.

35. *Baltimore Sun, July 3 and 8,1908.*

36. *Baltimore Sun,* July 6, 1908; *Washington Post,* July 9, 1908; Hanes Walton, Jr. and C. Vernon Gray, "Black Politics at the National Republican and Democratic Conventions, 1868-1972," *Phylon,* Vol. 36, No. 3, p. 269.

37. Milton W. Blumenberg, *Official Report of the Proceedings of the Democratic National Convention Held in Denver, Colorado, July 7, 8, 9 and 10, 1908,* (Chicago: Press of Western Newspaper Union, 1908) [hereafter "*Democratic Proceedings of 1908*"], pp. 14-15.

38. *Washington Post,* July 6, 1908.

39. *Democratic Proceedings of 1908,* pp. 31-35; *Baltimore Sun,* July 8, 1908.

40. Robert Lewallen, "Let the People Rule: William Jennings Bryan and the Oklahoma Constitution," (*The Chronicles of Oklahoma,* Autumn, 1995), pp. 287-92.

41. *Rocky Mountain News,* July 9, 1908; *Democratic Proceedings of 1908,* pp. 41-43.

42. *Baltimore Sun,* July 10, 1908.

43. *Democratic Proceedings of 1908,* pp. 120-22; *Baltimore Sun,* July 8, 1908; *New York Times,* July 9, 1908.

44. *Rocky Mountain News,* July 8, 1908; *Democratic Proceedings of 1908,* p. 151.

45. *Herald Democrat,* July 10, 1908.

46. *Democratic Proceedings of 1908,* pp. 176-84.

47. *Herald Democrat,* July 10, 1908; *Rocky Mountain News,* July 10, 1908; *Democratic Proceedings of 1908,* p. 182, *Philadelphia Inquirer,* July 11,1908.

48. *Democratic Proceedings of 1908,* pp. 200-04.

49. *Democratic Proceedings of 1908,* pp. 159 to 174.

50. *Democratic Proceedings of 1908,* pp. 183 to 248; *Rocky Mountain News,* July 10, 1908.

51. *Democratic Proceedings of 1908,* pp. 250-81.

52. Eaton, p. 207.

53. "1908: Taft v. Bryan," www.harpweek.com, viewed November 12, 2023.

54. Lorant, pp. 504-06; "1908: Taft v. Bryan," www.harpweek.com, viewed November 12, 2023.

55. Nasaw, p. 220; Lorant, p. 502.

56. Lorant, p. 507, 1076.

57. Brands, p. 632; Goodwin, p. 556.

Chapter 3

1. Goodwin, pp. 106-08; 134-35.

2. James Chace, *1912: Wilson, Roosevelt, Taft & Debs—The Election That Changed the Country* (New York: Simon & Schuster, 2004), pp. 105-06; Paolo E. Coletta, *The Presidency of William Howard Taft* (Lawrence: The University Press of Kansas, 1973), pp. 226-30.

3. Chace, pp. 100-05; Coletta, 218-22; Geoffrey Cowan, *Let the People Rule: Theodore Roosevelt and the Birth of the Presidential Primary* (New York: W. W. Norton & Company, 2016), pp. 64, 69-71.

4. Cowan, pp. 35-42.

5. Chace, pp. 109-13; Coletta, pp. 231-36.

6. Chace, 110-12; Coletta, pp. 233-34.

7. Edmund Morris, *Colonel Roosevelt* (New York: Random House, 2010), pp. 193-94; Eaton, pp. 216-19; Chace, p. 116; Bain and Parris, pp. 179-80.

8. *New York Times*, June 16, 1912; Morris, pp. 195-96.

9. Geoffrey Cowan, "Riots, Guns, Bribes: TR's Contested Convention," *The Atlantic*, April 23, 2016. *Baltimore Sun*, June 17 and 18, 1912.

10. *New York Times*, June 16, 17, and 18, 1912; *Baltimore Sun*, June 15, 16, and 17, 1912; Anderson, p. 236; Eaton, p. 220.

11. *Chicago Tribune*, June 18, 1912.

12. Sidney M. Milkis, *Theodore Roosevelt, the Progressive Party, and the Transformation of American Democracy* (Lawrence: The University Press of Kansas, 2009), pp. 111-12; *Baltimore Sun*, June 18, 1912; Chace, pp. 117-18.

13. *Baltimore Sun*, June 16, 1912; Cowan, pp. 193-94.

14. Judith Anderson, *William Howard Taft: An Intimate History* (New York: W. W. Norton Company, 1981), p. 236; Eaton, pp. 220-21.

15. Milton Blumenberg, *Official Report of the Proceedings of the Fifteenth Republican National Convention Held in Chicago, Illinois, June 18,19.20, 21 and 22, 1912*, (New York: The Tenny Press, 1912) [hereafter "*Republican Proceedings of 1912*"], pp. 29-41.

16. *Republican Proceedings of 1912*, pp. 42-43; *Baltimore Sun*, June 16, 1912.

17. Haynes, *President-Making in the Gilded Age*, pp. 91-93.

18. *Republican Proceedings of 1912*, pp. 43-61; *Chicago Tribune*, June 19, 1912; *New York Times*, June 19, 1912; Eaton, pp. 220-21; Cowan, pp. 221-22; Bain and Parris, pp. 180-81; Milkis, pp. 113-14.

19. Cowan, pp. 218-220.

20. *Republican Proceedings of 1912*, pp. 105-166; *Chicago Tribune*, June 20, 1912; Morris, pp. 201-05; Bain and Parris, p. 82.

21. *Republican Proceedings of 1912*, p. 143; Eaton, pp. 221-23; Cowan, pp. 223-26; Eaton 222-23; Cowan, pp. 230-31; Morris, pp. 202-05.

22. *Chicago Tribune*, June 20, 1912; Morris, pp. 203-05; Cowan, pp. 226-27; Haynes, *President-Making in the Gilded Age*, p. 230.

23. *Republican Proceedings of 1912*, p. 167; *Chicago Tribune*, June 21, 1912.

24. *Republican Proceedings of 1912*, pp. 167-238; Cowan, pp. 233-37; *Chicago Tribune*, June 22, 1912.

25. *Republican Proceedings of 1912*, pp. 239-335; Eaton, pp. 223-24; Cowan, pp. 240-43, Goodwin, pp. 708-09.

26. Goodwin, pp. 708-09; Cowan, pp. 240-43.

27. *Republican Proceedings of 1912*, pp. 342-74; *Chicago Tribune*, June 23, 1912; *New York Times*, June 23, 1912; Bain and Parris, p. 183; Coletta, pp. 237-38.

28. Francis Russell, *The Shadow of Blooming Grove: Warren G. Harding in His Times* (New York: McGraw-Hill Book Company, 1968), pp. 223-34; *Republican Proceedings of 1912*, pp. 377-86; Anderson, p. 239.

29. *Republican Proceedings of 1912*, pp. 386-90; *Chicago Tribune*, June 23, 1912.

30. *Republican Proceedings of 1912*, pp. 391-403; Coletta, p. 238; Eaton, p. 224; Goodwin, pp 710-11; Cowan, p. 252.

31. *Republican Proceedings of 1912*, pp. 403-07; *Chicago Tribune*, June 23, 1912; Chace, pp. 235-36.

32. *Chicago Tribune*, June 23, 1912.

33. *Chicago Tribune*, June 23, 1912.

34. Goodwin, pp. 718-21; Brands, pp.718-19.

35. Morris p. 207.

36. *New York Times*, June 23, 1912.

37. Milton Blumenberg, *Official Report of the Proceedings of the Democratic National Convention Held in Baltimore, Maryland, July 25,26,27,28,29 and July 1 and 2, 1912*, (Chicago: The Linotyping Co., 1912) [hereafter "*Democratic Proceedings of 1912*"], pp. 98 and 111; *Baltimore Sun*, June 28, 1912; Richard A. Morton, "It Was Bryan and Sullivan Who Did the Trick," (*Journal of the Illinois State Historical Society*, Vol. 108, No. 2, Summer, 2015, pp. 147-81), p. 157.

38. Lewis L. Gould, *The First Modern Clash Over Federal Power: Wilson Versus Hughes in the Presidential Election of 1916* (Lawrence: University Press of Kansas, 2016, p. 82; Morton, p. 152.

39. Eaton, p. 227; Chace, pp. 125-26.

40. Smith, pp. 86-89.

41. Stan Haynes, "When Baltimore Was Convention Central," *Baltimore Sun*, June 25, 1912; Morton, p. 156.

42. Eaton, p. 231; Chace, p. 142; Gould, 87; *Baltimore Sun*, June 26, 1912.

43. Walter Lord, "The Wild Convention Scrap a Professor Won," *LIFE*, May 16, 1960, pp. 126-38, at p. 128; Henry Bourguignon, "Bryan's Influence on Wilson's Nomination in 1912," Master's Thesis, 1364, Loyola University Chicago, 1956, pp. 21-23; Eaton, pp. 232-33; A. Scott Berg, *Wilson*, (New York: G. P. Putnam Sons, 2013), pp. 230-31.

44. *Democratic Proceedings of 1912*, pp. 3-19; Lord, p. 129.

45. Eaton, pp. 233-35; Chase, pp. 148-49, Bourguignon, pp. 31-36.

46. Chase at pp. 148-49, Bourguignon, pp. 31-36.

47. *Democratic Proceedings of 1912*, pp. 129-38; Morton, pp. 161-62; Lord, pp. 130-31.

48. *Baltimore Sun,* June 28, 1912.

49. *Democratic Proceedings of 1912*, pp. 139-44.

50. *Democratic Proceedings of 1912*, pp. 144-51; Lord, p. 132.

51. *Democratic Proceedings of 1912*, pp. 157-58.

52. *Democratic Proceedings of 1912*, pp. 160-61.

53. *Democratic Proceedings of 1912*, pp. 162-98; *Baltimore Sun*, June 28 and 29, 1912; Eaton, pp. 236-38; Lord, p. 132.

54. *Democratic Proceedings of 1912*, pp. 219-22; Haynes, *The First American Political Conventions*, pp. 80-86; Eaton, pp. 238-39.

55. *Democratic Proceedings of 1912*, pp 222-28; Eaton, pp. 238-39.

56. Chace, pp. 154-55; Lord, p. 134-36, Berg, pp. 232-33. William F. McCombs, *Making Woodrow Wilson President* (New York: Fairview Publishing Co., 1921), pp.143-46.

57. *Baltimore Sun*, June 30, 1912; *Democratic Proceedings of 1912*, pp. 232-43; Eaton, p. 240-41.

58. *Democratic Proceedings of 1912*, pp. 273-77; Champ Clark, *My Quarter Century in American Politics, Volume 2*, (New York: Harper and Brothers Publishers, 1920), pp. 427-28.

59. Lord, p. 136; *Baltimore Sun*, July 1 and 2, 1912.

60. *Democratic Proceedings of 1912*, pp. 273-77, 329-33.

61. *Democratic Proceedings of 1912*, pp. 334-53; Eaton, pp. 242-44; Chase, 156-58; Morton, pp. 172-73.

62. *Democratic Proceedings of 1912*, pp. 365-76; Chace, p. 158.

63. Stan Haynes, "Why Have There Been So Many Vice Presidential Candidates from Indiana of All Places?," *History News Network*, January 17, 2017; *Democratic Proceedings of 1912*, pp. 354-64, 377-89; Berg, p. 234, Chase, p. 158, Eaton, pp. 244-45.

64. Boyce House, "Bryan at Baltimore: The Democratic National Convention of 1912," *Nebraska History* 41, 1960, pp. 29 -51; *Baltimore Sun*, July 2, 1912.

65. Clark, pp. 392-430.

66. Chace, pp. 219-21.

67. Lorant, p. 530.

68. Chace, pp. 229-33; Oliver Remey, Henry Cochems, and Wheeler Bloodgood, *The Attempted Assassination of Ex-President Theodore Roosevelt* (Milwaukee: The Progressive Publishing Company, 1912), *see generally*.

69. Sidney Milkis, *Theodore Roosevelt, the Progressive Party, and the Transformation of American Democracy* (Lawrence: The University Press of Kansas, 2009), pp. 229-31.

70. Chace, pp. 235-36; Coletta, pp. 243-44.

71. Chace, pp. 238-40; Lorant, p. 532.

Chapter 4

1. Lorant, pp. 535-37.

2. Lorant, pp. 536-38; *New York Times*, June 16, 1916.

3. Lorant, p. 537; *New York Times*, June 16, 1916.

4. Marcella K. Alverson, "The Attitudes and Activities of the Republican Party in the Election of 1916," Loyola University Chicago, Master's Thesis, 30, 1939, at pp. 4-5, 24.

5. Eaton, p. 247

6. Wesser, pp. 25-48, 49-69, and 226-51.

7. Gould, pp. 45-46; Wesser, pp. 209-225; James F. Simon, *FDR and Chief Justice Hughes* (New York, Simon & Schuster, 2012), p. 100.

8. Alverson, p. 11; Eaton, p. 249.

9. Gould, Appendix A; Eaton, pp. 249-51.

10. George Hart, *Official Report of the Proceedings of the Sixteenth Republican National Convention Held in Chicago, Illinois June 7, 8, 9 and 10, 1916* (New York: The Tenny Press, 1916) [hereafter "*Republican Proceedings of 1916*"], pp. 9, 11-13; *Washington Post*, June 8, 1916; *New York Times*, June 5, 1916; Eaton, p. 252.

11. Alverson, p. 13.

12. *Republican Proceedings of 1916*, pp. 7-13; *Washington Post*, June 8, 1916.

13. *Republican Proceedings of 1916*, pp. 13-28, 32-37; Eaton p. 253, *New York Times*, June 8, 1916.

14. *Republican Proceedings of 1916*, p. 16; "December Highlight: Founding Fathers?," *Declaration Resources Project, Course of Human Events*, December 4, 2016, declaration.fas.harvard.edu, viewed August 3, 2023.

15. Alverson, p. 22; *New York Times*, June 8, 1916; Eaton, p. 253.

16. *New York Times*, June 7, 1916; *Washington Post*, June 8, 1916.

17. *New York Times*, June 8, 1916; Lucas Bensley, "Suffer Not the Rain: The 1916 Suffrage Parade in Chicago," www.suffrage-2020illinois.org. viewed July 29, 2023.

18. *Republican Proceedings of 1916*, pp. 38-68, 79; *New York Times*, June 9, 1916.

19. *Republican Proceedings of 1916*, pp. 88-102.

20. *Republican Proceedings of 1916*, pp. 103-06.

21. *Republican Proceedings of 1916*, p. 110-11.

22. *Republican Proceedings of 1916*, p. 118.

23. *Republican Proceedings of 1916*, pp. 111-16; *Washington Post*, June 10, 1916.

24. *Republican Proceedings of 1916* pp. 119-56; *Washington Post*, June 10, 1916; Eaton p. 247.

25. *Republican Proceedings of 1916*, pp. 181-90.

26. *Washington Post*, June 10, 1916; *New York Times*, June 11, 1916, Eaton, pp. 255-56.

27. Eaton, p. 255.

28. *Republican Proceedings of 1916* pp. 191-202; *Washington Post*, June 11, 1916.

29. *Republican Proceedings of 1916*, pp. 204-13; Stan Haynes, "Why Have There Been So Many Vice Presidential Candidates from Indiana of All Places?" *www.historynewsnetwork.org*; Eaton, p. 257.

30. *New York Times*, June 11, 1916; Gould, p. 71.

31. *Baltimore Sun*, June 11, 1916.

32. *Washington Post*, June 11, 1916.

33. *Washington Post*, June 13, 1916; *New York Times*, June 11, 1916.

34. *Washington Post*, June 15, 1916.

35. Haynes, *President-Making in the Gilded Age*, p. 78.

36. Margot McMillen, *The Golden Lane: How Missouri Women Gained the Vote and Changed History*, (Charleston, SC: The History Press, 2011), ch. 9; *Washington Post*, June 15, 1916.

37. Louis Granat, Official Reporter, *Official Report of the Proceedings of the Democratic National Convention Held in Saint Louis, Missouri June 14, 15 and 16th, 1916*, [hereafter *Democratic Proceedings of 1916*], pp. 9-14; *Washington Post*, June 15, 1916.

38. *Democratic Proceedings of 1916*, pp. 14-21.

39. *Democratic Proceedings of 1916*, pp. 22-24.

40. *Democratic Proceedings of 1916*, p. 26.

41. Arthur Link, *Wilson: Campaigns for Progressivism and Peace, 1916-17, Volume 5*, (Princeton: Princeton University Press, 1965), pp. 43-45.

42. *Democratic Proceedings of 1916*, pp. 41-52.

43. *Democratic Proceedings of 1916*, pp. 53-79.

44. *Democratic Proceedings of 1916*, p. 88; *Baltimore Sun*, June 18, 1916.

45. *Democratic Proceedings of 1916*, pp. 92-93.

46. *Democratic Proceedings of 1916*, pp. 101-04; *Washington Post*, June 16, 1916.

47. Morton, p. 141; *Democratic Proceedings of 1916*, p. 107.

48. *Democratic Proceedings of 1916*, p. 107; Morton, pp. 138-39; *Washington Post*, June 15, 1916.

49. *Washington Post*, June 16, 1916; Jeffrey Graf, "What This Country Needs is a Really Good Five-Cent Cigar," *Indiana University Libraries*, Bloomington, Scholars' Commons, pp. 1-33.

50. *Democratic Proceedings of 1916*, pp. 121-48; *Baltimore Sun*, June 16 and 17, 1916; *New York Times*, June 17, 1916.

51. *Democratic Proceedings of 1916*, pp. 134-35, 146-48; *New York Times*, June 17, 1916.

52. *Washington Post*, June, 16, 1916.

53. Lorant, pp. 541-43; Gould, pp. 80-86.

54. Gould, pp. 85-86.//
55. Lorant, p. 1078.

Chapter 5

1. Lorant, pp. 547-52.
2. Lorant, pp. 547-52.
3. David Pietrusza, *1920: The Year of Six Presidents* (New York: Basic Books, 2007), pp. 63-71.
4. Mencken, p. 15; Russell, 325-29; Pietrusza, pp. 167-72; Sobel, pp.164-65.
5. Eaton, pp. 260-62; Pietrusza, pp. 167-75.
6. Sobel, pp. 164-67.
7. Pietruska, pp. 177-80; Russell, p. 330; Sobel, pp. 164-65.
8. Mencken, pp. 10-11; Eaton, p. 280; Pietrusza, pp. 7; Russell, pp. 166-71; 287-93, 323; Pietrusza, pp. 74-81; Sobel, p. 168.
9. Sobel, pp. 135-44, 151-58; Pietrusza, pp. 99-102.
10. Russell, p. 350.
11. Eaton, p. 266.
12. Pietrusza, pp. 184-85; Russell, pp. 351-52.
13. Sobel. pp. 170-71.
14. Russell, p. 363.
15. *Baltimore Sun*, June 6 and 10, 1920; *Washington Post*, June 7 and 10, 1920; George Hart, Official Reporter, *Official Report of the Proceedings of the Seventeenth Republican National Convention Held in Chicago, Illinois June 8, 9, 10, 11 and 12, 1920* (New York: The Tenny Press, 1920), [hereafter *Republican Proceedings of 1920*], p. 81.
16. Russell, pp. 355-58; *Washington Post*, June 7, 1920.
17. *Washington Post*, June 7, 1920; Russell, p. 363.
18. Russell, p. 365; *Republican Proceedings of 1920*, pp. 7-41.
19. Russell, p. 272, Pietrusza, pp. 369-71.
20. *Republican Proceedings of 1920*, pp. 42-76.
21. *Republican Proceedings of 1920*, pp. 76-80; *Baltimore Sun*, June 10, 1920.
22. *Republican Proceedings of 1920*, pp 81-82.
23. *Baltimore Sun*, June 11, 1920; *Republican Proceedings of 1920*, pp. 83-85.
24. *Republican Proceedings of 1920*, pp. 96-97.
25. *Republican Proceedings of 1920*, pp. 85-114; Russell, p. 367; *Baltimore Sun*, June 11, 1920; Pietrusza, pp. 211-12.
26. *Republican Proceedings of 1920*, p. 116.
27. *Republican Proceedings of 1920*, pp. 117-26; Eaton, p. 269; Pietrusza, pp. 213-14.
28. *Republican Proceedings of 1920*, pp. 126-29; Pietrusza, p. 214.
29. *Republican Proceedings of 1920*, pp. 132-40; Pietruska, p. 214.
30. *Republican Proceedings of 1920* pp. 148-68.
31. *Republican Proceedings of 1920*, pp. 168-70; *Baltimore Sun*, June 12, 1920; Pietrusza, pp. 216-17; Russell, pp. 358-60.
32. *Republican Proceedings of 1920*, pp., 172-83.
33. *Republican Proceedings of 1920*, p. 185; Eaton, pp. 270.
34. *Republican Proceedings of 1920*, pp. 186-95; Pietruska, pp., 219-21; Eaton, pp. 270-71.
35. *Republican Proceedings of 1920*, pp. 197-213; Pietruska, pp. 227-30; Eaton, pp. 274-75.

36. *Baltimore Sun*, June 13, 1920; *Republican Proceedings of 1920*, pp. 213-219; Russell, pp. 392-94; Pietrusza, pp. 231-34.

37. *Republican Proceedings of 1920*, pp. 219-24; Pietrusza, pp. 232-38; Russell, pp. 394-95; *Baltimore Sun*, June 13, 1920.

38. Pietrusza, p. 224-27; Russell, pp. 379-83.

39. Pietrusza, p. 224-27; Russell, pp. 379-83.

40. Russell, p. 386.

41. Russell, pp. 371-72, 379; *Baltimore Sun*, June 13, 1920; Pietrusza, p. 222.

42. Russell, pp. 384-85; Laton McCartney, *The Teapot Dome Scandal* (New York: Random House, 2008), pp. 3-26.

43. *Republican Proceedings of 1920*, pp. 224-26; Russell, p. 395; Sobel, p. 186; Pietrusza, pp. 238-39.

44. *Republican Proceedings of 1920*, pp. 225-240.

45. Russell, pp. 395-96; Sobel, pp. 185-90; Pietrusza, pp. 238-41.

46. Sobel, pp. 189-90; Pietrusza, pp. 240-41.

47. Charles Werling, "The Nomination of James M. Cox: The Democratic Convention of 1920," Masters Thesis, 2046, Loyola University Chicago, 1965, pp. 28-30; Pietrusza, pp. 191-92; Eaton, p. 285-86; *Baltimore Sun*, June 28, 1920.

48. Pietrusza, pp. 187-90.

49. Werling, pp. 30-37; Pietrusza, pp. 190-93.

50. Mencken, pp. 10-11; Eaton, p. 280; Pietrusza, pp. 192-94.

51. Werling, pp. 10-19; Stone, pp. 34-41.

52. Stone, pp. 33-41; Pietrusza, pp. 195-97; Werling, pp.10-19.

53. *Baltimore Sun*, June 29, 1920.

54. William Harbaugh, *Lawyer's Lawyer: The Life of John W. Davis* (New York: Oxford University Press, 1973), pp. 168-75; Robert Slayton, *Empire Statesman: The Rise and Redemption of Al Smith* (New York: The Free Press, 2001), pp. 365-66.

55. Bain and Parris, p. 209; *Baltimore Sun*, June 26 and 27, 1920; *Washington Post*, June 28, 1920; Eaton, pp. 280-823.

56. *Baltimore Sun*, June 28, 1920; *Baltimore Evening Sun*, June 29, 1920; *Washington Post*, June 29 and 30, 1920.

57. "The 1920 Democratic Convention in San Francisco: An Epic, Illegal Booze Party," June 7, 2020. www.sfgate.com, viewed December 12, 2023; Marion E. Rodgers, *Mencken: The American Iconoclast* (Oxford: Oxford University Press, 2005), p. 222; *Washington Post*, June 30, 1920; *Baltimore Evening Sun*, June 29, 1920 and July 1, 1920; S. T. Joshi, Editor, *From Baltimore to Bohemia: The Letters of H. L. Mencken and George Sterling* (Cranbury, NJ: Associated University Presses, 2001), p. 13.

58. *Washington Post*, June 29, 1920; Harry Couch, Official Reporter, *Official Report of the Proceedings of the Democratic National Convention Held in San Francisco, California June 28, 29, 30, July 1, 2, 3, 5, and 6, 1920* (Indianapolis: Bookwalter-Ball Printing Co., 1920), p. 3 [hereafter "*Democratic Proceedings of 1920*"], *Baltimore Sun*, June 29, 1920; *Washington Post*, June 29, 1920.

59. *Democratic Proceedings of 1920*, pp. 3-26.

60. *Democratic Proceedings of 1920*, pp. 26-38.

61. *Washington Post*, June 30, 1920; *Democratic Proceedings of 1920*, pp. 39-94.

62. *Democratic Proceedings of 1920*, pp. 95-149.

63. *Democratic Proceedings of 1920*, pp. 113-19.

64. *Democratic Proceedings of 1920*, pp. 128-32.

65. *Democratic Proceedings of 1920*, pp. 142; *Reedy's Mirror*, Vol. 29, No. 28, July 8, 1920, p. 542.

66. *Washington Post*, June 30, 1920; *Baltimore Evening Sun*, July 1, 1920.

67. Haynes, *President-Making in the Gilded Age*, pp. 189-90; *Democratic Proceedings of 1920*, pp. 135-40; *Baltimore Evening Sun*, July 1, 1920.

68. *Baltimore Evening Sun*, July 1, 1920; *Democratic Proceedings of 1920*, pp. 140-41.

69. *Democratic Proceedings of 1920*, pp. 150-68.

70. *Democratic Proceedings of 1920*, pp. 168-77.

71. Eaton, pp. 284-85; *Democratic Proceedings of 1920*, pp. 180-200.

72. *Democratic Proceedings of 1920*, p. 182.

73. *Democratic Proceedings of 1920*, pp. 201-05.

74. *Democratic Proceedings of 1920*, pp. 255-65.

75. *Democratic Proceedings of 1920*, pp. 266-74.

76. *Democratic Proceedings of 1920*, pp. 275-338.

77. Eaton, p. 287, Werling, p. 108.

78. *Democratic Proceedings of 1920*, pp. 339-56.

79. *New York Times*, July 5, 1920; Pietrusza, pp. 243 and 255; *Washington Post*, July 5, 1920.

80. *Baltimore Sun*, July 5, 1920; Eaton, p. 286; Werling, pp. 93-94.

81. *Democratic Proceedings of 1920*, pp. 360-98; Werling, p. 114.

82. *Democratic Proceedings of 1920*, pp. 399-420; Eaton, pp. 288-89; Werling, pp.118-26; Pietrusza, p. 257.

83. James MacGregor Burns, *The Definitive FDR: The Lion and the Fox* (New York: Open Road Media, 1912), ch. 4; Lorant, p. 557; Pietrusza, pp. 258.

84. Pietrusza, pp. 258-59; Haynes, *President-Making in the Gilded Age*, pp. 241-42.

85. *Democratic Proceedings of 1920*, pp. 438-53.

86. Jeanne Demling, "Personalities and Issues of the Presidential Election of 1920," (1950). Master's Thesis, 751, Loyola University Chicago, pp. 49-50; *Literary Digest*, Vol. 66, July 24, 1920, p. 41; Stone, p. 42; Pietrusza, pp. 259-60.

87. Stone, pp. 42-43.

88. Russell, pp. 405-16; Lorant, pp. 557-58; Pietrusza, pp, 369-85.

89. Russell, pp. 405-16; Lorant, pp. 557-58.

90. Lorant, pp. 557-59; Sobel, pp. 206-07; Russell, p. 418.

Chapter 6

1. *Baltimore Sun*, June 11, 1920; Russell, p, 571; Sobel, pp. 227-33.

2. Sobel, p. 237.

3. Sobel, pp. 252-53; 260-68.

4. Ferrell, Robert, *The Presidency of Calvin Coolidge* (Lawrence: University Press of Kansas, 1998), pp. 51-53; Sobel, pp. 255-56, 277-78; Bain and Parris, p. 215.

5. *Baltimore Sun*, June 9, 1920; M. C. Murphy, *Calvin Coolidge: The Presidency and Philosophy of a Progressive Conservative*

(Jefferson, NC: McFarland & Company, Inc., 2023), pp. 83-84.

6. *Washington Post*, June 8, 9, and 10, 1924; Eaton, p. 312; *New York Times*, June 9, 1924.

7. *Baltimore Sun*, June 8 and 9, 1924; Murphy, p. 85-86.

8. Mencken, pp. 77-78; *New York Times*, June 9, 1920; Murphy, p. 86.

9. Murphy, p. 86; *Baltimore Sun*, June 9 and 11, 1924.

10. George Hart, Official Reporter, *Official Report of the Proceedings of the Eighteenth Republican National Convention Held in Cleveland, Ohio June 10, 11 and 12, 1924* (New York: The Tenny Press, 1924) [hereafter "*Republican Proceedings of 1924*"], pp. 7-16; *Baltimore Sun*, June 9, 1924; *New York Times*, June, 11, 1924.

11. *Baltimore Sun*, June 10, 1924; *Washington Post*, June 10, 1924; *New York Times*, June 11, 1924; *Republican Proceedings of 1924*, p. 90.

12. *Baltimore Sun*, June 11, 1924.

13. *Republican Proceedings of 1924*, pp. 17-37.

14. *Baltimore Sun*, June 11, 1924; Murphy, p. 84.

15. *Republican Proceedings of 1924*, pp. 85-89; *New York Times*, June 12, 1924.

16. *Republican Proceedings of 1924*, pp. 98-115.

17. *Republican Proceedings of 1924*, pp. 116-24; *Baltimore Sun*, June 12, 1924.

18. *Republican Proceedings of 1924*, pp. 134-52.

19. *New York Times*, June 13, 1924; *Republican Proceedings of 1924*, pp. 152-165.

20. William Allen White, *A Puritan in Babylon: The Story of Calvin Coolidge* (London: Papamoa Press, 2018), ch. 27; Murphy, p. 86; Ferrell, pp. 55-57; Sobel, pp. 286-89.

21. *Republican Proceedings of 1924*, pp. 167-87.

22. Haynes, *The First American Political Conventions*, pp. 87-88; *Republican Proceedings of 1924*, pp. 187-90; White, ch. 27.

23. *Republican Proceedings of 1924*, pp. 190-94; *New York Times*, June 13, 1924.

24. Robert K. Murray, *The 103rd Ballot: Democrats and the Disaster in Madison Square Garden* (New York: Harper Collins, 1976), pp. xv-xvi.

25. Lee Allen, "The McAdoo Campaign for the Presidential Nomination in 1924," *The Journal of Southern History*, Vol. 29, No. 2, May, 1963, pp. 211-228, pp. 220-22; Murray, pp. 53-61.

26. Murray, pp. 15-24; 105-08; Allen, pp. 217-19.

27. Murray, pp. 71-80; Slayton, pp. 154-55.

28. Slayton, pp. 202-06; Murray, pp. 67-71.

29. Murray, pp. 61-66; Allen, p. 217.

30. Harbaugh, pp. 181-200; Murray, pp. 93-97.

31. Eaton, p. 295.

32. Murray, pp. 103-11; Allen, pp. 215-19; Eaton, p. 293.

33. Murray, pp. 111-12; Harbaugh, p. 213.

34. Haynes, *The First American Political Conventions*, pp. 208-15; Murray, pp. 117-21, 130.

35. Louis Granat, Official Reporter, *Official Report of the Proceedings of the Democratic National Convention held in Madison Square Garden New York City June 24, 25, 26, 27, 28, 30, July 1, 2, 3, 4, 5, 7, 8 and 9, 1924* (Indianapolis: Bookwalter-Ball-Greathouse

Printing Co., 1924) [hereafter "*Democratic Proceedings of 1924*"], pp. 3-25; Eaton, p. 297.

36. *Democratic Proceedings of 1924*, pp. 106-16; Eaton, p. 298; Murray, pp. 154-55; Murray, pp.154-57.

37. Slayton, pp. 209-10; Murray, pp. 159-60.

38. Slayton, pp. 209-11; Murray, p. 159.

39. *Democratic Proceedings of 1924*, pp. 122-29; Slayton, pp. 209-11; Murray, pp. 159-61.

40. Murray, pp. 159-65; Slayton, pp. 209-11; *Democratic Proceedings of 1924*, p. 129.

41. *Democratic Proceedings of 1924*, pp. 212-15; Murray, p. 172.

42. *Democratic Proceedings of 1924*, pp. 245-248.

43. Eaton, p. 300; *Democratic Proceedings of 1924*, pp. 294-98.

44. *Democratic Proceedings of 1924*, p. 298.

45. *Democratic Proceedings of 1924*, pp. 303-09.

46. Eaton, p. 299.

47. *Democratic Proceedings of 1924*, pp. 310-30.

48. *Democratic Proceedings of 1924*, pp. 228-47, 259-79, 334.

49. *Democratic Proceedings of 1924*, pp. 335-410; Eaton, pp. 300-01.

50. *Democratic Proceedings of 1924*, pp. 411-91; Eaton, pp. 301-02; *TIME*, July 14, 1924.

51. *Democratic Proceedings of 1924*, pp. 492-559; Eaton, pp. 302-04; *TIME*, July 14, 1924.

52. *Democratic Proceedings of 1924*, pp. 560-650; Eaton, pp. 304-05.

53. *Democratic Proceedings of 1924*, pp. 651-730; Eaton, pp. 305-06.

54. *Democratic Proceedings of 1924*, pp. 731-79; Eaton, p. 306.

55. *Democratic Proceedings of 1924*, pp. 780-851; Eaton, pp. 306-07.

56. *Democratic Proceedings of 1924*, pp. 852-947; Eaton, pp. 307-09.

57. *Democratic Proceedings of 1924*, pp. 852-947; Eaton, pp. 307-09.

58. *Democratic Proceedings of 1924*, pp. 46, 998-1039; Eaton, pp. 310-11; *Long Beach Post*, August 31, 2020; Harbaugh, pp. 218-19.

59. *Democratic Proceedings of 1924*, pp. 1022-24 and 1012-15; Eaton, pp. 310-11; *TIME*, July 21, 1924; *New York Times*, July 10, 1924; Harbaugh, p. 218.

60. Garland S. Tucker, III, *The High Tide of American Conservatism: Davis, Coolidge, and the 1924 Election* (Austin: Emerald Book Company, 2010), pp. 85-87.

61. *New York Times*, July 10, 1924.

62. *New York Times*, July 10, 1924.

63. Sobel, p. 300, Tucker, pp. 219-239.

64. Sobel, pp. 300-03.

65. Tucker, pp. 232-34; Sobel, pp. 303-04; Harbaugh, pp. 244-47.

66. Lorant, p. 571; Sobel, pp. 305-06; Tucker, pp. 233-35.

67. Harbaugh, p. 248.

Chapter 7

1. Glen Jeansonne, *Herbert Hoover: A Life* (New York: New American Library, 2016), pp. 186-87; Robert Sobel, *Coolidge: An American Enigma* (Washington, D. C.: Regnery Publishing, Inc., 1998), pp. 368-71.

2. Richard Norton Smith, *An Uncommon Man: The Triumph of Herbert Hoover* (New York: Simon and Schuster, 1984), pp. 59-96; Jeansonne, pp. 1-151.

3. Jeansonne, pp. 138, 152-185; Smith, pp. 97-102; *TIME*, March 26, 1928, p. 8.

4. Jeansonne, p. 188, Eaton p. 316, Bain and Parris, p. 228.

5. Sobel, pp. 152-53; Bain and Parris, p. 228; Jeansonne, pp. 189-90, Eaton, p. 315-16.

6. Eaton, p. 316; Sobel, p. 374.

7. *New York Times*, June 10, 11, 12, 13, and 14, 1928.

8. *New York Times*, June 9 and 11, 1928.

9. Robert J Rusnak, "Andrew Mellon: Reluctant Kingmaker," *Presidential Studies Quarterly*, Vol. 13, No. 2 (Spring 1983, pp. 269-78; *Washington Post*, June 13, 1928; *Baltimore Sun*, June 14, 1928; Eaton, p. 317; Clements, p. 408.

10. *New York Times*, June 13, 1928.

11. *New York Times*, June 13, 1928.

12. Kendrick A. Clements, *The Life of Herbert Hoover: Imperfect Visionary, 1918-1928* (New York: Palgrave McMillan, 2010), p. 408; *Baltimore Sun*, June 14, 1928.

13. *New York Times*, June 13 and 14, 1928; Clements, p. 409.

14. *New York Times*, June 14, 1928; Donald Lisio, *Hoover, Blacks, and Lily-Whites: A Study of Southern Strategies* (Chapel Hill, NC: University of North Carolina Press, 1985), pp. 50-63; "Black Politics at the National Republican and Democratic Conventions, 1868-1972, Walton and Gray, p. 273.

15. Wayne Thorburn, *The Republican Party of Texas: A Political History* (Austin: University of Texas Press, 2021), ch. 3; Bain and Parris, pp. 239-31; *New York Times*, June 14, 1928; Lisio, pp. 50-63; Heersink and Jenkins, Table 1.

16. *New York Times*, June 14, 1928; *Baltimore Sun*, June 14, 1928.

17. *New York Times*, June 10, 1928; Emily White, "Senator William E. Borah's Dry Campaign: Its Effect on the Presidential Election of 1928," University of Richmond, Honors Thesis, 1971, Honors Thesis 1081, pp. 1-25.

18. *Washington Post*, June 15, 1928; *Baltimore Sun*, June 15, 1928; Bain and Parris, pp. 229-31.

19. *Washington Post*, June 15, 1928.

20. *Baltimore Sun*, June 15, 1928; *Washington Post*, June 15, 1928.

21. Bain and Parris, p. 231; *Baltimore Sun*, June 15, 1928.

22. Eaton, pp. 317-18; Bain and Parris, p. 231; *Washington Post*, June 15, 1928; *Baltimore Sun*, June 15, 1928; Jeansonne, pp.193-94.

23. *Baltimore Sun*, June 15 and 16, 1928; *Washington Post*, June 16, 1928; Eaton, p. 318; Clements, p. 410.

24. *Baltimore Sun*, June 16, 1928; Eaton, p. 318; Jeansonne, p. 194.

25. Slayton, pp. 232-44; Paul Carter, "The Other Catholic Candidate: The 1928 Presidential Bid of Thomas J. Walsh," *The Pacific Northwest Quarterly*, Vol. 55, No. 1, January, 1964, pp. 1-8.

26. *Washington Post*, June 24, 1928.

27. Jon L. Gillum, "Parley of Prominence: The Houston Democratic Convention of 1928," *Houston History Magazine*, November 8, 2012; Slayton, pp. 244-45.

28. *Washington Post*, June 24, 1928; *New York Times*, June 26, 1928.

29. *Baltimore Sun*, June 24, 1928; *Washington Post*, June 29, 1928; *New York Times*, June 28, 1928; Slayton, pp. 250-51.

30. *Baltimore Sun*, June 26 and 28, 1928; Slayton, p. 249.

31. Slayton, p. 250-51.

32. *Baltimore Sun*, June 27, 1928; Slayton, pp. 251-52.

33. *New York Times*, June 27, 1928; *Washington Post*, June 27, 1928, *Baltimore Sun*, June 27, 1928; *TIME*, July 9, 1928.

34. *Baltimore Sun*, June 28, 1928.

35. *Baltimore Sun*, June 28, 1928; Slayton, pp. 254-55.

36. *TIME*, July 9, 1928.

37. *Baltimore Sun*, June 29, 1928; *Washington Post*, June 29, 1928.

38. *Washington Post*, June 27, 1928; *Baltimore, Sun*, June 29 and 30, 1928; Slayton, p. 256; Eaton, p. 319-20; Congressional Quarterly, Inc. *National Party Conventions: 1831-1996* (Washington, D. C.: Congressional Quarterly, Inc., 1997), pp. 82-82.

39. *Baltimore Sun*, June 29, 1928, Eaton, p. 320.

40. *Baltimore Sun*, June 30, 1928; Slayton p. 257-59.

41. *Washington Post*, June 30, 1928.

42. *Washington Post*, June 30, 1928; Slayton, pp. 258-59.

43. *Washington Post*, June 30, 1928; Slayton, pp. 246-48; Bain and Parris, p. 233.

44. *Baltimore Sun*, June 30, 1928.

45. Jeansonne, pp. 200-02. Slayton, pp. 222-75; Lorant, pp. 579-81.

46. Slayton, pp. 1, 274-82; Jeansonne, p. 202, Lorant, pp. 581-83.

47. Lorant, pp., 583, 1079; Jeansonne, p. 204; Slayton, p. 322-23.

Chapter 8

1. David C. King, *Herbert Hoover* (Tarrytown, NY: Marshall Cavendish Corp., 2010), pp. 74-75.

2. Jeansonne, pp. 228-42.

3. *New York Times*, June 12, 1932.

4. "The Fascinating Senator France . . . of Maryland," *Mad Politics: The Bizarre, Fascinating, and Unknown of American Political History*, fascinatingpolitics.com, April 25, 2020), viewed on September 1, 2023; Donald A. Ritchie, *Electing FDR: The New Deal Campaign of 1932* (Lawrence: University Press of Kansas, 2007), pp. 96-97; Bain and Parris, pp. 234-35; *Baltimore Sun*, June 12, 1932

5. Neal, pp. 206-14; *New York Times*, June 12, 1932.

6. Eaton, p. 322; *Baltimore Sun*, June 13, 1932; *see generally* Paul M. Peterson, *Chicago Stadium* (Charleston, SC: Arcadia Publishing, 2011); *New York Times*, June 12, 1932.

7. Heersink and Jenkins, Tables 1 and 2; *New York Times*, June 12, 1932; *Baltimore Sun*, June 14, 1932; *Baltimore Sun*, June 16, 1932; Ritchie, p. 97.

8. *Baltimore Sun*, June 14 and 15, 1932, *Washington Post*, June 16, 1932.

9. Ritchie, pp. 97-98; *Baltimore Sun*, June 12, 13 and 14, 1932.

10. *Baltimore Sun*, June 15, 1932.

11. Loretto C. Marsh, "The Presidential Campaign of 1932," (1937). Loyola University Chicago, Master's Thesis, 575, pp. 33-34; *Washington Post*, June 15, 1932.

12. *Baltimore Sun*, June 16, 1932, *TIME*, June 27, 1932.

13. *New York Times*, June 16 1932.

14. Haynes, *President-Making in the Gilded Age*, pp. 57-62; *New York Times*, June 16, 1932.

15. Bain and Parris, pp. 235-36; *New York Times*, June 15 and 17, 1932.

16. Bain and Parris, pp. 236-37; *Baltimore Sun*, June 16, 1932; *Washington Post*, June 16, 1932.

17. *New York Times*, June 17, 1932.

18. *New York Times*, June 17, 1932; "Republicans: Dutch Take Holland," *TIME*,

June 27, 1932; Donald T. Critchlow, *When Hollywood Was Right: How Movie Stars, Hollywood Moguls, and Big Business Remade American Politics* (New York: Cambridge University Press, 2013), p. 14.

19. *New York Times,* June 17, 1932; Eaton, pp. 323-34; Bain and Parris, p. 257.

20. *New York Times*, June 17, 1932, Eaton, p. 324; Congressional Quarterly, Inc., p. 232.

21. *New York Times*, June 16 1932; Bain and Parris, pp. 237-38.

22. *New York Times*, June 17, 1932.

23. Mencken, p. 260; Frank Freidel, *Franklin D. Roosevelt: A Rendezvous with Destiny* (Boston: Little, Brown and Company, 1990), pp. 67-68.

24. Donald A. Ritchie, *Electing FDR: The New Deal Campaign of 1932* (Lawrence: University Press of Kansas, 2007, pp. 67-76.

25. Ritchie, pp. 67-76.

26. Friedel, pp. 33-67.

27. Eaton, pp. 325-30; James A. Farley, *Jim Farley's Story: The Roosevelt Years* (New York: Whittlesey House, 1948), ch. 1 and 2; Mencken, p. 259.

28. Slayton, pp. 365-66; Neal, pp. 108-120.

29. Neal, pp. 133-39.

30. Ritchie, pp. 67-76; C. H. Cramer, *Newton D. Baker: A Biography* (Cleveland: The World Publishing Company, 1961), pp. 235-51.

31. Neal, pp. 54-64, 80-95; Eaton, pp. 326-27.

32. Eaton, pp. 32; Ritchie, pp. 88-90.

33. Neal, pp. 35-48; Eaton, pp. 329-32.

34. *New York Times*, June 26, 1932.

35. *New York Times,* June 24 and 25, 1932.

36. Farley, ch. 2, Friedel, p. 71, Neal, pp. 179-81.

37. Haynes, *The First American Political Conventions*, p. 36; Neal, pp. 181-98; Eaton, pp. 337-38.

38. James Tobin, *The Man He Became: How FDR Defied Polio to Win the Presidency* (New York: Simon & Schuster Paperbacks, 2013), p. 299, Neal, pp. 164-75.

39. *Baltimore Sun*, June 28, 1932; Eaton, pp. 338-39; *New York Times*, June 28, 1932.

40. *New York Times*, June 29, 1932; Bain and Parris, pp. 239-40; Eaton, pp. 339-40; Neal, pp. 220-35.

41. Eaton, p. 340; Neal, p. 305; Peter Carlson, "Although as Crooked as They Come, This Boston Politician Was Beloved, *American History*, Autumn, 2023; *New York Times*, June 24 and July 3, 1932.

42. Eaton, p. 333, 340-41.

43. *New York Times*, June 30, 1932.

44. Farley, ch. 3; Eaton, pp.343-46; Neal, pp. 275-77.

45. Eaton pp. 346, 355-56.

46. *Baltimore Sun*, June 30, 1932; Eaton, pp. 341-42; Bain and Parris, pp. 241-42.

47. Eaton, pp. 341-43; Neal, pp. 242-49; Bain and Parris, pp. 241-42.

48. Eaton, pp. 341-43; Neal, pp. 242-49; Bain and Parris, pp. 241-42.

49. Smith, p. 268; *Washington Post*, July 1, 1932.

50. Eaton, pp. 346-47.

51. Eaton, p. 347

52. Eaton, pp. 347-48; Ritchie, p. 104; Neal, pp. 260-66.

53. Eaton, pp. 349-55; Bain and Parris, p. 243; Ritchie, pp. 104-05.

54. Eaton, pp. 348-49; Neal, p. 270; Cramer, pp. 249-54] Neal, pp. 271-72; Ritchie, pp. 107-08; Nasaw, pp. 455-56.

55. Eaton, pp. 349-56; Neal, pp. 279-86.

56. Eaton, p. 357; Neal, pp. 288-89.

57. Eaton, pp. 357-60; Neal, pp.290-93; Bain and Parris, 243-44; Slayton, pp. 372-73.

58. Cramer, p. 254; Eaton, pp. 359-60; Neal, pp. 286-87.

59. Freidel, p. 73; Neal, pp. 295-97.

60. Baird Wonsey and Marguerite Wonsey, "American Airways Ford Trimotor Transports FDR to Chicago Democratic Convention," Virginia Aviation History Project, pp. 12-16, *www.vahsonline.com*, viewed September 27, 2023; Neal, pp. 295-310.

61. *New York Times*, July 3, 1932; *Baltimore Sun*, July 3, 1932.

62. Ritchie, pp.109-10; Wonsey, pp. 16-17; Neal, pp. 308-09; *New York Times*, July 3, 1932.

63. *Baltimore Sun*, July 3, 1932.

64. *New York Times*, July 3, 1932.

65. Freidel, p. 74; Ritchie, p. 110.

66. Ritchie, pp. 102-03.

67. *Big Fork Eagle*, August 12, 2019; *Madera Tribune*, July 19, 1933; Freidel, pp. 87-88; *The Oklahoman*, August 23, 2023; *The Times-Picayune*, September 8, 1910.

68. Lorant, pp. 594-99; Freidel, pp. 74-78; Ritchie, p. 153.

69. Lorant, pp. 599-600; Freidel, p. 78; Ritchie, p. 157.

Chapter 9

1. *Washington Post*, June 28, 1936

2. Irving Stone, *They Also Ran: The Story of the Men Who Were Defeated for the Presidency* (New York: Signet, 1968), pp. 337-40; *TIME*, May 8, 1936.

3. *TIME*, May 8, 1936, Stone, pp. 337, 340-42.

4. Pietrusza, pp. 187-92.

5. Pietrusza, pp. 196-98.

6. Pietrusza, pp. 192-96.

7. Jeansonne, pp. 297-309; *TIME*, May 25, 1936.

8. Eaton, p. 362; Pietrusza, pp. 226-229; *TIME*, May 8, 1936.

9. Eaton, p. 364, Pietrusza, pp. 228-30; Paul M. Warden, "Reorganize or Perish: William Edgar Borah and the Republican Civil War, 1930-36," Thesis in History, Washington State University, 2011, pp. 52-55.

10. *Baltimore Sun*, June 5 and 6, 1936; *Washington Post*, June 6, 1936.

11. Pietrusza, p. 238; *TIME*, June 22, 1936; Heersink and Jenkins, Table 2; *Baltimore Sun*, June 5 and 6, 1936.

12. *Baltimore Sun*, June 7, 1936; *Cleveland Plain Dealer*, June 10, 1936.

13. "An Exclusive Look at the Leaked PR Agenda of the 1936 Republican National Convention," Atlas Obscura website, *www.atlasobscura.com/articles*, viewed October 23, 2023; *Baltimore Sun*, June 7, 1936.

14. *Washington Post*, June 10, 1936; "Great Lakes Exposition," *Encyclopedia of Cleveland History*, Case Western Reserve University, *www.case.edu/ech/artlices/g/great-lakes-exposition*, viewed on October 30, 2023.

15. *Baltimore Sun*, June 7 and 10, 1936.

16. *Washington Post*, June 10 and 12, 1936; *Baltimore Sun*, June 10, 1936; *TIME*, June 22, 1936.

17. *Baltimore Sun*, June 11, 1936.

18. Richard Norton Smith, p. 222, 225-71; *TIME*, June 22, 1936; Pietrusza, pp. 240-41.

19. *Baltimore Sun*, June 11, 1936; Richard Allen Smith, pp. 227-28; Pietrusza, pp. 240-41.

20. "Republican Party Platform of 1936," *The American Presidency Project, www.*

presidency. ucsb.edu, viewed October, 27, 2023; *Baltimore Sun*, June 12, 1936.

21. *Baltimore Sun*, June 12, 1936.
22. *TIME*, June 22, 1936; *Baltimore Sun*, June 12, 1936.
23. *Baltimore Sun*, June 12, 1936; *Washington Post*, June 12, 1936; Eaton p. 365.
24. *Baltimore Sun*, June 12, 1936; *Washington Post*, June 10, 1936.
25. *TIME*, June 22, 1936; Bain and Parris, p. 247; Pietrusza, p. 245.
26. Freidel, p. 197.
27. *Washington Post*, June 23, 1936.
28. *Baltimore Sun*, June 20, 21, 22, and 23, 1936.
29. Slayton, pp. 379-89; *Washington Post*, June 28, 1936; *Baltimore Sun*, June 23, 1936; Si Sheppard, *The Buying of the Presidency? Franklin D. Roosevelt, The New Deal, and The Election of 1936* (Santa Barbara, CA: Praeger, 2014), p. 62.
30. *TIME*, July 6, 1936; Freidel, pp. 200-01; Sheppard, p. 69.
31. *New York Times*, June 25, 1936; Walton and Gray, p. 274; Pietrusza, p. 258-59; Sheppard, p. 65; Bain and Parris, p. 248; *TIME*, July 6, 1936.
32. *Baltimore Sun*, June 25 and 26, 1936; TIME July 6, 1936; Sheppard, pp. 65-66; Pietrusza, pp. 259-60; Eaton, p. 430; Bain and Parris, pp. 275-77.
33. *New York Times*, June 24, 1936, *Baltimore Sun*, June 24, 1936, Bain and Parris, p. 248.
34. *New York Times*, June 24, 1936, *Baltimore Sun*, June 24, 1936, Bain and Parris, p. 248.
35. *Baltimore Sun*, June 25, 1936.
36. *Baltimore Sun*, June 26, 1936; Bain and Parris, p. 249; Eaton, p. 366.
37. *Baltimore Sun*, June 26, 1936; Bain and Parris, pp. 249-50; Sheppard, p. 70-71.
38. *Baltimore Sun*, June 26, 1936; *TIME*, July 6, 1936; Pietrusza, p. 164.
39. *Baltimore Sun*, June 28, 1936.
40. Sheppard, p. 63; *New York Times*, June 25, 1936; *New York Times*, June 26, 1936; *Baltimore Sun*, June 26, 1936; Pietrusza, pp. 76, 262.
41. *Washington Post*, June 27, 1936; *Baltimore Sun*, June 22, 1936.
42. *Baltimore Sun*, June 26, 1936; *New York Times*, June 26, 1936; *TIME*, July 6, 1936.
43. *New York Times*, June 28, 1936.
44. *TIME*, July 6, 1936; *New York Times*, June 28, 1936; *Washington Post*, June 28, 1932; Sheppard, pp. 72-73.
45. Freidel, pp. 201-02; Sheppard, pp. 73-74; Michael Waldman, *My Fellow Americans* (Naperville, IL: Sourcebooks, 2010), p. 102.
46. *Washington Post*, June 28, 1936; *Baltimore Sun*, June 28, 1936; Pietrusza, pp. 266-68.
47. *Washington Post*, June 28, 1936; *New York Times*, June 28, 1936; Sheppard, pp. 76-78.
48. Freidel, pp. 202-03.
49. Lorant, pp.620-25.
50. Lorant, p.624.
51. Pietrusza, pp. 271-93.
52. Pietrusza, p. 420; Lorant, pp. 624-25; Freidel, pp. 206-07.

Chapter 10

1. Haynes, *President-Making in the Gilded Age*, pp. 44-64.
2. *See* Chapter 3 of this book.
3. Freidel, pp. 321-40.
4. John W. Jeffries, *A Third Term for FDR: The Election of 1940*, (Lawrence: University of

Kansas Press, 2017), pp. 47-8; Susan Dunn, *1940 FDR, Willkie, Lindbergh, Hitler—the Election amid the Storm* (New Haven: Yale University Press, 2013), ch. 6; Eaton, p. 369.

5. Jeffries, pp. 45-6; Dunn, ch. 6.

6. Jeffries, pp. 48-49; Dunn, ch. 6; William L. Hafer, "Robert Alfonzo Taft: And the Quest for the Presidency," Masters Theses, Western Michigan University, 2090 (1978), pp. 29-35.

7. Jeffries, p. 51-52.

8. Jeffries, pp. 55-59; Dunn, ch. 6.

9. Charles Peters, *Five Days in Philadelphia* (New York: PublicAffairs, 2005), pp. 46-49; Jeffries, pp. 55-59; Dunn, ch. 6; Eaton, pp. 372-74.

10. Eaton, pp. 369-70; Hafer, pp. 30-32, 39-40.

11. Dunn, ch. 6 and 8; Peters, pp. 40-41.

12. Peters, pp. 57-61; Steve Neal, *Dark Horse: A Biography of Wendell Willkie* (Lawrence: University of Kansas Press, 1989), p. 99; Dunn, ch. 8.

13. Neal, p. 86; Peters, p. 61.

14. Peters, pp. 63-65; Neal, p 87-89.

15. *New York Times*, June 27, 1940.

16. Peters, p. 75; Neal, pp. 98-99, 123.

17. *New York Times*, June 25, 1940; Peters, pp. 74-75; Neal, p. 100; Eaton, p. 378.

18. Peters, p. 76; Neal, p. 100; Eaton, p. 378.

19. *New York Times*, June 26, 1940; Peters, pp. 78-79,82; Neal, pp. 100-02.

20. Peters, pp. 82-83, Neal, p. 102.

21. Neal, pp. 83-84; Peters, pp. 91-92; Paul Starobin, "Fake News and Election Meddling—1940s Style," March 23, 2018, www.historynet.com, viewed December 10, 2023.

22. Haynes, *The First American Political Conventions*, p. 173; *see* Chapter 6 of this book; Neal, p. 165; Peters, pp. 96-97; *New York Times*, June 27, 1940.

23. Peters, p. 91; *TIME*, July 1, 1940.

24. *New York Times*, June 27, 1940; Peters, p. 94.

25. *New York Times*, June 27, 1940; Peters, p. 94; Neal, pp. 104-05.

26. *New York Times*, June 27, 1940; Eaton, p. 382, Peters, pp. 94-95; Neal, pp. 105-07.

27. Hafer, p. 49; Eaton, p. 383.

28. Congressional Quarterly, Inc., p. 234; Eaton, p. 383; Hafer, p. 49.

29. Eaton, pp. 383-84; Hafer, p. 50.

30. Eaton, pp. 384-5; Hafer, p. 51.

31. Congressional Quarterly, Inc., p. 234; Eaton, p. 385; Hafer, p. 51.

32. Eaton, p. 385.

33. Congressional Quarterly, Inc., p. 234; Eaton, pp. 385-86; Hafer, p. 51.

34. Congressional Quarterly, Inc., p. 234; Eaton, pp. 386-87; Peters, pp. 106-08; Neal, pp. 114-16.

35. Eaton, p. 387; Peters, pp. 110-112; Neal, pp. 117-19.

36. *New York Times*, June 29, 1940; Neal, p. 121; Peters, pp. 112-13.

37. *Washington Post*, June 29, 1940; *New York Times*, June 29, 1940; *Baltimore Sun*, June 28 and 29, 1940.

38. *Washington Post*, June 29, 1940.

39. Richard Moe, *Roosevelt's Second Act: The Election of 1940 and the Politics of War* (Oxford: Oxford University Press, 2013), ch. 2.

40. Peters, pp. 123-25; Moe, intro. and ch. 9.

41. *New York Times*, February 6, 1940; *Chicago Tribune*, February 6, 1940; R. Craig Sautter and Edward Burke, *Inside the Wigwam:*

Chicago Presidential Conventions, 1860-1996 (Chicago: Wild Onion Books, 1996), p. 180.

42. Lorant, pp. 638-39; Moe, ch.5; Freidel, p. 327.

43. Peters, pp. 126-29; Eaton, p. 390; Moe, ch. 9.

44. Moe, ch. 11.

45. Christopher D. O'Sullivan, *Harry Hopkins: FDR's Envoy to Churchill and Stalin* (Lanham, MD: Rowman & Littlefield, 2015), pp. 49-51; *Baltimore Sun*, July 12, 1940; Peters, pp. 136-37.

46. Eaton, p. 389; Peters, pp. 123-24.

47. Sautter and Burke, pp. 18; Dunn, ch. 10; *Chicago Tribune*, July 16, 1940.

48. *Baltimore Sun*, July 16; Peters, p. 138.

49. *Chicago Tribune*, July 16, 1940; Dunn, ch. 10; Moe, ch. 11.

50. *Baltimore Sun*, July 17, 1940; Sautter and Burke, pp. 181-82; Peters, pp. 140-41.

51. Bain and Parris, p. 258; Eaton, p. 391; Sautter and Burke, pp. 181-82; Peters, p. 142; Moe, ch. 11; Dunn, ch. 10.

52. *Chicago Tribune*, July 17, 1940; Sautter and Burke, pp. 181-84; Peters, p. 142.

53. Bain and Parris, pp. 258-59; *Baltimore Sun*, July 18, 1940.

54. Sautter and Burke, p. 182; *Baltimore Sun*, July 18, 1940.

55. Sautter and Burke, p. 182; Peters, pp. 138, 143-44; *Baltimore Sun*, July 18, 1944.

56. Eaton, p. 391-92.

57. *Washington Post*, July 18, 1940.

58. Mark L. Kleinman, "Searching for the 'Inner Light': The Development of Henry A. Wallace's Experimental Spiritualism," *The Annals of Iowa*, Vol. 53 (Summer, 1994), *see generally*; Bill Kelter, *Veeps* (Atlanta: Top Shelf Productions, 2008), pp. 167-71; David McCullough, *Truman* (New York: Touchstone, 1992), p. 294.

59. Peters, pp. 148-51; Eaton, 392.

60. Peters, p. 147.

61. *Baltimore Sun*, July 19, 1940; Sautter and Burke, p. 183; Peters, pp. 148-49.

62. "Speech to the 1940 Democratic Convention in Chicago, July 18, 1940," *Eleanor Roosevelt Speeches*, www2.gwu.edu, viewed October 4, 2023; Sautter and Burke, p. 183.

63. "Speech to the 1940 Democratic Convention in Chicago, July 18, 1940," *Eleanor Roosevelt Speeches*, www2.gwu.edu, viewed October 4, 2023.

64. *Baltimore Sun*, July 19, 1940; Eaton, p. 392; Peters, p. 150; Freidel, p. 346.

65. Peters, p. 150; *Washington Post*, July 21, 1940.

66. *Baltimore Sun*, July 20, 1940; Sautter and Burke, p. 184; Peters, p. 161.

67. *Baltimore Sun*, July 19, 1940.

68. *Baltimore Sun*, July 19, 1940; *Life*, July 29, 1940; Peters, pp 151-52.

69. Freidel, pp. 352-55; Lorant, pp. 645-49; Peters, pp. 174-79.

70. Lorant, pp. 649-52; Freidel, pp. 354-57.

71. Peters, p. 176; Freidel, pp. 353-54; Neal, pp. 144-45.

72. Lorant, pp. 653, 1081.

Chapter 11

1. Freidel, pp. 359-428.

2. David M. Jordan, *FDR, Dewey, and the Election of 1944* (Bloomington, IN: Indiana University Press, 2011, pp. 15-21.

3. David Brinkley, *Washington Goes to War* (New York: Alfred A. Knopf, 1988), p. 259; Jordan, p. 27; Jordan, pp. 22-28.

4. Neal, pp. 199-207, 231-66, 277-85; Jordan, pp. 40-41.

5. Neal, p. 62; Jordan, pp. 29-34; Neal, p. 281; Richard N. Smith, pp. 400-01.

6. Jordan, pp. 35-40; Eaton, pp. 394-95.

7. Eaton, pp. 394-96; Neal, pp. 286-97.

8. Neal, pp. 279-98; Eaton, pp. 395-97.

9. Neal, pp. 299-305.

10. Eaton, pp. 398-99; Neal, pp. 305-07; Sautter and Burke, pp. 188-89.

11. Eaton, p. 399; *New York Times*, June 25, 1944.

12. *New York Times*, June 25 and 26, 1944; Eaton, p. 399.

13. Sautter and Burke, p. 190; *New York Times*, June 25 and 27, 1944.

14. *New York Times*, June 27, 1944; Sautter and Burke, pp. 190-91; Michael Davis, "Politics as Usual: Franklin Roosevelt, Thomas Dewey and the Wartime Presidential Campaign of 1944," dissertation for doctorate of philosophy, University of Arkansas, 2005, *www.digitalcommons.liberty.edu*, pp. 107-09; *Washington Post*, June 27, 1944.

15. *New York Times*, June 28, 1944, Sautter and Burke, pp. 190-91; Davis, pp. 105-07.

16. Eaton, p. 400; *New York Times*, June 28, 1944.

17. Michael Davis, *Politics as Usual: Thomas Dewey, Franklin Roosevelt, and the Wartime Presidential Campaign of 1944* (DeKalb, IL: Northern Illinois University Press, 2014), pp. 100-01; James Baughman, *Henry R. Luce and the Rise of the American News Media* (Baltimore: The Johns Hopkins University Press, 2001), p. 141; Eaton, p. 400.

18. *New York Times*, June 29, 1944; Richard N. Smith, pp. 403; Sautter and Burke, p. 193; Davis, p. 110.

19. Richard N. Smith, p. 402; Sautter and Burke, pp. 193-94.

20. Sautter and Burke, p. 193; Eaton, pp. 400-01; *New York Times*, June 29, 1944.

21. *New York Times*, June 29, 1944; Sautter and Burke, p. 194; Davis, pp. 110-11.

22. *New York Times*, June 29, 1944; Sautter and Burke, p. 194; Eaton, p. 401.

23. *New York Times*, June 29, 1944.

24. *New York Times*, June 29, 1944.

25. *New York Times*, June 29, 1944.

26. *New York Times*, June 29, 1944.

27. *New York Times*, June 29, 1944.

28. *New York Times*, June 30, 1944; Sautter and Burke, p. 195.

29. Robert Ferrell, *Choosing Truman: The Democratic Convention of 1944* (Columbia, MO: University of Missouri Press, 1994), pp. 1-3; McCullough, pp. 295-96.

30. Ferrell, pp. 2-3; McCullough, pp. 295-96.

31. Ferrell, pp. 3-4.

32. Ferrell, pp. 4-5, 12-33; McCullough, pp. 297.

33. Ferrell, pp. 5-12.

34. Ferrell, p. 5; McCullough, p. 300.

35. Ferrell, pp. 6-7.

36. Michael Janeway, *The Fall of the House of Roosevelt: Brokers of Ideas and Power from FDR to LBJ* (New York: Columbia University Press, 2004), p. 54.

37. Ferrell, pp. 11-15; McCullough, pp. 299-301.

38. McCullough, p. 302; Ferrell, pp. 22-3.

39. Ferrell, pp. 26-34; McCullough, pp. 302-04.

40. Ferrell, pp. 36-41; McCullough, pp. 305-08; *Baltimore Sun*, July 20, 1920.

41. Ferrell, pp. 30-31, 44-45.

42. Ferrell, pp. 36-76; McCullough, pp. 306-14; *Washington Post*, July 20, 1944.

43. Ferrell, p. 64; McCullough, p, 313; *Washington Post*, July 20, 1944.

44. *Washington Post*, July 20, 1928; Richard Norton Smith, *Thomas E. Dewey and His Times* (New York: Simon and Schuster, 1982), p. 404; *Baltimore Sun*, July 20, 1928.

45. *Washington Post*, July 20, 1944; *Baltimore Sun*, June 20, 1944.

46. *Baltimore Sun*, June 21, 1944.

47. *Washington Post*, July 19, 1944; Ferrell, p. 78; *Baltimore Sun*, July 18, 1944.

48. *Baltimore, Sun*, July 21, 1944.

49. *Baltimore Sun*, July 21, 1944; Ferrell, p. 77; Bain and Parris, p. 266.

50. *Baltimore Sun*, July 16, 1944.

51. *Washington Post*, July 21, 1944; McCullough, p. 316; Freidel, 537-38.

52. John C. Culver and John Hyde, *American Dreamer: The Life and Times of Henry A. Wallace* (New York: W. W. Norton & Company, 2000), pp. 362-64; McCollough, pp. 315-173; Ferrell, pp. 78-81.

53. Culver and Hyde, pp. 363-64.

54. Ferrell, pp. 84-87; McCollough, p. 318.

55. McCollough, p. 318-19; Ferrell, pp. 86-87; Eaton, pp. 408-09.

56. Eaton, p. 409; Ferrell, pp, 87-88; *Baltimore Sun*, July 22, 1944.

57. *Baltimore Sun*, July 22, 1944.

58. McCullough, p. 321.

59. Ferrell, p. 91.

60. Davis, pp. 147-213; Lorant, pp. 664-65, 671-76; Richard N. Smith, pp. 409-37.

61. Lorant, pp. 661-71; Freidel, pp. 556-68.

62. Lorant, pp. 676-79, 1081; Freidel, p. 567; Davis, pp. 321-32.

Conclusion

1. "FDR: The Long Goodbye," *Atlanta Magazine*, August 2, 2010; "Franklin D. Roosevelt and the Spirit of Warm Springs," *www.nationalww2museum.org*, viewed December 15, 2023.

2. Freidel, pp. 603-06; "FDR: The Long Goodbye," *Atlanta Magazine*, August 2, 2010; "Franklin D. Roosevelt and the Spirit of Warm Springs," *www.nationalww2museum.org*, viewed December 15, 2023.

3. Congressional Quarterly, *National Party Conventions, 1831-1996*, pp. 94-95; Eaton, pp. 429-31.

4. Congressional Quarterly, *National Party Conventions, 1831-1996*, pp. 98-99; Eaton, pp. 478-81.

5. Congressional Quarterly, *National Party Conventions, 1831-1996*, pp. 113-14.

6. Congressional Quarterly, *National Party Conventions, 1831-1996*, pp. 127-28, 249;137-38, 250.

7. John F. Kennedy: "Address Accepting the Democratic Nomination for President at the Memorial Coliseum in Los Angeles, California," The American Presidency Project, www.presidency.ucsb.edu, viewed January 12, 2024; Ronald Reagan: "Address Accepting the Presidential Nomination at the Republican National Convention in Detroit," The American Presidency Project, www.presidency.ucsb.edu, viewed January 12, 2024; Barack Obama: "Address Accepting the Presidential Nomination at the Democratic National Convention in Denver," The American Presidency Project, www.presidency.ucsb.edu, viewed January 12, 2024.

8. Congressional Quarterly, Inc., *National Party Conventions, 1831-1996*, pp. 102-180.

9. Haynes, *The First American Political Conventions*, p. 243.

10. Gerald Pomper, "The New Role of the Conventions as Political Rituals," *Rewiring Politics: Presidential Nominating Conventions in the Media Age*, Costas Panagopoulos, Editor (Baton Rouge: Louisiana State University Press, 2007), p. 198.

www.ingramcontent.com/pod-product-compliance
Lightning Source LLC
Chambersburg PA
CBHW082150070526
44585CB00020B/2154